O|S Ordn...

STREE...

Berkshire

Contents

III	Key to map symbols
IV	Key to map pages
VI	Route planning
VIII	Administrative and Postcode boundaries
1	Street maps
154	Index of hospitals, industrial estates, railway stations, schools, shopping centres, street names and universities

PHILIP'S

First edition published 1990
First colour edition published 1996
Second colour edition published 2000 by

George Philip Ltd, a division of
Octopus Publishing Group Ltd
2-4 Heron Quays, London E14 4JP

ISBN 0-540-07679-1 (pocket)

**The mapping between pages 1 and 153 (inclusive) in this
atlas is derived from Ordnance Survey® OSCAR® and
Land-Line® data and Landranger® mapping.**

Ordnance Survey, OSCAR, Land-line and Landranger are
registered trade marks of Ordnance Survey, the national
mapping agency of Great Britain.

Printed and bound in Spain by Cayfosa

Digital Data

The exceptionally high-quality mapping found
in this book is available as digital data in TIFF
format, which is easily convertible to other
bit-mapped (raster) image formats. The data
can be provided as pages or, in some regions,
as larger extracts of up to 200 sq km. The
larger extracts can also be supplied on paper.

The index is also available in digital form as a
standard database table. It contains all the
details found in the printed index together with
the National Grid reference for the map square
in which each entry is named.

For further information and to discuss your
requirements, please contact Philip's on
020 7531 8440 or
george.philip@philips-maps.co.uk

Also available in various formats

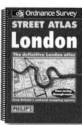

*'Very clear mapping.
Great in scope and value'*
BEST BUY, AUTO EXPRESS

- ◆ Bedfordshire
- ◆ Birmingham and West Midlands
- ◆ Bristol and Avon
- ◆ Buckinghamshire
- ◆ Cannock, Lichfield, Rugeley
- ◆ Cardiff, Swansea and Glamorgan
- ◆ Cheshire
- ◆ Derbyshire
- ◆ Derby and Belper
- ◆ Durham
- ◆ Edinburgh and East Central Scotland
- ◆ North Essex
- ◆ South Essex
- ◆ Glasgow and West Central Scotland
- ◆ North Hampshire
- ◆ South Hampshire
- ◆ Hertfordshire
- ◆ East Kent
- ◆ West Kent

- ◆ Lancashire
- ◆ Leicestershire and Rutland
- ◆ London
- ◆ Greater Manchester
- ◆ Merseyside
- ◆ Northamptonshire
- ◆ Northwich, Winsford, Middlewich
- ◆ Nottinghamshire
- ◆ Oxfordshire
- ◆ Peak District Towns
- ◆ Staffordshire
- ◆ Stafford, Stone, Uttoxeter
- ◆ Surrey
- ◆ East Sussex
- ◆ West Sussex
- ◆ Tyne and Wear
- ◆ Warrington, Widnes, Runcorn
- ◆ Warwickshire
- ◆ South Yorkshire
- ◆ West Yorkshire

◆ Colour regional atlases (hardback, spiral, wire-o, pocket)   Colour local atlases (paperback)
◆ Black and white regional atlases (hardback, softback, pocket)

The Street Atlases are available from all good bookshops or by mail order direct from the publisher. Orders can be made by ringing our special Credit Card Hotline on
01933 443863 during office hours (9am to 5pm), or leave a message on the answering machine, quoting your full credit card number plus expiry date and your full name
and address. Before placing an order on the answering machine, please telephone to check availability and prices.

(22a)	Motorway with junction number	Railway station *Walsall*
	Primary route - dual carriageway and single	London Underground station
	A road - dual carriageway and single	Private railway station
	B road - dual carriageway and single	Bus, coach station
	Minor road - dual carriageway and single	Ambulance station
	Other minor road - dual carriageway and single	Coastguard station
	Road under construction	Fire station
	Pedestrianised area	Police station
DY7	Postcode boundaries	Accident and Emergency entrance to hospital
	County and Unitary Authority boundaries	H Hospital
	Railway	Places of worship
	Tramway, miniature railway	Information Centre (open all year)
	Rural track, private road or narrow road in urban area	P Parking
	Gate or obstruction to traffic (restrictions may not apply at all times or to all vehicles)	P&R Park and Ride
	Path, bridleway, byway open to all traffic, road used as a public path	PO Post Office
	The representation in this atlas of a road, track or path is no evidence of the existence of way	Camping site
126		Caravan site
94	Adjoining page indicators	Golf course
		Picnic site
		Important buildings, schools, colleges, universities and hospitals *Prim Sch*
		River Medway Water name

Allot Gdns	Allotments	Meml	Memorial	Stream
Acad	Academy	Mon	Monument	
Cemy	Cemetery	Mus	Museum	River or canal - minor and major
C Ctr	Civic Centre	Obsy	Observatory	
CH	Club House	Pal	Royal Palace	Water
Coll	College	PH	Public House	
Crem	Crematorium	Recn Gd	Recreation Ground	Tidal water
Ent	Enterprise	Resr	Reservoir	
Ex H	Exhibition Hall	Ret Pk	Retail Park	Woods
Ind Est	Industrial Estate	Sch	School	
Inst	Institute	Sh Ctr	Shopping Centre	Houses
Ct	Law Court	TH	Town Hall/House	
L Ctr	Leisure Centre	Trad Est	Trading Estate	*House* Non-Roman antiquity
LC	Level Crossing	Univ	University	
Liby	Library	Wks	Works	*VILLA* Roman antiquity
Mkt	Market	YH	Youth Hostel	

The dark grey border on the inside edge of some pages indicates at the mapping does not continue onto the adjacent page

■ The small numbers around the edges of the maps identify the 1 kilometre National Grid lines

The scale of the maps is 3.92 cm to 1 km
2½ inches to 1 mile 1: 25344

0	¼		½		¾		1 mile
0	250m	500m	750m	1 kilometre			

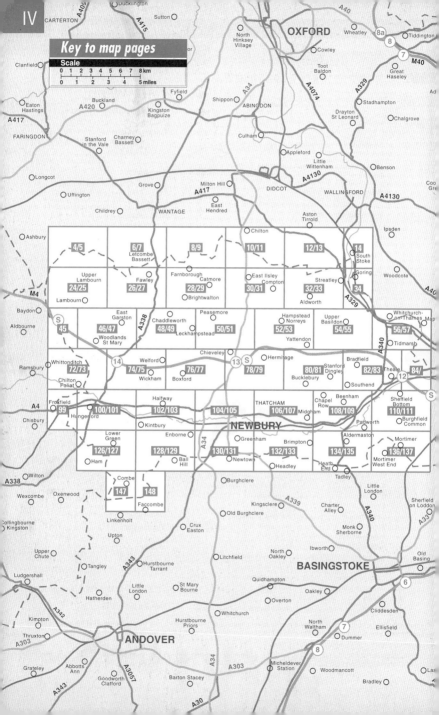

IV

Key to map pages

Scale

0 1 2 3 4 5 6 7 8 km
0 1 2 3 4 5 miles

CARTERTON
Ducklington
Sutton
A415
A40
OXFORD
Wheatley
8a
8
Tiddington
7
M40
Clanfield
North Hinksey Village
Cowley
Toot Baldon
Great Haseley
Ad
Eaton Hastings
A420
Buckland
A417
FARINGDON
Kingston Bagpuize
Fyfield
Shippon
A34
ABINGDON
A4074
Stadhampton
Drayton St Leonard
Chalgrove
Longcot
Stanford in the Vale
Charney Bassett
Grove
A417
Milton Hill
Culham
Appleford
Little Wittenham
Benson
Coo
Gre
Uffington
DIDCOT
A4130
WALLINGFORD
A4130
Childrey
WANTAGE
East Hendred
Aston Tirrold
Ipsden
Ashbury
Chilton
4/5
6/7 Letcombe Bassett
8/9
10/11
12/13
14 South Stoke
Goring
Woodcote
A4
Upper Lambourn
24/25
Fawley
26/27
Farnborough
Catmore
28/29
Brightwalton
East Ilsley
Compton
30/31
Streatley
32/33
Aldworth
34
A329
Lambourn
M4
Baydon
45
S
East Garston
46/47
A338
Chaddleworth
48/49
Leckhampstead
Peasemore
50/51
Hampstead Norreys
52/53
Yattendon
Upper Basildon
54/55
Whitchurch-on-Thames
Map
56/57
A340
Tidmarsh
Aldbourne
Woodlands St Mary
Ramsbury
Whittonditch
72/73
Chilton Foliat
14
Welford
74/75
Wickham
Chieveley
76/77
Boxford
13
S
Hermitage
78/79
Stanford Dingley
80/81
Bucklebury
Bradfield
Southend
82/83
Theale
84/
12
S
Froxfield
99
Hungerford
100/101
Kintbury
Halfway
102/103
104/105
THATCHAM
106/107
Midgham
Chapel Row
Beenham
108/109
Padworth
Sheffield Bottom
110/111
Burghfield Common
Chisbury
A4
Lower Green
126/127
Ham
Enborne
128/129
Ball Hill
A34
130/131
Newtown
Greenham
Brimpton
132/133
Headley
NEWBURY
Aldermaston
134/135
Heath End
Mortimer
136/137
Mortimer West End
Wilton
A338
Combe
147
Faccombe
148
Burghclere
Tadley
Little London
Sherfield on Loddon
Wexcombe
Oxenwood
Linkenholt
Kingsclere
A339
Old Burghclere
Charter Alley
A340
Monk Sherborne
A33
Collingbourne Kingston
Upton
Crux Easton
Litchfield
North Oakley
Ibworth
Old Basing
Upper Chute
Tangley
A343
Hurstbourne Tarrant
Quidhampton
Oakley
BASINGSTOKE
6
Ludgershall
Little London
St Mary Bourne
Overton
Cliddesden
Ellisfield
Hatherden
A342
Whitchurch
Hurstbourne Priors
North Waltham
7
Dummer
Kimpton
Thruxton
A303
ANDOVER
A34
A303
Micheldever Station
Woodmancott
8
Las
Grateley
Abbotts Ann
A3057
Goodworth Clatford
Barton Stacey
A30
Bradley
A343

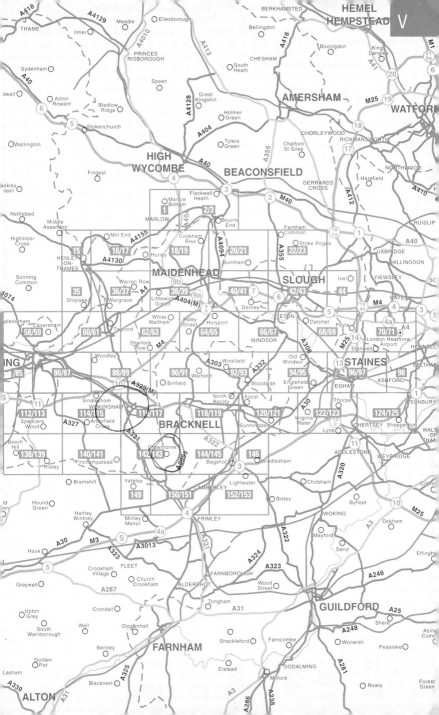

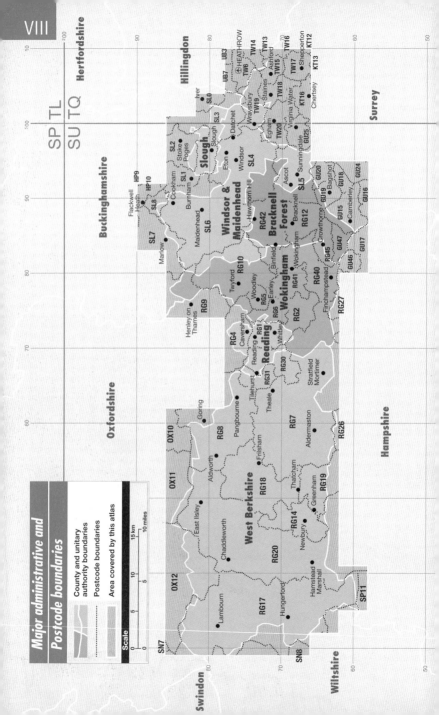

Nuttings Wood
High Heavens Wood
Wymers Wood
Burroughs Grove Hill
Linzees Firs
Little Manor
Hatches Wood
Widmere Farm
Munces Wood
Three Horseshoes (PH)
Burroughs Grove
Wood Barn Farm
Juniper
Coldharbour
Juniper Hill
Marlow Bottom
Kiln House
Highruse Wood
Capel Cillia
Burford Cty Comb Sch
Brucewood Par
Bencombe Farm
Seymour Court
End Farm
High Rews Farm
Kingswood Par
SL7
Stowe
Woodland
Great Marlow Sch
Stapleton Cl
The Old Workhouse
MUNDAYDEAN LA
Blount's Wood
Woodside Farm
Bovingdon Green
Blount's
Marlow CE Inf Sch
Foxes Piece Comb Sch
The Royal Oak (PH)
Marefield
St Peter's RC Comb Sch
Holy Trinity Sch
Marlow Com
MARLOW
Spinfield Cty Comb Sch
Langley Way
Sir William Borlase's Gram Sch
Marlow
Thames Ind Est
Fieldhouse Ind Est
Forty Green
Little House Farm
Liby
Spinfield
Marlow Weir
Court Garden L Complex
The Thames Path
River Thames
PH

MARLOW RD
SEYMOUR COURT RD
A4155 HENLEY RD
WEST ST
CHAPEL ST
SPITTAL ST
LITTLE MARLOW RD
A4155

← 18

B1
1 BRAEMAR CT
2 CHISWICK LODGE
3 LISTON CT
4 LIME BARN
5 MORRIS PL
6 BARLEY WAY
7 MALTHOUSE WAY
8 PORTLANDS MEWS

C1
1 BEECH CT
2 VICTORIA CT
3 GLADE HO
4 ST JAMES CTYD
5 LEIGHTON HO
6 MONKSWOOD CT
7 LITTLE BOLTONS
8 PENN CT
9 TEMPLARS PL

10 TIERNEY CT
11 DUNSTABLE HO
C2
1 EASTWOOD CT
2 WILTSHIRE RD
3 MILE ELM
4 BEECHINGSTOKE
5 BUTLER CT
6 BYRON CL
7 MEAD CL

8 WILLOWMEAD RD
9 WILLOWMEAD SQ
10 WILLOWMEAD CL
11 ROMNEY CT
12 SHELLSEY RD

2 →

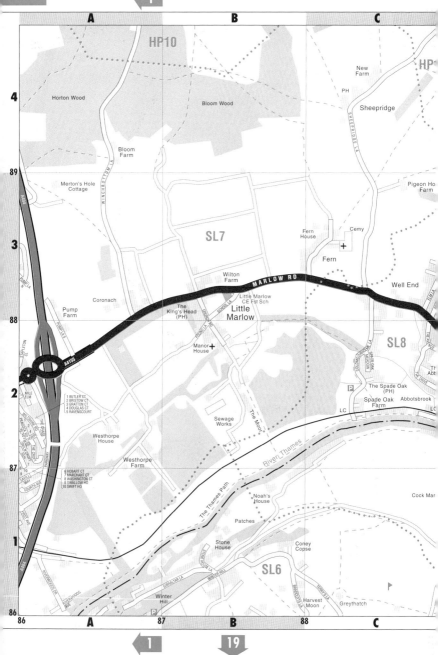

A B C

HP10

4

Horton Wood

Bloom Wood

New Farm

HP

PH

Sheepridge

89

Bloom Farm

Merton's Hole Cottage

SHEEPRIDGE LA

Pigeon Ho Farm

3

SL7

Fern House

Cemy

Fern

Wilton Farm

MARLOW RD

Well End

88

Coronach

The King's Head (PH)

Little Marlow CE Fst Sch

Little Marlow

SL8

Pump Farm

STATION LA

A4155

Manor House

SL7

COLDMOORHOLM LA

SPADE OAK

MARLOW

The Spade Oak (PH)

2

MILE ELM

1 BUTLER CT
2 BRISTOW CT
3 GRATTON CT
4 DOUGLAS CT
5 RAVENSCOURT

Sewage Works

The Moor

P

Spade Oak Farm

Abbotsbrook

LC

The Cruise

Th Abt

LC

Westhorpe House

87

THE PASSAGE

6 HOBART CT
7 MARCHANT CT
8 WASHINGTON CT
9 SWALLOW HO
10 SWIFT HO

Westhorpe Farm

River Thames

FOURTH AVE

Noah's House

Cock Mar

The Thames Path

Patches

1

Stone House

Coney Copse

SL6

Winter Hill

GIBRALTAR LA

WINTER HILL

Harvest Moon

Greythatch

86

P

86 A 87 B 88 C

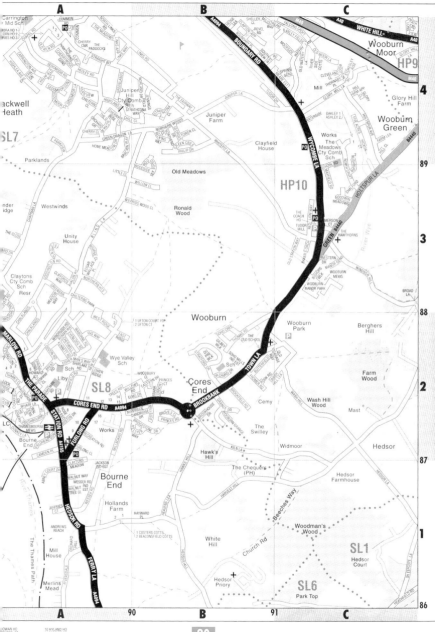

A   B   C

Ridgeway

SN7   Uffington Down

Long Plantation

4

Woolstone Hill Barn

SN6

Pingoose Covert

85

Kingston Warren

Jacknen Barren

Gallops

OX12

Gallops

Kingston Warren Down

3

Gallops

Gallops

Woolstone Down

84

Compton Close

Knighton Down

Gallops

2

Whit Coombe

Wellbottom Down

Gallops

83

Knighton Bushes Plantation

RG17

Lambourn Valley Way

1

Baldback Covert

Post D

Maddle Farm

Post O Bore

Parkfarm Down

Gallops

82

Weathercock Hill

29   A   30   B   31   C

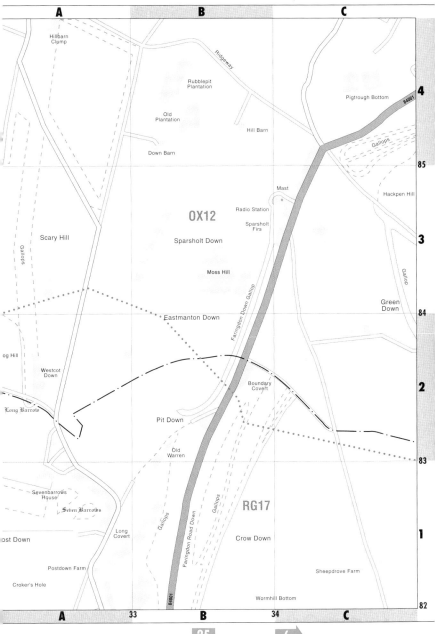

A B C

Hillbarn
Clump

Ridgeway

Rubblepit
Plantation

4

Old
Plantation

Pigtrough Bottom

B4001

Hill Barn

Gallops

Down Barn

85

Mast

Hackpen Hill

OX12

Radio Station

Sparsholt
Firs

Scary Hill

Sparsholt Down

3

Gallops

Moss Hill

Gallop

Green
Down

Eastmanton Down

84

Faringdon Down Gallop

og Hill

Westcot
Down

Boundary
Covert

2

Long Barrow

Pit Down

Old
Warren

83

Sevenbarrows
House

RG17

Seven Barrows

Gallops

Long
Covert

Crow Down

1

ost Down

Gallops

Faringdon Road Down

Postdown Farm

Sheepdrove Farm

Croker's Hole

B4001

Wormhill Bottom

82

A 33 B 34 C

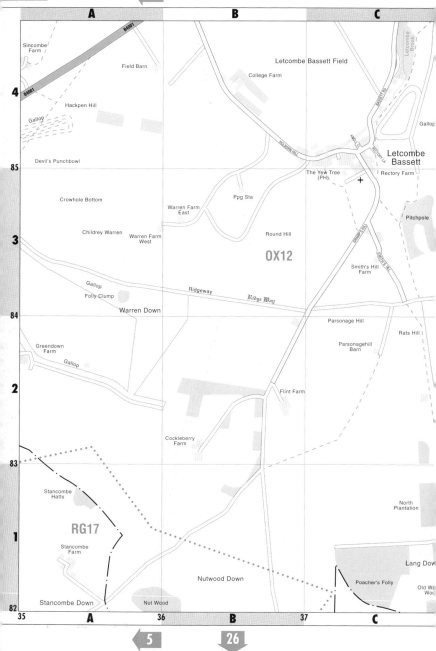

5

A

B

C

B4001

Sincombe
Farm

B4001

Field Barn

Letcombe Bassett Field

College Farm

Letcombe
Brook

4

Hackpen Hill

Gallop

Gallop

BASSETT RD

85

Devil's Punchbowl

HOLBORN HILL

MAND

The Yew Tree
(PH).

LA

BECTON LA

Letcombe
Bassett

Rectory Farm

+

Crowhole Bottom

Ppg Sta

Warren Farm
East

Pitchpole

3

Childrey Warren

Warren Farm
West

Round Hill

OX12

GRAMP STREET

SMITHS RD

Smith's Hill
Farm

Gallop

Ridgeway

Ridge Way

Folly Clump

84

Warren Down

Parsonage Hill

Rats Hill

Greendown
Farm

Parsonagehill
Barn

Gallop

2

Flint Farm

Cockleberry
Farm

83

Stancombe
Hatts

North
Plantation

RG17

1

Stancombe
Farm

Lang Dov

Poacher's Folly

Old Wa
Woc

Nutwood Down

82

Stancombe Down

Nut Wood

35

A

36

B

37

C

5

26

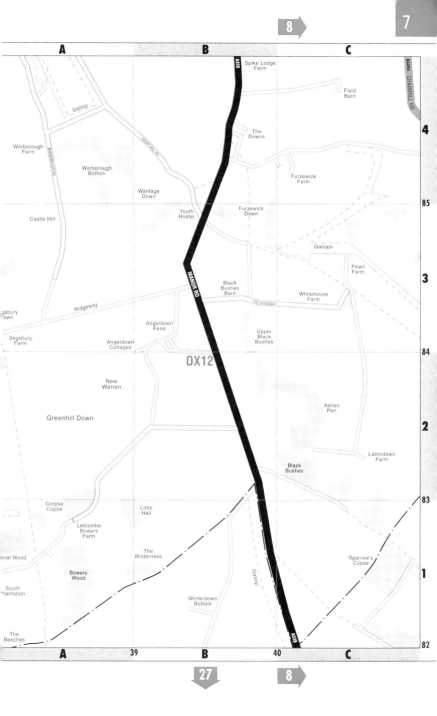

A   B   C

A358

B4494 CHAINHILL RD

Spike Lodge Farm

Field Barn

4

The Downs

Furzewick Farm

CHAIN HILL RD

Warborough Farm

Warborough Bottom

Wantage Down

Furzewick Down

85

Youth Hostel

Castle Hill

Gallops

Pewit Farm

3

MANOR RD

Black Bushes Barn

Whitehouse Farm

gsbury own

Ridgeway

THE RIDGEWAY

Segsbury Farm

Angeldown Farm

Upper Black Bushes

Angeldown Cottages

84

OX12

New Warren

Ashen Pen

Greenhill Down

2

Lattindown Farm

Corpse Copse

Little Hall

83

Letcombe Bowers Farm

Black Bushes

nal Wood

The Wilderness

Sparrow's Copse

Bowers Wood

Gallop

1

South Plantation

Winterdown Bottom

The Beeches

A358

82

A   39   B   40   C

A   B   C

Droveway Hill

Coldharbour Road

4   CHANN HILL RD   B4494

Goddard's Road

Chalkhill
Barn

Resr

Long Valley
Down

Co
P
W

Gallop

BITHAM RD

Jew's
Harp

Ardington
Down

The
Sycamores

85

Midsummer
Wood

Resr

3
Ridgeway

Ridgeway
Down

Middlehill
Down

* Monument

Betterton
Down

Wether
Down

Old Street

P

Yew
Down

84

OX12

Mead Platt

The Warren

Lattin
Down

Triangle
Wood

Betterton Copse

2

Mast

Lockinge
Kiln Farm

Farnborough
Furze Down

Lockinge
Down

83

Little Coombe
Farm

Moonlight
Barn

1

Coombe
Down

DOWNSLANE RD

Coombe
Lodge

B4494

Farnborough
Hall

82

41   A   42   B   43   C

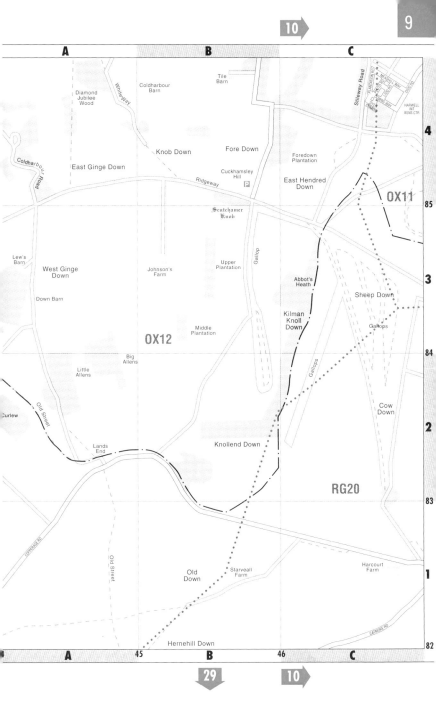

A

B

C

Diamond
Jubilee
Wood

White Way

Coldharbour
Barn

Tile
Barn

Shefford Road

Silleway Road

MERRICK WAY
BLANDFORD WAY
PRIMROSE WAY
PORTWAY

HARWELL
INT
BSNS CTR

4

Coldharbour Road

East Ginge Down

Knob Down

Fore Down

Ridgeway

Cuckhamsley
Hill
P

Foredown
Plantation

East Hendred
Down

Foredown

OX11

85

Lew's
Barn

West Ginge
Down

Johnson's
Farm

Scutchamer
Knob

Upper
Plantation

Gallop

Abbot's
Heath

Sheep Down

3

Down Barn

OX12

Middle
Plantation

Kilman
Knoll
Down

Gallops

Gallops

84

Big
Allens

Little
Allens

Curlew

Old Street

Lands
End

Knollend Down

Cow
Down

2

RG20

83

DUNSTABLE RD

Old Street

Old
Down

Starveall
Farm

Harcourt
Farm

1

CATMORE RD

Hernehill Down

82

A

45

B

46

C

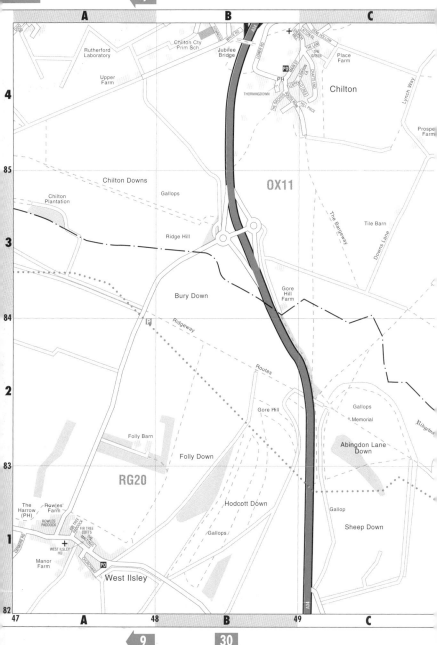

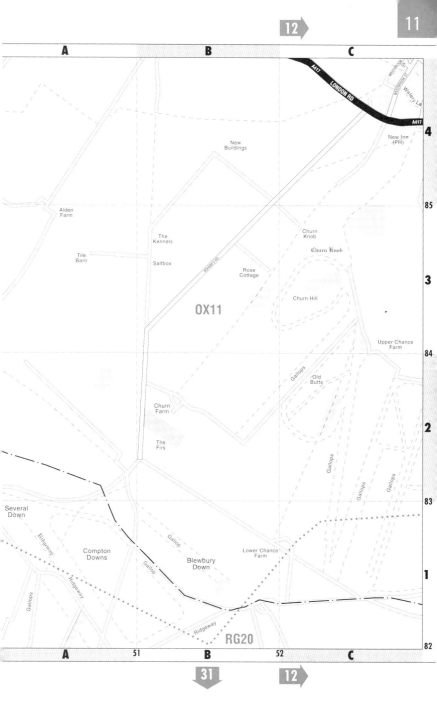

A   B   C

4

85

3

84

2

83

1

82

OX11

RG20

New
Buildings

Alden
Farm

The
Kennels

Tile
Barn

Saltbox

Rose
Cottage

Churn
Knob

Churn Knob

Churn Hill

Upper Chance
Farm

Gallops

Old
Butts

Churn
Farm

The
Firs

Gallops

Gallops

Gallops

Several
Down

Ridgeway

Compton
Downs

Gallop

Gallop

Blewbury
Down

Lower Chance
Farm

Ridgeway

Gallops

Ridgeway

New Inn
(PH)

A417

LONDON RD

A417

WESTBROOK DR

WESTBROOK ST

Watery La

| A | B | C |

RECTORY LA

Copsestile Farm

PO

THE CLOSE DOWNS VIEW

Aston Tirrold

CHURCH END WATT'S LA

+ Blewbury

PH

A4016

A417 LONDON RD

TREBLE HO TERR

BLEWBURY HILL

Hunt's Grave

Golf Driving Range

Blewbury Barn

4

DOWNMOOR DR

WHITE SHOT

Downside Farm

Baldon Hill

Lid's Down

Gallop

Carrimers Farm

85

Riddle Hill

OX11

Chalk Hill Bottom

Sheepcot Farm

3

Woodway Hostel

Woodway

Lower Hill Barn

Hogtrough Bottom

84

Gallop

Upper Hill Barn

Big Bull Hill

The Plantation

2

Oven Bottom

Langdon Hill

Gallop

Gallops

Aston Upthorpe Downs

83

The Fair Mile

Unhill Bottom

Gallops

Gallop

Fuller's Firs

1

RG20

Lowbury Hill

RG8

Dean's Bottom

Ridgeway

82

| A | B | C |
| 53 | 54 | 55 |

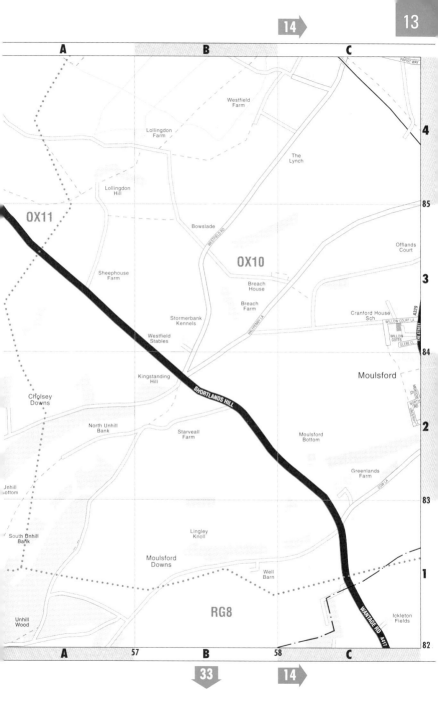

13

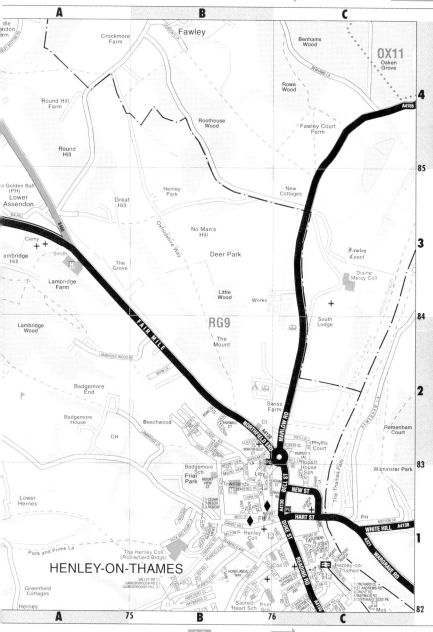

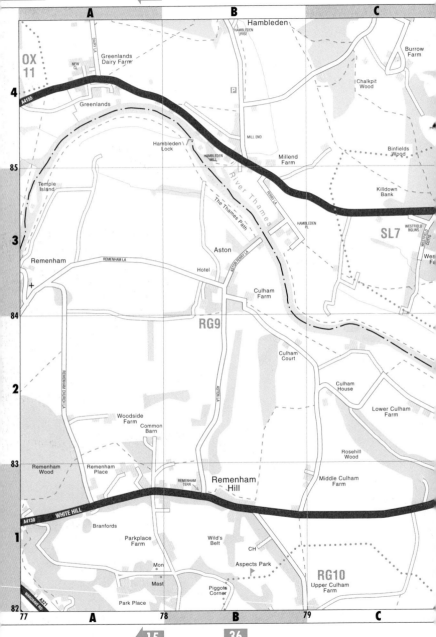

OX
11

A4155

Hambleden

HAMBLEDEN RISE

Burrow
Farm

NEW
GL

Greenlands
Dairy Farm

Chalkpit
Wood

Greenlands

P

Hambleden
Lock

MILL END

HAMBLEDEN
MILL

Millend
Farm

Binfields
Wood

Temple
Island

River Thames

Killdown
Bank

WESTFIELD
BGLWS

SL7

The Thames Path

HAMBLEDEN
PL

WESTFIELD
COTTS

Aston

Wes
Fe

Remenham

REMENHAM LA

Hotel

ASTON FERRY LA

Culham
Farm

RG9

ASTON LA

Culham
Court

Culham
House

Lower Culham
Farm

REMENHAM CHURCH LA

Woodside
Farm

Common
Barn

Rosehill
Wood

Remenham
Wood

Remenham
Place

REMENHAM
TERR

Remenham
Hill

Middle Culham
Farm

A4130

WHITE HILL

Branfords

Parkplace
Farm

Wild's
Belt

CH

Mon

Aspects Park

RG10

Mast

Piggots
Corner

Upper Culham
Farm

Park Place

A321

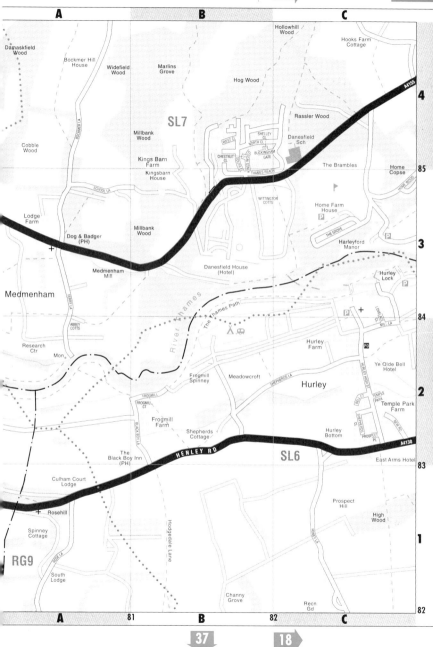

18

A · B · C

Damaskfield Wood

Bockmer Hill House

Widefield Wood

Marlins Grove

Hollowhill Wood

Hog Wood

Hooks Farm Cottage

A4155

SL7

Rassler Wood

Cobble Wood

Millbank Wood

SHELLEY CL
NORTH CL
WEST CL
BUCKINGHAM GATE
CHESTNUT CL

Danesfield Sch

Kings Barn Farm

Kingsbarn House

Thames Reach

The Brambles

Home Copse

HOME WOOD

SCHOOL LA

WITTINGTON COTTS

Home Farm House

Lodge Farm

Dog & Badger (PH)

Millbank Wood

THE GROVE

Harleyford Manor

Medmenham Mill

Danesfield House (Hotel)

Hurley Lock

Medmenham

River Thames

The Thames Path

Hurley Farm

ABBEY COTTS

P

LONG DEL CL
MILL LA

PO

Research Ctr

Mon

Ye Olde Bell Hotel

FERRY LA

Frogmill Spinney

Meadowcroft

SHEPHERDS LA

HURLEY

HURLEY HIGH ST

FREES CT
TEMPLE PARK

Temple Park Farm

FROGMILL CT
FROGMILL

BLACK BOY LA

Frogmill Farm

Shepherds Cottage

Hurley Bottom

SHEPHERDS

PROSPECT PL

WEIR RD

A4130

The Black Boy Inn (PH)

HENLEY RD

SL6

East Arms Hotel

Culham Court Lodge

Rosehill

Prospect Hill

High Wood

HONEY LA

Hodgedale Lane

RG9

ROSE LA

Spinney Cottage

South Lodge

Channy Grove

Recn Gd

A · 81 · B · 82 · C

37
18

4
85
3
84
2
83
1
82

A   B   C

HIGHFIELD PARK
THE RUSHES
POUND LA
PIKE LA
TICKET CL
PERCH CL
BEECHWOOD DR
HENLEY RD
Hooks Corner
A4155
THE HEIGHTS
Sentry Hill
Lower Lodge
LOWER POUND LA
Pens Place
RIVERMEAD
QUARRY WOOD RD
Lock Island
Longr Scout B Activit
STONEY WARE RD
MARLOW RD

4

East Lodge
Harleford Lane
Stoney Ware
Bisham CE Prim Sch
Bisham Abbey National Sports Ctr
PH
Town Farm
Bisham

85

HOMEWOOD
Lake Grounds Farm
THE LAKES
SL7
Bisham Abbey
BISHAM GN
Fultness Wood
EAST PADDOCK
Th Hoo

The Garden Cottage
The Thames Path
River Thames
TEMPLE LA
MILL WAY
A404

3

Marina
Temple Lock
TEMPLE MILL ISLAND
TEMPLE MILL COTTS
Temple Park
Temple
Princess Elizabeth's Well
Inkydown Wood
Park Farm

Weir
STABLE COTTS
BUCKINGHAM LA

84

Temple Farm
Park Wood

Sewage Works

2

HURLEY LA
MARLOW RD
The Lodge
Goulding's Wood

Hyde Farm

83

HENLEY RD
CH
A4130
Black Horse Lodge
Dungrovehill Wood
DUNGROVEHILL LA
SL6
Lee Farm

1

Speen Hill
A404
Carpenter's Wood
St Timoth

Applehouse Hill
Red Lion (PH)
Pinkneys Court
LEE LA
DARLING LA

Berkshire Coll of Agriculture
Applehouse Farm
BURCHETTS GREEN RD
A4130

82

83   A   84   B   85   C

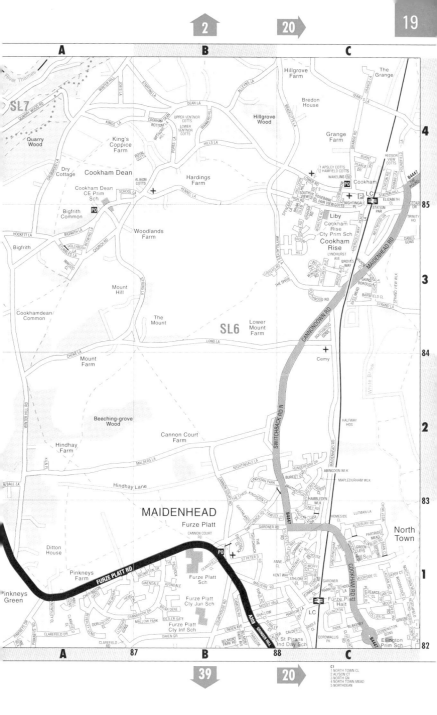

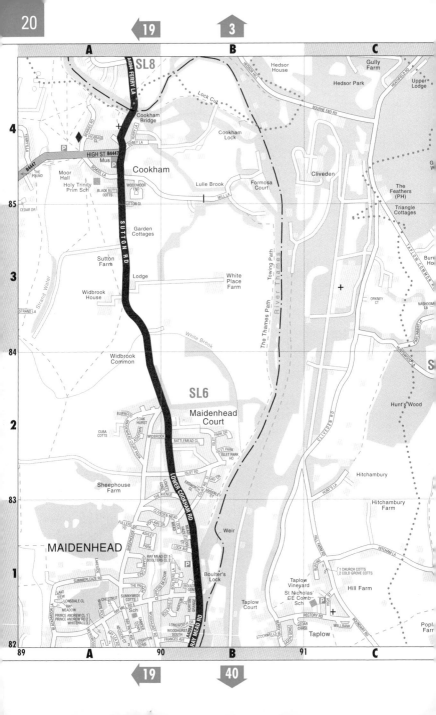

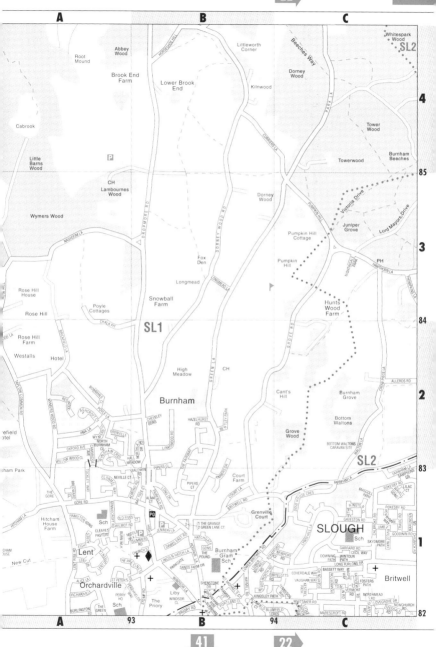

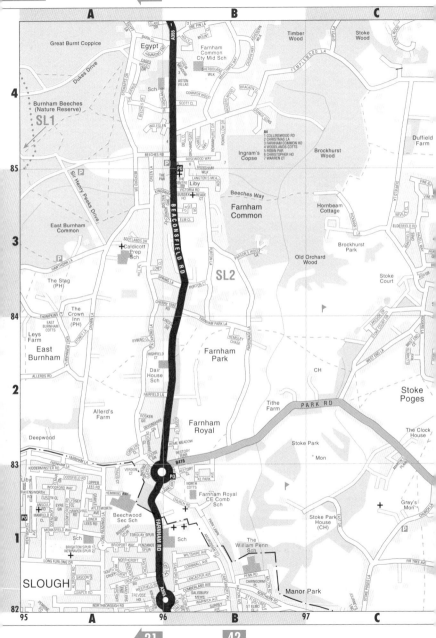

A B C

Great Burnt Coppice

Egypt

Farnham Common Cty Mid Sch

Timber Wood

Stoke Wood

Dukes Drive

4

Burnham Beeches
(Nature Reserve)

SL1

Sch

ASTON VILLAS

Ingram's Copse

Brockhurst Wood

Duffield Farm

85

Sir Henry Peeks Drive

Beeches Rd

Rosewood Way

Liby

SUSSEX READE CT

Beeches Way

Farnham Common

Hornbeam Cottage

East Burnham Common

3

Caldicott Prep Sch

BEACONSFIELD RD

SL2

Parson's Wood La

Old Orchard Wood

Brockhurst Park

Stoke Court

The Stag (PH)

Springe La

Cherry Tree La

Purton Ct

84

The Crown Inn (PH)

Leys Farm

East Burnham

Farnham Park La

Kemsley Chase

Farnham Park

CH

Park Rd

2

Allerds Rd

Dair House Sch

Fairfield La

Allerd's Farm

Deepwood

Rosken Gr

Devonshire Av

Farnham Royal

Tithe Farm

Stoke Poges

Stoke Park

Mon

The Clock House

Home Meadow

83

Kidderminster Rd

Farnham La

Ravensworth

Liby

Woodford Way

Dodsfield Rd

Upper Lees Rd

Verdon Ct

Hemming Way

B416

PO

Rectory Terr

North Cotts

Ke Park

Stoke Park House (CH)

Gray's Mon

PO

Mansfield Cl

Eyre Gn

Hawkshill Rd

Lower Lees Rd

Beechwood Sec Sch

Church Rd

Farnham Royal CE Comb Sch

1

Sch

Brighton Spur

Newhaven Spur 2

Bridport Way

Torquay Spur

Penzance Spur

FARNHAM RD

Sch

Wiltshire Ave

The William Penn Sch

Penn Rd

Cairngorm Pl

Stoke Poges La

PO

Long Furlong Dr

Northcroft

Cornwall Ave

Lancaster Ave

Manor Park

Fir Tree Ave

SLOUGH

Cowper Rd

Westfield Rd

Trevuse Rd

Cumberland Ave

Salisbury Mews

Warwick Ave

Surrey Ave

St Elmo

82

Northborough Rd

A355

95 A 96 B 97 C

B4
1 COLLINSWOOD RD
2 CHRISTMAS LA
3 FARNHAM COMMON HO
4 WOODLANDS COTTS
5 ROBIN PAR
6 CHRISTOPHER HO
7 WARREN CT

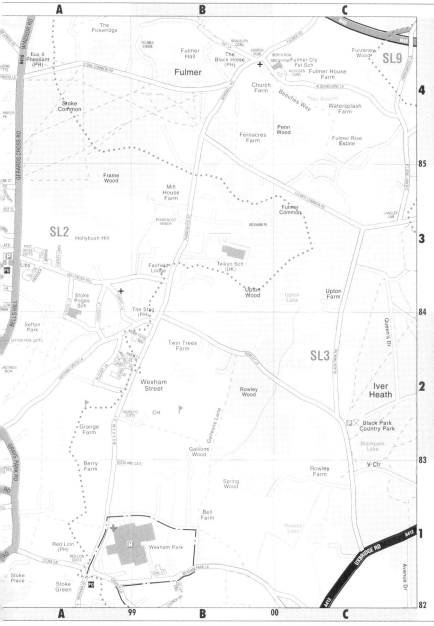

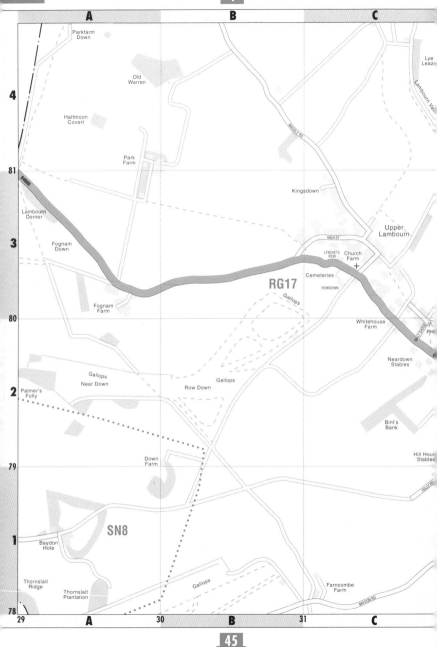

A   B   C

4

81

3

80

2

79

1

78

29   A   30   B   31   C

Parkfarm Down

Old Warren

Halfmoon Covert

Park Farm

Lambourn Corner

Fognam Down

Fognam Farm

Gallops

Near Down

Palmer's Folly

Down Farm

SN8

Baydon Hole

Thornslait Ridge

Thornslait Plantation

Gallops

Row Down

Gallops

MARSH RD

Kingsdown

Upper Lambourn

HIGH ST

LYNCHETS VIEW

Church Farm

Cemeteries

ROWDOWN

RG17

Gallops

Whitehouse Farm

Neardown Stables

Bint's Bank

Hill House Stables

FOLLY RD

Farncombe Farm

BAYDON RD

Lye Leaze

Lambourn Valley

MALT SHOVEL LA

PH

B4000

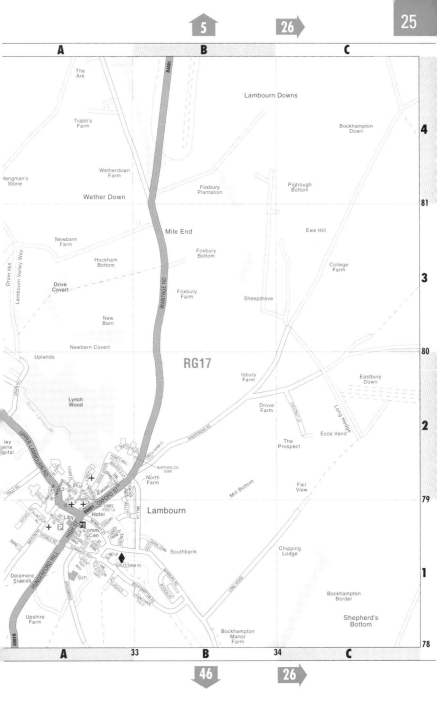

A
B
C

4

The Ark

Lambourn Downs

Bockhampton Down

Trabb's Farm

Hangman's Stone

Wetherdown Farm

Wether Down

Foxbury Plantation

Pigtrough Bottom

81

Newbarn Farm

Mile End

Ewe Hill

Drain Hill

Lambourn Valley Way

Hockham Bottom

Foxbury Bottom

College Farm

3

Drive Covert

Foxbury Farm

Sheepdrove

New Barn

Newbarn Covert

Uplands

80

RG17

Isbury Farm

Eastbury Down

Lynch Wood

River Lambourn

Drove Farm

Long Hedge

2

SHEEPDROVE RD

NORTH FARM CL

The Prospect

Ecce Venit

CHESTNUT CL

UPPER LAMBOURN RD

HONEY'S HILL

NORTHFIELDS TERR

North Farm

Fair View

79

ley ine pital

B4001 OXFORD ST

P

ST Liby

PO

Hotel

Comm Cen

Lambourn

Mill Bottom

MILL LA

THREE POST LA

Southbank

Chipping Lodge

1

HUNGERFORD HILL

Delamere Stables

Sch

WALES FARM RD

END LA

LONG HEDGE

Bockhampton Border

Shepherd's Bottom

Upshire Farm

B4000

Bockhampton Manor Farm

78

A
33
B
34
C

A   B   C

Warren Farm
(Beef Testing Centre)

Cockcrow
Bottom

Mere End
Down

4

Stancombe
Down

OX12

81

Littleworth
Cottage

Old
Warren

3

Warren Down

Eastbury
Bottom

Warren
Farm

Warren
Plantation

Washmore
Hill

Cranes
Copse

Grange
Farm

80

Eastbury
Grange

Eastbury
Down

Cranes
Farm

Gallop

RG17

Pound's
Farm

2

Poors'
Furze

East Garston
Down

79

Oakhe
Cop

1

Eastbury Fields

Winterdown
Bottom

Gallops

Hasham
Copse

78

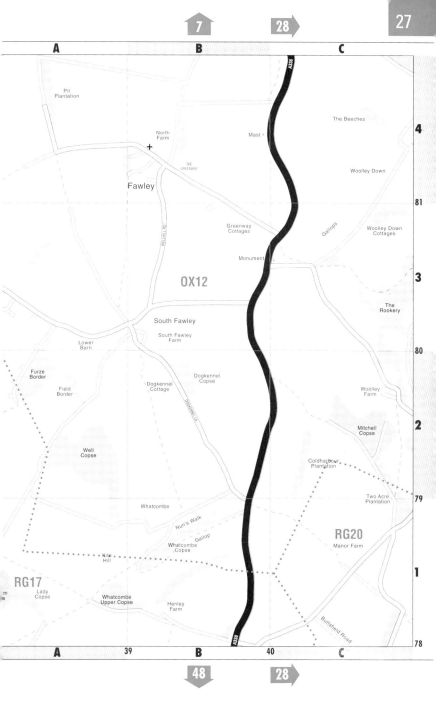

A
B
C

4

The Beeches

Pit
Plantation

Mast

Woolley Down

North
Farm

Trd
GREENWAY

81

Fawley

Greenway
Cottages

Gallops

Woolley Down
Cottages

WELL END RD

Monument

OX12

3

South Fawley

The
Rookery

Lower
Barn

South Fawley
Farm

80

Furze
Border

Dogkennel
Copse

Field
Border

Dogkennel
Cottage

Woolley
Farm

DOGKENNEL LA

Mitchell
Copse

2

Well
Copse

Coldharbour
Plantation

Two Acre
Plantation

79

Whatcombe

Nun's Walk

RG20

Whatcombe
Copse

Gallop

Manor Farm

Kite
Hill

1

RG17

Lady
Copse

Whatcombe
Upper Copse

Henley
Farm

Buttsfield Road

A338

78

A
39
B
40
C

A   B   C

Farnborough Down

Keepers
Cottage

B4494

Lower
Farm

Upper
Farm

Farnborough

Farnborough
Downs
Farm

Upper
Grove

4

COOMBE HILL

Boardhouse
Plantation

81

California
Farm

Common
Plantation

Liddiard's
Green

OX12

Nine Acre
Wood

Lower
Barn

3

Coombefield
Plantation

Brightwalton
Common

Deer Park

COMMON LA

Brown's Lane

Woolley
House

80

Woolley
Park

Woolley Home
Farm

Chalkpit
Clump

RG20

2

The
Rectory

LONG LA

Long
Plantation

Water Tower

Brightwalton CE
Prim Sch

Manor
Farm

BLUETTS
LEG LANE

Dunmore
Barn

Brightwalton

79

Sparrowbill
Copse

1

Spray
Wood

HONESTY BOTTOM

Malthouse
Farm

SPARROWBILL

Green
Farm

Brightwalton
Green

FUDDING LA

Folly
Farm

HOLT LA

SPRAY LA

Lime Tree
Farm

78

Southend

A
B
C

OX12

Whiteshute Row

Parkwood

The Barracks

4

Old Street

Old Down Row

Heath Copse

CATMORE RD

Hodcott Copse

81

Wickslett Copse

Wickslett Row North

Hodcott Buildings

3

Woolvers Borders

Catmore

High Robins

Old Street

Woolvers Barn

+
Catmore Farm

Dark Lane

80

RG20

Parson's Row

Round Copse

Lilley

Warren Row

Redlane Barn

Fox & Cubs (PH)

Witnam's Copse

Wilkins Barne

Redlane Wood

Redlane Road

Green Lane

2

ley pse

Hunham Copse

LONG LA

Witnam's Barn

The Broadway

79

Earl's Grove

Larches

Heath Barn

Old Street Lane

SHEEP LEAS LA

Barrow Hill

Whitelands

SPARROWBILL

Rowdown Farm

1

REEDS RD

Hailey Copse

PEASEMORE HILL

HALL LA

78

A
45
B
46
C

A
B
C

4

Hodcott
House

West Ilsley
Stables

Windmill
House

A34

81

Inn

FIDLER'S LA

COW LA

STANMORE RD

THE GALLOPS

Sch

CHURCH

East Ilsley

Woolvers Road

Yewtree
Hill

Beechtree
Hedge
Farm

Windmill
Down

3

BALLEY RD

Ilsley
Barn

RG20

80

Nutfield
Down

Shrill
Down

Dennistor

Green Han

Lower
Copse

2

Redlane Road

William's
Wood

Little Ashridge
Wood

North Stanmore
Farm

79

ILSLEY RD

Stanmore

South Stanmore
Farm

STANMORE RD

Halfpenny Catch Lane

1

Ashridge
Farm

Cemy

Beedon
Manor

78
47

A

48

B

49

C

A34

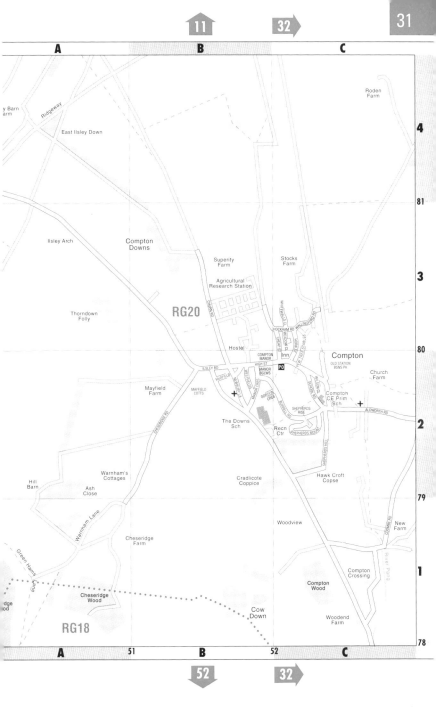

A   B   C

Roden
Downs

Warren
Farm

Town
Copse

4

Ridgeway

81

Starveall

Streatley
Warren

3

Crows
Foot

Bower
Farm

RG20   RG8

Grey
Ladies

80

Lower
Farm

The Bell Inn
(PH)

Hungerford
Green

The
Red Lion
(PH)

Applepie
Hill

Parsonage
Green

PO

BELL LA

THE GITER

2

DOWNE RD

PARSONAGE RD

Dumworth
Farm

Pibworth
Farm

Aldworth

79

Woodrows
Farm

Fayley
Borde

Aces
High

The
Four Points
(PH)

Four
Points

Foxborough
Copse

1

Southfield
Shaw

HAW LA

Lower Point
Cottage

De La
Beche

B4009

Thorn
Hill

RG18

78

53   A 54   B 55   C

33
14

A
B
C

A329
Streatley Farm
Cleeve Lock
B4009
WALLINGFORD RD

4
SPRINGHILL RD
IONFIELD RD
Battle Farm
Wroxhills Wood

TOWNSEND RD
SIDNEY RD
ICKNIELD RD
PO
ELVENDON RD
Battle House

THREE GABLES LA
Cleeve Mill
MILL
Lower Bungalows
Goring CE Prim Sch
THE RISE
BATTLE RD

Streatley
CLEEVE
CROFT CL
Battle Plantation

A417
A329
Cleeve
Gri Wo

NARTIMER RD
HOWGATE DR
MILLDOWN RD

81
CLEEVE
ELMHURST RD
MILLDOWN AVE
FERNE CL

Goring Lock
MALLERS CT
NUN'S ACRE
UPPER RED CROSS RD
FARNE CL
MEADOW CL

Hotel
The Birches
GLEBE RIDE
WALNUT TREE CT
FARM RD SLOAN
VALLEY CL
READING RD
North Cottage
B4

A329
MAPLE CT
B4009
B4526

B4009 STREATLEY HILL
HIGH ST
Streatley & Goring Bridge
HIGH ST
ST ANDREWS GREEN
WHITEHILLS GREEN
Goring
Burntwood

HILL GDNS
THE BULL MEADOW
PO
THE ARCADE
P
Cemy

YH
READING RD
FERRY LA
STATION RD
LIME TREE RD

3
THE BIRCHES
GABLES CL
LITTLE CROFT RD
VICTORIA RD
Goring & Streatley

GATEHAMPTON RD
Upper Gatehampton Farm

80
RG8
Gatehampton Farm
Primrosehill Shaw

Holies Hanging
River Thames
Gatehampton Manor
Hattonhill Shaw

Hotel
The Grotto
Towing Path
The Thames Path

2
Church Farm
Lower Hartslo Wooc

Rottendown Hill Plantation
Grove Farm
The Crown Inn (PH)

79
Basil Corner
Lower Basildon

Howe Grove Wood
GARSTOCK VIEW

Harecroft Wood
Hill Fields Farm
PARK WALL LA

1
RIDGE END LA
Basildon Park

Tomb Farm
Harley Hill Wood
Basildon House
Basildon Park
Beale Park Wildlife Park

78
WHITEMOOR LA
THE RIDGE

59
A
60
B
61
C

33
55

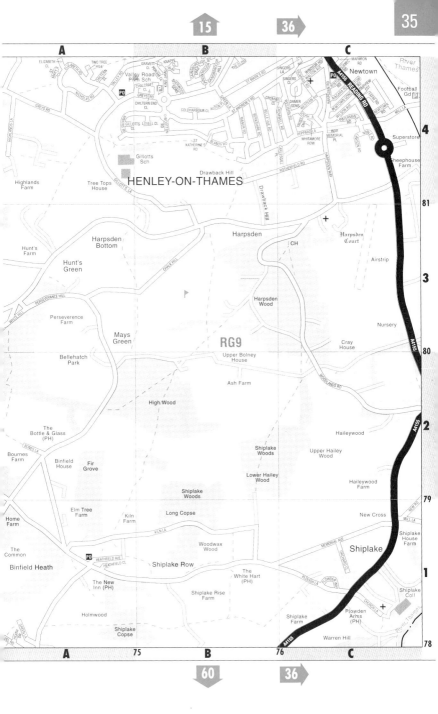

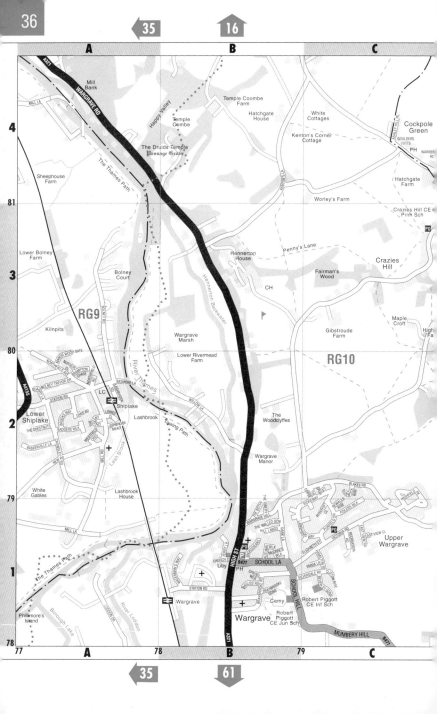

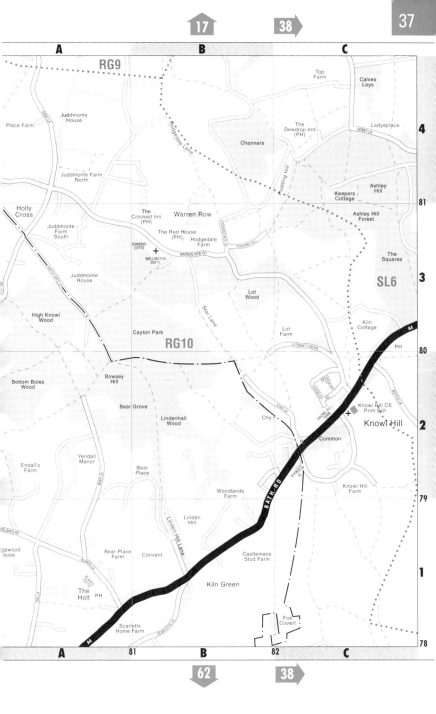

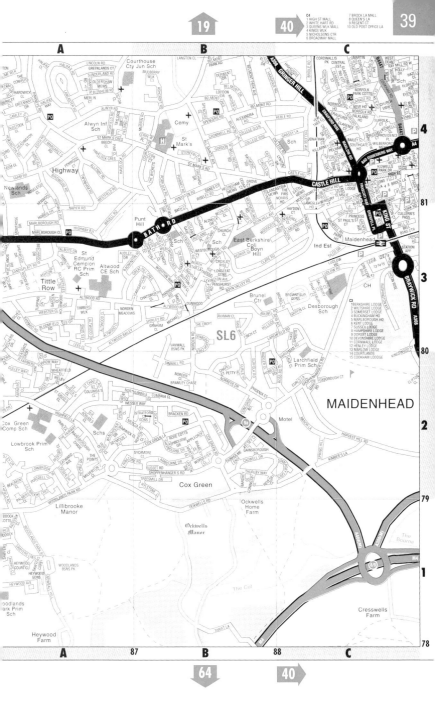

SL6

MAIDENHEAD

Flood Relief Scheme
Due for completion
Late 2001

River Thames

The Thames Path

Bray Wick

Bray

SL4

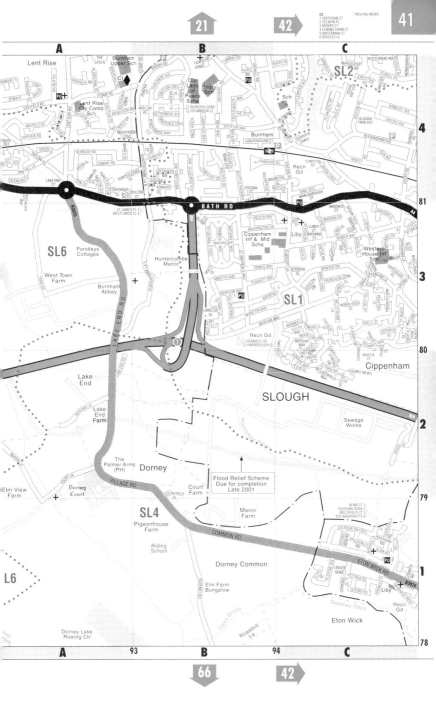

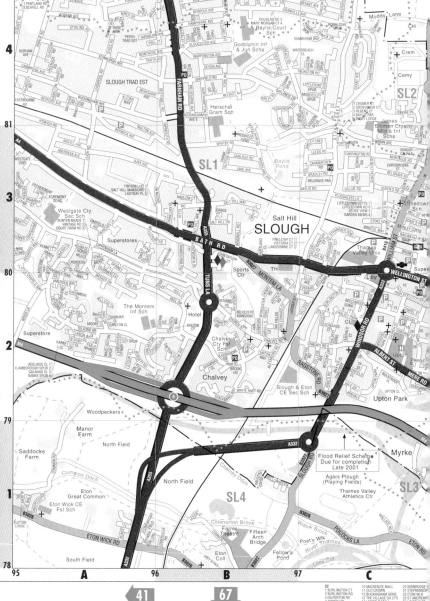

SL2

SL1

SLOUGH
Salt Hill

SL3
Myrke

SL4

C2
1 BURLINGTON CT
2 BURLINGTON RD
3 HILPERTON RD
4 TOWER HO
5 ASHBOURNE HO
6 SHAFTESBURY CT
7 MOUNSTOWN CT
8 PRUDENTIAL BLDGS
9 MACKENZIE ST
10 MACKENZIE MALL
11 OLD CROWN
12 BUCKINGHAM GDNS
13 THE VILLAGE SH CTR
14 LEOPOLD MALL
15 CURZON MALL
16 CHANDOS MALL
17 TOWN SQ
18 VICTORIA ST
19 BISHAM CT
20 BEMBRIDGE C
21 STEPHENSON
22 ETON WLK
23 ST ANDREW
24 LINCOLN CT
25 LOCKSLEY C
26 SPRUCE CT
27 DARTMOUTH
28 ALBERT CL
29 MANOR CT

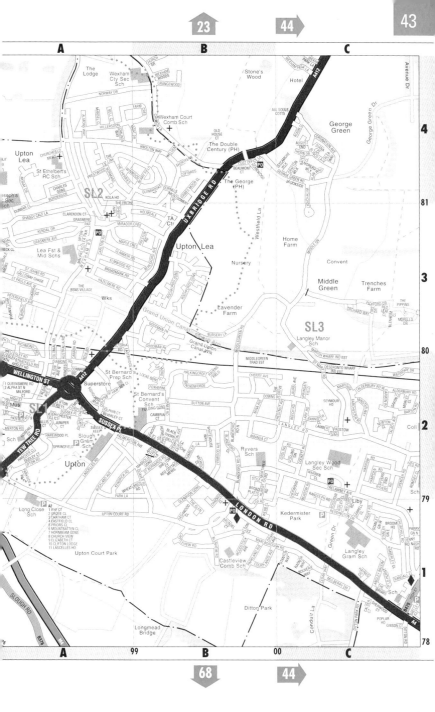

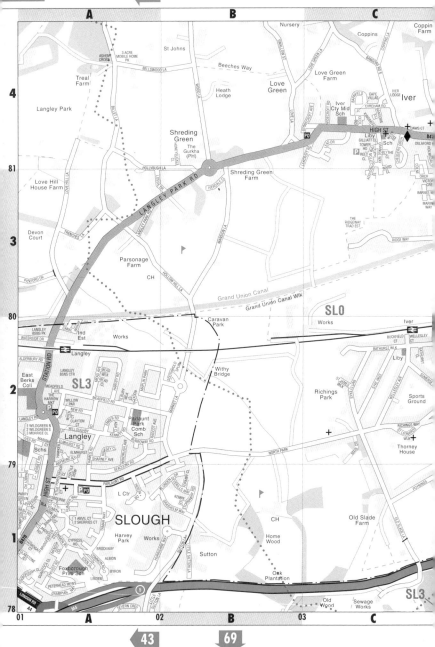

A B C

4

81

3

80 SL0

2 SL3

79

1 SLOUGH

78

01 A 02 B 03 C

Nursery
Coppins
Coppin Farm
St Johns
Beeches Way
Love Green Farm
3 ACRE MOBILE HOME PK
ASHEN CROSS
Treal Farm
BELLSWOOD LA
Love Green
Iver Cty Mid Sch
EVREHAM RD
Iver Lodge
CAPE VILLAS
Iver
Langley Park
Heath Lodge
WOOD LA
HIGH ST
Liby
Sch
DELAFORD
DAWS CT
B470
Shreding Green
The Gurkha (PH)
GILLIATT CL
TOWER RD
REED CL
VICTORIE
DROH
BARNES WI
MARINE WAY
Love Hill House Farm
HOLLYBUSH LA
Shreding Green Farm
IVERDALE CL
LANGLEY PARK RD
THE RIDGEWAY TRAD EST
RIDGE WAY
Devon Court
TRENCHES
Parsonage Farm
CH
HOLLOW HILL LA
MANSION LA
Grand Union Canal
Grand Union Canal Wlk
Works
Iver
PIXFORD DR
Caravan Park
WELLESLEY CT
BUCKFIELD CT
Liby
Langley BSNS PK
WATERSIDE DR
CANAL
Ind Est
Works
Withy Bridge
BATHURST WLK
East Berks Coll
Langley
STATION RD
LANGLEY BSNS CTR
SL3
MEAD
THE HARROW MKT
MAIN PK
Richings Park
ST JAMES CL
Sports Ground
ALDERBURY RD
MEADFIELD AVE
WILLOW PAR
NEW RD
CLAYTON
WILLOUGHBY
Parlaunt Park Comb Sch
MARKET LA
RICHINGS WAY
ST LEONARDS WLK
Thorney House
Langley
Schs
1 WILDGREEN N
2 WILDGREEN S
3 MOHRICE CL
ELMHURST CL
SHARNEY AVE
CASEY CL
SEACCOME RD
BURROWAY RD
NORTH PARK
Old Slade Farm
HIGH ST
L Ctr
PARLAUNT RD
CHURCHILL WAY
KENNEDY
Harvey Park
Works
SLOUGH
1 ANVIL CT
2 SKERRIES CT
CYPRESS HO
BROCKWAY
ALBION
BYRON
CONGREVE WAY
Sutton
Home Wood
CH
Old Slade Farm
Foxborough Prim Sch
PETERHEAD MEWS
CRAMPIAN
LINDEN
Oak Plantation
OLD SLADE LA
Old Wood
Sewage Works
SL3
LONDON RD
A4
M4
SEVERN CRES
SUTTON LA
5

A
B
C

SN8

Farncombe Down
Gallops
Gallops

Windmill Farm

Farn Combe

Hatchets Cornor

B4000

Lodge Down

Coppington Down

4

Lodge Farm
Lodge Copse

Dean Stubbing Copse

Kingwood House

The Kingwood Stud

77

Woodlands Lodge

PLATT LA
Gallop

FARM ST

Rookery

rickkiln opse

Great West Wood

Little West Wood

Great Noakes Copse

3

Common Barn Copse

Hadley Farm

Fox Farm

Lambourn Woodlands

eygre ose

Badger Hole

Mast

Membury Service Area

Batten's Farm

76

RG17

Baydon Wood
St John's Green

Works

Works

The Hare and Hounds (PH) Lyedowns

B4000
LEDOWN LA

Copse Ground Wood

Membury Airfield (disused)

Dixon's Farm

2

Hillier's Copse

Paxlet Plantation

Walls Copse

Membury

AERIAL BSNS PK

Works

M4

Membur

Cuckoo Copse

75

SN8

Membury

Petteville Copse

ridge Hill cken Farm

Membury Farm

Leigh Farm

Membury House

Moon's Copse

Lyckweed Farm

HALF MILE RD

1

Balak Farm

ard's pse

White House

Membury Lodge

Pit Cottage

Marridge Hill Wood

Witcha Copse

Pit (dis)

74

A
30
B
31
C

A
B
C

Winterdown
Barn

Jimmy's
Farm

Lone Barry
Farm

Coldborough Hill

Furze
Border

4

Lambourn Valley Way
Manor
Farm

+

77

Coldborough
Farm

Westfield
Farm

ROGER'S LA

+

PO

COLL

East
Garston

3

Queen's Arms (PH)

Parsonage
Farm

River Lambourn

Peake's
Border

Maidencourt
Farm

76

RG17

Gold Hill

River
Mead

2

Bottom
Copse

Dore's
Farm

Manor
Farm

Goodings

GOODINGS LA

East Garston
Woodlands

Gallop

75

Grasscroft
Copse

hild's
m

Greenlands Copse

Potter's Cottage

South Hidden
Farm

1

Fieldridge
Copse

A338

HUNGERFORD HILL

Fieldridge Lane

MAN ROAD

N ST

Coldridge
Copse

A338

74

A
36
B
37
C

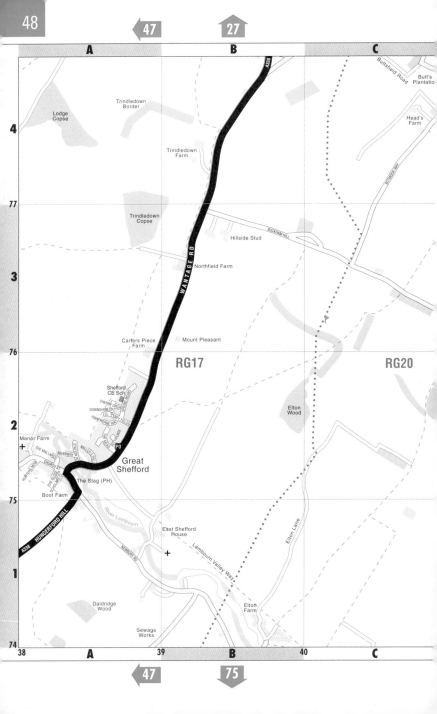

A   B   C

Buttsfield Road
Butt's
Plantatio

4

Lodge
Copse

Trindledown
Border

Head's
Farm

Trindledown
Farm

77

Trindledown
Copse

BUCKHAM HILL

Hillside Stud

WANTAGE RD

Northfield Farm

3

Carters Piece
Farm

Mount Pleasant

76

RG17

RG20

Shefford
CE Sch

Elton
Wood

CHERRY ORCH
DOWNSHIRE
GL. PLACE FIELD CL.
HAWTHORNE WAY

2

Manor Farm
+

THE MALLARD
RIVERWAY
CHURCH ST
MILLERS LEA

PO

Great
Shefford

HUNTS MEW
THE CLOSE
SCHOOL RD
THE TERRACE

The Stag (PH)

Boot Farm

75

Elton Lane

HUNGERFORD HILL

River Lambourn

A338

East Shefford
House

NEWBURY RD

+

Lambourn Valley Way

1

Daldridge
Wood

Elton
Farm

Sewage
Works

74
38   A   39   B   40   C

A
B
C

+ Chaddleworth House
Norris's Farm

UPPER END

NORRIS LA

NORRIS FIELD

HOLT LA

BARR

Brightwalton Holt

Chaddleworth

Yew Tree Farm

Cotswold Farm

GLEBE FIELD

TURNER FIELD

The Ibex (PH)

Chaddleworth St Andrews CE Prim Sch

PO

Tyneys Green

Oak Ash Farm

Grovepit Green

NODMORE

Purley Farm

Wick Lane

+

Leckhampstead Thicket

SHEPHERDS WAY

Wicklane Copse

Leckhampstead Farm

NUTTINGTONS

3

Highfield House

The Green

Leckhampstead

Field Copse

Highfield Farm

PH

PO 3

Hall

Lower Barn

GOOSE LA

JOHNS

HANGMAN'S STONE LA

Stirt Copse

Manor Farm

Hill Farm

76

MILLER CL

Rooksnest Copse

EISENHOWER AVE

RG20

MANOR LA

+

Down Copse

Nodmore Corner

Bassdown Copse

New Barn

2

Poughley Farm

Little Copse

Stony Croft

Rowbury Farm

Paine's Copse

75

Hangman's Stone

Rowbury Farm Cottages

1

Courtoak Farm

74

A
42
B
43
C

A

B

C

Haley
Copse

PEASEMORE HILL

Eastley
Copse

Little Hailey
Copse

WEST VIEW

FIELD RD

HAILEY LA

4

Lower Hailey
Copse

Eastley
House

HATT
CL

PALMER
CL

Fox and Hounds
(PH)

BOLTON
ROW

Drake's
Farm

MEAD CL

HALL GREEN LA

Peasemore

THE ROOKERY

Nightingale
Farm

Prince's
Farm

+

Peasemore House

77

Widows'
Farm

Old Street Lane

PRINCE'S LA

3

Egypt

Bushy
Leaze

Hillgreen
House

MUD LA

Woods Folly
Bungalow

Hillgreen

Windmill
Place

Gidley
Farm

76

Chapel
Farm

RG20

Prior's
Wood

Gidley
Copse

2

New Road

Gidley Lane

75

Chapel
Wood

Hazelhanger
Farm

Ward's
Copse

North Heath
Farm

1

Pope's
Wood

**North
Heath**

Green Lane

SCHOOL RD

Penclose
Wood

B4494

Blue Boar Inn
(PH)

74

B4494

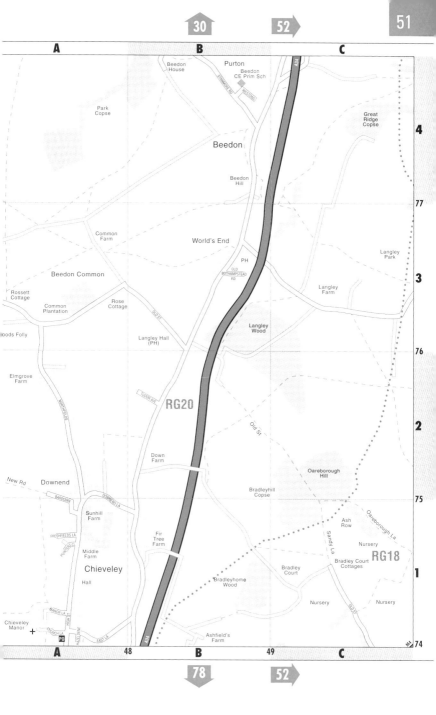

Purton

Beedon House

Beedon CE Prim Sch

Park Copse

Great Ridge Copse

Beedon

4

Beedon Hill

77

Common Farm

World's End

PH

Langley Park

Beedon Common

3

Rossett Cottage

Rose Cottage

OLD ST

Langley Farm

Common Plantation

OLD BOTHAMPSTEAD RD

Langley Wood

Woods Folly

Langley Hall (PH)

76

Elmgrove Farm

TUDOR AVE

RG20

NORTHFIELD RD

Old St

2

Down Farm

Oareborough Hill

New Rd

Downend

Bradleyhill Copse

75

BAYDOWN

DOWNEND LA

Sunhill Farm

Ash Row

Oareborough La

FRESHFIELDS LA

Sandy La

Nursery

RG18

POINTERS CL

Middle Farm

Bradley Court Cottages

Chieveley

Fir Tree Farm

1

Hall

Bradleyhome Wood

Bradley Court

Nursery

OLD ST

Nursery

Chieveley Manor

MANOR LA SCH

HAZEL LANE

CHURCH LA

EAST LA

PO

A29

Ashfield's Farm

M4

74

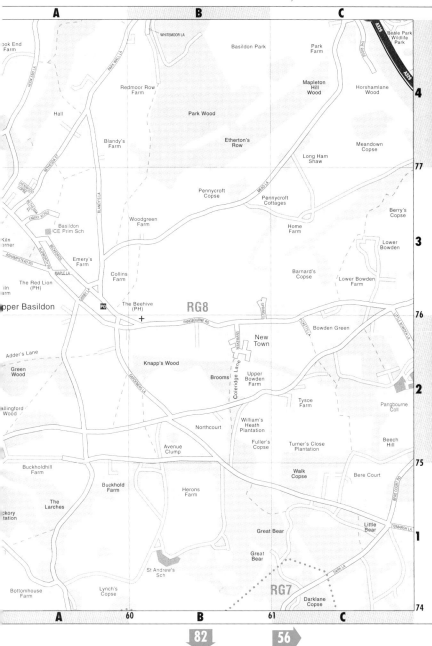

A329
Beale Park
Wildlife Park
A329

WHITEMOOR LA

Basildon Park

Park
Farm

THE RIDGE

4

Redmoor Row
Farm

Mapleton
Hill
Wood

Horshamlane
Wood

Hall

Park Wood

Blandy's
Farm

Etherton's
Row

Meadown
Copse

Long Ham
Shaw

77

Pennycroft
Copse

Pennycroft
Cottages

Berry's
Copse

MAPLE LA

Woodgreen
Farm

Home
Farm

Lower
Bowden

3

Basildon
CE Prim Sch

Kiln
orner

Emery's
Farm

Barnard's
Copse

Lower Bowden
Farm

ASHAMPSTEAD RD

MAPLE LA

Collins
Farm

The Red Lion
(PH)

iln
rm

BLANDY'S LA
BROCKS LA

AMBER LA

pper Basildon

The Beehive
(PH)

RG8

PANGBOURNE RD

SPRINGS

76

Bowden Green

LITTLE BOWDEN LA

STREET

New
Town

BRADMANS

Adder's Lane

Knapp's Wood

Brooms

Upper
Bowden
Farm

Green
Wood

Coleridge Lane

GARDENERS LA

2

Pangbourne
Coll

allingford
Wood

Tysoe
Farm

Northcourt

William's
Heath
Plantation

Avenue
Clump

Fuller's
Copse

Turner's Close
Plantation

Beech
Hill

Buckholdhill
Farm

75

Walk
Copse

Bere Court

Buckhold
Farm

Herons
Farm

BERE COURT RD

The
Larches

ckory
tation

Little
Bear

TIDMARSH LA

Great Bear

1

Bottomhouse
Farm

Lynch's
Copse

St Andrew's
Sch

Great
Bear

DARK LA

RG7

Darklane
Copse

74

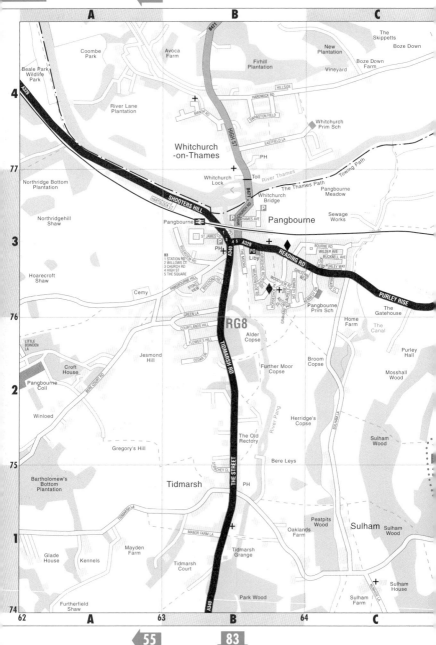

55

A **B** **C**

4

The Skippetts
Boze Down
Coombe
Park
Avoca
Farm
New
Plantation
Boze Down
Farm
Beale Park
Wildlife
Park
Firhill
Plantation
Vineyard
River Lane
Plantation
HILLSIDE
HARDWICK RD
MANOR RD
HIGH ST
GRANISTON FIELD
Whitchurch
Prim Sch
Whitchurch
-on-Thames
EASTFIELD LA

77

PH
River Thames
Towing Path
Northridge Bottom
Plantation
Whitchurch
Lock
Toll
The Thames Path
Pangbourne
Meadow
Whitchurch
Bridge
SHOOTERS HILL
HARTSLOCK CT
Northridgehill
Shaw
Pangbourne
P
THAMES AVE
P
Pangbourne
Sewage
Works

3

St JAMES CL
PH
PO
Liby
BOURNE RD
WILDER AVE
BUCKNELL AVE
READING RD
PURLEY WAY
Hoarecroft
Shaw
83
1 STATION RD
2 WILLOWS CT
3 CHURCH RD
4 HIGH ST
5 THE SQUARE
Cemy
PANGBOURNE HILL
STOKES
VIEW
BEEDONS RD
Pangbourne
Prim Sch
Home
Farm
The Gatehouse
PURLEY RISE

76

GREEN LA
RG8
Alder
Copse
The
Canal
Purley
Hall
COURTLANDS HILL
FLOWER'S LA
CEDAR LA
Jesmond
Hill
Further Moor
Copse
Broom
Copse
Mosshall
Wood
LITTLE
BOWDEN
LA
BERE COURT RD
TIDMARSH RD

2

Croft
House
Pangbourne
Coll
River Pang
Herridge's
Copse
BUCKNELL LA
Sulham
Wood
Winloed

75

Gregory's Hill
The Old
Rectory
Bere Leys
Bartholomew's
Bottom
Plantation
STROHEY CLOSE
THE STREET
Tidmarsh
PH

1

LOMBARDS LA
MANOR FARM LA
Glade
House
Kennels
Mayden
Farm
Tidmarsh
Grange
Tidmarsh
Court
Oaklands
Farm
Peatpits
Wood
Sulham
Sulham
Wood
Furtherfield
Shaw
Park Wood
A340
Sulham
Farm
Sulham
House

74

62 **A** **63** **B** **64** **C**

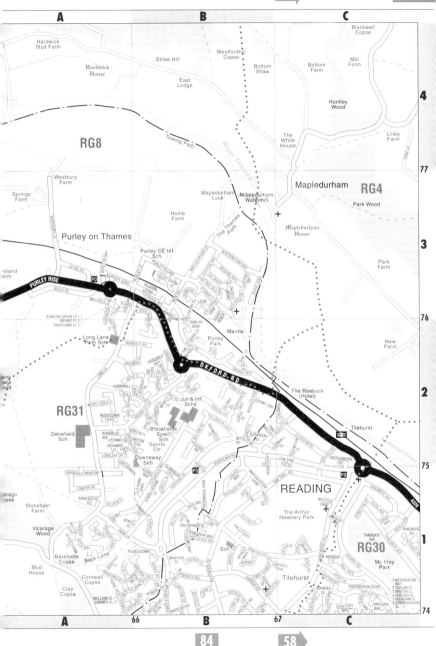

4

77

RG8

Towing Path

River Thames

Mapledurham RG4

Park Wood

Springs Farm

Westbury Farm

Purley on Thames

Home Farm

Mapledurham Lock

Mapledurham Watermill

Mapledurham House

Park Farm

3

Purley CE Inf Sch

Purley Village

The Thames Path

Hardwick Stud Farm

Hardwick House

Straw Hill

East Lodge

Westfordhill Copse

Bottom Shaw

Bottom Farm

Mill Farm

Blackwell Copse

Huntley Wood

The White House

Lilley Farm

7SDD LA

PURLEY RISE

PO

76

Long Lane Prim Sch

Highfield Rd

Purley Park

Marina

New Farm

OXFORD RD

The Roebuck (Hotel)

2

RG31

Denefield Sch

White Lodge

Addiscombe Chase

Rosemead Ave

Cranmer

Brookfields Spec Sch Sports Ctr

Jun & Inf Schs

Longleat Dr

Downsway Sch

Tilehurst

Overlanders

PO

75

Barbara's Meadow

Conifer Dr

Ridgemount Cl

PO

Oak Tree Copse

READING

The Arthur Newbery Park

RG30

1

Stoneham Farm

Vicarage Wood

Barefoots Copse

Mud House

Back Lane

Clay Copse

Cornwell Copse

Thistledown

Bracken Cl

Southernwent

Ringwood Way

Sch

Swansea Terr

Tilehurst

Mc Ilroy Park

Sandgate Ave

Ringwood Rd

A329

Hornsea

Portmeirion Gdns

Coalport Way

Pottery Rd

Dresden Way

1 WEDGEWOOD WAY
2 TUSCAN CL
3 MISTON CL
4 CHELSEA CL
5 HOLKHAM CL
6 STAFFORDSHIRE CL

74

A   B   C

4

Trench Green
Pithouse Farm

Currs
Copse

Greendean
Farm

Newell's
Copse

SABRIES VIEW
DYSONSWOOD LA

BARDOLPH'S CL
ROKEBY DR

Tokers
Green

Dysons Wood
Farm

CH

GASKELLS
END
RUSSELL RD
ROSEBERY RD

Tokers Green
Farm

Tanners
Lane
Farm

Chazey
Heath

BEECH RD

ELM RD

Fox Hill
Farm

Middle
Farm

Page's
Shaw

Pack Saddle
Inn
(PH)

77

Newell's Lane

Farthingworth
Green

RG4

Noke End
Shaw

Rose Farm

SHEPHERDS LA

Shipnell's
Cottages

MIDSUMMER
MEADOW

3

Sandy Hill

Jacksons Lane

HILLTOP RD

CARLTON RD

MORECAMBE
AVE

UPPER WOODCOTE RD

CONISBORO
WAY

UPLANDS RD

Hemdean
Bottom

76

Grain Store

Chazey Wood

Blagrave
Farm

PO

PINCROFT RD

KING'S HILL

HEWETT
CL

WOBURN RD

ST ANDREW'S RD

OAKLEY RD

2

Gravel Hill

CHAZEY RD

UPPER WARREN AVE

The Warren

WOODCOTE RD

HIGHMOOR RD

Caversham
Heights

ST PETER'S HILL

75

Chazey Farm

The
Chase

The
Fishery

St Mary's
Island

The Warren

River Thames

The Thames Path

Thames Side Promenade

Poplar Island

Appletree
Eyot

Upper
Large

Towing Path

Aliot
Gdns

Coombe
Bank

CLIFTON
RD

A4074 DW

1

OXFORD RD

RINGWOOD RD

RIPLEY RD

KINSON RD

DEACON WAY

STADIUM WAY

Little John's
Farm

WIGMORE LA

BROUGHTON CL

RG30

RG1

Rivermead
LCtr

RICHFIELD AVE

DENBIGH

BRAMSHAW RD

MOWBRAY DR

RYDENE

WESTBROOK RD

OVERDOCK RD

Reading West
Junction

CREMYLL RD

CARDIFF RD

ROMANY LA

A329

A329

74

68   A   69   B   70   C

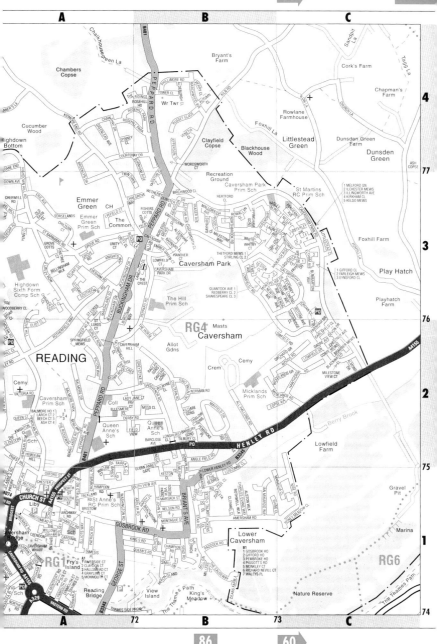

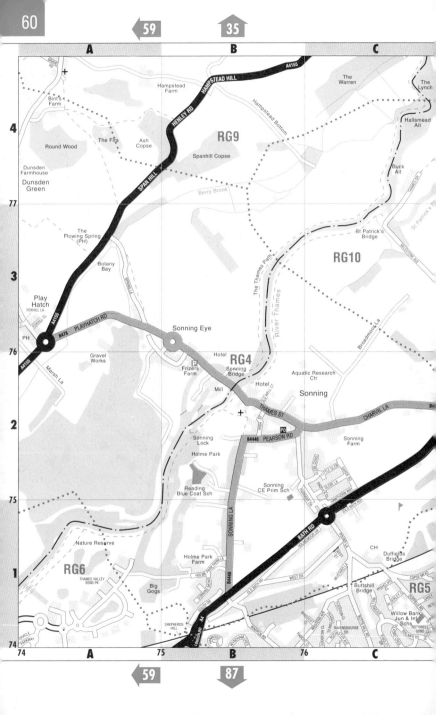

A B C

A4155

The Warren
The Lynch

Hampstead Farm
HAMPSTEAD HILL

HENLEY RD

Hampstead Bottom

Hallsmead Ait

4

RG9

Round Wood
The Firs
Ash Copse
Spanhill Copse

Buck Ait

SPAN HILL

Dunsden Farmhouse

Dunsden Green

77

Berry Brook

St Patrick's Ctr

St Patrick's Bridge

RG10

The Flowing Spring (PH)

Botany Bay

3

RG10

The Thames Path

River Thames

Broadmoor La

Play Hatch
FOXHILL CL

PLAYHATCH RD

Sonning Eye

A4155

B478

PH

A4155

Marsh La

76

Gravel Works

Hotel

RG4

Sonning Bridge

Frizers Farm

Aquatic Research Ctr

Mill

Hotel

Sonning

CHARVIL LA

2

Sonning Lock

THAMES ST

Sonning Farm

Holme Park

PO

PEARSON RD

B4446

Reading Blue Coat Sch

Sonning CE Prim Sch

SONNING LA

75

Nature Reserve

Holme Park Farm

BATH RD

CH

Duffields Bridge

B4446

WEST DR

COPSE MEAD

1

RG6

THAMES VALLEY BSNS PK

Big Gogs

Buttshill Bridge

RG5

Willow Bank Jun & Inf Schs

SHEPHERDS HILL

A4

LINKENHOLT

74

A 75 B 76 C

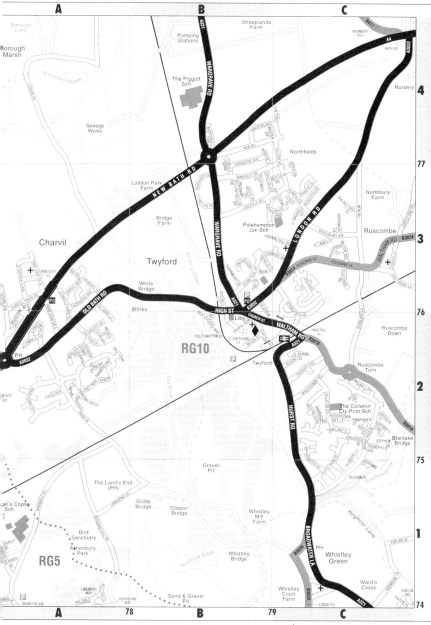

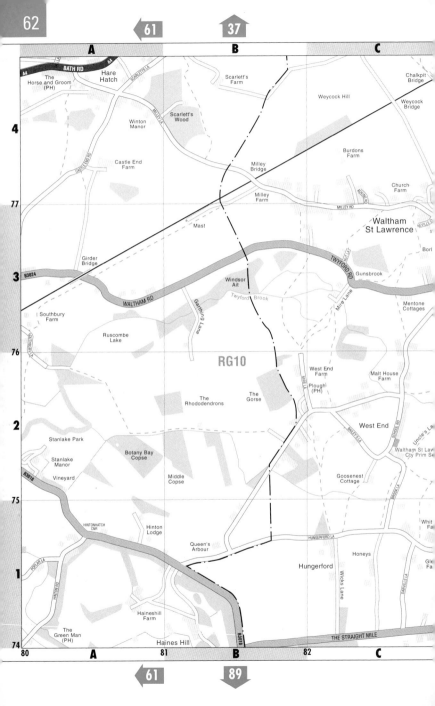

A
B
C

BATH RD
A4
A4

The Horse and Groom (PH)

Hare Hatch

Scarlett's Farm

Weycock Hill

Chalkpit Bridge

Weycock Bridge

Winton Manor

Scarlett's Wood

4

Castle End Farm

Milley Bridge

Burdons Farm

Church Farm

77

Milley Farm

MILLEY RD

Waltham St Lawrence

Mast

Girder Bridge

3

B3024

WALTHAM RD

Windsor Ait

Twyford Brook

TWYFORD RD

Gunsbrook

Mire Lane

Borl

Mentone Cottages

Southbury Farm

Garthing Lane

Ruscombe Lake

76

RG10

West End Farm

Malt House Farm

Mire La

Plough (PH)

The Rhododendrons

The Gorse

2

West End

Stanlake Park

Uncle's La

Stanlake Manor

Botany Bay Copse

BELLE LA

Waltham St Law Cty Prim Se

B3018

Vineyard

Middle Copse

SCHOOL RD

Goosenest Cottage

75

HINTONHATCH CNR

Hinton Lodge

Whit Fa

Queen's Arbour

HUNGERFORD LA

Honeys

Gle Fa

POPLAR LA

Hungerford

Wicks Lane

DARVILLE'S LA

1

HINTON RD

The Green Man (PH)

Haineshill Farm

B3018

THE STRAIGHT MILE

74

80
A
81
B
82
C

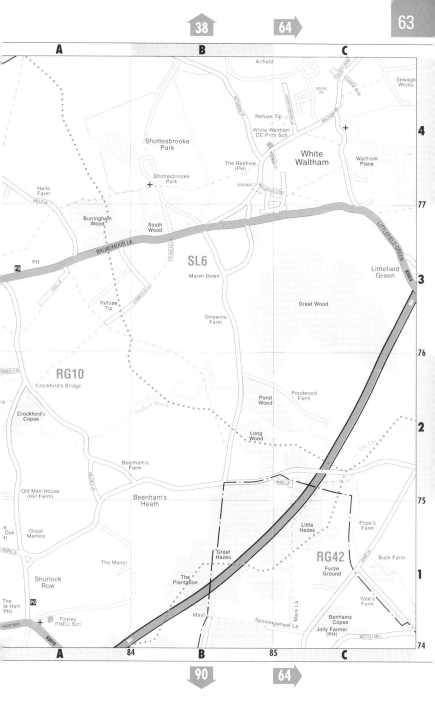

A B C

4

Belmont Farm

Thimble Farm

Stud Green

ASCOT RD

Paddock Wood

Foxley Green Farm

Holyport Manor Sch

The Jolly Gard (PH)

77

Paley Street Farm

B3024 FOREST GREEN RD

SNOWBALL HILL

PALEY ST

Longchase Farm

Little Foxley

Gad Fa

The Bourne

Win Agins Inn (PH)

Short Lane Farm

A330

Touchen-end

LONG LA

3

Whitehouse Farm

B3024

Whites Farm

B3024

Paley Street

SL6

LITTLEFIELD GREEN

Duell Farm

Littlefield Farm

The Royal Oak (PH)

The Bridge House (PH)

Long Lane Farm

GREEN LA

76

How Lane Farm

SHEEPCOTE LA

The Cut

Windmills

Blee

LONG LA

Hay Hill Farm

Howlane Bridge

2

Braywoodside

Braywood Farm

75

DRIFT RD

Hornbuckle Farm

Silver Springs Farm

CH

Crych La

1

RG42

Fernygrove Copse

Hawthorn Hill

Cruchfield Manor House

Lordland's Farm

Hazelwood La

Pendry's La

A3095 MAIDENHEAD RD

ASCOT RD

A330

74

86 A 87 B 88 C

A B C

RD A330

PO

Holyport
CE Prim
Sch

John
Gays
House

PH

Holyport

Moneyrow
Green

Stroud
Farm

The Guild
House

The Queen's
Head (PH)

Water Oakley

WINDSOR RD

A308

FERNDALE PARK

A308

4

77

Old
Beams

Green Lane

Coningsby
Farm

Fifield

SL6

Grove
House

FOREST VIEW
COTTS

The Rising Sun
(PH)

FOREST GREEN RD

Ledger
Farm

FIFIELD
COTTS

The Retreat
Farm

The Hare and Hounds
(PH)

Pond Farm

Fifield
House

Braywood
CE Fst
Sch

Kimbers
Farm

OAKLEY GREEN RD

B3024

3

76

Mount Scipett
Copse

nt Scipett
Farm

Banham
Farm

Longfields
Farm

Braywood
House

Haws Hill
Farm

The Bourne

The
Foresters
(PH)

Wakers
Farm

DRIFT RD

SL4

Lakeside
Farm

New Lodge
Farm

New
Lodge

Nobbscrook

Darthole Ride

2

75

Foliejon
Park

Hogoak Lane

Chawridge
Bourne

Chawridge
Gorse

Lawn
Hill

Windsor
Hill

Home
Farm

Nobbscrook
Copse

Nobbscrook
Farm

Home
Covert

1

74

G42

A 90 B 91 C

A · B · C

4

Dorney Lake Rowing Ctr

Boveney

Roasthill La

Boveney Court Farm

LOCK PATH

Boveney Lock

Oakley Court Hotel

Down Place Farm

Boveney Court

Weir

Royal Windsor Race Course

Marina

River Thames

The Thames Path

A308

WINDSOR RD

Mill Stream

Works PH

Oak View Farm

Cemy

Windsor Marina

The Willows

SUTHERLAND GRANGE

BALLARD GREEN

GRASMERE

77

MAIDENHEAD RD

B3383

1 GUARDS WLK
2 CHARLTON PL
3 CHARLTON SQ
4 CHARLTON ROW
5 CHARLTON ROW
6 FURNESS SQ
7 FURNESS WLK
8 FURNESS PL
9 FURNESS ROW
10 KENNEALLY WLK
11 KENNEALLY CL
12 KENNEALLY PL
13 KENNEALLY ROW
14 LIDELL SQ

HAYSE HILL

HANLEY CL

CLIFTON RISE

WHITELEY

ASTON MEAD

SAWYER'S CL

HALE

BROAD LEY'S

PO

HYTHE

WINWOOD

DEDWORTH MANOR

THAMES MEAD

HARCOURT

Works

Willows Path

Homer Fst Sch

HOMERS RD

BUTLERS CL

Dedworth

Dedworth Mid Sch

ST GEORGE'S CL

JUTLAND HO

3

Kimbers Lane Farm

Oakley Place Farm

Bishops Farmhouse

B3024

BISHOPS CL

PH

OAKLEY GREEN RD

NEWBERRY CRES

BARRY VIEW

HELEN COTTS

Dedworth Green Fst Sch

CRES

Braywood Cotts

B3024

Forest Farm

Fair Acres Farm

FAIRACRES IND EST

CHARLTON

DEDWORTH RD

DEACON

Superstore

CASTLE FARM CARAVAN SITE

PO

CRANBOURNE AVE

Ye Old Red Lion (PH)

Oakley Green

FURNESS

FILMER RD

IRVINE WLK

SHEPHERDS CL

76

FOREST RD

BRUCE WLK

STIRLING

KEEPERS LN

LUZENES WLK

MANOR FARM HO

Gale House Farm

Alexander Fst Sch

KENNEALLY

LIDELL

TOZER WLK

MONKS RD

BURHAM CL

DEAN

MERWIN CT

KEEPERS FARM CL

TINER COTTS

Hilltop Fst Sch

2

Tarbay Farm

LIDELL PL 1
LIDELL WAY 2
NICHOLLS WLK 3
LYELL PLACE E 4
LYELL WALK E 5
LYELL WALK W 6
LYELL PLACE W 7
WRIGHT WAY 8
WRIGHT SQ 9

SIDNEY RD

WRIGHT

DUNCANNON CRES

HOWLAND CL

STROUD CL

REDWING

GILMAN CRES

BRANKLYN

WASHINGTON DR

POOLMANS RD

ST LEONARDS HILL

ILLINGWORTH

DURHAM PARK

WOODLAND AVE

SL4

Darkhole Bridge

SNOWDEN CL

Clewer Green

CHESTNUT DR

75

Holliday's Plain

St Leonard's

St Leonard's Farm

Legoland Windsor

WINKFIELD RD

1

Forbe's Ride

Darkhole Ride

ST LEONARDS RD

Queen Adelaide's Ride

B3022

Forest Park

Prince Consort's Dr

High Standinghill Woods

74

Orchard Lea

WINKFIELD LA

Forbe's Fields

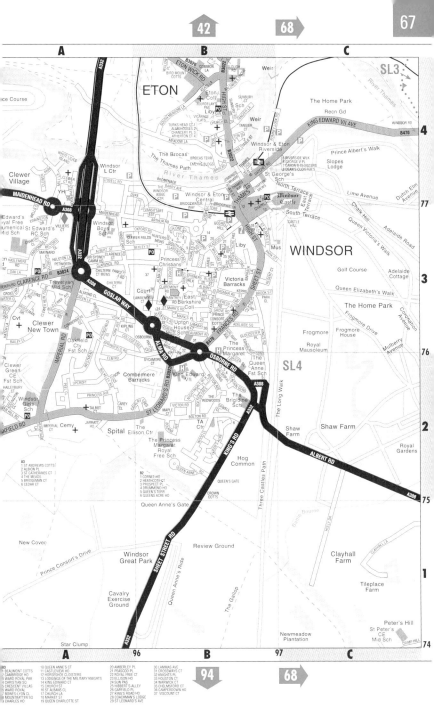

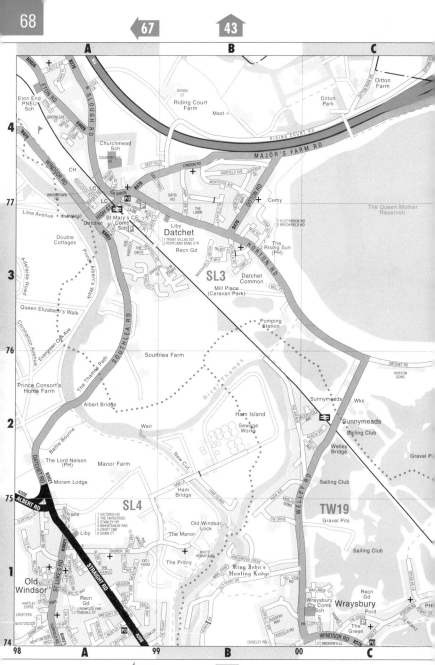

Grid references: A, B, C (columns); 4, 77, 3, 76, 2, 75, 1, 74 (rows); 98, 99, 00 coordinates.

Place names and labels:

- B3024, B376, M4, CASTLE AVE, ETON RD
- Ditton Farm
- Ditton Park
- Eton End PNEU Sch
- GREENLEAF
- SLOUGH RD
- WINDSOR RD
- Riding Court Farm, RIDING CT
- Mast
- MAJOR'S FARM RD
- RIDING COURT RD
- The Queen Mother Reservoir
- Churchmead Sch
- COUNTRY LIFE AVE
- DEEP FIELD
- LONDON RD
- FAIRFIELD AVE
- MONTROSE AVE
- CH
- LC, VC
- THE GREEN
- PO
- B470
- SATIS HO
- LAWN
- Cemy
- DITTON RD
- INNISSHOWN HO
- Lime Avenue
- St Mary's CE Comb Sch
- Datchet
- HIGH ST
- Liby, Datchet
- 1 TRENT VILLAS EST, 2 PORTLAND BSNS CTR
- THE LAWN
- 1 FLEETBROOK HO, 2 BROOKFIELD HO
- The Rising Sun (PH)
- Double Cottages
- Prince Albert's Walk
- THE DRIVE
- Recn Gd
- TALBOT PL
- B WLK
- ELM PL
- SL3
- HORTON RD
- Datchet Common
- Mill Place (Caravan Park)
- MILL PL
- Adelaide Road
- Queen Elizabeth's Walk
- Coronation Avenue
- Evergreen Oak Ave
- SOUTHLEA RD
- Pumping Station
- DATCHET RD
- HORTON GDNS
- Southlea Farm
- The Thames Path
- River Thames
- Prince Consort's Home Farm
- Albert Bridge
- Ham Island
- Sewage Works
- Weir
- Sunnymeads, Wks
- Sunnymeads
- Sailing Club
- Gravel P
- Battle Bourne
- New Cut
- ACACIA AVE
- Welley Bridge
- WELLEY RD
- The Lord Nelson (PH)
- Manor Farm
- Moram Lodge
- DATCHET RD
- B3021
- Sailing Club
- A308, ALBERT RD
- CLARVILLE LA
- SL4
- HAM LA
- Ham Bridge
- 1 VICTORIA HO, 2 THE TAPESTRIES, 3 STANLEY HO, 4 WHEATSHEAF PAR, 5 CROFT CNR, 6 SHAW CT
- Old Windsor Lock
- ENGLISH GDNS
- THE DRIVE
- Gravel Pits
- TW19
- ST LUKE'S RD
- Liby
- CHURCH RD
- The Manor
- WHITE HERMITAGE
- The Priory
- Old Windsor
- STRAIGHT RD
- MASON
- THE AVENUE
- CELL FARM
- Kingswood Creek
- King John's Hunting Lodge
- HILL VIEW RD
- WAYLANDS
- Recn Gd
- Wraysbury Cty Comb Sch
- Wraysbury
- Ford
- PH
- Hartley Copse, Crofters, Newtonside
- Recn Gd, 1 LYNDWOOD PAR, 2 RANDALL CT
- GREGORY DR
- MEADOW
- OLD FERRY DR
- NURSERY WAY
- FAIRFIELD RD
- POUND COTT
- The Green
- STATION DR
- WINDSOR RD, B376
- PO
- ST ANDREW'S CL
- OUSELEY RD
- A308
- ORCHARD

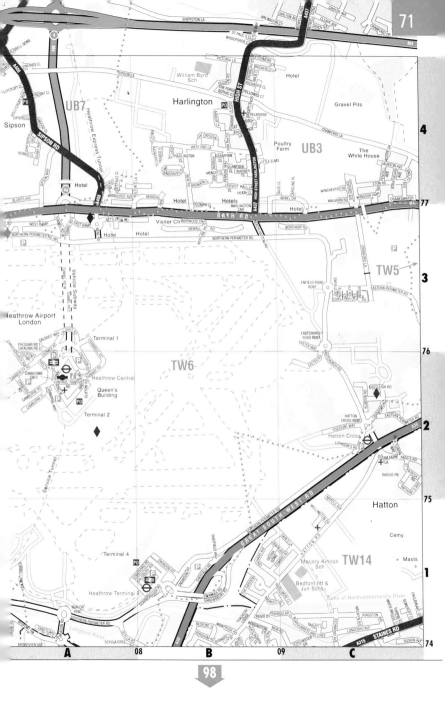

A　　　　　　B　　　　　　C

Marridge Hill Wood

Ragnal

Hunt's Copse

Witcha Cottage

Witcha Farm

4

Hails Grove

Oaken Coppice

73

Eastridge House

Eastridge Farm

Bower Wood

West Soley Farm Cottages

Woodlands

Whittonside Farm

West Soley Farm

Crooked Soley

3

The Lodge

Balaam's Wood

Whittonditch

Foxbury Wood

Old Farm West Soley

SN8

Oaken Coppice

RG17

72

Elm Border

Queen's Coppice

Fewley Coppice

Coal Brake

Princess Copse

2

Upper Dwarf Brake

Daffy Copse

King's Copse

Knighton

71

Dwarf Brake

River Kennet

Manor Farm

Park Coppice

Stev Clos

1

Littlecote Park

Littlecote

East Lodge

70

29　　　　A　　　　30　　　　B　　　　31　　　　C

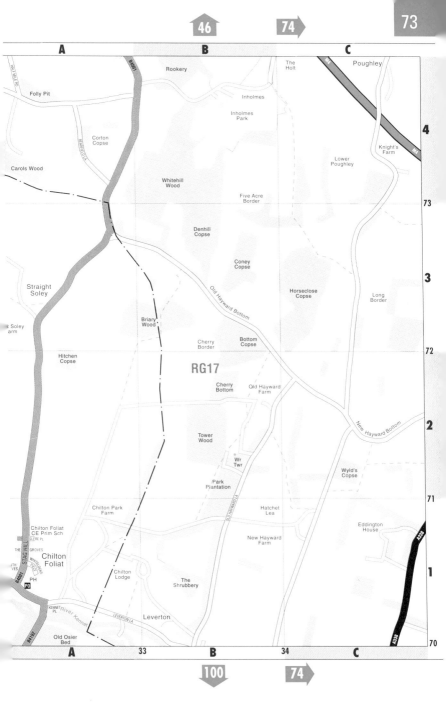

4

73

3

72

RG17

2

71

1

70

The Holt
Poughley
Rookery
Inholmes
Inholmes Park
Knight's Farm
Folly Pit
Lower Poughley
Corton Copse
Carols Wood
Whitehill Wood
Five Acre Border
Denhill Copse
Coney Copse
Straight Soley
Horseclose Copse
Long Border
Soley arm
Briary Wood
Old Hayward Bottom
Hitchen Copse
Cherry Border
Bottom Copse
Cherry Bottom
Old Hayward Farm
New Hayward Bottom
Tower Wood
Wr Twr
Wyld's Copse
Park Plantation
Chilton Park Farm
Hatchet Lea
Eddington House
Chilton Foliat CE Prim Sch
New Hayward Farm
GLEBE PL
THE
GROVES
WHITELOCKE
STAG HILL
Chilton Foliat
Chilton Lodge
The Shrubbery
PH
PO
KENNET PL
River Kennet
LEVERTON LA
Leverton
Old Osier Bed

A

B

C

B4000

ERMIN ST

Fisher's Farm

Somercourt

A338

Tommylands
Copse

The Pheasant Inn
(PH)

ERMIN ST

B4000

Shefford
Woodlands

Templars
Farm

4

M4

B4000

BARN
COTTS

73

A338

14

Newtown Lodge
Farm

Breach
Copse

Lovelocks

3

North Hidden
Farm

Norbin's
Wood

North Hidden
Cottages

72

RG17

Hungerford
Newtown

Wickfield
Copse

Windingwo...
La

Lower
Farm

Jeffrey's
Border

2

The Tally-ho
(PH)

RADLEY
BOTTOM

HUNGERFORD NEWTOWN

PO

Little Hidden
Farm

71

Winding
Wood

Windingwood
Bottom

A338

North
Denford Farm

Dunkin's
Copse

Heath Hanger La

Three Gate
Copse

1

Heath Hanger
Copse

Stibbs
Wood

Radley Farm

Great
Hidden
Farm

The
Hassock

70

35

A

36

B

37

C

A B C

Daldridge
Barn

Weston

Weston Farm

Mill

The
Rookery

4

Royal Ground
Border

field
m

Oakhanger
House

River Lambourn

Lambourn Valley Way

Welford
Park

73

Blindman's
Border

Scroggin's
Copse

Highwood
Copse

Queen's
Plantation

Home
Farm

Mantclose
Copse

Buck's
Copse

3

M4

RG20

Tullock
Farm

WHITE GATES

Mast

72

Wickham

St SWITHUN CL

PH

ERMIN ST

Welford
& Wickham
CE Prim Sch

Wickham
Green

G17

Grey's
Copse

PO

Windingwood La

Mast

Resr

2

Wickham
Rails

New
Copse

g
er

Wormstall

Wormstall
Wood

71

Orpenham
Farm

Lip La

B4000

1

Clapton

Harrod's
Border

Harrod's
Barn

on

Lower
Farm

70

A 39 B 40 C

Bradleywood
Farm

4

Grove
Corner

Welford
Farm

Welford

73

M4

3

Tullock
Bottom

Easton
Farm

Westbrook
Farm

Bo
C

Easton

River Lambourn

Knapps
Farm

Westbrook

72

ROAD HILL

RG20

EASTON HILL

Lambourn Valley Way

Sole
Border

SHEPHERD'S
HILL

Boxford
Farm

2

The Bell
Inn
(PH)

SCHOOL LA

WINTERBOURNE RD

Sole
Farm

Boxford

SOUTHFIELDS

High Street
Farm

Woodmansfield
Cottages

Hoar
Hill

71

HIGH ST

Moorbridge
Farm

Sole
Plantation

Ownham
Old Farm

1

Upper
Farm

Ownham

B4000

Ownham
Lower Farm

COOMBESBURY LA

Coombesbury
Farm

ERMIN ST

Ownham
Plantation

William's
Copse

Jann

B4000

Hunt's
Green

70

A
B
C

SCHOOL RD

Fir Tree
Cottage

Hop
Castle

Penclose
Farm

Penclose
Cottage

Ogdown
House

4

Wyfield Manor
Farm

73

M4

New Found Out
Cottages

Pound
Cottage

Winterbourne Stream

Philip's Hill

Bussock Wood

borough
Hill

Bussock
Mayne

3

Lower
Farm

Winterbourne Arms
(PH)

Winterbourne
Farm

Pebble La

Wyfield
Copse

Winterbourne

Vauxhall
Copse

Beans
Hill

72

Mud Hall
Cottage

Winterbourne
Manor

+

COUNCIL
HOS

RG20

RG14

Winterbourne
Wood

Mapleash
Copse

WINTERBOURNE RD

Bussock Hill
House

Holly
Copse

Home
Farm

2

Boxford
Common

Leonard's
Plantation

Winterbourne
Holt

The Mary Hare
Gram Sch
for the Deaf

Pit King
Farm

71

P

Snelsmore Common
Country Park

Barrett's
Wood

Broomclose
Border

Withy
Copse

Sheppard's
Copse

Honeybottom

1

Swilly
Copse

Copse
Barn

Mount
Hill

Bagnor
Marsh

gnor
ood

Ashpiece
Copse

Hill's
Pightle

Snelsmore
House

A34

B4494

A34

B4494

A
45
B
46
C
70

Chieveley
Prim Sch
SCHOOL RD

Wheatsheaf
(PH)

GRACES LA

SOUTHFIELDS

Priorscourt
Park

Priorscourt
Wood

Priors Court
Specl Sch

Priorscourt
Farm

Baker's
Row

Church
Farm

Horsemoor

PRIORS COURT RD

4

RG20

Sch of
Military Survey

Radnall
Farm

GREEN LA

73

M4

13

Hotel

Depot

Osmond's
Pightle

Copyhold
Farm

Faircross
Plantation

High
Wood

Kite's
Abbey

Chieveley
Service
Area

3

Curridge

The Bunk
(PH)

Snelsmore
Farm

Breach
Copse

Marsh La

HOLLANDS DR

KILN DR

Park
Farm

KILN
TERR

72

Chalky La

Spring
Copse

RG18

Lanolee
Farm

Grigg's
Copse

CHAPEL LA

Curridge
Prim Sch

RG14

Orchard
Copse

Oaklands
Farm

The Old
Parsonage

Rookery
Farm

Arlington Grange
Farm

Oaklands

CURRIDGE GREEN

2

Grange
Cottages

CURRIDGE RD

71

Snelsmore East
Common

Woodside

Dolman's
Row

LONG LA

Fisher's Lane
Crossing

Fox and Hounds
(PH)

Grange
Farm

FISHER'S LA

Fisher's
Farm

Ash
Plantation

1

A4009

Angel's
Hill

Shaw Dene
House

Long Lane
Poultry Farm

Big
Copse

B4009

70

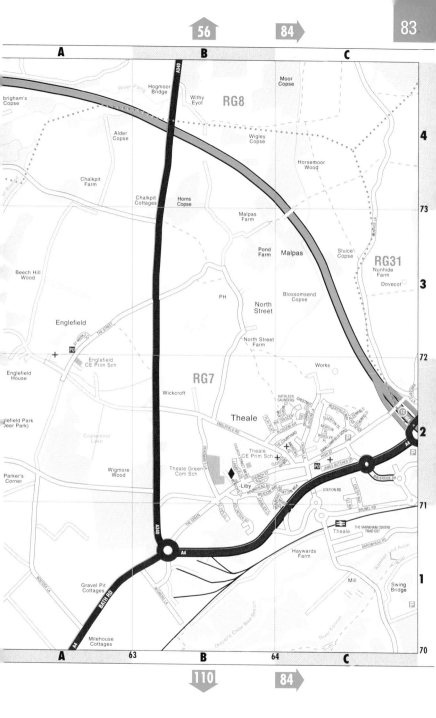

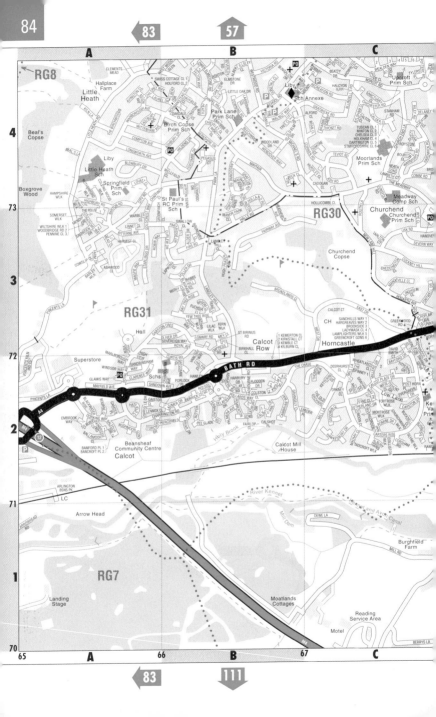

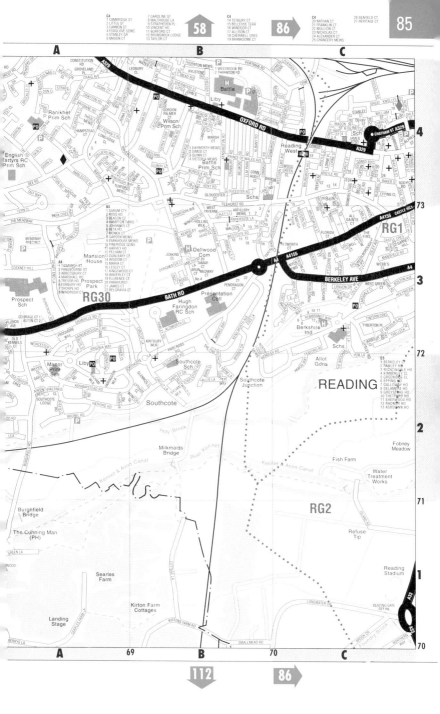

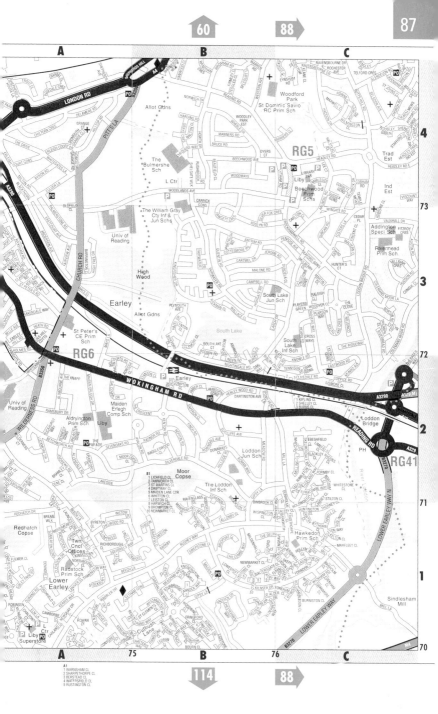

87
61

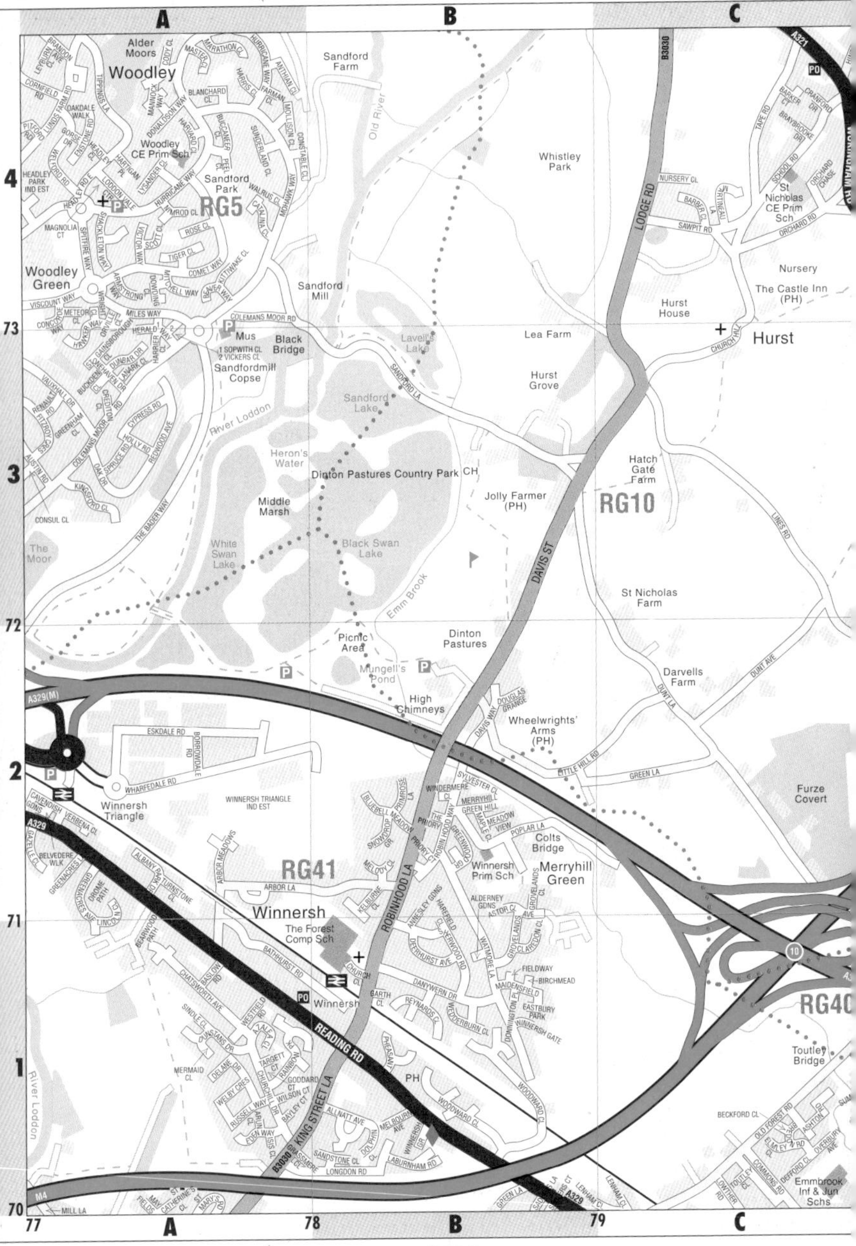
A
B
C
4
73
3
72
2
71
1
70
77
78
79
Alder Moors
Woodley
BRANDON CL
LEYBURN CL
CORNFIELD RD
TIPPINGS LA
CODY CL
MASTER CL
MARATHON CL
HURRICANE WAY
ANTHIAN CL
HARRIS CL
FARMAN CL
MANNOCK WAY
BLANCHARD CL
DONALDSON WAY
MOLLISON CL
OAKDALE WALK
LUNDS FARM RD
PITFORD RD
GORSE DR
ENSTONE RD
HEADLEY RD
WILFORD RD
HARTIGAN PL
Woodley CE Prim Sch
HARVARD CL
BUCCANEER CL
SUNDERLAND CL
CONSTABLE CL
HEADLEY PARK IND EST
LODDON VALE
LYSANDER CL
Sandford Park
PEEL CL
WALRUS CL
MOHAWK WAY
CATALINA CL
HURRICANE WAY
MROD CL
RG5
MAGNOLIA CT
SPITFIRE WAY
SHACKLETON WAY
VICTOR WAY
SCOTT CL
ROSE CL
TIGER CL
COMET WAY
KITTIWAKE CL
Woodley Green
ARMSTRONG WAY
DOWDING CL
MITCHELL WAY
BEAVER WAY
VISCOUNT WAY
METEOR CL
WRIGHT CL
CONCORDE WAY
MILES WAY
HAWKER WAY
ORVILLE CL
GAINSBOROUGH
HERALD WAY
HARRIER CL
COLEMANS MOOR RD
Mus
1 SOPWITH CL
2 VICKERS CL
Sandfordmill Copse
Black Bridge
DUNBAR DR
LANARK CL
BUCKDEN CL
VAUXHALL DR
RENAULT RD
FITZROY CRES
GREENHAM CL
CREDITON CL
CYPRESS RD
COLEMANS MOOR RD
REDWOOD AVE
HOLLY RD
SPRUCE RD
OAK DR
AUSTIN RD
KINGSFORD CL
CONSUL CL
THE BADER WAY
The Moor
River Loddon
Sandford Farm
Old River
Sandford Mill
Lavell's Lake
SANDFORD LA
Sandford Lake
Heron's Water
Dinton Pastures Country Park
CH
Middle Marsh
White Swan Lake
Black Swan Lake
Emm Brook
Picnic Area
Mungell's Pond
High Chimneys
Dinton Pastures
Whistley Park
B3030
LODGE RD
Lea Farm
Hurst Grove
Jolly Farmer (PH)
DAVIS ST
A321
PO
BARKER CT
CRANFORD DR
TAPE RD
BRAYBROOKE DR
SCHOOL RD
ORCHARD CHASE
NURSERY CL
BARBER CL
MARTINEAU LA
St Nicholas CE Prim Sch
SAWPIT RD
ORCHARD RD
Nursery
The Castle Inn (PH)
Hurst House
CHURCH HILL
Hurst
Hatch Gate Farm
RG10
LINES RD
St Nicholas Farm
Darvells Farm
DUNT LA
DUNT AVE
Wheelwrights' Arms (PH)
DOUGLAS GRANGE
DAVIS WAY
LITTLE HILL RD
GREEN LA
Furze Covert
A329(M)
ESKDALE RD
BORROWDALE RD
WHARFEDALE RD
Winnersh Triangle
WINNERSH TRIANGLE IND EST
CAVENDISH GDNS
VERBENA CL
A329
BELVEDERE WLK
GAZELLE CL
GREENACRES LA
GREENACRES AVE
DROME PATH
LINCOLN CL
ALBANY PARK DR
TURNSTONE CL
ARBOR MEADOWS
RG41
ARBOR LA
Winnersh
The Forest Comp Sch
BEARWOOD PATH
BATHHURST RD
CHATSWORTH AVE
BASLOW RD
CHURCH CL
PO
Winnersh
GARTH CL
READING RD
WESTFIELD RD
SINDLE CL
DUNSTANS DR
MERMAID CL
DELANE DR
TARGETT CT
RAINBOW
GODDARD CT
WILSON CT
BAYLEY CT
WELBY CRES
RUSSELL WAY
CHURCHILL DR
EDEN WAY
KING STREET LA
B3030
ROBINHOOD LA
PHEASANT
PH
ALLNATT AVE
DOLPHIN
MELBOURNE AVE
WINNERSH GR
WOODWARD CL
SANDSTONE CL
LONGDON RD
LABURNHAM RD
M4
MILL LA
ST CATHERINE'S CL
ST MARY'S RD
MAY FIELDS
GREEN LA
LENHAM CL
A329
River Loddon
PRIMROSE LA
BLUEBELL MEADOW
SNOWDROP GR
WINDERMERE CL
SYLVESTER CL
MERRYHILL GREEN HILL
MAPLE CL
MEADOW VIEW
POPLAR LA
THE PRIORY
PRIORY CT
ROBIN HOOD WAY
GREENWOOD GR
Colts Bridge
Winnersh Prim Sch
Merryhill Green
MELODY CL
KELBURNE CL
ANNESLEY GDNS
HAREFIELD CL
ALDERNEY GDNS
ASTOR CL
GROVELANDS AVE
GROVELANDS CL
CLAREDON CL
DEERHURST AVE
HERWOOD RD
WATMORE LA
FIELDWAY
BIRCHMEAD
DANYWERN DR
REYNARDS CL
WEDDERBURN CL
MAIDENSFIELD
DONNINGTON PL
EASTBURY PARK
WINNERSH GATE
WOODWARD CL
10
A329(M)
RG40
Toutley Bridge
BECKFORD CL
OLD FOREST RD
ASHTON RD
ELMLEY RD
OVERBURY AVE
COMMONS RD
DEFFORD CL
TOUTLEY CL
LOWTHER RD
Emmbrook Inf & Jun Schs
A
B
C

87
115

A
B
C

4
73
3
72
2
71
1
70

B3018

Surrells Wood

Charity Wood

Park Farm

Bushy Lees

Grange Farm

Buckland Farm

BROAD COMMON RD

RG10

Broad Common

Warren Copse

THE STRAIGHT MILE

Grange Farm

Oakley Farm

Pound Lane Farm

POUND LA

NESTLE LA

Birch Plantation

Penn Bushes

North Ockett Wood

Churchmans Farm

Mount Farm

Beech Wood

Straight Mile Stud

Warren Farm

Pond Wood

RG40

Ashridge Wood

Tippen's Wood

BILL HILL PK

Harp Farm

Targetts Farm

B3034

FOREST RD

B3034

Pike's Farm

Bill Hill

Ashridge Manor

Warren Inn (PH)

OLD FOREST RD

Ashridgewood House

Ashridgewood Farm

Rushton's Farm

TWYFORD RD

WARREN HOUSE RD

RG41

TRIMBLECOMBE CL

Bell Farm

BELL FOUNDRY LA

Ashridge Water Reclamation Plant

Pebblestone Copse

A329 (M)

A
81
B
82
C

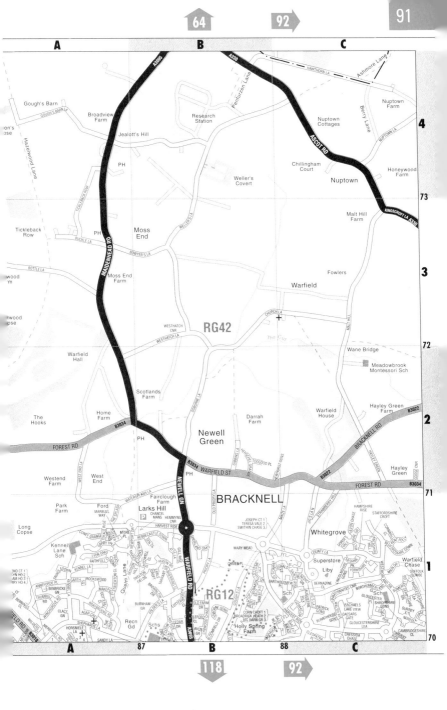

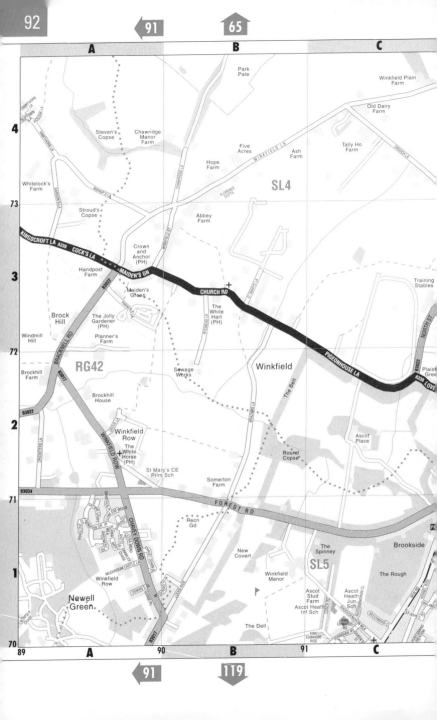

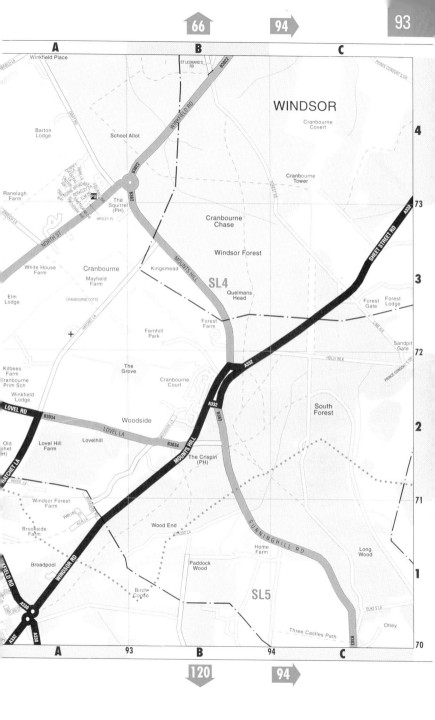

93
67

A   **B**   **C**

Flemish Farm

Bear's Rails

Cemy

Rush Pond

BEARS RAILS PK

4

Prince of Wales Pond

Bear's Rails Pond

Pickleherring Pond

SHEET STREET RD

A332

Ranger's Lodge

Beehive Hill

Seymours Plantation

Battle Bourne

The Gallop

The Long Walk

73

Russel's Pond

PRINCE CONSORTS DR

Fiddle Covert

Statue

Snow Hill

Spring Hill

Copkes Hill

3

Richardson's Lawn

SL4

Three Castles Path

The Village

RICHARDSONS LAWN COTTS

OLD PARK SQ

PO

Isle of Wight Pond

Poets Lawn

Deepstrood

Royal Lodge

+

The Ho

72

Windsor Great Park

Queen Anne's Ride

Dark Wood

The Royal Prim Sch

Bishopsga

Cow Pond

Chapel Wood

PARK COTT

2

MEZEL HILL COTTS

CUMBERLAND LODGE

Mezel Hill

The S (PH

DUKE'S LA

Hilton's Covert

Wilderness

THE LONG WALK

Park Close

71

Square Covert

The Savill Gardens

Par H

Slans Hill

Leiper Hill

Great Meadow Pond

Temple Hill

TW20

P

1

SL5

Norfolk Plantation

Norfolk Farm

Mill Pond

Statue

Smith's Lawn

Obelisk

Rosy Bottom

Obelisk Pond

70

Polo Gds

95   **A**   **96**   **B**   **97**   **C**

93
121

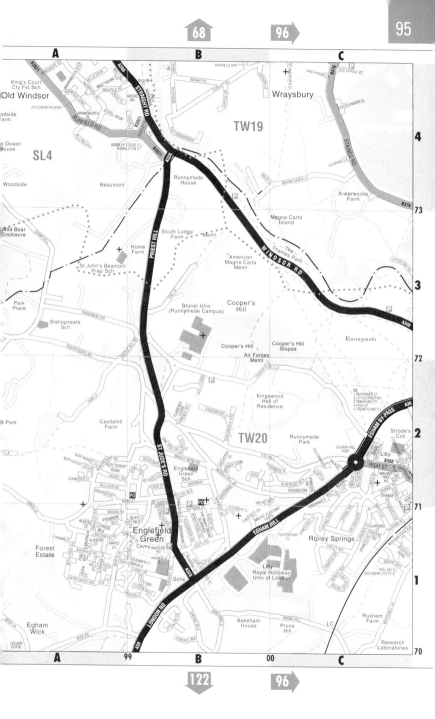

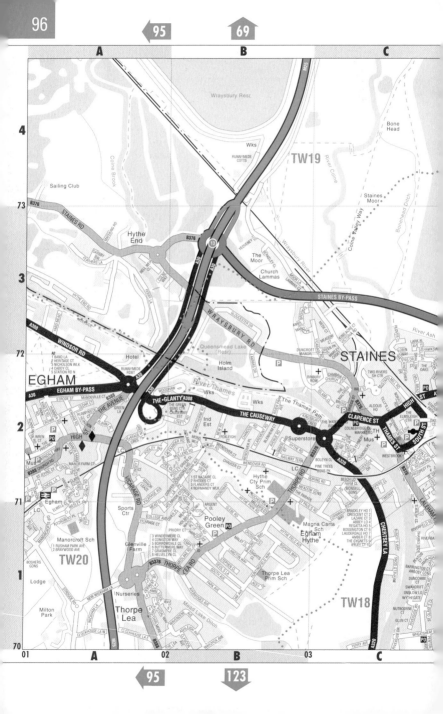

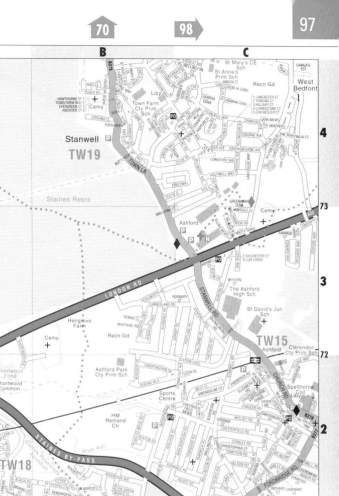

A

B

C

St Mary's CE Sch

CAMGATE EST

West Bedfont

St Anne's Prim Sch

Recn Gd

1 LANCASTER CT
2 TENSING CT
3 HILLARY CT
4 LIVINGSTONE CT
5 CHICHESTER CT

Liby

Cemy

HAWTHORNE CT 1
TOWN FARM WAY 2
EVERGREEN CT 3
ANDOVER CT 4

Town Farm Cty Prim Sch

King George VI Resr

Stanwell

TW19

4

Staines Resrs

TOWN LA

Cemy

73

Ashford

The Ashford High Sch

LONDON RD

1 SILCHESTER CT
2 LUD LODGE

3

St David's Jun Sch

Hengrove Farm

Cemy

Recn Gd

TW15

Ashford

Clarendon Cty Prim Sch

72

Shortwood Inf Sch

Birch Green

Ashford Park Cty Prim Sch

Spelthorne Coll Liby

LONDON RD

Shortwood Pond

Shortwood Common

Sports Centre

2

Staines

STAINES BY-PASS

HM Remand Ctr

River Ash

FORDBRIDGE RD

Knowle Green L Ctr

TW18

71

Kingscroft Cty Jun Sch

The Matthew Arnold Sch

ASHFORD

Ashford Manor

Our Lady of the Rosary RC Sch

Mast

1

LALEHAM RD

KINGSTON RD

A308

Buckland Cty Jun & Inf Sch

Works

Queen Mary Resr

River Ash

70

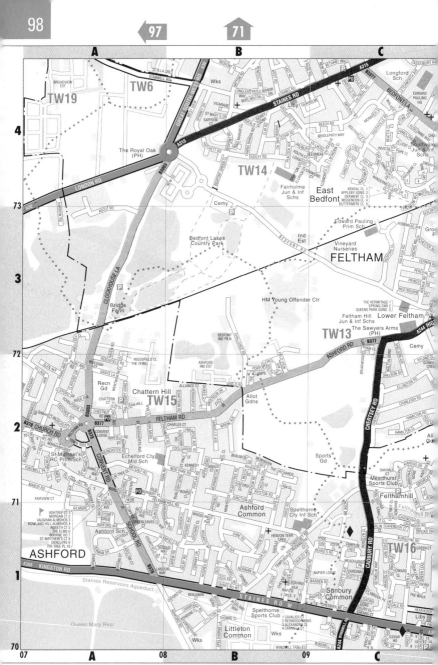

TW19
BROADVIEW EST
TW6
STANWELL ROW
Wks
Longford Sch
EDWARD PAULING HO
Southville Jun & Inf Schs

LONGFORD RD
Vicarage
ST MARY'S DR
SAFFRON
BURLINGTON CL
STAINES RD
Liby
FAIRHOLME
BEECH RD
BRIDLEPATH WAY

The Royal Oak (PH)
LONDON RD
TW14

Cemy

Fairholme Jun & Inf Schs

East Bedfont

KENDAL CL 1
APPLEBY GDNS 2
DERWENT CL 3
MISSENDEN CL 4
BUTTERMERE CL 5

Edward Pauling Prim Sch
ROSEMEAD AVE

Bedfont Lakes Country Park

Vineyard Nurseries
FELTHAM

THE HERMITAGE 1
SPRING CNR 2
QUEENS PARK GDNS 3

Bridge Farm
CLOCKHOUSE LA

HM Young Offender Ctr

Feltham Hill Jun & Inf Schs
Lower Feltham

TW13
The Sawyers Arms (PH)
B377
Cemy

BEDFONT IND PK N

ASHFORD RD

REEDSFIELD CL
THE YEWS

Ashford Ind Est

REESFIELD RD
GRAYS LA
Recn Gd

Chattern Hill
CHATTERN HILL
TW15

Allot Gdns

CHERTSEY RD

CHURCH RD
B378
B3003
PO

CONVENT LODGE
FELTHAM RD

OAKFIELD RD

St Michael's RC Prim Sch

Echelford Cty Mid Sch

Sports Gd

Meadhurst Sports Club
Felthamhill

CONVENT RD
B378

Ashford Sch
SCHOOL RD

Ashford Common

Spelthorne Cty Inf Sch

CADBURY RD
TW16

FAIRVIEW CT

ASHTREE CT 1
MORGAN CT 2
VAUGHAN ALMSHOS 3
ROWLAND HILL ALMSHOS 4
ROXETH CT 5
THE ELMS 6
BOURNE HO 7
ST MATTHEW'S CT 8
DENCLIFFE 9
FIR TREE PL 10

ASHFORD
A308 KINGSTON RD
Staines Reservoirs Aqueduct

HENDON TERR
BEARD'S RD
HYDE TERR
HYDE
CHAPLIN CRES
MEADHURST

Napier Lodge
WARREN RD

Sunbury Common

STAINES RD W

Spelthorne Sports Club
1 CAVALIER CL
2 REDWOOD MEWS
3 ALEXANDRA CL
4 CARMEL CT

Littleton Common

Queen Mary Resr

Wks

Wks
WINDMILL TRAD EST
A244 WINDMILL RD

Liby
THE PAR

HEATHCROFT

C1
1 TASMAN CT
2 WILLOW CT
3 CATLE CL
4 KILLIGREW HO
5 GRANTHAM HO
6 ASH LODGE
7 LIME LODGE
8 OAK LODGE
9 ELM CT
10 WILLOW LODGE EDWARD
11 SYCAMORE LODGE
12 ISOBEL HO
13 PRISCILLA HO
14 SUNBURY CROSS CTR

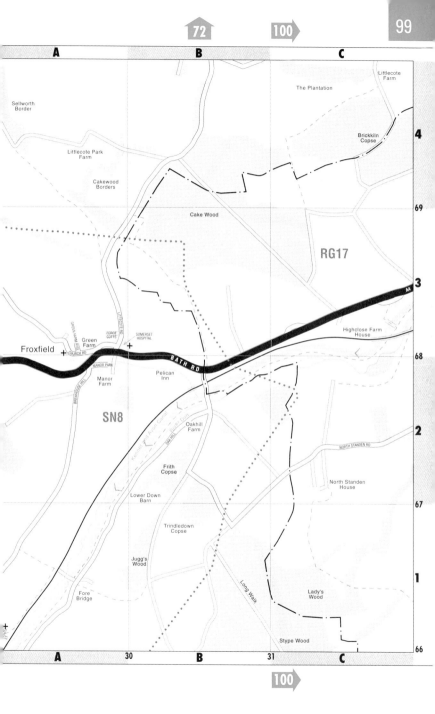

A   B   C

Littlecote
Farm

The Plantation

Sellworth
Border

Brickkiln
Copse

4

Littlecote Park
Farm

Cakewood
Borders

69

Cake Wood

RG17

3
A4

Highclose Farm
House

GREEN FARM ROAD

LITTLECOTE RD

FORGE
COTTS

SOMERSET
HOSPITAL

Froxfield

Green
Farm

68

CHURCH RD

BATH RD

MANOR PARK

Pelican
Inn

Manor
Farm

BREWERS HILL

2

SN8

Kennet & Avon Canal

North Standen
Road

NORTH STANDEN RD

Oakhill
Farm

North Standen
House

River Dun

OAK HILL

Frith
Copse

67

Lower Down
Barn

Trindledown
Copse

Jugg's
Wood

1

Long Walk

Lady's
Wood

Fore
Bridge

RIVER DUN

Stype Wood

66

A   30   B   31   C

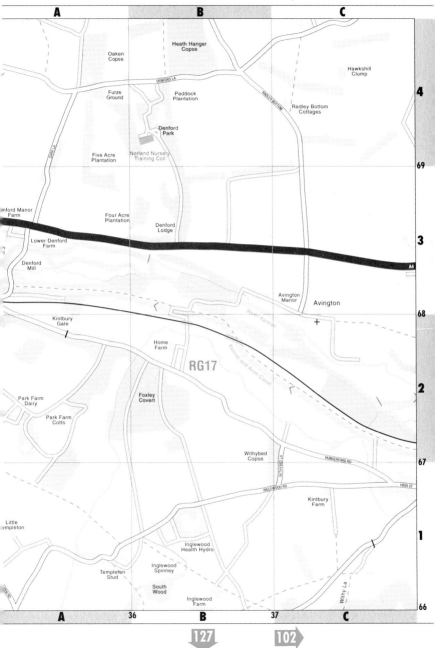

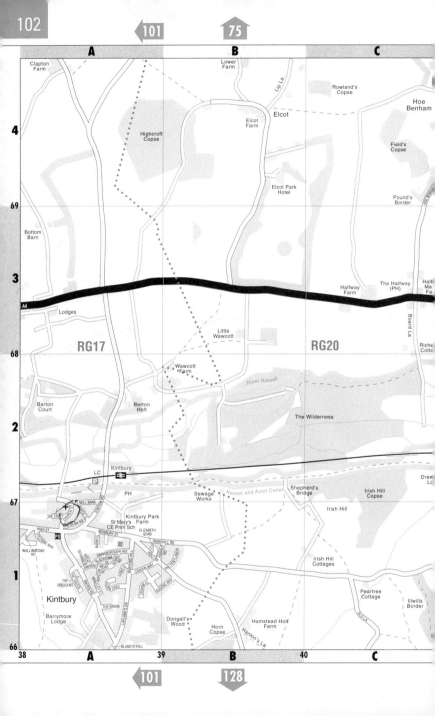

Clapton
Farm

Lower
Farm

Lip La

Rowland's
Copse

Hoe
Benham

4

Highcroft
Copse

Elcot
Farm

Elcot

Field's
Copse

Elcot Park
Hotel

69

Pound's
Border

HOE BENHAM

Bottom
Barn

3

A4

The Halfway
(PH)

Halfway
Farm

Half
Ma
Fa

Lodges

Board La

Riche
Cotta

RG17

Little
Wawcott

RG20

68

Wawcott
Farm

River Kennel

Barton
Court

Barton
Holt

The Wilderness

2

Kintbury

LC

Drew
Lo

67

PH

Sewage
Works

Kennet and Avon Canal

Shepherd's
Bridge

Irish Hill
Copse

THE CROFT
MILL BANK

Irish Hill

P

Kintbury Park
Farm
St Mary's
CE Prim Sch

Elizabeth
GDNS

HIGH ST

P

NEWBURY ST

IRISHHILL RD

Irish Hill
Cottages

WALLINGTONS
RD

GAINSBOROUGH AVE
GLADSTONE
LAWRENCE MEAD

CRAVEN WAY

1

THE
CRESCENT

BARR CL

BRISTINE WAY

THE PADDOCKS

QUEENS WAY

Peartree
Cottage

Illwills
Border

Kintbury

Barrymore
Lodge

THE GREEN

LADY LANE RD

Dongall's
Wood

Horn
Copse

Hamstead Holf
Farm

Hankin's La

OLD LA

66

A   B   C

B4000

COOMBESBURY LA

Benham
Farm

Wickham
Heath

Nalder
Plantation

Cecil
(old & new)

Priddle's
Farm

Huntsgreen
Farm

River Lambourn

4

Woodspeen
Farm

Nalderhill
Copse

Scotch
Wood

ERMIN ST

Shepherd's
Farm

Spring
Wood

69

Nalderhill
House

Pique

CHAPEL RD
BROOKWOOD

Stockcross
CE Prim
Sch

SMALE LA

CROFTERS

Grange
Farm

Common
Wood

Furze
Hill

The
Dismals

Stockcross

PO

CHURCH RD

GLEBE

B4000

3

ham
ange

Bradford's
Farm

BENHAM CHASE

GRAVEL HILL

Benham
Dairy

A4

68

Bradford's
Gorse

RG20

West
Meadows

MILKHOUSE RD

Magdalen
Plantation

Benham
Park

River Kennet

Marsh
Benham

Benham
Gardens

2

Red House
(PH)

Benham
Stud

Hamstead
Crossing

Hamstead
Lock

Kennet and Avon Canal

Benham Marsh
Farm

67

More Wood

Mill

Barnett's
Lock

Ivy
House

PARK LA

Hamstead
Gardens

1

Hamstead
Park

Enborne Copse

Craven
Hill

The
Mews

66

A   42   B   43   C

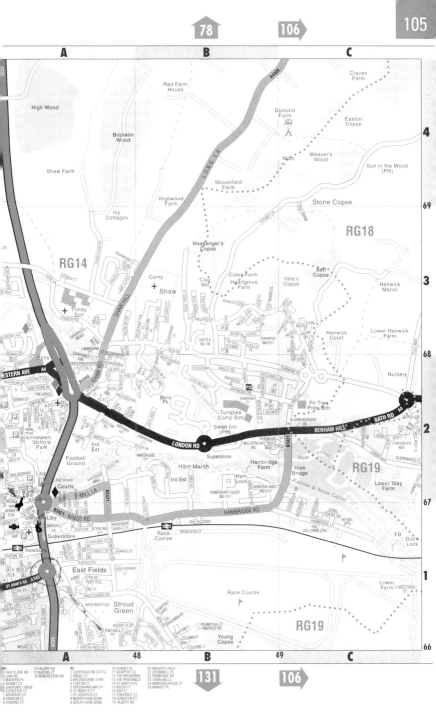

A B C

4

69

Craven Farm

High Wood

Red Farm House

Brickkiln Wood

Dymond Farm

Easton Copse

Shaw Farm

Mast

Weaver's Wood

Sun in the Wood (PH)

Mousefield Farm

Highwood Farm

Stone Copse

RG18

Ivy Cottages

RG14

Messenger's Copse

Cemy

Shaw

Clay Hill

Coley Farm Heartgrove Farm

Yate's Copse

Sett Copse

3

Henwick Manor

Trinity Sch

Church Rd

Lower Henwick Farm

Henwick Court

Castle Ind Pk

WESTERN AVE A4

Turnpike Ind Est

68

Nursery

Bsns Pk

Fir Tree Prim Sch

Turnpike Comp Sch

BATH RD A4

BENHAM HILL

Swan Inn (PH)

2

LONDON RD

Superstore

Victoria Park

Ind Est

River Kennet

RG19

Ham Marsh

Hambridge Farm

Football Ground

Ind Est

Ham Lock

Ham Bridge

Kennet & Avon Canal

Lower Way Farm

Libv

Courts

MILL LA

Kingfisher Court Ind Est

HORIZON WEST IND EST

67

Liby

KINGS RD

HAMBRIDGE RD

Mayors La

Superstore

Race Course

THE PADDOCK

MANDARIN CT

Bull's Lock

FB

Newbury

STATION RD

A343

East Fields

CHRISTOPHER CT

1

Race Course

Lower Farm

Stroud Green

Young Copse

RG19

66

A 48 B 49 C

A1
FAIR CLOSE HO
LINK HO
MADEIRA PL
KENNET CT
SHEFFORD LODGE
ILCHESTER CT
ASHRIDGE CT
GORDON CT
ROMANO CT

10 HILARY HO
11 QUEENS CT
12 WINCHESTER HO

A2
1 CORPORATION COTTS
2 ANGEL CT
3 WESTBOURNE TERR
4 LYNTON CT
5 SPEENHAMLAND CT
6 ST MARY'S CT
7 ST JOSEPH'S CT
8 NORTH VIEW GDNS
9 SOUTH VIEW GDNS

10 KENNET PL
11 NEWPORT CL
12 THE BROADWAY
13 THE PENTANGLE
14 ST MARY'S PL
15 BEECH CT
16 ASH CT
17 CHESTNUT CT
18 CONISTON CT
19 ALBERT RD

20 WEAVER'S WLK
21 CROMWELL PL
22 PEMBROKE RD
23 TOWN MILLS
24 MANSION HOUSE ST
25 MARKET PL

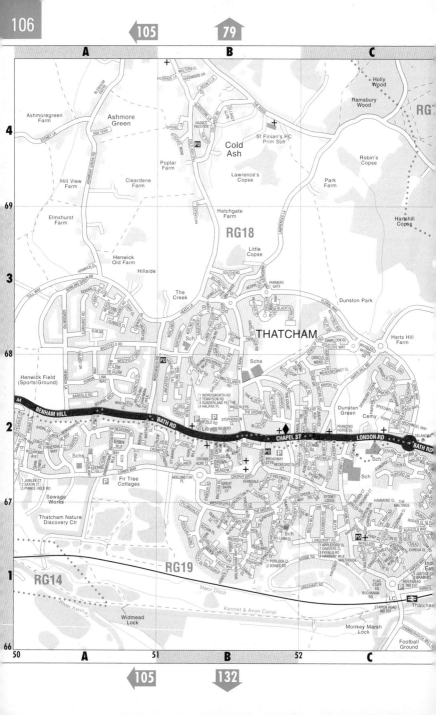

A   B   C

4

Ashmoregreen Farm

Ashmore Green

Holly Wood

Ramsbury Wood

RG

St Finian's RC Prim Sch

Cold Ash

Robin's Copse

Poplar Farm

Hill View Farm

Cleardene Farm

Lawrence's Copse

Park Farm

Hartshill Copse

69

Elmshurst Farm

Hatchgate Farm

RG18

Little Copse

Henwick Old Farm

Hillside

The Creek

Southend

Dunston Park

Harts Hill Farm

3

THATCHAM

68

Henwick Field (Sports Ground)

Schs

Dunstan Green

Cemy

2

BENHAM HILL   BATH RD

Liby

CHAPEL ST   LONDON RD   BATH RD

Pranging Horse Cl

67

Fir Tree Cottages

Sewage Works

Thatcham Nature Discovery Ctr

The Moors

The Maltings

Ind Est

1

RG14

RG19

Moor Ditch

Widmead Lock

Kennet & Avon Canal

Monkey Marsh Lock

Thatcha

Station Road Ind Est

66

50   A   51   B   52   C

Football Ground

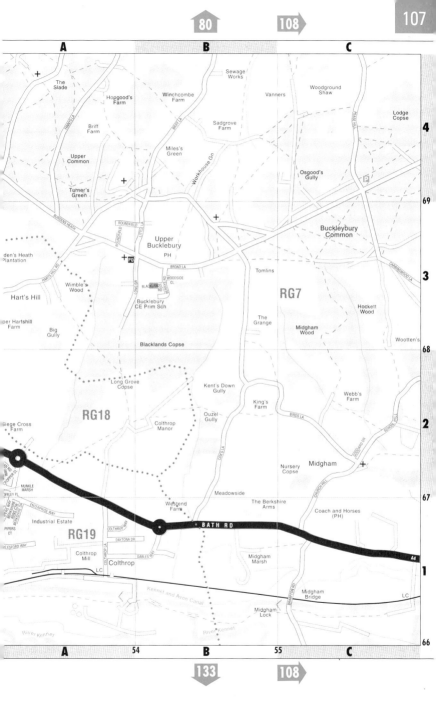

80
108

A
B
C

The Slade

Hopgood's Farm

Winchcombe Farm

Sewage Works

Vanners

Woodground Shaw

Lodge Copse

4

Briff Farm

Sadgrove Farm

Upper Common

Miles's Green

Osgood's Gully

Turner's Green

Workhouse Gn

P

69

BURDENS HEATH

ROUNDFIELD

Upper Bucklebury

PH

Buckleybury Common

CARBINSWOOD LA

den's Heath Plantation

PO

BROAD LA

Tomlins

RG7

3

Wimble's Wood

WOODSIDE CL

BLACKLANDS RD

Hart's Hill

Bucklebury CE Prim Sch

The Grange

Midgham Wood

Hockett Wood

per Hartshill Farm

Big Gully

Blacklands Copse

Wootten's

68

Long Grove Copse

Kent's Down Gully

King's Farm

Webb's Farm

RG18

Siege Cross Farm

Colthrop Manor

Ouzel Gully

COX'S LA

BIRDS LA

SCHOOL HILL

2

Nursery Copse

Midgham

CHURCH RD

67

MUNKLE MARSH

RFLEY PL

ENTERPRISE WAY

Westend Farm

Meadowside

The Berkshire Arms

Coach and Horses (PH)

Industrial Estate

RG19

COLTHROP LA

COLTHROP WAY

DAYTONA DR

GABLES WAY

BATH RD

BRIMPTON RD

PIPERS CT

LESFORD WAY

Colthrop Mill

Colthrop

Midgham Marsh

A4

1

LC

Kennet and Avon Canal

Midgham Bridge

LC

River Kennet

River Kennet

Midgham Lock

66

A
54
B
55
C

133
108

A

B

C

Scotland

Gunnells
Farm

Hilliers

St Annes
Farm

Chapelrow
Common

The
Blade Bone
(PH)

Beenham
Hatch

The
Bourne

4

Chapel Row

The Bourne

Paradise La

Long Gully

Lower
Common

Middle Wood

Ironmongers
Copse

Withy
Copse

Awbery's
Farm

69

Six Bells
(PH)

Beenham
Cty Prim
Sch

Copyhold
Farm

Greyfield
Wood

Horn's
Copse

Reading's Gully

Kiff Green

Beenham

3

High Wood

Old
Copse

CARBINSWOOD LA

Bucklebury
Place

Channel
Wood

Oakwood
Farm

Ferrises

WINDMILL LA

Douai Abbey
(Benedictine)

68

Douai Sch

Lodge

Midgham
Green

Malthouse
Farm

Gravelpit
Copse

SCHOOL HILL

Woolhampton
CE Prim Sch

Webcroft
Copse

RG7

2

Midgham Park

Upper
Woolhampton

Beenham
Lodge

NEW ROAD

Elstree
Sch

Hallcourt
Farm

The
Court

Home
Farm

Jennings's
Copse

Woolhampton Park

67

Great Mounts
Copse

Inn

Woolhampton

Gateways

ORCHARD CL

Midgham

Rising Sun
(PH)

BATH RD

WATERMILL CT

Oxlease
Bridge

LC

A4

Woolhampton
Lock

Kennet & Avon Canal

River Kennet

Swing-bridge

Heales Lock

1

Woolhampton Bridge

Gravel
Pit

River Enborne

66

A
B
C

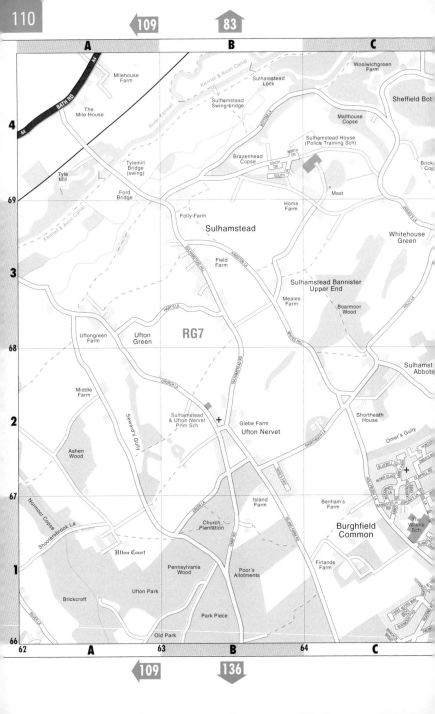

A B C

Woolwichgreen Farm

Milehouse Farm

BATH RD

The Mile House

Sheffield Bot

Kennet & Avon Canal

Sulhamstead Lock

4

Sulhamstead Swing-bridge

Malthouse Copse

River Kennet

Sulhamstead House (Police Training Sch)

Tylemill Bridge (swing)

Brazenhead Copse

NORTH DR

Brick Cop

Tyle Mill

SOUTH DR

SOUTH

Mast

Ford Bridge

69

Home Farm

Kennet & Avon Canal

Folly Farm

JACKET'S LA

Sulhamstead

Whitehouse Green

Field Farm

3

KINGSTON LA

SULHAMSTEAD HILL

Sulhamstead Bannister Upper End

Meales Farm

Boarmoor Wood

HART'S LA

HOLLY LA

Uftongreen Farm

Ufton Green

RG7

Sulhamst Abbots

68

NOTTON HILL

CHURCH LA

SULHAMSTEAD RD

Middle Farm

Omer's Gully

Seward's Gully

Sulhamstead & Ufton Nervet Prim Sch

Glebe Farm

Shortheath House

HUNTER

BLUEBELL DR

OMER'S DR

2

+

Ufton Nervet

SHORTHEATH LA

ALDER GLADE

CLENHILL RD

Ashen Wood

MARY LA

JOHN'S LA

67

RIDGE'S RD

Island Farm

Benham's Farm

BANNISTER RD

Normoor Copse

GREEN LA

ISLAND FOREST RD

FALLOWFIELD

Shootersbrook La

Church Plantation

CAMP RD

Burghfield Common

The Willink Sch

BLANT'S DR

Ufton Court

Pennsylvania Wood

Poor's Allotments

Firlands Farm

1

Ufton Park

Park Piece

THREE GABLES WAY

BROAD OAKS

BILLEY'S LA

Brickcroft

Old Park

TOTTERIDGE LA

BRACKEN WAY

PATIM

66

62 A 63 B 64 C

A B C

Reading Service Area

Jame's Copse

Dean's Copse

4

Amner's Farm

Fehill Farm

Trash Green

Green Farm

69

FOLLY LA

Burghfield St Mary's CE Prim Sch

The Old Rectory

3

Sewage Works

Pilgrims

Burghfield

Manor House

The Six Bells (PH)

Brook House

POST OFFICE LA

RG30

Stud Farm

Hillfields

Burghfield Place

68

Clayhill Copse

Pondhouse Farm

Scratchface Copse

Works

G7

HORNBEAM PIGHTLE

Simpson's Farmhouse

2

Highwoods

Chandlers Farm

PALMER'S LA

Garland Jnr Sch

Hill Farm

Burghfield Hill

Jame's Farm

Culverlands

67

HIGHFIELD CT

Culverlands Farm

Pitchkettle Wood

PO

GREAT AUCLUM PL

Great Auclum

Goddard's Green

Pierce's Farm

1

SPRING WOOD LA

Kennels

Rookery Wood

Oakfield

PALMER'S LA

Burghfield Slade

Pullen's Pond

Wokefield Common

Milham Pond

GORING LA

LOCKRAM LA

66

A 66 B 67 C

111
85

A   B   C

Knight's Farm

BERRYS LA

KITTONS FARM RD

Kirtons Farm Country Club

Small Mead Farm

BROOK DR

Madejski Stadium

ASCOT RD

NOTH MILL RD

SHOOT

ASCOT END BISCUIT WAY 2

HURS

Works

M4

4

LONG WATER DR

SOUTH OAK WAY

RG2

Pingewood

RG30

Brewery

PINGEWOOD RD S

Moores Farm

69

Pinge Wood

Hartley Court Farm

Hartley Court

HARTLEY COURT RD

Amner's Wood

Burghfield Brook

Hopkiln Farm

3

BURNTHOUSE LA

CUFES LA

Burnthouse Farm

Great Lea Farm

Works

Burnthouse Bridge

68

RIDGE LA

RG7

Foudry Brook

MEREOAK LA

FULLERS LA

Manor Farm

Grazeley Court Farm

Gravelly Bridge Farm

2

PALMER'S

Poundgreen Farm

Bell Copse

Poundgreen

Gravelly Bridge

The Old Bell (PH)

B3349 CHURCH LA

67

Rapleys

Shepherdton La

The Wheatsheaf (PH)

Lambwoodhill Common

Grazeley Parochial Prim Sch

Grazeley

Woodcock Lane

Highlands

Diddenham Manor Farm

1

GOODDIES LA

Lambwoodhill Farm

LAMBWOOD HILL

Thurley Farm

BROOMFIELD DITCH LA

A33

66

68   A   69   B   70   C

111
138

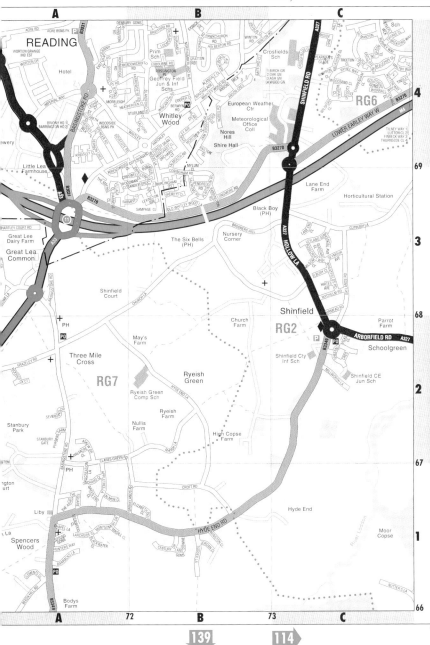

READING

RG6

RG2

Shinfield

RG7

Three Mile Cross

Ryeish Green

Spencers Wood

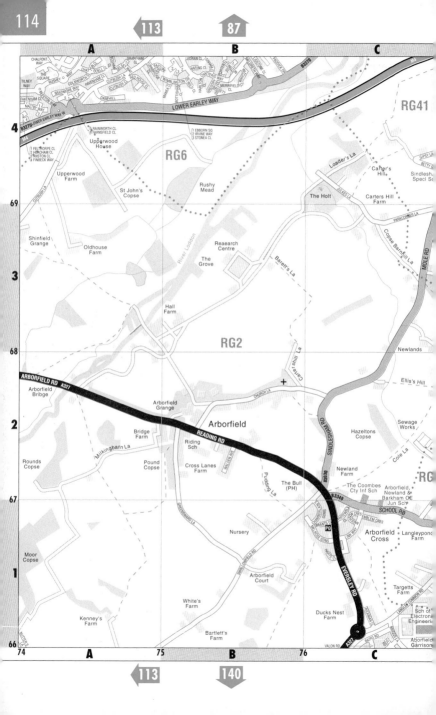

RG41

RG6

RG2

RG

ARBORFIELD RD A327

READING RD

SINDLESHAM RD B3030

EVERSLEY RD

Arborfield Bribge

Arborfield Grange

Arborfield

Bridge Farm

Riding Sch

Cross Lanes Farm

Pound Copse

Rounds Copse

Moor Copse

Kenney's Farm

White's Farm

Bartlett's Farm

Arborfield Court

Nursery

The Bull (PH)

Newland Farm

The Coombes Cty Inf Sch

Arborfield, Newland & Barkham OE Jun Sch

Arborfield Cross

Langleypond Farm

Targetts Farm

Ducks Nest Farm

Sch of Electronic Engineering

Arborfield Garrison

SCHOOL RD

VALON RD A327

Hazeltons Copse

Sewage Works

Cole La

Newlands

Ellis's Hill

The Holt

Loader's La

Carter's Hills

Carters Hill Farm

Sindlesham Specl Sc

Copse Barn Hill La

MOLE RD

PARKCORNER LA

Barett's La

Carters Hill La

CHURCH LA

Research Centre

The Grove

Hall Farm

River Loddon

Rushy Mead

St John's Copse

Upperwood Farm

Shinfield Grange

Oldhouse Farm

Upperwood House

LOWER EARLEY WAY

B3270

M4

① FELTHORPE CL
② HORNCHAM CL
③ INGSTON CL
④ FINBECK WAY

① RAINWORTH CL
② TARNSFIELD CL

① EBBORN SQ
② IRVINE WAY
③ STONEA CL

Milkingbarn La

Pudding La

GREENSWARD LA

SWALLOWFIELD RD

BRAMBLE CRES

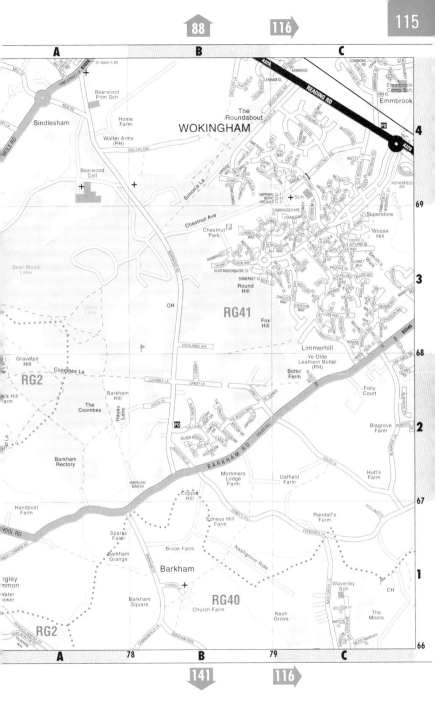

A   B   C

ST MARY'S RD
KING STREET LA
MILL LA
B3030
NEW RD
Bearwood Prim Sch
Home Farm
Sindlesham
Walter Arms (PH)
SADLERS END
Bearwood Coll
MOLE RD

The Roundabout
WOKINGHAM

Simon's La

Chestnut Ave

Chestnut Park

Bear Wood Lake

Upper Lake

CH

RG41

REMBRANDT CL
TIEPOLO CL
HUNTINGDONSHIRE CL
CAMBRIDGESHIRE CL
RUSKIN WAY
TRAFALGAR
SOMERSET CL
Round Hill
Fox Hill

Superstore

Woose Hill

Smith's Walk

CHAUCER WAY
SHERIDAN WAY

ROWAN

Limmerhill

Ye Olde Leathern Bottel (PH)

Bottel Farm

Folly Court

HIGHLANDS AVE

Gravelpit Hill
Coombes La
RG2

Barkham Hill
The Coombes

Hayes Lane

COOMBES LA
SANDY LA
LAMMAS CT
ST JAMES
ALMOND CL

Blagrove Farm

DOLES LA

Hutt's Farm

Barkham Rectory

SILVER BIRCHES
ASH WAY
RUSSELL DR
BARKHAM MANOR

THE LILAC
HORNBEAM

Mortimers Lodge Farm

Daffield Farm

BARKHAM RD

Handpost Farm

Sparks Farm

Barkham Grange

Coppid Hill

Ednys Hill Farm

Nashgrove Ride

Randall's Farm

EVENDON'S LA

Brook Farm

Barkham

REDLANDS DR

Langley Common
Water Tower

Barkham Square

CHURCH LA

RG40

Church Farm

Nash Grove

Waverley Sch

GOLDSMITH

WATSON CL

The Moors

CH

RG2

PRINCE OF WALES DR
ISAAC NEWTON WAY
HILBORN

COMMONFIELD LA

BARKHAM RIDE

A   78   B   79   C

4

69

3

68

2

67

1

66

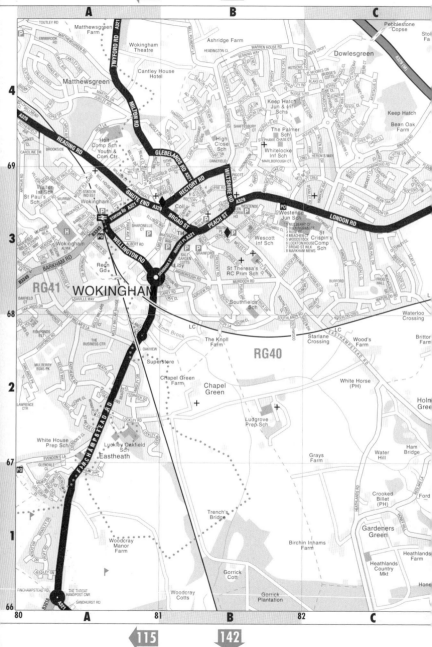

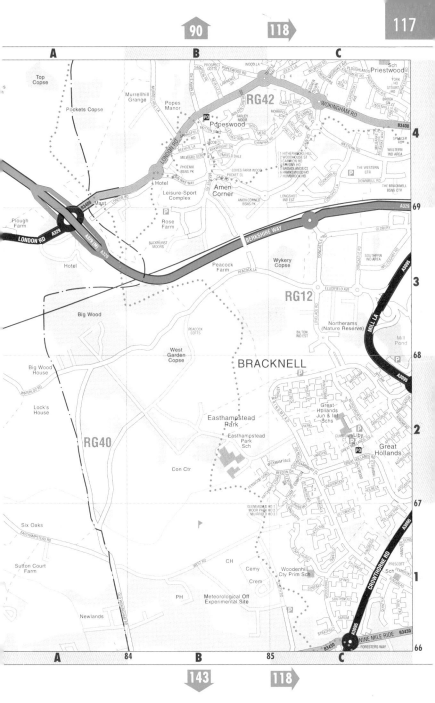

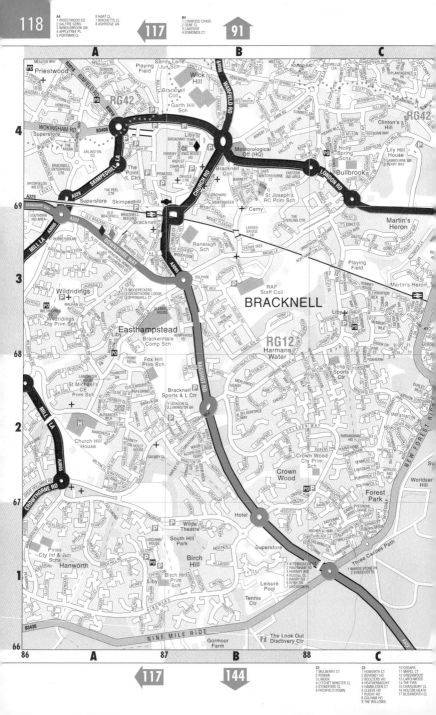

A   B   C

Chavey
Down

Big
Wood

MAIN DR

B3017

PRIORY RD

Pump
Rough

SANDY LA

Windsor
Forest

THE GROVE

NORTH RD

CHURCH RD

Mast

P

Ascot
Priory

Cemy

Heathfield
Sch

Hotel

The
Brackens

LAVENDER
PK

FOREST RD

Hereford
House
P

Whitmoor
Bog

Sewage
Wks

RG12

Blacksmith's
Hill

Icehouse
Hill

Swinley
Park

CLAYHILL CL

Three Castles Path

WINDSOR RD

B3017

SWINLEY RD

Passmore's
Plantation

CROWN
COTTS

BLANE'S LA

Tower
Hill

Blane's
Allotment

Bright's
Allotment

A   90   B

WOODEND CL 1
KING EDWARDS RISE 2
QUEENS CL 3
KING EDWARDS CL 4

ROYAL HUNT HO 1
OAK LEAF CT 2

CH   PO

Liby

BURLEIGH LA

1 DRUCE WOOD
2 BOWYER WLK

1 MARSTON WAY
2 CHERINGTON WAY

ST CHRISTOPHERS
GDNS

BRACKEN BANK

FERNBANK

WENTWORTH WAY

WENTWORTH AVE

GOATERS RD

NAPPER CL

NORTH LODGE DR

THE CLOSE

WARREN
ROW

MANSFIELD

AUDLEY WAY

THE LAWNS

LICKTON
CHASE

VALLEY CR

QUEENS RIDE

North
Ascot

Papplewick
Sch

WINDSOR RD

A332

CHURCHILL RD

London Rd   Ascot
                                   Race Course

LONDON RD

Englemere
Pond

Englemere Pond
Nature Trail   Woodstock

Englemere

HIGH ST   A329

H

Heatherwood

KING'S RIDE

SL5

PRINCE CONSORT DR

PRIORY RD

LC

King's Ride
House

Green
Acres

BEAUMONT
CT

68

P

Kingsride

WOODLANDS
RIDE

2

WOODLANDS CL

WRIGHT RD

67

Butterstep
Hill

Swinley Forest
CH

WODENS RIDE

Butterstep
Allotments

Butterstep
House

A332

BUTTERSTEEP RISE

1

66

A   90   B   91   C

69

4

3

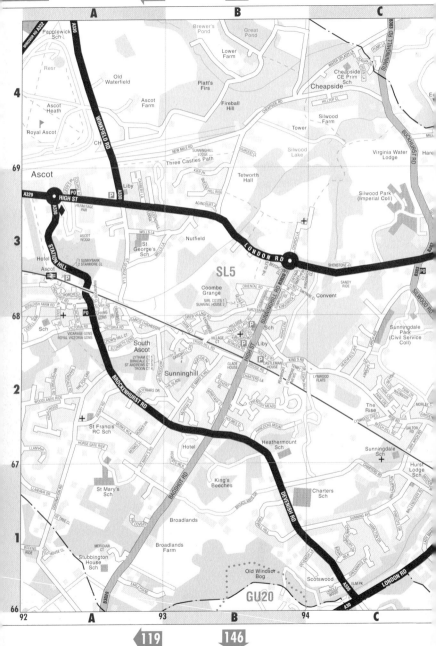

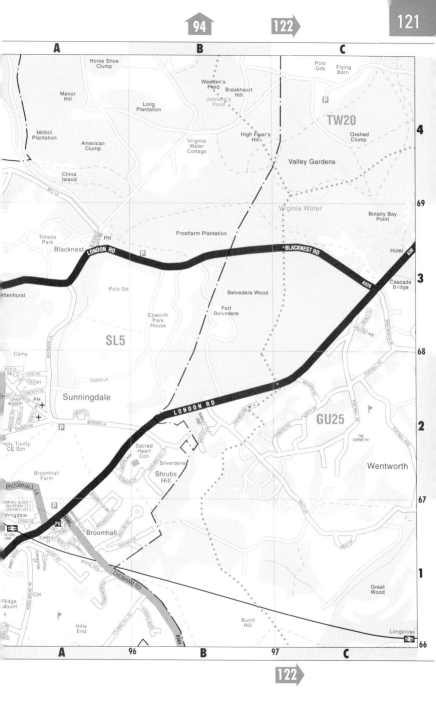

A   B   C

Horse Shoe
Clump

Weeden's
Field
Breakheart
Hill

Polo
Gds
Flying
Barn

Manor
Hill

Long
Plantation

Johnson's
Pond

P

Millhill
Plantation

American
Clump

Virginia
Water
Cottage

High Flyer's
Hill

TW20

Oxshed
Clump

4

China
Island

MILL LA

Valley Gardens

Virginia Water

69

Titness
Park

PH

Frostfarm Plantation

Botany Bay
Point

LONDON RD

BLACKNEST RD

Hotel

A30

Blacknest

P

Cascade
Bridge

A329

3

ettenhurst

Polo Gd

Belvedere Wood

CHESTNUT AVE

WENTWORTH DR

Coworth
Park
House

Fort
Belvedere

68

SL5

Cemy

WHITMORE LA

CHURCH LA

MANOR RD

PORTNALL RD

KILN LA
DALE CL
LODGE RD

SANDY
NURSERY

PH

WENTWORTH RD

LONDON RD

SHRUBS HILL LA

RIDGEMOUNT RD

PORTNALL DR

PORTNALL RISE

GU25

THE
DORMY HO

2

CHURCH RD
BEDFORD LA

HEATHWOOD RD

WESTERN RD

Wentworth

Sunningdale

Holy Trinity
CE Sch

P

Sacred
Heart
Coll

WELLS RD

Silverdene

WEST DR

67

Broomhall
Farm

BROOMHALL LA

SUNWOOD RD

Shrubs
Hill

BROOMFIELD RD

WEST DR

BROOMHALL BLDGS 1
HALFPENNY CT 2
STATION FLATS 3

Sunningdale

CEDAR DR

P

Broomhall

WEATHER DR

WEST DR

STATION
PARK

CLAREFIELD

ABBEY WOOD

PRIORY CT

BRIDGE VIEW

CHOBHAM RD

1

Ridge
Mount

CH

CHERISTON
COURT

Hills
End

Burnt
Hill

Great
Wood

Longcross

66

A   B   C
96   97

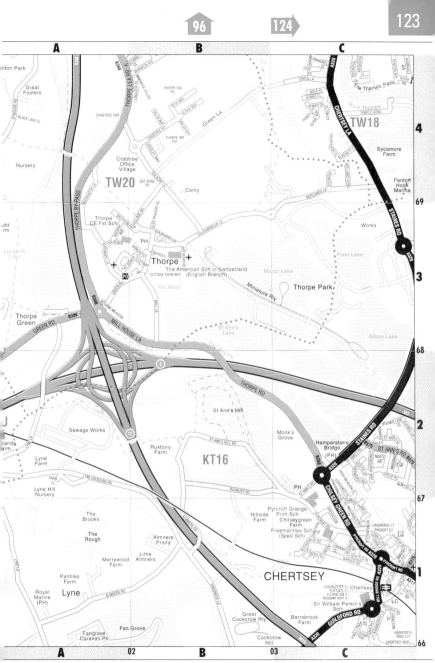

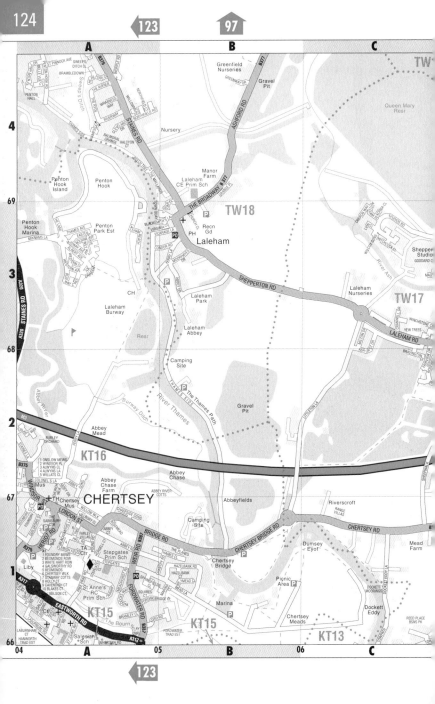

123
97

A   B   C

TW

Queen Mary Resr

Greenfield Nurseries

Gravel Pit

4

Nursery

Manor Farm

Laleham CE Prim Sch

THE BROADWAY

TW18

69

Shepperton Studio

GODDARD C

Penton Hook Island

Penton Hook

River Ash

Penton Hook Marina

Penton Park Est

Recn Gd

PH

Laleham

3

BLACKSMITH

VICARAGE LA

PO

CONDOR RD

SHEPPERTON RD

Laleham Nurseries

TW17

Laleham Burway

CH

Laleham Park

Laleham Abbey

LALEHAM RD

WINCHSTONE C

VIEW TREES

68

Resr

Camping Site

The Thames Path

River Thames

Gravel Pit

2

M3

Abbey Mead

BURLEY ORCHARD

KT16

Abbey Chase Farm

Abbey Chase

ABBEY RIVER COTTS

Abbeyfields

Riverscroft

RANGE VILLAS

COLONELS LA

Mus

67

TH Chertsey Mus

CHERTSEY

WILLOW WLK

CHASESIDE GDNS

Camping Site

CHERTSEY RD

Mead Farm

LONDON ST

PO

BRIDGE RD

WEIR RD

Dumsey Eyot

THE SAINSBURY

CHERTSEY BRIDGE RD

HEROD RD

Chertsey Bridge

THE PLANES

HAZELBANK RD

HAZELBANK

Y MEAD CL

Stepgates Prim Sch

1

Liby

1 FOUNDRY MEWS
2 BEOMONDS ROW
3 WHITE HART ROW
4 GALSWORTHY RD
5 BEOMONDS
6 CHERTSEY WLK
7 STANWAY COTTS
8 HOLLY CT
9 CAVENDISH CT
10 BLAKES CT.
11 NELSON CT.

St Anne's RC Prim Sch

SQUIRES

FORDWATER RD

Picnic Area

Marina

DOCKETT MOORINGS

Dockett Eddy

REED PLACE BSNS PK

A317

EASTWORTH RD

KT15

The Bourn

Salesian Sch

WHITEACRE RD

A317

Chertsey Meads

KT15

KT13

FORDWATER TRAD EST

LABURNHAM CT

HANWORTH TRAD EST

66

04   A   05   B   06   C

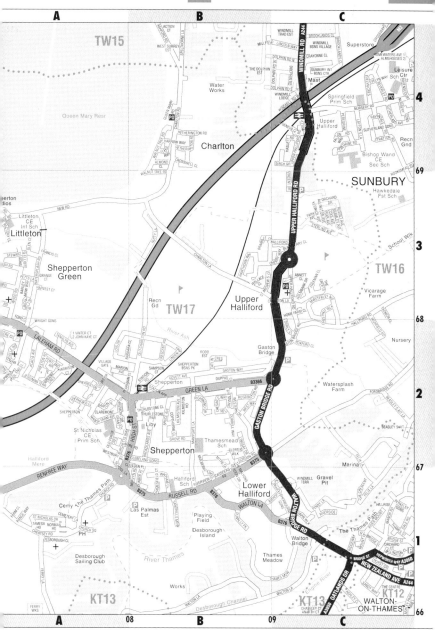

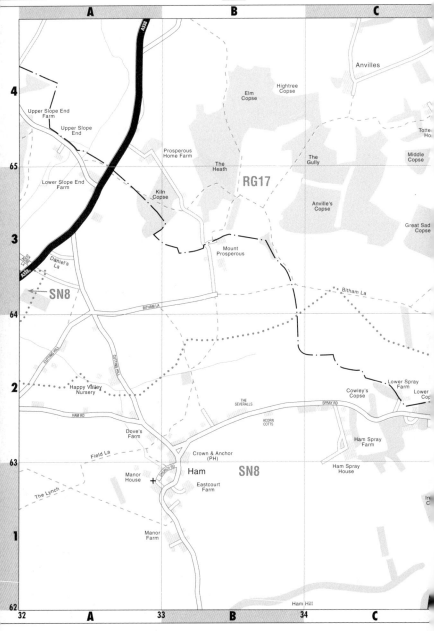

A   B   C

4

Anvilles

Upper Slope End
Farm

Upper Slope
End

Hightree
Copse

Elm
Copse

Totte
Ho

Prosperous
Home Farm

The
Heath

The
Gully

Middle
Copse

65

Lower Slope End
Farm

RG17

Kiln
Copse

Anville's
Copse

Great Sad
Copse

3

Daniel's
La

Mount
Prosperous

SN8

Bitham La

64

BITHAM LA

Lower Spray
Farm

2

Happy Valley
Nursery

Cowley's
Copse

Lower
Cop

HAM RD

THE
SEVERALLS

SPRAY RD

Dove's
Farm

ACORN
COTTS

Ham Spray
Farm

Field La

Crown & Anchor
(PH)

63

Manor
House

Ham

SN8

Ham Spray
House

In
C

The Lynch

Eastcourt
Farm

1

Manor
Farm

62

Ham Hill

32   A   33   B   34   C

A   B   C

St Cassian's

Templeton
Border

High
Trees

Winterly
Copse

Catmore
Copse

Winterly La

New Templeton
Gorse

erdown
opse

Titcomb
Manor

Cherrytree
Copse

Pond
Close

Follygully
Copse

Titcomb

4

Balsdon
Farm

BACK LA

ttle
mmon
rs

The
Firs

Finch's
Copse

Blandy's
Corner

Pondgully
Wood

Holly
Copse

Titcomb
Farm

65

The
Folly

ANTHILL RD

Clayground
Copse

Moss
Farm

CRAVEN RD

Northcroft
Farm

The
Folly

Inkpen
Prim Sch

FOLLY RD

SPRINGFIELD

THE OLD
SAWMILLS

Fox
Hill

Vale
Farm
The
Swan Inn
(PH)

WEAVERS LA

Gully
Copse

BRACKEN
COPSE

3

Sands Dro

Lower
Green

The
Plantation

Great
Plantation

Manor
Farm

Inkpen

THE FIRS

POST OFFICE RD

64

RG17

POTTERY LA

Wergs
Barn

The Wansdyke

+

PH

B 17HAM LA

The Drove

Rolf's
Farm

SPRAY RD

Trapshill

2

+

INGLES
EDGE

Upper
Green

Bungum La

Kirby
Farm

Rookery
Copse

BELL LA

Kirby
House

63

SN8

Red
Woods

Oldlands
Copse

1

Gallows
Down

RG20

Little Rivar
Copse

Combe
Gibbet

Rivar
opse

Inkpen
Hill

Test Way

Wayfarers Wlk

P

62

A   36   B   37   C

A   **B**   **C**

Horn Copse

Kintbury Holt Farm

Hankin's La

Mason's Farm

Barr's Farm

OLD LA

Queenhills Copse

4

Cowleaze

Godfreys

Hightree Copse

Old Hat

The Oaks

Wergs Copse

Crossways Country Club

Kintbury

BACK LA

Cemy

FORBURY LA

Mount Pleasant

KINTBURY RD

Curr Copse

Little Holt Copse

Great Holt Copse

65

Kintbury Cross Ways

Forbury House

PEBBLE HILL

RG17

Holt Lodge

Skew-whiff

Milkhouse Copse

Waterman's Copse

New Mill

Rooksnest

The Adlers

BRIDGES LA

Holt Manor Farm

Waterman's Farm

3

ROOKSNEST LA

Burgess Farm

HEADS LA

Nature Reserve

Inkpen Great Common

Hell Corner

Furze Parks

WATERY LA

64

Middle Furze Park

Holly La

Bricklayers Farm

Malt House

Holly Copse

Prosser's Farm

Prosser's Hanging

RG20

Haz Ho

2

Great Farm

Brickplace Copse

Green Farm Copse

Malthouse Farm

Smart's Copse

West Woodhay House

Fishponds Farm

Ansell' Copse

West Woodhay

63

Chalky Close

Wilmot's Farm

Green Plantation

Park House

Bagnell's Copse

Old Rectory

Hatch House Farm

North

Hatch House Plantations

1

Berries Copse

North

Highwood Farm

Woodcut Copse

Hayes

North Farm

Berries Farm

62

38   **A**   **39**   **B**   **40**   **C**

A   B   C

White Hill
Farm

Hamstead
Marshall

Elm
Farm

White Hart Inn
(PH)

Plumb
Farm

Ashtree
Plantation

Wise's
Border

Spicer's
Copse

PARK LA

ASH TREE GR

4

Hamstead Park

Enborne Copse

Enborne

Church
Farm

Avery's Pightle
(Nature Reserve)

CHURCH LA

65

Briff's
Copse

Mayhouse
Gullies

Holtwood
Farm

Smith's
Bridge

Holtwood

Gore End
Bridge

Gore End

Hillier's
Farm

Ball Hill

Burlyns
Farm

Burlyns

orth
End

Heath
End

Little
Farm

Red Hill

Redhill Wood

The Craven Arms
(PH)

Redhill
Plantation

RG20

Crockhamheath
Farm

Vanner's
Farm

Round
Copse

River Enborne

Hatt Common

Knight's
Farm

Ball Hill
Farm

Lane End
Farm

Yew
Tree
Farm

STROUD LAND
IND EST

KNIGHTS LA

GORE END RD

PH

Hatt Farm

WELLINGTON
COTTS

Burley
Moor
Farm

Oakhurst

Woolton House
Farm

Woolton
House

Farm
Copse

Woolton House
Stud

Hobley La

FULLERS LA

HOLT WOOD RD

WATERY LA

GRAVEL LA

CHURCH CL

VANNERS LA

Enborne Street
Farm

Enborne
Prim Sch

Braylands
Copse

Crockham
Heath

Long
Copse

BARKERS LA

CHURCH LA

3

Bigg's Hill

Bourne
Farm

Bourne
House

East Woodhay
House

Slade Hill

Harwood
Farm

Harwood
Lodge

ENBORNE ST

STATION RD

WOOLTON LODGE GDNS

HARWOOD RISE

ELM COTTS

PH

Broad
Laying

GREENWAYS

GREENMORE

GREEN CL

GREEN ACRE

LONGMEAD

ELM BANK VIEW

MASON
CT

62

64

2

63

1

42   43

A   B   C

A   B   C

4

Skinners
Green
Farm

Skinners Green La

Skinners
Green

Round Hill

NEWBURY

John Rankin
Cty Jun & Inf
Schs

BARTLEMY RD

BARTLEMY

MEADOW RD

Oaken
Copse

COPSE HALL LA

65

Foxgrove

Wash
Common
Farm

ESSEX ST

PO

Falkland Meml

RG14

Crook's
Copse

WHEATLANDS LA

WILMOT WLK 1
GOODWIN WLK 2
VILLIERS WLK 3
NORTON CL 4

Wr Twr

Falkland
Prim Sch

Slockett's
Copse

ANDOVER RD

3

Wheatlands
Farm

Redding's
Copse

Redding's
Copse

Enborne
Lodge Sch

KINGS
MEAD

JOHN
BOYS'
RD

LEWIS
WLK

SPENCER RD

PHOENIX
WLK

Park House
Sch

Warren
Lodge

Boame's
Farm

BOAMES LA

THE CHANDLERS

WARREN RD

KENDRICK RD

Wash
Common

Gorse Covert

64

ENBORNE ST

BELL HILL

WILLOWMEAD CL

CONIFER CREST

NORMAY RISE

BADGERS RD

SMALLRIDGE

Bunker's Hill

ANDOVER DRO

Enborne
Row

Wash Water
House

The
Woodpecker
(PH)

SANDPIT HILL

River Enborne

Oakleaze
Farm

2

WASH WATER

Wash Water

Falkland
Farm

Common
Farm

STATION RD

Riding
Centre

PENWOOD RD

Horris Hill
Sch

63

The Chase

Poultry
Farm

Woodedge
Farm

RG20

Horris Hill

SHEEPWA

1

Sewage
Works

Wheatlands
Farm

SNELSMORE

WOODBINE

62

A343

Great Pen Wood

Brown Hill
Plantation

P

Deadman's
Bottom

Tot Hill

Tot Hill
Farm

A34

B4640

Woodbin
Farm

44   A   45   B   46   C

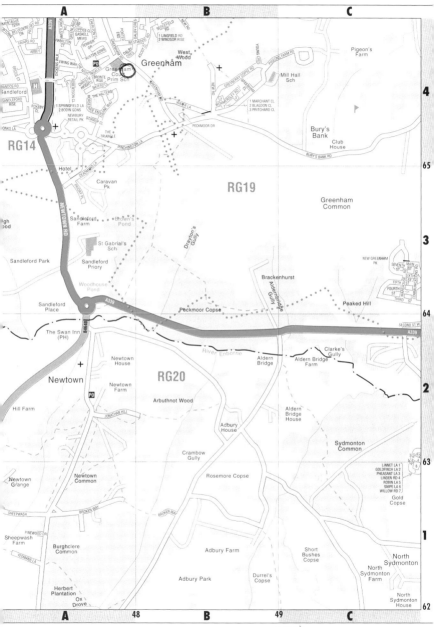

RG14

RG19

Greenham

West
Wood

Pigeon's
Farm

Mill Hall
Sch

1 LINGFIELD RD
2 WINDSOR RISE

1 SPRINGFIELD LA
2 BODIN GDNS

NEWBURY
RETAIL PK

THE HALTERS

1 MARCHANT CL
2 BLAGDON CL
3 PRITCHARD CL

PECKMOOR DR

Bury's
Bank

Club
House

BURY'S BANK RD

Greenham
Common

Hotel

Caravan
Pk

Sandleford
Farm

Brown's
Pond

St Gabriel's
Sch

Sandleford Park

Sandleford
Priory

Woodhouse
Pond

Drayton's
Gully

Brackenhurst

Aldermbridge
Gully

NEW GREENHAM
PK

SEVENTH
ST

MAIN
ST

SIXTH
ST

FIFTH
ST

FOURTH
ST

THIRD
ST

Peaked Hill

Sandleford
Place

A339

Peckmoor Copse

SECOND ST W

A339

NEWTOWN RD

The Swan Inn
(PH)

B4640

River Enborne

Clarke's
Gully

Aldern
Bridge

Aldern Bridge
Farm

Newtown
House

Newtown
Farm

Newtown

RG20

Arbuthnot Wood

Aldern
Bridge
House

Hill Farm

JONATHAN HILL

Adbury
House

Sydmonton
Common

Crambow
Gully

Rosemore Copse

LINNET LA 1
GOLDFINCH LA 2
PHEASANT LA 3
LINDEN RD 4
ROBIN LA 5
SNIPE LA 6
WILLOW RD 7

Gold
Copse

Newtown
Grange

Newtown
Common

SHEEPWASH

BROKEN WAY

BROKEN WAY

Sheepwash
Farm

Burghclere
Common

PINEWOOD DR

YEOMANS LA

Adbury Farm

Adbury Park

Durrel's
Copse

Short
Bushes
Copse

North
Sydmonton
Farm

North
Sydmonton

North
Sydmonton
House

Herbert
Plantation

Ox
Drove

4

65

3

64

2

63

1

62

131
106

A   B   C

Football Ground
CHAMBERHOUSE MILL LA

Bowdown Farm
Cakeball Copse
Sayer's Copse
River Kennet
Chamberhouse Farm
Avenell's Cottages

4

Bowdown House
Ashen Copse
Conduit Copse
Highfield Copse

Longlane Gully

65

Great Wood
Nature Reserve
The Round House
BURY'S BANK RD

Crookham Court

Thornford Hights

Greenham Common

3

RG19

Crookham Common

George's Farm

Goldfinch Bottom

Boar's Gully

64

Head's Hill
Head's Hill Farm
Foxhold House
Foxhold Farm
THORNFORD RD
Ford
South Lands
Low Cop

A339
Martindale Farm
River Enborne
George's Wood

2

Ppg Sta
Knight's Bridge
Knightsbridge Farm
The Oven
Folly Farm

Sewage Works

Bishop's Green

Knightsbridge House

THORNFORD RD

Mill Green

63

Bishop's Green Farm
KNIGHTSBRIDGE DR
THORNFIELD

Bishop's Green Farm
Upper Knightsbridge Farm
Forge Farm
Holly Bush Farm
ASHFORD HILL RD

CROOKSFIELD
PO
Cherry Tree Farm

1

RG20
Pitts Farm
Hill View Farm
ST PETERS LD
Longcross Farm
Headley
Nursery

HYDE LA
The Harrow (PH)
Fuces Farm

North Ecchinswell Farm
Headley House
Headley Stud
A339

62

50   A   51   B   52   C

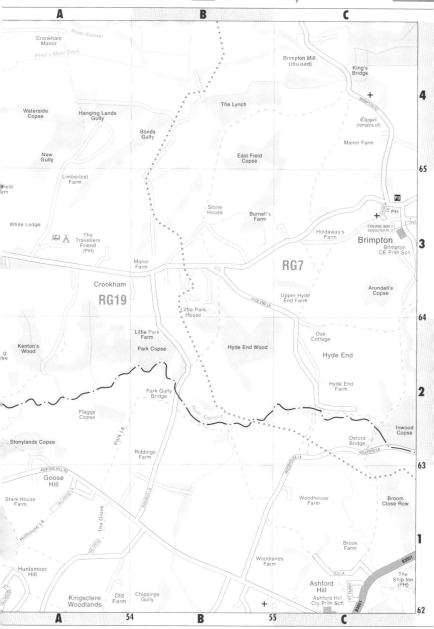

A   B   C

Crookham Manor
River Kennet
Prior's Moor Ditch

Brimpton Mill
(disused)
King's Bridge

4

Waterside Copse
Hanging Lands Gully
The Lynch

Chapel
(remains of)
Manor Farm

Bonds Gully

New Gully
East Field Copse

65

Limberlost Farm

White Lodge
Stone House
Burnell's Farm
Holdaway's Farm

Brimpton
ENBORNE WAY 1
BANNISTER PL 2

Brimpton CE Prim Sch

The Travellers Friend (PH)

Manor Farm

RG7

3

Crookham

RG19
Upper Hyde End Farm

Arundell's Copse

Little Park House

Oak Cottage

64

Little Park Farm
Park Copse
Hyde End Wood
Hyde End

Kenton's Wood

Hyde End Farm

2

Park Gully Bridge
River Enborne

Flaggy Copse

Inwood Copse

Stonylands Copse
Park La
Riddings Farm
Oxford Bridge
ROCKFORD LA

63

Goose Hill
ASHFORD HILL RD
HILLHOUSE LA

Woodhouse Farm
Broom Close Row

Stark House Farm
Hillhouse La
The Drove

1

Huntsmoor Hill

Brook Farm

B3051
OLD LA

Kingsclere Woodlands
Old Farm
Chippings Gully
Woodlands Farm

Ashford Hill
Ashford Hill Cty Prim Sch

The Ship Inn (PH)

62

A   54   B   55   C

A **B** **C**

4

River Kennet

Bottle Cottage

Malthouse Cottages

Hinc
Aldermaston Hea
CE Prim Sch (PH-

Landing Strip

FORST

Wasing Lower Farm

Wasing Lodge

65

WASING LA

River Enborne

Shalford Lodge

Forster
Farm

Shalford Farm

Wasing Park

3

Bannister's Wood

RG7

Breaches Gully

Chaplin's Wood

Garden Piece

+ Wasing

Able Bridge

HOME FARM LA

Wasing Home Farm

Paices Wood

64

BACK LA

Stockwell Farmhouse

Howell's Wood

Broom Close

YOUN
ND H

Boot Farm

2

Paice's Gully

Wasing Wood

Inwood Copse

Old Stock Farm

Brimpton Common

BRIMPTON LA

PAICES HILL

Blacknest Farm

Burnha
Cops

63

MOORFORD LA

Larkwhistle Farm

Lodge

Wr Twr

CALLEVA PARK

A340

Burnh
Planta

A340

Ashford Hill Farr

The Pineapple Inn (PH)

B3051

A340

Broom Close Row

LITTLE KNIGHSBY

Borson Cottages

FOREST CL

PLANTATION RD

BIRCH RD

SURZE RD

BURNHAM RD

1

RG26

The Hurst Com Sch

LONG GR

HEATS CNR

FIR TREE CNR

PO

PORTWAY

BISHOPSWOOD

NEWCHURCH RD

HANGE
MINTER
CT

B3051

Baughurst Common

BRIMPTON RD

SHYSHACK LA

Heath End
Tadley

RG19

HAUGHURST HILL

STOKES LA

PO

BISHOPSWOOD RD

HALSTEAD
RD

WIGMORE RD

+

+

Haughurst Hill

HAZEL GREEN

1 HEATHLANDS
2 HEPPLEWHITE CL
3 CHIPPEDALE CL

INHURST WAY

HARTSHILL
RD

Redlands Copse

HEATHROW COPSE

DOURO CL

62

56 **A** 57 **B** 58 **C**

A   B   C

Aqua Vitae
Copse

Fisherman's
Cottage

Upper Lodge
Farm

The Old
Rectory

Sawmill

Upper Church
Farm

Padworth
Gully

4

Aldermaston
Church
Farm

Springhill
Farm

Wrays
Farm

Hatch
Farm
House

CONGREVE CL   CHURCH RD

SPRING LA

RECTORY RD

65

Portland
House

The Birches

BIGHAM HILL

Court
Farm

RAGHILL

Raghill
Farm

Wr Twr

DELTA

Black
Pightle

Old Warren

3

Harbourhill
Copse

PACES HILL

RG7

CHAP LA

WELSHMAN'S RD

64

Little Heath

VALENTINE WOOD
IND EST

2

Decoy
Pond

SOKE RD

Aldermaston
Soke

63

Upper Moor's
Gully

THIRD AVE
SECOND AVE
FIRST AVE
RAVENSWING
MOBILE HOME PK

Soke
Pig Farm

PH

FALCON FIELDS

A340

KENNINGTON LA

White House
Farm

PELICAN RD

WAKEFORD CT

1

ALMSWOOD RD

BRACKENWOOD DR

MULFORDS HILL A340

Liby

STACEY'S
IND EST

SILCHESTER RD

RG26

SPENCER CL

PO

PAMBER HEATH RD

CHURCH RD

WAKEFORD CL
KNOLLYS RD

Pamber
Heath

FRANKLIN AVE

BISHOPS

GLENDALE

THE
PARADE

Tadley
Court

BRACKNELL PL

TADLEY COMMON RD

Tadley Common

CHURCH RD

VALLEY WAY

SPRING CL

THE GLEN

RUSSELL RD

NEWCHURCH RD

OAK TREE
CL

SILVERDALE RD

BLAMES LA

GORSELANDS

SIMPSON RD

ARNEWOOD AVE

WESTLYN
RD

EASTLYN
RD

HEATH RD

BURNEY BIT

62

SOUTHDOWN RD

STANFIELD

A   60   B   61   C

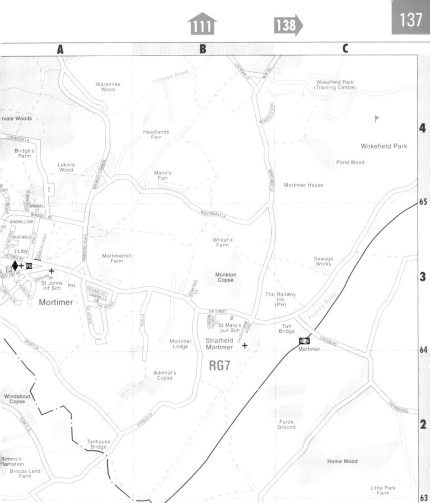

A   B   C

Lockram Brook

Warennes Wood

Wokefield Park (Training Centre)

rvale Woods

4

Headlands Farr

Wokefield Park

LONGMOOR LA

Pond Wood

Bridge's Farm

Mortimer House

Lukin's Wood

Mann's Farr

WINDMILL CT
WINDMILL RD

NIGHTINGALE LA

65

WINDMILL CNR

HEATHFIELD

Liby

Wheat's Farm

Sewage Works

Mortimerhill Farm

Monkton Copse

3

P ◆ PO

St Johns Inf Sch   PH

The Railway Inn (PH)

CAMPBELLS
THE AVENUE

Foundry Brook

Mortimer

THE STREET

GORDON PALMER

St Mary's Jun Sch

Tun Bridge

Mortimer Lodge

Stratfield Mortimer ✛

STATION RD

64

Admiral's Copse

RG7

⇆ Mortimer

DRURY LA

PITFIELD LA

Windabout Copse

Furze Ground

THE FORBHEAD

2

TULL'S LA

Tanhouse Bridge

Simms's Plantation

Home Wood

Brocas Land Farm

Little Park Farm

63

Sheepgrove Farm

Slinchester Brook

TICKLECORNER LA

Hogs Plat

Butlers Lands

Park Lane
The Devils Highway

e Devil's ighway

PARK LA

1

Butlers Land Copse

MORTIMER LA

Wigmore Farm

Garden Copse

62

A   66   B   67   C

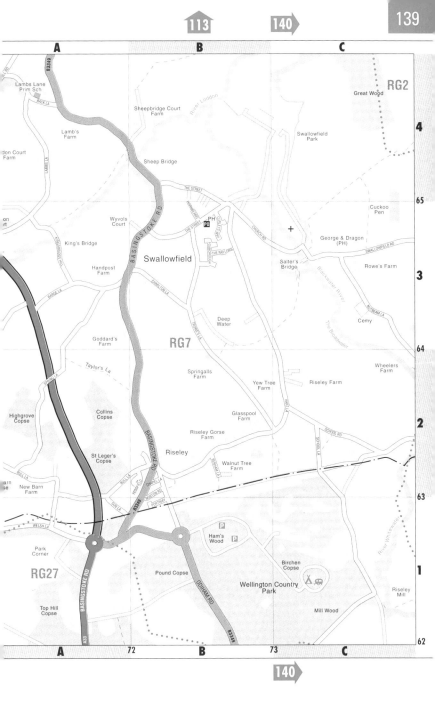

A   B   C

RG2

Great Wood

Lambs Lane
Prim Sch

BACK LA

Lamb's
Farm

Sheepbridge Court
Farm

Swallowfield
Park

4

don Court
Farm

Sheep Bridge

LAMBS LA

THE STREET

65

Cuckoo
Pen

Wyvols
Court

PO

on
rt

King's Bridge

BASINGSTOKE RD

THE STREET

PH

GEORGE & DRAGON

CHURCH RD

Salter's
Bridge

George & Dragon
(PH)

SWALLOWFIELD RD

Rowe's Farm

THUNDRIDGE LA

Swallowfield

TO THE NAYLORS

+

3

Handpost
Farm

BARGE LA

CHARLTON LA

Blackwater River

The Bourwater

NETBEAM LA

Cemy

Deep
Water

RG7

Goddard's
Farm

FROME LA

64

Taylor's La

Springalls
Farm

Yew Tree
Farm

Riseley Farm

Wheelers
Farm

Highgrove
Copse

Collins
Copse

PART LA

2

SCHOOL RD

Glasspool
Farm

St Leger's
Copse

Riseley Gorse
Farm

SCHOOL LA

arn
se

BULL LA

Riseley

BULL LA

FROME RD

New Barn
Farm

BASINGSTOKE RD

B3349

SUN LA

BENGAL LA

Walnut Tree
Farm

63

WELSH LA

MORTON RD

PORTWAY

River Whitewater

Park
Corner

P

Ham's
Wood

P

RG27

Pound Copse

ODIHAM RD

Birchen
Copse

Wellington Country
Park

Riseley
Mill

1

Top Hill
Copse

A33

Mill Wood

B3349

62

A   72   B   73   C

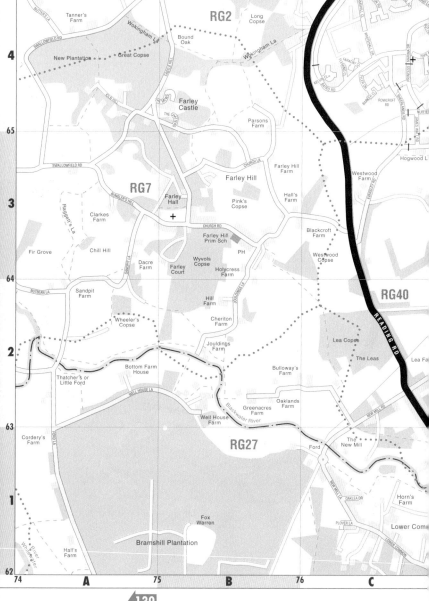

A   B   C

RG2

Tanner's Farm

Long Copse

Bound Oak

Wokingham La

New Plantation

Great Copse

4

Farley Castle

Parsons Farm

65

Farley Hill Farm

Hogwood L

Swallowfield Rd

Farley Hill

Westwood Farm

RG7

Clarkes Farm

Farley Hall

Pink's Copse

Hall's Farm

3

Fir Grove

Chill Hill

Dacre Farm

Farley Court

Wyvols Copse

Farley Hill Prim Sch

PH

Holycress Farm

Blackcroft Farm

Westwood Copse

RG40

64

Nutbean La

Sandpit Farm

Hill Farm

Cheriton Farm

Reading Rd

Wheeler's Copse

Jouldings Farm

Lea Copse

2

Thatcher's or Little Ford

Bottom Farm House

Bulloway's Farm

The Leas

Lea Fa

Well House La

Oaklands Farm

Greenacres Farm

Blackwater River

New Mill Rd

63

Cordery's Farm

Well House Farm

RG27

Ford

The New Mill

Ford La

Fox Warren

Horn's Farm

1

Plover La

Oaklea Dr

Lower Com

Bramshill Plantation

Hall's Farm

River Whitewater

Lower Common

62

74   A   75   B   76   C

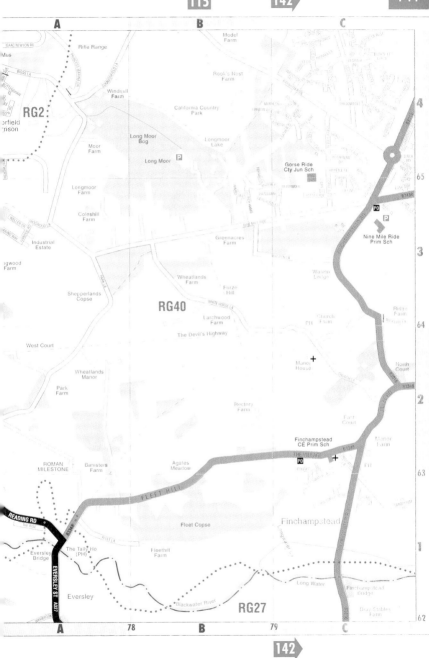

A B C

ISAAC NEWTON RD

Mus

RG2

orfield
rrison

Rifle Range

Windmill
Farm

Rook's Nest
Farm

Model
Farm

California Country
Park

Long Moor
Bog

Longmoor
Lake

Long Moor P

Gorse Ride
Cty Jun Sch

4

65

Moor
Farm

Longmoor
Farm

Coleshill
Farm

Industrial
Estate

PO

P

Nine Mile Ride
Prim Sch

3

gwood
Farm

Shepperlands
Copse

Greenacres
Farm

Wheatlands
Farm

Furze
Hill

RG40

Larchwood
Farm

WHITE HORSE LA

Warren
Lodge

Church
Farm

PH

Ridge
Farm

64

The Devil's Highway

West Court

Wheatlands
Manor

Park
Farm

Manor
House

North
Court

B3348

2

Rectory
Farm

Fayt
Court

Finchampstead
CE Prim Sch

Manor
Farm

ROMAN
MILESTONE

Banisters
Farm

Agates
Meadow

THE VILLAGE PO

63

FH

READING RD

FLEET HILL

Fleet Copse

Finchampstead

Eversley
Bridge

The Tally Ho
(PH)

Fleethill
Farm

Long Water

Finchampstead
Bridge

1

EVERSLEY ST A327

Eversley

Blackwater River

RG27

Drey Stables
Farm

62

A 78 B 79 C

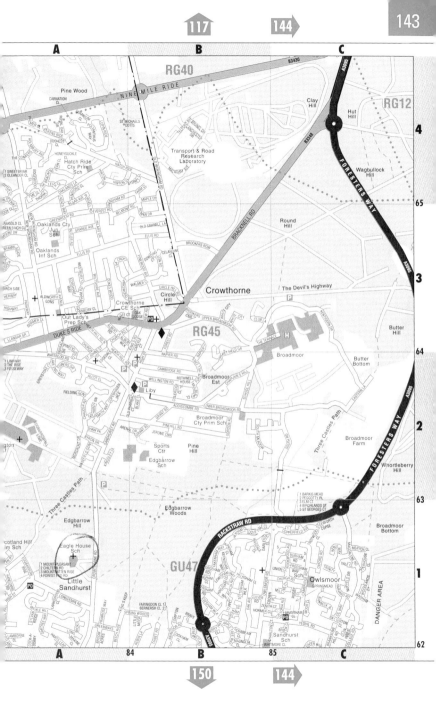

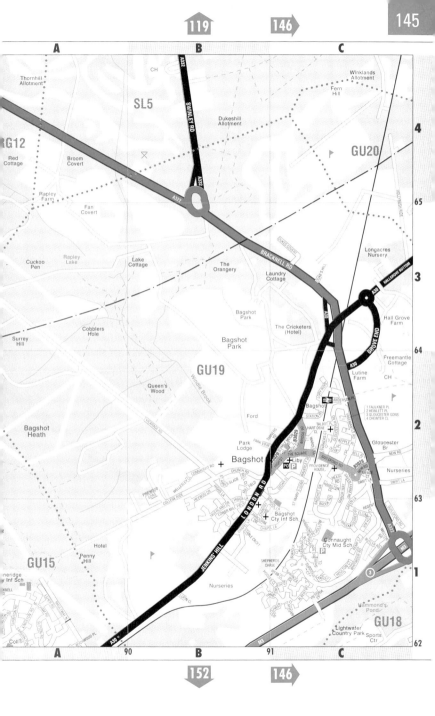

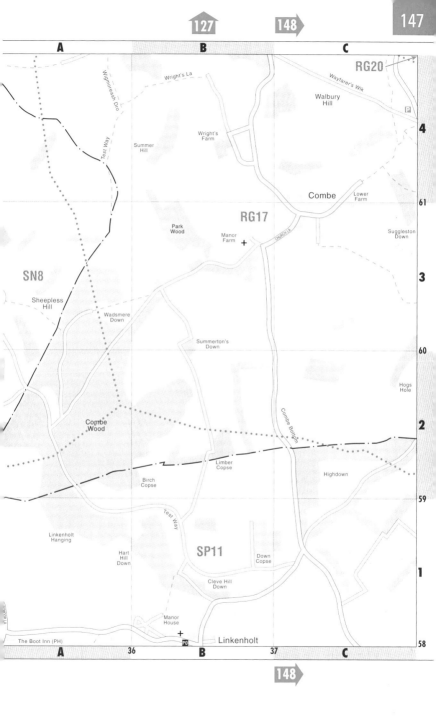

127
148

A   **B**   **C**

RG20

Waylarer's Wlk

Wright's La

Walbury
Hill

P

4

Wigmoreash Dro

Test Way

Wright's
Farm

Summer
Hill

Combe

Lower
Farm

61

Park
Wood

RG17

Manor
Farm

CHURCH LA

Suggleston
Down

SN8

3

Sheepless
Hill

Wadsmere
Down

Summerton's
Down

60

Hogs
Hole

Combe
Wood

Combe Bough

2

Limber
Copse

Highdown

Birch
Copse

59

Test Way

Linkenholt
Hanging

SP11

Down
Copse

1

Hart
Hill
Down

Cleve Hill
Down

Manor
House

The Boot Inn (PH)

PO

Linkenholt

58

A   36   **B**   37   **C**

148

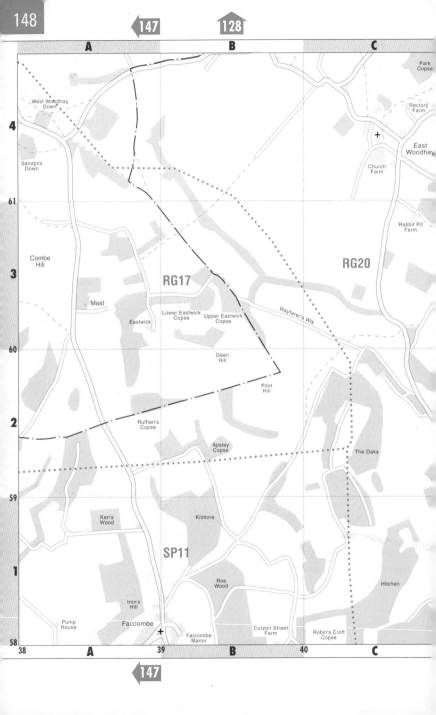

Park Copse

West Woodhay Down

Rectory Farm

East Woodhay

Sandpits Down

Church Farm

Rabbit Pit Farm

RG20

Combe Hill

RG17

Mast

Lower Eastwick Copse

Upper Eastwick Copse

Eastwick

Waylarer's Wik

Dean Hill

Pilot Hill

Ruffian's Copse

Apsley Copse

The Oaks

Ken's Wood

Kilmore

SP11

Hitchen

Roe Wood

Iron's Hill

Pump House

Faccombe

Faccombe Manor

Curzon Street Farm

Robin's Croft Copse

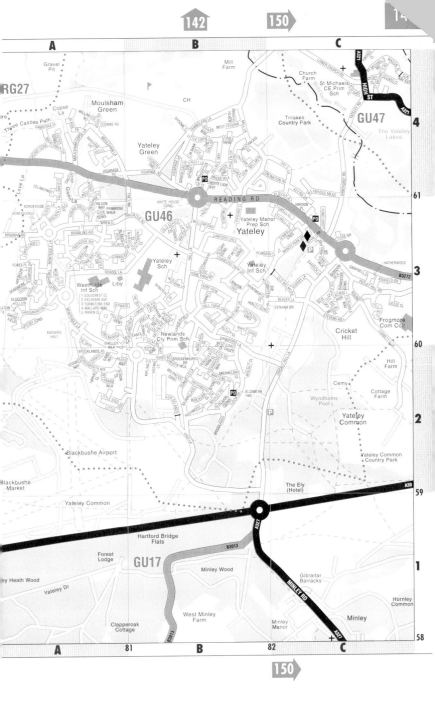

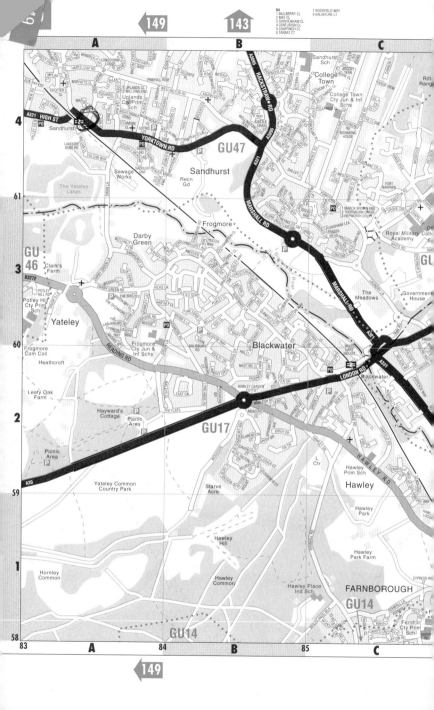

B4
1 MULBERRY CL
2 MAY CL
3 SHRIVENHAM CL
4 CENTURION CL
5 CHAFFINCH CL
6 TARBAT CT

7 ROCKFIELD WAY
8 BALINTORE CT

A   B   C

College Town

Sandhurst Sch

4 A321 HIGH ST
   Sandhurst
   YORKTOWN RD
   GU47
   Sandhurst

61

GU
46

3 Clark's Farm
   B3272
   Yateley
   Darby Green
   Frogmore

Frogmore
Com Coll
Heathcroft

60 Leafy Oak Farm

   Blackwater

   Royal Military Coll Academy

   The Meadows

   Government House

GU

2 Hayward's Cottage
   Picnic Area
   GU17

   Picnic Area
   A30

59 Yateley Common Country Park
   Starve Acre

   Hawley Prim Sch
   Hawley
   Hawley Park

1 Hornley Common
   Hawley Hill
   Hawley Common
   Hawley Park Farm

   Hawley Place Ind Sch
   FARNBOROUGH
   GU14

58 GU14
   Fernhill Cty Prim Sch

83   A   84   B   85   C

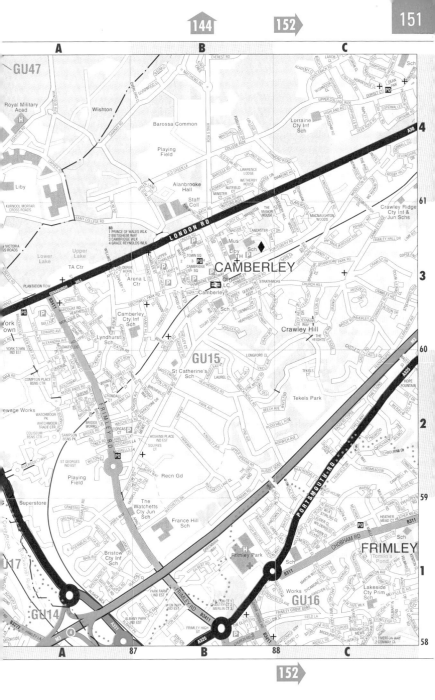

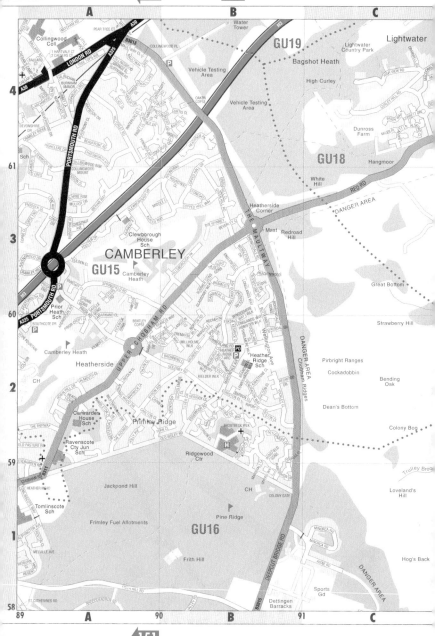

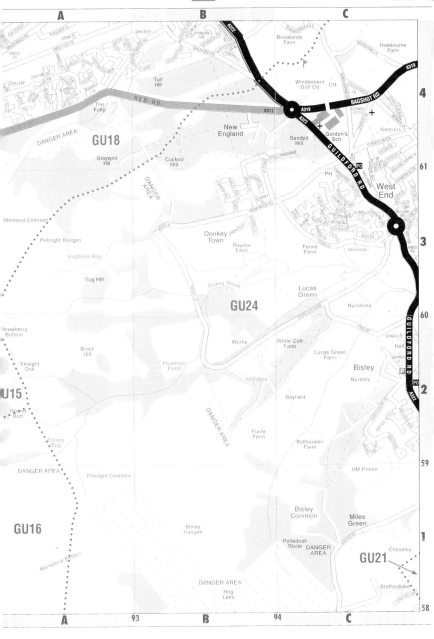

A B C

Fox Covert · Ridgeway Ct · Highal Pl · Oakleigh
Macdonald Rd · Maple Dr · Marbledale Rd · Park Dr · Sbk Dr · Osborne Ave
Deer Leap · Osborne Cl · Farnham Ave
The Folly
Turf Hill
RED RD
DANGER AREA
GU18
Grayspot Hill
Cuckoo Hill
DANGER AREA
Westend Common
Pirbright Ranges
Hagthorn Bog
Dog Hill
Strawberry Bottom
Straight Oak
U15
Round Butt
Colony Bog
DANGER AREA
Pirbright Common
GU16
Mainstone Bottom

Blackstroud La E
Brooklands Farm
Halebourne Farm
A322
Windlemere Golf Ctr.
CH
Hindhead La
A319
B311
A319
Bagshot Rd
New England
Sandpit Hill
Gordon's Sch
Council Cotts
Fairfield La
Streets Heath
61
PH
West End
GUILDFORD RD
Donkey Town
Rounce Farm
Fenns Farm
3
Lucas Green
Nurseries
GU24
Trulley Brook
RED LA
School Cl
Hall
60
Works
White Cott Farm
FORD RD
Lucas Green Farm
Brock Hill
Peatmoor Pond
LUCAS GREEN
Bisley
Nursery
2
PO
A322
Bayfield
DANGER AREA
Furze Farm
Bullhousen Farm
HM Prison
59
Bisley Ranges
Bisley Common
Miles Green
1
Polledoak Slade
DANGER AREA
GU21
Chaseley
DANGER AREA
Hog Lees
Staffordlake
58

A 93 B 94 C

Index

Street names are listed alphabetically and show the locality, the Postcode District, the page number and a reference to the square in which the name falls on the map page

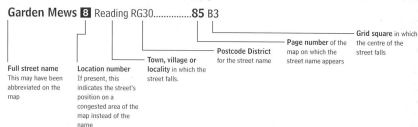

Garden Mews **8** Reading RG30.............**85 B3**

Full street name — This may have been abbreviated on the map

Location number — If present, this indicates the street's position on a congested area of the map instead of the name

Town, village or locality in which the street falls.

Postcode District for the street name

Page number of the map on which the street name appears

Grid square in which the centre of the street falls

Abbreviations used in the index

App	Approach	Cl	Close	Espl	Esplanade	N	North	S	South
Arc	Arcade	Comm	Common	Est	Estate	Orch	Orchard	Sq	Square
Ave	Avenue	Cnr	Corner	Gdns	Gardens	Par	Parade	Strs	Stairs
Bvd	Boulevard	Cotts	Cottages	Gn	Green	Pk	Park	Stps	Steps
Bldgs	Buildings	Ct	Court	Gr	Grove	Pas	Passage	St	Street, Saint
Bsns Pk	Business Park	Ctyd	Courtyard	Hts	Heights	Pl	Place	Terr	Terrace
Bsns Ctr	Business Centre	Cres	Crescent	Ind Est	Industrial	Prec	Precinct	Trad	Trading Est
Bglws	Bungalows	Dr	Drive		Estate	Prom	Promenade	Wlk	Walk
Cswy	Causeway	Dro	Drove	Intc	Interchange	Ret Pk	Retail Park	W	West
Ctr	Centre	E	East	Junc	Junction	Rd	Road	Yd	Yard
Cir	Circus	Emb	Embankment	La	Lane	Rdbt	Roundabout		

Town and village index

Aldermaston........135 A3
Aldworth...........32 A2
Arborfield.........114 B1
Ascot.............120 A1
Ashampstead.......54 A3
Ashford............97 A3
Aston Tirrold......12 C4
Bagshot...........145 B1
Ball Hill.........129 C1
Barkham...........115 A1
Beech Hill........138 A1
Beedon............51 B4
Beenham...........108 C3
Binfield...........90 A1
Bisham.............18 A1
Bisley............153 C2
Blackwater........150 A2
Blewbury...........12 A3
Bourne End..........3 A1
Boxford............76 A1
Bracknell.........118 B2
Bradfield..........82 A1
Brands Hill........69 A4
Brightwalton.......28 B1
Brimpton..........133 C3
Bucklebury.........80 A1
Burchett's Green....38 A3
Burghfield Common..110 B1
Burnham............21 A1
Camberley.........151 A1
Caversham..........59 A1
Chaddleworth.......49 A2
Charlton..........125 B4
Charvil............61 A1
Chertsey..........124 A1
Chieveley..........51 A1

Chilton............10 B4
Chilton Foliat.....73 A4
Cholsey............14 A4
Cold Ash..........106 A4
Colnbrook..........69 A3
Combe............147 C3
Compton...........31 B2
Cookham............20 A3
Crowthorne........143 A4
Datchet............68 A3
Dorney.............41 A2
Earley.............87 A1
East Bedfont.......98 A3
East Garston.......47 A2
East Isley.........30 A3
Egham.............96 A1
Englefield Green...95 A1
Eton..............67 B4
Farnborough (Berks)..28 A4
Farnborough (Hants)..150 C1
Farnham Common.....3 A3
Fawley (Berks).....27 B2
Fawley (Bucks).....15 A3
Feltham............98 B2
Finchampstead.....141 A1
Flackwell Heath.....3 A3
Frimley...........151 B1
Froxfield..........99 A1
Fulmer.............23 A3
Goring.............34 A3
Great Shefford.....48 A1
Greenham..........131 B4
Ham..............126 A2
Hambleden..........16 A4
Hampstead Norreys..52 C3
Hamstead Marshall..129 A4

Harlington.........71 A1
Harmondsworth......70 A2
Hatton.............71 B1
Headley...........132 C1
Henley-on-T........15 A2
Hermitage..........79 A1
Holyport..........65 A4
Horton.............69 A1
Hungerford........100 A2
Hungerford Newtown..74 A2
Hurley.............17 A1
Hurst..............88 B2
Inkpen...........127 B2
Iver..............44 A3
Iver Heath.........23 B1
Kintbury..........102 A1
Knowl Hill.........37 A3
Laleham..........124 A4
Lambourn...........25 A1
Leckhampstead......49 C3
Letcombe Bassett....6 B4
Lightwater........152 C4
Linkenholt.......147 A1
Little Marlow.......2 A2
Littleton.........125 A2
Littlewick Green....38 A2
Lower Basildon.....34 A1
Lower Halliford...125 A1
Lyne.............123 A1
Maidenhead.........39 A1
Mapledurham........57 C3
Marlow..............1 A1
Marlow Bottom......1 A3
Medmenham.........17 A2
Mortimer.........137 A3
Moulsford..........13 B2

Newbury...........104 B1
Newell Green.......92 A3
Newtown...........131 C1
North Ascot.......119 C4
Oakley Green.......66 A1
Old Windsor........95 A3
Padworth.........109 B2
Pangbourne.........56 A1
Peasemore..........50 A4
Poyle..............69 B3
Purley on T........57 A1
Reading............86 A2
Remenham Hill......16 A1
Sandhurst.........150 A4
Shefford Woodlands..74 B4
Shepperton.......125 A1
Shinfield.........113 A1
Shiplake...........35 A1
Silchester.......136 A1
Slough.............42 A3
Sonning............60 C1
South Stoke........14 A2
Staines............96 B3
Stanford Dingley....81 B2
Stanwell...........97 A3
Stockcross.......104 A4
Stoke Poges........22 C1
Streatley..........34 A3
Sulham.............56 C3
Sulhamstead.......110 B1
Sunbury..........125 C3
Sunningdale.......121 A1
Swallowfield......139 A1
Tadley...........134 A1
Taplow.............20 C1
Thatcham.........106 A1

Theale.............83 A1
Thorpe...........123 A3
Thorpe Lea.........96 A1
Tidmarsh...........56 A1
Twyford............61 A3
Upper Basildon.....55 A3
Upper Halliford...125 B3
Virginia Water....122 A2
Waltham St Lawrence..62 A4
Walton-on-T.......125 C1
Wargrave...........36 B1
Wentworth........121 A1
West End..........153 C3
West Ilsley........10 A1
West Woodhay.....128 A3
Whitchurch-on-T....56 B4
White Waltham......63 A3
Wickham............75 B2
Windlesham.......146 A2
Windsor............67 A2
Winkfield..........92 A1
Winnersh...........88 A3
Winterbourne.......77 B3
Wokingham........116 A1
Wooburn Green.......3 B2
Wooburn Moor........3 C4
Woodley............88 A3
Woolhampton......108 B1
Wraysbury..........68 B2
Yateley...........149 A2
Yattendon..........53 A1

Acre Mobile Home Pk SL0 ... 44 A4

A

Abattoirs Rd RG1 ... 86 A4
Abberbury Cl RG14 ... 104 C3
Abbetts La GU15 ... 151 A2
Abbey Cl Bracknell RG12 ... 118 B2
Newbury RG14 ... 131 A4
Slough SL1 ... 41 C3
Wokingham RG40 ... 116 B4
Abbey Cotts SL7 ... 17 A2
Abbey Ct Camberley GU15 ... 151 B3
Chertsey KT16 ... 124 A1
Abbey Dr TW18 ... 124 B3
Abbey Gdns KT16 ... 124 A1
Abbey Gn KT16 ... 124 A2
Abbey Jun Sch RG1 ... 86 B3
Abbey Lodge TW18 ... 96 C2
Abbey Pk RG7 ... 110 C2
Abbey Rd Bourne End SL8 ... 2 C3
Chertsey KT16 ... 124 A1
Lower Halliford TW17 ... 125 A1
Virginia Water GU25 ... 122 B3
Abbey River Cotts KT16 ... 124 B2
Abbey Sq RG1 ... 86 A4
Abbey Way SL1 ... 84 A4
Abbey Wood SL5 ... 121 A1
Abbot Cl TW18 ... 97 B1
Abbot's Wlk SL4 ... 66 C3
Abbots Dr GU25 ... 122 B3
Abbots Rd
Burghfield Common RG7 ... 110 C1
Newbury RG14 ... 105 A1
Abbots Way KT16 ... 123 C1
Abbots Wlk RG1 ... 86 A4
Abbots Way RG2 ... 117 C2
Abbotsbury ⬛ RG30 ... 85 A4
Abbotsmead Pl RG4 ... 59 A1
Abbotts Way SL1 ... 41 B3
Abelia Cl GU24 ... 153 C3
Abell Gdns SL6 ... 19 A1
Aberaman RG4 ... 58 C3
Aberdeen Ave SL1 ... 42 A3
Aberford Cl RG30 ... 85 B4
Abex Rd RG14 ... 105 B2
Abingdon Cl RG12 ... 118 C2
Abingdon Dr RG4 ... 59 B3
Abingdon Rd
East Isley RG20 ... 30 C4
Sandhurst GU47 ... 143 C1
Abingdon Wlk SL6 ... 19 C2
Abney Court Dr SL8 ... 3 A1
Abotts Mead OX10 ... 14 A4
Abrahams Rd RG9 ... 15 B2
Acacia RG9 ... 15 B1
Acacia Ave Littleton TW17 ... 125 A2
Sandhurst GU47 ... 143 B1
Wraysbury TW19 ... 68 C2
Acacia Ct SL3 ... 118 A3
Acacia Mews UB7 ... 70 B4
Acacia Rd Reading RG1 ... 86 B3
Staines TW18 ... 97 A2
Academy Cl GU15 ... 151 C4
Accommodation La UB7 ... 70 B4
Acer Dr GU24 ... 153 C3
Ackrells Mead GU47 ... 142 C1
Acorn Cotts SN6 ... 1 C4
Acorn Dr Thatcham RG18 ... 106 B3
Wokingham RG40 ... 116 B4
Acorn Gr UB3 ... 71 C4
Acorn Rd GU17 ... 150 A3
Acre Cl WR31 ... 84 B3
Acre Bsns Pk RG2 ... 113 A4
Acre Pas SL4 ... 67 B3
Acre Rd RG2 ... 113 A4
Acre The SL7 ... 1 C1
Acton Ct TW15 ... 125 B4
Adam Cl Slough SL1 ... 42 A3
Tadley RG26 ... 134 C1
Adam Ct RG9 ... 15 C1
Adams Way RG6 ... 86 C1
Addington La SL4 ... 67 A2
Addington Rd RG1 ... 86 B3
Addington Specl Sch RG5 ... 87 C3
Addiscombe Chase RG31 ... 57 A2
Addiscombe Rd RG45 ... 143 B2
Addison Cl SL0 ... 44 C3
Addison Ct SL6 ... 20 A1
Addison Rd RG1 ... 59 A1
Adelaide Cl SL1 ... 42 A2
Adelaide Rd Ashford TW15 ... 97 B2
Reading RG6 ... 87 A3
Adelaide Sq SL4 ... 67 B3
Adelphi Gdns SL1 ... 42 C2
Adey's Cl RG14 ... 105 A1
Adkins Rd RG10 ... 62 C4
Admirals Ct RG2 ... 86 A3
Admiralty Way GU15 ... 150 C2
Admoor La RG7 ... 82 B1
Admoor Dr RG6 ... 87 C1
Adwell Sq RG9 ... 15 B1
Adwood Ct RG19 ... 106 C2
Aerial Bsns Pk RG17 ... 45 C2
Agars Cres RG42 ... 91 A1
Agars Pl SL3 ... 68 C4
Agate Cl RG41 ... 115 C4
Aggisters La RG41 ... 115 A3
Agincourt Cl RG41 ... 115 C3
Agincourt Pl SL5 ... 120 B3
Agricola Way RG19 ... 106 C1

Ainsdale Cres RG30 ... 85 A2
Aintree RG12 ... 25 A1
Aintree Cl Newbury RG14 ... 105 B1
Poyle SL3 ... 69 C3
Air Forces Meml TW20 ... 95 B2
Airport Way TW19 ... 70 A2
Aisne Rd GU16 ... 152 C1
Ajax Ave SL1 ... 42 A3
Alan Pl RG30 ... 85 A3
Alan Way SL3 ... 43 C4
Alandale Cl RG2 ... 113 B4
Albain Cres TW15 ... 97 C3
Albany Cl GU16 ... 151 B1
Albany Park Dr RG41 ... 88 A2
Albany Park Ind Est GU15 ... 151 B1
Albany Pk Ind Est Poyle SL3 ... 69 B4
Albany Pl TW20 ... 96 A2
Albany Rd Old Windsor SL4 ... 68 A1
Reading RG30 ... 85 A2
Windsor SL4 ... 67 B3
Albert Ave KT16 ... 124 A3
Albert Cl ⬛ SL1 ... 42 C2
Albert Illsley Cl RG31 ... 84 B4
Albert Pl SL4 ... 42 C2
Albert Rd Ashford TW15 ... 97 C2
Bagshot GU19 ... 145 C1
Bracknell RG42 ... 118 A4
Camberley GU15 ... 151 B3
Caversham RG4 ... 58 C2
Crowthorne RG45 ... 143 A3
Englefield Green TW20 ... 95 B1
Henley-on-T RG9 ... 15 C1
⬛ Newbury RG14 ... 105 A1
Windsor SL4 ... 67 C2
Wokingham RG40 ... 116 A3
Albert St Maidenhead SL6 ... 39 C4
Slough SL1 ... 42 C2
Windsor SL4 ... 67 A3
Albert Wlk RG45 ... 143 A3
Albion Cl SL2 ... 43 A1
Albion Ct SL6 ... 19 B4
Albion Pl ⬛ SL4 ... 67 A3
Albury Rd RG47 ... 150 A4
Albury Terr RG1 ... 86 B4
Albury Cl RG30 ... 58 B1
Alcot Cl RG45 ... 143 A2
Aldborough Spur SL1 ... 42 C4
Aldbourne Ave RG6 ... 87 B1
Aldbourne Cl RG17 ... 100 B3
Aldbourne Rd SL1 ... 41 A4
Aldeburgh Cl RG6 ... 59 B4
Aldebury Rd SL6 ... 19 C1
Alden View SL4 ... 66 B3
Alderbourne La SL3 ... 23 C4
Alderbrook Cl RG45 ... 142 C2
Alderbury Rd SL3 ... 43 C2
Alderbury Rd W SL3 ... 43 C2
Alderfield Cl RG7 ... 83 C2
Alderley Cl RG5 ... 60 C1
Alder Bridge Steiner Sch RG7 ... 109 B2
Alder Cl
Englefield Green TW20 ... 95 C2
Newbury RG14 ... 105 B2
Slough SL1 ... 41 C3
Alder Ct RG12 ... 118 A3
Alder Dr Earley RG6 ... 87 B1
Reading RG31 ... 84 B3
Alder Glade RG7 ... 110 C2
Alder Gr GU46 ... 149 B3
Alderman Willey Cl RG41 ... 116 A3
Aldermaston CE Prim Sch RG7 ... 134 C4
Aldermaston Rd RG7 ... 109 B2
Aldermaston Sta RG7 ... 108 C3
Alderney Gdns RG41 ... 88 B1
Alders The RG18 ... 106 B2
Alderside Wlk TW20 ... 95 C2
Aldin Ave N SL1 ... 43 A2
Aldin Ave S SL1 ... 43 A2
Aldous Ho TW18 ... 96 C2
Aldridge Rd SL2 ... 22 A1
Aldryington Prim Sch RG6 ... 87 A2
Aldwick Dr SL6 ... 39 B3
Aldworth Cl Bracknell RG12 ... 118 A3
Reading RG30 ... 85 B3
Aldworth Gdns RG45 ... 143 A3
Aldworth Rd
Compton RG20 ... 31 C2
Upper Basildon RG8 ... 55 A3
Alexander Cl TW20 ... 95 A1
Alexander Ct RG42 ... 85 C4
Alexander Fst Sch SL4 ... 66 B2
Alexander Rd Egham TW20 ... 96 B2
Thatcham RG18 ... 106 C1
Alexander Wlk RG12 ... 118 A3
Alexandra Cl GU46 ... 151 A3
Alexandra Ct Ashford TW15 ... 98 B1
Staines TW18 ... 97 B1
Alexandra Ct TW15 ... 97 B1
Alexandra Rd
Ashford TW15 ... 98 C1
Englefield Green TW20 ... 95 B1
Maidenhead SL6 ... 39 B4
Reading RG1 ... 86 B3
Slough SL1 ... 42 B2
Windsor SL4 ... 67 B3
Alford Cl RG30 ... 84 B4

Alfred Davis Ct SL7 ... 1 B2
Alfred St RG1 ... 85 C4
Alfred Sutton Prim Sch RG1 ... 86 C3
Alice Gough Memorial Homes RG12 ... 118 A3
Alison Cl SL1 ... 21 A1
Alison Ct RG7 ... 110 C1
Alison Dr GU15 ... 151 C3
All Hallows Rd RG4 ... 59 B2
All Saints' Ave SL6 ... 39 A3
All Saints CE Inf Sch RG1 ... 85 C4
All Saints CE Jun Sch SL6 ... 39 B3
All Saints Cl RG40 ... 116 C4
All Saints Cres GU14 ... 150 C1
All Saints Ct RG30 ... 85 C4
All Saints Rd GU18 ... 146 B1
All Saints Rise RG42 ... 91 C1
All Souls Cotts SL3 ... 43 A1
All Souls' Rd SL5 ... 120 A3
Allanson Rd SL7 ... 1 C2
Allcot Cl TW14 ... 98 C4
Allcroft Rd RG1 ... 86 B3
Allenby Rd Maidenhead SL6 ... 39 A4
Sandhurst GU15 ... 151 A3
Allendale Cl GU47 ... 143 A1
Allendale Rd RG6 ... 87 A2
Allerds Rd SL2 ... 22 A2
Alleyns La SL4 ... 19 B4
Allhusen Gdns SL3 ... 23 C4
Alliance Ct TW15 ... 98 B2
Allington Ctr RG1 ... 117 C2
Allington Cl SL2 ... 42 C3
Allison Ct ⬛ RG1 ... 85 C4
Allison Gdns RG8 ... 57 B3
Allkins Ct SL4 ... 67 B3
Allnatt Ave RG41 ... 88 B1
Allonby Cl RG6 ... 87 B1
Allsmoor La RG12 ... 118 C3
Allyn Cl TW18 ... 96 C1
Alma Ct Burnham SL1 ... 21 C1
Alma Ct SL4 ... 41 C1
Wokingham RG41 ... 116 A3
Alma Rd Eton SL4 ... 42 C1
Windsor SL4 ... 67 B3
Alma St RG30 ... 85 B4
Almners Rd KT16 ... 123 A1
Almond Ave RG14 ... 105 A3
Almond Cl Charlton TW17 ... 125 B4
Englefield Green TW20 ... 95 A1
Reading RG6 ... 87 A2
Wokingham RG41 ... 115 B2
Almond Dr Caversham RG4 ... 59 C2
Thatcham RG18 ... 106 B2
Almond Rd SL1 ... 21 B1
Almons Way SL2 ... 43 A4
Almshouses Eton SL4 ... 67 B2
Reading RG1 ... 86 A4
Slough SL2 ... 23 A4
Alpha Ho ⬛ RG1 ... 86 B3
Alpha St N SL1 ... 42 C2
Alpha St S SL1 ... 42 C2
Alpha Way TW20 ... 123 B4
Alphington Ave GU16 ... 151 C1
Alphington Gn GU16 ... 151 C1
Alphington Rd RG2 ... 113 A4
Alpine Ct SL1 ... 41 B3
Alsace Wlk GU15 ... 151 A1
Alsford Cl GU18 ... 152 C4
Alston Gdns SL6 ... 39 C4
Alston Mews RG19 ... 106 B1
Alston Wlk RG4 ... 59 B3
Altmore SL6 ... 38 C4
Alton Cl TW18 ... 123 C4
Alton Ride GU17 ... 150 B3
Altona Way SL1 ... 42 A4
Altwood Bailey SL6 ... 39 B2
Altwood CE Comp Sch SL6 ... 39 A3
Altwood Cl Maidenhead SL6 ... 39 A2
Slough SL1 ... 41 C4
Altwood Dr SL6 ... 39 A3
Altwood Rd SL6 ... 39 A3
Alvista Ave SL6 ... 40 B4
Alwyn Inf Sch SL6 ... 39 A4
Alwyn Rd SL6 ... 39 A4
Alyson Ct ⬛ RG1 ... 19 C1
Amanda Ct Ashford TW15 ... 97 C3
Slough SL3 ... 43 A3
Ambarrow Cres GU47 ... 142 C1
Ambarrow La GU47 ... 142 C2
Ambassador RG12 ... 117 C2
Amber Cl RG6 ... 87 B1
Amber Ct TW18 ... 96 C2
Amber Hill GU15 ... 152 B2
Amberley Cl RG14 ... 104 C2
Amberley Ct SL6 ... 20 B2
Amberley Dr RG10 ... 61 B3
Amberley Pl ⬛ SL4 ... 67 B3
Amberley Rd SL2 ... 22 A1
Amberwood Dr GU15 ... 151 C4
Ambleside Rd RG45 ... 87 C4
Ambleside Cl RG18 ... 106 B2
Ambleside Dr TW14 ... 98 C4
Ambleside Way TW20 ... 96 A1
Ambrook Rd RG2 ... 113 B2
Ambrose Pl RG1 ... 85 C4
Ambury Rd RG8 ... 33 C2
Amen Corner Bsns Pk RG12 ... 117 B4
Amerden Cl SL6 ... 40 A4
Amerden La SL6 ... 40 A4
Amerden Way SL1 ... 42 A2

American Comm Sch GU25 ... 122 B4
American Magna Carta Meml TW20 ... 95 B3
American Sch in Switzerland (English Branch) The TW20 ... 123 B3
Amersham Rd RG4 ... 59 A3
Amethyst Cl RG41 ... 115 B4
Amethyst La RG30 ... 85 B3
Amherst Rd RG6 ... 87 A3
Amity Rd RG1 ... 86 C4
Amity St RG1 ... 86 C4
Ammanford RG4 ... 58 C3
Amners Farm Rd RG30 ... 112 A4
Ampere Rd RG14 ... 105 A2
Amport Ct RG13 ... 125 C1
Ancaster Dr SL5 ... 119 C4
Ancastle Gr RG9 ... 15 C1
Anderson Ave RG6 ... 87 A3
Anderson Cres RG42 ... 114 C1
Anderson Dr TW15 ... 98 B2
Anderson Pl GU19 ... 145 C2
Andover Cl
East Bedfont TW14 ... 98 C4
Reading RG2 ... 57 B1
Andover Dro RG20 ... 130 A2
Andover Rd
Blackwater GU17 ... 150 B3
Newbury RG14 ... 130 B3
Andrew Cl RG40 ... 116 C3
Andrews Cl RG7 ... 83 C2
Andrews Rd RG6 ... 87 A2
Andrews Reach SL8 ... 3 A4
Andrews Way SL7 ... 1 B4
Angel Ct ⬛ RG14 ... 105 A2
Angel Mead RG7 ... 108 B1
Angel Pl RG42 ... 91 C1
Angers Cl GU15 ... 152 B4
Angle Field Rd RG4 ... 59 B2
Anglesey Cl TW15 ... 98 A2
Angus Cl RG31 ... 84 C2
Annadale RG18 ... 79 B1
Anne Cl SL6 ... 19 C1
Anneforde Pl RG42 ... 91 A1
Annes Ct SL6 ... 20 C3
Annesley Gdns RG41 ... 88 B2
Annett Cl TW17 ... 125 C3
Annie Brookes Cl TW18 ... 96 B3
Anscuff Rd SL2 ... 22 A2
Ansell Rd GU16 ... 151 C1
Anslow Pl SL1 ... 41 A4
Anson Cres RG2 ... 113 B4
Anson Rd GU14 ... 151 A3
Anson Wlk RG2 ... 113 B4
Anstey Pl RG7 ... 111 A2
Anston Cl RG6 ... 114 A4
Antares Cl RG41 ... 115 C3
Anthian Cl RG5 ... 88 A4
Anthony Wall RG42 ... 118 C4
Antrim Rd RG5 ... 87 B3
Anvil Ct Slough SL3 ... 44 A1
Thatcham RG18 ... 106 B2
Apex Dr GU16 ... 151 B1
Aplin Way GU18 ... 146 A1
Apple Cl Purley on T RG31 ... 57 A2
Wokingham RG41 ... 115 B2
Apple Tree Way GU47 ... 143 B1
Appleby Cl GU15 ... 151 A3
Appleby Gdns TW14 ... 98 B4
Appleby Rd SL6 ... 39 B2
Applecroft SL6 ... 39 B2
Appledore RG12 ... 117 B1
Appleford Cl RG19 ... 106 B1
Appleford Rd RG30 ... 85 A3
Appleton Ho ⬛ RG1 ... 86 B4
Appletree La
Shinfield RG7 ... 113 A1
Slough SL3 ... 43 B2
Appletree Pl ⬛ RG42 ... 118 A4
Appley Dr GU15 ... 151 B4
Approach Rd
Ashford TW15 ... 98 B1
Tadley RG26 ... 135 A1
April Cl GU15 ... 151 B1
Apsey Ct RG42 ... 90 C1
Apsley Cotts SL6 ... 19 A4
Apsley Ho SL1 ... 43 A2
Aquila Cl RG41 ... 115 C3
Aragon Cl TW16 ... 98 C1
Aragon Ct RG12 ... 118 B3
Arbor La RG41 ... 88 A2
Arbor Mdws RG41 ... 88 A2
Arborfield SL3 ... 42 C2
Arborfield, Newland & Barkham CE Jun Sch RG2 ... 114 C1
Arborfield Rd RG2 ... 114 A1
Arbour Cl RG41 ... 85 C3
Arbour Vale Sch SL2 ... 42 C4
Arc The RG1 ... 86 A4
Arcade The Goring RG8 ... 34 B3
Newbury RG14 ... 105 A2
Archangel Way RG18 ... 106 A2
Archer Cl SL6 ... 20 B2
Archway Rd RG4 ... 58 C3
Arden Cl RG12 ... 119 A4
Ardingly RG12 ... 117 C1
Ardler Rd RG4 ... 59 B2
Ardrossan Ave GU15 ... 152 A3
Ardrossan Cl SL2 ... 22 B1
Ardwell Cl RG45 ... 142 C3

Arena L Ctr GU15 ... 151 B3
Arena The RG12 ... 118 A4
Arenal Dr RG45 ... 143 B2
Arethusa Way GU24 ... 153 C2
Argent Ct TW20 ... 96 B1
Argent Terr GU47 ... 150 C4
Argosy Gdns TW18 ... 96 C1
Argosy La TW19 ... 97 B4
Argyle Rd Newbury RG14 ... 104 C1
Reading RG1 ... 85 C4
Argyle St SL1 ... 85 C3
Argyll Ave SL1 ... 42 A3
Aries Ho HP10 ... 3 A4
Arkle Ave RG19 ... 105 C2
Arkley Ct SL6 ... 40 B1
Arkwright Dr RG42 ... 117 B4
Arkwright Rd Poyle SL3 ... 69 C3
Reading RG2 ... 86 A2
Arlington Cl
Bracknell RG42 ... 118 A4
Maidenhead SL6 ... 39 B4
Arlington Rd TW15 ... 97 C2
Arlington Sq RG12 ... 118 A4
Armadale Cl RG30 ... 85 B3
Armitage Ct SL5 ... 120 B2
Armitage Dr GU16 ... 151 C1
Armour Hill RG31 ... 57 B1
Armour Rd RG31 ... 57 B1
Armour Wlk RG31 ... 57 B1
Armstrong Rd TW20 ... 95 B1
Armstrong Way RG5 ... 88 A4
Arncliffe RG12 ... 118 A2
Arndale Way ⬛ TW20 ... 96 A2
Arnett Ave RG40 ... 141 C4
Arnewood Ave RG26 ... 135 B1
Arnhem Rd RG14 ... 105 A2
Arnold Rd TW18 ... 97 B1
Arnside Cl RG10 ... 61 B4
Arnwood Rd RG41 ... 115 C4
Arrowhead Rd RG7 ... 83 C1
Arrowsmith Way RG19 ... 106 C1
Artemis Ho RG1 ... 86 A4
Arthur Cl GU19 ... 145 C1
Arthur Pl RG1 ... 86 B3
Arthur Rd Newbury RG14 ... 104 C1
Slough SL1 ... 42 B2
Windsor SL4 ... 67 B3
Wokingham RG41 ... 116 A3
Arthurstone Birches RG42 ... 90 B2
Artillery Mews RG30 ... 85 B3
Arun Cl RG41 ... 88 A1
Arun Ct RG6 ... 86 C3
Arundel Cl SL6 ... 39 B4
Arundel Ct SL3 ... 43 B1
Arundel Rd Frimley GU15 ... 152 B2
Woodley RG5 ... 87 C4
Ascot Heath Inf Sch SL5 ... 92 C1
Ascot Heath Jun Sch SL5 ... 92 C1
Ascot Race Course SL5 ... 119 C3
Ascot Rd
East Bedfont TW14 ... 98 A3
Holyport SL6 ... 65 A4
Newell Green RG42 ... 91 C4
Ascot Sta SL5 ... 120 A3
Ascot Twrs SL5 ... 119 C4
Ash Cl Blackwater GU17 ... 150 B3
Brightwalton RG20 ... 28 B2
Slough SL3 ... 43 C2
Ash Copse RG4 ... 59 C4
Ash Ct SL6 ... 98 B2
Caversham RG4 ... 59 A2
⬛ Reading RG6 ... 87 A3
Ash Gate RG18 ... 106 C2
Ash La SL6 ... 38 C1
Ash Lodge ⬛ TW16 ... 98 B3
Ash Rd Littleton TW17 ... 125 A3
Newtown RG20 ... 131 C1
Reading RG30 ... 84 C3
Ash Terr RG18 ... 106 A4
Ash Tree Gr RG20 ... 129 A4
Ash Way RG41 ... 115 B2
Ashampstead Rd
Bradfield RG7 ... 82 A4
Reading RG30 ... 85 A3
Upper Basildon RG8 ... 55 A3
Ashbourne RG12 ... 117 C2
Ashbourne Gr SL6 ... 39 B2
Ashbourne Ho ⬛ SL1 ... 42 B2
Ashbrook Rd SL4 ... 95 A4
Ashburton Rd RG2 ... 86 A1
Ashbury Dr
Farnborough (Hants) GU17 ... 151 A1
Reading RG31 ... 84 A4
Ashby Ct SL6 ... 39 C1
Ashby Way UB7 ... 71 A4
Ashcroft Cl RG4 ... 58 C3
Ashcroft Ct SL1 ... 21 C1
Ashcroft Rd SL6 ... 39 B4
Ashdale Cl TW19 ... 97 C3
Ashdale Pk RG40 ... 142 B3
Ashdene Cl TW15 ... 98 B2
Ashdene Ho TW20 ... 95 B3
Ashdown SL6 ... 20 A2
Ashdown Cl RG12 ... 119 A4

Ashdown Ho 13 RG30 ...85 C3
Ashen Cross SL3 ...44 A4
Ashenden Wlk SL2 ...22 B4
Asher Dr SL5 ...119 B4
Ashes The RG7 ...113 A1
Ashfield Gn UG46 ...149 C3
Ashford Ave TW15 ...98 A1
Ashford CE Prim Sch TW15 ...98 A1
Ashford Cl TW15 ...97 C2
Ashford Cres TW15 ...97 C3
Ashford High Sch The TW15 ...97 C3
Ashford Hill Cty Prim Sch RG19 ...133 C1
Ashford Hill Rd RG19 ...132 C1
Ashford Hospl TW15 ...97 C2
Ashford Ind Est TW15 ...98 B2
Ashford La SL4 ...41 A2
Ashford Manor Golf Club TW15 ...97 B2
Ashford Rd
  Feltham TW13, TW15 ...98 C3
  Littleton TW15 ...98 B1
  Staines TW18 ...124 B4
Ashford Sta TW15 ...97 C3
Ashlea Ho TW15 ...97 C2
Ashleigh Ave TW20 ...96 B1
Ashley HP10 ...3 C4
Ashley Cl Earley RG6 ...87 A1
  Walton-on-KT12, KT13 ...125 C1
Ashley Ct SL6 ...40 A4
Ashley Dr GU17 ...150 B2
Ashley Hill Pl RG10 ...36 C4
Ashley Park Ave KT12 ...125 C1
Ashley Pk SL6 ...20 A1
Ashley Rd RG1 ...85 C3
Ashley Way GU24 ...153 B3
Ashman Rd RG2 ...107 A2
Ashmead Sch RG2 ...86 B1
Ashmere Cl RG31 ...84 B2
Ashmere Gdns RG30 ...85 C4
Ashmore Green Rd RG18 ...106 A4
Ashmore Rd RG2 ...86 B1
Ashridge Ct 7 RG14 ...105 A1
Ashridge Gn 8 RG42 ...118 A4
Ashridge Rd RG40 ...116 B4
Ashton Cl RG31 ...84 A4
Ashton Pl Kintbury RG17 ...102 A1
  Maidenhead SL6 ...39 A3
Ashton Rd Newbury RG14 ...105 A1
  Wokingham RG41 ...88 C1
Ashtree Ct TW15 ...98 A2
Ashtrees Rd RG5 ...87 C4
Ashurst Dr TW17 ...124 C3
Ashview Cl RG30 ...85 A1
Ashview Gdns TW15 ...97 C2
Ashville Way RG41 ...116 A3
Ashwell Ave GU15 ...151 C3
Ashwell Ct TW15 ...97 C3
Ashwood RG5 ...87 B2
Ashwood Cl RG31 ...84 A3
Ashwood Dr RG14 ...105 B2
Ashworth Dr RG19 ...106 B1
Askew Dr RG7 ...113 A2
Aspect Park Golf Ctr RG ...16 B1
Aspen Cl Slough SL2 ...42 A4
  Staines TW18 ...96 C3
Aspen Gdns TW15 ...98 B2
Aspin Way GU17 ...150 A3
Astleham Rd TW17 ...124 C3
Astley Cl RG41 ...115 C4
Aston Ave RG31 ...84 A4
Aston Cl SL6 ...56 B3
Aston Ct RG30 ...85 A3
Aston Ferry La RG9 ...16 B3
Aston La RG9 ...16 B3
Aston Mead SL4 ...66 C3
Aston St OX11 ...12 C4
Aston Villas SL2 ...22 B4
Aston Cl Maidenhead SL6 ...40 A3
  Winnersh RG41 ...88 A3
Astra Mead RG42 ...92 A1
Atfield Gr GU20 ...146 B2
Atherton Cl Reading RG30 ...84 C4
  Stanwell TW19 ...70 B1
Atherton Cres RG17 ...100 B3
Atherton Ct SL4 ...67 B4
Atherton Pl RG17 ...25 A2
Atherton Rd RG17 ...100 B3
Athlone Cl SL6 ...19 C1
Attenborough Rd GU47 ...143 B1
Atte La RG42 ...91 B1
Attebrouche Ct RG22 ...118 B1
Auburn Ct RG4 ...59 A1
Auckland Cl SL6 ...40 A4
Auckland Rd RG6 ...87 A3
Auclum Cl RG7 ...111 A1
Auclum La RG7 ...111 A1
Audley Cl RG14 ...105 B3
Audley Dr SL6 ...39 A3
Audley St RG30 ...85 C4
Audley Way SL5 ...119 B3
Augur Cl TW18 ...96 C2
August End Reading RG30 ...85 B4
  Slough SL3 ...43 C4
Augustine Cl SL3 ...69 C2
Augustine Wlk RG42 ...91 C1
Augustus Gdns GU15 ...152 B3
Austen Gdns RG14 ...130 A4

Austin Rd RG5 ...87 C3
Austins Gate SL6 ...38 C4
Australia Ave SL6 ...39 C4
Australia Rd SL1 ...43 A2
Auton Pl RG9 ...35 B4
Autumn Cl Caversham RG4 ...59 B4
  Slough SL1 ...41 C3
Autumn Wlk
  Maidenhead SL6 ...39 A3
  Wargrave RG10 ...36 B1
Avalon Rd Bourne End SL8 ...3 A3
  Earley RG6 ...87 B2
Avebury Bracknell RG12 ...118 A2
  Slough SL1 ...42 A3
Avebury Sq RG1 ...86 B3
Aveley Wlk 20 RG1 ...86 A3
Avenue Rd Egham TW18 ...96 B4
  Feltham TW13 ...98 C3
  Maidenhead SL6 ...40 A3
Avenue Sch The RG6 ...86 B2
Avenue Sucy GU15 ...151 A2
Avenue The Bourne End SL8 ...3 A2
  Camberley GU15 ...151 A3
  Crowthorne RG45 ...143 A3
  Datchet SL3 ...68 A3
  Egham TW20 ...96 A2
  Farnham Common SL2 ...22 A4
  Lightwater GU18 ...146 A1
  Maidenhead SL6 ...20 B2
  Mortimer RG7 ...137 A3
  North Ascot SL5 ...92 C1
  Old Windsor SL4 ...68 A3
  Staines TW18 ...124 A4
  Wraysbury TW19 ...68 B2
Averil Cl SL6 ...41 B4
Avery Cl RG40 ...141 C3
Avington Cl RG31 ...84 A4
Avocet Cres GU47 ...150 C4
Avocet Ct 4 RG1 ...86 A3
Avon Cl Reading RG31 ...84 C3
  Slough SL1 ...41 C3
Avon Cr RG12 ...91 B1
Avon Pl RG1 ...86 B4
Avon Rd TW16 ...98 C1
Avon Way RG7 ...109 C3
Avondale SL6 ...19 B1
Avondale Ave TW16 ...98 C1
Avondale Rd TW15, TW19 ...97 B3
Aveyway RG14 ...105 B2
Axbridge RG12 ...118 C2
Axbridge Rd RG2 ...86 B1
Ayebridges Ave TW20 ...96 B1
Aylesbury Cres SL1 ...42 B4
Aylesford Way RG19 ...107 A1
Aylesham Way GU46 ...149 A3
Aylesworth Ave SL2 ...22 A1
Aylesworth Spur SL4 ...95 A4
Aylsham Cl RG30 ...84 C4
Aymer Cl TW18 ...123 C4
Aymer Dr TW18 ...123 C4
Ayrton Senna Rd RG31 ...84 B4
Aysgarth RG12 ...118 A2
Aysgarth Pk SL6 ...40 A1
Azalea Cl RG41 ...88 A1
Azalea Way Frimley GU15 ...152 A3
  Slough SL3 ...43 C4

B

Babbington Rd RG2 ...113 B3
Bachelors Acre SL4 ...67 B3
Back La Beenham RG7 ...109 A4
  Brimpton RG7 ...134 B2
  Kintbury RG17 ...127 C4
  Shinfield RG7 ...139 A4
  Silchester RG7 ...136 B2
  Stanford Dingley RG7 ...81 C2
Back St RG17 ...47 B3
Backsidelans RG10 ...36 B1
Bacon Cl GU47 ...150 B3
Bad Godesberg Way SL6 ...39 C4
Baden Cl TW18 ...97 A1
Baden Gdns SL1 ...42 A2
Bader Way The RG5 ...88 A3
Badgebury Rise SL7 ...1 B4
Badgemoor La RG9 ...15 B2
Badgemore Cty Prim Sch GU9 ...
Badger Cl SL6 ...39 B2
Badger Dr
  Lightwater GU18 ...146 A1
  Twyford RG10 ...61 B4
Badgers Cl TW15 ...97 C2
Badgers Copse GU15 ...151 C2
Badgers Croft RG7 ...137 A3
Badgers Glade RG7 ...111 A1
Badgers Hill GU25 ...122 B2
Badgers Holt GU46 ...149 A3
Badgers Ridge RG20 ...130 B2
Badgers Rise RG4 ...59 A3
Badgers Sett RG45 ...142 C3
Badgers Way
  Bracknell RG12 ...118 C4
  Marlow Bottom SL7 ...1 B4
Badgers Wlk RG9 ...36 A2
Badgers Wood SL2 ...22 B4
Badgerwood Dr GU16 ...151 B1
Badminton Rd SL6 ...39 A3
Bagnols Way RG14 ...104 C1
Bagshot Cty Inf Sch GU19 ...145 C1
Bagshot Gn GU19 ...145 C2
Bagshot Rd Ascot SL5 ...120 B1
  Bracknell RG12 ...118 B2
  Englefield Green TW20 ...95 B1
  West End GU24 ...153 C4
Bagshot Sta GU19 ...145 C2

Baigents La GU20 ...146 B2
Bailey Cl Maidenhead SL6 ...39 C4
  Windsor SL4 ...67 A3
Bailey Ho 7 SL8 ...3 A2
Bailey's La RG10 ...62 C2
Baileys Cl GU17 ...150 A4
Baileys Cl GU17 ...150 A4
Baily Ave RG18 ...106 A2
Bain Ave GU15 ...151 A1
Bainbridge Rd RG31 ...84 A2
Bainhurst Cotts SL6 ...38 A3
Baird Cl SL1 ...42 B2
Baird Rd RG2 ...140 C4
Bakeham La TW20 ...95 B1
Baker St Aston Tirrold OX11 ...12 C4
  Reading RG1 ...85 C4
Baker's Orch HP10 ...3 C3
Bakers Ct TW19 ...70 B1
Bakers La SL6 ...38 C4
Baldwin Rd SL1 ...21 B1
Baldwin's Shore SL4 ...67 B4
Balfour Cres
  Bracknell RG12 ...118 A2
  Newbury RG14 ...130 B3
Balfour Dr RG31 ...84 A2
Balfour Pl SL7 ...1 C2
Balintore Cl 3 GU47 ...150 B4
Ball Pit Rd RG20 ...28 A3
Ballamoor Cl RG31 ...84 A2
Ballard Cl GU15 ...152 A4
Ballard Gn SL4 ...66 C4
Ballard Rd GU15 ...152 A4
Ballencrieff Rd SL5 ...120 C1
Balliol Rd RG4 ...58 B2
Balliol Way GU47 ...143 C1
Balme Cl RG10 ...61 A2
Balmoral SL6 ...19 A1
Balmoral Cl SL1 ...42 A4
Balmoral Gdns SL4 ...67 B2
Balmoral Grange TW18 ...124 A4
Balmore Dr RG4 ...59 A2
Balmore Ho RG4 ...59 A2
Balmore Pk RG4 ...59 A2
Bambrugh Cl RG2 ...86 C2
Bamford Pl RG31 ...84 A2
Banbury RG12 ...118 C1
Banbury Ave SL1 ...41 C4
Banbury Cl RG41 ...116 A3
Banbury Gdns RG4 ...59 C2
Bancroft Cl TW15 ...98 A2
Bancroft Pl RG31 ...84 A2
Band La 1 TW20 ...96 A2
Bangors Cl SL0 ...44 C4
Bangors Rd S SL0 ...44 C4
Bank Side RG40 ...141 C3
Banks Spur SL1 ...42 A2
Bankside RG1 ...86 B1
Bannard Rd SL6 ...39 A3
Bannister Cl SL3 ...43 C2
Bannister Gdns GU46 ...149 C3
Bannister Pl RG7 ...134 C3
Bannister Pl RG7 ...110 C1
Barbara Cl TW17 ...125 A2
Barbaras Mdw RG31 ...57 B2
Barbel Cl RG6 ...87 A4
Barber Cl RG10 ...88 C4
Barberry Way GU17 ...150 C1
Barbon Cl GU15 ...152 B2
Barbrook Cl RG31 ...57 B2
Barchester Rd SL3 ...43 C2
Barclay Rd RG31 ...84 B2
Barclose Ave RG4 ...59 B2
Bardney Cl SL6 ...39 B2
Bardolphs Cl RG4 ...58 B4
Bardown RG20 ...51 A1
Barefoot Cl RG31 ...57 A1
Barfield Rd RG18 ...106 A2
Barge La RG7 ...139 A3
Bargeman Rd SL6 ...39 C3
Barholm Cl RG6 ...87 C1
Barkby RG6 ...87 B1
Barker Ct RG42 ...140 C4
Barker Cl RG4 ...88 C4
Barker Gn RG12 ...118 A2
Barker Rd RG18 ...123 C1
Barkham Manor RG41 ...115 B2
Barkham Rd
  Barkham RG41 ...115 B2
  Wokingham RG41 ...116 A4
Barkham Ride
  Barkham RG40 ...115 B1
  Wokingham RG40 ...141 C4
Barkham St RG40 ...115 B1
Barkhart Dr RG40 ...116 B4
Barkhart Gdns RG40 ...116 B4
Barkis Mead GU47 ...143 C1
Barkwith Cl RG6 ...87 C1
Barley Cl RG10 ...106 C1
Barley Fields HP10 ...3 C4
Barley Mead RG42 ...91 C1
Barley Mow Rd TW20 ...95 B2
Barley Wlk RG31 ...84 A3
Barley Way 6 SL7 ...1 B1
Barn Cl Ashford TW15 ...98 A2
  Bracknell RG12 ...118 A4
  Camberley GU15 ...151 C3
  Farnham Common RG7 ...22 A4
  Kintbury RG17 ...102 A1
  Maidenhead SL6 ...19 C1
  Reading RG30 ...85 B3
Barn Cotts SL17 ...74 B4
Barn Cres RG14 ...130 B4
Barn Dr SL6 ...39 A2
Barn La RG9 ...15 B1
Barn Owl Way RG7 ...111 A2
Barnard Cl RG4 ...59 B3
Barnards Hill SL7 ...1 B1
Barnes Way SL0 ...44 C3

Barnett Ct RG12 ...118 B4
Barnett Gn RG12 ...118 A2
Barnett La GU18 ...152 C4
Barnfield Iver SL0 ...44 C4
  Slough SL1 ...41 B3
Barnfield Cl SL7 ...1 B2
Barnhill Gdns SL7 ...1 B2
Barnhill Rd SL7 ...1 B2
Barnsdale Rd RG2 ...86 B2
Barnway SL4 ...95 B2
Barnwood Ct RG30 ...85 C4
Baroma Way RG9 ...15 C1
Baron Ct RG30 ...85 C4
Barons Mead RG9 ...15 B1
Barons Way TW20 ...96 B1
Barossa Rd GU15 ...151 B3
Barr's Rd SL6 ...41 A4
Barracane Dr RG45 ...143 A3
Barrack La SL4 ...67 B3
Barracks La RG7 ...113 A1
Bartelotts Rd SL2 ...21 C1
Barrington Cl RG6 ...87 A3
Barrington Ho RG2 ...113 A4
Barrington Rd RG30 ...85 C3
Barrington Way RG30 ...85 C3
Barry Ave SL4 ...67 B4
Barry Pl RG1 ...86 A4
Barry Sq RG12 ...118 B1
Barry Terr TW15 ...97 C3
Barry View SL4 ...66 B3
Bartholomew Pl RG42 ...91 C1
Bartholomew Ct RG14 ...104 C1
Bartholomew St RG14 ...104 C1
Bartlemy Cl RG14 ...130 C4
Bartlemy Rd RG14 ...130 C4
Bartletts La SL6 ...65 A4
Barton Cl TW17 ...125 A2
Barton Rd Reading RG31 ...84 A4
  Slough SL3 ...43 C2
Bartons La RG6 ...88 A4
Barwell Cl RG45 ...142 C2
Basemoors RG12 ...118 C3
Basford Way SL4 ...66 B2
Basil Cl RG6 ...86 C1
Basildon CE Prim Sch RG8 ...55 A3
Basingstoke Rd
  Aldermaston RG7 ...109 A1
  Reading RG2 ...86 A2
  Swallowfield RG7 ...139 B3
Baskerville La RG9 ...36 A2
Baslow Rd RG41 ...88 A1
Basmore La RG9 ...36 A2
Bass Mead SL6 ...19 C3
Bassett Cl RG6 ...114 B4
Bassett Rd OX12 ...6 C4
Bassett Way SL2 ...21 C1
Batcombe Mead RG12 ...118 C1
Bates Cl SL3 ...43 C4
Bath Ct SL6 ...39 A3
Bath Rd Camberley GU15 ...151 A3
  Froxfield SN8,RG17 ...99 B2
  Harlington TW6, UB3 ...71 B3
  Harmondsworth TW6, UB7 ...71 A4
  Hungerford RG17 ...100 C4
  Knowl Hill RG10 ...37 B2
  Littlewick Green SL6 ...38 B3
  Maidenhead SL6 ...39 B3
  Newbury RG14 ...104 B2
  Poyle SL3, UB7 ...69 C3
  Reading RG30, RG31 ...85 B3
  Slough SL1,SL6 ...41 B3
  Sonning RG4 ...60 C1
  Thatcham RG7,RG19 ...107 B1
  Woolhampton RG7 ...108 B1
Bathurst Cl SL0 ...44 C2
Bathurst Rd RG41 ...88 B1
Bathurst Wlk SL0 ...44 C2
Battery End RG14 ...130 B3
Battle Cl RG14 ...104 B2
Battle Hospl RG30 ...85 B4
Battle Prim Sch RG30 ...85 B4
Battle Rd Goring RG8 ...34 C4
  Newbury RG14 ...130 B3
Battle St RG1 ...85 C4
Battlemead Cl SL6 ...20 B2
Batty's Barn Cl RG40 ...116 B3
Baxendales The RG14 ...105 B1
Baxter Cl SL1 ...42 C2
Bay Cl RG6 ...86 C1
Bay Dr RG12 ...118 C4
Bay Rd RG12 ...118 C4
Bay Tree Ct SL1 ...21 B1
Bay Tree Rise RG31 ...84 B3
Baydon Dr RG1 ...85 C3
Baydon Rd RG17 ...24 C1
Bayfield Ave GU16 ...151 C1
Bayford Cl GU17 ...151 A1
Bayford Dr RG31 ...142 A4
Bayford Dr RG31 ...142 A4
Bayleys Cres SL1 ...41 A4
Bayley Ct RG41 ...88 A1
Baylis Court Sch SL1,SL2 ...42 B4
Baylis Par SL1 ...42 C3
Bayliss Rd RG10 ...36 C1
Baysfarm Ct TW6, UB7 ...70 B3
Beach's Ho TW18 ...96 C3
Beacon Ct Colnbrook SW3 ...69 B4
Beacon Rd TW19 ...71 A1
Beacon Rdbt TW6 ...71 A1
Beaconsfield Cotts SL8 ...3 A1
Beaconsfield Rd SL2 ...22 B3
Beaconsfield Way RG6 ...87 A1
Beacontree Plaza RG2 ...86 B2
Beal's La RG31 ...84 A4

Beale Cl RG40 ...116 A4
Beale Park Wildlife Pk RG8 ...55 C4
Beales Farm Rd SL4 ...25 A1
Bean Oak Rd RG40 ...116 C3
Beancroft Rd RG19 ...106 B1
Bear La Newbury RG14 ...105 A3
  Wargrave RG10 ...37 A4
Beard's Rd TW15 ...98 C2
Bearfield La RG17 ...73 A4
Bears Rails Pk SL4 ...94 C4
Bearwood Cl RG40 ...141 B3
Bearwood Coll RG41 ...115 A4
Bearwood Path RG41 ...88 A4
Bearwood Prim Sch RG41 ...115 A4
Bearwood Rd RG41 ...115 B3
Beasley's Ait La TW16,TW17 ...125 C2
Beattie Cl TW14 ...98 C4
Beatty Dr RG30 ...84 B4
Beauchief Cl RG6 ...113 C4
Beaufield Cl RG5 ...87 B4
Beaufort Cl SL7 ...1 C1
Beaufort Gdns Marlow SL7 ...1 C1
  North Ascot SL5 ...119 C4
Beaufort Pl SL6 ...40 B2
Beauforts TW20 ...95 B3
Beaufront Cl GU15 ...152 A4
Beaufront Rd GU15 ...152 A4
Beaulieu Cl
  Bracknell RG12 ...119 A3
  Datchet SL3 ...68 A2
Beaulieu Gdns GU17 ...150 B3
Beaumaris Ct SL1 ...42 B4
Beaumont Cl SL6 ...39 A2
Beaumont Cotts 1 SL6 ...41 A1
Beaumont Ct Ascot SL5 ...119 C1
  Slough SL3 ...43 B4
Beaumont Dr TW15 ...98 B2
Beaumont Gdns RG12 ...118 C3
Beaumont Rd Slough SL2 ...42 B4
  Windsor SL4 ...67 B3
Beaumont Rise SL7 ...1 C1
Beaver Cl RG41 ...116 A3
Beaver La GU46 ...149 C3
Beaver Way RG5 ...88 A3
Beavers Cl RG26 ...135 A1
Beck Ct RG1 ...86 C3
Beckett Cl RG40 ...116 C3
Beckford Ave RG12 ...118 A2
Beckford Cl RG41 ...88 C1
Beckford Ct RG10 ...106 B2
Beckfords RG8 ...55 A1
Beckins Way HP10 ...3 B4
Bede Wlk RG2 ...86 B2
Bedfont Cl Feltham TW14 ...71 B1
Bedfont Court Est TW19 ...70 C3
Bedfont Ct TW19 ...70 C3
Bedfont Green Cl TW14 ...98 B4
Bedfont Ho TW14 ...71 C1
Bedfont Ind Pk N TW15 ...98 B2
Bedfont Jun Sch TW14 ...71 C1
Bedfont La TW14, TW13 ...98 C4
Bedfont Lakes Cntry Pk TW14 ...98 B3
Bedfont Rd
  Feltham TW13, TW14 ...98 B1
  Stanwell TW19 ...70 C1
Bedford Ave SL1 ...42 A4
Bedford Cl Maidenhead SL6 ...39 A3
  Newbury RG14 ...130 B2
Bedford Dr SL2 ...22 B4
Bedford Gdns RG41 ...115 C4
Bedford La SL5 ...121 A2
Bedford Rd SL6 ...85 C4
Bedfordshire Down RG42 ...91 C2
Bedfordshire Way RG41 ...115 C3
Bedwins La SL6 ...19 A3
Beech Ave GU15 ...151 B3
Beech Cl Ashford TW15 ...98 B2
  Burghfield Common RG30 ...111 A1
  Hampstead Norreys RG18 ...53 A4
  Maidenhead SL6 ...39 A4
  Stanwell TW19 ...97 B4
Beech Ct Caversham RG4 ...59 A2
  Newbury RG14 ...105 A2
Beech Dr GU17 ...150 B2
Beech Glen RG12 ...118 A3
Beech Hill Rd
  Beech Hill RG7 ...138 C2
  Sunningdale SL5 ...120 C2
Beech La RG6 ...87 A1
Beech Lodge TW18 ...96 C2
Beech Rd
  East Bedfont TW14 ...98 C4
  Mapledurham RG4 ...58 B4
  Newtown RG20 ...132 A2
  Purley on T RG8 ...57 A3
  Reading RG2 ...86 C3
  Slough SL3 ...43 C2
Beech Ride GU47 ...143 A1
Beech Tree La SL4 ...124 A4
Beech Wlk RG19 ...106 C3
Beecham Rd RG30 ...85 B4
Beechbrook Ave GU46 ...149 B1
Beechcroft Cl SL5 ...121 A3
Beechcroft Ct RG12 ...120 B3
Beechcroft Rd RG12 ...118 A3
Beeches Dr SL2 ...22 A4
Beeches Rd SL2 ...22 A4
Beeches The Goring RG8 ...34 A1
Beeches The
  Reading RG31 ...57 B2
  Staines TW18 ...97 A2

eechfield RG18 ...80 B4
eechingstoke 4 SL7 ...1 C2
eechnut Ave GU25 ...122 B2
eechnut Cl RG41 ...115 C3
eechnut Dr GU17 ...150 B4
eechtree Ave
　Englefield Green TW20 ...95 A1
　Marlow Bottom SL7 ...1 B3
eechwood Ave
　Reading RG31 ...84 B4
　Staines TW18 ...97 A1
　Woodley RG5 ...87 B4
eechwood Ct SL5 ...92 C1
eechwood Dr
　Marlow SL7 ...39 A3
　Marlow SL7 ...56 A2
eechwood Gdns SL1 ...42 C2
eechwood Prim Schs
　RG5 ...87 C4
eechwood Sec Sch SL2 ...22 A1
eedon CE Prim Sch
　RG20 ...51 B4
eedon Dr RG12 ...117 C2
eehive La RG12 ...117 B4
eehive Rd
　Bracknell RG12, RG42 ...117 B4
　Staines TW18 ...96 C2
eeham Cty Prim Sch
　RG7 ...108 C3
eeston Way RG6 ...114 A4
eeggars Hill Rd RG10 ...61 A1
eeighton Cl RG8 ...113 C4
elfast Ave SL1 ...42 B4
elford Ct 15 RG1 ...86 A3
elgrave Ct GU17 ...150 B2
elgrave Par SL1 ...42 C3
elgrave Rd SL1 ...42 C2
elgrava Ct 22 RG30 ...85 B3
ell Bridge Rd KT16 ...123 C1
ell Cl SL2 ...39 C3
ell Cnr KT16 ...123 C1
ell Ct SL6 ...17 C2
ell Foundry La RG40 ...116 B4
ell Hill RG14 ...130 A2
ell Holt RG14 ...130 B3
ell House Gdns RG41 ...116 A3
ell La Aldworth RG8 ...32 C2
　Blackwater GU17 ...150 B3
　Eton SL4 ...41 C1
　Henley-on-T RG9 ...15 C2
　Inkpen RG17 ...127 B2
ell St Henley-on-T RG9 ...15 C1
　Maidenhead SL6 ...39 C3
elle View SL4 ...66 C3
elle Vue SL4 ...66 C3
elle Vue Rd
　Henley-on-T RG9 ...15 C1
　Reading RG1 ...85 C4
elleisle RG8 ...57 A3
ellever Hill GU15 ...151 C3
ellevue Terr 15 RG1 ...85 C4
ellingham Cl GU15 ...152 B2
ellingham Wlk RG4 ...59 A3
ellman Ct 8 RG1 ...86 A4
ells Hill Ct SL2 ...23 A2
ells Hill Gn SL2 ...23 A3
ells La SL3 ...69 A2
ellsfield Ct SL4 ...44 A4
ellswood La SL3 ...44 A4
elmont Cl SL3 ...69 B4
elmont Cotts SL3 ...69 A4
elmont Cres SL6 ...39 B4
elmont Dr SL6 ...39 B4
elmont Mews GU15 ...151 B2
elmont Park Ave SL6 ...39 B4
elmont Park Rd SL6 ...39 B4
elmont Rd
　Camberley GU15 ...151 B2
　Crowthorne RG45 ...143 A3
　Maidenhead SL6 ...39 B4
　Reading RG30 ...85 A4
elmont Vale SL6 ...39 B4
elton Rd SL3 ...151 C3
elvedere Ct GU17 ...150 B2
elvedere Dr RG14 ...131 A4
elvedere Mans SL1 ...42 B2
elvedere Wlk RG41 ...88 A2
elvoir Cl GU16 ...151 C1
embridge Cl 20 SL1 ...42 C2
embridge Pl RG1 ...86 B4
enbrickle Gn RG42 ...91 A1
ence The TW20 ...123 A3
encombe Rd SL7 ...1 C2
enedict Dr TW14 ...98 B4
enedict Gn RG42 ...91 C1
enen-Stock Rd TW19 ...70 A1
enett Cl RG14 ...104 C3
enett Gdns RG42 ...90 A2
enett Rd RG2 ...86 A1
enham Chase RG20 ...103 C3
enham Hill
　Newbury RG14 ...105 C2
　Thatcham RG18 ...106 A2
enham La RG7 ...82 A1
enhams La RG9 ...15 C4
enjamin Ct TW15 ...98 B1
enner La GU24 ...153 C2
ennet Cl RG42 ...86 A1
ennet Rd RG2 ...86 A1
ennet Cl GU15 ...151 B3
ennetts Cl SL1 ...42 A3

Bennetts Hill RG7,RG30 ...111 B4
Benning Cl SL4 ...66 B2
Bennings Cl RG42 ...91 A1
Bensington Ct TW14 ...71 B1
Benson Cl Reading RG2 ...86 B2
　Slough SL2 ...43 A3
Benson Rd RG45 ...142 C3
Bentley Copse GU15 ...152 A2
Bentley Dr SL1 ...42 C2
Bentley Rd SL1 ...42 A2
Benyon Ct RG1 ...85 C3
Benyon Mews RG1 ...85 C3
Beomonds 8 KT16 ...124 A1
Beomonds Row 2 KT16 ...124 A1
Bere Court Rd RG8 ...56 A2
Bere Rd RG12 ...118 C2
Beresford Ave SL2 ...43 B3
Beresford Rd RG30 ...85 B3
Bergenia Ct GU24 ...153 C3
Berkeley Ave RG1 ...85 C3
Berkeley Ct TW19 ...96 B3
Berkeley Cl 1 RG1 ...85 C3
Berkeley Dr SL4 ...93 A4
Berkeley Gdns KT12 ...125 C1
Berkeley Mews SL7 ...1 C1
Berkeley Rd RG14 ...104 C1
Berkley Cl SL6 ...39 A4
Berkshire Bsns Ctr RG19 ...107 A1
Berkshire Coll of
　Agriculture SL6 ...18 A1
Berkshire Coll of
　Agriculture (Hall Place)
　SL6 ...38 A4
Berkshire Dr Reading RG31 ...84 B4
　Thatcham RG19 ...107 A1
Berkshire Ind Hospl RG1 ...85 C3
Berkshire Lodge 1 SL6 ...39 C3
Berkshire Rd
　Camberley GU15 ...151 C4
　Henley-on-T RG9 ...35 A4
Berkshire Way RG12 ...117 B3
Bernadine Cl RG42 ...91 C1
Bernard Ct GU15 ...151 A2
Berners Cl SL1 ...41 C3
Bernersh Cl GU47 ...143 B1
Berries Rd SL6 ...20 A4
Berry Field SL3 ...43 B4
Berry Hill SL6 ...20 A4
Berry Hill Ct SL6 ...40 B4
Berrybank GU47 ...150 C3
Berrycroft RG12 ...118 B4
Berrylands Rd RG41 ...59 A2
Berrys La RG30 ...85 A1
Berrys Rd RG7 ...107 B3
Berryscroft Ct TW18 ...97 B1
Berryscroft Rd TW18 ...97 B1
Berstead Cl 3 RG6 ...87 A1
Berwick Ave SL1 ...42 A3
Berwick Cl SL7 ...1 B2
Berwick La SL7 ...1 B2
Berwick Rd SL7 ...1 B2
Berwyn Ho RG2 ...113 B4
Beryl Cl RG41 ...115 C4
Bessels Way OX11 ...12 A4
Bestobell Rd SL1 ...42 B4
Beswick Gdns RG12 ...118 C3
Beta Ho 6 RG30 ...85 B3
Beta Way TW20 ...123 A2
Betam Rd RG1 ...86 B4
Betchworth Ave RG6 ...87 A2
Bethany Waye TW14 ...98 B4
Bethesda Cl RG8 ...55 A3
Bethesda St RG8 ...55 A3
Betjeman Wlk GU46 ...149 A2
Betteridge Rd RG19 ...106 C1
Betty Grove La RG41 ...114 C4
Beverley Cl Frimley GU15 ...152 B3
　Marlow SL7 ...1 A1
　Thatcham RG18 ...106 B2
Beverley Ct SL1 ...43 A2
Beverley Gdns
　Maidenhead SL6 ...19 A1
　Wargrave RG10 ...36 C3
Beverley Rd Reading RG31 ...57 B1
　Sunbury TW16 ...125 C4
Bevers The RG7 ...137 A3
Bexley Ct RG30 ...85 A4
Bexley St SL4 ...67 B3
Bibury Cl RG5 ...87 B2
Bicknell Rd GU16 ...151 C1
Biddles Cl 6 SL1 ...41 C3
Bideford Cl RG5 ...87 B2
Bideford Spur SL2 ...22 C1
Bier Path The RG8 ...55 B3
Bietighefen Way 2 GU15 ...151 B3
Big Barn Gr RG42 ...91 A2
Big La RG17 ...25 B2
Bigbury Gdns RG2 ...86 B2
Bigfrith La SL6 ...19 A3
Biggs La RG2,RG40 ...141 A4
Bill Hill Pk RG41 ...89 A2
Billet La SL3 ...43 C4
Billet Rd TW18,TW19 ...97 A3
Billing Ave RG40 ...141 C3
Billingbear La RG42 ...89 B2
Billingbear Way RG28 ...106 B3
Bilton Ind Est RG12 ...117 C3
Binbrook Cl RG6 ...87 A1
Binbury Row TW18 ...96 C2

Binghams The SL6 ...40 A2
Bingley Gr RG5 ...60 C1
Binsted Dr GU17 ...150 B3
Birch Ave RG30 ...85 A4
Birch Cl GU15 ...151 C4
Birch Copse Prim Sch
　RG31 ...84 B4
Birch Dr GU17 ...150 B2
Birch Gn Reading RG2 ...113 B4
　Staines TW18 ...97 A2
Birch Gr Bracknell RG12 ...118 B3
　Slough SL3 ...43 C4
　Upper Halliford TW17 ...125 C4
　Windsor SL4 ...66 B3
Birch Hill Prim Sch
　RG12 ...118 A1
Birch Hill Rd RG12 ...118 A1
Birch La Martinez RG7 ...136 C3
　West End GU24 ...153 B4
　Winkfield RG12, SL5 ...119 A4
Birch Platt GU24 ...153 B3
Birch Rd
　Burghfield Common RG7 ...111 A1
　Tadley RG26 ...134 C1
　Windlesham GU20 ...146 C2
　Wokingham RG40 ...142 A4
Birch Side RG45 ...143 A3
Birch Tree View GU18 ...146 A1
Birch View RG2 ...86 C2
Birchen Cl SL3 ...69 C3
Birches The
　Blackwater GU17 ...150 A3
　Goring RG8 ...34 A3
Birchetts Cl 2 RG42 ...118 A4
Birchfields GU15 ...151 B2
Birchland Cl RG7 ...136 C3
Birchland Ct SL5 ...67 A3
Birchlands Ct GU47 ...143 C1
Birchmead RG41 ...88 B1
Birchview Cl GU46 ...149 B2
Birchwood Cl RG4 ...59 B3
Birchwood Dr GU18 ...146 B1
Birchwood Rd RG14 ...105 B2
Birchwoods The RG41 ...88 A4
Bird Mews RG40 ...116 A3
Bird Mount Cotts SL4 ...67 B4
Birdhill Ave RG2 ...86 B3
Birds La RG7 ...107 C2
Birdwood Rd
　Maidenhead SL6 ...39 A4
　Sandhurst GU15 ...150 C3
Birkbeck Pl GU47 ...143 C1
Birkdale RG12 ...117 C1
Birkdale Cl SL6 ...120 B2
Birkhall Cl RG31 ...84 B3
Birley Rd SL1 ...42 B4
Biscuit Way RG2 ...112 C4
Bisham Abbey National
　Sports Ctr SL7 ...18 B4
Bisham CE Prim Sch SL7 ...18 A4
Bisham Ct Bisham SL7 ...13 C3
　19 Slough SL1 ...42 C2
Bisham Gn SL7 ...18 A4
Bishop Ct SL6 ...39 B3
Bishop Dr SL6 ...39 B3
Bishop Ctr The SL6 ...39 B3
Bishop Duppas Pk TW17 ...125 C2
Bishop Wand CE Sec Sch
　TW16 ...125 C4
Bishop's Cl SL4 ...92 A4
Bishopdale RG12 ...118 A3
Bishops Cl RG26 ...135 A1
Bishops Ct TW19 ...98 C1
Bishops Dr
　East Bedfont TW14 ...71 B1
　Wokingham RG40 ...116 B4
Bishops Farm Cl SL4 ...66 A3
Bishops Gr GU20 ...146 B2
Bishops Orch SL2 ...22 A1
Bishops Rd Bradfield RG7 ...82 A3
Bishops Way TW20 ...96 B1
Bishops Wlk HP10 ...3 C2
Bishopsgate Sch TW20 ...95 A3
Bishopsgate Rd TW20 ...95 A3
Bishopswood La RG26 ...134 C1
Bishopswood Rd RG26 ...134 C1
Bispham Ct 2 RG1 ...86 B3
Bissley Dr SL6 ...39 A3
Bitham La Ham RG17 ...126 A3
　Inkpen RG17 ...127 A2
Bittam Rd OX12 ...9 B4
Bittern Cl GU47 ...150 A3
Bitterne Ave RG31 ...84 A3
Bix Hill HP9 ...15 A3
Bix La SL6 ...38 C4
Black Boy La SL6 ...17 B2
Black Butts Cotts SL6 ...20 A4
Black Horse Cl SL4 ...66 B3
Black Lake Cl TW20 ...123 A4
Black Park Ctry Pk SL3 ...23 C2
Black Park Rd SL3 ...23 C2
Blackamoor La SL6 ...40 A4
Blackberry Cl TW17 ...125 C3
Blackbird Cl
　Burghfield Common RG7 ...111 A1
　Sandhurst GU47 ...143 C1
Blackbird Ho RG12 ...118 B2
Blackburn Trad Est TW19 ...70 C1
Blackcap Pl GU47 ...150 C4
Blackdown Way RG19 ...106 B1
Blackett Cl TW18 ...123 C4
Blacklands Rd RG7 ...107 B3
Blackley Cl RG6 ...87 C2
Blackmeadows RG12 ...118 B3
Blackmoor Cl SL5 ...119 B4
Blackmoor Wood SL5 ...119 B4
Blacknest Gate Rd SL5 ...121 A3
Blacknest Rd GU25,SL5 ...121 C3
Blackpond La SL2 ...22 A2

Blacksmith Row SL3 ...44 B1
Blacksmith's La TW18 ...124 B1
Blacksmiths La KT16 ...124 B1
Blackstroud La E
　GU18,GU24 ...153 C4
Blackstroud La W GU18 ...153 B4
Blackthorn Cl Earley RG6 ...87 A4
　Purley on T RG31 ...57 A1
Blackthorn Dell SL3 ...43 B2
Blackthorn Dr
　Lightwater GU18 ...153 A4
　Thatcham RG18 ...106 B3
Blackthorne Cres SL3 ...69 C3
Blackthorne Rd SL3 ...69 C2
Blackwater
　Caversham RG4 ...59 C2
　Shinfield RG7 ...113 A1
Blackwater Rise RG41 ...115 C2
Blackwater Sta GU17 ...150 C2
Blaenant RG4 ...58 C3
Blaenavon RG4 ...58 C3
Blagdon Cl RG19 ...131 B4
Blagdon Rd RG2 ...86 B1
Blagrave La RG4 ...58 B2
Blagrave Rise RG31 ...84 B3
Blagrave St RG1 ...86 A4
Blagrove Dr RG41 ...115 C2
Blagrove La RG41 ...115 C2
Blair Rd SL1 ...42 C3
Blaire Pk GU46 ...149 A4
Blake Cl Crowthorne RG45 ...143 B2
　Wokingham RG40 ...116 C4
Blakeney Cl SL6 ...19 C1
Blakeney Fields RG7 ...48 A2
Blakes Cl 10 KT16 ...124 A1
Blakes La Tadley RG26 ...135 B1
　Wargrave RG10 ...37 A1
Blakes Cotts Reading RG1 ...86 B4
Blakes Lock Mus RG1 ...86 B4
Blakes Rd RG10 ...36 C2
Blakes Ride GU46 ...149 A3
Blamire Dr RG42 ...90 C1
Blanchard Cl RG5 ...88 A4
Blandford Cl SL3 ...41 B2
Blandford Dr RG41 ...115 C2
Blandford Rd N SL3 ...43 B2
Blandford Rd S SL3 ...43 B2
Blands Cl RG7 ...110 C1
Blandy Rd RG9 ...35 B4
Blandys Hill RG17 ...128 A4
Blandys La RG8 ...55 A3
Blane's La SL5 ...119 B2
Blatchs Cl RG7 ...136 C3
Blay's La TW20 ...95 A1
Blays Cl TW20 ...95 B1
Bledlow Cl RG12 ...130 B3
Blenheim Cl Slough SL3 ...43 C3
　Wokingham RG41 ...115 C3
Blenheim Cotts RG18 ...106 A4
Blenheim Ho RG2 ...86 A3
Blenheim Gdns RG4 ...58 C3
Blenheim Rd
　Caversham RG4 ...59 A2
　Maidenhead SL6 ...39 A4
　Newbury RG14 ...104 C1
　Reading RG1 ...86 A3
　Slough SL3 ...43 B1
Blenheim Terr 1 RG1 ...86 A3
Bletchmore Cl UB3 ...71 B3
Blewburton Wlk RG12 ...118 C3
Blewbury Dr RG31 ...84 A4
Blewbury Hill OX11 ...12 A4
Blinco La SL3 ...43 C4
Blind La
　Bourne End HP10, SL8 ...3 A3
　Lambourn RG17 ...25 C1
Blomfield Dale RG42 ...117 B4
Blondell Cl UB7 ...70 B4
Bloomfield Dr RG12 ...91 B3
Bloomfieldhatch La
　Beech Hill RG7 ...138 A4
　Shinfield RG7 ...112 C1
Bloomsbury Way GU17 ...150 B2
Blossom Ave RG7 ...83 C2
Blossom La RG2 ...87 A3
Blount Cres RG42 ...90 C1
Bloxworth Cl 11 RG12 ...118 C3
Blue Ball La TW20 ...95 C2
Blue Coat Wlk RG12 ...118 A3
Bluebell Dr RG7 ...110 C2
Bluebell Hill RG12 ...118 C4
Bluebell Mdw RG41 ...88 A3
Bluebell Rise GU18 ...153 A4
Bluebell Way RG18 ...106 B3
Bluecoats RG18 ...106 B3
Bluethroat Cl GU47 ...150 C4
Blundell Cl RG41 ...88 A3
Blunden Dr SL3 ...44 B2
Blunts Ave UB7 ...71 A4
Blyth Ave RG19 ...106 C1
Blyth Wlk 7 RG1 ...86 A3
Blythe Rd SL10 ...44 C4
Blythewood La SL5 ...119 C4
Blythwood Dr GU16 ...151 C1
Boames La RG20 ...129 C3
Boarlands Cl SL1 ...41 C3
Boathouse Reach RG9 ...15 C1
Bobgreen Ct RG2 ...113 B3
Bobmore La SL7 ...1 C2
Bockhampton Rd RG17 ...25 B1
Bockmer La SL7 ...17 A4
Bodens Ride SL5 ...119 C1

Bodin Gdns RG14 ...131 A4
Bodmin Ave SL2 ...42 A4
Bodmin Cl RG19 ...106 B1
Bodmin Rd RG5 ...87 B3
Body Rd RG1 ...85 C4
Bog La RG12 ...119 A3
Bohams Rd OX11 ...11 B3
Bold's Ct SL2 ...23 A3
Bolding House La GU24 ...153 C4
Boldrewood RG7 ...110 C1
Boleyn Cl TW18 ...96 C2
Bolingbroke Way RG19 ...106 C2
Bolney Rd RG9 ...36 A3
Bolney Trevor Dr RG9 ...36 A2
Bolton Ave SL4 ...67 B2
Bolton Cres SL4 ...67 B2
Bolton Rd SL4 ...67 B2
Bolton Row RG20 ...50 B4
Bolton's La RG43 ...71 B4
Boltons La RG42 ...90 C1
Bolwell Cl RG10 ...61 C2
Bomer Cl UB7 ...71 B3
Bomford Cl RG18 ...78 C3
Bond St TW20 ...95 B2
Bone La RG14 ...105 B2
Bonemill La RG20 ...104 B1
Bones La RG9 ...35 A2
Boot End RG2 ...112 C4
Booth Dr TW18 ...97 B4
Borderside Slough SL2 ...43 A4
　Yateley GU46 ...149 A3
Borrowdale Cl TW20 ...96 A1
Borrowdale Gdns GU15 ...152 B2
Borrowdale Rd RG41 ...88 A2
Boscombe Cl TW20 ...123 A4
Boscowen Way RG19 ...107 A1
Bosham Cl RG6 ...87 C2
Boshers Gdns TW20 ...95 C1
Bosman Dr GU20 ...146 A3
Bossington Ct TW18 ...96 C2
Bostock La RG7 ...83 A1
Boston Ave RG1 ...85 C3
Boston Dr SL8 ...3 A2
Boston Rd RG9 ...35 B4
Boston Rd RG19 ...131 C4
Bosworth Gdns RG5 ...87 C2
Botany Cl RG19 ...131 C4
Botham Dr SL1 ...42 C2
Bothy The RG10 ...36 B1
Botmoor Way RG20 ...49 A4
Bottisham Cl RG6 ...114 B4
Bottle La Knowl Hill SL6 ...38 A1
　Newell Green RG42 ...91 A3
Bottom La RG7 ...110 B4
Bottom Waltons
　Caravan Site SL3 ...21 C2
Bouldish Farm Rd SL5 ...120 A3
Boult St RG1 ...86 B4
Boulters Cl
　Maidenhead SL6 ...20 B1
　Slough SL1 ...42 A2
　Woodley RG5 ...87 C4
Boulters Gdns SL6 ...20 B1
Boulters Ho 3 RG12 ...118 C3
Boulters La SL6 ...20 B1
Boulters Rd RG12 ...86 A2
Boults Wlk RG2 ...86 B1
Boundary Cl RG31 ...84 A4
Boundary La RG4 ...58 C2
Boundary Pl HP10 ...3 B4
Boundary Rd
　Newbury RG14 ...105 A1
　Staines TW15 ...97 B2
　Taplow SL6 ...40 C4
　Wooburn Green HP10 ...3 B4
Bourn Cl RG6 ...87 A3
Bourne Arch RG18 ...106 A2
Bourne Ave
　Chertsey KT16 ...124 A1
　Reading RG2 ...86 A2
　Windsor SL4 ...67 C3
Bourne Cl Bourne End SL8 ...3 A3
　Reading RG31 ...84 B4
Bourne End Bsns Ctr 6
　SL8 ...3 A2
Bourne End Rd SL6,SL8 ...20 C4
Bourne End Sta SL8 ...3 A2
Bourne Ho TW15 ...98 A3
Bourne Mdw TW20 ...123 A3
Bourne Rd Pangbourne RG8 ...56 C3
　Slough SL1 ...41 C2
　Thatcham RG19 ...106 A2
　Wentworth GU25 ...122 B2
Bourne- Stevens Ct RG1 ...86 B4
Bourne Vale RG17 ...100 B3
Bourneside GU25 ...122 A1
Bourton Cl RG30 ...84 C4
Bouverie Way SL3 ...43 C1
Boveney Cl SL1 ...42 A2
Boveney Ho 2 RG12 ...118 C3
Boveney New Rd SL4 ...41 C1
Boveney Rd SL4 ...41 A2
Boveridge Hts SL7 ...1 A1
Bowden Cl TW14 ...98 C4
Bowden Rd SL5 ...120 C4
Bowdown Ct RG14 ...104 C1
Bower Cl 8 SL1 ...41 C3
Bower Way SL1 ...41 C3
Bowes Rd Egham TW18 ...96 B3
　Thatcham RG19 ...106 B2
Bowes-Lyon Cl 7 SL4 ...67 B3
Bowfell Cl RG31 ...57 B1
Bowland Dr RG12 ...118 C1
Bowling Ct RG9 ...15 B2

Bowling Green La RG8 . . . . . .57 A3
Bowling Green Rd RG18 . . .106 A3
Bowlings The GU15 . . . . . . .151 B3
Bowman Ct RG45 . . . . .142 C2
Bowmans Cl SL1 . . . . .21 A2
Bowry Dr TW19 . . . . .68 C1
Bowyer Cres RG40 . . . . .116 B4
Bowyer Dr SL1 . . . . .41 C3
Bowyer Wlk SL5 . . . . .119 C4
Bowyers La RG42 . . . . .91 B3
Boxford Ridge RG12 . . . . . . .118 A3
Boxshall Ct RG14 . . . . .104 C1
Boyd Ct RG42 . . . . .118 A4
Boyn Ave SL6 . . . . .39 B3
Boyn Hill Cl SL6 . . . . .39 B3
Boyn Hill Ave SL6 . . . . .39 B3
Boyn Valley Rd SL6 . . . . .39 B3
Boyndon Rd SL6 . . . . .39 B4
Boyne Hill CE Inf Sch SL6 . . .39 B3
Bracebridge GU15 . . . . .151 A3
Bracken Bank SL5 . . . . .119 B4
Bracken Cl Ashford TW16 . . . .98 C1
Farnham Common SL2 . . . . . .22 B4
Purley on T RG31 . . . . .57 B1
Bracken Copse RG17 . . . . . .127 C3
Bracken La GU46 . . . . .149 A3
Bracken Rd SL6 . . . . .39 A4
Bracken Way
Burghfield Common RG7 . . .111 A1
Flackwell Heath HP10 . . . . . . .3 A4
Brackendale Cl GU15 . . . . . .151 C2
Brackendale Rd GU15 . . . . .151 B2
Brackenforde SL3 . . . . .43 B2
Brackenhale Comp Sch
RG12 . . . . .118 A3
Brackens The RG45 . . . . . . .143 A4
Brackenwood
Burghfield Common RG7 . . .110 C1
Frimley GU15 . . . . .152 B3
Brackenwood Dr RG26 . . . . .135 A1
Brackley Ho TW18 . . . . .96 C2
Bracknell Beeches RG12 . . .118 A3
Bracknell Bsns Ctr The
RG12 . . . . .117 C4
Bracknell Cl GU15 . . . . .144 C1
Bracknell Coll
Bracknell RG12 . . . . .118 B4
Bracknell, Wick Hill RG12 . . .118 B4
Bracknell Enterprise Ctr
RG12 . . . . .118 A4
Bracknell Rd
Bagshot GU19 . . . . .145 C3
Camberley GU15 . . . . .145 A1
Crowthorne RG45 . . . . .143 B3
Winkfield RG42 . . . . .92 A3
Bracknell Sports & L Ctr
RG12 . . . . .118 B2
Bracknell Sta RG12 . . . . . . .118 A3
Brackstone Cl RG4 . . . . .59 B1
Bradbury Gdns SL3 . . . . .23 B4
Bradcutts La SL6 . . . . .19 C4
Bradenham La SL7 . . . . .18 B3
Bradfield CE Prim Sch
RG7 . . . . .82 A1
Bradfield Coll RG7 . . . . .82 B3
Bradfields RG12 . . . . .118 B2
Bradford Rd SL1 . . . . .42 A4
Brading Way RG8 . . . . .57 B3
Bradley Cl RG17 . . . . .102 A1
Bradley Dr RG40 . . . . .116 A1
Bradley Rd SL1 . . . . .42 C3
Bradley-Moore Sq RG18 . . .106 C3
Bradmore Way RG6 . . . . . . .114 A4
Bradshaw Cl SL4 . . . . .66 C3
Bradwell Rd RG31 . . . . .57 B2
Braemar St6 . . . . .63 B4
Braemar Ct SL1 . . . . .1 B1
Braemar Gdns SL1 . . . . .42 A2
Braemore Cl RG19 . . . . .106 B1
Brakendale Way RG6 . . . . . . .87 A3
Bramber Cl SL1 . . . . .42 A3
Bramber Mews RG4 . . . . .59 C2
Bramble Cl TW17 . . . . .125 B3
Bramble Cres RG30 . . . . .84 C4
Bramble Dr SL6 . . . . .39 A2
Brambledown TW18 . . . . . . .124 A4
Bramblegate RG45 . . . . .143 A3
Brambles The
Crowthorne RG45 . . . . .142 B3
Newbury RG14 . . . . .130 C4
Bramblings RG4 . . . . .58 C3
Bramcote GU15 . . . . .152 B3
Bramley Ave TW17 . . . . .125 C3
Bramley Chase SL6 . . . . .20 B2
Bramley Cl Chertsey KT16 . .124 A1
Earley RG6 . . . . .87 A2
Maidenhead SL6 . . . . .39 B3
Staines TW18 . . . . .97 B1
Bramley Gr RG45 . . . . .142 B3
Bramley La GU17 . . . . .150 A3
Bramley Rd
Camberley GU15 . . . . .151 A1
Silchester RG7 . . . . .136 A1
Bramling Ave GU46 . . . . . . .149 A3
Brammas Cl SL1 . . . . .42 B2
Brampton Chase RG9 . . . . . . .36 A2
Brampton Ct SL6 . . . . .40 A2
Bramshaw Rd RG30 . . . . .58 A1
Bramshill Cl RG22 . . . . .140 C4
Bramwell Rd RG19 . . . . .106 C1
Bran Cl RG30 . . . . .84 C4
Brandon Ave RG5 . . . . .88 A4
Brandon Cl GU15 . . . . .152 B2
Brands Rd SL3 . . . . .69 A4
Bransome Cl GU15 . . . . .151 C4

Bransome Ct RG10 RG1 . . . . .85 C4
Bransome Hill Rd GU47 . .150 C4
Bransome Park Rd
GU15 . . . . .151 C3
Brants Bridge RG12 . . . . . . .118 C4
Brants Cl RG2 . . . . .114 C1
Braunfels Wlk RG14 . . . . . . .104 C1
Bravington Cl TW17 . . . . . . .124 C2
Bray Cl SL6 . . . . .40 B2
Bray Ct SL6 . . . . .40 B1
Bray Rd Maidenhead SL6 . . . .40 B2
Reading RG30 . . . . .85 A2
Braybank SL6 . . . . .40 B2
Braybrooke Dr RG10 . . . . . . .88 C4
Braybrooke Gdns RG10 . . . . .36 B1
Braybrooke Rd
Bracknell RG42 . . . . .91 A1
Wargrave RG10 . . . . .36 B1
Braye Cl GU47 . . . . .143 B1
Brayfield Rd SL6 . . . . .40 B2
Brayford Rd RG2 . . . . .113 B4
Braywick Park
& Nature Ctr SL6 . . . . .40 A2
Braywick Rd SL6 . . . . .40 A2
Braywood Ave TW20 . . . . .96 A1
Braywood CE Fst Sch SL4 . . .65 C3
Braywood Cotts SL4 . . . . .66 A3
Braziers La SL4, SL5 . . . . .92 B2
Breach Sq RG17 . . . . .100 B2
Breadcroft La SL6 . . . . .38 C2
Breadcroft Rd SL6 . . . . .38 C2
Bream Cl SL7 . . . . .18 B4
Bream Wlk RG6 . . . . .87 A1
Brechin Ct ☐ RG1 . . . . .86 B3
Brecon Ct SL1 . . . . .42 B2
Brecon Rd RG5 . . . . .87 C4
Bredon Rd RG41 . . . . .115 B4
Bredward Cl SL1 . . . . .21 A1
Breech The GU47 . . . . .150 C4
Breedons Hill RG8 . . . . .56 B3
Bremer Rd TW18, TW19 . . . . .97 A3
Brendon Cl Harlington UB3 . . .71 B4
Reading RG30 . . . . .57 C1
Brent Cl RG19 . . . . .106 B1
Brent Gdns RG2 . . . . .86 A2
Brent Rd SL8 . . . . .3 A2
Brentmoor Rd GU24 . . . . . . .153 B3
Brerewood RG6 . . . . .86 C1
Bret Harte Rd GU16 . . . . . . .151 C1
Brew Tower SL7 . . . . .1 B1
Brewery Comm RG7 . . . . . . .137 A4
Brewhouse Hill SN8 . . . . .99 A2
Briants Ave RG4 . . . . .59 B1
Briants Piece RG18 . . . . .79 A3
Briar Ave GU18 . . . . .153 A4
Briar Cl Burnham SL6 . . . . . . .41 A4
Caversham RG4 . . . . .59 A3
Briar Dene SL6 . . . . .19 C3
Briar Glen SL6 . . . . .19 C2
Briar Rd TW17 . . . . .125 A2
Briar Way SL2 . . . . .42 A4
Briarlea Rd RG7 . . . . .136 C3
Briars Cl RG8 . . . . .56 C2
Briars The Slough SL3 . . . . . . .43 C1
Stanwell TW19 . . . . .70 A1
Briarwood RG40 . . . . .141 C3
Briarwood Cl TW13 . . . . .98 B3
Brickfield La Burnham SL1 . . .21 A2
Harlington UB3 . . . . .71 B4
Brickfields Ind Ctr RG12 . . .118 A4
Bridge Ave Cookham SL6 . . . .19 C3
Maidenhead SL6 . . . . .40 A4
Bridge Cl Slough SL1 . . . . .41 C3
Staines TW18 . . . . .96 C2
Walton-on-T KT12 . . . . .125 C1
Bridge Ct SL6 . . . . .40 B4
Bridge End GU15 . . . . .151 A2
Bridge Gdns TW15 . . . . .98 B1
Bridge La GU25, KT16 . . . . .122 C2
Bridge Rd Ascot SL5 . . . . . . .120 B2
Bagshot GU19 . . . . .145 C2
Camberley GU15 . . . . .151 A2
Chertsey KT16 . . . . .124 A1
Maidenhead SL6 . . . . .40 A4
Bridge St Caversham RG4 . . .59 A1
Colnbrook SL3 . . . . .69 B4
Hungerford RG17 . . . . .100 B3
Maidenhead SL6 . . . . .40 A4
Newbury RG14 . . . . .105 A2
Reading RG1 . . . . .86 A4
Staines TW18 . . . . .96 C2
Walton-on-T KT12 . . . . .125 C1
Bridge View SL5 . . . . .121 A1
Bridge Walk GU46 . . . . .149 B4
Bridge Works GU15 . . . . . . .151 A2
Bridgeman Ct ☐ SL4 . . . . . . .67 A3
Bridgeman Dr SL4 . . . . .67 A3
Bridges Cl RG41 . . . . .115 C4
Bridges The RG7 . . . . .136 B3
Bridgestone Dr SL8 . . . . .3 B2
Bridgewater Cl RG30 . . . . . . .58 B1
Bridgewater Ct SL3 . . . . .44 A1
Bridgewater Terr SL4 . . . . . . .67 A3
Bridgewater Way SL4 . . . . . . .67 B3
Bridle Cl SL6 . . . . .19 C1
Bridle Rd SL6 . . . . .19 C1
Bridlepath Way TW14 . . . . . . .98 B4
Bridlington Spur SL1 . . . . . . .42 A2
Bridport Cl RG6 . . . . .87 B1
Bridport Way SL2 . . . . .22 A1
Brierley Pl RG31 . . . . .57 B2
Briff La RG7 . . . . .107 B4
Brigham Rd RG1 . . . . .59 A1
Brighton Rd RG6 . . . . .87 A3
Brighton Spur SL2 . . . . .22 A1
Brightside Ave TW18 . . . . . . .97 B1
Brightwalton CE Prim Sch
RG20 .28 B2

Brigidine Sch The SL4 . . . . . .67 B2
Brill Cl Caversham RG4 . . . . . .59 A2
Maidenhead SL6 . . . . .39 B2
Marlow SL7 . . . . .1 B1
Brimblecombe Cl RG41 . . . . .89 A1
Brimpton CE Prim Sch
RG7 .133 C3
Brimpton La RG7 . . . . .134 A2
Brimpton Rd
Brimpton RG7 . . . . .133 C4
Reading RG30 . . . . .85 B2
Tadley RG26 . . . . .134 B1
Brinkworth Pl SL4 . . . . .95 A4
Brinn's La GU17 . . . . .150 B3
Briony Ho RG2 . . . . .113 A4
Brisbane Rd RG30 . . . . .85 A4
Bristol Cl TW19 . . . . .70 C1
Bristol Ct ☐ TW19 . . . . .70 C1
Bristol Way SL1 . . . . .42 C3
Bristow Ct Caversham RG4 . . .59 A1
Marlow SL7 . . . . .2 A2
Bristow Cty Inf Sch
GU15 . . . . .151 A1
Bristow Rd GU15 . . . . .151 A2
Britannia Ind Est SL3 . . . . . . .69 C3
Britannia Way TW19 . . . . .97 B4
Brittain Ct GU47 . . . . .150 B4
Britten Rd RG2 . . . . .86 A3
Britwell Rd SL1 . . . . .21 B1
Brixham Rd RG2 . . . . .86 A1
Broad Hinton RG10 . . . . .61 C2
Broadacre RG12 . . . . .118 B3
Bradbury RG7 . . . . .107 B3
Wooburn Green HP10 . . . . . . .3 C3
Broad Ley's SL4 . . . . .68 B4
Broad Oak Ashford TW16 . . . .98 C1
Slough SL2 . . . . .22 B3
Broad Oak Ct SL2 . . . . .22 B1
Broad Platts SL3 . . . . .43 B2
Broad St East Isley RG20 . . . .30 C4
Reading RG1 . . . . .86 A4
West End GU24 . . . . .153 B1
Wokingham RG40 . . . . .116 B3
Broad St Wlk RG40 . . . . .116 B3
Broad Street Mall The
RG1 . . . . .86 A4
Broad Way RG7 . . . . .138 B2
Broad Wlk GU16 . . . . .151 C1
Broadacre TW18 . . . . .97 A2
Broadcommon Rd RG10 . . . .89 A4
Broadhalfpenny La RG26 . . .135 B1
Broadlands Ave TW17 . . . . . .125 B2
Broadlands Cl RG31 . . . . .84 B3
Broadlands Ct RG42 . . . . . . .117 C4
Broadlands Dr SL5 . . . . .120 B1
Broadley Gn GU20 . . . . .146 B2
Broadmark Rd SL2 . . . . .43 A3
Broadmeadow End
RG18 . . . . .106 C2
Broadmoor Cty Prim Sch
RG45 . . . . .143 B2
Broadmoor Hospl RG45 . . . .143 C3
Broadmoor La RG10, SL6 . . . .63 A3
Broadrick Heath RG42 . . . . . .91 C1
Broadview Est TW17 . . . . . . .125 B3
Broadwater Cl TW19 . . . . .95 C4
Broadwater La RG10 . . . . . . .61 C1
Broadwater Pk SL6 . . . . .40 C2
Broadwater Rd RG10 . . . . . . .61 C2
Broadway
Bracknell RG12 . . . . .118 B4
Maidenhead SL6 . . . . .39 C4
Staines TW19 . . . . .97 A1
Thatcham RG19 . . . . .106 B2
Winkfield SL4 . . . . .93 A4
Broadway Ctyd RG19 . . . . . .106 B2
Broadway Mall ☐ SL6 . . . . . .39 C4
Broadway Rd GU18,GU20 . . .146 B3
Broadway The
Laleham TW18 . . . . .124 B4
Lambourn RG17 . . . . .25 A2
☐ Newbury RG14 . . . . .105 A2
Sandhurst GU47 . . . . .150 A4
Theale RG7 . . . . .83 C1
Brunel Ret Pk RG2 . . . . .86 C2
Brocas Rd RG7 . . . . .133 B4
Brocas St SL4 . . . . .67 B4
Brocas Terr SL4 . . . . .67 B4
Brock Gdns RG30 . . . . .85 B4
Brock La SL6 . . . . .39 C4
Brock La Mall ☐ SL6 . . . . .39 C4
Brock Way GU25 . . . . .122 B3
Brockenhurst Dr GU46 . . . . .149 C3
Brockenhurst Rd
Ascot SL5 . . . . .120 C3
Bracknell RG12 . . . . .119 A3
Brockhurst & Marlston
House Prep Schs RG18 . . . .79 C2
Brocklands GU46 . . . . .149 A2
Brockley Cl RG30 . . . . .85 A4
Brocks La RG7 & RG18 . . . . . .80 A2
Brocks Way RG9 . . . . .36 A2
Broken Furlong SL4 . . . . .42 A1
Broken Way RG20 . . . . .131 A1
Bromley Wlk RG30 . . . . .84 C4
Brompton Cl ☐ RG6 . . . . .87 B1
Brompton Dr SL6 . . . . .38 B1
Bromycroft Rd SL2 . . . . .22 A1
Bronte Rise RG14 . . . . .131 A4
Brook Cl Sandhurst GU47 . . .143 C1
Stanwell TW19 . . . . .97 C4
Wokingham RG41 . . . . .116 B4
Brook Cres SL1 . . . . .41 C4
Brook Dr Ashford TW16 . . . . . .98 C1
Bracknell RG12 . . . . .118 B1
Brook La RG10 . . . . .62 C2
Brook Mo SL1 . . . . .42 B2
Brook Path SL1 . . . . .41 C3

Brook Rd Bagshot GU19 . . . .145 C1
Camberley GU15 . . . . .151 A2
Brook St Twyford RG10 . . . . . .61 B2
Windsor SL4 . . . . .67 B3
Brook St W RG1 . . . . .86 A3
Brookbank HP10 . . . . .3 B2
Brookdene Cl SL6 . . . . .19 C1
Brooke Furmston Pl SL7 . . . . .1 C2
Brooke Pl RG42 . . . . .90 B2
Brookers Cnr RG45 . . . . .143 B3
Brookers Hill RG2 . . . . .113 B3
Brookers Row RG45 . . . . . . .143 B3
Brookfield Ho SL3 . . . . .68 B3
Brookfield Rd HP10 . . . . .3 B2
Brookfields Specl Sch
RG31 .57 B2
Brookhouse Dr HP10 . . . . .3 B2
Brooklands Cl TW16 . . . . . . .125 C4
Brooklyn Dr RG4 . . . . .59 A3
Brookmill The RG1 . . . . .85 C3
Brooks Rd RG18 . . . . .106 C2
Brooksby Cl RG12 . . . . .150 A3
Brooksby Rd RG31 . . . . .57 B1
Brookside Ave
Staines TW15 . . . . .97 B2
Wraysbury TW19 . . . . .69 B3
Brookside Cl RG6 . . . . .87 B1
Brookway RG14 . . . . .105 C1
Broom Acres GU47 . . . . .143 A1
Broom Cl
Blackwater GU17 . . . . .150 C2
Reading RG31 . . . . .84 B3
Broom Field RG18 . . . . .153 A4
Broom Gr RG41 . . . . .115 B2
Broom Hill Cookham SL6 . . . .19 C3
Stoke Poges SL2 . . . . .22 C2
Broom Ho SL3 . . . . .43 C3
Broome Cl GU46 . . . . .149 B4
Broome Ct RG12 . . . . .118 A3
Broome Lodge TW18 . . . . . . .97 A2
Broomfield TW18 . . . . .97 A2
Broomfield Cl SL5 . . . . .121 A1
Broomfield Dr SL5 . . . . .121 A1
Broomfield Pk SL5 . . . . .121 A1
Broomfield Rd RG30 . . . . .84 C4
Broomhall Bldgs SL5 . . . . . . .121 A1
Broomhall La SL5 . . . . .121 A1
Broomsquires Rd GU19 . . . .145 C1
Broughton Cl RG30 . . . . .84 C4
Broughton Mews GU16 . . . .151 C1
Brownfield Gdns SL6 . . . . . . .40 A3
Browngraves Rd UB3 . . . . . . .71 B4
Browning Cl
Frimley GU15 . . . . .152 B2
Thatcham RG18 . . . . .106 B2
Brownlow Dr RG42 . . . . .91 B1
Brownlow Rd RG1 . . . . .85 C4
Brownrigg Cres RG12 . . . . . .118 C4
Brownrigg Rd TW15 . . . . .98 A2
Browns Cl SL1 . . . . .41 C3
Brownsfield Rd RG18 . . . . . .106 B2
Bruan Rd RG14 . . . . .130 C4
Bruce Ave TW17 . . . . .125 B2
Bruce Cl SL1 . . . . .42 A3
Bruce Rd RG5 . . . . .87 B4
Bruce Wlk SL4 . . . . .66 B3
Brucewood Par SL7 . . . . .1 C2
Brudenell SL4 . . . . .66 C2
Brummell Rd RG14 . . . . .104 C2
Brunel Cl GU15 . . . . .39 C3
Brunel Rd Maidenhead SL6 . . .39 C3
Theale RG7 . . . . .83 C1
Brunel Dr
Crowthorne RG45 . . . . .143 B4
Woodley RG5 . . . . .60 C1
Brunel Univ (Runnymede
Campus) TW20 . . . . .95 B3
Brunel Way SL1 . . . . .42 C3
Brunswick RG12 . . . . .118 A1
Brunswick Cl SL6 . . . . .125 A2
Brunswick Lodge ☐ RG1 . . .85 C4
Brunswick St RG1 . . . . .85 C3
Bruton Way RG12 . . . . .118 C1
Bryant Ave SL2 . . . . .42 C4
Bryants La RG18 . . . . .53 C1
Bryants Pl RG8 . . . . .57 A2
Brybur Cl RG2 . . . . .113 B4
Bryer Pl SL4 . . . . .66 B2
Bryony Ho RG42 . . . . .117 C4
Bryony Way TW16 . . . . .98 C1
Bsns Village The SL2 . . . . . . .43 A3
Buccaneer Cl RG5 . . . . .88 A4
Buccleuch Rd SL3 . . . . .68 A4
Buchan The GU15 . . . . .152 A4
Buchanan Dr RG40 . . . . .141 C4
Buchanan Sq RG19 . . . . .106 C1
Buck Side RG4 . . . . .59 A1
Buckden Cl RG5 . . . . .88 A3
Buckfield Ct SL0 . . . . .44 C2
Buckham Hill
RG17 & RG20 . . . . .7 A3
Buckhurst Gr RG40 . . . . .116 C3
Buckhurst Hill RG12 . . . . . . .118 C3
Buckhurst La SL5 . . . . .121 A3
Buckhurst Moors RG12 . . . . .117 B3
Buckhurst Rd SL5 . . . . .120 C4
Buckhurst Way RG6 . . . . .87 B1
Buckingham Ave SL1 . . . . . . .42 A4
Buckingham Ave E SL1 . . . . . .42 B4

Buckingham Ct
Staines TW18 . . . . .97 A1
Wokingham RG40 . . . . .116 B1
Buckingham Dr RG4 . . . . .59 A4
Buckingham Gate SL7 . . . . . . .17 B1
Buckingham Gdns ☐ SL1 . . .42 C3
Buckingham Ho RG14 . . . . . .130 C4
Buckingham Rd RG14 . . . . . .104 C2
Buckingham Way GU16 . . . .151 C1
Buckland Ave SL2 . . . . .43 A3
Buckland Cres SL4 . . . . .66 C2
Buckland Cty Jun & Inf Sch
TW18 .97 B1
Buckland Gate SL3 . . . . .23 A4
Buckland Rd RG2 . . . . .86 A1
Buckle La RG42 . . . . .91 A4
Bucklebury RG12 . . . . .118 A1
Bucklebury CE Prim Sch
RG7 .107 B2
Bucklebury Cl SL6 . . . . .40 A1
Bucklebury Farm Pk RG7 . . .80 B2
Buckleuch Ave SL6 . . . . .56 C2
Bucknell Cl RG31 . . . . .84 C1
Buckthorn Cl RG40 . . . . .116 C3
Budebury Rd TW18 . . . . .97 A3
Budge's Cl RG40 . . . . .116 C4
Budge's Gdns RG40 . . . . . . .116 C4
Budge's Rd RG40 . . . . .116 C4
Budham Way RG12 . . . . .118 A2
Buffins SL6 . . . . .20 C
Bulbrook Row RG12 . . . . . . .118 C
Bulkeley Ave SL4 . . . . .67 A3
Bulkeley Cl TW20 . . . . .95 B
Bull La Bracknell RG42 . . . . .118 A
Swallowfield RG7 . . . . .139 A
Bull Meadow The RG8 . . . . . .33 C
Bullbrook Dr RG12 . . . . .118 C
Bullfinch Cl GU47 . . . . .150 C
Bulmershe Rd RG1 . . . . .86 C
Bulpit La RG17 . . . . .100 B
Bulstrode Pl SL1 . . . . .42 C
Bunby Rd SL2 . . . . .22 C
Bunces Cl SL4 . . . . .42 C
Bunces La RG7 . . . . .111 A
Bundy's Way TW18 . . . . .96 C
Bungalow Dr RG31 . . . . .84 B
Bunglers Hill RG7 . . . . .140 A
Bunkers Hill RG14 . . . . .105 A
Bunten Meade SL1 . . . . .42 A
Bunyan Ct ☒ RG1 . . . . .86 A
Burbage Gn RG12 . . . . .118 C
Burbidge Cl RG31 . . . . .84 C
Burbidge Rd TW17 . . . . .125 C
Burbury Woods GU15 . . . . . .151 C
Burchell Rd RG14 . . . . .104 C
Burchett Copse RG40 . . . . . .141 C
Burchett's Green
CE Inf Sch SL6 . . . . .38 A
Burchett's Green Rd SL6 . . . .38 A
Burchetts Green La SL6 . . . . .38 A
Burchetts Green Rd SL6 . . . . .38 A
Burcombe Way RG4 . . . . .59 A
Burcot Gdns SL6 . . . . .20 A
Burdens Heath RG7 . . . . . . .107 A
Burdett Ct RG2 . . . . .86 B
Burdock Cl
Burghfield Common RG7 . . .111 A
Lightwater GU18 . . . . .153 A
Burfield Rd SL4, TW19 . . . . . .95 A
Burford Cl SL7 . . . . .1 B
Burford Ct ☐ Reading RG1 . . .85 C
Wokingham RG40 . . . . .116 C
Burford Cty Comb Sch SL7 . . .1 B
Burford Gdns SL1 . . . . .41 C
Burford Rd RG12 . . . . .151 A
Burfords RG7 . . . . .82 C
Burges Way TW18 . . . . .97 A
Burgess Cl RG5 . . . . .88 B
Burgess La RG17,RG20 . . . . .128 B
Burgett Rd SL1 . . . . .42 A
Burghead Cl GU47 . . . . .150 B
Burghfield Cl RG30 . . . . .85 A
Burghfield St Mary's
CE Prim Sch RG30 . . . . .111 B
Burgoyne Rd
Ashford TW16 . . . . .98 C
Camberley GU15 . . . . .152 A
Burleigh Gdns TW15 . . . . . . .98 B
Burleigh La SL5 . . . . .119 C
Burleigh Mews RG4 . . . . .59 B
Burleigh Rd SL5 . . . . .119 C
Burley Orch KT16 . . . . .124 A
Burley Way GU17 . . . . .150 B
Burlingham Cl RG2 . . . . .113 B
Burlings The SL5 . . . . .119 C
Burlington Ave SL1 . . . . .42 C
Burlington Cl TW14 . . . . .98 B
Burlington Ct
Blackwater GU17 . . . . .150 B
☐ Slough SL1 . . . . .42 C
Burlington Rd
Burnham SL1 . . . . .21 A
Reading RG30 . . . . .84 C
☒ Slough SL1 . . . . .42 C
Burnbank RG12 . . . . .118 A
Burn Moor Chase RG12 . . . .118 A
Burn Wlk SL1 . . . . .21 A
Burne-Jones Dr GU47 . . . . . .150 B
Burnetts Ct GU24 . . . . .153 C
Burnetts Rd SL4 . . . . .66 B
Burney Bit RG26 . . . . .135 C
Burnham Beeches
(Nature Reserve) SL2 . . . . . .22 A
Burnham Cl Bourne End SL8 . .3 A
Windsor SL4 . . . . .66 B
Burnham Copse Jun &
Inf Schs RG26 . . . . .135 A

nham Gr RG42 .... 91 B1
nham Gram Sch SL1 .... 21 B1
nham La SL1 .... 41 C4
nham Manor RG45 ..... 152 A4
nham Rd RG26 .... 134 C1
nham Rise RG4 .... 59 B4
nham Sta SL1 .... 41 A4
nham Upper Sch SL1 ... 41 A4
niston CI RG6 .... 87 C1
nmoor Mdw RG27 ..... 141 C1
ns CI RG5 .... 87 C2
nthouse La RG18 ..... 106 B2
nt Oak Cosham St6 .... 19 C4
ningham RG40 .... 141 C4
nt Portland La GU18 .. 146 C2
nthouse Gdns RG42 ... 91 C1
nthouse La RG72 ..... 112 A3
ncroft Rd RG30 .... 85 A3
rell Rd RG20 .... 31 C2
roughs Cres SL8 ...... 3 A2
roway Rd SL3 .... 44 A2
rows Hill CI
r19. TW6 .... 70 B2
rows The RG26 ...... 135 A1
ton CI Twyford RG10 .. 61 C1
ndlesham GU20 ...... 146 B2
ton Way SL4 .... 66 C2
tons Hill RG17 ...... 102 A1
way Cres KT16 ...... 124 A3
well CI RG6 .... 87 B1
ys Bank Rd RG19 .... 132 B3
h Rd TW17 .... 124 C2
h Wlk RG40 .... 116 B3
ness Ctr The RG41 ... 116 A2
ichers La SL6 .... 63 B4
st SL RG30 .... 85 A3
er CI SL 5 SL7 ..... 1 C2
er Rd Bagshot GU19 . 145 C1
wthorne RG45 ...... 143 A3
ers CI SL4 .... 66 B3
son CI RG14 .... 104 C2
renshaw Ave RG2 .. 141 A4
renshaw CI RG2 ... 141 A4
er Market RG1 ..... 86 A4
tercup CI RG40 .... 117 A3
tercup PI RG18 .... 106 B2
tercup Sq TW19 .... 97 B4
terfield
mberley GU15 ..... 151 A2
oburn Green HP10 .. 3 B2
termere Ave SL1 ... 41 B4
termere CI TW14 ... 98 C1
termere CI TW15 .. 152 B2
termere Gdns RG12 . 118 B3
termere Way TW20 . 96 A1
rsteep Rise
20, SL5 .... 119 B1
ts Furlong RG20 .... 28 B2
ts Hill Rd RG5 ..... 87 C4
ton Ave RG4 ...... 58 C2
ton Rd TW15 ..... 97 B2
ton St SL2 .... 22 A2
field Rd RG30 .... 85 A2
ways CI Rc10 ..... 37 C2
and Dr SL6 ...... 40 A1
eton CI RG6 ..... 87 A1
on SL3 .... 44 A1
on Ave GU15 .... 152 A2
on CI 3 Marlow SL7 . 1 C2
wbury RG14 ..... 130 C4
ford RG10 .... 61 C2
eley GU46 .... 149 A2
on Dr RG45 ..... 143 A2
on Rd Earley RG6 . 87 A4
ford RG10 ...... 61 C2
horn CI RG2 .... 87 C1
rays Burnham SL1 . 41 A4
eley GU46 ...... 149 A3
rood CI RG2 .... 118 A1
orth CI RG2 .... 113 A4

in Moss RG12 .... 118 C1
rera Ave GU25 ... 122 B2
rera CI GU25 .... 122 B2
bury CI TW16 .... 98 C1
bury Rd TW16 ... 98 C1
dy CI 4 TW20 .... 96 A2
ogan CI Holyport SL6 . 65 A4
ading RG30 ..... 84 C4
well Dr SL6 ..... 39 B2
sar's Camp Rd GU15 . 152 A4
sar's CI GU15 ... 152 B4
sar's Way TW17 .. 125 B2
sars Gate RG42 .. 91 C1
sers CI GU15 .... 152 A4
es Wood Dr SL2 .. 22 A4
n Rd RG12 RG42 .. 117 C4
's La TW17 ...... 124 C1
n CI GU15 ...... 152 A2
ngorm PI SL2 .... 22 B1
ngorm Rd RG19 .. 106 B1
stor CI RG31 .... 84 A2
nor Rd RG18 .... 106 A3
ourne Dr RG11 .. 84 B2
roke Rd SL2 .... 21 C1
cot CI RG31 .... 84 C3
cot Place Dr RG31 . 84 C2
dbeck Dr RG5 .. 87 B4
der CI Maidenhead SL6 . 19 C1
ading RG30 .... 84 C4
der Ct Maidenhead SL6 . 19 C1
ough SL3 ...... 43 C1
der Way SL3 .... 43 B3
dicott Prep Sch SL2 . 22 A3
dwell Rd GU20 .. 146 B3

Caledonia Rd TW19 ... 97 C4
Caleta CI RG4 .... 59 B1
Calfridus Way GU12 .. 118 C3
California Ctry Pk RG2 . 141 B4
Calleva Mus RG7 .... 136 A1
Calleva Pk RG7 ..... 134 C1
Calleva Roman Town
  RG7 .... 136 B1
Callington Rd RG21 .. 86 B1
Callins La RG10 ..... 63 A2
Callis Farm CI TW19 .. 70 C1
Callow Hill GU25, TW20 . 122 B4
Calshot PI RG31 .... 84 B2
Calshot Rd TW4 .... 71 A3
Calshot Way TW6 ... 71 A3
Calvin CI GU15 ..... 152 A2
Camberley Cty Inf Sch
  GU15 .... 151 B3
Camberley Heath
  Golf Course GU15 . 152 A3
Camberley Rd TW6 .. 71 A2
Camberley Sta GU15 . 151 B3
Camberley Towers GU15 . 151 B3
Camborne CI Earley RG6 . 87 A1
  Harmondsworth TW6 . 71 A2
Camborne Cres TW6 . 71 A2
Camborne Rd TW6 .. 71 A2
Camborne Way TW6 . 71 A2
Cambria CI Slough SL3 . 43 B2
  Staines TW18 ..... 96 C2
Cambria Gdns TW19 . 97 C4
Cambrian CI GU15 .. 151 A3
Cambrian Way
  Reading RG31 .... 84 B2
  Wokingham RG40 . 142 A4
Cambridge Ave
  Burnham SL1 .... 21 A4
  Slough SL1 ...... 42 A4
Cambridge CI UB7 .. 70 B4
Cambridge Ho 2 SL4 . 67 B3
Cambridge Rd
  Crowthorne RG45 .. 143 B2
  Littleton TW15 ... 98 B1
  Marlow SL7 ..... 1 B1
  Sandhurst GU47 .. 143 C1
Cambridge Sq GU15 . 151 B3
Cambridge St 1 RG1 . 85 C4
Cambridge Wlk 3 GU15 . 151 B3
Cambridgeshire CI
  Bracknell RG42 .. 91 C1
  Wokingham RG41 . 115 C3
Camden PI Bourne End SL8 . 3 A2
  Reading RG31 .... 84 A2
Camden Rd SL6 .... 19 B1
Camelford CI RG2 ... 86 A1
Camellia CI GU24 ... 153 C3
Camellia Way RG41 .. 115 B4
Camgate Est TW19 .. 97 C4
Camilla CI TW16 .... 98 C1
Camley Gdns SL6 ... 39 A4
Camley Park Dr SL6 . 38 C4
Camm Ave SL4 ..... 66 C2
Camp Rd RG7 ...... 110 B1
Campbell CI GU46 ... 149 C1
Campbell PI GU16 ... 151 C2
Campbell Rd RG5 ... 87 B3
Campbells Gn RG7 .. 137 A3
Camperdown SL6 ... 20 A1
Camperdown Ho 30 SL4 . 67 B3
Campion CI GU17 ... 150 C2
Campion Ho RG7 ... 117 C4
Campion Way RG40 . 116 C4
Canada Rd SL1 ..... 43 A2
Canal View Rd RG14 . 105 B2
Canal Walk RG17 ... 100 B3
Canal Way RG1 .... 86 B4
Canal Wharf SL3 ... 44 A2
Canberra CI GU46 .. 149 A4
Canberra Rd TW6 .. 71 A2
Candleford CI RG12 . 91 B1
Candover CI UB7 ... 70 B4
Canford CI RG30 ... 85 A3
Cannock CI SL6 .... 40 A3
Cannock Way RG6 .. 87 B1
Cannon CI GU47 ... 150 C4
Cannon Court Rd SL6 . 19 C2
Cannon Hill RG12 .. 118 B2
Cannon Hill CI SL6 . 40 B1
Cannon La SL6 .... 38 C2
Cannon St 8 RG1 ... 85 C4
Cannondown Rd SL6 . 19 C3
Canon Hill Dr SL6 .. 40 A2
Canon Hill Way SL6 . 40 A1
Canon's Cloisters SL4 . 67 B4
Canopus Way TW19 . 97 C4
Cansfield End RG14 . 104 C2
Canterbury Ave SL2 . 22 B1
Canterbury Ct TW15 . 97 C2
Canterbury Rd RG12 . 86 B2
Cantley Cres RG41 .. 116 A4
Cantley House Hotel
  RG40 .... 116 A4
Cape Villas SL4 .... 44 C4
Capper Rd GU15 ... 151 A4
Capricorn Ho HP10 . 3 A4
Captains Gorse RG8 . 54 C3
Caraway Rd RG4 ... 87 A1
Carbery La SL5 .... 123 A3
Carbiswood La RG7 . 108 A3
Cardiff Rd RG1 .... 58 C1
Cardigan CI SL1 ... 41 C3
Cardigan Gdns RG1 . 86 C3
Cardigan Rd RG1 .. 86 C3
Cardinal CI RG4 ... 59 A1
Cardinal's Wlk TW16 . 98 C1
Cardinals Wlk SL6 . 41 B4
Cardwell Cres SL5 . 120 B2
Carew Rd TW15 ... 98 B1

Carey CI SL4 .... 67 A2
Carey Rd RG40 ..... 116 B3
Carey St RG1 ...... 85 C4
Cariad Ct RG8 ..... 34 A4
Carisbrooke CI
  Caversham RG4 ... 59 B3
  Maidenhead SL6 .. 39 B3
Carisbrooke Ct SL1 . 42 C3
Carland CI RG6 .... 87 A1
Carlesgill PI RG9 ... 35 C4
Carlile Gdns RG10 .. 61 B3
Carlinwark Dr GU15 . 151 C4
Carlisle Rd Reading RG1 . 57 C2
  Slough SL1 ...... 42 B3
Carlton CI Frimley GU15 . 152 A2
  Woodley RG5 .... 87 C3
Carlton Ct TW18 ... 97 A4
Carlton Ho TW19 .. 70 B1
Carlton Rd Ashford TW16 . 98 C1
  Caversham RG4 ... 58 C3
  Slough SL2 ...... 43 A3
Carlyle CI RG45 .... 143 B3
Carlyle Rd TW18 ... 97 A1
Carmarthen Rd SL1 . 42 C3
Carmela Ct TW15 .. 98 B1
Carnarvon Rd RG1 . 86 C3
Carnation CI RG45 . 143 A4
Carnation Dr RG42 . 92 A1
Carnegie Rd RG14 . 105 A1
Carnoustie RG12 ... 117 C1
Carnoustie Ct 22 RG1 . 86 B4
Carolina PI RG40 ... 141 C4
Caroline Ct Ashford TW15 . 98 A1
  Marlow SL7 ..... 1 C2
Caroline Dr RG41 .. 116 A4
Caroline PI UB3 ... 71 C4
Caroline St 7 RG1 .. 85 C4
Carrick Gdns RG5 .. 87 B4
Carrick La GU46 ... 149 C3
Carrington Ave HP10 . 3 A4
Carrington House Sch
  GU15 .... 152 A2
Cary CI RG14 ..... 130 B3
Casey Ct RG7 ..... 81 B2
Cassia Dr RG6 .... 86 C1
Cassiobury Ave TW14 . 98 C4
Cassocks Sq TW17 . 125 B1
Castle Ave SL3 .... 68 A4
Castle CI 3 Charlton TW16 . 98 C1
  Frimley GU15 .... 151 C2
Castle Cres RG1 ... 85 C3
Castle Ct SL6 ..... 39 B4
Castle Dr SL6 ..... 39 B4
Castle End Rd RG10 . 60 C4
Castle Farm Caravan Site
  SL4 .... 66 B3
Castle Gr RG14 .... 104 C3
Castle Hill Maidenhead SL6 . 39 C4
  Reading RG1 ..... 85 C3
  Swallowfield RG7 . 140 B4
  Windsor SL4 ..... 67 B3
Castle Hill Rd TW20 . 95 B3
Castle Hill Terr SL6 . 39 C4
Castle Ind Pk RG14 . 105 B3
Castle La RG14 ... 104 C3
Castle Lodge SL6 . 39 C4
Castle Mews SL6 . 39 C4
Castle Rd GU15 .. 151 C2
Castle St Reading RG1 . 86 A4
  Slough SL1 ..... 42 C2
Castlecraig Ct GU47 . 150 B4
Castleman Ho SL5 . 120 B2
Casteton Ct SL7 .. 1 C1
Castleview Comb Sch SL3 . 43 B1
Castleview Ho 11 SL4 . 67 B3
Castleview Rd SL3 . 43 A4
Castor Ct GU46 ... 149 A4
Caswall CI RG42 .. 90 B1
Caswall Ride GU46 . 149 C3
Catalina CI RG5 ... 88 A4
Catalina Rd TW6 .. 71 A2
Catcliffe Way RG6 . 114 B2
Catena Rise GU18 . 146 A1
Catesby Gdns GU46 . 149 A3
Catherine Dr TW16 . 98 C1
Catherine Rd RG14 . 105 A1
Catherine St RG30 . 85 B4
Catlin Cres TW17 .. 125 B2
Catmore Rd RG20 .. 29 B4
Caunter Rd RG14 .. 104 B2
Causeway Est TW20 . 96 B2
Causeway The
  Caversham RG4 .. 59 B1
  Egham TW18, TW20 . 96 B2
  Maidenhead SL6 . 40 B2
  Marlow SL7 .... 1 B2
Causmans Way RG31 . 57 B1
Cavalier CI
  Newbury RG14 .. 105 B3
  Theale RG7 .... 83 B1
Cavalier Ct TW15 . 97 A4
Cavalry Cres SL4 . 67 B2
Cavendish CI
  Ashford TW16 .. 98 C1
  Burnham SL6 .. 41 A4

Cavendish Ct
  Ashford TW16 ... 98 C1
  Blackwater GU17 . 150 B2
  9 Chertsey KT16 . 124 A1
  Newbury RG14 .. 105 C3
  Poyle SL3 ..... 69 C3
Cavendish Gdns RG41 . 88 A2
Cavendish Meads SL5 . 120 B2
Cavendish Rd
  Ashford TW16 ... 98 C1
  Caversham RG4 .. 59 B3
  Maidenhead SL6 . 39 A2
Caversham Hill RG4 . 59 A2
Caversham Park Dr RG4 . 59 B3
Caversham Park Prim Sch
  RG4 .... 59 B3
Caversham Park Rd RG4 . 59 C3
Caversham Prim Sch RG4 . 59 A2
Caversham Rd RG1 . 59 A1
Caversham Wharf RG1 . 59 A1
Caves Farm CI GU47 . 150 A4
Cawcott Dr SL4 ... 66 C3
Cawsam Gdns RG4 . 59 B2
Caxton CI RG30 ... 58 B1
Caxton Ct RG9 .... 15 C1
Cecil Aldin Dr RG31 . 57 B2
Cecil CI TW15 .... 98 B1
Cecil Rd Ashford TW15 . 98 B1
  Iver SL0 .... 44 C4
Cecil Way SL2 .... 21 C1
Cedar CI RG6 .... 15 B1
Cedar Ave GU17 .. 150 B3
Cedar Chase SL6 . 20 B1
Cedar CI Bagshot GU19 . 145 C2
  Laleham TW18 .. 124 B3
  Wokingham RG40 . 116 B3
Cedar Ct Egham TW20 . 96 A2
  Maidenhead SL6 . 39 B4
  Marlow SL7 .... 1 C1
  6 Windsor SL4 .. 67 A3
Cedar Dr Bracknell RG42 . 91 B1
  Cookham SL6 ... 19 C4
  Marlow Bottom SL7 . 1 B4
  Pangbourne RG8 . 56 B2
  Sunningdale SL5 . 121 A1
Cedar Gr RG19 ... 106 B2
Cedar Ho TW16 .. 98 C1
Cedar Mount RG14 . 130 C4
Cedar Rd SL5 .... 87 C3
Cedar Rd
  East Bedfont TW14 . 98 B4
  Reading RG2 ... 86 C1
Cedar Way Charlton TW16 . 98 C1
  Slough SL3 .... 43 C2
Cedar Wood Cres RG4 . 59 A2
Cedars 10 RG12 .. 118 C3
Cedars CI GU47 .. 149 C4
Cedars Rd SL6 ... 40 A4
Cedars The RG31 . 57 B1
Celandine CI RG45 . 143 B3
Celandine CI GU46 . 149 A4
Celandine Gr RG18 . 106 C2
Celia Cres TW15 . 97 B1
Cell Farm SL4 ... 68 A1
Cell Farm Ave SL4 . 68 A1
Celsea PI RG10 .. 14 A4
Cemetery La TW17 . 125 A1
Centenary Bsns Pk RG9 . 15 C1
Central Dr SL1 ... 41 C3
Central Est SL6 .. 39 C4
Central La SL4 ... 93 A4
Central Way SL4 . 93 A4
Central Wlk RG40 . 116 B3
Centre The
  Farnham Common SL2 . 22 B3
  Walton-on-t KT12 . 125 C1
  4 Sandhurst GU47 . 150 B4
Centurion CI Reading RG1 . 86 A3
Century Dr RG7 .. 113 B1
Century Rd TW20 . 96 B2
Cerotus PI KT16 .. 123 C1
Chackfield Dr RG41 . 115 B4
Chaddsworth St Andrews
  CE Prim Sch
    RG20 .... 49 A4
Chaffinch CI
  Reading RG31 .. 84 A4
  5 Sandhurst GU47 . 150 B4
  Wokingham RG41 . 115 C3
Chagford Rd RG2 . 86 A1
Chain St RG1 .... 86 A4
Chainhill Rd 0x12 . 8 A4
Chalcott SL1 .... 42 C2
Chalcraft CI RG9 . 35 B4
Chalfont CI RG6 . 87 A1
Chalfont Ct RG6 . 87 A1
Chalfont Way RG6 . 87 A1
Chalford HP10 ... 3 C3
Chalford Rd RG14 . 104 C1
Chalgrove CI SL6 . 40 A3
Chalgrove Way RG4 . 59 A3
Chalk Hill
  Aston Tirrold OX11 . 12 C4
  Shiplake RG9 ... 35 B3
Chalk Pit La SL1 . 21 A2
Chalklands SL8 .. 3 A2
Chalkpit La SL7 .. 1 A2
Challenge Rd TW15 . 98 B3
Challenor CI RG40 . 141 C4
Challis PI RG42 .. 117 C4
Challow Ct SL6 .. 19 B3
Chalmore Gdns RG6 . 98 A2
Chalmers Rd E TW15 . 98 B1
Chalvey City Fst Sch SL1 . 42 B2
Chalvey Gdns SL1 . 42 C2
Chalvey Gr SL1 .. 42 A2
Chalvey Pk SL1 .. 42 C2
Chalvey Rd E SL1 . 42 C2
Chalvey Rd W SL1 . 42 B2

Chamberhouse Mill Rd
  RG19 .... 106 C1
Chamberlains Gdns RG2 . 114 C1
Chambers The 2 RG1 . 86 A4
Champion Rd RG4 . 59 B1
Chancel Mans RG42 . 91 B1
Chancellors Way The
  RG6 .... 86 C2
Chancery Mews 22 RG1 . 85 C4
Chancery PI SL4 . 67 B4
Chanctonbury Dr SL5 . 120 C1
Chandlers CI TW14 . 98 C4
Chandlers La GU46 . 149 B4
Chandos Mall 8 SL1 . 42 C2
Chandos Rd Egham TW18 . 96 B2
  Newbury RG14 .. 131 A4
Chantry CI SL4 .. 67 A3
Chantry Ct GU16 . 151 B1
Chantry Mead RG17 . 100 B3
Chantry Rd Bagshot GU19 . 145 B1
  Chertsey KT16 .. 124 B1
Chapel Arches SL6 . 40 A4
Chapel CI Bracknell RG12 . 118 B3
  South Stoke RG8 . 14 B2
Chapel Ct
  Hungerford RG17 . 100 B3
  Maidenhead SL6 . 39 B2
  18 Reading RG1 . 86 A4
  Reading RG18 .. 106 C2
Chapel Hill Reading RG31 . 84 B4
  Windsor SL4 ... 67 B3
Chapel La
  Ashampstead RG8 . 54 A4
  Bagshot GU19 .. 145 B1
  Binfield RG42 .. 90 B1
  Blewbury OX11 . 12 A4
  Farnborough (Hants) GU14 . 151 A1
  Headley RG19 .. 133 C1
  Hermitage RG18 . 79 B4
  Hermitage, Curridge RG18 . 78 C2
  Lambourn RG17 . 25 A2
  Shinfield RG7 .. 113 A1
  Silchester RG7 . 135 C3
  Stoke Poges SL2 . 23 A3
  Swallowfield RG7 . 139 B2
  Yattendon RG18 . 53 C1
Chapel Rd
  Camberley GU15 . 151 A3
  Flackwell Heath HP10 . 3 A4
  Silchester RG7 . 136 B3
  Stockcross RG20 . 103 C3
Chapel Row RG10 . 61 B2
Chapel Sq
  Sandhurst GU15 . 150 C3
  Virginia Water GU25 . 122 C3
Chapel St Marlow SL7 . 1 C1
  Slough SL1 .... 42 C2
  Thatcham RG18 . 106 B2
Chapels CI SL1 .. 41 C3
Chaplain's Hill RG45 . 143 B2
Chaplin Cres TW16 . 98 C1
Chapman La HP10, SL8 . 3 A3
Chapman Wlk RG18 . 106 A2
Chapter Mews SL4 . 67 B4
Charadon CI RG2 . 86 A3
Charcroft Ct RG1 . 86 C3
Charfield Ct RG1 . 86 C4
Charlbury CI 16 RG12 . 118 C3
Charlecombe Ct TW18 . 97 A2
Charles Ct TW15 . 98 B2
Charles Evans Way RG4 . 59 B1
Charles Gdns SL2 . 43 A4
Charles Ho 9 SL4 . 67 B3
Charles PI 22 RG1 . 86 A4
Charles Rd Cholsey OX10 . 14 A4
  Staines TW18 .. 97 B1
Charles Sq RG12 . 118 B4
Charles St Chertsey KT16 . 123 C1
  Newbury RG14 . 130 B3
  Reading RG1 ... 85 C4
  Windsor SL4 ... 67 B3
Charlock CI RG18 . 106 C3
Charlotte CI RG18 . 79 A3
Charlton SL4 .... 66 B3
Charlton CI SL1 .. 42 A2
Charlton Ct GU47 . 143 B1
Charlton La
  Swallowfield RG7 . 139 B3
  Upper Halliford TW17 . 125 B3
Charlton PI
  Newbury RG14 . 105 A2
  8 Windsor SL4 . 66 B3
Charlton Rd TW17 . 125 B4
Charlton Row 6 SL4 . 66 B3
Charlton Sq 4 SL4 . 66 B3
Charlton Way SL4 . 66 B3
Charlton Wlk 5 SL4 . 66 B3
Charlville Dr RG31 . 84 A2
Charnwood CI RG14 . 130 C4
Charnham La RG17 . 100 B3
Charnham Park RG17 . 100 B3
Charnham St RG17 . 100 B3
Charnwood SL2 .. 120 C2
Charrington Rd RG31 . 84 B2
Charta Rd TW20 . 96 B2
Charter CI SL1 ... 42 C2
Charter Rd Newbury RG14 . 130 C4
  Slough SL1 .... 41 C3
Charterhouse CI RG12 . 118 C2
Charters La SL5 . 120 B2
Charters Rd SL5 . 120 C1
Charters Sch SL5 . 120 C1
Charters Way SL5 . 120 C1
Charvil House Rd RG10 . 61 A3

Charvil La RG4 . . . . .60 C2
Charvil Meadow Rd RG10 . .61 A3
Charwood Rd RG40 . . . . .116 C4
Chase Gdns RG42 . . . . .90 B2
Chase The
Crowthorne RG45 . . . . .143 A3
Maidenhead SL6 . . . . .19 B2
Marlow SL7 . . . . .2 A2
Newbury RG14 . . . . .104 C4
Reading RG31 . . . . .113 B2
Chaseley Ct KT13 . . . . .125 C1
Chaseside Ave RG10 . . . . . . .61 B4
Chaseside Gdns KT16 . . . . .124 A1
Chatfield SL2 . . . . .42 A4
Chatham Ct **3** SL1 . . . . . . .43 A2
Chatham St RG1 . . . . .85 C4
Chatsworth Ave RG41 . . . . . .88 A1
Chatsworth Cl
Caversham RG4 . . . . .59 B3
Maidenhead SL6 . . . . .20 B2
Chatsworth Hts GU15 . . . . .152 A4
Chatteris Way RG6 . . . . . . .114 B4
Chattern Ct TW15 . . . . .98 A2
Chattern Hill TW15 . . . . .98 A2
Chattern Rd TW15 . . . . .98 B2
Chatters The RG7 . . . . .140 B4
Chatton Cl RG6 . . . . .114 A4
Chaucer Cl Caversham RG4 . . .59 A3
Windsor SL4 . . . . .67 B2
Wokingham RG40 . . . . .116 C4
Chaucer Cres RG24 . . . . . . .104 C3
Chaucer Ct TW18 . . . . .96 B2
Chaucer Gr GU15 . . . . .151 B3
Chaucer Rd Ashford TW15 . . .97 C2
Crowthorne RG45 . . . . .143 A2
Chauntry Cl SL6 . . . . .40 B3
Chauntry Rd SL6 . . . . .40 B3
Chavey Down Rd RG42 . . . .92 A1
Chawridge La SL4 . . . . .92 B4
Chazey Cl RG4 . . . . .58 B4
Chazey Rd RG4 . . . . .58 B2
Cheam Cl RG12 . . . . .118 B2
Cheap St Compton RG20 . . . .31 C3
Newbury RG14 . . . . .105 A1
Cheapside RG1 . . . . .86 A4
Cheapside CE Prim Sch
SL5 .120 C4
Cheapside Rd SL5 . . . . .120 B4
Cheddar Rd TW6 . . . . .71 A3
Cheddington Cl RG30 . . . . . .84 C3
Cheeseman Cl RG40 . . . . . .116 B4
Chelford Way RG4 . . . . .58 C2
Chelmsford Ct **3** SL4 . . . .67 B3
Chelsea Cl RG30 . . . . .84 C4
Chelwood Dr GU47 . . . . . . .142 C1
Chelwood Rd RG6 . . . . .87 A1
Cheney Cl RG42 . . . . .90 B1
Cheniston Ct SL5 . . . . .121 A1
Cheniston Gr SL6 . . . . .38 C4
Chepstow Rd RG31 . . . . .57 B2
Chequer La RG7 . . . . .138 C1
Chequers Orch SL0 . . . . .44 C4
Chequers Way RG5 . . . . .87 B4
Cherbury Cl RG12 . . . . .118 C3
Cherington Gate SL6 . . . . . . .19 A1
Cherington Way SL5 . . . . . .119 C4
Cheriton Ave RG10 . . . . .61 B3
Cheriton Cl RG14 . . . . .131 A4
Cheriton Ct **2** RG1 . . . . . . .86 A3
Cheriton Way GU17 . . . . . . .150 B3
Cherries The SL2 . . . . .22 C4
Cherry Ave SL3 . . . . .43 B2
Cherry Cl Caversham RG4 . . . .59 B4
Flackwell Heath HP10 . . . . . .3 A4
Newbury RG14 . . . . .104 C2
Cherry Cnr HP10 . . . . .3 A4
Cherry Garden La SL6 . . . . . .38 C2
Cherry Gr RG17 . . . . .100 B3
Cherry Orch
Great Shefford RG17 . . . . . .48 A2
Staines TW18 . . . . .97 A2
Stoke Poges SL2 . . . . .23 A3
Cherry Rise HP10 . . . . .3 A4
Cherry Tree Ave TW18 . . . . .97 A1
Cherry Tree Cl GU47 . . . . . .143 B1
Cherry Tree Dr RG12 . . . . . .118 B3
Cherry Tree Gr RG41 . . . . . .115 B2
Cherry Tree La SL3 . . . . .23 C3
Cherry Tree Rd SL2 . . . . .22 B3
Cherry Way Horton SL3 . . . . .69 B2
Upper Halliford TW17 . . . . .125 C3
Cherrydale Rd GU15 . . . . . .152 B3
Cherrygarden La SL6 . . . . . . .63 C4
Cherrywood Ave TW20 . . . . .95 A1
Cherrywood Gdns HP10 . . . . .3 A4
Chertsey Bridge Rd
KT16, TW18 . . . . .124 B1
Chertsey Bvd KT16 . . . . . . .123 C1
Chertsey La TW18 . . . . .96 C1
Chertsey Mus KT16 . . . . . . .124 A1
Chertsey Rd
Ashford TW15 &TW16 . . . . .98 B1
Feltham TW13 &TW14 . . . . .98 C2
Lower Halliford TW17 . . . . .125 A1
Shepperton TW17 . . . . .124 C1
Windlesham GU20 . . . . .146 C3
Chertsey Sta KT16 . . . . .123 C1
Chertsey Wlk **6** KT16 . . . .124 A1
Chervil Way RG7 . . . . .111 A1
Cherwell Cl Brands Hill SL3 . . .69 A4
Maidenhead SL6 . . . . .40 A4
Cherwell Cres **2** RG1 . . . . .85 C4
Cherwell Rd Bourne End SL8 . . .3 A2
Caversham RG4 . . . . .59 A3

Cheseridge Rd RG20 . . . . . . .31 B2
Cheshire Ct SL1 . . . . .43 A2
Cheshire Pk RG42 . . . . .91 C1
Chessholme Ct TW16 . . . . . .98 C1
Chessholme Rd TW15 . . . . . .98 B1
Chester Cl Ashford TW15 . . . .98 B2
Maidenhead SL6 . . . . .19 B2
Chester Rd Harlington TW6 . . .71 A2
Slough SL1 . . . . .42 B4
Chester St Caversham RG4 . . .59 A1
Reading RG30 . . . . .85 B4
Chesterblade La RG12 . . . . .118 C1
Chesterfield Mews TW15 . . . .97 C2
Chesterfield Rd
Ashford TW15 . . . . .97 C2
Newbury RG14 . . . . .105 A1
Chesterman St RG1 . . . . .86 A4
Chesterment Way RG6 . . . . .87 B1
Chesters Rd GU15 . . . . .152 A3
Chesterton Dr TW19 . . . . . . .97 C4
Chesterton Rd RG18 . . . . . .106 C3
Chestnut Ave
Camberley GU15 . . . . .152 A3
Caversham RG4 . . . . .59 C2
Slough SL3 . . . . .43 C2
Wentworth GU25 . . . . .121 C3
Wokingham RG41 . . . . .115 C4
Chestnut Cl
Ashford, Chattern Hill TW15 . . .98 A2
Ashford, Felthamhill TW16 . . . .98 C1
Blackwater GU17 . . . . .150 C2
Englefield Green TW20 . . . . .95 B1
Harlington UB7 . . . . .71 A4
Maidenhead SL6 . . . . .40 A4
Medmenham SL7 . . . . .17 B4
Theale RG7 . . . . .83 C2
Chestnut Cres
Ashford TW15 . . . . .105 A2
Shinfield RG2 . . . . .113 C2
Chestnut Ct **3** RG14 . . . . .105 A2
Chestnut Dr
Burghfield Common RG30 . .111 A2
Englefield Green TW20 . . . . .95 B1
Windsor SL4 . . . . .66 C2
Chestnut Gr
Purley on T RG8 . . . . .57 B3
Staines TW18 . . . . .97 B1
Chestnut La RG17 . . . . .25 C2
Chestnut Manor Cl TW18 . . .97 A2
Chestnut Pk SL4 . . . . .40 C2
Chestnut Rd TW15 . . . . .98 A2
Chestnut Wlk
Englefield RG17 . . . . .100 B2
Upper Halliford TW17 . . . . .125 C2
Chestnuts The RG9 . . . . .36 A2
Chetwode Cl RG40 . . . . .116 C3
Cheveley Gdns SL1 . . . . .21 B2
Cheviot Cl Frimley GU15 . . . .152 B2
Harlington UB3 . . . . .71 B4
Maidenhead SL6 . . . . .40 A3
Newbury RG14 . . . . .130 B3
Cheviot Rd
Sandhurst GU47 . . . . .142 C1
Slough SL3 . . . . .44 A1
Chewter Cl GU19 . . . . .145 C2
Chewter La GU20 . . . . .146 A3
Cheylesmore Dr GU16 . . . . .152 B2
Cheyne Rd TW15 . . . . .98 B1
Chichester Ct Slough SL1 . . . .43 A2
Stanwell TW19 . . . . .97 C4
Chichester Rd RG30 . . . . . . .84 C4
Chicory Cl RG6 . . . . .86 C1
Chieveley Cl RG31 . . . . .84 B4
Chieveley Prim Sch RG20 . . .78 A4
Chilbolton TW20 . . . . .95 C2
Chilcombe Way RG6 . . . . . . .87 B1
Child Cl RG40 . . . . .116 B4
Child St RG17 . . . . .25 A2
Childrey Way RG31 . . . . .84 A4
Chillingham Way GU15 . . . .151 B2
Chilsey Green Rd KT16 . . . .123 C1

Chive Rd RG6 . . . . .87 A1
Chivers Pl RG40 . . . . .141 C4
Chivers Pl RG42 . . . . .91 B1
Chobham La GU25 . . . . .122 A1
Chobham Rd
Frimley GU16 . . . . .151 C1
Sunningdale SL5 . . . . .121 A1
Choke La SL6 . . . . .19 A2
Cholmeley Pl RG1 . . . . .86 C4
Cholmeley Rd RG1 . . . . .86 C4
Cholmeley Terr RG1 . . . . . . .86 C4
Cholsey Rd RG10 . . . . .106 C2
Choseley Cl RG10 . . . . .37 C2
Choseley Rd RG10 . . . . .37 C2
Chrislaine Ct TW19 . . . . .70 B1
Christ the King
RC Prim Sch RG2 . . . . . . .113 B4
Christ the King RC Sch
TW19 . . . . .70 C1
Christchurch CE Fst Sch
GU25 . . . . .122 A3
Christchurch Cotts
GU25 . . . . .122 A3
Christchurch Ct RG1 . . . . . .86 B3
Christchurch Dr GU17 . . . . .150 B3
Christchurch Gdns RG2 . . . . .86 B3
Christchurch Rd
Harlington TW6 . . . . .71 A2
Reading RG2 . . . . .86 B3
Virginia Water GU25 . . . . . .122 B3
Christian Sq SL4 . . . . .67 B3
Christie Cl GU18 . . . . .146 B1
Christie Hts RG14 . . . . .131 A4
Christie Wlk GU46 . . . . .149 B2
Christmas La **2** SL2 . . . . . . .22 B4
Christopher Ct
Ashford TW15 . . . . .97 C2
Newbury RG14 . . . . .105 A1
Christopher Ho **5** SL2 . . . . .22 B4
Chudleigh Gdns RG2 . . . . . . .86 B1
Church App TW20 . . . . .123 B3
Church Ave RG9 . . . . .15 C1
Church Cl Eton SL4 . . . . .67 B4
Hampstead Marshall RG20 . .129 C3
Lakenham TW18 . . . . .124 B3
Lambourn RG17 . . . . .25 B1
Maidenhead SL6 . . . . .39 B3
Winnersh RG41 . . . . .88 B1
Church Cotts SL6 . . . . .20 C1
Church Croft RG17 . . . . .100 B3
Church Dr SL6 . . . . .39 A3
Church End La RG30 . . . . . . .84 C4
Church Farm Barns RG7 . . .137 B3
Church Gate RG19 . . . . .106 B2
Church Gr SL3 . . . . .43 B4
Church Hams RG40 . . . . . . .141 B3
Church Hill Binfield RG42 . . . .90 B3
Camberley GU15 . . . . .151 C3
Chilton OX11 . . . . .10 B4
Hermitage RG18 . . . . .79 A3
Wooltington RG7 . . . . .88 C2
Woolhampton RG7 . . . . . . .107 C2
Church Hill House Hospl
RG12 . . . . .118 A2
Church La Arborfield RG2 . . .114 B3
Ascot SL5 . . . . .120 B3
Ashamstead RG8 . . . . .54 A3
Barkham RG40 . . . . .115 B1
Binfield RG42 . . . . .90 B2
Bisley GU24 . . . . .153 C2
Brimpton RG7 . . . . .133 C3
Burghfield Common RG30 . .111 C3
Caversham RG4 . . . . .59 C4
Chieveley RG20 . . . . .51 A1
Combe RG17 . . . . .147 C3
Hampstead Marshall RG20 . .129 C4
Hungerford RG17 . . . . .100 B3
Maidenhead SL6 . . . . .40 B2
Newell Green RG42 . . . . . . .91 B3
Padworth RG7 . . . . .110 B2
Reading RG2 . . . . .113 B3
Shiplake RG9 . . . . .35 C1
Silchester RG7 . . . . .136 C1
Slough SL2, SL3 . . . . .43 B4
Stoke Poges SL2 . . . . .22 C1
Sunningdale SL5 . . . . .121 A2
Swallowfield RG7 . . . . .140 B3
Thatcham RG19 . . . . .106 B2
Twyford RG10 . . . . .61 C3
Wexham SL3 . . . . .44 B3
Yattendon RG18 . . . . .53 C1
Church Mews
Purley on T RG8 . . . . .57 B3
Woodley RG5 . . . . .87 C4
Church Par TW15 . . . . .97 C2
Church Path SL6 . . . . .40 B2
Church Rd
Aldermaston RG7 . . . . .135 A4
Arborfield RG7 . . . . .140 B3
Ascot SL5 . . . . .120 B3
Ashford TW15 . . . . .97 C2
Bagshot GU19 . . . . .145 B2
Blewbury OX11 . . . . .12 A4
Bracknell RG12 . . . . .118 B4
Caversham RG4 . . . . .59 A1
Cookham SL6 . . . . .19 A3
Earley RG6 . . . . .87 A1
Egham TW20 . . . . .96 A2
Farnham Common SL2 . . . . .22 B1
Frimley GU16 . . . . .151 C1
Little Marlow SL7 . . . . .2 B4
Lower Halliford TW17 . . . . .125 A1
Maidenhead SL6 . . . . .40 B2
Newbury RG14 . . . . .105 A3
Old Windsor SL4 . . . . .68 A1

Church Rd continued
Reading RG6 . . . . .56 B3
Sandhurst GU15 . . . . .150 C4
Sandhurst,
Owlsmoor GU47 . . . . .143 C1
Silchester RG26 . . . . .135 C1
Stockcross RG20 . . . . .103 C3
Sunningdale SL5 . . . . .121 A2
Swallowfield RG7 . . . . .139 B3
West End GU24 . . . . .153 C4
Windlesham GU20 . . . . . . .146 B2
Winkfield SL4 . . . . .92 B3
Winkfield, Chavey Down
SL5 . . . . .119 A4
Woodley RG5 . . . . .87 C4
Church Rd E RG45 . . . . .143 A3
Church Row SL3 . . . . .68 C4
Church Side RG20 . . . . .30 C3
Church Sq TW17 . . . . .125 A1
Church St Burnham SL1 . . . . .21 B1
Caversham RG4 . . . . .59 A1
Crowthorne RG45 . . . . .143 A2
Froxfield SN8 . . . . .99 B3
Great Shefford RG17 . . . . . .48 A2
Hampstead Norreys RG18 . . .52 C3
Henley-on-T RG9 . . . . .15 B1
Hungerford RG17 . . . . .100 B3
Kintbury RG17 . . . . .102 A1
Reading RG1 . . . . .86 A3
Slough SL1 . . . . .42 B2
Slough, Upton Park SL1 . . . .42 C2
Staines TW18 . . . . .96 C2
Theale RG7 . . . . .83 B2
Twyford RG10 . . . . .61 B2
Wargrave RG10 . . . . .36 B1
Windsor SL4 . . . . .67 B3
Church Street Mews RG7 . . .83 B2
Church Terr
8 Reading RG1 . . . . .86 A4
Windsor SL4 . . . . .66 C3
Church View
Beenham RG7 . . . . .109 A3
8 Slough SL1 . . . . .43 A2
White Waltham SL6 . . . . . . .63 A4
Yateley GU46 . . . . .149 B4
Church Views SL6 . . . . .39 C4
Church Way RG10 . . . . .100 B3
Church Wlk KT16 . . . . .124 A2
Chennell Prim Sch
RG30 . . . . .84 C3
Churchfield Mews SL3 . . . . .44 A2
Churchill Cl
East Bedfont TW14 . . . . . . .98 C4
Flackwell Heath HP10 . . . . . .3 A4
Reading RG2 . . . . .86 B1
Churchill Cres GU46 . . . . . .149 B3
Churchill Dr Marlow SL7 . . . . .1 C2
Newbury RG14 . . . . .130 B3
Churchill Rd
North Ascot SL5 . . . . .119 C4
Slough SL3 . . . . .43 C1
Churchmead Sch SL3 . . . . . .68 A4
Churchview Rd RG31 . . . . . . .84 C2
Churchway RG20 . . . . .10 A1
Churn Rd RG20 . . . . .31 B3
Cinnamon Cl RG6 . . . . .86 C1
Cintra Ave RG2 . . . . .86 B3
Cintra Cl RG1 . . . . .86 B3
Cippenham Inf Sch SL1 . . . .41 B3
Cippenham La SL1 . . . . .42 A3
Cippenham Mid Sch SL1 . . .41 C3
Circle Hill Rd RG45 . . . . . . .143 B3
Circuit La RG30 . . . . .85 B3
City Rd RG31 . . . . .84 A4
Clacy Gn RG42 . . . . .91 A1
Claires Court Sch SL6 . . . . . .20 A1
Clandon Ave TW20 . . . . .96 B1
Clanfield Cres RG31 . . . . . . .57 B1
Clanfield Ride GU17 . . . . . .150 B3
Clappers Farm Rd RG7 . . . .136 C1
Clappers Mdw SL6 . . . . .20 B2
Clapps Gate Rd RG26 . . . . .135 C1
Clapton App HP10 . . . . .3 B4
Clare Ave RG40 . . . . .116 B4
Clare Dr SL2 . . . . .22 A4
Clare Gdns TW20 . . . . .96 A2
Clare Rd Maidenhead SL6 . . . .39 B3
Slough SL6 . . . . .41 B4
Stanwell TW19 . . . . .97 C4
Clare Wlk RG14 . . . . .130 B3
Claredon Cl RG41 . . . . .88 B1
Clarefield Cl SL6 . . . . .19 A1
Clarefield Ct SL5 . . . . .121 A1
Clarefield Dr SL6 . . . . .19 A1
Claremont Caversham RG4 . . .59 B3
Egham TW20 . . . . .95 B2
Claremont Lodge TW20 . . . .95 B2
Claremont Rd
Henley-on-T RG9 . . . . .15 B1
Marlow SL7 . . . . .1 C2
Windsor SL4 . . . . .67 B3
Clarence Cres Egham TW20 . .95 C1
Camberley SL4 . . . . .39 C4
Maidenhead SL6 . . . . .39 C4
Windsor SL4 . . . . .67 A3
Clarence Dr
Camberley GU15 . . . . .152 A4
Englefield Green TW20 . . . . .95 B2
Clarence Lodge TW20 . . . . .95 B2
Clarence Rd
Henley-on-T RG9 . . . . .15 B1
Windsor SL4 . . . . .67 A3
Clarence St Egham TW20 . . . .95 C1
Staines TW18 . . . . .96 C2
Clarence Way RG31 . . . . .84 A2

Clarendon Ct
Blackwater GU17 . . . . .150 C3
Slough SL1 . . . . .43 A1
Clarendon Cty Prim Sch
TW15 . . . . .97 C2
Clarendon Gdns RG14 . . . . .105 A1
Clarendon Rd
Ashford TW15 . . . . .97 C2
Reading RG6 . . . . .87 A3
Clares Green Rd RG7 . . . . . .111 C2
Clarewood Dr GU15 . . . . . . .151 C4
Clarke Cres GU15 . . . . .151 C4
Clarks Gdns RG17 . . . . .100 C4
Classics The RG17 . . . . .25 C2
Claverdon RG12 . . . . .118 A2
Clay Cl Flackwell Heath HP10 . . .3 A4
Purley on T RG31 . . . . .57 B2
Clay Cnr KT16 . . . . .124 B2
Clay Hill Cres RG14 . . . . . . .105 A3
Clay La Beenham RG7 . . . . .108 B4
Wokingham RG40 . . . . .116 C4
Claycots Inf Sch SL2 . . . . . . .22 C4
Claycots Jun Sch SL2 . . . . . .22 C4
Claydon Ct
2 Caversham RG4 . . . . . . .59 A1
Staines TW18 . . . . .97 A3
Claydon Gdns GU17 . . . . . .150 C1
Clayhall La SL4 . . . . .66 B1
Clayhill Cl RG12 . . . . .118 C3
Clayhill Rd RG7,RG30 . . . . .111 C3
Clayton Ct SL3 . . . . .44 A3
Clayton Gr RG12 . . . . .118 C4
Clayton La SL4 . . . . .68 C4
Clayton Rd SL4 . . . . .150 C4
Clayton Wlk RG2 . . . . .86 C1
Claytons Cty Comb Sch
SL8 . . . . .3 A2
Claytons Mdw SL8 . . . . .3 A2
Cleares Pasture SL1 . . . . .21 A1
Clearspring GU18 . . . . .153 A3
Cleeve Ct TW14 . . . . .98 C4
Cleeve Down RG8 . . . . .34 C4
Cleeve Ho **6** RG12 . . . . . . .118 C4
Cleeve Rd RG8 . . . . .34 C4
Clements Cl Shinfield RG2 . .113 C2
Slough SL1 . . . . .42 C2
Clements Mead RG31 . . . . . .57 B2
Clements Rd RG9 . . . . .15 B2
Clent Rd RG2 . . . . .86 B4
Cleopatra Pl RG42 . . . . .91 C2
Clerewater Pl RG19 . . . . . . .106 B2
Clerics Wlk TW17 . . . . .125 B3
Cleve Ct RG40 . . . . .34 C4
Clevedon Dr RG6 . . . . .87 A1
Clevedon Rd RG31 . . . . .57 B1
Clevehurst Cl SL2 . . . . .22 C4
Cleveland Cl
Maidenhead SL6 . . . . .40 A4
Wooburn Green HP10 . . . . . .3 B2
Cleveland Dr TW18 . . . . . . .124 A1
Cleveland Gr RG14 . . . . .104 C2
Cleveland Pk TW19 . . . . .70 C1
Clevemede RG8 . . . . .34 B3
Cleves Ct SL4 . . . . .66 C2
Cleves Way TW16 . . . . .98 C1
Clewborough Dr GU15 152
Clewborough House Sch
GU15 . . . . .152 B4
Clewer Ave SL4 . . . . .67 A3
Clewer Ct Rd SL4 . . . . .66 C4
Clewer Fields SL4 . . . . .67 A3
Clewer Green CE Fst Sch
SL4 .66 C2
Clewer Hill Rd SL4 . . . . .66 B2
Clewer New Town SL4 . . . . . .67 A3
Clewer Park SL4 . . . . .66 C4
Clifford Gr TW15 . . . . .98 A3
Clifford Way SL8 . . . . .3 A3
Clifton Cl SL6 . . . . .40 A4
Clifton Ct **2** TW19 . . . . .70 C1
Clifton Lodge Eton SL4 . . . . .43 C1
10 Slough SL1 . . . . .42 C2
Clifton Park Rd RG4 . . . . . . .59 A2
Clifton Rd Harlington TW6 . . . .71 A2
Newbury RG14 . . . . .105 A1
Slough SL1 . . . . .42 C2
Wokingham RG41 . . . . .116 A3
Clifton Rise
Wargrave RG10 . . . . .36 B1
Windsor SL4 . . . . .66 B3
Clifton St SL1 . . . . .42 C2
Clive Ct SL1 . . . . .42 B2
Clive Gn RG12 . . . . .118 A3
Clivedale Rd RG5 . . . . .87 C4
Cliveden Mead SL6 . . . . .39 C4
Cliveden Pl TW17 . . . . .125 B3
Cliveden Rd SL6 . . . . .20 A4
Clivemont Rd SL6 . . . . .39 C4
Clockhouse La
TW14,TW15 . . . . .98 B4
Clockhouse La E TW20 . . . . .96 B1
Clockhouse La W TW20 . . . . .96 A1
Cloister Mews RG7 . . . . .83 C2
Cloisters The
Caversham RG4 . . . . .59 A2
Frimley GU16 . . . . .152 C1
Clonmel Cl RG4 . . . . .59 A2
Clonmel Way SL1 . . . . .21 A1
Clopton Dr RG6 . . . . .87 C1
Close The
Aston Tirrold OX11 . . . . . . .13 C4
Bourne End SL8 . . . . .3 A2
Bracknell RG12 . . . . .118 B4
Burghfield Common RG7 . . .111 C4
Burnham SL1 . . . . .21 A1
Great Shefford RG17 . . . . . .48 A2

Hampstead Norreys RG18 . . . . . . 52 C3
Henley-on-T RG9 . . . . 35 B4
Lightwater GU18 . . . . 146 A1
North Ascot SL5 . . . . 119 B4
Sandhurst GU47 . . . . 150 C4
Thatcham RG18 . . . . 106 A2
Virginia Water GU25 . . . . 122 B2
Woodley RG5 . . . . 87 C3
Dough Dr RG18 . . . . 78 C3
ove Cl RG6 . . . . 86 C1
over Cl RG40 . . . . 116 C4
over La GU46 . . . . 149 A3
ub La RG45 . . . . 143 B3
umps The TW13,TW15 . . . . 98 B2
lyde Rd TW19 . . . . 97 C4
yve Way TW18 . . . . 123 C4
oach Ho The HP10 . . . . 3 C3
oach House Cl GU16 . . . . 151 C2
oach Rd SL5 . . . . 92 C1
oach Ride SL7 . . . . 1 B2
oachman's Lodge **28** SL4 . . . . 67 B3
oachmans Ct RG41 . . . . 105 A2
oachmans Gr GU47 . . . . 150 A4
oalport Way SL1,SL6 . . . . 41 A4
oalport Way RG30 . . . . 57 C1
obb Cl SL3 . . . . 43 C2
obbetts La GU46,GU17 . . . . . . 149 C3
obblers Cl SL2 . . . . 22 A2
obham Cl SL1 . . . . 41 C3
obham Rd RG5 . . . . 87 C4
ochrane Cl RG9 . . . . 106 C2
ochrane Pl GU20 . . . . 146 B3
ock La RG7 . . . . 82 A1
ock's La RG42,SL4 . . . . 92 B3
ock-A-Dobby GU47 . . . . 143 A1
ockett Rd SL3 . . . . 44 A3
ockney Hill RG30 . . . . 84 C3
ody Cl RG5 . . . . 88 A4
oe Spur SL1 . . . . 42 C3
oftards SL3 . . . . 43 B4
okers Ct **2** SL8 . . . . 3 A2
old Ash Hill RG18 . . . . 106 B4
old Ash St Mark's
  CE Prim Sch RG18 . . . . 79 B1
old Grove Cotts SL6 . . . . 20 C1
oldharbour Cl
  Henley-on-T RG9 . . . . 35 B4
Thorpe TW20 . . . . 123 B3
oldharbour La
  Thorpe TW20 . . . . 123 B3
  West End GU24 . . . . 153 A4
oldharbour Rd RG17 . . . . 100 B2
oldicutt St SL4 . . . . 59 B1
oldmoorholme La SL8 . . . . 2 C2
olemans Moor La RG5 . . . . 3 A4
olemans Moor Rd RG5 . . . . . . 88 A3
olenorton Cres SL4 . . . . 41 C1
oleridge Ave GU46 . . . . 149 C2
oleridge Cl
  Crowthorne RG45 . . . . 143 B2
  Twyford RG10 . . . . 61 C3
oleridge Cres SL3 . . . . 69 C3
oleridge Rd TW15 . . . . 97 C2
oley Ave RG1 . . . . 85 C3
oley Ave RG1 . . . . 85 C3
oley Park Rd RG1 . . . . 85 C3
oley Park Rd RG1 . . . . 85 C3
oley Pl RG1 . . . . 86 A3
oley Prim Sch RG1 . . . . 86 A3
olin Way SL1 . . . . 42 A2
oliseum Bsns Ctr GU15 . . . . . 151 A2
ollaroy Glen GU18 . . . . 106 B4
ollaroy Rd RG10 . . . . 61 A3
ollege Ave Egham TW20 . . . . . . 96 A1
  Maidenhead SL6 . . . . 39 C4
  Slough SL1 . . . . 42 C2
ollege Cl GU15 . . . . 151 B4
ollege Cres
  Sandhurst GU47 . . . . 150 C4
  Windsor SL4 . . . . 67 B3
ollege Glen SL6 . . . . 39 B4
ollege Piece RG31 . . . . 136 C3
ollege Rd
  Bracknell RG12 . . . . 118 B3
  Maidenhead SL6 . . . . 39 C4
  Reading RG6 . . . . 86 C3
  Sandhurst GU47 . . . . 150 C4
  Slough SL1 . . . . 41 C3
ollege Ride
  Bagshot GU19 . . . . 145 B1
  Camberley GU15 . . . . 151 B4
ollege Rose SL6 . . . . 19 C1
ollege Town Cty Inf Sch
  GU47 . . . . 150 C4
ollege Town Cty Jun Sch
  GU47 . . . . 150 C4
ollege Way Ashford TW15 . . . . . 97 C2
  East Garston RG17 . . . . 47 B3
olleton Cty Prim Sch The
  RG10 . . . . 61 C2
olleton Dr RG10 . . . . 61 C2
olliar Cl SL6 . . . . 19 C1
olliers Way RG30 . . . . 85 A4
ollingwood Coll GU15 . . . . . . 152 A4
ollingwood Grange Cl
  GU15 . . . . 152 A4
ollingwood Mount
  GU15 . . . . 152 A4
ollingwood Pl GU15 . . . . 152 A4
ollingwood Rd RG30 . . . . 84 C3
ollingwood Wlk RG31 . . . . 84 A4
ollins Dr RG18 . . . . 78 C3
ollinswood Rd **1** SL2 . . . . . . 22 B4
ollis St RG2 . . . . 86 A4
ollishin Wlk RG31 . . . . 84 C2
ollum Green Rd SL2 . . . . 23 A4

Coln Cl SL6 . . . . 39 C4
Coln Trad Est SL3 . . . . 69 C3
Colnbrook By-Pass
  Colnbrook SL3,UB7 . . . . 69 B4
  Harmondsworth UB7 . . . . 70 B4
Colnbrook CE Prim Sch
  SL3 . . . . 69 B4
Colnbrook Ct SL3 . . . . 69 C3
Colndale Rd SL3 . . . . 69 C3
Colne Bank SL3,TW19 . . . . 69 B2
Colne Orch SL0 . . . . 44 C3
Colne Reach TW19 . . . . 69 C1
Colne Way TW19 . . . . 96 A3
Colnebridge Cl TW18 . . . . 96 C2
Colnedale Rd UB8 . . . . 44 A4
Colonel's La KT16 . . . . 124 A2
Colonial Rd
  East Bedfont TW14 . . . . 98 C4
  Slough SL1 . . . . 43 A2
Colonnade SL6 . . . . 40 A4
Colony Gate GU16 . . . . 152 B1
Colston Cl RG31 . . . . 84 B2
Colthrop La RG19 . . . . 107 A1
Colthrop Way RG19 . . . . 107 A1
Coltsfoot Cl RG7 . . . . 111 A2
Columbia Ct RG40 . . . . 141 C4
Colville Gdns GU18 . . . . 153 B4
Colwyn Cl GU46 . . . . 149 B3
Colyer Cl RG18 . . . . 79 B4
Colyton Way RG8 . . . . 57 B3
Combe Rd RG30 . . . . 84 C4
Combe View RG17 . . . . 100 B2
Combermere Ct SL4 . . . . 67 A3
Comet Rd TW19 . . . . 97 B4
Comet Way RG5 . . . . 88 A4
Comfrey Cl RG40 . . . . 116 C4
Commercial Rd
  Reading RG2 . . . . 86 A1
  Staines TW18 . . . . 97 A1
Common Hill RG7 . . . . 82 C2
Common La
  Brightwalton RG20 . . . . 28 B3
  Eton SL4 . . . . 42 B1
Common Rd Dorney SL4 . . . . . . 41 B1
  Eton SL4 . . . . 42 B1
  Flackwell Heath HP10 . . . . 3 A4
  Headley RG19 . . . . 132 C1
  Slough SL3 . . . . 44 A1
Common The HP10 . . . . 3 A4
Common Wood SL2 . . . . 22 B4
Commonfield La RG40 . . . . . . 141 A4
Commonfields GU24 . . . . 153 C3
Commons Rd RG41 . . . . 88 C1
Communications Rd
  RG19 . . . . 131 C3
Compton Ave RG31 . . . . 84 A4
Compton CE Prim Sch
  RG20 . . . . 31 C2
Compton Cl
  Bracknell RG12 . . . . 117 C2
  Earley RG6 . . . . 87 B2
  Sandhurst GU47 . . . . 143 B1
Compton Ct SL1 . . . . 41 C4
Compton Dr SL6 . . . . 39 A4
Compton Manor RG20 . . . . 31 B2
Compton Place Bsns Ctr
  GU15 . . . . 152 A3
Comsaye Wlk RG12 . . . . 118 B2
Concorde Rd SL6 . . . . 39 A1
Concorde Way Slough SL1 . . . . 42 B2
  Woodley RG5 . . . . 88 A4
Condor Cl RG31 . . . . 57 B2
Condor Rd TW18 . . . . 124 B3
Conegar Ct SL1 . . . . 42 C3
Coney Grange RG42 . . . . 91 A1
Coneygree Cl RG6 . . . . 87 A1
Coneygree Cr RG7 . . . . 135 A4
Conifer Cl RG26 . . . . 134 C1
Conifer Crest RG14 . . . . 130 B2
Conifer Dr
  Camberley GU15 . . . . 152 A3
  Reading RG31 . . . . 57 A1
Conifer La TW20 . . . . 96 B2
Conifers The
  Crowthorne RG45 . . . . 143 A4
  Maidenhead SL6 . . . . 39 A4
Coningham Rd RG2 . . . . 113 B3
Coningsby RG12 . . . . 118 B3
Coningsby Cl SL6 . . . . 39 B2
Coningsby La SL6 . . . . 65 B3
Conisboro Ave RG4 . . . . 58 C3
Conisboro Way RG4 . . . . 58 C3
Coniston Cl Frimley GU15 . . . . 152 B2
  Thatcham RG19 . . . . 106 A2
  Woodley RG5 . . . . 87 C3
Coniston Cres SL1 . . . . 41 B4
Coniston Ct
  Lightwater GU18 . . . . 146 A1
  16 Newbury RG14 . . . . 105 A2
Coniston Dr RG30 . . . . 57 C1
Coniston Way TW20 . . . . 96 A1
Conkers SL6 . . . . 40 A4
Connaught Ave TW15 . . . . 97 C2
Connaught Cl
  Crowthorne RG45 . . . . 142 C2
  Maidenhead SL6 . . . . 19 C1
  Reading RG30 . . . . 85 B4
  Yateley GU46 . . . . 149 B3
Connaught Cty Mid Sch
  GU19 . . . . 145 C1
Connaught Rd
  Bagshot GU19 . . . . 145 B2
  Camberley GU15 . . . . 151 A2
  Newbury RG14 . . . . 105 A2
  Reading RG30 . . . . 85 B4
  Slough SL1 . . . . 43 A4
Conniston Cl SL7 . . . . 1 A1
Connop Way GU16 . . . . 151 C2

Consort Dr GU15 . . . . 152 B4
Constable Cl RG5 . . . . 88 A4
Constable Way GU47 . . . . 150 C3
Constitution Rd RG30 . . . . 85 A4
Consul Ct RG5 . . . . 88 A3
Control Tower Rd TW6 . . . . 71 A2
Convent Lodge TW15 . . . . 98 A2
Convent Rd Ashford TW15 . . . . 98 A2
  Windsor SL4 . . . . 67 A3
Conway Cl GU16 . . . . 151 C1
Conway Dr Ashford TW15 . . . . . 98 B1
  Thatcham RG18 . . . . 106 A3
Conway Rd Burnham SL6 . . . . . 41 A4
  Harlington TW6 . . . . 71 A2
  Reading RG31 . . . . 84 B2
Cooke Rise RG42 . . . . 91 A1
Cookham Cl GU47 . . . . 150 C3
Cookham Dean Bottom La
  SL6 . . . . 19 B4
Cookham Dean CE Prim Sch
  SL6 . . . . 19 A4
Cookham Lodge **15** SL6 . . . . 39 C3
Cookham Rd
  Bracknell RG12 . . . . 117 C4
  Maidenhead SL6 . . . . 19 C2
Cookham Rise Cty Prim Sch
  SL6 . . . . 19 C4
Coolarne Rise GU15 . . . . 152 A3
Coolgardie Rd TW15 . . . . 98 B2
Coombe Cl RG19 . . . . 106 C2
Coombe Hill Cl OX12 . . . . 28 A4
Coombe Pine RG12 . . . . 118 B2
Coombe Rd Compton RG20 . . . 31 C1
  Yateley GU46 . . . . 149 A4
Coombe Sq RG19 . . . . 106 C2
Coombe The RG8 . . . . 33 C3
Coombes Cty Inf Sch The
  RG2 . . . . 114 C2
Coombes La RG41 . . . . 115 B2
Coomesbury La RG20 . . . . 76 B1
Cooper Cl RG2 . . . . 113 B4
Cooper Rd Henley-on-T RG9 . . 15 B2
  Windlesham GU20 . . . . 146 B2
Cooper Way SL1 . . . . 42 A2
Cooper's Hill La TW20 . . . . 95 B2
Coopers Cl TW18 . . . . 96 C2
Coopers Cres RG18 . . . . 106 B2
Cope Ct SL6 . . . . 39 B4
Cope Hall La RG14 . . . . 130 B4
Copelands Cl GU15 . . . . 152 B2
Copenhagen Cl RG2 . . . . 113 B2
Copenhagen Wlk RG45 . . . . . . 143 A2
Copped Hall Dr GU15 . . . . 152 B3
Copped Hall Way GU15 . . . . . 152 B3
Copper Beech Cl SL4 . . . . 66 B3
Copperage Rd OX12 . . . . 9 A1
Copperdale Cl RG6 . . . . 86 C2
Copperfield Ave GU47 . . . . . . 143 C1
Copperfields
  Ashford TW16 . . . . 98 C1
  Reading RG4 . . . . 58 B2
Coppermill Rd TW19 . . . . 69 A1
Coppice Cl RG14 . . . . 131 A4
Coppice Dr TW19 . . . . 95 B4
Coppice Gdns
  Crowthorne RG45 . . . . 142 C3
  Yateley GU46 . . . . 149 B3
Coppice Gn RG42 . . . . 90 C1
Coppice Rd RG5 . . . . 87 C2
Coppins The TW15 . . . . 98 A1
Coppins La SL0 . . . . 44 C4
Copse Ave RG4 . . . . 59 C2
Copse Cl Camberley GU15 . . . 152 A3
  Marlow SL7 . . . . 1 B1
  Purley on T RG31 . . . . 57 B2
  Slough SL1 . . . . 43 C3
Copse Dr RG41 . . . . 116 A4
Copse End GU15 . . . . 152 A3
Copse Mead RG5 . . . . 60 C1
Copse The RG14 . . . . 36 C2
Copse Way RG40 . . . . 141 C4
Copthall Rd SL6 . . . . 40 A4
Copthorn Cl SL6 . . . . 39 A2
Copthorne Chase TW15 . . . . . . 97 C2
Copthorne Cl TW17 . . . . 125 B2
Copthorne Dr GU18 . . . . 146 A1
Corbett Dr GU18 . . . . 152 C4
Corbett Gdns RG5 . . . . 87 C4
Corbridge Rd RG2 . . . . 86 B2
Corby Cl RG5 . . . . 61 A1
Corby Dr TW20 . . . . 95 C3
Cordelia Croft RG42 . . . . 118 C4
Cordelia Gdns TW19 . . . . 97 C4
Cordelia Rd TW19 . . . . 97 C4
Corderoy Cl RG19 . . . . 106 C1
Corderoy Pl KT16 . . . . 123 C2
Cordwalles Cty Jun Sch
  GU15 . . . . 151 A4
Cordwalles Rd GU15 . . . . 151 C4
Cordwallis Est SL6 . . . . 39 C4
Cordwallis Pk SL6 . . . . 39 C4
Cordwallis Rd SL6 . . . . 39 C4
Cordwallis St SL6 . . . . 39 C4
Cores End Rd SL8 . . . . 3 A2
Corfe Gdns Frimley GU16 . . . . 151 C1
  Slough SL1 . . . . 42 A3
Corfe Mews RG4 . . . . 59 C2
Corfe Pl SL6 . . . . 39 B4
Corfield Cl RG40 . . . . 141 C2
Coriander Way RG6 . . . . 86 C1
Corinne Cl RG2 . . . . 86 A1
Cormorant Cl GU47 . . . . 150 B4
Corn Croft RG42 . . . . 91 A1
Cornbunting Cl GU47 . . . . 150 B4
Cornel Ho **1** SL4 . . . . 84 B3
Cornerside TW15 . . . . 98 B1
Cornfield Gn RG41 . . . . 115 C4

Cornfield Rd RG5 . . . . 88 A4
Cornfields GU46 . . . . 149 A2
Cornflower Cl RG41 . . . . 115 B4
Cornwall Ave SL2 . . . . 22 B1
Cornwall Cl Bracknell RG42 . . 91 C1
  Camberley GU15 . . . . 151 C4
  Eton SL4 . . . . 41 C1
  Maidenhead SL6 . . . . 19 C1
  Purley on T RG31 . . . . 57 A2
  Wokingham RG41 . . . . 115 B3
Cornwall Gdns **11** SL6 . . . . . 39 C3
Cornwall Way TW18 . . . . 96 C1
Cornwell Rd SL4 . . . . 68 A1
Cornwood Gdns RG2 . . . . 86 B2
Coronation Ave SL3 . . . . 43 C4
Coronation Rd Ascot SL5 . . . . 120 A1
  Littlewick Green SL6 . . . . 38 A3
  Yateley GU46 . . . . 149 C4
Coronation Sq
  Reading RG30 . . . . 85 A2
  Wokingham RG40 . . . . 116 B4
Corporation Cotts **1**
  RG14 . . . . 105 A2
Corrie Gdns GU25 . . . . 122 B1
Corsair Cl TW19 . . . . 97 C4
Corsair Rd TW19 . . . . 97 C4
Corsham Rd RG31 . . . . 84 C2
Corsham Way RG45 . . . . 143 A3
Corwen Rd RG30 . . . . 84 C4
Coster Cl RG14 . . . . 104 B3
Costers Cotts SL4 . . . . 93 C1
Cotswold Cl
  Maidenhead SL6 . . . . 40 A3
  Slough SL1 . . . . 42 A2
  Staines TW18 . . . . 97 A2
Cotswold Rd GU47 . . . . 142 C1
Cotswold Way RG31 . . . . 57 A3
Cottage Farm Way TW20 . . . . 123 B3
Cottage La RG30 . . . . 85 B1
Cotterell Cl RG42 . . . . 91 A1
Cotterell Gdns RG10 . . . . 61 C2
Cottesbrooke Cl SL3 . . . . 69 B3
Cottesloe Cl GU24 . . . . 153 C2
Cottesmore RG12 . . . . 118 A1
Cottesmore Rd RG5 . . . . 87 B3
Coulson Way SL1 . . . . 41 A4
Council Cotts GU24 . . . . 153 C4
Council Hos RG18 . . . . 77 B3
Country Life Ho SL3 . . . . 68 A4
County La RG42 . . . . 91 C1
Courage Ct RG30 . . . . 85 B4
Courage Shire Horse Ctr
  SL6 . . . . 38 B3
Course Rd SL5 . . . . 120 A3
Court Cl SL6 . . . . 40 B1
Court Cres SL1 . . . . 42 B4
Court Dr SL6 . . . . 20 B2
Court Farm Ho SL1 . . . . 42 A3
Court Farm Ind Est TW19 . . . . . 70 C1
Court Garden L Complex
  SL7 . . . . 1 B2
Court Gdns GU15 . . . . 151 B3
Court Hill Rd OX12 . . . . 7 A4
Court La Burnham SL1 . . . . 21 B1
  Dorney SL4 . . . . 41 A2
  Iver SL0 . . . . 44 C3
Court Rd SL6 . . . . 20 B2
Court The RG18 . . . . 106 B2
Courtenay Dr RG4 . . . . 59 A4
Courtfield Dr SL6 . . . . 39 B3
Courtfield Rd TW15 . . . . 98 A1
Courthouse Cty Jun Sch
  SL6 . . . . 39 A4
Courtlands **14** SL6 . . . . 39 C3
Courtlands Ave SL3 . . . . 43 B1
Courtlands Hill RG8 . . . . 56 B2
Courtlands Rd RG14 . . . . 105 A1
Courtney Rd TW6 . . . . 71 A2
Courts Rd RG6 . . . . 87 A2
Courtyard The
  17 Borne End SL8 . . . . 3 A2
  Theale RG7 . . . . 83 C2
Coventry Rd RG1 . . . . 86 C4
Coverdale Way SL2 . . . . 21 C1
Covert La RG12 . . . . 118 A2
Covert The SL5 . . . . 120 A2
Cowes Farm Wood RG42 . . . . 117 B4
Cow La East Isley RG20 . . . . . . 30 C4
  Moulsford OX10 . . . . 13 C2
  Reading RG1 . . . . 58 C1
Cowley Ave KT16 . . . . 123 C1
Cowley La KT16 . . . . 123 C1
Coworth Cl SL5 . . . . 121 A2
Coworth Rd SL5 . . . . 121 A2
Cowper Cl KT16 . . . . 123 C2
Cowper Rd SL2 . . . . 22 A1
Cowper Way RG30 . . . . 85 B2
Cowslade RG14 . . . . 104 B3
Cowslip Cl RG31 . . . . 84 A3
Cowslip Cres RG18 . . . . 106 C2
Cox Green Comp Sch SL6 . . . . 39 B2
Cox Green La SL6 . . . . 39 B2
Cox Green Rd SL6 . . . . 39 B2
Coxborrow Cl SL6 . . . . 19 C4
Coxeter Rd RG14 . . . . 104 C2
Coxgreen GU47 . . . . 150 B3
Coxs Ave TW17 . . . . 125 C3
Coxs La RG7 . . . . 107 B2
Crabtree Cl RG18 . . . . 78 C3
Crabtree Cnr TW20 . . . . 123 A3
Crabtree La RG18 . . . . 78 C3
Crabtree Office Village
  TW20 . . . . 123 B4
Crabtree Rd
  Camberley GU15 . . . . 151 A1
  Thorpe TW20 . . . . 123 B4
Craddock Rd RG2 . . . . 86 A2

Crafnant Ct TW15 . . . . 97 C2
Crafts End OX11 . . . . 10 C4
Craig Ave RG30 . . . . 85 A4
Craigwell Cl TW18 . . . . 123 C4
Crail Cl RG41 . . . . 116 A2
Crake Pl GU47 . . . . 150 B4
Cramond Ct TW14 . . . . 98 C4
Cranbourne Ave
  Reading RG1 . . . . 84 B2
  Windsor SL4 . . . . 66 C3
Cranbourne Cl SL1 . . . . 42 B3
Cranbourne Cotts SL4 . . . . 93 A3
Cranbourne Gdns RG30 . . . . . 58 C1
Cranbourne Prim Sch
  SL5 . . . . 93 A2
Cranbourne Rd SL1 . . . . 42 B3
Cranbrook Dr SL6 . . . . 19 B1
Cranbury Rd RG30 . . . . 85 B4
Crane Ct GU47 . . . . 150 B4
Crane Rd TW19 . . . . 71 A1
Crane Wharf **11** RG1 . . . . . . 86 A4
Craneswater UB3 . . . . 71 C4
Cranford Ave TW19 . . . . 97 C4
Cranford Cl Hurst RG10 . . . . . . 88 C4
  Stanwell TW19 . . . . 97 C4
Cranford House Sch
  OX10 . . . . 13 C3
Cranford La
  Harlington TW6 . . . . 71 C3
  Harlington UB3 . . . . 71 C4
  Hatton TW6 . . . . 71 C2
Cranford Mews **10** RG1 . . . . 86 A3
Cranford Park Dr GU46 . . . . . 149 B3
Cranleigh Rd TW13 . . . . 98 C2
Cranmer Cl RG31 . . . . 57 A2
Cranwell Dr
  Lightwater GU18 . . . . 152 C4
  Littleton TW17 . . . . 124 C3
Cranwell Rd TW6 . . . . 71 A3
Craufurd Ct SL6 . . . . 39 C4
Craufurd Rise SL6 . . . . 39 C4
Craven Cl RG17 . . . . 102 A1
Craven Dene RG14 . . . . 105 A2
Craven Rd Inkpen RG17 . . . . . 127 A3
  Newbury RG14 . . . . 104 C1
  Reading RG1 . . . . 86 B3
Craven Way RG17 . . . . 102 A1
Crawford Cl RG6 . . . . 87 A2
Crawford Gdns GU15 . . . . 151 A3
Crawford Pl RG14 . . . . 104 C2
Crawley Chase RG42 . . . . 92 A1
Crawley Dr GU15 . . . . 151 C3
Crawley Hill GU15 . . . . 151 C3
Crawley Ridge GU15 . . . . 151 C3
Crawley Ridge Cty Inf Sch
  GU15 . . . . 151 C3
Crawley Ridge Cty Jun Sch
  GU15 . . . . 151 C4
Crawley Wood Cl GU15 . . . . . 151 C3
Crawshay Dr RG4 . . . . 59 A4
Crayle St SL2 . . . . 22 A1
Crayonne Cl TW16 . . . . 125 C4
Crazies Hill CE Prim Sch
  RG10 . . . . 36 A1
Crecy Cl RG41 . . . . 115 C3
Crediton Cl RG5 . . . . 88 A3
Cree's Mdw GU20 . . . . 146 B2
Creighton Ct RG2 . . . . 86 B2
Cremyll Rd RG1 . . . . 58 C1
Crendon Ct RG4 . . . . 59 A1
Crescent Ct TW18 . . . . 96 C2
Crescent Dale SL6 . . . . 39 C3
Crescent La RG18 . . . . 79 A4
Crescent Rd
  Reading, Tilehurst RG31 . . . . . 57 B1
  Reading, Whiteknights RG1 . . 86 C2
  Shepperton TW17 . . . . 125 B2
  Wokingham RG40 . . . . 116 B3
Crescent The
  Ashford TW15 . . . . 97 C2
  Bracknell RG12 . . . . 118 B3
  Chertsey KT16 . . . . 124 A3
  Earley RG6 . . . . 87 B2
  Egham TW20 . . . . 95 C1
  Harlington UB3 . . . . 71 B4
  Kintbury RG17 . . . . 102 A1
  Lower Halliford TW17 . . . . 125 C1
  Maidenhead SL6 . . . . 39 C4
  Mortimer RG7 . . . . 137 A3
  Padworth RG7 . . . . 109 B2
  Shiplake RG9 . . . . 36 A2
  Slough SL1 . . . . 42 C2
  Theale RG7 . . . . 83 C2
Crescent Villas **5** SL4 . . . . . 67 B3
Cress Rd SL1 . . . . 42 A3
Cressex Cl RG42 . . . . 90 B1
Cressida Chase RG42 . . . . 91 C1
Cressingham Rd RG2 . . . . 86 B1
Cressington Pl SL8 . . . . 3 A2
Cresswell Rd RG14 . . . . 105 B2
Cresswell Row SL7 . . . . 1 A1
Cresswells Mead SL6 . . . . 40 B1
Crest Cl RG10 . . . . 61 C3
Crest Ho TW19 . . . . 98 B4
Crest The RG4 . . . . 59 B2
Creswell Cl RG2 . . . . 113 B3
Cricket Field Gr RG45 . . . . . . 143 B2
Cricket Hill La
  GU17,GU46 . . . . 149 C2
Cricketers RG20 . . . . 103 C3
Cricketers La
  Windlesham GU20 . . . . 146 B2
  Winkfield RG42 . . . . 92 A2
Crimp Hill SL4, TW20 . . . . 95 A3
Crisp Gdns RG42 . . . . 90 C1

Crisp Rd RG9 . . . . 15 B2
Crispin Cl RG4 . . . . 58 B3
Crispin Way SL2 . . . . 22 B4
Crocker Cl SL5 . . . . 119 C4
Crockford Pl RG42 . . . . 90 C1
Crockhamwell Rd RG5 . . . . 87 C3
Crocus Mead RG18 . . . . 106 C2
Crocus Way RG41 . . . . 115 B4
Croft Cl Harlington UB3 . . . . . 71 B4
Wokingham RG41 . . . . 116 A1
Croft Cnr SL4 . . . . 68 A1
Croft La Newbury RG14 . . . . . 104 C2
Yateley GU46 . . . . 149 B4
Croft Rd Goring RG8 . . . . 34 B3
Hungerford RG17 . . . . 100 B3
Mortimer RG7 . . . . 136 C3
Newbury RG14 . . . . 130 C4
Shinfield RG7 . . . . 113 B1
Wokingham RG40 . . . . 116 A1
Croft The Bracknell RG42 . . . . 91 A1
Kintbury RG17 . . . . 102 A1
Maidenhead SL6 . . . . 39 B3
Marlow SL7 . . . . 2 A2
Croft Way RG12 . . . . 151 C1
Crofter's Cl GU47 . . . . 150 A4
Crofters SL4 . . . . 68 A1
Crofthill Rd SL2 . . . . 22 A1
Crofton Cl RG12 . . . . 118 C2
Crofts The TW17 . . . . 125 C3
Cromer CI RG31 . . . . 57 B1
Cromer Ct SL1 . . . . 42 C4
Cromer Rd TW6 . . . . 71 A3
Cromwell Cl RG9 . . . . 35 C4
Cromwell Dr SL1 . . . . 42 C4
Cromwell Gdns SL7 . . . . 1 C1
Cromwell Pl RG42 RG14 . . . . 105 A2
Cromwell Rd Ascot SL5 . . . . . 120 A2
Camberley GU15 . . . . 151 B4
Caversham RG4 . . . . 59 A1
Henley-on-T RG9 . . . . 35 C4
Maidenhead SL6 . . . . 39 B4
Marlow SL7 . . . . 1 C1
Newbury RG14 . . . . 105 B3
Crondall St GU15 . . . . 151 A2
Crondall End GU46 . . . . 149 B4
Cropper Cl RG19 . . . . 107 A2
Crosby Gdns GU46 . . . . 149 A4
Crosby Hill Dr GU15 . . . . 151 C4
Crosfields Sch RG2 . . . . 113 C4
Cross Fell RG12 . . . . 118 A3
Cross Gates CI RG12 . . . . 118 C3
Cross Keys Rd RG8 . . . . 14 B2
Cross La RG7 . . . . 138 B4
Cross Oak SL4 . . . . 67 A3
Cross Rd SL5 . . . . 121 A1
Cross St Reading RG1 . . . . 86 A4
Wokingham RG40 . . . . 116 B3
Crossfields CI RG22 . . . . 113 C4
Crossland Rd RG1 . . . . 86 A4
Crossway RG12 . . . . 118 A4
Crossways Charlton TW16 . . . 98 C1
Egham TW20 . . . . 96 B1
Woodley RG5 . . . . 87 C3
Crossways Ct 5 SL4 . . . . 67 B3
Crosswell Cl TW17 . . . . 125 B4
Crosthwaite Way SL1 . . . . 41 B4
Crouch La SL4 . . . . 92 C4
Crow Piece La SL2 . . . . 21 C2
Crowfield Dr RG19 . . . . 106 A2
Crowle Rd RG17 . . . . 25 A1
Crown Acre Cl RG19 . . . . 106 B2
Crown Cl SW3 . . . . 69 B4
Crown Colonnade RG1 . . . . . . 86 C4
Crown Cotts
Bracknell SL5 . . . . 119 B2
Englefield Green TW20 . . . . . . 95 A1
Windsor SL4 . . . . 67 B2
Crown Ct RG10 . . . . 106 B2
Crown Hill Ct SL5 . . . . 120 A2
Crown La Burnham SL2 . . . . . . 22 A2
Maidenhead SL6 . . . . 40 A4
Theale RG7 . . . . 83 C2
Wentworth GU25 . . . . 122 B2
Crown Mdw SL3 . . . . 69 A4
Crown Mead RG9 . . . . 106 B2
Crown Pl Reading RG1 . . . . . . 86 B3
Sandhurst GU47 . . . . 150 A4
Crown Rd Marlow SL7 . . . . 1 C1
Wentworth GU25 . . . . 122 B2
Crown Rise KT16 . . . . 123 C1
Crown Row RG12 . . . . 118 B2
Crown St Egham TW20 . . . . . . 96 A2
Reading RG1 . . . . 86 A3
Crown Wood Cty Prim Sch
RG12 . . . . 118 C2
Crowsley Rd RG9 . . . . 36 A2
Crowthorne CE Sch
RG45 . . . . 143 B3
Crowthorne Lodge RG12 . . . 118 A3
Crowthorne Rd
Bracknell RG40, RG12 . . . . . 117 C1
Bracknell,
Easthampstead RG12 . . . . . 118 A3
Sandhurst GU47 . . . . 143 A1
Crowthorne Rd N RG12 . . . . . 118 A4
Crowthorne Sta RG45 . . . . . . 142 C2
Croxley Rise SL6 . . . . 39 B3
Croydon Rd TW6 . . . . 71 A2
Cruikshank Lane GU47 . . . . . 150 C3
Crummock Cl SL1 . . . . 41 B4
Crutchley Rd RG40 . . . . 116 B4
Cuba Cotts SL6 . . . . 20 A2
Cuckoo La GU24 . . . . 153 B3
Cuckoo Vale GU24 . . . . 153 B3

Culford Cl RG6 . . . . 87 B1
Culham Ct RG30 . . . . 85 A2
Culham Dr SL6 . . . . 19 C1
Culham Ho 8 RG12 . . . . 118 C3
Cullen Cl GU46 . . . . 149 B3
Cullern's Pass SL6 . . . . 39 C3
Culley Way SL6 . . . . 39 A2
Culloden Way RG41 . . . . 115 C3
Culver Croft RG42 . . . . 90 C1
Culver La RG6 . . . . 87 A4
Culver Rd Newbury RG14 . . . 130 C4
Reading RG6 . . . . 86 C1
Sandhurst GU47 . . . . 143 B1
Cumberland Ave SL2 . . . . 22 B1
Cumberland Dr RG12 . . . . . . 118 C4
Cumberland Lodge SL4 . . . . . 94 B2
Cumberland Rd
Ashford TW15 . . . . 97 B3
Frimley GU15 . . . . 152 B2
Reading RG1 . . . . 86 C4
Cumberland St TW18 . . . . 96 B2
Cumberland Way RG41 . . . . . 115 B3
Cumbernauld Gdns TW16 . . . 98 C2
Cumbrae CI SL2 . . . . 43 B2
Cumbria CI SL6 . . . . 39 B2
Cumnor Way RG12 . . . . 118 C3
Cunworth Ct RG12 . . . . 118 A3
Curfew Bell Rd KT16 . . . . 123 C1
Curl Way RG41 . . . . 116 A3
Curlew Cl RG19 . . . . 106 B2
Curlew Dr RG31 . . . . 84 B3
Curley Hill Rd GU18 . . . . 152 C4
Curleys Way RG7 . . . . 139 B3
Curling Way RG14 . . . . 105 B2
Curls La SL6 . . . . 39 C2
Curls Rd SL6 . . . . 39 B2
Curnock Ct RG14 . . . . 104 C1
Curridge Gn RG18 . . . . 78 C2
Curridge Piece RG18 . . . . 78 C2
Curridge Prim Sch RG18 . . . . 78 B2
Curridge Rd RG18 . . . . 78 B2
Curriers La SL1 . . . . 21 A4
Curtis Cl RG5 . . . . 152 B4
Curtis Rd RG31 . . . . 84 B2
Curzon Mall 18 SL1 . . . . 42 C4
Curzon St RG30 . . . . 85 C4
Cutbush Cl RG6 . . . . 114 A4
Cutbush La RG2 & RG6 . . . . . 114 A4
Cutting Hill SN8,RG17 . . . . . 126 A2
Cuttings The RG42 . . . . 91 A1
Cwmcarn RG4 . . . . 58 C3
Cygnet Cl RG19 . . . . 106 A2
Cygnets The TW18 . . . . 96 C2
Cypress Cl GU14 . . . . 150 C4
Cypress Ho SL3 . . . . 44 A1
Cypress Rd RG5 . . . . 88 A3
Cypress Way GU17 . . . . 150 A3
Cypress Wlk TW20 . . . . 95 A1

D

Dacre Ave RG4 . . . . 59 C2
Dagmar Rd SL4 . . . . 67 B3
Dair House Sch SL2 . . . . 22 B2
Dairy Ct SL6 . . . . 40 A4
Dairy La RG4 . . . . 16 A4
Dalby Cres RG14 . . . . 131 A4
Dalcross RG12 . . . . 118 C2
Dale Cl SL5 . . . . 121 A1
Dale Ct SL1 . . . . 42 B2
Dale Gdns GU47 . . . . 150 A4
Dale Lodge Rd SL5 . . . . 121 A2
Dale Rd Ashford TW16 . . . . . . 98 C1
Reading RG2 . . . . 86 A3
Walton-on-T KT12 . . . . 125 C3
Daleham Ave TW20 . . . . 96 A1
Dalley Ct GU47 . . . . 150 B4
Dalston Cl GU15 . . . . 152 B2
Dalton Cl RG30 . . . . 84 C4
Damask Cl GU24 . . . . 153 C3
Damer Gdns RG9 . . . . 35 C4
Damson La SL4 . . . . 42 B2
Dandridge Cl SL3 . . . . 43 B1
Dandridge Dr SL8 . . . . 3 B2
Dane Rd TW15 . . . . 98 B1
Danefield Rd RG8 . . . . 116 B3
Danehill RG6 . . . . 114 A4
Danehurst Ct TW20 . . . . 95 C1
Danes Ct SL6 . . . . 39 B4
Danes Gdns SL6 . . . . 39 C3
Danesfield Sch SL7 . . . . 17 C4
Danvers Cl RG19 . . . . 106 B1
Danywern Dr RG41 . . . . 88 B1
Darby Green La GU17 . . . . . . 150 A3
Darby Green Rd GU17 . . . . . . 150 A3
Darby La RG8 . . . . 55 A3
Darby Vale RG42 . . . . 91 A1
Darell Rd SL4 . . . . 58 C2
Dark La Bradfield RG7 . . . . 82 B4
Purley on T RG31 . . . . 57 A2
Wargrave RG10 . . . . 36 B1
Wickham RG17 . . . . 101 A4
Darleydale CI GU47 . . . . 143 B1
Darling's La SL6 . . . . 18 C1
Darracott Cl GU15 . . . . 152 C4
Darrell CI SL3 . . . . 43 C1
Dart CI Brands Hill SL3 . . . . . . 69 A4
Thatcham RG18 . . . . 106 A3
Wokingham RG40 . . . . 141 C3
Dartington Ave RG5 . . . . 87 B2
Dartington CI RG30 . . . . 84 C4
Dartmouth CI RG12 . . . . 118 C3
Dartmouth Ct 27 SL1 . . . . 42 C2
Dartmouth Terr 1 RG1 . . . . . . 86 B3
Darvill's La RG10 . . . . 62 C1

Darwall Dr SL5 . . . . 119 B4
Darwin Cl RG2 . . . . 86 A1
Darwin Rd SL3 . . . . 43 C2
Dashwood Cl
Bracknell RG12 . . . . 118 B4
Slough SL3 . . . . 43 B1
Datchet Pl SL3 . . . . 68 A3
Datchet Rd Horton SL3 . . . . . . 68 C2
Old Windsor SL4 . . . . 68 A2
Slough SL3 . . . . 42 C1
Windsor SL4 . . . . 67 B4
Datchet Sta SL3 . . . . 68 A3
Dauntless Rd RG7 . . . . 111 A2
Davenport Rd RG12 . . . . 118 C4
Daventry Cl SL3 . . . . 69 C3
Daventry Ct RG42 . . . . 118 A4
David Cl UB3 . . . . 71 C4
David Ct TW18 . . . . 97 A2
David Rd SL3 . . . . 69 C3
David Smith Ct RG31 . . . . 84 C3
Davis Cl SL7 . . . . 1 C1
Davis Gdns GU47 . . . . 150 C4
Davis St RG10 . . . . 88 B3
Davy Cl RG40 . . . . 116 B3
Dawes East Rd SL1 . . . . 21 B1
Dawes Moor Cl SL2 . . . . 43 B4
Dawley Ride SL3 . . . . 69 C3
Dawlish Rd RG2 . . . . 86 B1
Dawn Redwood Cl SL3 . . . . . . 69 A2
Dawnay Cl SL5 . . . . 119 C4
Daws Ct SL0 . . . . 44 C4
Dawsmere CI GU15 . . . . 152 B3
Daxton Cl SL4 . . . . 67 A3
Dayton Dr RG19 . . . . 107 A1
Dayworth Mews RG30 . . . . . . 85 B4
De Beauvoir Rd RG1 . . . . 86 C3
De Bohun Rd RG1 . . . . 86 A4
De Havilland Way TW19 . . . . . 70 C1
De Montfort Gr RG17 . . . . . . 100 B2
De Montfort Rd
Newbury RG14 . . . . 104 C3
Reading RG1 . . . . 59 A1
De Ros Pl TW20 . . . . 70 C1
De-Vitre Gn RG40 . . . . 116 C4
Deacon Cl RG40 . . . . 116 B4
Deacon Ct SL4 . . . . 66 B3
Deacon Way RG30 . . . . 58 A1
Deaconfield RG8 . . . . 14 B2
Deacons La RG18 . . . . 79 B4
Deadman's La RG7 . . . . 83 B2
Deadmans La RG14, RG19 . . 131 A3
Deadmoor La RG20 . . . . 130 C1
Deal Ave SL1 . . . . 41 C4
Dean Cl SL4 . . . . 66 B2
Dean Gr RG40 . . . . 116 B4
Dean La SL6 . . . . 19 B4
Dean Par GU15 . . . . 151 C4
Dean St SL7 . . . . 1 B1
Dean's Cloisters SL4 . . . . 67 B4
Deanfield Ave RG9 . . . . 15 B1
Deanfield Cl SL7 . . . . 1 B1
Deanfield Rd RG9 . . . . 15 B1
Deans Cl GU20 . . . . 146 B2
Deans Farm RG4 . . . . 59 B1
Deansfield Cl SL3 . . . . 43 B1
Deansgate RG12 . . . . 118 A1
Deansgate Rd RG1 . . . . 86 A3
Decies Way SL2 . . . . 23 A2
Dedmere Ct SL7 . . . . 1 C1
Dedmere Rise SL7 . . . . 1 C1
Dedmere Rd SL7 . . . . 1 C1
Dedworth Dr SL4 . . . . 66 C3
Dedworth Green Fst Sch
SL4 . . . . 66 C3
Dedworth Manor SL4 . . . . 66 C3
Dedworth Mid Sch SL4 . . . . . 66 B3
Dedworth Rd SL4 . . . . 66 B3
Dee Rd RG30 . . . . 85 A4
Deena Cl SL1 . . . . 41 A3
Deep Field SL3 . . . . 68 A4
Deep Well Dr GU15 . . . . 151 C3
Deepcut Bridge Rd
GU16 . . . . 152 B1
Deepdale RG12 . . . . 118 A3
Deepdene Cl RG1 . . . . 85 C4
Deepfield Rd RG12 . . . . 118 B4
Deer Leap GU18 . . . . 153 A4
Deer Rock Hill RG12 . . . . 118 B2
Deer Rock Rd GU15 . . . . 151 C4
Deerhurst Ave RG41 . . . . 88 B1
Deerhurst Ct RG31 . . . . 84 C2
Deerswood RG5 . . . . 20 A1
Defford Cl RG41 . . . . 88 C1
Delafield Dr RG31 . . . . 84 B3
Delaford Cl SL0 . . . . 44 C4
Delamere Ho 8 RG41 . . . . 67 A3
Delamere Rd RG6 . . . . 87 A4
Delane Dr RG41 . . . . 88 A1
Delaney Cl RG30 . . . . 84 C4
Dell Cl RG30 . . . . 84 C4
Dell Ct SL1 . . . . 42 A3
Dell Gr GU15 . . . . 152 C1
Dell Rd
Finchampstead RG40 . . . . . . 142 A2
Purley on T RG31 . . . . 57 A1
Dell The
Englefield Green TW20 . . . . . . 95 A3
Maidenhead SL6 . . . . 38 C1
9 Reading RG1 . . . . 86 B4
Yateley GU46 . . . . 149 B3
Deller St RG42 . . . . 90 C1
Dellwood Com Hospl
RG30 . . . . 85 A4
Delph The RG6 . . . . 87 B1
Delta Way TW20 . . . . 123 B4

Delwood Pk RG4 . . . . 58 C2
Denbeigh Pl RG41 . . . . 115 C2
Denborough Cres SL6 . . . . 39 B2
Denbury Gdns RG2 . . . . 113 B4
Denby Way RG30 . . . . 57 C1
Dencliffe TW15 . . . . 98 A2
Dene Cl 2 Bracknell RG12 . . 118 B4
Earley RG6 . . . . 87 A1
Dene Hollow SL11 . . . . 10 C4
Dene Way RG14 . . . . 105 A3
Denefield Sch RG31 . . . . 57 A2
Denford La RG17 . . . . 101 B4
Denham Cl SL6 . . . . 39 B3
Denham Dr GU46 . . . . 149 B3
Denham Gr RG12 . . . . 118 B2
Denham Rd TW20 . . . . 96 A2
Denison Rd TW13 . . . . 98 C2
Denly Way GU18 . . . . 146 B1
Denman Dr TW15 . . . . 98 A1
Denmark Ave RG5 . . . . 61 A1
Denmark Rd
Newbury RG14 . . . . 105 A2
Reading RG1 . . . . 86 B3
Denmark St
Maidenhead SL6 . . . . 39 C4
Wokingham RG40 . . . . 116 B3
Denmead Ct RG12 . . . . 118 C2
Dennis Cl TW15 . . . . 98 B1
Dennis Way SL1 . . . . 41 B3
Dennistoun Cl GU15 . . . . 151 B3
Dennose Cl RG6 . . . . 87 A1
Denny Rd SL3 . . . . 43 C1
Denton Cl RG19 . . . . 106 B1
Denton Rd RG40 . . . . 116 B3
Denton Way GU16 . . . . 151 B1
Depot Rd SL6 . . . . 40 A3
Derby Cl RG17 . . . . 25 A1
Derby Rd Caversham RG4 . . . . 59 A2
Newbury RG14 . . . . 105 A2
Derby St RG1 . . . . 85 C4
Derbyshire Gn RG42 . . . . 91 C1
Derek Horn Ct GU15 . . . . 151 A3
Derek Rd SL6 . . . . 40 B4
Deri Dene Cl 2 TW19 . . . . 70 C1
Derrick Cl RG31 . . . . 84 B2
Derry Rd GU14 . . . . 150 C1
Derwent Ave RG30 . . . . 57 C1
Derwent Cl
East Bedfont TW14 . . . . 98 C4
Wokingham RG41 . . . . 115 C3
Derwent Dr Burnham SL1 . . . . 41 B4
Maidenhead SL6 . . . . 39 B4
Derwent Rd
Lightwater GU18 . . . . 153 A4
Thatcham RG19 . . . . 106 A2
Thorpe Lea TW20 . . . . 96 A1
Desborough Cl TW17 . . . . . . 125 A1
Desborough Sch SL6 . . . . 1 C2
Deseronto Wharf Ind Est
SL3 . . . . 43 C2
Desford Way TW15 . . . . 97 C3
Devenish La SL5 . . . . 120 B1
Devenish Rd SL5 . . . . 120 B1
Devereux Rd SL4 . . . . 67 B3
Deverills Way SL3 . . . . 44 B1
Devereon Dr RG30 . . . . 85 A3
Devil's La TW20 . . . . 96 B1
Devils Highway The
RG45 . . . . 142 C3
Devon Ave SL1 . . . . 42 B2
Devon Dr SL1 . . . . 42 B4
Devon Chase RG42 . . . . 91 C1
Devon Cl Sandhurst GU47 . . 150 B4
Wokingham RG41 . . . . 115 C3
Devon Dr RG4 . . . . 59 C2
Devonshire Dr GU15 . . . . 151 C4
Devonshire Gdns RG31 . . . . . 57 A2
Devonshire Gn SL2 . . . . 22 A2
Devonshire Lodge 10 SL6 . . . . 39 C4
Devonshire Pk RG2 . . . . 86 C1
Dewberry Down RG18 . . . . . . 106 C2
Dewe La RG30 . . . . 84 C1
Dhoon Rise SL6 . . . . 39 C3
Diamedes Ave TW19 . . . . 70 C1
Diamond Cotts RG10 . . . . 37 B3
Diamond Hill GU15 . . . . 151 C4
Diamond Rd SL1 . . . . 43 A2
Diamond Ridge GU15 . . . . . . 151 C4
Diana Cl SL3 . . . . 43 C4
Dianthus Cl KT16 . . . . 123 C1
Dianthus Pl RG42 . . . . 90 C2
Dick Turpin Way TW14 . . . . . . 71 C2
Dickens Cl RG4 . . . . 59 B1
Dickens Way GU46 . . . . 149 B3
Dickens Wlk RG14 . . . . 131 A4
Dido Rd OX11 . . . . 9 A4
Dieppe Cl RG41 . . . . 115 C3
Digby Rd RG14 . . . . 104 C2
Dines Way RG18 . . . . 79 B4
Dingle Rd TW15 . . . . 98 A2
Dinton Pastures Ctry
Pk RG10 . . . . 88 B3
Disraeli Ct SL3 . . . . 69 A4
Ditchfield La RG40 . . . . 141 C4
Ditchling RG12 . . . . 118 A1
Ditton Park Rd SL3 . . . . 68 A4
Ditton Rd Datchet SL3 . . . . . . 68 B4
Slough SL3 . . . . 69 A4
Dittons The RG40 . . . . 141 C3
Divine Mercy Coll RG19 . . . . . 15 B1
Dobson's La RG9 . . . . 15 A4
Dockett Eddy La TW17 . . . . . 124 C1
Dockett Moorings KT16 . . . . 124 C1
Doctors La RG18 . . . . 79 A3
Doddington Cl RG6 . . . . 87 B1

Dodsells Well RG40 . . . . 141 C2
Dodsfield Rd SL2 . . . . 22 A2
Dog La RG8 . . . . 54 A2
Doghurst Ave UB3 . . . . 71 A4
Doghurst Dr UB7 . . . . 71 A4
Dogkennel La OX12 . . . . 27 A2
Doles Hill RG41 . . . . 115 B3
Doles La RG41 . . . . 115 B3
Dolman Rd RG14 . . . . 105 A4
Dolphin Cl Brimpton RG7 . . 134 C1
Winnersh RG41 . . . . 88 B1
Dolphin Ct Bracknell RG12 . . 118 C3
Slough SL1 . . . . 43 A2
Stanwell TW19 . . . . 97 C4
Dolphin Ct N TW19 . . . . 97 A4
Dolphin Est The TW16 . . . . . . 125 A4
Dolphin Rd
Charlton TW16 . . . . 125 C4
Slough SL1 . . . . 43 A3
Dolphin Rd N SL1 . . . . 125 C4
Dolphin Rd S TW16 . . . . 125 C4
Dolphin Rd W TW16 . . . . 125 C4
Doman Rd GU15 . . . . 151 A2
Domoney Cl RG19 . . . . 106 C1
Don Cl RG30 . . . . 85 A3
Donaldson Way RG5 . . . . 88 A3
Doncastle Rd RG12 . . . . 117 C3
Donegal Cl RG4 . . . . 59 B3
Donkey Dr SL3 . . . . 68 C3
Donkey La SL3 . . . . 68 C3
Donkin Hill RG4 . . . . 59 B1
Donnington Castle RG14 . . . 104 C2
Donnington Cl
Buckleberry RG7 . . . . 108 B1
Camberley GU15 . . . . 151 A2
Donnington Gdns
Maidenhead SL6 . . . . 19 C2
Reading RG1 . . . . 86 C3
Donnington Lodge RG14 . . . 104 C2
Donnington Pl RG41 . . . . 88 B1
Donnington Rd RG1 . . . . 86 C3
Donnington Sq RG14 . . . . . . 104 C2
Donnybrook RG12 . . . . 118 A2
Dorcas Ct GU15 . . . . 151 B2
Dorchester Cl SL6 . . . . 19 A4
Dorchester Ct
Reading RG30 . . . . 85 B3
Staines TW18 . . . . 97 A3
Dorchester Dr TW14 . . . . 71 C2
Dorian Dr SL5 . . . . 120 C4
Doris Rd TW15 . . . . 98 B3
Dorking Way RG31 . . . . 84 A4
Dorly Cl TW17 . . . . 125 C3
Dormer Cl
Crowthorne RG45 . . . . 143 A4
Reading RG1 . . . . 86 A4
Dormy Ho The GU25 . . . . 122 C1
Dornels SL2 . . . . 23 B3
Dorney Ct SL4 . . . . 41 A1
Dorney Cty Comb Sch
SL4 . . . . 40 C2
Dorney Lake Rowing Ctr
SL4 . . . . 66 A2
Dorney Reach Rd SL4 . . . . 40 C2
Dorney Wood Rd SL1 . . . . 21 C4
Dorothy Ct RG14 . . . . 105 B4
Dorothy St 5 RG1 . . . . 86 B3
Dorset Cl RG15 . . . . 151 C1
Dorset Lodge 9 SL6 . . . . 39 C4
Dorset Rd Ashford TW15 . . . . 97 B3
Windsor SL4 . . . . 67 B2
Dorset St RG30 . . . . 85 B4
Dorset Vale RG42 . . . . 91 C1
Dorset Way RG41 . . . . 115 C3
Douai Sch RG7 . . . . 108 C2
Doublet Cl RG19 . . . . 106 C2
Douglas Ct Earley RG6 . . . . . . 87 A2
Marlow SL7 . . . . 2 A2
Douglas Grange RG10 . . . . 88 C3
Douglas La TW19 . . . . 68 C1
Douglas Rd
Caversham RG4 . . . . 59 C2
Slough SL2 . . . . 42 B2
Stanwell TW19 . . . . 70 B1
Doultons The TW18 . . . . 97 A2
Douro Cl RG26 . . . . 134 B1
Dove Cl RG6 . . . . 113 C2
Dove Ct TW19 . . . . 97 C3
Dove House Cres SL2 . . . . 21 C2
Dovecote Rd RG2 . . . . 113 A4
Dovedale Cl
Caversham RG4 . . . . 59 B2
Sandhurst GU47 . . . . 143 B1
Dover Rd SL1 . . . . 41 C4
Dover St RG1 . . . . 86 A3
Doveton Way RG14 . . . . 105 A4
Dowding Cl RG5 . . . . 88 A3
Dowding Ct RG45 . . . . 143 B4
Dower Pk SL4 . . . . 94 A4
Down Pl SL4 . . . . 66 A4
Downe House Sch RG18 . . . . . 79 A4
Downend La RG20 . . . . 51 A4
Downfield La SL4 . . . . 66 A4
Downfield Rd RG10 . . . . 62 A3
Downham Ct RG2 . . . . 86 C1
Downing Path SL2 . . . . 21 C1
Downing Rd RG31 . . . . 84 A4
Downlands Rd RG17 . . . . 47 B4
Downmill Rd RG12 . . . . 117 C3
Downs Cl RG17 . . . . 46 C1
Downs Rd Aldworth RG20 . . . 32 A3
Slough SL3 . . . . 43 B1
Downs Sch The RG20 . . . . 31 B1
Downs View OX11 . . . . 12 C1
Downs Way Chilton OX11 . . . . 9 C1
Purley on T RG31 . . . . 57 A1
Downshire CI RG17 . . . . 48 A1
Downshire Sq RG1 . . . . 85 C3

wnshire Way
racknell, Priestwood RG12 .118 A3
racknell, Skimpedhill
cwnside OX11 ....10 B4
wnsway Sch RG41 ....57 B2
yle Gdns RG42 ....149 B2
ain Hill RG17 ....25 A2
ake Ave Slough SL3 .....43 B1
baines TW18 ....96 C2
ake CI Bracknell RG12 ..118 A2
aper CI RG19 ....106 B1
akroft RG12 ....118 C2
ayhorse Dr GU19 ....145 C1
ayton CI RG12 ....118 B4
ayton Rd RG30 ....85 A4
esden Way RG30 ....57 C1
ew Mdw SL2 ....22 B4
ewell CI RG2 ....113 B3
ilt Rd Holyport SL4,SL6 .65 B2
akley Green SL4 ....66 A1
ift Way SL3 ....69 B4
iftway CI 4 RG6 ....87 B1
ill Hall Rd RG14 ....124 A1
ive The Ashford TW15 ..98 B1
ourne End SL8 ....2 C2
atchet SL3 ....68 A3
ury La RG7 ....87 A2
ly Arch Rd SL5 ....120 C2
yden RG12 ....118 A1
yden Ct RG18 ....106 B3
n Pre Wlk HP10 ....3 B2
chess CI RG45 ....143 A4
chess St SL4 ....41 C3
dley CI RG31 ....57 C1
dley Ct SL1 ....43 A2
dley Mews RG31 ....57 C1
ny Rd Ashford TW15,TW14 ..97 C2
eet Bedfont TW14 ....98 B4
affield La SL2 ....22 C3
affield Pk SL2 ....23 A1
affield Rd RG5 ....60 C1
ogdale Ho TW20 ....96 C2
Duke Of Cornwall Ave
U15 ....144 B1
ake St Eton SL4 ....67 B4
henley-on-T RG9 ....15 C1
eading RG1 ....86 A4
ake's Hill GU19 ....145 C3
ld Windsor SL4, SL5 .....94 A2
inkfield SL5 ....93 C1
ake's Ride RG45 ....143 A3
akes CI TW15 ....98 A2
akes Covert GU19 .....145 C3
akes Pl SL7 ....1 B1
akes Ride RG7 ....136 A1
akes Wood RG45 ....143 A3
akeshill Rd RG42 ....89 A4
aman Ct RG30 ....85 A4
alverton Gdns RG2 .....86 B1
amas CI GU46 ....149 B3
ambarton Way RG4 .....59 C3
anbally Pk TW17 .....125 B1
anaways CI RG6 ....87 B2
anbar CI SL2 ....43 A3
anbar Dr RG5 ....88 A3
anboe PI TW17 ....125 B1
ancan Dr RG40 ....116 C3
ancan Gdns
urley on T RG8 ....57 B2
canes TW18 ....97 A1
ancan Rd RG5 ....60 C1
ancannon Cres SL4 ....66 B2
anconbe Ct TW18 .....96 C1
ancroft SL4 ....66 A3
anleary Ct RG30 ....85 B3
antuce Gdns RG6 ....56 C3
ann Cres RG17 ....102 A1
annock Way RG10 .....36 C2
annock CI RG31 ....84 C4
ansfold Rd RG30 ....84 C4
ansmore Gdns GU46 ...149 A3
anstable Ho 3 SL7 .....1 C2
anstall CI RG31 ....84 B4
anstan Ct TW18 ....97 A2
anstan Park Inf Sch
G18 ....106 B2

Dunstan Rd RG18 ....106 C2
Dunstans Dr RG41 ....88 A1
Dunster Cl RG4 ....59 B3
Dunster Gdns SL1 ....42 A3
Dunt Ave RG10 ....88 C2
Dunt La RG10 ....88 C2
Dunwood Ct SL6 ....39 B3
Duppas Ct TW17 ....125 B2
Dupre Cl SL1 ....41 C2
Durand Rd RG6 ....87 A1
Durant Way RG31 ....57 B2
Durham Ave SL1 ....42 A4
Durham Cl Reading RG2 .113 B4
Wokingham RG41 ....115 C3
Durham Rd GU47 ....143 C1
Durley Mead RG12 .....118 C2
Durrell Way TW17 .....125 B2
Dutch Barn Cl TW19 ....70 B1
Dutton Way SL0 ....44 C4
Duval Pl GU19 ....145 C2
Dwyer Rd RG2 ....85 A2
Dyer Straits OX12 .....9 C4
Dyers Ct RG5 ....87 B4
Dyson Cl SL4 ....67 A2
Dysons CI RG14 ....104 C2
Dysonswood La RG4 ....58 C4

E

Eagle CI Crowthorne RG45 .143 A4
Wokingham RG41 ....115 C3
Eagle House Sch GU47 .143 A1
Eagle Rd RG20 ....132 A1
Eagles Nest GU47 .....143 A1
Earle Croft RG42 ....91 B1
Earley Hill Rd RG6 .....87 A3
Earley Pl RG1 ....86 A4
Earley Sta RG6 ....87 B2
Earleydene SL5 ....120 A1
Earls Gr GU15 ....151 C3
Earls La SL1 ....41 C3
Earlsfield SL6 ....40 B1
Earlsfield Cl RG4 .....59 C2
Earlswood RG12 ....118 A1
Easby La RG6 ....87 A2
Easington Dr RG6 .....87 C1
East Berkshire Coll
Maidenhead SL6 ....39 B3
Slough SL3 ....43 A4
Windsor SL4 ....67 B3
East Burnham Cotts SL2 .22 A2
East Burnham La SL2 ...22 A2
East Cres SL4 ....66 C3
East Dr Reading RG31 ...84 C1
Stoke Poges SL2 ....22 C1
Wentworth GU25 ....122 A2
East Gn GU17 ....150 B2
East La RG20 ....51 A1
East Paddock SL6 .....18 C3
East Ram Farm Dr RG10 .61 A2
East Ramp TW6 ....71 A3
East Rd East Bedfont TW14 .98 B4
Maidenhead SL6 ....39 C4
East Ridge SL8 ....3 A2
East St RG1 ....86 A4
East Stratton Cl RG12 .118 C2
East View OX10 ....36 C1
East View Rd RG10 .....36 C1
Eastbourne Rd SL1 .....42 A4
Eastbridge SL2 ....43 A3
Eastbury Ave RG31 .....84 A4
Eastbury Ct RG42 ....90 C1
Eastbury Pk RG41 .....88 B1
Eastbury Shute RG17 ...46 C1
Eastchurch Rd TW6 .....71 C3
Eastchurch Road Rdbt
TW6 ....71 C3
Eastcourt Ave RG6 .....87 A3
Eastcroft SL2 ....22 A1
Eastern Ave
Chertsey KT16 ....124 A3
Reading RG1 ....86 C3
Eastern Dr SL8 ....3 A2
Eastern Ind Area RG12 .118 B4
Eastern La RG45 ....143 C2
Eastern Perimeter Rd
Hatton TW14 ....71 C2
Hatton TW6 ....71 C3
Eastfield OX11 ....12 A4
Eastfield Cl 3 SL1 .....43 A2
Eastfield La RG9 ....56 B4
Eastfield Rd SL1 ....41 A4
Easthampstead Park Sch
RG12 ....117 B2
Easthampstead Rd
Bracknell RG12 ....118 A4
Wokingham RG40 ....116 C2
Eastheath Ave RG41 ...116 A2
Eastheath Gdns RG41 ..116 A2
Eastleigh Rd TW6 .....71 C2
Eastman Cl RG30 .....135 C1
Easton Hill RG20 ....76 C2
Eastwood Cl 1 SL1 .....1 C2
Eastwood Rd RG5 .....88 A2
Eastworth Rd KT15, KT16 .124 A1
Eaton Pl RG1 ....85 C4
Eaton Rd GU15 ....151 A2
Ebborn Sq RG6 ....114 B4
Ebsworth Cl SL6 ....20 B2
Eccles Ct SL4 ....59 B1
Echelford Cty Mid Sch
TW15 ....98 A2
Echelforde Dr TW15 ...98 A2
Eddington Hill RG17 ..100 C4
Eddington Rd RG12 ...117 C2
Eddystone Wlk TW19 ...97 C4

Eden CI SL3 ....44 A1
Eden Way RG41 ....88 A1
Edenhall CI RG31 ....57 B2
Edenham CI RG6 ....87 C4
Edenham Cres RG1 .....85 C3
Edgar Milward Cl RG30 .58 A1
Edgar Wallace Pl SL8 ...3 A3
Edgbarrow Rise GU47 .143 A1
Edgbarrow Sch RG45 ..143 B2
Edgbarrowhill Star
RG45 ....143 A2
Edgcumbe Park Dr
RG45 ....143 A3
Edgecombe La RG14 ..105 B3
Edgedale Cl RG45 .....143 A3
Edgehill St RG1 ....86 A3
Edgell Cl GU25 ....122 C3
Edgell Rd TW18 ....96 C2
Edgemoor Rd GU16 ...152 B2
Edgewood Cl RG45 ....143 A3
Edinburgh Ave SL1 .....42 A4
Edinburgh Dr TW18 ....97 B1
Edinburgh Rd
Maidenhead SL6 ....19 C1
Marlow SL7 ....1 C2
Reading RG30 ....85 C4
Edith Rd SL6 ....39 A4
Edmonds Ct 4 RG12 ..118 B4
Edmunds Way SL2 .....43 A4
Edneys Hill RG41 .....115 B1
Edward Ave GU15 .....151 A3
Edward Ct TW18 ....97 A1
Edward Pauling Ho TW14 .98 C4
Edward Pauling Prim Sch
TW13 ....98 C4
Edward Pl 2 RG1 ....86 B4
Edward Rd Hatton TW14 .71 C1
Twyford RG10 ....61 A3
Windlesham GU20 .....146 B2
Edward Way TW15 .....97 C2
Edwards Ct SL1 ....42 C2
Edwards Hill RG17 .....25 A1
Edwin Cl RG19 ....106 C2
Eeklo Pl RG14 ....105 A1
Egerton Rd Reading RG2 .86 C1
Sandhurst GU15 ....150 C4
Slough SL2 ....21 C1
Egham By-Pass TW20 ..96 A2
Egham Hill TW20 ....96 A1
Egham Hill Rdbt TW20 .95 C2
Egham Mus TW20 ....96 A2
Egham Sta TW20 ....96 A2
Eghams Ct 9 SL8 ....3 A3
Egremont Dr RG6 ....87 B2
Egremont Gdns RG1 ...42 A3
Egypt La SL2 ....22 A1
Eight Acres SL1 ....21 A1
Eight Bells RG14 .....104 C1
Eisenhower Ave RG20 ..49 A2
Elan Cl RG30 ....84 C4
Elbow Mdw SL3 ....69 C3
Eldart Cl RG30 ....85 A4
Elder Cl RG31 ....57 B1
Elderberry Way RG6 ...87 B1
Elderfield Cres OX11 ..10 B4
Elderfield Rd SL2 .....22 C2
Eldon Pl RG1 ....86 B4
Eldon Rd RG1 ....86 B4
Eldon Sq RG1 ....86 B4
Eldon Terr RG1 ....86 B4
Eldrick Ct TW14 ....98 B4
Elford Cl RG6 ....87 B1
Elgar Ave RG45 ....143 A4
Elgar Rd RG2 ....86 A3
Elgar Rd S RG2 ....86 A2
Elgarth Dr RG40 .....141 C3
Elgin Ave TW15 ....98 B1
Elgin Cres TW6 ....71 C3
Elgin Ho RG3 ....69 C3
Eliot Ct Camberley GU15 .152 A4
Caversham RG4 ....59 A2
Thatcham RG18 ....106 B3
Elizabeth Ave
Bagshot GU19 ....145 C1
Newbury RG14 ....130 B4
Staines TW18 ....97 B1
Elizabeth Cl
Bracknell RG12 ....118 B3
Cookham SL6 ....19 C4
Henley-on-T RG9 ....35 A4
Elizabeth Ct 4 Slough SL1 .43 A2
Wargrave RG10 ....36 C1
Elizabeth Gdns Ascot SL5 .120 A2
Kintbury RG17 ....102 A1
Elizabeth Ho TW15 ....97 C2
Elizabeth Mews 16 RG1 .86 A3
Elizabeth Par GU46 ...149 B2
Elizabeth Rd
Henley-on-T RG9 ....35 A4
Marlow SL7 ....1 C2
Wokingham RG40 ....116 B3
Elizabeth Rout Cl RG7 .113 B1
Elizabeth Way SL2 .....22 C2
Elizabeth Wlk 28 RG1 .86 A3
Elizabethan Cl TW19 ...97 B4
Elizabethan Way TW19 .97 B4
Ellenborough Cl RG12 .118 B4
Ellerton Cl RG7 ....83 C2
Ellesfield Ave RG12 ..117 C3
Ellesmere Cl RG4 ....59 A2
Ellies Mews TW15 .....97 C3
Elliman Ave SL2 ....42 C3
Ellington Cl SL6 ....40 B4
Ellington Pk SL6 ....19 C1
Ellington Prim Sch SL6 .19 C1
Ellington Rd Feltham TW13 .98 C2

Ellington Rd continued
Taplow SL6 ....40 B4
Elliot Dr SL7 ....1 C2
Elliot Rd SL5 ....119 B4
Elliot Rise SL5 ....119 A4
Elliots Way RG4 ....59 A1
Elliott Gdns TW17 ...125 A3
Ellis Ave SL1 ....42 C2
Ellis Rd RG45 ....143 A3
Ellison Cl SL4 ....67 B3
Ellison Ho 2 SL4 ....67 B3
Ellison Way RG40 .....116 A3
Elm Bank GU46 ....149 B4
Elm Cl
Farnham Common SL2 ...22 B3
Stanwell TW19 ....97 B4
Elm Cotts RG20 ....129 C1
Elm Croft SL3 ....68 B3
Elm Ct 9 Charlton TW16 .98 C1
Sandhurst GU47 ....143 C1
Elm Dr
Burghfield Common RG30 .111 A3
Winkfield SL4 ....93 A4
Elm Gr Maidenhead SL6 ...39 C4
Thatcham RG18 ....106 A3
Elm La Bourne End SL8 ...2 C3
Earley RG6 ....86 C1
Elm Lodge Ave RG30 ...85 B4
Elm Park Rd RG30 .....85 B4
Elm Pk Reading RG30 ...85 B4
Summingdale SL5 .....120 C1
Elm Rd Earley RG2 & RG6 ...86 C1
East Bedfont TW14 .....98 B4
Maplesurham RG4 .....58 B4
Windsor SL4 ....67 A2
Elm Tree Cl TW15 .....98 A2
Elmar Gn SL2 ....22 A1
Elmbank Ave TW20 .....95 A1
Elmcroft SL6 ....34 B3
Elmcroft Cl TW14 .....71 C1
Elmcroft Dr TW15 .....98 A2
Elmdon Rd TW6 ....71 C2
Elmhurst Ballet Sch
GU15 ....151 B3
Elmhurst Ct SL3 ....44 A2
Elmhurst Rd Goring RG8 .34 B4
Reading RG1 ....86 B3
Slough SL3 ....44 A2
Thatcham RG18 ....106 A3
Elmleigh Ct RG4 ....59 B2
Elmley Cl RG41 ....88 C1
Elms Ave RG19 ....106 C2
Elms Dr SL8 ....3 B2
Elms Rd RG40 ....116 A3
Elms The TW15 ....98 A2
Elmshott La SL1 ....41 C3
Elmsleigh Ctr The TW18 .96 C2
Elmsleigh Rd TW18 ....96 C2
Elmslie Ct SL6 ....39 C4
Elmstone Dr RG31 .....57 B1
Elmsway TW15 ....98 A2
Elmwood SL6 ....20 A2
Elmwood Rd SL6 ....20 A2
Elsenwood Cres GU15 .152 A3
Elsenwood Dr GU15 ...152 A4
Elsinore Ave TW19 .....97 C4
Elsley Rd RG31 ....57 C2
Elstow Ave RG4 ....59 B3
Elstree Cl RG31 ....57 B1
Elstree Sch RG7 ....108 B2
Elsworth Cl TW14 .....98 C4
Eltham Ave Caversham RG4 .59 C2
Slough SL1 ....42 C2
Elton Dr SL6 ....39 B4
Elvaston Way RG30 ....85 A4
Elveden Cl RG6 ....87 C1
Elvendon Rd RG8 ....34 B4
Elwell Cl TW20 ....96 A1
Ely Ave SL1 ....42 B4
Ely Rd Hatton TW6 .....71 C3
Theale RG7 ....83 C2
Embankment The TW19 .95 B4
Ember Rd SL3 ....44 A2
Emblem Cres RG2 .....114 C1
Embrook Way RG41 ....84 A2
Emerald Cl SL1 ....42 C2
Emerald Ct SL1 ....43 A2
Emerson Ct HP10 ....3 C3
Emery Acres RG8 ....55 A3
Emery Down Cl RG12 .119 A3
Emlyns Bldgs SL4 ....67 B4
Emma Cl RG10 ....36 C1
Emma La RG10 ....36 C1
Emmbrook Comp
Sch RG41 ....115 C4
Emmbrook Ct RG2 .....86 C1
Emmbrook Gate RG41 .115 C4
Emmbrook Inf Sch RG41 .88 C1
Emmbrook Jun Sch RG41 .88 C1
Emmbrook Rd RG41 ...115 C4
Emmbrook Vale RG41 ...89 A1
Emmer Green Ct RG4 ...59 A3
Emmer Green Prim
Sch RG4 ....59 A3
Emmets Nest RG42 .....90 B1
Emmets Pk RG42 ....90 B1
Emmview Cl RG41 ....115 C4
Empress Rd RG31 ....84 B3
Enborne Cl RG31 ....84 B4
Enborne Gate RG14 ...104 B1
Enborne Gdns RG12 ...91 B1
Enborne Gr RG14 .....104 C1
Enborne Lodge
Sch RG14 ....130 A3
Enborne Pl RG14 .....104 B1
Enborne Prim Sch RG20 .129 C3
Enborne Rd RG14 .....104 B1
Enborne St
Hamstead Marshall RG20 .130 A2

Enborne St continued
Newbury RG14 ....130 B3
Enborne Way RG7 .....133 C3
Enfield Rd TW6 ....71 C3
Enfield Road Rdbt TW6 .71 C3
Engineers Rd RG2 .....112 A2
Englefield CE Prim Sch
RG7 ....83 A2
Englefield Cl TW20 .....95 B1
Englefield Green Sch
TW20 ....95 B2
Englefield Rd RG2 .....95 B1
Engleheart Dr TW14 ...71 C1
Englehurst TW20 ....95 B1
Englemere Pk SL5 ...119 B3
Englemere Pond
Nature Trail SL5 .....119 B3
Englemere Rd RG42 ...90 C1
Englesfield GU15 .....152 B3
English Gdns TW19 ....68 B1
English Martyrs
RC Prim Sch RG30 ...85 A4
Enid Wood Ho RG12 ..118 B4
Ennerdale RG12 ....118 A3
Ennerdale Cl TW14 .....98 C4
Ennerdale Cres SL1 ...41 B4
Ennerdale Rd RG2 .....86 B2
Ennerdale Way RG18 .106 A2
Ensign Cl TW19 ....97 B4
Ensign Way TW19 .....97 B4
Enstone Rd RG5 ....88 A4
Enterprise Way RG19 ..107 A1
EP Collier Prim Sch RG1 .59 A1
Epping Cl RG1 ....85 C4
Epping Way RG12 .....118 C3
Epsom Cl GU15 ....151 B4
Epsom Cres RG45 .....105 A1
Epsom Ct RG1 ....85 C3
Epsom Sq TW6 ....71 C3
Equine Way RG14 .....131 A4
Eric Ave RG4 ....59 A3
Erica Cl Slough SL1 ....41 C3
West End GU24 ....153 C3
Erica Dr RG40 ....116 B3
Eriswell Cl RG6 ....87 C1
Erkenwald Cl KT16 ...123 C2
Erleigh Court Dr RG6 ...87 A4
Erleigh Court Gdns RG6 .87 A4
Erleigh Dene RG14 ...104 C1
Erleigh Rd RG1 ....86 B3
Ermin St Lambourn RG17 .46 B1
Stockcross RG20 .....103 B4
Wickham RG20 ....75 B2
Ermin Wlk RG19 .....106 A2
Errington Dr SL4 ....67 A3
Erskine Ct RG26 .....135 C1
Escot Rd TW16 ....98 C1
Esher Cres TW6 ....71 C3
Esher Rd GU15 ....145 A1
Eskdale Gdns SL6 .....40 A1
Eskdale Rd RG41 ....88 A2
Eskdale Way GU15 ...152 B2
Eskin Cl RG30 ....85 A4
Essame CE RG40 .....116 B3
Essex Ave SL2 ....42 B4
Essex Pl RG17 ....25 A2
Essex Rise RG42 ....91 C1
Essex St Newbury RG14 .130 B4
Reading RG2 ....86 A1
Ethel Rd TW15 ....97 C2
Eton Cl SL3 ....68 A4
Eton Coll SL4 ....67 B4
Eton Ct Eton SL4 ....67 B4
Staines TW18 ....96 C2
Eton End PNEU Sch SL3 .68 A4
Eton Pl SL7 ....1 B1
Eton Porny CE Comb Sch
SL4 ....67 B4
Eton Rd Datchet SL3 ...68 A4
Harlington UB3 ....71 C4
Eton Sq SL4 ....67 B4
Eton Wick CE Fst Sch SL4 .42 A1
Eton Wick Rd SL4 .....42 A1
Eton Wlk 28 SL1 ....42 C2
European Weather Ctr
RG2 ....113 B4
Eustace Cres RG40 ...116 B4
Evedon RG12 ....118 A1
Evelyn Cres TW16 ....125 C4
Evelyn Ct RG5 ....87 C3
Evelyn Way TW16 ....125 C4
Evendon's Cl RG41 ...116 A2
Evendon's La
Barkham RG41 ....115 C1
Wokingham RG41 ....116 A2
Evenlode SL6 ....39 C4
Evenlode Rd SL8 ....3 A2
Evenlode Way GU47 ..150 B4
Everard Ave SL1 ....42 C2
Everest Rd
Camberley GU15 .....151 B4
Crowthorne RG45 .....143 A3
Stanwell TW19 ....97 C4
Evergreen Ct TW19 ....97 B4
Evergreen Dr RG31 ...84 C2
Evergreen Rd GU16 ..152 A2
Evergreen Way
Stanwell TW19 ....97 B4
Wokingham RG41 ....115 C3
Everington La RG17 ...33 A1
Everland Rd RG17 ....100 B3
Eversley Rd
Arborfield RG2 ....114 C1
Barkham RG40 ....140 C3

Eversley St RG27 . . . . .141 A1
Eversley Way TW20 . . . . .123 B4
Evesham Rd RG4 . . . . .59 A3
Evesham Wlk GU47 . . . . .143 B1
Evreham Rd SL0 . . . . .44 C4
Evreux Cl RG19 . . . . .106 C1
Ewing Way RG4 . . . . .131 A4
Exbourne Rd RG2 . . . . .113 B4
Exchange Rd SL5 . . . . .120 B2
Exeforde Ave TW15 . . . . .98 A2
Exeter Ct RG1 . . . . .113 A4
Exeter Gdns GU46 . . . . .149 A4
Exeter Rd TW6 . . . . .71 C2
Exeter Way Hatton TW6 . . . . . .71 C1
Theale RG7 . . . . .83 C2
Exmoor Rd RG19 . . . . .106 B2
Explorer Ave TW19 . . . . .97 C4
Expressway RG14 . . . . .105 C1
Exwick Sq RG2 . . . . .113 B4
Eylham RG8 . . . . .57 A3
Eynsford Cl RG4 . . . . .59 C3
Eynsham Rd RG5 . . . . .87 C4
Eyre Gn SL2 . . . . .22 A1

F

Fagg's Rd TW14 . . . . .71 C2
Fair Close Ho **1** RG14 . . . .105 A1
Fair Lawn Gn RG2 . . . . .86 C1
Fair Mile RG9 . . . . .15 B2
Fair Mile Mospl OX10 . . . . . . .14 A4
Fair View Cotts SL6 . . . . .19 C4
Fairacre SL6 . . . . .39 B2
Fairacres Ind Est SL4 . . . . . . .66 B3
Faircroft SL2 . . . . .22 A1
Faircross RG12 . . . . .118 A3
Faircross Quarters RG18 . . . .78 C3
Faircross Rd RG30 . . . . .85 B3
Fairfax RG42 . . . . .118 A4
Fairfax Cl RG4 . . . . .59 A2
Fairfax Pl RG14 . . . . .105 C3
Fairfield RG20 . . . . .31 B2
Fairfield App TW19 . . . . .68 B1
Fairfield Ave Datchet SL3 . . . .68 B4
Farnham Common SL2 . . . . . . .22 A2
Staines TW18 . . . . .96 C2
Fairfield Cl SL3 . . . . .68 B4
Fairfield Dr GU16 . . . . .151 C2
Fairfield La GU24 . . . . .153 C4
Fairfield Rd Burnham SL1 . . . .21 B1
Goring RG8 . . . . .34 B4
Wraysbury TW19 . . . . .68 B1
Fairfields RG17 . . . . .100 B3
Fairford Rd
Maidenhead SL6 . . . . .39 A4
Purley on T RG31 . . . . .57 B1
Fairhaven TW20 . . . . .95 C2
Fairhaven Ct **1** TW20 . . . . . .95 C2
Fairholme TW14 . . . . .98 C4
Fairholme Jun & Inf
Schs TW14 . . . . .98 B4
Fairholme Rd TW15 . . . . .97 C2
Fairlawn Pk SL4 . . . . .66 C2
Fairlawns Cl TW18 . . . . .97 A1
Fairlea SL6 . . . . .39 A2
Fairlight Ave SL4 . . . . .67 B3
Fairlop Cl RG31 . . . . .84 B2
Fairmead Cl GU47 . . . . .150 C4
Fairmead Rd RG2 . . . . .113 C3
Fairmile RG9 . . . . .15 B2
Fairoak Way RG26 . . . . .134 B1
Fairsted Cl RG30 . . . . .85 A4
Fairview RG14 . . . . .130 C4
Fairview Ave RG6 . . . . .87 C3
Fairview Cotts GU25 . . . . .122 B2
Fairview Ct TW15 . . . . .98 A2
Fairview Dr TW17 . . . . .124 C2
Fairview Est RG9 . . . . .35 C4
Fairview Rd Burnham SL6 . . . .41 A4
Hungerford RG17 . . . . .100 B3
Slough SL2 . . . . .21 C1
Wokingham RG40 . . . . .116 B3
Fairwater Dr RG5 . . . . .87 B3
Fairway KT16 . . . . .124 A1
Fairway Ave RG30 . . . . .84 B3
Fairway Dr RG10 . . . . .61 A3
Fairway The Burnham SL1 . . . .21 B2
Flackwell Heath HP10 . . . . .3 B4
Frimley GU15 . . . . .152 A2
Maidenhead SL6 . . . . .39 A2
Fairways TW15 . . . . .98 A1
Faithfull Cl RG42 . . . . .91 A1
Fakenham Cl RG6 . . . . .114 A4
Fakenham Way GU47 . . . . . .143 B1
Falaise TW20 . . . . .95 C2
Falcon Ave RG2 . . . . .86 C1
Falcon Cl GU18 . . . . .152 C4
Falcon Ct GU16 . . . . .151 B1
Falcon Dr TW19 . . . . .70 C1
Falcon Fields RG26 . . . . .135 A1
Falcon House
Gdns RG20 . . . . .129 C1
Falcon Way
Sunbury TW16 . . . . .125 C4
Wokingham RG41 . . . . .115 C3
Yateley GU46 . . . . .149 A3
Falcons Croft HP10 . . . . .3 C4
Falconwood TW20 . . . . .95 C2
Falkland Dr RG14 . . . . .130 C4
Falkland Garth RG14 . . . . . . .130 B4
Falkland Ho SL6 . . . . .39 C4
Falkland Prim Sch RG14 . . . .130 B3

Falkland Rd
Caversham RG4 . . . . .59 A1
Newbury RG14 . . . . .130 B3
Fallowfield GU46 . . . . .149 A4
Fallowfield Cl RG4 . . . . .59 A2
Falmouth Cl GU15 . . . . .152 A2
Falmouth Rd
Reading RG2 . . . . .113 B4
Slough SL1 . . . . .42 A4
Falmouth Way RG19 . . . . . . .106 C2
Falstaff Ave RG6 . . . . .86 C1
Fane Way SL6 . . . . .39 B3
Fanes Cl RG42 . . . . .117 C4
Fannys La RG7 . . . . .80 B1
Faraday Cl Arborfield RG2 . .140 C4
Slough SL2 . . . . .42 A4
Faraday Rd
Newbury RG14 . . . . .105 A2
Slough SL2 . . . . .42 A4
Farcrosse Cl GU47 . . . . .150 A4
Fareham Dr GU46 . . . . .149 A4
Faringdon Cl GU47 . . . . .143 B1
Faringdon Dr RG12 . . . . .118 B2
Faringdon Wlk RG30 . . . . .85 A2
Farleigh Mews RG4 . . . . .59 C3
Farley Copse RG42 . . . . .117 C4
Farley Ct RG1 . . . . .86 C4
Farley Moor RG42 . . . . .117 B4
Farley Villas KT16 . . . . .124 A1
Farm Cl Ascot SL5 . . . . .120 B2
Bracknell RG42 . . . . .117 C4
Crowthorne RG45 . . . . .143 B4
Egham TW18 . . . . .96 C2
Lower Halliford TW17 . . . . . . .125 A1
Lyne KT16 . . . . .123 A2
Maidenhead SL6 . . . . .40 B1
Maidenhead, Highway SL6 . . .39 A4
Purley on T RG8 . . . . .57 B3
Yateley GU46 . . . . .149 B3
Farm Cres SL2 . . . . .43 B4
Farm Dr Old Windsor SL4 . . . .68 A1
Reading RG1 . . . . .84 A3
Farm Lea HP10 . . . . .3 C4
Farm Rd Bourne End SL8 . . . . .2 C2
Burnham SL6 . . . . .41 A3
Frimley GU16 . . . . .151 C1
Goring RG8 . . . . .34 B3
Henley-on-T RG9 . . . . .35 C4
Maidenhead SL6 . . . . .39 A4
Staines TW18 . . . . .97 A1
Farm View GU46 . . . . .149 B3
Farm Way RG19 . . . . .69 C1
Farm Yd SL4 . . . . .67 B4
Farman Cl RG5 . . . . .88 A4
Farmer's Rd TW18 . . . . .96 C2
Farmers Cl Maidenhead SL6 .39 A2
Reading RG2 . . . . .113 B3
Farmers End RG10 . . . . .61 A2
Farmers Gate RG18 . . . . .106 B3
Farmers Way SL6 . . . . .39 A2
Farmiloe Cl RG8 . . . . .57 B2
Farnburn Ave SL1 . . . . .42 A4
Farnell Rd TW18 . . . . .97 A3
Farnham Cl RG12 . . . . .118 B4
Farnham Common
Cty Inf Sch SL2 . . . . .22 A4
Farnham Common
Cty Jun Sch SL2 . . . . .22 A4
Farnham Dr RG4 . . . . .59 C2
Farnham La SL2 . . . . .22 A2
Farnham Park La SL2 . . . . .22 B2
Farnham Rd SL1, SL2 . . . . .42 A4
Farningham RG12 . . . . .118 C2
Farningham Ho RG12 . . . . . . .118 C2
Farnsfield Cl RG6 . . . . .114 A4
Farrell Cl GU15 . . . . .151 B2
Farrer Theatre SL4 . . . . .42 A1
Farrier Ct **11** SL8 . . . . .3 A2
Farriers Cl RG5 . . . . .87 C4
Farriers Rd TW18 . . . . .96 A3
Farrowdene Rd RG2 . . . . .113 B4
Farthing Green La SL2 . . . . . . .23 A2
Farthingales The SL6 . . . . .40 A4
Fatherson Rd RG1 . . . . .86 C4
Faulkner Pl GU19 . . . . .145 C2
Faversham Rd GU47 . . . . .143 B1
Fawcett Cres RG5 . . . . .87 B3
Fawcett Rd SL4 . . . . .67 A3
Fawler Mead RG12 . . . . .118 C3
Fawley Bottom Rd RG9 . . . . . .15 A4
Fawley Cl SL6 . . . . .19 B1
Fawley Ct RG9 . . . . .15 C4
Fawley Mews **2** RG1 . . . . . .85 C3
Fawley Rd RG30 . . . . .85 B3
Fawns Manor Cl TW14 . . . . . .98 B4
Fawns Manor Rd TW14 . . . . . .98 B4
Fawsley Cl SL3 . . . . .69 C4
Faygate Way RG6 . . . . .87 A1
Feathers La TW19 . . . . .96 A3
Felbridge Cl GU16 . . . . .151 B1
Felbridge Ct U83 . . . . .71 B4
Felix La TW17 . . . . .125 C2
Felixstowe Cl RG6 . . . . .87 B1
Fellow Gn GU24 . . . . .153 C3
Fellow Green Rd GU24 . . . . .153 C3
Fellowes Ct U83 . . . . .71 B4
Fells The RG31 . . . . .84 A3
Felstead Cl RG6 . . . . .86 C2
Feltham Hill Jun & Inf Schs
TW13 .98 C2
Feltham Hill Rd TW15 . . . . . . .98 B1
Feltham Rd TW15 . . . . .98 B1
Felthorpe Cl RG6 . . . . .87 A1
Felton Way RG31 . . . . .84 B4
Fencote RG12 . . . . .118 B2

Fennel Cl Earley RG6 . . . . .86 C1
Newbury RG14 . . . . .105 B3
Fenns La GU24 . . . . .153 C3
Fennscombe Ct GU24 . . . . . .153 C3
Fenton Ave TW18 . . . . .97 B2
Fern Cl Crowthorne RG45 . . .143 A4
Frimley GU16 . . . . .152 B2
Reading RG1 . . . . .84 B3
Fern Dr SL6 . . . . .41 A4
Fern Glen RG31 . . . . .57 B1
Fern Wlk Ashford TW15 . . . . . .97 B2
Reading RG1 . . . . .84 B3
Fernbank RG40 . . . . .141 B4
Fernbank Cres SL5 . . . . .119 B4
Fernbank Pl SL5 . . . . .119 B4
Fernbank Rd SL5 . . . . .119 B4
Fernbrook Rd RG4 . . . . .58 C3
Ferndale Ave RG30 . . . . .85 A2
Ferndale Cl RG31 . . . . .57 C2
Ferndale Ct RG19 . . . . .106 B2
Ferndale Pk SL6 . . . . .41 A2
Ferndale Rd TW15 . . . . .97 C2
Ferne RG12 . . . . .34 B4
Fernery The TW18 . . . . .96 C2
Fernhill Cl Bracknell RG42 . . .90 C1
Farnborough (Hants) GU17 . .150 C1
Fernhill Comp Sch GU14 . . .150 C1
Fernhill Cty Prim Sch
GU14 .150 C1
Fernhill La GU17 . . . . .150 C1
Fernhill Rd GU14,GU17 . . . . .150 C1
Fernhill Wlk GU17 . . . . .150 C1
Fernhurst Rd
Ashford TW18 . . . . .98 B2
Reading RG1 . . . . .113 B4
Ferniehurst GU15 . . . . .151 C2
Fernley Ct SL6 . . . . .19 B1
Ferrard Cl SL5 . . . . .119 B4
Ferrers Cl SL1 . . . . .41 C3
Ferriby Ct RG12 . . . . .118 C1
Ferrier Gr RG14 . . . . .131 A4
Ferry Ave TW18 . . . . .96 C1
Ferry End SL6 . . . . .40 B2
Ferry La Bourne End SL8 . . . . .3 A1
Chertsey KT16 . . . . .124 A1
Cookham SL6 . . . . .20 A4
Goring RG8 . . . . .34 A3
Hambleden RG9 . . . . .16 B3
Laleham TW18 . . . . .96 A1
Lower
Halliford TW16,TW17 . . . . . .125 A1
Medmenham SL6 . . . . .17 A3
South Stoke RG8 . . . . .14 A2
Wargrave RG10 . . . . .36 B1
Wraysbury TW19 . . . . .96 A3
Ferry Rd Maidenhead SL6 . . . .40 B2
South Stoke RG8 . . . . .14 B2
Ferry Wks TW17 . . . . .125 A1
Festival Cotts SL3 . . . . .44 B4
Fettiplace RG17 . . . . .48 A2
Fidlers La RG20 . . . . .30 C4
Fidlers Wlk RG10 . . . . .36 C1
Field Cl
Burghfield Common RG7 . . . .111 A1
Harlington UB3 . . . . .71 B4
Field End GU47 . . . . .143 B4
Field House Cl SL5 . . . . .120 A1
Field Hurst SL3 . . . . .43 C1
Field La GU16 . . . . .151 C1
Field Pk RG12 . . . . .118 B4
Field Rd
Farnborough (Hants) GU14 . .150 C1
Peasemore RG20 . . . . .29 B1
Reading RG1 . . . . .86 B4
Field View Caversham RG4 . . .59 A2
Egham TW20 . . . . .96 B2
Feltham TW13 . . . . .98 B4
Felden **7** RG12 . . . . .118 B4
Fieldfare Ave GU46 . . . . .149 A3
Fieldhead Gdns SL8 . . . . .3 A2
Fieldhouse Ind Est SL7 . . . . . .1 C1
Fieldhouse La SL7 . . . . .1 C1
Fieldhouse Way SL7 . . . . .1 C1
Fielding Gdns
Crowthorne RG45 . . . . .143 A2
Slough SL3 . . . . .43 B2
Fielding Rd
Maidenhead SL6 . . . . .39 A4
Sandhurst GU47 . . . . .143 C4
Fieldings The SL6 . . . . .65 A4
Fieldridge RG14 . . . . .105 B3
Fields The SL1 . . . . .42 C4
Fieldview TW18 . . . . .97 A1
Fieldway RG41 . . . . .116 A4
Fifehead Cl TW15 . . . . .97 C1
Fifield Cotts SL6 . . . . .65 A2
Fifield La SL4,SL6 . . . . .65 B2
Fifield Rd SL6 . . . . .65 B4
Fifth Rd RG14 . . . . .104 C1
Fifth St RG19 . . . . .131 C3
Filbert Dr RG31 . . . . .84 B4
Filey Rd RG1 . . . . .86 C4
Filmer Rd SL4 . . . . .66 B3
Finbeck Way RG6 . . . . .113 C4
Finch Cl SL5 . . . . .39 B3
Finch Rd RG6 . . . . .87 B2
Finch Way RG7 . . . . .111 A1
Fincham End Dr RG45 . . . . . .142 C2
Finchampstead
CE Prim Sch RG40 . . . . .141 C2
Finchampstead Rd
Finchampstead RG40 . . . . . . .141 C3
Finchampstead RG40, RG40 . .116 A2
Wokingham RG41, RG40 . . . .116 A2
Findhorn Cl GU47 . . . . .150 B4
Fineleigh Ct SL1 . . . . .42 C3
Finmere RG12 . . . . .118 B1

Finney Dr GU20 . . . . .146 B2
Finstock Cl RG6 . . . . .87 B1
Finstock Gn RG12 . . . . .118 C3
Fir Cottage Rd RG40 . . . . . . .141 C4
Fir Dr GU17 . . . . .150 B2
Fir Tree Ave SL2 . . . . .22 C1
Fir Tree Cl SL5 . . . . .120 A1
Fir Tree Cnr RG26 . . . . .134 C1
Fir Tree Cotts RG20 . . . . .28 B1
Fir Tree La RG14 . . . . .105 C2
Fir Tree Paddock RG20 . . . . . .10 A1
Fir Tree Pl TW15 . . . . .98 A2
Fir Tree Prim Sch RG14 . . . . .105 C2
Firbank Pl TW20 . . . . .95 A1
Fircroft Cl Reading RG31 . . . . .57 B1
Stoke Poges SL2 . . . . .23 A3
Fireball Hill SL5 . . . . .120 B1
Firglen Dr GU46 . . . . .149 B4
Firgrove Rd RG27,GU46 . . . .149 B3
Firlands RG12 . . . . .118 B2
Firlands Ave GU15 . . . . .151 B3
Firmstone Cl RG6 . . . . .87 B1
Firs Ave SL4 . . . . .66 C2
Firs Cl RG40 . . . . .141 C4
Firs Dr SL3 . . . . .43 C2
Firs End RG7 . . . . .111 A1
Firs La Maidenhead SL6 . . . . .38 C2
Reading RG30 . . . . .85 B3
Firs Rd RG31 . . . . .57 B2
Firs The **2** Bracknell RG12 .118 C3
Inkpen RG17 . . . . .127 C3
Maidenhead SL6 . . . . .39 C4
Reading RG30 . . . . .85 C3
Thatcham RG18 . . . . .106 A2
First Ave Marlow SL7 . . . . .2 A2
Tadley RG7 . . . . .135 B1
First Cres SL1 . . . . .42 B4
First St RG19 . . . . .132 A3
Firtree Cl GU47 . . . . .142 C1
Firwater Cl SL7 . . . . .1 C1
Firwood Cl GU15 . . . . .151 B3
Firwood Dr GU15 . . . . .151 B3
Firwood Rd GU25 . . . . .121 C2
Fisher Gn RG42 . . . . .90 A1
Fisherman's Way SL8 . . . . .3 A2
Fishermans La RG7 . . . . .135 A4
Fishermans Retreat SL7 . . . . . .1 C1
Fishers Cotts RG4 . . . . .59 B3
Fishers Ct RG4 . . . . .59 B3
Fishers La RG18 . . . . .79 A1
Fishers Wood SL5 . . . . .123 B3
Fishery Rd SL6 . . . . .40 B3
Fishguard Spur SL1 . . . . .43 A2
Fishponds Cl RG41 . . . . .116 A2
Fishponds Est RG41 . . . . .116 A2
Fishponds Rd RG41 . . . . .116 A2
Fitzrobert Pl TW20 . . . . .96 A1
Fitzroy Cres RG5 . . . . .88 A3
Five Acre RG31 . . . . .57 A1
Five Acres HP10 . . . . .3 C4
Five Fields Cl SL1 . . . . .43 C1
Flambards RG4 . . . . .59 B1
Flamborough Cl RG6 . . . . .87 C1
Flamborough Spur SL1 . . . . . .42 A2
Flamingo Cl RG41 . . . . .115 C3
Flanders Ct TW20 . . . . .96 B3
Flats The GU17 . . . . .150 B2
Flaxman Cl RG6 . . . . .86 C1
Flecker Cl RG18 . . . . .106 B3
Fleet Cl RG41 . . . . .115 C3
Fleet Hill RG40 . . . . .141 B1
Fleet La RG40 . . . . .141 C1
Fleetbrook Ho SL3 . . . . .68 B3
Fleetham Gdns RG6 . . . . .87 B1
Fleetway TW20 . . . . .123 B3
Fleetwood Cl RG14 . . . . .105 B3
Fleetwood Ct **7** TW19 . . . . .70 C1
Fleetwood Rd SL2 . . . . .42 C3
Fleming Cl RG42 . . . . .140 C4
Fleming Dr RG14 . . . . .105 A2
Flemish Fields KT16 . . . . .124 A1
Fletcher Gdns RG42 . . . . .117 B4
Flexford Gn RG12 . . . . .117 C2
Flintgrove RG12 . . . . .118 B4
Flintjack Pl RG17 . . . . .25 A1
Flintlock Cl TW19 . . . . .70 A2
Floddan Dr RG31 . . . . .84 B2
Floral Ho KT16 . . . . .123 C1
Floral Way RG18 . . . . .106 A3
Floreat Gdns RG14 . . . . .104 C1
Florence Ave SL6 . . . . .40 A4
Florence Cl GU46 . . . . .149 B3
Florence Cotts SL4 . . . . .92 B4
Florence Ct **10** RG30 . . . . . . .85 C4
Florence Gdns TW18 . . . . .97 A1
Florence Rd GU47 . . . . .150 C4
Florence Wlk RG1 . . . . .86 B4
Florian Gdns RG30 . . . . .85 A3
Florida Ct Reading RG30 . . . . .85 C3
Staines TW18 . . . . .97 A2
Flowers Hill RG8 . . . . .56 B3
Flowers Piece RG8 . . . . .54 A3
Fobney St RG1 . . . . .86 A4
Fokerham Rd RG19 . . . . .106 C1
Folder's La RG42 . . . . .91 B1
Foliejohn Way SL6 . . . . .38 A3
Folkestone Ct SL3 . . . . .44 A1
Follet Cl SL4 . . . . .68 A1
Folly La RG7,RG30 . . . . .110 C3
Folly Rd Inkpen RG17 . . . . . . .127 C3
Lambourn RG17 . . . . .25 B2
Folly The RG14 . . . . .105 A1
Fontmell Cl TW15 . . . . .98 A1
Fontmell Pk TW15 . . . . .98 A1
Fontwell Cl SL6 . . . . .39 A4
Fontwell Dr RG14 . . . . .105 A1
Forbes Chase GU47 . . . . .150 B4

Forbury Ho **6** RG30 85
Forbury La RG17,RG20 128
Forbury Rd RG1 86
Forbury Ret Pk RG1 86
Forbury The RG1 86
Ford Cl Ashford TW15 97
Littleton TW17 125
Ford La RG7 140
Ford Rd Ashford TW15 97
Bisley GU24 153
Chertsey KT16 124
Fordbridge Ct TW15 97
Fordbridge Rd
Ashford TW15 97
Upper Halliford
TW16, TW17 125
Fordham Way RG6 87
Fordingbridge Cl KT16 124
Fordwater Rd KT15, KT16 . . .124
Fordwater Trad Est
KT16 .124
Fordwells Dr RG12 118
Forehead The RG7 137
Forest Cl Bracknell SL5 119
Forest Dean RG26 134
Forest Comp Sch The
RG41 88
Forest Dean RG2 113
Forest Dr TW16 98
Forest End Rd GU47 150
Forest Gn RG12 118
Forest Green Rd SL6 57
Forest Hill RG30 57
Forest Hills GU15 151
Forest Rd Binfield RG42 90
Crowthorne RG45 143
Windsor SL4 93
Windsor, Dedworth SL4 66
Winkfield RG42, SL5 92
Forest View Cotts SL6 40
Foresters Sq RG12 118
Foresters Way RG45 143
Forge Cl Caversham RG4 59
Kintbury RG17 102
Forge Cotts SN8 99
Forge Dr SL2 22
Forge Hill RG18 53
Forge The Harlington UB3 71
Hungerford RG17 100
Forlease Cl SL6 40
Forlease Dr SL6 40
Forlease Rd SL6 40
Formby Cl Earley RG6 87
Slough SL3 44
Forndon Cl RG6 87
Forsters RG27 134
Fort Narrien GU15 150
Fortrose Cl GU47 150
Fortrose Wlk RG31 84
Forty Green Dr SL7 1
Fosseway RG45 143
Fossewood Dr GU15 151
Foster Ave SL4 66
Fosters Gr GU20 146
Fosters La RG5 87
Fosters Path SL2 21
Fotherby Ct SL6 40
Fotheringay Gdns SL1 42
Foundation Pk SL6 38
Foundry Ct KT16 124
Foundry La SL1 42
Foundry La SL3 69
Foundry Mews **1** KT16 124
Foundry Pl **6** RG1 86
Fountain Gdns SL4 67
Fountains Garth RG12 118
Fourth Ave SL7 2
Fourth St RG19 131
Fowler Cl RG6 87
Fowlers La RG42 118
Fox Cl RG7 111
Fox Covert GU18 153
Fox Covert Cl SL5 120
Fox Dr GU46 149
Fox Hill Prim Sch RG12 118
Fox La RG27 149
Fox La N KT16 123
Fox La S KT16 123
Fox Rd Bracknell RG12 118
Slough SL3 43
Foxborough RG7 139
Foxborough Cl SL3 44
Foxborough Ct SL6 39
Foxborough Prim
Sch SL3 44
Foxbury RG17 25
Foxcombe Dr RG31 84
Foxcote RG40 142
Foxdown Cl GU15 151
Foxes Piece SL7 1
Foxes Piece Comb Sch SL7 . . .1
Foxes Wlk RG10 61
Foxglove Cl Stanwell TW19 . . .97
Winkfield RG42 92
Wokingham RG41 115
Foxglove Gdns **4** RG1 85
Foxglove Way
Thatcham RG18 106
Thatcham RG18 106
Foxhays Rd RG2 113
Foxheath RG12 118
Foxherne SL3 43
Foxhill Cres GU15 152
Foxhill La RG4 59
Foxhill Rd RG1 86
Foxhollow Dr SL2 22
Foxhunt Gr RG31 84

xhunter Rd WG19 . . . . . 105 C2
xleigh Cl TW18 . . . . 96 B2
xley Cl GU17 . . . . 150 B3
xley La RG42 . . . . 90 B1
xley PNEU Sch RG10 . . 63 A1
amewood Manor SL2 . . 23 B3
amewood Rd SL2 . . . . . 22 B3
amlingham Dr RG4 . . . . 59 C3
ampton Cl RG5 . . . . 60 C1
ance Hill Dr GU15 . . . . 151 B3
ance Hill Sch GU15 . . . 151 B1
ances Ave SL6 . . . . 20 B1
ances Rd SL4 . . . . 67 B3
ances Rd SL4 . . . . 67 B3
ances Baily Prim Sch
RG19 . . . . 106 C2
ancis Chichester Cl
SL5 . . . . 120 A2
ancis Cl TW17 . . . . 125 A3
ancis Gdns RG42 . . . . . . 91 B1
ancis St RG1 . . . . 86 A3
ancis Way Burnham SL1 . 41 B3
rimley GU15 . . . . 152 B2
ancomes Field RG17 . . . 25 B1
ank Lunnon Cl SL8 . . . . 3 B2
ank Sutton Way SL1 . . . 42 B3
anklin Ave Slough SL2 . . 42 A4
adley RG26 . . . . 135 A1
anklin Ct 21 RG1 . . . . . 85 C4
anklin St RG1 . . . . 85 C4
anklyn Cres SL4 . . . . . . 66 B2
ascati Way SL6 . . . . 39 C4
aser Ave RG4 . . . . 59 B3
aser Mead GU47 . . . . . . 150 C3
aser Rd RG42 . . . . 118 B3
ederick Ho TW15 . . . . . . 97 C2
ederick Pl RG41 . . . . . 116 A3
ee Prae Rd KT16 . . . . . . 124 A1
eeborn Way RG42 . . . . 118 C4
eeman Cl TW17 . . . . . . 125 C3
eemans Cl
ungerford RG17 . . . . . 100 B3
toke Poges SL2 . . . . 23 A3
eemantle Rd GU47 . . . 145 C2
eemantles Sch
Spec! Sch) KT16 . . . . . 123 C1
besia Cl RG41 . . . . 115 B4
ench Gdns GU17 . . . . . 150 B2
enchum Gdns SL1 . . . . . 41 C3
ensham RG12 . . . . 118 B2
ensham Cl GU46 . . . . . 149 A3
ensham Gn RG2 . . . . . . 86 C1
ensham Rd RG45 . . . . . 143 A4
ensham Wlk SL2 . . . . . . 22 B3
eshfield Cl RG6 . . . . 87 C2
eshfields La RG20 . . . . . 51 A1
eshwater Rd RG1 . . . . . 86 C4
eshwood Dr GU46 . . . 149 B2
ewin Rd SL4 . . . . 86 A4
iars Keep RG12 . . . . . . 118 A3
iars Rd Newbury RG14 . 131 A4
rginia Water GU25 . . . . 122 B3
iars Way KT16 . . . . 124 A2
iars Wlk 3 RG1 . . . . . . 86 A4
iary Dr TW17 . . . . 68 B1
iary Rd Ascot SL5 . . . . 120 A2
rrayabury TW17 . . . . . 125 A4
iary The SL4 . . . . 68 B1
day St RG9 . . . . 15 E1
endship Way RG12 . . . 118 A3
eth Cl RG6 . . . . 87 A1
Isham Rd RG30 . . . . 85 A2
mley Cl RG5 . . . . 60 C1
mley Grove Gdns
GU16 . . . . 151 C1
mley Hall Dr GU15 . . . 151 B3
mley High St GU15 . . 151 B1
mley Park Hospl
GU16 . . . . 151 B1
mley Rd
amberley GU15 . . . . . 151 A2
mley GU15 . . . . 151 A2
ngford Cl RG30 . . . . 87 B1
th Hill Rd GU16 . . . . . . 152 A1
bisher RG12 . . . . 118 B1
bisher Cres Stai TW19 . 97 C4
bisher Gdns TW19 . . . 97 C4
dsham Way GU47 . . . . 143 C1
og Hall RG40 . . . . 116 C3
og Hall Dr RG40 . . . . . 116 C2
oggy La RG12 . . . . 118 A3
gmill SL6 . . . . 17 B2
gmill Ct SL6 . . . . 17 B2
gmore Cl SL1 . . . . 42 A2
gmore Com Coll
SL6 . . . . 149 C3
gmore Cty Inf Sch SL7 . 150 B2
gmore Cty Inf Sch
SL7 . . . . 150 A3
gmore Cty Jun Sch
SL7 . . . . 150 A3
gmore Gr GU17 . . . . . . 150 B2
gmore Park Dr GU17 . 150 B2
gmore Rd GU17 . . . . . . 150 B2
gmore Way RG30 . . . . . 85 A3
omor Rd HP10 . . . . 3 C3
omont Dr RG10 . . . . . 106 B2
omor Gdns GU20 . . . . 146 B2
ont St RG17 . . . . 25 B1
buds Bridge Marina
SL8 . . . . 3 B2
gmore Cty SL7 . . . . . . 108 C1
buds La RG7 . . . . 109 A1
oxfield Ave RG2 . . . . . . 85 C3
oxfield Down 5 RG12 . 118 C2
uen Rd TW14 . . . . 98 C4
or Ct RG4 . . . . 59 A2

Frymley Hill SL4 . . . . 66 B3
Frys La GU46 . . . . 149 C4
Fuchsia Cl RG31 . . . . . . 84 B3
Fuchsia Way GU24 . . . . 153 C3
Fullbrook Cl
Maidenhead SL6 . . . . . 40 A4
Wokingham RG41 . . . . . 89 A1
Fullbrook Cres RG31 . . . 57 B2
Fullers Cl RG14 . . . . . . 106 C1
Fullers La Ball Hill RG20 . 129 B1
Burghfield Common RG7 . 112 A2
Fullers Yd SL6 . . . . 20 A1
Fulmead Rd RG30 . . . . . 85 B4
Fulmer Chase SL3 . . . . . 23 B4
Fulmer Cl RG6 . . . . 87 B1
Fulmer Common Rd SL3 . 23 C3
Fulmer Cty Fst Sch SL3 . 23 C4
Fulmer Rd SL3 . . . . 23 C4
Furlong Cl SL8 . . . . 3 A2
Upper Halliford TW17 . . 125 B2
Gatehampton Rd RG8 . . 34 B3
Gatwick Cl SL1 . . . . 42 C3
Gatward Ave SL6 . . . . . . 39 A2
Gaveston Rd SL2 . . . . . . 22 A2
Gayhurst Cl RG4 . . . . . . 59 B3
Gays La SL6 . . . . 65 A4
Gaywood Dr RG14 . . . . 105 B2
Gazelle Cl RG41 . . . . 88 A2
Geffers Ride SL5 . . . . . . 119 C4
Gelder Dr RG6 . . . . 87 B2
Genesis Cl TW19 . . . . . . 97 C4
Geneva Cl TW17 . . . . . . 125 C4
Geoffrey Field
Jun & Inf Schs RG2 . . 113 B4
Geoffreyson Rd RG4 . . . 58 C3
George Cl SL7 . . . . 22 A1
George Green Rd SL3 . . 43 C4
George Palmer Inf Sch
RG2 . . . . 86 B2
George Palmer Jun Sch
RG2 . . . . 86 B2
George St Caversham RG4 . 59 A1
Reading RG1 . . . . 85 C4
Staines TW18 . . . . 96 C4
George V Pl SL4 . . . . 67 B4
Georgeham Rd GU47 . . 143 B1
Georges Dr HP10 . . . . 3 B4
Georgian Cl
Camberley GU15 . . . . . 151 C4
Staines TW18 . . . . 97 A2
Geranium Cl GU47 . . . . 143 A4
Gerrards Cross Rd SL2 . . 23 A4
Gervaise Cl SL1 . . . . 41 C3
Gibbet La GU15 . . . . . . 152 A4
Gibbins La RG42 . . . . . . 91 B3
Gibbons Cl GU47 . . . . . 150 B4
Gibbs Cl RG40 . . . . 141 C3
Gibbs Way RG40 . . . . . 149 A2
Gibraltar La SL6 . . . . 2 B1
Gibson Cl SL3 . . . . 43 C1
Gibson Pl TW19 . . . . . . 70 B1
Gifford Cl RG4 . . . . 59 C3
Gifford Ho 2 RG4 . . . . . 59 B1
Gilbert Cl RG18 . . . . . . 106 B2
Gilbert Rd GU15 . . . . . . 151 B1
Gilbert Way RG40 . . . . 141 C4
Gilbey Wlk HP10 . . . . 3 A2
Gilchrist Way SL6 . . . . . . 38 A3
Giles Travers Cl TW20 . . 123 B3
Gill Rise RG42 . . . . 91 C3
Gillette Way RG2 . . . . . . 86 A1
Gilliat Rd SL1 . . . . 42 C3
Gilliatt Cl SL1 . . . . 44 C4
Gillotts Cl RG9 . . . . 35 A4
Gillotts La RG9 . . . . 35 A4
Gillotts Sch RG9 . . . . . . 35 A4
Gilman Cres SL4 . . . . . . 66 B2
Gilmore Cl SL3 . . . . 43 B2
Gilmore Cres TW15 . . . . 98 A1
Gilpin Way UB3 . . . . 71 B4
Gilroy Cl RG14 . . . . . . 130 B3
Gilson Cl SL4 . . . . 94 B3
Gingells Farm Rd RG10 . 63 A1
Gipsy La Arborfield RG41 . 114 C4
Bracknell RG12 . . . . . . 118 B4
Earley RG6 . . . . 87 B2
Hungerford RG17 . . . . 100 C4
Reading RG30 . . . . 85 A2
Wokingham RG40,
Sindlesham RG41 . . . . 115 A4
Girton Cl GU47 . . . . 143 C1
Glade Ho Ascot SL5 . . 120 B2
3 Marlow SL7 . . . . 1 C1
Glade Rd SL7 . . . . 1 C1
Glade The Ascot SL5 . . 120 B2
Maidenhead SL6 . . . . . 39 B3
Purley on T RG8 . . . . . . 57 B2
Staines TW18 . . . . 97 A1
Gladridge Cl RG6 . . . . . . 87 A1
Gladstone Cl SL7 . . . . . 102 A1
Gladstone Ind Est SL6 . . 39 C4
Gladstone La SL6,SL8 . . . . 2 A2
Gladstone Way SL1 . . . . 42 A3
Glaisdale RG12 . . . . . . 118 B1
Glamis Way RG31 . . . . . 84 A2
Glanmor Rd SL2 . . . . 22 A3
Glany The TW20 . . . . . . 123 A3
Glasgow Rd SL1 . . . . . . 42 A4
Glassonby Wlk GU15 . . 152 A3
Glebe Cl Dorney SL4 . . . 40 C2
Glebe Cotts RG18 . . . . . 14 B2
Glebe Field RG20 . . . . . 50 C4
Glebe Gdns RG4 . . . . . . 60 C2
Glebe La Sonning RG4 . . 60 C2

Garrick Cl TW18 . . . . . . 97 A1
Garson La TW19 . . . . . . 95 B4
Garson's La SL4 . . . . 92 A4
Gascon's Gr SL2 . . . . . . 22 A1
Garston Cl RG30 . . . . . . 85 A2
Garston Cres RG31 . . . . 84 A3
Garston Gr RG40 . . . . . 115 C1
Garswood RG12 . . . . . . 118 B2
Garth Cl RG41 . . . . 88 B1
Garth Hill Sch RG12 . . 118 B4
Garth Rd RG7 . . . . 137 A3
Garth Sq RG42 . . . . 91 A1
Gas La SL6 . . . . 40 A2
Gas Works Rd RG1 . . . . 86 B4
Gascon's Gr SL2 . . . . . . 22 A1
Gaskell Mews RG14 . . . 131 A4
Gaskells End RG4 . . . . . 58 B4
Gaston Bridge Rd
Shepperton TW17 . . . . 125 B2
Gaston Way TW17 . . . . 125 B2
Gatcombe Cl RG31 . . . . 84 B2

Glebe La continued
Stockcross RG20 . . . . . 103 C3
Glebe Pl RG17 . . . . 73 A1
Glebe Rd Egham TW20 . . 96 B1
Maidenhead SL6 . . . . . 40 A3
Old Windsor SL4 . . . . . 68 A1
Purley on T RG8 . . . . . . 57 A3
Reading RG2 . . . . 86 B3
Staines TW18 . . . . 96 C3
Glebe Ride RG8 . . . . 34 B4
Glebe The Aldworth RG8 . 32 C2
Blackwater GU17 . . . . . 150 C2
Glebefields RG14 . . . . . 105 A3
Glebeland Gdns TW17 . 125 B2
Glebeland Rd GU15 . . . 150 C2
Glebelands RG19 . . . . . 106 B2
Glebelands Rd RG40 . . 116 B4
Glebewood RG12 . . . . . 118 B2
Glen Ave TW15 . . . . 98 A2
Glen Cl TW17 . . . . 125 A3
Glen Ct RG18 . . . . 96 C1
Glen Innes GU47 . . . . . 143 C1
Glen The Ascot SL5 . . . 120 B3
Silchester RG26 . . . . . . 135 C1
Slough SL3 . . . . 43 B3
Glenahmond Ho TW15 . 97 C3
Glenapp Grange RG7 . . 114 A4
Glenavon Gdns Slough SL3 . 43 B2
Yateley GU46 . . . . 149 B2
Glenbeigh Terr RG1 . . . . 85 C3
Glendale Ave RG41 . . . . 116 A2
Glendale Cl RG41 . . . . . 116 A2
Glendale Rd RG26 . . . . 135 A1
Glendevon Rd RG5 . . . . 87 C4
Gleneagles Cl TW19 . . . 70 B1
Gleneagles Ct 5 RG1 . . 86 B4
Gleneagles Ho RG12 . . 117 C2
Glenfield Ho RG12 . . . . 118 B3
Glenfield Rd TW15 . . . . 98 B1
Glenhaven Dr TW19 . . . 70 B2
Glenhurst Cl GU17 . . . . 150 C2
Glenmore Cl RG19 . . . . 106 B1
Glenmore Pl 4 RG14 . . 105 A2
Glennon Cl RG30 . . . . . . 85 B2
Glenhorndale RG4 . . . . . 58 C3
Glenrosa Rd RG30 . . . . . 84 C4
Glenshee Cl RG45 . . . . 143 A2
Glentworth Pl SL1 . . . . . 42 A3
Glenwood Dr RG31 . . . . 84 B4
Glebe Farm La GU47 . . 150 A3
Gloster Cl TW15 . . . . . . 98 A1
Glory Cl HP10 . . . . 3 C4
Glory Hill La HP9 . . . . 3 C4
Glory Mill La HP10 . . . . . 3 C4
Gloucester Ave SL1 . . . . 42 B4
Gloucester Cres TW18 . . 97 B1
Gloucester Ct RG30 . . . . 85 B4
Gloucester Dr TW18,TW19 . 96 B3
Gloucester Gdns GU15 . 145 C2
Gloucester Pl
Bracknell RG42 . . . . . . 91 C1
Windsor SL4 . . . . 67 B3
Gloucester Rd
Bagshot GU19 . . . . . . 145 C2
Maidenhead SL6 . . . . . 19 C1
Newbury RG14 . . . . . . 104 C1
Reading RG30 . . . . 85 B4
Gloucestershire Lea RG42 . 91 C1
Glyme Wlk RG31 . . . . . . 84 C2
Glyncastle Rd RG4 . . . . 58 C3
Glynswood GU15 . . . . . 151 C2
Glynwood Ho SL6 . . . . . 40 A4
Goaters Rd SL5 . . . . . . 119 B4
Goddard Cl
Littleton TW17 . . . . . . 124 C3
Shinfield RG2 . . . . 113 C3
Goddard Ct RG41 . . . . . 88 B1
Goddard Dr RG7 . . . . . 107 C2
Goddards La GU47 . . . . 150 A4
Godfrey Cl GU47 . . . . . 150 B4
Godolphin Inf Sch SL1 . 42 B4
Godolphin Jun Sch SL1 . 42 B4
Godolphin Rd SL1 . . . . . 42 B4
Godstow Cl RG5 . . . . . . 87 C4
Goffs Rd TW15 . . . . 98 C1
Gogmore Farm Cl KT16 . 123 C1
Gogmore La KT16 . . . . 123 C1
Gold Cup La SL5 . . . . . 119 B4
Goldcrest Cl GU46 . . . . 149 A3
Goldcrest Way RG31 . . . 84 A3
Golden Ball La SL6 . . . . 19 A2
Golden Oak 1 SL2 . . . . . 22 C4
Golden Orb Wood RG42 . 117 B4
Goldfinch La RG20 . . . . 131 C2
Golding Cl RG19 . . . . . 106 C2
Goldney Rd GU15 . . . . . 152 B2
Goldsmid Rd RG1 . . . . . 85 C4
Goldsmith Cl
Thatcham RG18 . . . . . 106 B3
Wokingham RG40 . . . . 115 C1
Goldsmith Way RG45 . . 143 A2
Goldsworthy Way SL1 . . 41 B4
Goldthorpe Gdns RG6 . 113 C4
Goldwell Dr RG14 . . . . 104 C2
Golf Dr GU15 . . . . 151 C2
Gooch Cl RG10 . . . . 61 C2
Goodboys La RG7 . . . . 112 A2
Goodchild Rd RG40 . . . 116 C3
Goodings Gn RG40 . . . 116 C3
Goodings La RG7 . . . . . 139 A4
Goodliffe Gdns RG31 . . 57 B2
Goodman Pk SL2 . . . . . . 43 B3
Goodman Pl TW18 . . . . 96 C4
Goodrich Cl RG4 . . . . . . 59 C3
Goodways Dr RG12 . . . 118 B4
Goodwin Cl SL6 . . . . . . 38 C4
Goodwin Mdws HP10 . . . 3 C3

Goodwin Rd SL2 . . . . . . 21 C1
Goodwin Wlk RG14 . . . 130 B3
Goodwood Cl
Burghfield Common RG7 . 111 A1
Camberley GU15 . . . . . 151 B4
Goodwood Rise SL7 . . . . 1 B4
Goodwood Way RG14 . 105 B1
Goose Cnr RG42 . . . . . . 91 C2
Goose Gn
Farnham Common SL2 . 22 A2
Lambourn RG17 . . . . . . 25 A2
Goose Green Way RG19 . 106 B2
Goose La SL6 . . . . 49 C3
Gordon Ave GU15 . . . . 151 B2
Gordon Cl TW18 . . . . . . 97 A1
Gordon Clifford Ct RG42 . 118 A4
Gordon Cres
Camberley GU15 . . . . . 151 B3
Compton RG20 . . . . 31 B2
Gordon Ct 8 RG14 . . . . 105 A2
Gordon Dr TW17 . . . . . 125 B1
Gordon Palmer Cl RG7 . 137 B3
Gordon Palmer Ct RG30 . 85 B4
Gordon Pl RG30 . . . . 85 B4
Gordon Rd Ashford TW15 . 97 C1
Camberley GU15 . . . . . 151 B3
Crowthorne RG45 . . . . 143 A2
Maidenhead SL6 . . . . . 39 B4
Newbury RG14 . . . . . . 105 A1
Shepperton TW17 . . . . 125 B2
Thatcham RG18 . . . . . . 106 A3
Windsor SL4 . . . . 66 C3
Gordon Wlk GU46 . . . . 149 C3
Gordon's Sch GU24 . . . 153 C4
Gore End Rd RG20 . . . . 129 A2
Gore Rd SL1 . . . . 21 A1
Gore The SL1 . . . . 21 A4
Goring CE Prim Sch RG8 . 34 B4
Goring La RG7 . . . . 111 A1
Goring Rd RG8 . . . . 96 C2
Goring & Streatley
Sta RG8 . . . . 34 B3
Gorrick Sq RG41 . . . . . 116 A2
Gorse Bank GU18 . . . . 153 A4
Gorse Cottage Dr RG18 . 79 B1
Gorse Dr RG5 . . . . 88 A4
Gorse Hill La GU25 . . . 122 B3
Gorse Hill Rd GU25 . . . 122 B3
Gorse Meade SL1 . . . . . 42 A3
Gorse Pl RG42 . . . . 92 A1
Gorse Rd Cookham SL6 . 19 C2
Frimley GU15 . . . . 151 C1
Gorse Ride Cty Jun Sch
RG40 . . . . 141 C4
Gorse Ride N RG40 . . . 141 C4
Gorse Ride S RG40 . . . 141 C4
Gorselands
Caversham RG4 . . . . . . 59 A3
Newbury RG14 . . . . . . 130 B3
Tadley RG26 . . . . 135 B3
Yateley GU46 . . . . 149 B2
Gosbrook Ho 1 RG4 . . . 59 B1
Gosbrook Rd RG4 . . . . . 59 B1
Gosden Rd GU24 . . . . . 153 C3
Gosforth Cl RG6 . . . . 87 B1
Goslar Way SL4 . . . . 67 A3
Gosling Gn SL3 . . . . 43 C2
Gosling Rd SL3 . . . . 43 C2
Gosnell Cl GU16 . . . . . . 152 B2
Gossmore Cl SL7 . . . . . . 1 C1
Gossmore La SL7 . . . . . . 1 C1
Gossmore Wlk SL7 . . . . . 1 C1
Goswell Hill SL4 . . . . . . 67 B4
Goswell Rd SL4 . . . . 67 B4
Gothic Ct Harlington UB3 . 71 B4
Sandhurst GU47 . . . . . 150 A4
Gough's La
Bracknell RG12 . . . . . . 118 B4
Reading RG41 . . . . 91 B1
Gough's Mdw GU47 . . . 150 A4
Goughs Barn La RG42 . . 91 A4
Gould Cl RG14 . . . . 105 A2
Gould Rd TW14 . . . . 98 C4
Goulders Cotts RG10 . . . 36 C4
Governor's Rd GU15 . . 151 A3
Govett Ave TW17 . . . . . 125 B2
Govett Gr GU20 . . . . . . 146 B3
Gower Pk GU47 . . . . . . 150 B4
Gower Rd SL4 . . . . 85 C4
Gower The TW20 . . . . . 123 B3
Gowings Gn SL1 . . . . . . 41 C2
Grace Ct SL1 . . . . 42 B3
Grace Reynolds Wlk 4
GU15 . . . . 151 B3
Graces La RG20 . . . . 78 A4
Graffham Ct RG6 . . . . . 114 A4
Grafton Cl Maidenhead SL6 . 19 C1
Slough SL3 . . . . 43 C3
Grafton Ct TW14 . . . . . . 98 B4
Grafton Rd RG30 . . . . . . 85 B4
Graham Cl Blewbury OX11 . 12 A4
Maidenhead SL6 . . . . . 39 B3
Reading RG31 . . . . 84 C2
Graham Rd Cookham SL6 . 19 C2
Maidenhead SL6 . . . . . 39 B3
Grahame Ave RG8 . . . . . 56 B3
Grainford Ct RG40 . . . . 116 B3
Grampian Cl UB3 . . . . . . 71 B4
Grampian Rd GU47 . . . 143 A1
Grampian Way SL3 . . . . 44 A1
Gramps Hill OX12 . . . . . 10 C4
Granby Ct RG1 . . . . 86 C4
Granby End RG7 . . . . . 111 A2
Granby Gdns RG1 . . . . . 86 C4
Grand Ave GU15 . . . . . 151 B3

Grange Ave
Crowthorne RG45 . . . . .143 A3
Reading RG6 . . . . .87 A3
Grange Cl Goring RG8 . . . . . . .34 A3
Wraysbury TW19 . . . . .68 C1
Grange Ct Earley RG6 . . . . .87 A4
Egham TW20 . . . . .95 C2
Littleton TW17 . . . . .125 A3
Newbury RG14 . . . . .105 A1
Staines TW18 . . . . .97 A2
Grange Dr HP10 . . . . .3 B2
Grange Gdns SL2 . . . . .22 B4
Grange La SL6 . . . . .19 C4
Grange Pl TW18 . . . . .124 B4
Grange Rd Bracknell RG12 . . .118 B4
Camberley GU15 . . . . .151 C3
Cookham SL6 . . . . .19 C4
Egham TW20 . . . . .95 C2
Henley-on-T RG9 . . . . .15 C1
Grange The Burnham SL1 . . . . .21 B1
Caversham RG4 . . . . .58 B3
Newbury RG14 . . . . .130 B3
Old Windsor SL4 . . . . .68 A1
Grange Way SL0 . . . . .44 C4
Grangely Cl RG31 . . . . .84 B2
Grangewood SL3 . . . . .43 B4
Grant Ave SL1 . . . . .42 C4
Grant Cl TW17 . . . . .125 A2
Grant Ho 5 SL8 . . . . .3 A2
Grant Rd RG45 . . . . .143 B2
Grant Wlk SL5 . . . . .120 C1
Grantham Cl GU47 . . . . .143 C1
Grantham Ho 6 TW16 . . . . .98 C1
Grantham Rd RG30 . . . . .84 C2
Granthams The RG17 . . . . .25 A2
Grantley Hts 3 RG1 . . . . .86 B4
Granville Ave SL2 . . . . .42 B4
Granville Rd RG30 . . . . .85 A3
Grasholm Way SL3 . . . . .44 B3
Grasmere SL4 . . . . .66 C4
Grasmere Ave
Reading RG30 . . . . .57 C1
Slough SL2 . . . . .43 A3
Grasmere Cl
East Bedfont TW14 . . . . .98 C4
Thorpe Lea TW20 . . . . .96 A1
Grasmere Par SL2 . . . . .43 A3
Grasmere Rd GU18 . . . . .146 A1
Grass Hill RG4 . . . . .58 C2
Grassington Pl RG19 . . . . .106 B2
Grassmead RG19 . . . . .106 C1
Grassmere Cl RG41 . . . . .88 A1
Grassy La SL6 . . . . .39 C4
Grattan Ct SL7 . . . . .2 A2
Gratton Dr SL4 . . . . .66 C2
Gratton Rd RG2 . . . . .113 B4
Gratwicke Rd RG30 . . . . .84 C4
Gravel Hill Caversham RG4 . . . .59 A3
Henley-on-T RG9 . . . . .15 B1
Stockcross RG20 . . . . .103 C3
Gravel Rd RG9 . . . . .35 A1
Gravelly Cl RG20 . . . . .129 A2
Graveney Dr RG4 . . . . .58 C2
Gravett Ct RG9 . . . . .35 B4
Gray Ct SL4 . . . . .66 B3
Gray's Mon SL2 . . . . .22 C1
Gray's Pl SL2 . . . . .42 C3
Gray's Rd SL1 . . . . .42 C3
Grayling Ct SL7 . . . . .1 C3
Grayling Ct RG SL1 . . . . .59 A1
Grays Cres RG5 . . . . .87 B4
Grays Park Rd SL2 . . . . .23 A2
Grays La TW15 . . . . .98 A2
Grays Park Rd SL2 . . . . .23 A2
Grayshot Dr GU17 . . . . .150 B3
**Grazeley Parochial Prim
Sch** RG7 . . . . .112 C1
Grazeley Rd RG7 . . . . .111 A4
Great Auclum Pl RG2 . . . . .111 A1
Great Barn Ct RG19 . . . . .106 B2
Great Hill Cres SL6 . . . . .39 B3
**Great Hollands Jun &
Inf Sch** RG12 . . . . .117 C2
Great Hollands Rd RG12 . . . . .117 C2
Great Hollands Sq RG12 . . . . .117 C2
Great Knollys St RG1 . . . . .85 C4
Great Lea RG7 . . . . .113 A3
Great Marlow Sch SL7 . . . . . . .1 C2
Great Severals RG17 . . . . .102 A1
Great South-West Rd
East Bedfont TW14 . . . . .98 B4
Hatton TW6, TW14 . . . . .71 B1
Grebe Ct TW18 . . . . .97 A2
Green Acre Mount RG30 . . . . .84 B4
Green Bsns Ctr The TW20 . . . .96 B2
Green Cl Burnham SL6 . . . . .41 A4
Maidenhead SL6 . . . . .19 C1
Green Cres HP10 . . . . .3 B4
Green Croft RG40 . . . . .116 C4
Green Ct TW16 . . . . .116 C2
Green Dragon La HP10 . . . . .3 A4
Green End GU46 . . . . .149 B4
Green End Ct RG17 . . . . .113 A1
Green Farm Rd GU19 . . . . .145 C2
Green Farm Rise SN8 . . . . .99 A3
Green Finch Cl RG45 . . . . .142 C3
Green Hill Cl GU15 . . . . .152 B3
Green Hill Rd GU15 . . . . .152 B3
Green La Ascot SL5 . . . . .120 C4
Ashford TW16 . . . . .124 C2
Bagshot GU19 . . . . .145 C1
Blackwater GU17 . . . . .150 A2
Blackwater, Hawley GU17 . . . . .150 C2
Bradfield RG7 . . . . .81 C2
Burghfield Common RG30 . . . . .85 A1

Green La continued
Burnham SL1 . . . . .21 B2
Caversham RG9 . . . . .35 A1
Chieveley RG20 . . . . .78 A4
Datchet SL3 . . . . .68 A3
Egham TW20 . . . . .96 A2
Farnham Common SL2 . . . . .22 A3
Henley-on-T RG9 . . . . .35 A1
Holyport SL6 . . . . .64 A3
Hurst RG10 . . . . .88 C2
Littlewick Green SL6 . . . . .38 A3
Maidenhead SL6 . . . . .40 A3
Newbury RG14 . . . . .104 C1
Padworth RG7 . . . . .110 B1
Pangbourne RG8 . . . . .56 B3
Sandhurst GU47 . . . . .150 B4
Shepperton TW17 . . . . .125 B2
Thatcham RG19 . . . . .106 B2
Thorpe TW18 . . . . .123 C4
Windsor SL4 . . . . .67 A3
Wokingham RG41 . . . . .88 B1
Green Lane Cl GU15 . . . . .151 B4
Green Lane Ct SL1 . . . . .42 C4
Green Leas TW16 . . . . .98 C1
Green Leas Cl TW16 . . . . .98 C1
Green Leys SL6 . . . . .19 C1
Green Pk TW18 . . . . .96 C3
Green Rd Reading RG6 . . . . .87 A3
Thorpe TW20 . . . . .123 A3
Green The
Bracknell RG12 . . . . .118 A3
Burnham SL1 . . . . .21 A1
Chilton OX11 . . . . .10 C4
Datchet SL3 . . . . .68 A4
Kintbury RG17 . . . . .102 A1
Slough SL1 . . . . .42 B2
Staines TW18 . . . . .97 B2
Theale RG7 . . . . .83 B1
Wokingham RG41 . . . . .115 C4
Wooburn Green HP10 . . . . .3 C2
Wraysbury TW19 . . . . .68 C1
Green Verges SL7 . . . . .1 C2
Green Wood SL5 . . . . .119 B4
Greenacre SL4 . . . . .66 C3
Greenacre Ct TW20 . . . . .95 B1
Greenacres RG20 . . . . .129 C1
Greenacres Ave RG41 . . . . .88 A2
Greenacres La RG41 . . . . .88 A2
Greencroft Gdns RG30 . . . . . . .84 C2
Greendale Mews SL2 . . . . .43 A3
Greene Fielde End TW18 . . . . . .97 B1
Greenfern Ave SL1 . . . . .41 B4
Greenfield Way RG45 . . . . .143 A4
Greenfields SL6 . . . . .40 A3
Greenfields Rd RG2 . . . . .113 A4
Greenfinch Cl RG31 . . . . .84 A1
Greenham
Greenham RG19 . . . . .131 B4
Woodley RG5 . . . . .88 A4
Greenham Court Prim Sch
RG14 . . . . .131 A4
Greenham Mill RG14 . . . . .105 A2
Greenham Rd RG14 . . . . .105 A1
Greenham Wood RG12 . . . . . .118 B2
Greenholme GU15 . . . . .152 B3
Greenlands Rd RG12 . . . . .118 A3
Greenidge Cl 5 RG1 . . . . .85 C3
Greenlake Terr TW18 . . . . .97 A1
Greenlands Ball Hill RG20 . . . .129 C1
Flackwell Heath HP10 . . . . .3 A4
Greenlands Ct
Greenham RG19 . . . . .131 B4
Staines TW18 . . . . .39 A4
Greenlands Rd
Camberley GU15 . . . . .151 A1
Newbury RG14 . . . . .105 A1
Staines TW18 . . . . .97 B4
Greenleaf Ct SL3 . . . . .68 A4
Greenleas GU16 . . . . .151 C1
Greenleas Ave RG4 . . . . .59 A4
Greenleas Cl GU46 . . . . .149 B4
Greenleaves Ct TW15 . . . . .98 A1
Greeno Cres TW17 . . . . .125 A2
Greenock Rd SL1 . . . . .42 A4
Greenside Bourne End SL8 . . . . .3 A3
Crowthorne RG45 . . . . .142 C3
Slough SL2 . . . . .42 A4
Greensward La RG2 . . . . .114 B1
Greenview Ct TW15 . . . . .97 C2
Greenway Dr TW18 . . . . .124 B4
Greenway The
Fawley OX12 . . . . .27 A4
Slough SL1 . . . . .41 B3
Greenways Ball Hill RG20 . . . .129 C1
Egham TW20 . . . . .95 C2
Lambourn RG17 . . . . .25 A1
Sandhurst GU47 . . . . .143 A1
Greenways Dr
Maidenhead SL6 . . . . .39 A4
Sunningdale SL5 . . . . .120 C2
Greenwood 2 RG12 . . . . .118 C3
Greenwood Gr RG41 . . . . .88 B2
Greenwood Rd
Crowthorne RG45 . . . . .143 A3
Reading RG30 . . . . .84 C3
Gregory Cl SL6 . . . . .114 B4
Gregory Dr SL4 . . . . .68 A1
Grenfell Ave SL6 . . . . .39 C3
Grenfell Pl SL6 . . . . .39 C3
Grenfell Rd SL6 . . . . .39 C3
Grenville Ct SL1 . . . . .21 A2
Gresham Ct TW18 . . . . .97 A2
Gresham Rd Slough SL1 . . . . . .42 A4
Staines TW18 . . . . .97 A2
Gresham Way RG30 . . . . .58 A1

Greyberry Copse Rd
RG19 . . . . .131 B4
Greyfriars Dr SL5 . . . . .120 A2
Greyfriars Rd RG1 . . . . .86 A4
Greys Ct 8 RG2 . . . . .86 B4
Greys Hill RG9 . . . . .15 B1
Greys Rd RG9 . . . . .15 B1
Greystoke Ct RG45 . . . . .143 A2
Greystoke Ho 9 RG1 . . . . .85 C3
Greystoke Rd
Caversham RG4 . . . . .59 B2
Slough SL2 . . . . .41 C4
Griffin Cl Maidenhead SL6 . . . .39 C1
Slough SL1 . . . . .42 B2
Griffiths Cl RG19 . . . . .106 C1
Grindle Cl RG18 . . . . .106 B2
Gringer Hill SL6 . . . . .39 C2
Groombridge Pl RG14 . . . . . . .104 C3
Grosvenor Cl
Blackwater GU17 . . . . .150 B2
Slough SL1 . . . . .42 C4
Grosvenor Dr SL6 . . . . .40 B3
Grosvenor Lawn RG14 . . . . . . .104 C1
Grosvenor Rd
Caversham RG4 . . . . .59 B2
Staines TW18 . . . . .97 A3
Grove Cl Old Windsor SL4 . . . . .95 A4
Slough SL3 . . . . .43 A2
Wokingham RG40 . . . . .142 C4
Grove Cotts SL6 . . . . .2 A1
Grove Cross Rd GU16 . . . . . . .151 C1
Grove Ct Egham TW20 . . . . .96 A2
Maidenhead SL6 . . . . .39 C4
Slough SL3 . . . . .43 A2
Grove Cty Prim Sch The
GU16 . . . . .151 C1
Grove End GU19 . . . . .145 C3
Grove Hill RG4 . . . . .59 A2
Old Windsor SL4 . . . . .95 A4
Grove Ho Ashford TW15 . . . . . .97 C2
Slough SL3 . . . . .43 A2
Grove Pk SL6 . . . . .63 C4
Grove Rd Burnham SL1 . . . . . . .21 C2
Camberley GU15 . . . . .151 C3
Caversham RG4 . . . . .59 A3
Henley-on-T RG9 . . . . .15 C1
Maidenhead SL6 . . . . .39 C4
Newbury RG14 . . . . .104 C3
Shepperton TW17 . . . . .125 B2
Grove The Egham TW20 . . . . . .96 A2
Frimley GU16 . . . . .151 B1
Northmead SL5 . . . . .17 C3
North Ascot SL5 . . . . .119 B4
Reading RG1 . . . . .86 B4
Slough SL1 . . . . .43 A2
Twyford RG10 . . . . .61 B3
Grovebarns TW18 . . . . .97 A1
Grovefields Ave GU16 . . . . . . .151 B1
Groveland Pl RG30 . . . . .85 A4
Groveland Rd RG14 . . . . .104 C3
Grovelands Ave RG41 . . . . .88 B1
Grovelands Cl RG41 . . . . .88 B2
Grovelands Rd
Reading RG30 . . . . .85 A4
Shinfield RG7 . . . . .113 B1
Groveley Rd TW13, TW16 . . . . .98 C2
Groves Cl SL8 . . . . .3 B2
Groves Lea RG7 . . . . .136 C3
Groves The RG17 . . . . .73 A1
Groves Way SL6 . . . . .19 C3
Grubwood La SL6 . . . . .18 A4
Guards Club Rd SL6 . . . . .40 B4
Guards Ct SL5 . . . . .121 A1
Guards Rd SL4 . . . . .66 B3
Guards Wlk 1 SL6 . . . . .66 B3
Guerdon Pl RG12 . . . . .118 B1
Guildford Ave TW13 . . . . .98 C3
Guildford Rd
Bagshot GU19 . . . . .145 C1
Chertsey KT16 . . . . .123 C1
Lightwater GU18 . . . . .146 A1
Slough SL1 . . . . .42 A4
Guildford St
Chertsey KT16 . . . . .124 A1
Staines TW18 . . . . .97 A1
Gullane Ct 11 RG1 . . . . .86 A4
Gun St RG1 . . . . .86 A4
Gunthorpe Rd SL7 . . . . .2 A2
Gurney Cl RG42 . . . . .58 B3
Gurney Dr RG4 . . . . .58 B3
Gwendale SL6 . . . . .19 B1
Gwendoline Ct TW15 . . . . .97 C2
Gwent Cl SL7 . . . . .1 B2
Gwent Ct SL6 . . . . .39 A2
Gwyn Cl RG14 . . . . .130 C4
Gwynne Cl
Purley on T RG31 . . . . .57 B2
Windsor SL4 . . . . .66 C3
Gwyns Piece RG17 . . . . .25 C2
Gypsy La Marlow SL7 . . . . .1 C2
Stoke Poges SL2 . . . . .22 C4

H

Habershon Dr GU16 . . . . .152 B1
Haddon Cl RG42 . . . . .90 B1
Haddon Dr RG5 . . . . .87 C4
Haddon Rd SL6 . . . . .39 B3
Hadleigh Rise RG4 . . . . .59 C4
Hadley Ct SL3 . . . . .69 C3

Hadlow Ct SL1 . . . . .42 B3
Hadrian Cl TW19 . . . . .97 C4
Hadrian Way TW19 . . . . .97 B4
Hadrian Wlk E RG2 . . . . .86 B2
Hadrian Wlk W RG2 . . . . .86 B2
Hafod RG4 . . . . .58 C3
Hag Hill La SL6 . . . . .41 A4
Hag Hill Rise SL6 . . . . .41 A4
Hagley Rd RG2 . . . . .86 A2
Haig Dr SL1 . . . . .42 A2
Haig Rd GU15 . . . . .150 C3
Hailey La RG20 . . . . .29 C1
Haileybury Ct SL4 . . . . .42 C2
Hailsham Cl GU47 . . . . .143 B1
Halcyon Ct TW18 . . . . .124 A4
Halcyon Terr RG30 . . . . .84 C4
Haldane Rd RG4 . . . . .58 C3
Hale SL4 . . . . .66 C3
Hale End RG12 . . . . .118 C3
Hale St TW18 . . . . .96 C2
Halewood RG12 . . . . .117 C2
Half Mile Rd RG17 . . . . .46 A1
Half Moon St GU19 . . . . .145 C2
Halfacre Cl RG7 . . . . .113 A2
Halfpenny La SL5 . . . . .121 A1
Halfpenny La Cholsey OX10 . . .13 B3
Sunningdale SL5 . . . . .121 A1
Halfway Hos SL6 . . . . .18 C2
Halifax Cl SL6 . . . . .39 A4
Halifax Pl RG18 . . . . .106 B2
Halifax Rd SL6 . . . . .39 A4
Halifax Way SL6 . . . . .39 A4
Halkingcroft SL3 . . . . .43 B2
Hall Cl GU15 . . . . .151 C3
Hall Ct SL3 . . . . .68 A4
Hall Farm Cres GU46 . . . . .149 B3
Hall Grove (Sch) GU19 . . . . . . .146 A3
Hall La Harlington UB3 . . . . .71 B4
Yateley GU46 . . . . .149 B3
Hall Mdw SL1 . . . . .21 A2
Hall Pl La SL6 . . . . .38 A4
Hallbrook Gdns RG42 . . . . .90 C1
Halldore Hill SL6 . . . . .19 C4
Halley Dr SL5 . . . . .119 A4
Hallgrove Bottom GU19 . . . . .145 C3
Halliford Cl TW17 . . . . .125 C3
Halliford Rd TW16, TW17 . . . .125 C3
Halliford Sch TW17 . . . . .125 B3
Hallmark Cl GU47 . . . . .150 C4
Halls La Earley RG2 . . . . .86 C1
Waltham St Lawrence RG10 . . . .62 A4
Halls Rd RG30 . . . . .84 B3
Halpin Cl RG31 . . . . .59 A1
Halstead Cl RG5 . . . . .87 C4
Halstead Ho RG26 . . . . .134 C1
Halters The RG14 . . . . .131 A4
Ham Island SL4 . . . . .68 B2
Ham La
Englefield Green TW20 . . . . .95 A2
Old Windsor SL4 . . . . .68 B2
Hamble Ct 10 RG1 . . . . .86 A3
Hamblewood RG12 . . . . .118 C3
Hambleden Ct RG12 . . . . .118 C3
Hambleden Mill RG9 . . . . .16 B4
Hambleden Pl RG9 . . . . .16 B3
Hambledon Rise RG9 . . . . .16 B4
Hambledon Wlk SL6 . . . . .19 C1
Hambledon Cl RG6 . . . . .87 A1
Hambleton Ct GU16 . . . . .152 A2
Hambridge Mdw RG17 . . . . . .100 C4
Hambridge Rd RG14 . . . . .105 B1
Hamhaugh Island TW17 . . . . .125 B1
Hamfield Cotts SL6 . . . . .19 A4
Hamilton Ave RG9 . . . . .15 C1
Hamilton Ct GU19 . . . . .98 C2
Hamilton Ct
Farnborough (Hants) GU17 . . . .150 C1
Newbury RG14 . . . . .131 A4
Hamilton Dr SL5 . . . . .121 A4
Hamilton Gdns SL1 . . . . .21 A1
Hamilton Pk SL6 . . . . .39 A3
Hamilton Rd Feltham TW13 . . . .98 C2
Reading RG6 . . . . .86 C3
Slough SL1 . . . . .42 A4
Wargrave RG10 . . . . .36 C4
Hamlet St RG42 . . . . .118 C4
Hammond Cl RG19 . . . . .106 C1
Hammond Ct RG42 . . . . .91 A1
Hammond End SL2 . . . . .22 A4
Hammond Jun Sch
GU18 . . . . .146 A1
Hammond Way GU18 . . . . .146 A1
Hammonds Heath RG7 . . . . . .137 A3
Hammondswood Rd
GU18 . . . . .23 A1
Hampden Rd
Caversham RG4 . . . . .59 A2
Maidenhead SL6 . . . . .39 C4
Slough SL3 . . . . .43 C2
Hampdens The RG14 . . . . .130 B3
Hampshire Ave SL1 . . . . .42 B4
Hampshire Lodge 8 SL6 . . . . . .39 C3
Hampshire Rise RG42 . . . . .91 A1
Hampshire Way RG41 . . . . .88 A4
Hampshire Wlk RG31 . . . . .84 A4
Hampstead Ct RG30 . . . . .85 A4
Hampstead Norreys
CE Prim Sch** RG18 . . . . .52 C3
Hampstead Norreys Rd
RG18 . . . . .79 A1
Hampton Ho SL3 . . . . .43 A3
Hampton Rd RG2 . . . . .86 C2
Hampton Rd RG2 . . . . .104 C1
Hampton Twrs 4 RG30 . . . . . . .85 B3

Hanbury Cl SL1 41
Hanbury Dr RG31 84
Hanbury Way GU15 151
Hanbury Wlk RG19 106
Hancocks Mount SL5 120
Hancombe Rd GU47 143
Handford La GU46 149
Hanger Rd RG26 134
Hangerfield Cl GU46 149
Hangmans Stone La RG20 49
Hanley Cl SL4 66
Hannibal Rd TW19 97
Hanningtons Way RG7 111
Hanover Cl
Englefield Green TW20 95
Windsor SL4 151
Slough SL1 43
Windsor SL4 66
Hanover Ct Caversham RG4 59
Reading RG30 84
Hanover Gdns RG12 117
Hanover Mead
Maidenhead SL6 40
Newbury RG14 130
Hanover Way SL4 66
Hanson Cl GU15 152
Hanwood Cl RG5 87
Hanworth Cl RG12 118
Hanworth La KT16 123
Hanworth Rd RG12 118
Hanworth Trad Est KT16 123
Harborough Cl SL1 41
Harbury Cl RG42 105
Harcourt TW19 68
Harcourt Cl Dorney SL4 40
Egham TW20 96
Harcourt Dr RG6 87
Harcourt Rd
Bracknell RG12 118
Camberley GU15 151
Dorney SL4 40
Windsor SL4 66
Hardell Cl TW20 96
Harding Rd RG5 87
Hardwell Way RG12 118
Hardwick Cl SL6 39
Hardwick La KT16 123
Hardwick Rd Reading RG30 . . .84
Whitchurch-on-T RG8 56
Hardy Av GU46 149
Hardy Cl Caversham RG4 59
Slough SL1 42
Thatcham RG18 106
Hardy Gn RG45 143
Hare Shoots SL6 39
Harebell Dr RG18 106
Harefield Cl RG41 88
Harefield Rd SL6 39
Harewood Dr RG18 106
Harewood Pl SL1 43
Hargrave Rd SL6 39
Hargreaves Way RG31 84
Harkness Rd SL1 41
Harlech Ave RG4 59
Harlech Rd GU17 150
Harley Rd RG4 59
Harlington Cl UB3 71
Harlington Cnr UB3 71
Harlton Cl RG6 114
Harmans Water
Cty Inf Sch** RG12 118
Harmans Water Rd RG12 118
Harmar Cl RG40 116
Harmondsworth La UB7 70
Harmondsworth Prim Sch
UB7 70
Harness Cl RG2 113
Harold Rd RG17 102
Harpesford Ave GU25 122
Harpsden Rd RG9 35
Harpsden Way RG9 35
Harpton Cl GU46 149
Harrier Cl RG5 88
Harrington Cl Earley RG6 87
Windsor SL4 105
Harris Arc 5 RG1 86
Harris Cl Lambourn RG17 25
Woodley RG5 88
Harrison Cl RG10 61
Harrison Ct TW17 125
Harrison Way SL1 41
Harrogate Ct SL3 44
Harrogate Rd RG4 58
Harrow Bottom Rd GU25 122
Harrow Cl SL6 19
Harrow Ct RG1 85
Harrow La SL6 19
Harrow Mkt The SL3 44
Harrow Rd
Ashford TW14,TW15 98
Harrow Way TW17 125
Harry Tee Ct 11 RG1 85
Hart Cl RG42 90
Hart Dene Cl GU19 145
Hart Dyke Cl RG41 116
Hart St Henley-on-T RG9 15
Reading RG1 85
Hartford Rise GU15 151
Hartigan Pl RG5 88
Hartland Cl SL1 42
Hartland Ct RG2 86
Hartley Cl
Blackwater GU17 150

artley Cl continued
toke Poges SL3 . . . . 23 B2
artley Copse SL4 . . . . 68 A1
artley Court Rd RG7 . . . . . . 112 C3
artley Way RG18 . . . . 106 C2
artmead Rd RG19 . . . . 106 C2
arts Cl RG2 . . . . 114 C1
arts Hill Rd RG18 . . . . 106 C2
arts La RG7 . . . . 110 B3
arts Leap Cl GU47 . . . . 143 A1
arts Leap Rd GU47 . . . . 150 A4
artsbourne Rd RG6 . . . . 87 A2
artshill Rd RG26 . . . . 134 C1
artslock Ct RG8 . . . . 56 A3
artslock Way RG6 . . . . 34 C1
artslock Way RG31 . . . . 57 B1
artvale Ct GU15 . . . . 152 A4
arvard Cl RG5 . . . . 88 A4
arvard Rd GU47 . . . . 143 C1
arvest Cl Reading RG31 . . . . 84 A3
arvest Gn RG14 . . . . 104 C1
arvest Hill SL8 . . . . 3 B1
arvest Hill Rd SL6 . . . . 39 C2
arvest Rd TW20 . . . . 95 B1
arvest Ride
  rackneil RG42 . . . . 91 A1
  winkfield RG12, RG42, SL5 . 119 A4
arvey Ho 11 RG30 . . . . 85 B3
arvey Rd SL3 . . . . 43 B3
archurst Int Bsns Ctr OX11 . . . 9 C4
arwich Cl 8 RG6 . . . . 87 B1
arwich Rd SL1 . . . . 42 A4
arwood Gdns SL4 . . . . 95 A4
arwood Rd SL7 . . . . 1 B1
arwood Rise RG20 . . . . 129 C1
aslemere Cl GU16 . . . . 152 B2
aslemere Rd SL4 . . . . 67 A3
aslett Rd TW17 . . . . 125 C4
asting Cl SL6 . . . . 40 B1
astings Mdw SL2 . . . . 23 A2
atch Cl RG7 . . . . 108 B4
atch End GU20 . . . . 146 B2
atch La Bucklebury RG7 . . . 108 B4
  urgfield Common RG20 . . . 111 B3
  armondsworth TW6, UB7 . . . 70 B4
  Windsor SL4 . . . . 67 A3
atch Ride
  rowthorne RG45 . . . . 143 A4
  wokingham GU46 . . . . 142 C4
atch Ride Cty Prim Sch
  G45 . . . . 143 A4
atch The SL4 . . . . 66 B4
atchet La SL4, SL5 . . . . 93 A3
atchets La RG18 . . . . 80 B4
atchett Rd TW14 . . . . 98 B4
atchgate Cl RG18 . . . . 106 B4
atchgate Copse RG12 . . . . . 117 C2
atchgate Gdns SL1 . . . . 21 B1
atchgate Rd RG12 . . . . 113 B4
atfield Cl SL6 . . . . 39 B3
atfield Ct RG31 . . . . 84 A2
atfield Rd SL1 . . . . 43 A2
atford Rd RG30 . . . . 85 A2
atherley Rd RG1 . . . . 86 C3
atherwood GU46 . . . . 149 C1
att Cl RG20 . . . . 50 B4
atton Ave SL2 . . . . 22 C3
atton Cross Rdbt TW6 . . . . . 71 C2
atton Cross Sta TW6 . . . . . . 71 C2
atton Ct SL4 . . . . 67 B3
atton Hill
  ashampstead RG8 . . . . 54 A4
  undlesham GU20 . . . . 146 B3
atton Rd
  ast Bedfont TW14 . . . . 98 B4
  eltham TW14, TW6 . . . . 71 C1
  aughurst Hill RG26 . . . . . . 134 B1
avelock Cres SL6 . . . . 39 A4
avelock Rd
  Maidenhead SL6 . . . . 39 A4
  Wokingham RG41 . . . . 116 A3
avelock St SL4 . . . . 67 A3
aven Ct 8 RG1 . . . . 86 B4
aven Of Rest SL4 . . . . 40 A4
aven Rd TW15 . . . . 98 A3
aven The RG17 . . . . 102 A1
aversham Dr RG12 . . . . 118 A2
aw La Aldworth RG8 . . . . 32 C1
  ashampstead RG8,RG18 . . . 53 C4
awk La RG12 . . . . 118 B3
awkchurch Rd RG2 . . . . 113 B2
awkedale Fst Sch
  W16 . . . . 125 C3
awkedon Prim Sch RG6 . . . . 87 C1
awkedon Way RG6 . . . . 87 C1
awker Ct SL3 . . . . 44 A2
awker Way RG5 . . . . 88 A4
awkes Cl RG41 . . . . 116 A4
awkes Leap GU20 . . . . 146 A2
awkesbury Dr RG31 . . . . 84 C2
awksworth Dr GU19 . . . . . . 145 C1
awkins Cl RG12 . . . . 119 A4
awkins Way RG40 . . . . 116 C3
awkins Way RG12 . . . . 118 C3
awks Hill SL8 . . . . 3 B1
awkshill Rd SL2 . . . . 2 A4
awksway TW18 . . . . 96 C3
awkswood Ave GU16 . . . . . 151 C1
awkswood Ho RG42 . . . . . . 117 C4
awkswood La SL3 . . . . 23 C4
awksworth Rd RG7 . . . . 136 A4
awley Cl RG31 . . . . 84 B2
awley Garden Cotts
  GU17 . . . . 150 B2
awley Gn GU17 . . . . 150 C2

Hawley La GU14,GU17 . . . . 151 A1
Hawley Lodge GU17 . . . . . . 150 C1
Hawley Place Ind Sch
  GU17 . . . . 150 C1
Hawley Prim Sch GU17 . . . 150 C2
Hawley Rd GU17 . . . . 150 C2
Hawley Way SL1 . . . . 98 A2
Hawthorn Cl
  Bracknell RG42 . . . . 118 A4
  Marlow SL7 . . . . 1 C2
Hawthorn Gdns RG2 . . . . . . 86 C1
Hawthorn La Burnham SL2 . . 22 A3
  Newell Green, Hawthorn
  Hill RG42 . . . . 91 C4
  Newell Green,
  Nuptown RG42 . . . . 92 A4
Hawthorn Rd
  Frimley GU16 . . . . 151 C1
  Newbury RG14 . . . . 105 A2
Hawthorn Way
  Sonning RG4 . . . . 60 C2
  Upper Halliford TW17 . . . . 125 B3
Hawthorne Ave SL4 . . . . 93 A3
Hawthorne Cres
  Blackwater GU17 . . . . 150 C2
  Slough SL1 . . . . 42 C4
Hawthorne Ct TW19 . . . . 97 B4
Hawthorne Dr SL4 . . . . 93 A4
Hawthorne Rd
  Caversham RG4 . . . . 59 C2
  Egham TW20 . . . . 96 B2
Hawthorne Way
  Great Shefford RG17 . . . . . 48 A2
  Stanwell TW19 . . . . 97 B4
  Winkfield SL4 . . . . 93 A4
Hawthornes RG31 . . . . 57 A2
Hawthorns Prim Sch The
  RG41 . . . . 115 C4
Hawthorns The
  Charvil RG10 . . . . 61 A2
  Flackwell Heath HP10 . . . . . 3 A4
  Poyle SL3 . . . . 69 C3
  Wooburn Green HP10 . . . . . 3 C3
Hawtrey Cl SL1 . . . . 43 A2
Hawtrey Rd SL4 . . . . 67 B3
Hay La SL3 . . . . 23 B4
Hay Rd SL1 . . . . 85 C3
Haydon Cl SL6 . . . . 39 C3
Haydon Pl GU46 . . . . 149 C3
Hayes La RG41 . . . . 115 B2
Hayes Pl SL7 . . . . 1 B1
Hayfield Cl RG31 . . . . 84 A4
Hayfield Ct RG17 . . . . 46 C3
Hayley Gn RG42 . . . . 91 C2
Haymill Rd SL1,SL2 . . . . 21 B1
Haynes Cl SL3 . . . . 43 C1
Hayse Hill SL4 . . . . 66 B3
Hayward Pl SL8 . . . . 3 B1
Haywards Cl RG9 . . . . 15 B1
Haywards Mead SL4 . . . . . . 41 C1
Haywards The RG18 . . . . . . 106 B2
Haywood RG12 . . . . 118 B1
Haywood Ct RG1 . . . . 86 C4
Haywood Way RG30 . . . . . . 84 C4
Hazel Cl
  Burghfield Common RG30 . 111 A3
  Englefield Green TW20 . . . . 95 A1
  Marlow Bottom SL7 . . . . 1 B3
  Wokingham RG41 . . . . 115 C3
Hazel Cres RG2 . . . . 86 C1
Hazel Dr RG5 . . . . 87 B3
Hazel Gn RG26 . . . . 134 B1
Hazel Gr Stanes TW18 . . . . . 97 B1
  Thatcham RG18 . . . . 106 B3
Hazel Rd RG8 . . . . 57 B2
Hazelbank RG40 . . . . 141 C3
Hazelbank Ct KT16 . . . . 124 B1
Hazelbank Rd KT16 . . . . . . 124 B1
Hazeldene RG20 . . . . 51 A1
Hazelhurst Rd SL1 . . . . 21 B2
Hazell Cl SL6 . . . . 39 C4
Hazell Hill RG12 . . . . 118 B3
Hazell Way SL2 . . . . 22 C3
Hazelmere Ct TW14 . . . . 71 C1
Hazelmere Rd SL2 . . . . 43 A3
Hazels Paddock RG18 . . . . 106 B4
Hazelwood Cl RG31 . . . . 57 B1
Hazelwood La RG42 . . . . . . 90 C2
Heacham Cl RG6 . . . . 114 A4
Headington Cl
  Maidenhead SL6 . . . . 39 A4
  Wokingham RG40 . . . . 116 B4
Headington Dr RG40 . . . . . 116 B4
Headington Rd SL6 . . . . 39 A4
Headington Way
  Headley RG5 . . . . 88 A4
Headley Park Ind Est RG5 . . 87 C4
Headley Rd RG5 . . . . 87 C4
Headley Rd E RG5 . . . . 88 A4
Heads La RG17 . . . . 118 C2
Heardman Cl RG19 . . . . 106 C1
Hearmon Cl GU46 . . . . 149 C3
Hearn Rd RG5 . . . . 87 C3
Hearn Wlk RG12 . . . . 118 C4
Hearsey Gdns GU17 . . . . . . 150 B3
Heath Cl Harlington UB3 . . . . 71 B4
  Stanwell TW19 . . . . 70 B1
  Virginia Water GU25 . . . . . 122 B3
  Wokingham RG41 . . . . 116 A3
Heath Ct GU15 . . . . 152 A2
Heath Dr RG9 . . . . 15 A1
Heath End Rd RG26 . . . . . . 134 C1
Heath Gr TW16 . . . . 98 B1
Heath Hill Rd N RG45 . . . . . 143 A2
Heath Hill Rd S RG45 . . . . . 143 A2
Heath La RG18 . . . . 106 B3
Heath Rd Bagshot GU19 . . . 145 C2

Heath Rd continued
  Bradfield RG7 . . . . 82 A1
  Reading RG6 . . . . 87 A3
  Silchester RG26 . . . . 135 C1
Heath Rise
  Camberley GU15 . . . . 151 B3
  Virginia Water GU25 . . . . . 122 B3
Heathacre SL3 . . . . 69 C3
Heathcote SL6 . . . . 40 A1
Heathcote Ct 8 SL6 . . . . 67 B2
Heathcote Rd GU15 . . . . . . 151 B3
Heathcroft Ave TW16 . . . . . . 98 C1
Heather Cl RG40 . . . . 141 C4
Heather Dr
  Sunningdale SL5 . . . . 121 A1
  Tadley RG26 . . . . 134 C1
  Thatcham RG18 . . . . 106 B3
Heather Gdns RG14 . . . . . . 130 C4
Heather Mead SL6 . . . . 151 C1
Heather Mead Ct GU16 . . . 151 C1
Heather Ridge Arc GU15 . . 152 A2
Heather Ridge Cty Inf Sch
  GU15 . . . . 152 B2
Heatherdale Rd GU15 . . . . 151 B2
Heatherden Cl RG2 . . . . 113 B4
Heatherden Ave RG45 . . . . 142 C2
Heatherley Cl GU15 . . . . . . 151 A3
Heatherley Rd GU15 . . . . . . 151 A3
Heathermount 4 RG12 . . . 118 C3
Heathermount Dr RG45 . . . 143 A3
Heathermount Sch SL5 . . . 120 B2
Heathers The TW19 . . . . 97 C4
Heatherside Dr GU25 . . . . . 122 A2
Heatherway RG45 . . . . 143 A3
Heathermead Hospl SL5 . . 119 C3
Heathfield RG7 . . . . 137 A3
Heathfield Ave Ascot SL5 . . 120 C2
  Reading RG30 . . . . 84 B3
  Shiplake RG9 . . . . 35 A1
Heathfield Cl RG9 . . . . 35 A1
Heathfield Ct TW15 . . . . 97 C3
Heathfield Rd SL1 . . . . 3 C1
Heathfield Sch SL5 . . . . 119 A4
Heathfields RG20 . . . . 78 A4
Heathlands RG26 . . . . 134 C1
Heathlands Country Mkt
  RG40 . . . . 116 C1
Heathlands Dr RG40 . . . . . . 142 C4
Heathlands Dr SL6 . . . . 39 A3
Heathlands Rd RG40 . . . . . 116 C1
Heathmoors RG12 . . . . 118 B2
Heathpark Dr GU20 . . . . . . 146 C2
Heathrow Airport London
  TW6 . . . . 71 A3
Heathrow Airport
  Visitor Ctr TW6 . . . . 71 B3
Heathrow Bvd UB7 . . . . 70 C4
Heathrow Central Sta
  TW6 . . . . 71 A2
Heathrow Cl TW6 . . . . 70 B2
Heathrow Copse RG26 . . . . 134 B1
Heathrow Sch UB7 . . . . 70 C4
Heathrow Terminal 4 Sta
  TW6 . . . . 71 B1
Heathside Pk GU15 . . . . . . 152 B4
Heathway
  Camberley GU15 . . . . 151 B3
  North Ascot SL5 . . . . 119 C4
  Reading RG31 . . . . 84 B4
Heathway Cl GU15 . . . . 151 B3
Heathwood Cl GU46 . . . . . . 149 B4
Heavens Lea SL8 . . . . 3 A1
Hebbecastle Down RG42 . . . 91 A1
Hebden La RG12 . . . . 106 B1
Hedge Lea HP10 . . . . 3 A4
Hedgeway RG14 . . . . 130 B3
Hedingham Mews SL6 . . . . . 39 B4
Hedley Rd HP10 . . . . 3 A4
Hedsor Hill SL8 . . . . 3 B2
Hedsor La HP10,SL1 . . . . 3 C1
Hedsor Rd SL8 . . . . 3 B1
Hedsor View Cotts SL8 . . . . 19 C4
Heelas Rd RG41 . . . . 116 A3
Heights The
  Camberley GU15 . . . . 151 C3
  Marlow SL7 . . . . 1 B4
Helen Cotts SL4 . . . . 66 B3
Helena Rd SL4 . . . . 67 B3
Helgiford Gdns TW16 . . . . . . 98 C1
Helksham Cl GU47 . . . . 143 B1
Hellyer Way SL8 . . . . 3 B2
Helmsdale RG12 . . . . 118 C2
Helmsdale Cl RG30 . . . . 85 A4
Helston Gdns RG2 . . . . 86 A1
Helston La SL4 . . . . 67 A3
Helvellyn Cl TW20 . . . . 96 A1
Hemdean Hill RG4 . . . . 59 A2
Hemdean House Sch RG4 . . 59 A2
Hemdean Rd RG4 . . . . 59 A2
Hemdean Rise RG4 . . . . 59 A2
Hemming Way SL2 . . . . 22 A1
Hemmyng Gnr RG42 . . . . . . 91 B1
Hempson Ave SL3 . . . . 43 B2
Hemsdale SL6 . . . . 19 A1
Hemwood Rd SL4 . . . . 66 B2
Hencroft St N SL1 . . . . 42 C2
Hencroft St S SL1 . . . . 42 C2
Hendon Terr TW15 . . . . 98 B1
Hendon Way TW19 . . . . 70 B1
Hendons Way SL6 . . . . 40 A1
Hengrave Cl RG6 . . . . 87 C1
Hengrove Cres TW15 . . . . . . 97 B2
Henley Coll The
  (Deanfield Bldgs) RG9 . . . . 15 B1
Henley Coll The
  (Rotherfield Bldgs) RG9 . . . 15 B1

Henley Coll The
  (Southfield Bldgs) RG9 . . . 15 B1
Henley Gdns GU46 . . . . 149 B3
Henley Lodge 12 SL6 . . . . . 39 C3
Henley Rd Bisham SL6 . . . . 18 B4
  Caversham RG4 . . . . 59 B2
  Hurley SL6 . . . . 17 B2
  Marlow SL7 . . . . 18 A4
  Shiplake RG9 . . . . 60 B4
  Slough SL1 . . . . 41 C4
Henley Trinity Prim Sch
  RG9 . . . . 15 B1
Henley Wood Rd RG6 . . . . . 87 B2
Henley-on-Thames Sta
  RG9 . . . . 15 C1
Henry Ct 22 RG1 . . . . 86 B4
Henry Rd SL1 . . . . 42 B2
Henry St RG1 . . . . 86 A3
Henrys The RG18 . . . . 106 B2
Henshaw Cres RG14 . . . . . . 130 B4
Hensworth Rd TW15 . . . . . . 97 B2
Henwick Cl RG18 . . . . 106 A3
Henwick La RG18 . . . . 106 A2
Henwood Copse RG8 . . . . . 55 A3
Hepplewhite Cl RG26 . . . . . 134 C1
Hepworth Croft GU47 . . . . 150 C3
Hepworth Way KT12 . . . . . . 125 C1
Herald Way RG5 . . . . 88 A3
Herbert Cl RG12 . . . . 118 A2
Hereford Cl TW14 . . . . 124 A4
Herewood Cl RG14 . . . . 104 C2
Heriot Rd KT16 . . . . 124 A1
Heritage Ct
  2 Egham TW20 . . . . 96 A2
  27 Reading RG1 . . . . 85 C4
Hermitage Cl
  Frimley GU16 . . . . 151 C1
  Littleton TW17 . . . . 125 A3
  Slough SL3 . . . . 43 B2
Hermitage Ct TW16 . . . . 98 B1
Hermitage Cty Prim Sch
  RG18 . . . . 79 A4
Hermitage Dr
  North Ascot SL5 . . . . 119 C4
  Twyford RG10 . . . . 61 B3
Hermitage La SL4 . . . . 67 A2
Hermitage Par SL5 . . . . 120 A3
Hermitage Rd RG18 . . . . . . 79 A1
Hermitage The
  Feltham TW13 . . . . 98 C3
  Lambourn RG17 . . . . 46 C4
  Marlow SL7 . . . . 1 C2
  Mirists Hill RG17 . . . . 111 B2
Herndon Cl TW20 . . . . 96 A2
Heroes Wlk RG2 . . . . 113 A4
Heron Cl SL5 . . . . 119 B4
Heron Ct Stanes TW18 . . . . . 97 C4
  Stanwell TW19 . . . . 97 C4
Heron Dr Slough SL3 . . . . . . 44 A1
  Twyford RG10 . . . . 61 C3
Heron Ho RG14 . . . . 105 B2
Heron Island RG4 . . . . 59 B1
Heron Rd RG41 . . . . 115 C3
Heron Shaw RG8 . . . . 34 B4
Heron Way
  Burghfield Common RG1 . . . 85 C2
  Padworth RG7 . . . . 109 A2
  Thatcham RG19 . . . . 106 B2
Heron's Way RG40 . . . . 116 C4
Herondale RG12 . . . . 118 B1
Heronfield TW20 . . . . 95 B1
Herongate RG17 . . . . 100 B4
Herons Pl SL7 . . . . 1 C2
Heronscourt GU18 . . . . 153 B4
Herrick Cl GU16 . . . . 152 B2
Herrings La GU20 . . . . 146 B2
Herriot Ct GU46 . . . . 149 B2
Herschel Gram Sch SL1 . . . 42 B3
Herschel Grange RG42 . . . . 91 B2
Herschel Park Dr SL1 . . . . . 42 C2
Herschel St SL1 . . . . 42 C2
Hertford Cl Caversham RG4 . 59 B3
  Wokingham RG41 . . . . 115 C3
Hetherington Cl SL2 . . . . . . 21 C3
Hetherington Rd TW17 . . . 125 B4
Hever Cl SL6 . . . . 39 B3
Hewett Ave RG4 . . . . 58 B2
Hewett Cl RG4 . . . . 58 B2
Hewgate Ct RG9 . . . . 15 C1
Hewlett Pl GU19 . . . . 145 C2
Hexham Cl GU47 . . . . 143 B1
Hexham Rd RG2 . . . . 86 B2
Heynes Gn SL6 . . . . 39 A2
Heywood Dr GU19 . . . . 145 B2
Heywood Ave SL6 . . . . 39 A1
Heywood Court Cl SL6 . . . . 39 A1
Heywood Gdns SL6 . . . . 39 A1
Hibbert Rd SL6 . . . . 40 A2
Hibbert's Alley 2 SL4 . . . . . 67 B3
Hickox Cl HP10 . . . . 3 A3
Hicks La GU17 . . . . 150 A3
Higgs La GU19 . . . . 145 A2
High Beech RG12 . . . . 118 C3
High Beeches GU16 . . . . . . 151 B1
High Close Sch RG40 . . . . 116 B4
High Fields SL5 . . . . 120 C2
High Heavens Wood SL7 . . . 1 B4
High Mdw RG4 . . . . 58 B2
High Meadow Pl KT16 . . . . 123 C2
High Rd SL6 . . . . 19 B4
High St Ascot SL5 . . . . 120 A3
  Ascot, Sunninghill SL5 . . . 120 B2
  Bagshot GU19 . . . . 145 C2
  Boxford RG20 . . . . 76 A1
  Bracknell RG12 . . . . 118 B4
  Burnham SL1 . . . . 21 B1
  Camberley GU15 . . . . 151 B3
  Chieveley RG20 . . . . 51 A1

High St continued
  Colnbrook SL3 . . . . 69 B4
  Compton RG20 . . . . 31 B2
  Cookham SL6 . . . . 20 A4
  Crowthorne RG45 . . . . . . 143 B2
  Datchet SL3 . . . . 68 A3
  East Isley RG20 . . . . 30 C4
  3 Egham TW20 . . . . 95 C2
  Eton SL4 . . . . 67 B3
  Feltham TW13 . . . . 98 C3
  Goring RG8 . . . . 34 B3
  Harlington UB3 . . . . 71 B4
  Harmondsworth UB7 . . . . . 70 B4
  Hungerford RG17 . . . . . . 100 B3
  Iver SL0 . . . . 44 C4
  Kintbury RG17 . . . . 102 A1
  Lambourn RG17 . . . . 25 A4
  Lambourn, Upper Lambourn
  RG17 . . . . 24 C3
  Maidenhead SL6 . . . . 40 B2
  Marlow SL7 . . . . 1 C1
  Pangbourne RG8 . . . . 56 B3
  Reading RG1 . . . . 86 A4
  Sandhurst GU47 . . . . 149 C4
  Sandhurst, Little Sandhurst
  GU47 . . . . 143 A1
  Shepperton TW17 . . . . . . 125 B2
  Slough, Langley SL3 . . . . . 44 A1
  Slough, Upton SL1 . . . . . . 42 C2
  Sonning RG4 . . . . 60 B2
  Staines TW18 . . . . 96 C2
  Stanwell TW19 . . . . 70 B1
  Streatley RG8 . . . . 34 A3
  Sunningdale SL5 . . . . 121 A2
  Taplow SL6 . . . . 20 C1
  Thatcham RG19 . . . . 106 B2
  Theale RG7 . . . . 83 C2
  Twyford RG10 . . . . 61 B2
  Wargrave RG10 . . . . 36 B1
  West End GU24 . . . . 153 C4
  Whitchurch-on-T RG8 . . . . 56 B4
  Windsor SL4 . . . . 67 B3
  Wraysbury TW19 . . . . 68 C1
High Street Harlington
  UB3 . . . . 71 B4
High Town Rd SL6 . . . . 39 C4
High Tree Dr RG6 . . . . 87 A3
High View Cl SL7 . . . . 1 B4
High View Rd GU18 . . . . . . 152 C4
Highbeeches Cl SL7 . . . . 1 B4
Highbridge Cl RG4 . . . . 59 A4
Highbridge Wharf 10 RG1 . 86 A4
Highbury Cres GU15 . . . . . 152 A4
Highbury Rd SL1 . . . . 42 A3
Highclere SL5 . . . . 120 B2
Highclere Cl RG12 . . . . 118 C4
Highclere Dr GU15 . . . . 152 A4
Highcliffe Cl RG5 . . . . 60 C1
Highdown Ave RG4 . . . . 59 A3
Highdown Hill Rd RG4 . . . . . 59 A3
Highdown Sixth Form
  Comp Sch RG4 . . . . 59 A3
Higher Alham RG12 . . . . . . 118 C1
Highfield Bracknell RG12 . . 117 C2
  Earley RG6 . . . . 87 A1
Highfield Ave RG14 . . . . . . 105 A1
Highfield Cl
  Englefield Green TW20 . . . . 95 B1
  Wokingham RG40 . . . . 116 A3
Highfield Ct
  Burghfield Common RG7 . . 111 A2
  Burnham SL2 . . . . 22 A3
  Englefield Green TW20 . . . . 95 B1
Highfield La SL6 . . . . 39 A2
Highfield Pk Marlow SL7 . . . . 1 A1
  Wargrave RG10 . . . . 36 C2
Highfield Rd Bourne End SL8 . 3 B2
  Chertsey KT16 . . . . 124 A1
  Englefield Green TW20 . . . . 95 B1
  Flackwell Heath HP10 . . . . . 3 A4
  Maidenhead SL6 . . . . 39 A4
  Newbury RG14 . . . . 104 C1
  Purley on T RG31 . . . . 57 B2
  Upper Halliford TW16 . . . 125 C2
  Windsor SL4 . . . . 66 C2
Highgate Rd RG6 . . . . 87 B3
Highgrove Pk SL6 . . . . 39 C4
Highgrove Pl RG10 . . . . 61 C3
Highgrove St RG1 . . . . 86 B3
Highgrove Terr RG1 . . . . 86 A3
Highland Pk TW13 . . . . 98 C2
Highland Rd GU15 . . . . 151 C4
Highlands HP10 . . . . 3 A4
Highlands Ave RG41 . . . . . . 115 B3
Highlands La SL6 . . . . 39 A2
Highlands Sch The RG31 . . . 57 B1
Highlands The SL2 . . . . 22 B3
Highlea Ave HP10 . . . . 3 A4
Highmead Cl RG2 . . . . 86 C1
Highmoor Rd RG4 . . . . 58 C2
Highview GU21 . . . . 84 A3
Highview Cres GU15 . . . . . 144 C1
Highway RG45 . . . . 143 A3
Highway Ave SL6 . . . . 39 A3
Highway Rd SL6 . . . . 39 A3
Highwayman's Ridge
  GU20 . . . . 146 A3
Highwood Cl
  Newbury RG14 . . . . 105 A3
  Yateley GU46 . . . . 149 B2
Highwoods Cl SL7 . . . . 1 B4
Highwoods Dr SL7 . . . . 1 B4
Highworth Cotts RG26 . . . 134 B1
Highworth Way RG31 . . . . 57 A1

Hilary Cl RG2 . . . . .113 B4
Hilary Dr RG45 . . . . .143 A3
Hilary Ho **10** RG14 . . . . .105 A1
Hilborne Way RG2 . . . . .115 A1
Hilbury Rd RG6 . . . . .87 A2
Hilcot Rd RG30 . . . . .85 B4
Hildens Dr RG31 . . . . .84 B4
Hill Cl Newbury RG14 . . . . . . .130 B4
  Wooburn Green HP10 . . . . . . .3 C4
Hill Copse View RG12 . . . . . .118 C4
Hill Cres RG2 . . . . .108 B2
Hill Farm App HP10 . . . . .3 C4
Hill Farm Rd
  Marlow Bottom SL7 . . . . .1 C3
  Taplow SL6 . . . . .20 C1
Hill Gdns RG8 . . . . .34 A3
Hill Lands RG10 . . . . .36 B1
Hill Piece OX11 . . . . .10 C2
Hill Pl SL2 . . . . .22 A3
Hill Prim Sch The RG4 . . . . . . .59 B3
Hill Rd Arborfield RG2 . . . . . . .114 C1
  Newbury RG14 . . . . .104 C2
Hill Side RG1 . . . . .86 B3
Hill St RG1 . . . . .86 A3
Hill Top Dr SL7 . . . . .1 A1
Hill View Rd TW19 . . . . .68 B1
Hillary Ct TW19 . . . . .97 C4
Hillary Rd SL3 . . . . .43 C2
Hillberry RG12 . . . . .118 B1
Hillbrow RG2 . . . . .86 C1
Hillcrest
  Hampstead Norreys RG18 . . .52 C3
  Tadley RG26 . . . . .135 A1
Hillcrest Ave SL6 . . . . .19 C3
Hillcrest Rd GU15 . . . . .152 A4
Hilldrop La RG17 . . . . .46 A2
Hillersdon SL2 . . . . .43 A4
Hillfield GU46 . . . . .149 C3
Hillgreen La RG20 . . . . .50 B4
Hillhampton SL5 . . . . .120 C1
Hillhouse La RG19 . . . . .133 A1
Hillingdon Ave TW19 . . . . .97 C4
Hillmead Ct SL6 . . . . .40 C4
Hillrise Brands Hill SL3 . . . . . . .69 A4
  Walton-on-T KT12 . . . . .125 C1
Hills La SL6 . . . . .19 B4
Hillsborough Pk GU15 . . . . . .152 B3
Hillside Ascot SL5 . . . . .120 B2
  Burghfield Common RG7 . . . .111 B2
  East Garston RG17 . . . . .47 B3
  Maidenhead SL6 . . . . .39 B3
  Sandhurst GU15 . . . . .150 C4
  Slough SL1 . . . . .42 C2
  Wentworth GU25 . . . . .122 A3
  Whitchurch-on-T RG8 . . . . . . .56 B4
Hillside Dr RG42 . . . . .90 B1
Hillside Pk Earley RG6 . . . . .87 B2
  Sunningdale SL5 . . . . .120 C1
Hillside Rd Earley RG6 . . . . .87 B2
  Hungerford RG17 . . . . .100 B2
  Marlow SL7 . . . . .1 C2
Hilltop Cl SL5 . . . . .120 C4
Hilltop Fst Sch SL4 . . . . .66 C2
Hilltop Rd Caversham RG4 . . . .58 B3
  Earley RG6 . . . . .87 A4
  Twyford RG10 . . . . .61 C4
Hilltop View GU46 . . . . .149 A3
Hillview RG31 . . . . .57 A1
Hilmanton RG6 . . . . .113 C4
Hilperton Rd **3** SL1 . . . . .42 C2
Hindhead Rd RG6 . . . . .87 A2
Hinksey Cl SL3 . . . . .44 A2
Hinton Cl RG45 . . . . .143 A4
Hinton Dr RG45 . . . . .143 A4
Hinton Pk RG10 . . . . .61 C1
Hinton Rd Hurst RG10 . . . . .62 A1
  Slough SL1 . . . . .41 C3
Hintonhatch Cnr RG10 . . . . . . .62 A1
Hirstwood RG30 . . . . .57 C1
Hirtes Ave RG2 . . . . .113 C3
Hitcham Ho SL1 . . . . .21 A1
Hitcham La Burnham SL1 . . . . .21 A1
  Taplow SL1,SL6 . . . . .20 C1
Hitcham Rd SL1,SL6 . . . . .41 A4
Hitchcock Cl TW17 . . . . .124 C3
Hitherhooks Hill RG42 . . . . . . .90 C1
Hithermoor Rd TW19 . . . . .70 A1
Hobart Ct SL7 . . . . .1 C2
Hobbis Dr SL6 . . . . .39 A3
Hockett La SL6 . . . . .19 A3
Hockford La RG7 . . . . .134 A2
Hockham Rd RG20 . . . . .31 C3
Hockley La SL2 . . . . .23 A3
Hodge La SL3 . . . . .93 A2
Hodgedale La RG10 . . . . .37 B3
Hodges Cl GU19 . . . . .145 C1
Hodsoll Rd RG1 . . . . .85 C6
Hoe Benham La RG20 . . . . . . .102 C4
Hogarth Ave Ashford TW15 . . .98 B1
  Reading RG30 . . . . .84 C3
Hogarth Cl
  Sandhurst GU47 . . . . .150 C3
  Slough SL1 . . . . .41 C3
Hogfair La SL1 . . . . .21 C1
Hogmoor La RG10 . . . . .61 C1
Hogoak La SL4 . . . . .92 A4
Hogwood La RG40 . . . . .141 A4
Holbeche Cl GU46 . . . . .149 A3
Holbeck RG12 . . . . .117 C2
Holborton Rd RG2 . . . . .113 B4
Holburne Hill OX12 . . . . .6 B4
Holborne Cl RG14 . . . . .131 A3
Holbrook Ct TW20 . . . . .96 B2
Holbrook Mdw TW20 . . . . .96 B1
Holford Cl RG31 . . . . .84 B4

Holkam Cl RG30 . . . . .84 C4
Holkham Cl RG30 . . . . .57 C1
Holland Ct TW15 . . . . .97 C1
Holland Gdns TW20 . . . . .123 C4
Holland Pines RG12 . . . . .117 C1
Holland Rd Marlow SL7 . . . . . . .1 C2
  Reading RG30 . . . . .84 B4
Hollands The RG19 . . . . .106 C2
Hollicombe Cl RG30 . . . . .84 C4
Hollies The RG14 . . . . .130 B3
Hollington Pl RG19 . . . . .106 B2
Hollins Wlk RG30 . . . . .85 B3
Hollow Hill La SL0 . . . . .44 A3
Hollow La Shinfield RG2 . . . . .113 C3
  Virginia Water GU25 . . . . . . .122 B3
Holloway Dr GU15 . . . . .122 C3
Holloway La U87 . . . . .70 C4
Holly Ave GU16 . . . . .152 A2
Holly Cl
  Englefield Green TW20 . . . . . .95 A1
  Farnham Common SL2 . . . . . .22 B4
Holly Cres SL4 . . . . .66 B3
Holly Ct **8** SL6 . . . . .124 A1
Holly Dr Maidenhead SL6 . . . . .39 C4
  Windsor SL4 . . . . .67 C1
Holly Hedge Cl GU15 . . . . .151 C3
Holly Hedge Rd SL6 . . . . .151 C1
Holly Ho RG12 . . . . .118 A2
Holly La RG8 . . . . .54 A3
Holly Orch RG41 . . . . .115 C3
Holly Ridge GU24 . . . . .88 A3
Holly Spring Cty Inf Sch
  RG12 . . . . .118 C4
Holly Spring Cty Jun Sch
  RG12 . . . . .118 B4
Holly Spring La RG12 . . . . .118 B4
Holly Way GU17 . . . . .150 B2
Holly Wlk SL4 . . . . .93 C2
Hollybank GU24 . . . . .153 C3
Hollybush Hill SL2 . . . . .23 A3
Hollybush La Cookham SL6 . . . .4 A3
  Iver SL0 . . . . .44 A4
  Sulhamstead RG7 . . . . .110 C2
Hollybush Ride
  Windlesham GU19,GU20 . . . .145 C3
  Wokingham RG40,RG45 . . . .142 B3
Hollycombe TW20 . . . . .95 B2
Hollycroft Cl UB7 . . . . .71 A4
Hollycroft Gdns UB7 . . . . .71 A4
Hollydale Cl RG2 . . . . .86 C1
Hollyfields Cl GU15 . . . . .151 A3
Hollym Cl RG6 . . . . .87 C1
Holmbank Dr TW17 . . . . .125 C3
Holmbury Ave RG45 . . . . .143 A4
Holmdale SL2 . . . . .43 B3
Holme Ho RG45 . . . . .111 A2
Holme Cl RG45 . . . . .143 A4
Holme Park Farm La RG4 . . . . .60 A1
Holmemoor Dr RG4 . . . . .60 C1
Holmes Cl Ascot SL5 . . . . .120 B2
  Wokingham RG41 . . . . .116 A2
Holmes Cres RG41 . . . . .116 A2
Holmes Rd RG6 . . . . .87 A3
Holmewood Cl RG41 . . . . .116 A1
Holmlea Rd Datchet SL3 . . . . . .68 B3
  Goring RG8 . . . . .34 B3
Holmlea Wlk SL3 . . . . .68 B3
Holmsdale Cl SL0 . . . . .44 C4
Holmwood Ave RG30 . . . . .84 C2
Holmwood Cl RG6 . . . . .39 A3
Holsworthy Cl RG6 . . . . .87 C2
Holt Comp Sch RG41 . . . . .116 A4
Holt La
  Brightwalton RG20 . . . . .49 C4
  Wokingham RG41 . . . . .116 A4
Holt Rd RG17 . . . . .102 A1
Holt The RG8 . . . . .57 B2
Holton Heath **12** RG12 . . . . . .118 C3
Holtspur Ave HP10 . . . . .3 C4
Holtspur La HP10 . . . . .3 C3
Holtwood Rd RG20 . . . . .129 A3
Holy Family RC Sch SL3 . . . . . .43 C1
Holy Trinity CE Mid Sch
  SL7 . . . . .1 C1
Holy Trinity CE Sch SL5 . . . . . .121 A2
Holy Trinity Prim Sch SL6 . . . . .20 A3
Holybrook Cres RG30 . . . . .85 A2
Holybrook Rd RG1 . . . . .85 C6
Holyhook Cl RG45 . . . . .143 A3
Holyport CE Prim Sch
  SL6 . . . . .65 A4
Holyport Manor Sch SL6 . . . . .64 C3
Holyport Rd SL6 . . . . .40 A1
Holyport St SL6 . . . . .65 A4
Holyrood Cl RG4 . . . . .59 B3
Holywell Cl TW19 . . . . .97 C4
Holywell Ho RG12 . . . . .118 B4
Holywell Way TW19 . . . . .97 C4
Hombrook Dr RG42 . . . . .117 C4
Hombrook Ho RG42 . . . . .117 C4
Home Croft RG31 . . . . .57 A1
Home Farm
  Reading RG2 . . . . .86 B2
  Upper Halliford TW17 . . . . . .125 C3
Home Farm La RG17 . . . . .134 B3
Home Farm Way SL3 . . . . .22 B1
Home Mdw SL2 . . . . .23 B3
Home Mead Cl RG14 . . . . .130 C4
Home Meadow Dr HP10 . . . . . . .3 A4
Home Park Rd GU46 . . . . .149 B3
Home Wood SL7 . . . . .17 C3
Homefield Way RG17 . . . . .100 B4
Homelands Way RG9 . . . . .15 B1
Homer Fst Sch SL4 . . . . .66 B3
Homers Rd SL4 . . . . .66 B3
Homeside Cl SL6 . . . . .19 C1

Homestead Rd
  Maidenhead SL6 . . . . .39 B2
  Staines TW18 . . . . .97 A1
Homewaters Ave TW16 . . . . . .125 C4
Homewood SL3 . . . . .43 A4
Hone Hill GU47 . . . . .150 A4
Honesty Bottom RG20 . . . . .28 B1
Honey End La RG30 . . . . .85 A2
Honey Hill Lambourn RG17 . . . .25 A2
  Wokingham RG40 . . . . .117 A1
Honey La SL6 . . . . .17 C1
Honey Meadow Cl RG4 . . . . . . .59 C1
Honeybottom Rd RG26 . . . . . .135 A1
Honeyfields RG17 . . . . .100 B3
Honeyhill Rd RG42 . . . . .118 A4
Honeysuckle Cl
  Crowthorne RG45 . . . . .143 A4
  Iver SL0 . . . . .44 B4
  Yateley GU46 . . . . .149 A3
Honister Wlk GU15 . . . . .152 B2
Honiton Rd RG2 . . . . .86 B1
Honnor Rd TW18 . . . . .97 B1
Hook End La RG8 . . . . .34 A1
Hook La GU24 . . . . .153 B3
Hook Mill La GU18 . . . . .146 B1
Hookstone La GU24 . . . . .153 C4
Hoops Way RG2 . . . . .112 C4
Hop Gdns RG9 . . . . .15 B1
Hope Ave RG12 . . . . .118 C1
Hope Fountain GU15 . . . . .152 A2
Hopeman Cl GU47 . . . . .150 B4
Hopwood Cl RG14 . . . . .105 B2
Horatio Ave RG42 . . . . .118 C4
Horewood Rd RG12 . . . . .118 A2
Horizon West Ind Est
  RG14 . . . . .104 B3
Hormer Cl GU47 . . . . .143 B1
Horn St RG20 . . . . .31 C3
Hornbeam Cl
  Purley on T RG8 . . . . .57 B3
  Sandhurst GU47 . . . . .143 B1
  Wokingham RG41 . . . . .115 B2
Hornbeam Dr RG6 . . . . .87 A1
Hornbeam **7** SL1 . . . . .43 A2
Hornbeams RG7 . . . . .139 B3
Hornby Ave RG12 . . . . .118 B1
Horncastle Dr RG30 . . . . .84 C3
Horndean Rd RG12 . . . . .118 C2
Hornsea Cl RG30 . . . . .57 C1
Horris Hill Sch RG20 . . . . .130 C2
Horse Cl The RG4 . . . . .59 C4
Horse Gate RG45 . . . . .142 A4
Horsebrass Dr GU19 . . . . .145 C1
Horseguards Dr SL6 . . . . .40 A4
Horsemoor Cl SL3 . . . . .44 A1
Horsemoor Cl SL3 . . . . .44 A1
Horseshoe Cl GU15 . . . . .151 C4
Horseshoe Cloisters **12**
  SL4 . . . . .67 B3
Horseshoe Cres
  Burghfield Common RG7 . . . .111 A2
  Camberley GU15 . . . . .151 C4
Horseshoe End RG14 . . . . .131 A4
Horseshoe Hill SL1 . . . . .21 B4
Horseshoe Pk RG8 . . . . .56 B3
Horseshoe Rd RG8 . . . . .56 B3
Horsham Rd
  East Bedfont TW14 . . . . .71 B1
  Sandhurst GU47 . . . . .143 B1
Horsnape Gdns RG42 . . . . .90 A1
Horsneile La RG42 . . . . .118 A4
Horton Cl SL6 . . . . .20 B1
Horton Gdns SL3 . . . . .68 C2
Horton Grange SL6 . . . . .20 B1
Horton Rd Datchet SL3 . . . . . . .68 B3
  Horton SL3 . . . . .69 A3
  Poyle SL3,TW19 . . . . .69 C2
  Stanwell TW19 . . . . .70 A1
Horton Trad Est SL3 . . . . .69 A2
Hose Hill RG7,RG30 . . . . .111 A4
Hosier St RG1 . . . . .86 A6
Hoskins Place Ind Est
  GU15 .151 A2
Houlton Cl GU19 . . . . .145 C1
Houston Ct **3** SL4 . . . . .67 B3
Houston Way RG45 . . . . .142 B3
Howard Ave SL2 . . . . .42 C4
Howard Cl TW16 . . . . .98 C1
Howard Ct SL6 . . . . .3 A2
Howard Rd
  Newbury RG14 . . . . .105 A1
  Wokingham RG40 . . . . .116 B3
Howard St RG1 . . . . .85 C4
Howarth Rd SL6 . . . . .40 A3
Howe La RG42 . . . . .63 C1
Howell Cl RG42 . . . . .90 B1
Howgate Dr RG8 . . . . .34 B1
Howorth Ct **1** RG12 . . . . .118 C3
Howth Dr RG5 . . . . .87 B4
Hoylake Cl SL1 . . . . .41 C2
Hrmondsworth Moor
  Ctry Pk U87 . . . . .70 A4
Hubbard Cl RG10 . . . . .61 C1
Hubberholme RG12 . . . . .118 A3
Hubert Rd SL3 . . . . .43 B2
Huckleberry Cl RG8 . . . . .57 B2
Huddington Glade GU46 . . . .149 A3
Hudson Rd Harlington SL8 . . . .71 A4
  Woodley RG5 . . . . .87 C3
Hugh Faringdon RC Sch
  (Spec) Resource
  (Aspergers Syndrome)
  RG30 . . . . .85 B3
Hugh Fraser Dr RG31 . . . . .84 B3
Hughenden Rd SL1 . . . . .42 B4

Hughendon Cl SL6 . . . . .39 B3
Hughes Rd Ashford TW15 . . . . .98 B1
  Wokingham RG40 . . . . .116 C4
Hull Cl SL1 . . . . .42 B2
Humber Cl
  Thatcham RG18 . . . . .106 A3
  Wokingham RG41 . . . . .115 C4
Humber Way
  Sandhurst GU47 . . . . .150 B4
  Slough SL3 . . . . .44 A1
Hummer Rd TW20 . . . . .96 A2
Humphrays La RG17 . . . . .47 B3
Humphries Yd RG12 . . . . .118 B3
Hungerford Ave SL2 . . . . .42 C4
Hungerford Cl GU47 . . . . .150 B4
Hungerford Dr
  Maidenhead SL6 . . . . .19 C2
  Reading RG1 . . . . .85 C3
Hungerford Hill
  East Garston RG17 . . . . .47 C1
  Lambourn RG17 . . . . .25 A1
Hungerford La
  Bradfield RG7 . . . . .81 C1
  Waltham St Lawrence RG10 . .62 C1
Hungerford Newtown
  Newtown RG17 . . . . .74 A2
Hungerford Prim Sch
  RG17 .100 C2
Hungerford Rd RG17 . . . . .101 C2
Hungerford Sta RG17 . . . . . . .100 C2
Hunstanton Cl SL3 . . . . .43 C1
Hunt's La SL6 . . . . .20 C2
Hunter Cl SL1 . . . . .41 B4
Hunter's Ct RG5 . . . . .87 C3
Huntercombe Cl SL6 . . . . .41 B4
Huntercombe La N SL6 . . . . . .41 B4
Huntercombe La S SL6 . . . . . . .41 C3
Hunters Chase RG4 . . . . .58 C3
Hunters Hill RG7 . . . . .110 C2
Hunters Mdw SL6 . . . . .47 B3
Hunters Mews SL4 . . . . .67 B2
Hunters Way
  Shinfield RG2 . . . . .113 A1
  Slough SL1 . . . . .41 C2
Huntingdonshire Cl
  RG41 .115 B3
Huntingfield Way TW20 . . . . . .96 B1
Huntington Cl RG6 . . . . .87 C2
Huntley Cl RG1 . . . . .86 C3
Huntsgreen Ct RG12 . . . . .118 B4
Huntsmans Mdw SL5 . . . . . . .119 C4
Huntsmoor Rd RG26 . . . . .135 A1
Huntswood La SL1,SL6 . . . . . . .20 C2
Hurford Dr RG19 . . . . .106 C2
Hurley Cl RG12 . . . . .118 A3
Hurley High St SL6 . . . . .17 C2
Hurley La SL6 . . . . .18 A2
Hurricane Way Slough SL3 . . .44 B1
  Woodley RG5 . . . . .88 A4
Hursley Cl RG30 . . . . .85 A4
Hurst Com Sch The
  RG6 . . . . .134 B1
Hurst Gr KT12 . . . . .125 C1
Hurst La TW20 . . . . .123 A3
Hurst Lodge Sch SL5 . . . . .120 C1
Hurst Park Rd RG10 . . . . .61 C1
Hurst Rd Slough SL1 . . . . .41 B4
  Twyford RG10 . . . . .61 C4
Hurst Way RG2 . . . . .112 C4
Hurstdene Ave TW18 . . . . .97 A1
Hurstfield Dr SL6 . . . . .41 A4
Hurstwood SL5 . . . . .120 A2
Huscarle Way RG31 . . . . .57 B2
Huson Rd RG42 . . . . .91 B1
Hutsons Cl RG40 . . . . .116 B4
Hutton Cl Earley RG6 . . . . .87 A1
  Newbury RG14 . . . . .105 A2
  Windlesham GU20 . . . . .146 B2
Hyde Cl TW15 . . . . .98 C1
Hyde End La
  Brimpton RG7 . . . . .133 B3
  Shinfield RG7 . . . . .113 B2
Hyde End Rd RG7 . . . . .113 B1
Hyde Field Ave TW20 . . . . .96 B1
Hyde Park Rd TW20 . . . . .96 B1
Hyde Rd RG18 . . . . .106 B3
Hyde Terr TW15 . . . . .98 C1
Hydes The RG31 . . . . .57 B2
Hyland Ho **10** SL8 . . . . .3 A3
Hylle Cl SL4 . . . . .66 C3
Hyperion Way RG2 . . . . .86 A2
Hythe Cl RG12 . . . . .118 C2
Hythe Cty Prim Sch TW18 . . . .96 B2
Hythe End Rd TW19 . . . . .96 A3
Hythe Field Ave TW20 . . . . . . .96 B1
Hythe Park Rd TW20 . . . . .96 B2
Hythe Rd TW18 . . . . .96 B2
Hythe The TW18 . . . . .96 C2

I

Ian Mikardo Way RG4 . . . . .59 B1
Iberian Way GU15 . . . . .152 A3
Ibotson Ct SL3 . . . . .69 C3
Ibstock Cl RG30 . . . . .85 A4
Ibstone Ave RG4 . . . . .59 C3
Icarus Ct **18** RG1 . . . . .86 A3
Icknield Pl RG8 . . . . .34 B4
Icknield Rd RG8 . . . . .34 B4
Iden Ct RG14 . . . . .105 A2
Iffley Ct TW18 . . . . .96 C2
Ilbury Cl RG12 . . . . .115 A3
Ilchester Cl SL6 . . . . .39 B3
Ilchester Ct **4** RG14 . . . . . . .105 A1
Ilchester Mews SL4 . . . . .59 C3
Ilex Cl
  Englefield Green TW20 . . . . . .95 A1
  Silchester RG26 . . . . .135 C1

Ilex CI *continued*
  Yateley GU46 149
Ilfracombe Way RG6 87
Ilkley Rd RG4 58
Ilkley Way RG19 106
Illingworth SL4 66
Illingworth Ave RG4 59
Illingworth Gr RG12 118
Ilsley Prim Sch The RG20 30
Ilsley Rd RG20 31
Imperial Ct
  Henley-on-T RG9 15
  Windsor SL4 67
Imperial Ho GU25 122
Imperial Rd
  East Bedfont TW14 98
  Windsor SL4 67
Imperial Way RG2 113
Impstone Rd RG26 135
In The Ray SL6 40
Inchwood RG12 118
India Rd SL1 43
Ingle Dell GU15 151
Ingle Glen RG40 142
Ingleglen SL2 22
Ingleside SL3 69
Ingleton RG12 118
Inglewood Ave GU15 152
Inglewood Ct RG30 85
Inglewood Rd RG17 101
Inhurst La RG26 134
Inhurst Way RG26 134
Inkerman Rd SL4 41
Inkpen Cl RG30 85
Inkpen Prim Sch RG17 127
Inkpen Rd
  Hungerford RG17 100
  Inkpen RG17 127
  Kintbury RG17 102
Inner Ring E TW6 71
Inner Ring W TW6 71
Innings La
  White Waltham SL6 63
  Winkfield RG12 118
Inniscrown Ho SL3 43
Institute Rd Marlow SL7 1
Insync SL6 66
Instow Rd RG6 87
Invergordon Cl RG31 84
Inverness Way GU47 150
Invicta Cl TW14 98
Inwood Cl SL6 39
Iona Cres SL1 41
Ipswich Rd SL1 42
Irish Hill Rd RG17 102
Irvine Ho SL4 66
Irvine Pl GU25 122
Irving Way RG41 88
Isaac Newton Rd RG2 115
Isis Cl RG41 116
Isis Ct RG1 59
Isis Way Bourne End SL8 3
  Sandhurst GU47 150
Island Cl TW18 96
Island Farm Rd RG17 110
Island Rd RG2 113
Islandstone La RG10 89
Islet Park Dr SL6 20
Islet Park Ho SL6 20
Islet Pk SL6 20
Islet Rd SL6 20
Isobel Ho **12** TW16 98
Ivanhoe Rd RG40 141
Iveagh Ct RG12 118
Iver Cty Fst Sch SL0 44
Iver Cty Mid Sch SL0 44
Iver Lodge SL0 44
Iver Sta SL0 44
Iverdale Cl SL0 44
Iverna Gdns TW14 71
Ives Cl GU46 149
Ives Rd SL3 44
Ivy Cl SL6 65
Ivy Cres SL1 41
Ivy Dr GU18 153
Ivybank RG31 57
Ivydene Rd RG30 85

J

Jack Price Cl **23** RG1 86
Jack St RG14 105
Jackson Cl RG12 118
Jackson Ind Est SL8 3
Jacob Cl Bracknell RG42 117
  Windsor SL4 66
Jacob Rd GU15 151
Jakes Ho SL6 40
James Butcher Dr RG7 83
James Cl SL7 2
James Ct **8** RG30 85
James Elliman Cty Inf Sch
  SL2 42
James Elliman Cty Mid Sch
  SL2 42
James Rd GU15 151
James St Reading RG1 85
  Windsor SL4 67
James Watt Rd RG42 140
James Way GU15 151
James's La RG7,RG30 111
Jameston RG12 118
Jamnagar Cl TW18 96
Janson Ct RG1 85
Japonica Cl RG41 115
Jaques's La RG7 139
Jardine Cotts SL2 23

rratt Ho SL4 ....67 A2
rry Ct SL7 ....1 C2
rvis Dr RG10 ....61 B3
smine Cl RG41 ....115 B4
y Cl RG6 ....87 A1
ys Nest Cl GU17 ....150 B2
yworth Ho RG1 ....86 C4
dburgh Cl RG19 ....106 C2
fferson Cl
  Caversham RG4 ....59 B4
  Slough SL3 ....44 A1
fries Ct SL8 ....3 A1
llicoe Cl SL1 ....42 A2
nkins Cl RG30 ....85 B3
nkins' Hill London Rd
  GU19 ....146 B2
nner Wlk RG31 ....84 A4
nnery La SL1 ....21 B1
nnetts Cl RG7 ....81 C2
nnings Field HP10 ....3 A4
nnings Wharf SL4 ......67 B4
nnys Wlk GU46 ....149 C3
rome Cnr GU47 ....143 B2
rome Cl SL7 ....1 C2
rome Cnr GU47 ....143 B2
rracknell RG42 ....87 C3
rrymoor Hill RG40 ....104 C2
esmond Dene RG14 ...104 C2
esse Cl GU46 ....149 C3
esse Terr RG1 ....85 C4
essiman Terr TW17 ....125 A2
evington RG12 ....118 B1
g's La N RG42 ....91 C1
g's La S Bracknell RG42 ..91 C1
  Winkfield RG42 ....118 C4
ggs La SL6 ....19 A4
ock's La Binfield RG42 ..90 C1
el Cl RG6 ....87 A2
hannes Ct [5] RG30 ...85 B3
hn Balliol Ct [2] RG1 ..86 B4
hn Boys Ho RG14 .....130 B3
hn Childs Cl RG14 ....105 A1
hn Hunt Cl RG19 .....106 C1
hn Kaye Ct TW17 .....125 A2
hn Kimber's Almshouses
  RG14 ....104 C2
hn Nike Way RG14 ....117 B4
hn Norgate Ho RG18 ..105 A1
hn O'Gaunt Sch RG17 ..100 B2
hn Rankin Cty Inf Sch
  RG14 ....130 B4
hn Rankin Cty Jun Sch
  RG14 ....130 B4
hn Taylor Ct SL1 ....42 B3
hnson Dr RG40 ....142 A4
hnsons La RG18 ......106 B4
nathan Cl SL6 ....39 C4
nathan Hill RG20 .....131 A2
nathan Miller Sch The
  SL1 ....29 C4
nes Cnr SL5 ....119 C4
ordan Ct Caversham RG4 ..59 C3
  Shinfield RG7 ....113 C3
ordans Cl TW19 ....97 B4
ordans La RG7 ....110 C1
oseph Ct RG42 ....91 C1
osephine Ct RG1 ....85 C3
ouldings La RG7 ......140 B2
ourdelay's Pas SL4 ....67 B4
ourneys End SL2 ....42 C4
abilee Ave
  North Ascot SL5 ......119 C4
  Wokingham RG41 ....116 A4
abilee Cl
  North Ascot SL5 ......119 C4
  Silchester RG26 ......135 C1
  Stanwell TW19 ....97 A2
abilee Ct Bracknell RG12 ..118 B3
  Staines TW18 ....97 A2
  Thatcham RG19 ......106 A2
abilee Rd
  Finchampstead RG40 ..141 C2
  Littlewick Green SL6 ..38 A3
  Newbury RG14 ....105 A1
  Reading RG6 ....87 B3
Slough SL1 ....86 A3
Stoke Row SL6 ....86 A3
Stoke Row TW14 ....98 B1
udy's Pas SL4 ....42 B1
ulet Gdns RG42 ....118 C4
ulius Hill RG42 ....118 A2
ulkes La RG42 ....114 C4
unction Rd Ashford TW15 ..98 B2
  Lightwater GU18 .....146 A1
  Reading RG1 ....86 C3
uniper Ct SL4 ....67 B4
uniper Cl2 ....118 B1
uniper Ct SL1 ....43 A2
uniper Dr SL6 ....40 A4
uniper Way RG31 .....115 C3
ustice Cl RG1 ....104 B3
utland Cl RG41 ....115 C3
utland Ho SL4 ....67 B4
utland Pl TW20 ....96 B2

Kaynes Pk SL5 ....119 C4
Kaywood Cl SL3 ....43 B2
Keane Cl RG5 ....87 C4
Kearsley Rd RG30 .....85 B3
Keates Gn RG42 ......118 A4
Keats Cl RG5 ....87 C2
Keats La SL4 ....67 B4
Keats Rd RG5 ....87 C2
Keats Way
  Crowthorne RG45 ....143 A3
  Yateley GU46 ....149 A2
Keble Rd SL6 ....39 C4
Keble Way GU47 ......143 C1
Keel Dr SL1 ....42 B2
Keeler Cl SL4 ....66 C2
Keep Hatch Inf Sch
  RG40 ....116 B4
Keep Hatch Jun Sch
  RG40 ....116 B4
Keepers Combe RG12 ..118 B1
Keepers Farm Cl SL4 ..66 C3
Keepers Terr GU25 ...122 A2
Keepers Wlk GU25 ...122 B2
Keephatch Rd RG40 ..116 C4
Keighley Cl RG19 .....106 B1
Kelburne Cl RG41 .....88 B2
Keldholme RG12 ......118 A3
Kelly Cl TW17 ....125 C4
Kelmscott Cl RG4 .....58 C2
Kelpatrick Rd SL1 .....41 B4
Kelsey Ave RG40 .....141 C6
Kelsey Cl SL6 ....39 B2
Kelsey Gr GU46 ....149 C3
Kelso Mews SL4 ......59 C3
Kelton Cl RG6 ....87 C1
Kelvedon Way RG4 ...58 C3
Kelvin Cl RG2 ....140 C4
Kelvin Rd RG14 ......105 A2
Kemble Ct RG31 ......84 B2
Kemerton Cl RG31 ...84 B2
Kemp Ct GU19 ....145 C1
Kempe Cl SL3 ....44 B1
Kempton Cl RG14 ....105 B1
Kemsley Chase SL2 ...22 B2
Kenavon Dr RG1 ......86 B4
Kendal Ave Caversham RG4 ..59 C3
  Shinfield RG2 ....113 C3
Kendal Cl
  East Bedfont TW14 ..98 C4
  Slough SL2 ....43 A3
  Thatcham RG18 ......106 B2
Kendal Dr SL2 ....43 A3
Kendal Gr GU15 ......152 B2
Kendrick Cl RG40 ....116 B3
Kendrick Ct [5] RG1 ..86 B3
Kendrick Girls' Gram Sch
  RG1 ....86 B4
Kendrick Rd
  Newbury RG14 ....130 B3
  Reading RG1 ....86 B3
  Slough SL3 ....43 A2
Kenilworth Ave
  Bracknell RG12 ......118 B4
  Reading RG30 ....85 B3
Kenilworth Ct SL1 .....42 C2
Kenilworth Gdns TW18 ..97 B2
Kenilworth Rd
  TW15, TW19 ....98 B2
Kennally SL4 ....66 B3
Kenneally Ct [11] SL4 ..66 B3
Kenneally Pl [12] SL4 ..66 B3
Kenneally Row [13] SL4 ..66 B3
Kenneally Wlk [14] SL4 ..66 B3
Kennedy Cl
  Farnham Common SL2 ..22 B3
  Maidenhead SL6 .....39 B3
  Marlow SL7 ....1 C2
  Newbury RG14 ....105 A1
Kennedy Ct TW15 .....98 B2
Kennedy Dr RG8 ......56 C3
Kennedy Gdns RG6 ...87 A2
Kennedy Ho SL1 .....41 B3
Kennel Ave SL5 ......119 C4
Kennel Cl SL5 ....92 C1
Kennel Gn SL5 ....119 C4
Kennel La Bracknell RG42 ..91 A1
  Cookham SL6 ....19 B4
  Windlesham GU20 ..146 B3
Kennel Lane Sch RG42 ..91 A1
Kennel Ride SL5 ......92 C1
Kennel Wood SL5 ....119 C4
Kennet & Avon Canal
  Visitor Ctr RG7 ......109 B2
Kennet Cl RG19 ......106 C2
Kennet Ct
  Hungerford RG17 ...100 C4
  [4] Newbury RG14 ..105 A1
  Wokingham RG41 ...115 C3
Kennet Ctr The RG14 ..105 A1
Kennet Pl
  Burghfield Common RG7 ..111 A2
  Chilton Foliat RG17 ..73 A1
  [10] Newbury RG14 ..105 A2
Kennet Rd Kintbury RG17 ..102 A1
  Maidenhead SL6 .....39 C4
  Newbury RG14 ....104 C1
Kennet Sch RG19 ....106 C2
Kennet Side
  Newbury RG14 ....105 B2
  [12] Reading RG1 ...86 B4
Kennet St RG1 ....86 B4
Kennet Valley Prim Sch
  RG31 ....84 C2
Kennet Way RG17 ...100 C4
Kennett Rd Bourne End SL8 ..3 A2
  Slough SL3 ....44 A2
Kensington Cl RG6 ...87 A1
Kensington Rd RG30 ..85 B4

Kent Ave SL1 ....42 B4
Kent Cl Staines TW18 ..97 B1
  Wokingham RG41 ...115 B3
Kent Folly RG42 ......91 C1
Kent Lodge [3] SL6 ...39 C3
Kent Rd Reading RG30 ..85 B4
  Windlesham GU20 ..146 B3
Kent Way SL6 ....19 C1
Kentigern Dr RG45 ..143 C3
Kenton Cl Bracknell RG12 ..118 B4
  Frimley GU16 ....151 C1
  Marlow SL7 ....1 C1
Kenton Rd RG6 ....87 B2
Kenton's La SL4 ......66 C3
Kentons La RG30 .....36 B4
Kentwood Cl RG30 ...57 C1
Kentwood Hill RG31 ..57 C1
Kenwood Cl
  Harmondsworth UB7 ..71 A4
  Maidenhead SL6 .....39 A4
Kenworth Gr GU18 ..146 A1
Keppel Spur SL4 .....95 A4
Keppel St SL4 ....67 B3
Kepple Pl GU19 ......145 C2
Kernham Dr RG31 ...57 B2
Kerria Way GU24 ....153 C3
Kerris Way RG6 ......87 A1
Kersey Cres RG14 ...104 C3
Kesteven Way RG41 ..115 C3
Keston Cl RG4 ....59 B1
Kestrel Ave TW18 ....96 C3
Kestrel Cl RG19 .....106 A2
Kestrel Path SL2 .....21 C1
Kestrel Way
  Burghfield Common RG7 ..111 A2
  Reading RG30 ....85 A2
  Wokingham RG41 ...115 C3
Keswick Ave TW17 ..125 C2
Keswick Cl SL2 ....42 C2
Keswick Ct GU18 ....153 A4
Keswick Gdns RG5 ..87 C3
Keswick Rd TW20 ....96 A1
Ketcher Gn RG42 ....90 B2
Kettering Cl RG31 ...84 C4
Kevins Dr GU46 .....149 C4
Keynsham Way GU47 ..143 B1
Keys La SL6 ....39 C3
Kibble Gn RG12 .....118 A1
Kibblewhite Cres RG10 ..61 B3
Kidderminster Rd SL2 ..22 B1
Kidmore End Rd RG4 ..59 A4
Kidmore Rd RG4 ......58 C3
Kidwells Cl SL6 ......39 C4
Kidwells Park Dr SL6 ..39 C4
Kielder Wlk GU15 ...152 B2
Kier Pk SL5 ....120 B3
Kilburn Cl RG31 .....84 B2
Kildare Gdns RG4 ...59 B2
Kilarney Dr SL6 ......39 C4
Killigrew Ho [4] TW14 ..71 C1
Kilross Rd TW14 .....98 C1
Kilmartin Gdns GU16 ..151 C1
Kilmington Cl RG12 ..118 C1
Kilmiston Ave TW17 ..125 B2
Kilmiston Ho TW17 ..125 B2
Kilmore Dr GU15 ....152 A2
Kilmuir Cl GU47 .....150 B4
Kiln Cl Harrington SL3 ..71 B4
  Hermitage RG18 ......79 B4
Kiln Croft SL7 ....2 A2
Kiln Dr RG18 ....78 C3
Kiln Hill RG7 ....140 A4
Kiln La Bourne End SL8,HP10 ..3 B2
  Bracknell RG12 ......118 A4
  Mortimer RG7 ....137 B3
  Reading RG31 ....84 B4
  Shiplake RG9 ....35 B1
  Sunningdale SL5 ....121 A2
  Winkfield SL5 ....93 A1
Kiln Pl SL6 ....19 A2
Kiln Rd Caversham RG4 ..59 B4
  Newbury RG14 ....105 B3
Kiln Ride
  Upper Basildon RG8 ..54 C3
  Wokingham RG40 ...142 A4
Kiln Ride Extension RG40 ..142 A3
Kiln Terr RG18 ....78 C3
Kiln View Rd RG2 ....86 B1
Kilnsea Dr RG6 ....87 B1
Kilowna Cl RG10 .....61 A3
Kilross Rd TW14 .....98 C4
Kimber Cl SL4 ....67 A2
Kimber's Cl RG14 ...104 C2
Kimber's La SL6 .....39 C2
Kimberley RG12 .....118 B1
Kimberley Cl
  [6] Reading RG1 .....85 C3
  Slough SL3 ....43 C1
Kimbers Dr Burnham SL1 ..21 B3
  Newbury RG14 ....104 B3
Kimmeridge RG12 ...118 A1
Kimpton Cl RG6 .....113 C4
Kinburn Dr TW20 ....95 C2
King Acre Ct TW18 ..96 C3
King Edward Ct [14] SL4 ..67 B3
King Edward St SL1 ..42 B4
King Edward VII Ave SL4 ..67 C4
King Edward VII Hospl SL4 ..67 B2
King Edwards Cl SL5 ..119 C4
King Edwards Rd SL5 ..119 C4
King Edwards Rise SL5 ..119 C4
King George Cl TW16 ..98 C2
King James Way RG9 ..35 A4

King John's Cl TW19 ..68 B1
King John's Palace SL3 ..69 B3
King St Chertsey KT16 ..124 A1
  Maidenhead SL6 .....39 C3
  Mortimer RG7 ....137 B3
  Reading RG1 ....86 A4
King Stable St SL4 ...67 B4
King Street La RG41 ..88 B1
King's Ave TW16 .....98 C1
King's Cl TW18 ......96 C4
King's Court Cty Fst Sch
  SL4 ....95 A4
King's Gr SL6 ....39 C3
King's Keep GU47 ...143 A1
King's Rd Ascot SL5 ..120 C3
  Crowthorne RG45 ....143 B3
  Egham TW20 ....96 A2
  Henley-on-T RG9 .....15 B1
  Slough SL1 ....42 C2
  Windsor SL4 ....67 B3
King's Ride Bracknell SL5 ..119 B3
  Camberley GU15 ....151 B4
King's Road Ho [17] SL4 ..67 B3
King's Wlk GU15 ....150 C3
Kingfisher Cl RG12 ..109 A2
Kingfisher Court Ind Est
  RG14 ....105 B2
Kingfisher Ct Slough SL2 ..22 A1
  Twyford RG10 ....61 C2
Kingfisher Dr
  Staines TW18 ....96 C2
  Woodley RG5 ....87 B3
  Yateley GU46 ....149 A3
Kingfisher Pl RG1 ....86 A4
Kinghorn La SL6 ......19 B2
Kinghorn Pk SL6 .....19 B2
Kings Cl RG9 ....15 B1
Kings Cres GU15 ....151 B4
Kings La Cookham SL6 ..19 A4
  Englefield Green TW20 ..95 A2
  Windlesham GU20 ..146 C3
Kings Mead RG14 ...130 B3
Kings Meadow Rd RG1 ..86 A4
Kings Rd Caversham RG4 ..59 B1
  Newbury RG14 ....105 A1
  Reading RG1 ....86 B4
  Silchester RG7 ......136 A1
  West End GU24 ......153 C3
Kings Rd W RG14 ...105 A1
Kings Reach Ct [17] RG1 ..86 A4
Kings Terr SL5 ....119 A4
Kings Wlk
  [4] Maidenhead SL6 ..39 C4
  Reading RG1 ....86 A4
Kings Wood SL7 ......17 B4
Kingsbridge Cotts RG40 ..142 C4
Kingsbridge Hill RG9 ..139 A3
Kingsbridge Rd
  Newbury RG14 ....104 C1
  Reading RG2 ....86 B1
Kingsbury Cres TW18 ..96 B4
Kingsbury Dr SL4 ....95 A4
Kingsclear Pk GU15 ..151 B2
Kingscroft Cty Inf Sch
  TW18 ....97 A2
Kingscroft Cty Jun Sch
  TW18 ....97 A2
Kingscroft La RG42 ..92 A3
Kingsdown Cl RG6 ...87 A1
Kingsfield SL4 ....66 B3
Kingsford Cl RG5 ....88 A3
Kingsgate Pl [20] RG1 ..86 B4
Kingsgate St RG1 ....86 B4
Kingsland Grange RG14 ..130 C4
Kingsley Ave
  Camberley GU15 ....151 B2
  Englefield Green TW20 ..95 B1
Kingsley Cl Charvil RG10 ..61 A3
  Crowthorne RG45 ....143 A2
  Newbury RG14 ....105 A3
  Reading RG2 ....113 A4
Kingsley Dr SL7 ....2 A2
Kingsley Path SL2 ...21 B1
Kingsmere Rd RG42 ..117 C4
Kingston Ave TW14 ..71 C1
Kingston Cres TW15 ..97 B3
Kingston Gdns RG2 ..86 B1
Kingston La UB7 .....71 B4
Kingston Rd
  Ashford TW15, TW17 ..97 C1
  Camberley GU15 ....145 A1
  Staines TW15, TW18 ..97 A1
Kingsway
  Blackwater GU17 ....150 C3
  Caversham RG4 ......59 C3
  Farnham Common SL2 ..22 B3
  Iver SL0 ....44 C1
  Stanwell TW19 ....97 C4
  Thatcham RG19 ......106 C1
Kingswick Cl SL5 ....120 C3
Kingswick Dr SL5 ...120 B3
Kingswood Cl TW20 ..95 B2
Kingswood Creek TW19 ..68 B1
Kingswood Ct
  Maidenhead SL6 .....39 C3
  [17] Reading RG30 ..85 B4
Kingswood Hall of
  Residence TW20 .....95 B2
Kingswood Ho SL1 ..42 B4
Kingswood Par SL7 ..17 B4
Kingswood Rise TW20 ..95 B2
Kinnaird Cl SL1 ......41 B4
Kinross Ave SL5 .....119 C4
Kinross Cl TW16 .....98 C2
Kinross Ct SL5 ......119 C2
Kinross Dr TW16 ....98 C2
Kinson Rd RG30 .....58 A1

Jar–Lak 169

Kintbury Rd SL5 .....127 C3
Kintbury Sq RG17 ...102 A1
Kintbury Sta RG17 ..102 A2
Kinver Wlk [30] RG41 ..86 A3
Kipling Cl Thatcham RG18 ..106 B3
  Woodley RG5 ....87 C2
  Yateley GU46 ....149 B2
Kipling Ct SL4 ....67 A3
Kirkby Ct GU16 ......151 C1
Kirkfell Cl RG31 .....57 B1
Kirkham Cl Caversham RG4 ..59 C3
  Sandhurst GU47 .....143 B1
Kirkstall Ct RG31 ....84 B2
Kirkstone Cl GU15 ..152 B2
Kirkwall Spur SL1 ...42 C4
Kirkwood Cres RG7 ..110 C2
Kirton Cl RG30 ......85 A4
Kirtons Farm Rd
  RG2 & RG30 ....85 B1
Kitsmead La GU35 ..122 B1
Kittiwake Cl RG5 ....88 A4
Kitwood Dr RG6 .....87 C1
Klondyke SL7 ....1 B1
Knapp Rd TW15 .....97 C2
Knapp The RG6 ......87 A2
Knappe Cl RG9 ......35 B4
Knighton Cl RG4 ....59 A2
Knights Cl Egham TW20 ..96 B1
  Windsor SL4 ....66 B3
Knights La RG20 ....129 B2
Knights Lea RG20 ..129 A2
Knights Pl [12] SL4 ..67 B3
Knights Way
  Caversham RG4 ......59 A3
  Frimley GU15 ....152 A2
Knightsbridge Cres TW18 ..97 A1
Knightsbridge Dr RG19 ..132 A2
Knightsbridge Rd GU15 ..151 C4
Knightswood RG12 ..118 A1
Knole Wood SL5 ....120 C1
Knoll Cl OX12 ....6 C4
Knoll Park Rd KT16 ..123 C1
Knoll Rd GU15 ......151 B3
Knoll The Chertsey KT16 ..123 C1
  Purley on T RG31 ....57 A1
Knollmead RG31 ....84 B2
Knollys Rd RG26 ....135 C1
Knolton Way SL2 ....43 B4
Knossington Ct RG6 ..87 B1
Knott La RG7 ....109 A2
Knowl Hill CE Prim Sch
  RG10 ....37 C2
Knowl Hill Terr RG10 ..37 C2
Knowle Cl RG4 ......58 B2
Knowle Gn TW18 ...97 A2
Knowle Gr GU25 ...122 B1
Knowle Grove Cl GU25 ..122 B1
Knowle Hill GU25 ..122 B1
Knowle Park Ave TW18 ..97 A2
Knowle Rd RG5 ......87 C2
Knowles Ave RG45 ..142 C3
Knowsley Cl SL6 .....19 A1
Knowsley Rd RG31 ..57 B2
Knox Gn RG42 ......90 B2
Kola Ho SL2 ....43 A3
Korda Cl TW17 .....124 C3
Krooner Rd GU15 ..151 A2
Kurnool Mortar
  Cross Roads GU15 ..151 A3
Kybes La RG30 .....112 B3
Kyftle Court Flat RG14 ..104 C1
Kyle Cl RG12 ....118 A3

L

La Roche Cl SL3 .....43 B2
Laburham Ct KT16 ..124 A1
Laburnham Rd
  Maidenhead SL6 .....39 C3
  Wonersh RG41 ....88 B1
Laburnum Cl SL2 ......1 C2
Laburnum Gdns RG2 ..86 C1
Laburnum Gr
  Brands Hill SL3 ....69 A4
  Newbury RG14 ....105 A2
Laburnum Pl TW20 ..96 A1
Laburnum Rd KT16 ..124 A1
Laburnum Way TW19 ..97 C4
Laburnums The GU17 ..150 A3
Lacewood Gdns RG2 ..86 C1
Lacey Cl TW20 ......96 B1
Ladbroke Cl RG5 ....87 C3
Ladbrooke Rd SL1 ..42 B2
Ladwell Cl RG14 ....130 B3
Lady Jane Ct RG4 ...59 B2
Lady Margaret Rd SL5 ..120 C2
Ladybank RG12 .....118 A1
Ladyday Pl SL1 .....42 B3
Ladymask Cl RG31 ..84 C2
Lafords The RG2 ....82 A1
Laggan Rd SL6 ......19 C1
Laggan Sq SL6 .....19 C1
Laird Ct GU19 ......145 C1
Lake Ave SL1 ....42 A4
Lake End Rd SL4,SL6 ..41 A3
Lake End Way RG45 ..143 A2
Lake Rd GU25 ......122 A3
Lake Side The GU17 ..150 B2
Lakeland Dr GU16 ..151 C1
Lakes The SL7 ....18 A3
Lakeside
  [5] Bracknell RG42 ..118 B4

Lakeside *continued*
Earley RG6 ....87 A2
Maidenhead SL6 ....20 A1
Lakeside Bsns Pk GU47 ....150 A4
Lakeside Cty Prim Sch
 GU16 ....151 C1
Lakeside Dr SL2 ....22 C2
Lakeside Est SL3 ....70 A4
Lakeside Rd SL3 ....69 C4
Lalande Cl RG41 ....115 C3
Laleham CE Prim Sch
 TW18 ....124 B4
Laleham Rd
 Shepperton TW17 ....125 A2
 Staines TW18 ....96 C2
Laleham Reach KT16 ....124 A3
Laleys Gn RG18 ....78 C2
Lamb Cl RG18 ....106 A3
Lambdens Hill RG7 ....109 B4
Lambert Ave SL3 ....43 C2
Lambert Ct Caws GU17 .....150 B2
Lambeth Ct RG30 ....84 C4
Lambfields RG7 ....83 B2
Lambly Hill GU25 ....122 C3
Lamborne Cl GU47 ....143 A1
Lambourn Ct RG14 ....105 A2
Lambourn Rd RG14 ....25 A2
Lambourn Rd RG20 ....104 B3
Lambourne Cl RG31 ....84 B4
Lambourne Dr
 Bagshot GU19 ....145 B1
 Maidenhead SL6 ....39 B2
Lambourne Gdns RG6 ....87 B2
Lambourne Gr RG12 ....118 C4
Lambridge La RG9 ....15 A2
Lambridge Wood Rd RG9 ...15 A2
Lambs Cl SL6 ....39 A4
Lambs Lane Prim Sch
 RG7 ....139 A4
Lambwood Hill RG7 ....112 B1
Lamerton Rd RG2 ....86 B1
Lamesley Ho SL6 ....39 C3
Lammas Ave [52] SL4 ......67 B3
Lammas Ct Stanwell TW19 ..96 B3
 Windsor SL4 ....67 B3
Lammas Dr TW18 ....96 B2
Lammas Rd RG42 ....90 C1
Lammas Rd SL1 ....41 B4
Lamorna Cres RG31 ....57 B1
Lamp Acres RG14 ....105 A3
Lamplighters Wlk RG31 ....84 C2
Lamsden Way RG2 ....111 A2
Lanark Cl Frimley GU16 ...151 C1
 Woodley RG5 ....62 B3
Lancashire Hill RG42 .....91 C1
Lancaster Ave SL4 ....68 C3
Lancaster Cl
 Englefield Green TW20 ....95 B2
 [2] Reading RG1 ....86 B4
 Stanwell TW19 ....70 C1
 Thatcham RG18 ....106 B2
Lancaster Ct Bracknell RG2 ..86 C1
 Stanwell TW19 ....97 C4
Lancaster Dr GU15 ....151 B3
Lancaster Gdns RG6 ....87 A2
Lancaster Ho RG12 ....118 A2
Lancaster Rd SL6 ....39 A4
Lancaster Sq RG17 ....100 B2
Lancastria Mews SL6 ......39 B4
Lancelot Cl SL1 ....42 A4
Lanchester Dr RG45 ......143 B4
Lancing Cl RG30 ....85 B4
Lancing Rd TW13 ....98 C3
Landen Ct RG40 ....116 A2
Landon Way TW15 ....98 A1
Landrake Cres RG2 ....86 B1
Landseer Cl GU47 ....150 C3
Landsend La RG10 ....61 A1
Lane End Cl RG2 ....113 C3
Lane The Chertsey KT16 ...124 A3
 Chilton OX11 ....10 C4
 Virginia Water GU25 .....122 C2
Laneswood RG7 ....136 C3
Langborough Rd RG40 .....116 A3
Langdale Cl SL6 ....40 A3
Langdale Dr SL5 ....119 C4
Langdale Gdns RG6 ....86 C1
Langdon Cl GU15 ....152 B2
Langford Ct RG4 ....59 B3
Langham Pl RG10 ....95 C2
Langhams Way RG10 ....36 C1
Langley Broom SL3 ....44 C4
Langley Bsns Ctr SL3 ....44 A2
Langley Bsns Pk SL3 .....44 A2
Langley Cnr SL3 ....23 C3
Langley Common Rd
 RG2, RG40 ....114 C1
Langley Cres UB3 ....71 C4
Langley Dr GU15 ....151 C1
Langley Gram Sch SL3 ....43 C1
Langley Hill RG31 ....84 B3
Langley Hill Cl RG31 .....84 B3
Langley Manor Sch SL3 ...43 C3
Langley Park Rd SL0 .....44 B3
Langley Rd Slough SL3 ...43 C2
 Staines TW18 ....96 C1
Langley Sta SL3 ....44 A1
Langley Way SL7 ....1 B1
Langley Wood Sec Sch
 SL3 ....43 C2
Langton Cl Maidenhead SL6 ..39 B4
 Slough SL1 ....41 C3
Langton Way TW20 ....96 B1
Langton's Mdw SL2 ....22 B3
Langworthy End SL6 ....65 A4

Langworthy La SL6 ....65 A4
Laniver Cl RG6 ....87 A1
Lansdowne Ave SL1 ....42 C3
Lansdowne Ct SL1 ....42 C3
Lansdowne Gdns RG7 .....113 B1
Lansdowne Rd
 Reading RG30 ....84 B4
 Staines TW18 ....97 A1
Lanterns Wlk SL6 ....40 A4
Lapwing Cl RG31 ....84 B3
Larbert Cotts SL6 ....38 A3
Larch Ave Ascot SL5 .....120 C2
 Wokingham RG41 ....115 C2
Larch Cl
 Burghfield Common RG30 ..111 A2
 Camberley GU15 ....151 C4
 Newbury RG14 ....104 B3
 Slough SL2 ....42 A4
Larch Ct RG4 ....59 A4
Larch Dr RG2 ....87 C3
Larches Way GU17 ....150 A3
Larchfield Prim Sch SL6 ...39 C2
Larchfield Rd SL6 ....39 C3
Larchmoor Pk SL2 ....23 A4
Larchside Cl RG7 ....113 A1
Larchwood Cl RG12 ......118 C1
Larchwood Dr TW20 ......95 A1
Larchwood Glade GU15 ...152 A4
Larges Bridge Dr RG12 ...118 B3
Larges La RG12 ....118 B4
Larissa Cl RG31 ....57 C1
Lark Ave TW18 ....96 C3
Larkham Cl TW13 ....98 C3
Larkings La SL2 ....23 A2
Larks-Meade RG6 ....87 A1
Larksfield TW20 ....95 B1
Larkspur Cl RG41 ....115 B4
Larkspur Gdns RG18 ....106 C2
Larkswood Cl
 Reading RG31 ....57 B2
 Sandhurst GU47 ....143 A1
Lascelles Ho [1] SL1 .....43 A2
Lascelles Rd SL3 ....43 A2
Lashbrook Mead RG9 .....36 A2
Lashbrook Rd RG9 ....36 A2
Lassell Gdns SL6 ....40 B4
Lasswade Ct KT16 ....123 C1
Lasswade Rd KT16 ....123 C1
Lastingham Ct TW18 .....97 A1
Latham Ave GU16 ....151 C1
Latimer RG12 ....118 A1
Latimer Dr RG31 ....84 B2
Latimer Rd RG41 ....116 A3
Latton Cl OX11 ....10 C4
Laud Cl Newbury RG14 ...106 B3
 Reading RG2 ....86 A3
Laud Way RG40 ....116 C3
Laud's Cl RG9 ....15 B1
Lauder Cl GU16 ....151 C1
Lauderdale Ho TW18 .....96 C2
Launceston Ave RG4 .....59 C3
Launceston Cl RG6 ......87 A1
Laundry La GU47 ....150 C3
Lauradale RG12 ....118 A3
Laurel Ave
 Englefield Green TW20 ...95 A2
 Slough SL3 ....43 C2
Laurel Cl Camberley GU15 ..151 B2
 Poyle SL3 ....70 A4
 Wokingham RG41 ....115 C3
Laurel Dr RG31 ....84 A4
Laurels The RG8 ....56 B3
Laurence Ct SL7 ....1 B1
Lauser Rd TW19 ....97 B4
Lavender Pk SL5 ....119 B3
Lavenham Dr RG5 ....87 C4
Lawford Cres GU46 .....149 B3
Lawkland SL2 ....22 B1
Lawn Cl SL3 ....68 B3
Lawn The SL3 ....68 B3
Lawns The
 North Ascot SL5 ....119 B3
 Reading RG2 ....86 B2
Lawrence Cl RG40 ......116 B3
Lawrence Cres GU20 ....146 B2
Lawrence Ct SL4 ....67 B3
Lawrence Ctr RG41 .....116 A2
Lawrence Gr RG42 ......117 B4
Lawrence Lodge GU15 ...151 B4
Lawrence Mead RG17 ....102 A1
Lawrence Rd RG30 ......85 A4
Lawrence Way
 Camberley GU15 ....150 C2
 Slough SL1 ....41 B4
Lawrences La RG18 ......106 B3
Lawrences Way RG18 ....106 B3
Lawson Dr RG4 ....58 C3
Lawson La OX11 ....10 C4
Lawson Rd RG9 ....35 C4
Lawson Way SL5 ....121 A2
Laxton Gn SL6 ....39 B2
Layburn Cres SL3 ....44 A4
Laylands Gn RG17 ......102 A1
Layton Rise RG31 ....57 C2
Layton's La TW16 ......125 C4
Lazare Ct TW14 ....96 C2
Le Marchant Rd
 GU15, GU16 ....151 C2
Lea Marlow Bottom SL7 ...1 B3
 Reading RG30 ....85 A2
Lea Croft RG45 ....143 A3
Lea Fst Sch SL2 ....43 A3
Lea Mid Sch SL2 ....43 A3
Lea Rd GU15 ....151 A1
Lea The Thorpe Lea TW20 ...96 A3
 Wokingham RG40 ....141 C4
Lea View RG18 ....79 B4

Leacroft Staines TW18 ....97 A2
 Sunningdale SL5 ....121 A2
Leacroft Cl TW18 ....97 A2
Leacroft Rd SL0 ....44 A2
Leafield Copse RG12 ....118 C3
Leaholme Gdns SL1 ....41 B4
Leander Pl RG31 ....84 B3
Leas Dr SL0 ....44 C4
Leaver Rd RG9 ....15 A1
Leaves Gn RG12 ....118 B2
Ledbury Cl RG30 ....58 A1
Ledbury Dr RG31 ....84 B2
Ledger La SL6 ....65 B3
Ledger's Rd SL1 ....42 B4
Lee Ct RG6 ....87 C4
Lee La SL6 ....18 C1
Leeds Rd SL1 ....42 C3
Lees Cl SL6 ....39 A3
Lees Gdns SL6 ....39 A3
Lees Wlk SL7 ....1 B1
Leeson Gdns SL4 ....41 C1
Legoland Windsor SL4 ...66 B1
Leicester SL1 ....118 C1
Leicester Cl RG9 ....15 B2
Leigh Field RG7 ....136 C3
Leigh Pk SL3 ....68 A4
Leigh Rd SL1 ....42 A3
Leigh Sq SL4 ....66 B3
Leighton Gdns SL6 ......20 A1
Leighton Ho [5] SL7 .....1 A2
Leighton Park Sch RG2 ...86 C2
Leiston Cl [7] RG6 ......87 B1
Leiston Spur SL1 ....42 C4
Leith Cl Crowthorne RG45 ..143 A4
 Slough SL1 ....43 A3
Lemart Cl RG30 ....84 C4
Lemington Gr RG12 .....118 A2
Leney Cl RG40 ....116 B4
Lenham Cl RG41 ....88 C1
Lennox Cl RG31 ....84 A2
Lennox Rd RG6 ....87 A3
Lent Gn SL1 ....21 A1
Lent Green La SL1 ......21 A1
Lent Rise Cty Comb Sch
 SL1 ....41 A4
Lent Rise Rd SL1 ....21 A1
Leopold Mall [14] SL1 ...42 C2
Leopold Wlk RG1 ....86 B4
Leppington RG12 ....118 A1
Lerwick Dr SL1 ....42 C4
Lesford Rd RG1 ....86 A3
Lesley Ct RG30 ....85 B3
Leslie Southern Ct RG14 ..105 A2
Lesters Rd SL6 ....19 A3
Letchworth Ave TW14 ...98 C4
Letcombe Ct [17] RG1 ...86 A3
Letcombe Sq RG12 .....118 C3
Letcombe St RG1 ....86 A4
Leverkusen Rd RG12 ...118 A3
Leverton La SL7 ....73 A1
Levendon Rd RG14 ......104 C1
Lewington Mews RG17 ..100 B2
Lewins Farm Ct [4] SL1 ...41 C3
Lewins Way SL1 ....41 C3
Lewis Wlk RG14 ....130 B3
Lewisham Way GU47 ....143 B1
Lexington Ave SL6 ......39 B3
Lexington Gr RG2 ......113 B3
Leyburn Cl RG5 ....88 A4
Legland Gdns RG2 .....113 C3
Leylands La TW19 ....70 A1
Leys Gdns RG14 ....104 C2
Leyside RG45 ....143 A3
Libra Ho HP10 ....3 A4
Library Par RG5 ....87 C4
Licensed Victuallers Sch
 SL5 ....119 B3
Lichfield Cl [1] RG6 .....87 B1
Lichfield Rd SL3 ....68 B3
Lichfields RG12 ....118 C4
Liddell SL4 ....66 B2
Liddell Cl RG40 ....141 C2
Liddell Pl SL4 ....66 B2
Liddell Sq [4] SL4 ......66 B3
Liddell Way Ascot SL5 ..119 C2
 Windsor SL4 ....66 B2
Lido Rd OX11 ....9 C4
Lidstone Cl RG6 ....114 B4
Lieberwood Rd RG30 ....85 B4
Lightlands La RG6 .....119 C3
Lightwater Ctry Pk GU18 ..145 C1
Lightwater Mdw GU18 ...153 A4
Lightwater Rd GU18 ....153 B4
Lightwater Village Sch
 GU18 ....153 A4
Lightwood RG12 ....118 B2
Lilac Cl RG8 ....57 B3
Lilac Cl SL2 ....21 C1
Lilac Wlk RG31 ....84 B3
Lilacs The RG41 ....115 B2
Lilley Way SL1 ....41 C3
Lillibrooke Cres SL6 ....39 A2
Lily Hill Dr RG12 ......118 C4
Lily Hill Rd RG12 .....118 C4
Lima Ct RG1 ....85 C3
Lime Ave Camberley GU15 ..152 A3
 Winkfield SL4 ....93 C3
Lime Barn [4] SL7 ....1 B1
Lime Cl Newbury RG14 ..105 B2
 Wokingham RG41 ....115 C3
Lime Ct [2] TW16 ......98 C1
Lime Tree Rd RG8 ....34 A3
Lime Tree Wlk GU25 ....122 C3
Lime Wlk Bracknell RG12 ..118 B3
 Maidenhead SL6 ....39 A4

Limecroft GU46 ....149 B3
Limefield Cl RG6 ....87 C2
Limerick Cl RG42 ......118 A4
Limes Cl TW15 ....98 A2
Limes Rd TW20 ....95 C2
Limes The RG4 ....66 B3
Limmer Cl RG41 ....115 B2
Limmerhill Rd RG41 ....115 C3
Lincoln Cl Frimley GU15 ..152 A2
 Winnersh RG41 ....88 A2
Lincoln Ct Newbury RG14 ..104 C1
 [24] Slough SL1 ....42 C2
Lincoln Gdns RG10 ......61 B3
Lincoln Hatch La SL1 ....21 B1
Lincoln Rd
 Maidenhead SL6 ....39 A4
 Reading RG2 ....86 B2
Lincoln Way
 Charlton TW16 ....125 C4
 Slough SL1 ....43 B3
Lincolnshire Gdns RG42 ..91 C1
Lind Cl RG6 ....87 B1
Lindale Cl GU25 ....121 C3
Lindberg Way RG5 ....61 A1
Linden [3] Bracknell RG12 ..118 C2
 Slough SL3 ....43 A4
Linden Ave SL6 ....19 B1
Linden Cl Holyport SL6 ...64 C3
 Newbury RG14 ....104 C2
 Wokingham RG41 ....115 C2
Linden Ct
 Camberley GU15 ....151 C4
 Englefield Green TW20 ...95 A1
Linden Dr SL2 ....22 B2
Linden Pl TW18 ....97 A2
Linden Rd Newtown RG20 ..131 C2
 Reading RG2 ....86 C1
 Woodley RG5 ....87 B2
Linden Way TW17 ......125 B2
Lindenhill Rd RG42 ....117 C4
Lindores Rd SL6 ....66 A3
Lindsay Cl TW19 ....70 B1
Lindsay Dr TW17 ......125 B2
Lindsey Cl RG41 ......115 C3
Lindsey Gdns TW14 .....98 B4
Lines Rd RG10 ....88 C3
Ling Dr GU18 ....152 C4
Lingfield Rd RG14 .....131 B4
Lingholm Cl
 Maidenhead SL6 ....39 B3
 Reading RG30 ....85 A4
Lingwood RG12 ....118 B2
Link Ho RG41 ....105 A1
Link Rd Datchet SL3 .....68 B3
 East Bedfont TW14 .....98 C4
 Newbury RG14 ....105 A1
Link The Slough SL2 .....22 C1
 Yateley GU46 ....149 B4
Link Way Arborfield RG2 ..114 C1
 Staines TW18 ....97 A1
 Thatcham RG18 ....106 A2
Links Dr RG30 ....85 A3
Links Rd Ashford TW15 ...97 C2
 Flackwell Heath HP10 ....3 A4
Links The SL5 ....43 A3
Links Way RG14 ....98 A1
Linkscroft Ave TW15 ....98 A1
Linkswood Rd SL1 ....22 A3
Linkway Camberley GU15 ..151 B2
 Crowthorne RG45 ......142 C3
Linnet Cl RG31 ....84 A3
Linnet La RG20 ....131 C2
Linnet Wlk RG41 ....115 C3
Lintott Ct TW19 ....70 B1
Lion Cl TW17 ....124 C3
Lipscomb Cl RG18 ......79 A3
Lipscombe Cl RG14 ....104 C2
Liquel Cl RG17 ....100 B2
Liscombe RG12 ....118 A1
Liscombe Ho RG12 ....118 A1
Lisle Cl RG4 ....104 C3
Lismore Cl SL6 ....87 C2
Lismore Ct SL1 ....42 C4
Lismore Pk SL2 ....22 C3
Lisset Rd SL6 ....40 A3
Lister Cl RG8 ....57 B3
Liston Ct [5] SL7 ....1 B1
Liston Rd SL7 ....1 A1
Litcham Spur SL1 ....42 B4
Lithgow's Rd TW14, TW6 ..71 C2
Littington Cl RG6 .....114 B4
Little Aldershot La RG26 ..134 C4
Little Boltons [7] SL7 ....1 C1
Little Bowden La RG8 ...55 C2
Little Buntings SL4 .....66 C4
Little Chapels Way SL1 ..42 A2
Little Cl HP10 ....3 A3
Little Copse GU46 .....149 B4
Little Croft Rd RG8 ....34 B3
Little Elms UB3 ....71 B4
Little Fryth RG40 .....142 B3
Little Glebe RG4 ....60 C2
Little Heath Rd RG31 ...84 A4
Little Hatch Sch RG31 ...84 A4
Little Hill Rd RG10 ....88 B2
Little Johns La RG30 ...85 A4
Little London Rd RG7 ..136 A1
Little Marlow CE Fst Sch
 SL7 ....2 C3
Little Marlow Rd SL7 ....1 C2
Little Moor GU47 ......143 B1
Little Oak Dr RG31 .....84 A3
Little Paddock GU15 ...152 A4
Little Ridgdale RG18 ...118 C3
Little Saffron RG18 ....79 A3
Little St [2] RG1 ....86 A4

Little Sutton La
 Brands Hill SL3 69
 Slough, Sutton SL3 44
Little Vigo GU46 149
Little Woodlands SL4 66
Littlebrook Ave SL2 41
Littlecote Dr RG1 85
Littlecote Rd SN8 99
Littlecroft Rd [2] TW20 ...95
Littledale Cl RG12 118
Littledown Cotts SL1 42
Littledown Cotts SL1 42
Littledown Rd SL1 42
Littledown Sch SL1 42
Littlefield Ct UB7 70
Littlejohns La RG30 58
Littleport Spur SL1 42
Littlestead Cl RG4 59
Littlewick CE Inf Sch
 TW3 125
Littleton La TW17, TW18 ..124
Littleton Rd TW15 98
Littlewick Green
 Montessori Sch SL6 38
Litton Rd RG2 86
Liverpool Rd Reading RG1 ..86
 Slough SL1 42
Livery Cl RG1 86
Livingstone Ct TW19 97
Livingstone Gdns RG5 ...87
Livingstone Rd RG14 ...105
Llangar Gr RG45 143
Llanvair Cl SL5 120
Llanvair Dr SL5 119
Llewellyn Pk RG10 61
Lochinvar Cl SL1 42
Lochinver RG12 118
Lock Ave SL6 20
Lock Bridge Rd SL6 3
Lock La SL6 39
Lock Mead SL6 20
Lock Path SL4 66
Lock Pl RG1 86
Lock Rd SL7 1
Lockbridge Ct SL6 40
Locke Gdns SL3 43
Lockets Cl SL4 66
Lockram La RG7 111
Locks Ride SL5 92
Lockside Ct RG7 109
Locksley Ct [2] SL1 43
Lockstile Mead RG8 34
Lockstile Way RG8 34
Lockton Chase SL5 119
Lockton Ho RG40 116
Loddon Bridge Rd RG5 ...87
Loddon Cl GU15 152
Loddon Dr Charvil RG10 ..61
 Maidenhead SL6 39
Loddon Hall Rd RG10 61
Loddon Inf Sch The RG6 ..87
Loddon Jun Sch RG6 87
Loddon Rd SL3 3
Loddon Spur SL1 42
Loddon Vale Ctr RG5 88
Lodge Cl
 Englefield Green TW20 ...95
 Marlow SL7 1
 Slough SL1 42
Lodge Gr GU46 149
Lodge Rd RG10 88
Lodge The RG14 104
Lodge Way Ashford TW15 ..97
 Charlton TW17 125
 Windsor SL4 66
Lodgings of the Military
 Knights [8] SL4 67
Logan Cl RG30 85
Lois Dr TW17 125
Lomond Ave RG4 59
London Rd Ascot SL5 ...120
 Ashford TW15, TW18,
 TW19, TW14 97
 Bagshot GU15,GU19 145
 Bracknell RG12, SL5 119
 Bracknell, Binfield
 RG12, RG42 117
 Brands Hill SL3 69
 Camberley GU15 151
 Datchet SL3 68
 Earley RG6 87
 Englefield Green TW20 ...95
 Newbury RG14 105
 Reading RG1 86
 Slough SL3 43
 Sunningdale, Blacknest SL5 ..121
 Sunningdale, Shrubs Hill
 SL5, GU25 121
 Thatcham RG18 106
 Twyford RG10 61
 Virginia Water
 GU25, TW20 122
 Windlesham GU18,GU20,SL5
 GU19,GU20,SL5 146
 Woodley RG4,RG5 63
London St Chertsey KT16 ..124
 Reading RG1 86
Loneacre GU20 146
Long Barn La RG2 86
Long Cl
 Farnham Common SL2 22
 Kintbury RG17 102
Long Close Sch SL3 43
Long Dr SL1 21
Long Furlong Dr SL2 21
Long Gr RG26 134

ng Grove RG7 .... 107 B3
ng Half Acre SL6 .... 38 A2
ng Hedge RG17 .... 25 B1
ng Hill Rd RG12, SL5 ... 119 A4
ng La Brightwalton RG20 .. 28 C2
  :pokham SL6 .... 19 B3
  lermitage RG14, RG18 .... 78 C1
  lolyport, Bray Woodside SL6 64 B3
  lolyport, touchen-end SL6 . 64 C3
  lewbury RG18 .... 105 B4
  Purley on T RG31 ...... 57 A2
  Stanwell TW15, TW19 ... 97 C4
lng Lane Prim Sch
  RG31 .... 57 C3
lng Mickle SL6 .... 143 A1
lng Readings La SL2 ..... 22 A1
lng Water Dr RG30 ..... 112 B4
lng Wlk The SL4 .... 94 B4
lng's Way RG40 .... 116 C4
lngbourne Way KT16 .... 123 C2
lngbridge Rd RG19 ..... 106 C1
lngcroft Rd RG19 ...... 106 C1
lngcross Sta GU25 ..... 121 C1
lngdale Rd RG41 .... 88 B1
lngdown Lodge GU47 ... 150 A4
lngdown Rd GU47 ...... 143 A1
lngfield Rd RG10 ...... 61 B3
lngford Ave
  Feltham TW14 .... 71 C1
  Stanwell TW19 ...... 97 C4
lngford Cl GU15 .... 151 B2
lngford Rdbt TW6, UB7 .. 70 B1
lngford Sch TW14 ..... 98 C4
lngford Way TW19 ..... 97 C4
lnghurst Cl RG4 .... 59 A1
lnglands Way GU15 ..... 152 B3
lngleat Dr RG31 ...... 57 A2
lngleat Gdns SL1 ...... 39 B3
lngleat Way TW14 ..... 98 A4
lngmead Ball Hill RG20 .. 129 C1
  Windsor SL4 .... 66 C3
lngmead La SL1 .... 44 B3
lngmeadow GU15, GU16 . 151 C2
lngmoor La RG7 ...... 137 A4
lngmoors RG42 .... 117 C4
lngmore Rd RG2 ...... 113 B3
lngridge Cl RG30 ..... 85 A4
lngridge Scout Boating
  Activity Ctr SL7 ..... 18 C4
lngshot Ind Est RG12 .. 117 C4
lngshot La RG12 ...... 117 C4
lngside Cl TW20 ...... 123 B4
lngview HP9 .... 3 C4
lngwater Dr RG30 ..... 85 C1
lngwater La RG27,RG40 . 141 C2
lngwater Rd
  Bracknell RG12 ..... 118 B2
  Finchampstead RG40 .. 141 C1
lngworth Ave RG31 .... 84 A4
lngworth Dr SL6 ...... 20 B1
lnsdale Cl SL6 .... 20 A1
lnsdale Way SL6 ...... 40 B1
lok Out Discovery Ctr
  The RG12 .... 118 B1
loosen Dr SL6 .... 40 A2
lord Knyvett Cl TW19 .. 70 B1
loring Rd SL4 .... 66 C3
lorne Cl SL1 .... 42 A2
lorne Pl RG1 .... 85 C4
lorne St RG1 .... 85 C4
lorraine Cty Inf Sch
  GU15 .... 151 C4
lorraine Rd GU15 ..... 151 C4
lory Ridge GU19 ...... 145 C2
losfield Rd SL4 ...... 66 C3
loughborough RG12 .... 118 C2
loundyes Cl RG18 ..... 106 A2
lovatt Cl RG31 ...... 84 A4
love Green La SL0 .... 44 A3
love Hill La SL3 ..... 44 A3
love La Iver SL0 ..... 44 B4
  Newbury RG14 ...... 105 A3
lovedean Ct RG12 .... 118 C2
lovegrove Dr SL2 .... 21 C1
lovejoy La SL4 ...... 66 B3
lovel La SL5 .... 93 A2
lovel Rd SL5 .... 93 A2
lovelace Cl SL6 ..... 17 C2
lovelace Rd RG12 .... 117 C3
lovell Cl RG9 ...... 35 B4
lovells Cl GU18 ..... 146 A1
loverock Rd RG30 .... 58 B1
loves Cl RG7 .... 111 A2
lovett Cl RG31 ..... 136 C3
lovett Gdns SL6 .... 20 B2
lovett Rd TW20 ..... 30 B4
lowbrook Dr SL6 .... 39 A2
lowbrook Prim Sch SL6 . 39 A2
lowbury RG12 ...... 118 C2
lower Armour Rd RG31 . 57 B1
lower Bglws RG8 .... 34 B4
lower Boyndon Rd SL6 . 39 C3
lower Britwell Rd SL2 .. 21 B2
lower Broadmoor Rd
  RG45 .... 143 B2
lower Brook St RG1 ... 86 A3
lower Canes GU46 .... 149 A2
lower Charles St GU15 . 151 B3
lower Church Rd GU47 . 150 A2
lower Cippenham La SL1 . 41 C3
lower Common RG27 .. 140 C1
lower Cookham Rd SL6 . 20 B1
lower Earley Way (N)
  RG6 .... 87 C1
lower Earley Way (W)
  RG6 .... 113 C4

Lower Elmstone Dr RG31 . 57 B1
Lower Farm Ct RG19 ... 105 C1
Lower Field Rd RG1 .... 86 A3
Lower Henley Rd RG4 ... 59 B2
Lower Lees Rd SL7 .... 22 A1
Lower Meadow Rd RG2 .. 86 B4
Lower Mill Field GU19 .. 145 B1
Lower Mount RG1 ..... 86 A3
Lower Pound La SL7 .... 3 B1
Lower Rd Chilton OX11 .. 10 B4
  Cookham SL6 ...... 19 C4
Lower Ridge SL8 ..... 3 A2
Lower Sandhurst Rd
  RG40,GU47 .... 143 C4
Lower Ventnor Cotts SL6 . 19 B4
Lower Village Rd SL5 .. 120 B2
Lower Way RG19 ..... 106 A2
Lower Wokingham Rd
  RG40, RG45 ...... 143 C2
Lowes Cl RG9 .... 36 A2
Lowestoft Cl RG6 .... 87 B1
Lowestoft Dr SL1 .... 41 B4
Loweswater Wlk GU15 . 152 B2
Lowfield Cl GU18 .... 153 A4
Lowfield Gn RG4 .... 59 B3
Lowfield Gn RG4 .... 59 C2
Lowfield Rd RG4 .... 59 B3
Lowlands Rd
  Blackwater GU17 ... 150 B2
  Stanwell TW19 .... 70 B1
Lowry Cl GU47 ..... 150 B3
Lowther Cl RG41 .... 115 C4
Lowther Rd RG41 ... 115 C4
Loxwood RG6 ...... 87 B1
Loxwood Cl TW14 ... 98 C4
Lucan Dr TW18 ..... 97 B2
Lucas Cl GU46 ..... 149 B3
Lucas Gn GU24 ..... 153 B2
Lucas Green Rd GU24 . 153 C3
Lucey Cl RG31 ..... 57 A2
Lucie Ave TW15 .... 98 A1
Luckley Oakfield Sch
  RG40 .... 116 A2
Luckley Path RG40 .. 116 B3
Luckley Rd RG41 ... 116 A2
Luckley Wood RG41 . 116 A2
Luckmore Dr RG6 ... 87 A2
Lud Lodge TW15 .... 97 C3
Luddington Ave
  GU25, TW20 ..... 122 C4
Ludgrove Prep Sch
  RG40 .... 116 B2
Ludlow RG12 ...... 118 A1
Ludlow Cl RG14 .... 105 C3
Ludlow Ho SL6 .... 39 C3
Ludlow Rd SL6 .... 39 C3
Luff Cl SL4 ...... 66 C2
Luker Ave RG9 .... 15 B2
Lulworth Rd RG2 ... 113 B4
Lunds Farm Rd RG5 . 88 A4
Lundy Ct SL1 ..... 41 C3
Lundy La RG30 .... 85 B4
Lupin Cl GU19 .... 145 B1
Lupin Ride RG45 ... 143 A4
Luscombe Cl RG4 .. 59 B2
Lutman La SL6 .... 37 C3
Lutmans Haven RG10 . 37 C3
Lutterworth Cl RG42 . 91 B1
Lutton Cl RG4 .... 113 C4
Lych Gate Cl GU47 . 149 C4
Lycroft Cl RG8 ... 34 B4
Lydbury RG12 .... 118 C3
Lydford Ave SL2 .. 42 B4
Lydford Rd RG1 ... 86 C3
Lydney RG12 ..... 118 A1
Lydsey Cl SL2 .... 22 A1
Lyefield Ct RG4 .. 59 A3
Lyell Place E SL4 . 66 B2
Lyell Place W SL4 . 66 B2
Lyell Rd SL4 .... 66 B2
Lyell Walk E SL4 . 66 B2
Lyell Walk W SL4 . 66 B2
Lyme Gr RG31 .... 57 A2
Lymington Ave GU46 . 149 B3
Lymington Gate RG4 . 58 C3
Lynch Hill La SL2 . 21 C1
Lynch Hill Sch SL2 . 22 A2
Lynch La RG17 ... 25 A2
Lynchets View RG17 . 24 C3
Lynden Mews RG1 .. 86 A3
Lyndhurst Ave
  Blackwater GU17 .. 150 B3
  Cookham SL6 .... 19 C3
Lyndhurst Cl RG12 . 119 A3
Lyndhurst Rd Ascot SL5 . 120 A3
  Goring RG8 ..... 34 B3
  Reading RG30 ... 58 A1
Lyndhurst Sch GU15 . 151 A3
Lyndwood Dr SL4 .. 66 C2
Lyndwood Par SL4 . 66 C2
Lyne Cl GU25 .... 122 C2
Lyne Crossing Rd
  KT16, GU25 .... 123 A2
Lyne Ct GU25 .... 122 C1
Lyne La KT16,TW20,GU25 . 123 A2
Lyne Place Manor GU25 . 122 C1
Lyne Rd GU25 .... 122 B2
Lyngrove Ave TW15 . 98 A3
Lyneham Gdns SL6 . 19 A1
Lyneham Rd RG45 .. 143 A3
Lynmouth Ct RG1 . 59 A1
Lynmouth Rd RG1 . 59 A1
Lynn Cl TW15 .... 97 B3
Lynton Cl RG5 ... 87 B3
Lynton Ct 4 RG14 . 105 B3
Lynton Gn SL6 ... 39 C4
Lynwood Ave Egham TW20 . 95 C1
  Slough SL3 ..... 43 B2

Lynwood Chase ■ RG12 . 118 B4
Lynwood Cres SL5 .. 120 C2
Lynwood Ct SL1 ... 42 C4
Lynwood Flats SL5 . 120 C2
Lyon Cl RG19 .... 106 C1
Lyon Oaks RG42 .. 91 A1
Lyon Rd RG45 .... 143 B3
Lyon Sq RG30 .... 85 A4
Lyon Way Ind Est GU16 . 151 B1
Lysander Cl RG5 .. 88 A4
Lysander Mead SL6 . 40 B4
Lytchet Minster Cl 4
  RG12 .... 118 C3
Lytham RG12 .... 117 C2
Lytham Cl SL3 ... 85 B2
Lytham Ct SL5 ... 120 B2
Lytham End RG31 . 57 A2
Lytham Rd RG5 ... 87 C4

M

Macadam Ave RG45 . 143 C4
Macbeth Ct RG40 . 118 C4
Macdonald Rd GU18 . 153 A4
Mace Cl RG6 ..... 87 A1
Mackay Cl RG31 .. 84 C2
Mackenzie Mall 18 SL1 . 42 C2
Mackenzie St 8 SL1 . 42 C2
Macklin Cl RG17 . 100 B3
Macnaughton Woods
  GU15 .... 151 C3
Macphail Cl RG40 . 116 C4
Macrae Rd GU46 .. 149 B3
Maddle Rd RG17 .. 24 B4
Madeira Pl 3 RG14 . 105 A1
Madejski Stad RG2 . 112 C2
Madingley RG12 .. 118 A1
Madox Brown End GU47 . 150 C3
Mafeking Rd TW19 . 96 A3
Magdalene Rd
  Littleton TW17 .. 124 C3
  Sandhurst GU47 .. 143 C1
Magill Cl RG7 ... 113 A1
Magna Carta La TW19 . 96 B1
Magna Carta Sch TW18 . 96 B1
Magna Rd TW20 .. 95 A1
Magnolia Cl GU47 . 143 B1
Magnolia Ct RG5 . 88 A4
Magnolia Gdns SL3 . 43 B2
Magnolia Way RG41 . 115 C3
Magpie Cl RG19 .. 106 C1
Magpie Way Reading RG31 . 84 A3
  Slough SL2 ..... 21 C1
Maguire Dr GU16 . 152 B2
Mahonia Cl GU24 . 153 C3
Maiden Erlegh Comp Sch
  RG6 .... 87 A2
Maiden Erlegh Dr RG6 . 87 A2
Maiden Lane Ctr 5 RG6 . 87 B1
Maiden Pl RG6 ... 87 B1
Maiden's Gn SL4 . 92 A3
Maidenhead Coll
  Claires Court Girls SL6 . 39 C4
Maidenhead Court Pk
  SL6 .... 20 A2
Maidenhead Office Pk
  SL6 .... 38 C1
Maidenhead Rd
  Binfield RG40 .... 89 B2
  Cookham SL6 ... 19 C3
  Newell Green RG42 . 91 A3
  Windsor SL4 .... 66 C4
Maidenhead Sta SL6 . 40 A3
Maidensfield RG41 . 88 B1
Main Dr Bracknell RG42 . 91 C1
  Iver SL0 .... 44 C2
  Winkfield RG12, SL5 . 119 A4
Main St Chilton OX11 . 10 B4
  Greenham RG19 .. 131 C3
  Newtown RG19 .. 132 A2
  Yateley GU46 .... 149 B4
Mainprize Rd RG12 . 118 C4
Mainstone Rd GU24 . 153 A1
Maise Webster Cl TW19 . 97 B4
Maitland Rd RG1 . 85 C4
Maiwand Gdns RG31 . 84 B4
Maize La RG42 ... 91 C1
Majendie Cl RG14 . 104 B3
Major's Farm Rd
  Brands Hill SL3 .. 69 A4
  Datchet SL3 .... 68 C4
Makepiece Rd RG42 . 91 A1
Maker Cl RG30 ... 85 A2
Makins Rd RG9 .. 35 A4
Malders La SL6 .. 19 B2
Maldon Cl RG30 . 85 B3
Malet Cl TW20 .. 96 B1
Malham Fell RG12 . 118 A3
Malham Rd RG19 . 106 B2
Mallard Cl Earley RG6 . 87 A2
  Twyford RG10 ... 61 C2
Mallard Ct RG14 . 104 C2
Mallard Dr SL1 .. 41 C3
Mallard Row RG1 . 86 A4
Mallard Way
  Padworth RG7 ... 136 A1
  Yateley GU46 .... 149 A3
Mallards The
  Frimley GU16 ... 151 C1
  Great Shefford RG17 . 48 A2
  Laleham TW18 .. 124 A3
Mallards Way GU18 . 153 A4
Mallory Ave RG4 . 59 B3
Mallow Pk SL6 .. 19 B1
Mallowdale Rd RG12 . 118 C1
Malone Rd RG5 .. 87 B3

Malpas Rd SL2 ... 43 A3
Malt Hill Egham TW20 . 95 C2
  Newell Green RG42 . 91 C3
Malt Ho SL4 ..... 95 A4
Malt House Cl SL4 . 95 A4
Malt Shovel La RG12 . 24 C2
Maltby Way RG6 . 114 A4
Malthouse Cl RG9 . 106 C1
Malthouse La
  Reading RG1 .... 85 C4
  West End GU24 .. 153 C4
Malthouse Way 7 SL7 . 1 B1
Maltings Pl 8 RG1 . 86 A4
Maltings The Staines TW18 . 96 C2
  Thatcham RG19 .. 106 C1
  West Ilsley RG20 . 10 A1
Malton Ave SL1 . 42 A3
Malvern Cl RG5 .. 87 C3
Malvern Ct Brands Hill SL3 . 69 A4
  Newbury RG14 .. 104 C1
  Reading RG1 .... 86 B3
Malvern Rd Harlington UB3 . 71 C4
  Maidenhead SL6 . 19 B1
Malvern Way RG10 . 61 B4
Malyons The TW17 . 125 B2
Man's Hill RG7 .. 111 B1
Managua Cl RG4 . 59 C1
Manchester Rd RG1 . 86 C4
Mandarin Ct RG14 . 105 B1
Mandela Ct 6 RG1 . 86 B4
Mandeville Cl RG30 . 84 C3
Mandeville Ct TW20 . 96 A2
Mandeville Rd TW17 . 125 A2
Manea Cl RG6 ... 114 B4
Manfield Cl SL2 . 22 A2
Manners Rd RG5 . 87 B4
Mannock Way RG5 . 88 A4
Manor Bglws RG20 . 31 B2
Manor Cl RG42 .. 91 A1
Manor Cres RG20 . 31 B2
Manor Ct Marlow SL7 . 1 B2
  Slough, Cippenham SL1 . 41 C3
  Slough, Upton Park SL1 . 42 C2
Manor Farm Ave TW17 . 125 A2
Manor Farm Cl SL4 . 66 A4
Manor Farm Cotts SL4 . 68 A1
Manor Farm Cotts SL4 . 68 A3
Manor Farm Ct TW20 . 96 A2
Manor Farm Ho SL4 . 66 A3
Manor Farm La
  Egham TW20 ... 96 A2
  Tidmarsh RG8 ... 56 B3
Manor Farm Rd RG2 . 86 A1
Manor Gdns HP10 . 3 C3
Manor Gr SL6 .... 65 B3
Manor House Dr SL5 . 93 A1
Manor House La SL3 . 68 A3
Manor House The GU20 . 151 B3
Manor La Cheveley RG20 . 51 A1
  Harlington UB3 .. 71 B4
  Hermitage RG18 .. 79 A4
  Leckhampstead RG20 . 39 C2
  Newbury RG14 .. 105 C3
Manor Leaze TW20 . 96 A2
Manor Park Ct RG30 . 84 B3
Manor Park Dr
  Wokingham RG40 . 141 C3
  Yateley GU46 .... 149 A3
Manor Pk Froxfield SN8 . 99 A2
  Staines TW18 ... 96 B3
Manor Pl Newbury RG14 . 104 B3
  Staines TW18 ... 97 A2
Manor Prim Sch RG30 . 84 B3
Manor Rd Ashford TW15 . 98 A2
  Goring RG8 ..... 34 A3
  Henley-on-T RG9 . 35 B4
  Letcombe Bassett OX12 . 7 B3
  Maidenhead SL6 . 20 C2
  Walton-on-T KT12 . 125 C1
  Whitchurch-on-T RG8 . 56 B4
  Windsor SL4 .... 66 C3
  Wokingham RG40 . 116 B3
Manor Way Bagshot GU19 . 145 C2
  Egham TW20 .... 95 C1
  Holyport SL6 .... 65 A4
Manor Wood Gate RG9 . 36 A2
Manorcroft Rd TW20 . 96 A1
Manorcrofts Rd TW20 . 96 A1
Manse Cl UB3 ... 71 B4
Mansel Cl SL2 ... 43 A4
Mansell Cl SL4 .. 66 C3
Mansell Ct RG2 .. 86 C1
Mansell Dr RG14 . 130 B3
Mansfield Cl SL5 . 119 B4
Mansfield Cr RG12 . 118 A2
Mansfield Pl SL5 . 119 B4
Mansfield Rd
  Reading RG1 .... 85 C3
  Wokingham RG40 . 116 A3
Mansion House St 24
  RG14 .... 105 A2
Mansion La SL0 .. 44 B3
Manston Dr RG12 . 118 B2
Mant Cl RG20 ... 75 B3
Manygate La TW17 . 125 A1
Mapel Cl 1 RG12 . 118 C3
Maple Cl Blackwater GU17 . 150 B3
  Maidenhead SL6 . 39 B2
  Sandhurst GU47 .. 142 C1
  Winnersh RG41 .. 88 B2
Maple Cres
  Newbury RG14 .. 105 A2
  Slough SL2 ..... 43 A3
Maple Ct
  Englefield Green TW20 . 95 A1
  Goring RG8 ..... 34 A3
  Slough SL2 ..... 43 A3
  Windsor SL4 .... 67 B2

Maple Dr
  Crowthorne RG45 . 143 B4
  Lightwater GU18 . 152 C4
Maple Gdns Reading RG2 . 86 C1
  Stanwell TW19 .. 97 C3
  Yateley GU46 .... 149 B3
Maple La RG8 ... 55 A3
Maple Rise SL7 .. 1 C2
Mapledene RG4 .. 58 C2
Mapledurham Dr RG8 . 57 C3
Mapledurham Ho RG31 . 57 C3
Mapledurham View RG31 . 57 B1
Mapledurham Watermill
  RG31 .... 57 C3
Mapledurham Wlk SL6 . 19 C2
Maples The 8 SL8 . 3 A2
Maplin Pk SL3 ... 44 A2
Marathon Cl RG5 . 88 A4
Marbeck Cl SL4 . 66 B3
Marbull Way RG42 . 91 A1
Marchant Cl RG19 . 131 B4
Marchant Ct SL7 . 2 A2
Marcheria Cl RG12 . 118 A2
Marchwood Ave RG4 . 59 B4
Marcia Ct SL1 ... 41 C3
Marconi Rd RG14 . 105 A2
Marcus Cl RG30 . 85 A4
Mardale GU15 ... 152 B2
Mardy RG4 ..... 58 C3
Mare La RG10 ... 63 C2
Marefield RG6 ... 87 B1
Merefield Rd SL7 . 1 B1
Marescroft Rd SL2 . 21 C1
Mareshall Ave RG42 . 91 A1
Marfleet Cl RG6 . 87 C1
Margaret Cl Reading RG2 . 113 B4
  Wokingham RG41 . 116 A3
Maria Ct 11 RG30 . 85 A3
Marie Davis Ct 2 RG1 . 86 A4
Marigold Cl RG45 . 142 C3
Marina Cl KT16 . 124 B1
Marina Way SL1 . 41 B3
Mariners La RG7 . 82 A2
Marino Way RG40 . 141 A3
Marion Ave TW17 . 125 A2
Marish Ct SL3 ... 44 A2
Marish Cty Fst Sch SL3 . 44 A2
Marish Jun Sch SL3 . 44 A2
Marish Wharf Ind Est SL3 . 43 C2
Marjory Kinnon Sch
  TW14 .... 71 C1
Markby Way RG6 . 87 C1
Market La SL3 ... 44 B2
Market Pl Colnbrook SL3 . 69 B4
  Henley-on-T RG9 . 15 C1
  12 Newbury RG14 . 105 A2
  Reading RG1 .... 86 A4
  Wokingham RG40 . 116 B3
Market Sq Marlow SL7 . 1 B1
  Staines TW18 ... 96 C2
Market St Bracknell RG12 . 118 A4
  Maidenhead SL6 . 39 C4
  Newbury RG14 .. 105 A2
  18 Windsor SL4 .. 67 B3
Market Way 18 RG1 . 86 A4
Markham Centre Trad Est
  The RG7 .... 83 C1
Markham Ct GU15 . 151 B3
Markham Mews RG40 . 116 B3
Marks Rd RG41 .. 116 A4
Marlborough Ave RG6 . 87 B1
Marlborough Ct
  Reading RG1 .... 85 C3
  Slough SL1 ..... 41 C4
  Wokingham RG40 . 116 B4
Marlborough Ho
  5 Maidenhead SL6 . 39 C3
  Reading RG1 .... 86 B3
Marlborough Rd
  Ashford TW15 ... 97 C2
  Maidenhead SL6 . 39 A3
  Slough SL3 ..... 43 C1
Marlborough Rise GU15 . 151 C3
Marlborough Way RG31 . 84 A2
Marley Croft TW18 . 96 C3
Marlin Cl TW16 . 97 B1
Marlin Ct SL7 ... 1 B1
Marling Cl RG31 . 57 B1
Marlow Bottom SL7 . 1 B3
Marlow Bridge La SL7 . 1 B1
Marlow CE Inf Sch SL7 . 1 B2
Marlow Com Hospl SL7 . 1 C1
Marlow Lodge 10 SL6 . 39 C2
Marlow Mill SL7 . 1 C1
Marlow Rd Bisham SL7 . 1 B4
  Bisham SL6 ..... 2 A4
  Henley-on-T RG9 . 15 C2
  Little Marlow SL7,SL8 . 2 B3
  Maidenhead SL6 . 39 C4
  Marlow Bottom SL7 . 1 A4
  Marlow SL7 ..... 2 A1
Marlowes The RG14 . 130 C4
Marlston Rd RG18 . 79 B3
Marquis Pl RG1 .. 86 C4
Marriott Cl TW14 . 71 B1
Mars Cl RG41 ... 115 C3
Marsack St RG4 . 59 B1
Marsdale Rd RG4 . 58 C3
Marsh La
  Hungerford RG17 . 100 A3
  Newbury RG14 .. 105 A2
  Taplow SL6 ..... 40 C4
Marsh Rd RG18 .. 106 C2

rlands Ave RG30 . . . . .85 A3
rley Cl Slough SL3 . . . . .43 C2
rley Ct SL5 . . . . .120 C2
rley Pl RG17 . . . . .100 B3
rmington Ave RG40 . . . . . . .141 C4
rmington Cl RG26 . . . . .134 C1
rmington Rd TW15 . . . . .98 B2
rrpeth Cl RG2 . . . . .86 B2
rrell Ct TW18 . . . . .97 A2
rrice Cl SL3 . . . . .44 A1
rris Ct SL4 . . . . .66 C3
rris Pl 5 SL7 . . . . .1 B1
rriss Ct 14 RG1 . . . . .86 B4
rtaine Rd TW15 . . . . .97 B3
rtimer Cl RG2 . . . . .113 B4
rtimer La RG7 . . . . .137 B4
rtimer Rd SL3 . . . . .43 B2
rtimer Sta RG7 . . . . .137 C3
rton Pl RG7 . . . . .83 C2
ss Cl RG4 . . . . .59 B2
ssy Vale SL6 . . . . .19 B1
astyn Ho RG2 . . . . .91 A1
ulsford Prep Sch OX10 . .14 A3
ulsham Copse La
L46 . . . . .149 A4
ulsham La RG46 . . . . .149 A4
undield Way SL1 . . . . .41 C2
unt Cl
inham Common SL2 . . . . . .22 B4
ppleford RG8 . . . . .105 A1
unt Cl The GU25 . . . . .122 B2
unt Felix KT12 . . . . .125 C2
unt La Bracknell RG12 . . . .118 B4
haddleworth RG20 . . . . .49 A4
unt Lee TW20 . . . . .95 C2
unt Pleasant
racknell RG12 . . . . .118 B3
eading RG1 . . . . .86 A3
andhurst GU47 . . . . .149 A1
unt Pleasant RG20 . . . . . .135 A1
okingham RG41 . . . . .116 A3
unt Pleasant CI GU18 . .146 A1
unt Pleasant Cotts
2 Bourne End SL8 . . . . .3 A2
inglefield Green TW20 . . . . . .95 B1
unt Pleasant Gr RG1 . . . . .86 A3
unt Rd RG18 . . . . .106 C2
unt St RG2 . . . . .86 A3
unt The
aversham RG4 . . . . .58 C2
eading RG1 . . . . .86 B3
entworth GU25 . . . . .122 B2
unt View RG9 . . . . .15 B1
unt View Ct RG9 . . . . .15 B1
untain Ash SL1 . . . . .1 B3
untbatten Cl
ewbury RG14 . . . . .105 B3
3 Slough SL1 . . . . .43 A2
untbatten Rise GU47 . . .142 C1
urfield Cl RG1 . . . . .86 B4
urfield Ho RG12 . . . . .117 C2
ulberry Ave TW19 . . . . .97 B1
1 Sandhurst GU47 . . . . . . .150 B4
oodley RG5 . . . . .87 C3
ulberry Cl
1 Bracknell RG12 . . . . .118 C2
ewbury RG14 . . . . .104 C2
okingham RG40 . . . . .116 B3
ulberry Dr SL3 . . . . .43 C1
ulberry Ho RG42 . . . . .91 A1
ulberry Way RG7 . . . . .83 C2
ulberry Wlk SL7 . . . . .39 B4
ulfords Hill RG26 . . . . . . .135 A1
ulgrave Rd GU16 . . . . .151 C1
ullens Rd TW20 . . . . .95 C2
ullion Ct 2 RG1 . . . . .85 C4
ulroy Dr GU15 . . . . .152 A3
umbery Hill RG10 . . . . .36 C1
uncaster Cl TW15 . . . . .98 A2
uncaster Rd TW15 . . . . .98 A2
unces Rd SL7 . . . . .2 A1
unday Ct RG42 . . . . .90 C1
undaydean La SL7 . . . . .1 A2
undesley Spur SL1 . . . . . . .42 C4
undesley St RG1 . . . . .86 A3
unkle Marsh RG17 . . . . .25 C1
unnings Dr RG7 . . . . .150 C3
unro Ave RG5 . . . . .87 C2
urdoch Cl TW18 . . . . .97 A2
urdoch Rd RG40 . . . . .116 B3
urray Cl SL5 . . . . .120 B2
urray Ho RG41 . . . . .116 A3
urray Rd RG41 . . . . .116 A3
urrellhill La RG42 . . . . . . .117 B4
urrells La GU15 . . . . .151 C4
urrin Rd SL6 . . . . .39 B4
us of Berkshire Aviation
The RG5 . . . . .88 A3
us of English Rural Life
RG2 . . . . .86 C2
us of Reading RG1 . . . . . . .86 A4

Mushroom Castle La
RG42 . . . . .92 A1
Mustard La RG4 . . . . .60 C1
Mustard Mill Rd TW18 . . . .97 A3
Muswell Cl RG7 . . . . .83 C2
Mutton Oaks RG12 . . . . . . .117 B4
Myers Way GU16 . . . . .152 B1
Mylne Sq RG40 . . . . .116 B3
Mylum Cl RG12 . . . . .118 B3
Myrke The SL3 . . . . .42 C1
Myrtle Ave TW14 . . . . .71 C1
Myrtle Cl
Burghfield Common RG7 . . .111 A2
Lightwater GU18 . . . . .153 A4
Poyle SL3 . . . . .69 C3
Purley on T RG31 . . . . .57 B2
Myrtle Cres SL2 . . . . .42 C3
Myrtle Dr GU17 . . . . .150 B3
Myton Wlk SL6 . . . . .83 C2

N

Nabbs Hill Cl RG31 . . . . .84 B3
Nairn Cl GU16 . . . . .151 C1
Nalderhill Rd RG20 . . . . . . .103 A3
Napier Cl RG45 . . . . .143 B3
Napier Dr GU15 . . . . .152 A4
Napier Lodge TW15 . . . . . . .98 B1
Napier Rd Ashford TW15 . . .98 B1
Crowthorne RG45 . . . . .143 B2
Harmondsworth TW6 . . . . . . .70 B3
Maidenhead SL6 . . . . .39 A3
Reading RG1 . . . . .86 B4
Napier Wlk TW15 . . . . .98 B1
Napper Cl SL5 . . . . .119 B4
Narromine Dr RG31 . . . . . . .84 C2
Naseby RG12 . . . . .118 A1
Naseby Rise RG14 . . . . .105 B3
Nash Cl RG6 . . . . .87 A2
Nash Gdns SL5 . . . . .119 C4
Nash Grove La RG40 . . . . . .115 C1
Nash Pk RG42 . . . . .90 A1
Nash Rd SL3 . . . . .44 A1
Nashdom La SL1 . . . . .22 A4
Natalie Cl TW14 . . . . .98 B4
Nathan Ct 20 RG1 . . . . .85 C4
Naylors The RG7 . . . . .139 B3
Neath Gdns RG30 . . . . .84 C4
Needham Cl SL4 . . . . .66 C3
Neil Cl TW15 . . . . .98 B2
Nell Gwynn Ave TW17 . . . .125 B2
Nell Gwynne Ave SL5 . . . .120 B3
Nell Gwynne Cl SL5 . . . . . .120 B3
Nelson Cl Bracknell RG12 . .118 C4
East Bedfont TW14 . . . . .98 C4
Slough SL3 . . . . .43 B1
Nelson Ct KT16 . . . . .124 A1
Nelson Rd Ashford TW15 . . .97 C2
Caversham RG4 . . . . .59 B1
Harmondsworth TW6 . . . . . . .70 C2
Windsor SL4 . . . . .66 C2
Nelson Terr 22 RG1 . . . . . . .86 A3
Nelson Way SL1 . . . . .150 C2
Nelson's La RG10 . . . . .89 A3
Nene Rd TW6, UB7 . . . . .71 A3
Neptune Cl RG41 . . . . .115 C3
Neptune Rd TW6 . . . . .71 B3
Neptune Way SL1 . . . . .41 C2
Netherton RG12 . . . . .118 A3
Netley Cl RG4 . . . . .59 B3
Nettlecombe RG12 . . . . . . .118 B2
Nettleton Rd TW6 . . . . .71 A3
Neve Ho SL6 . . . . .39 C4
Nevelle Cl RG42 . . . . .117 B4
Neville Cl Stoke Poges SL2 . . .23 C3
Waltham St Lawrence RG10 . . .62 C3
Neville Ct SL1 . . . . .41 A1
Neville Dr RG19 . . . . .106 C2
Nevis Rd RG31 . . . . .57 B2
New Bath Rd RG10 . . . . .61 B3
New Bldgs RG7 . . . . .81 B2
New Bright St 5 RG1 . . . . . .86 A3
New Christ Church
CE Prim Sch RG1 . . . . .86 A3
New Cl RG6 . . . . .16 A4
New Forest Ride RG12 . . . .118 C2
New Greenham Pk RG19 . .131 C3
New Hill RG8 . . . . .34 C3
New Lane Hill RG30 . . . . . . .84 C3
New Mdw SL5 . . . . .119 C4
New Mile Rd SL5 . . . . .120 B4
New Mill La RG27 . . . . .140 C1
New Mill Rd RG27 . . . . .140 C2
New Par TW15 . . . . .97 C2
New Park Rd TW15 . . . . .98 A2
New Rd Bagshot GU19 . . . .145 C2
Blackwater GU17 . . . . .150 C2
Bourne End SL8 . . . . .3 A2
Bracknell RG42 . . . . .118 B4
Burghfield Common RG7 . . .111 C1
Cookham SL6 . . . . .19 C4
Crowthorne RG45 . . . . .143 B3
Datchet SL3 . . . . .68 B3
East Bedfont TW14 . . . . .71 B1
Egham TW18 . . . . .96 B2
Harlington UB3 . . . . .71 A4
Holyport SL6 . . . . .65 A4
Hurley SL6 . . . . .17 B4
Littleton TW17 . . . . .125 A3
Marlow Bottom SL7 . . . . .1 B3
Newbury RG14 . . . . .105 B3
North Ascot SL5 . . . . .92 C1
Reading RG1 . . . . .86 B3
Sandhurst GU47 . . . . .150 A4
Shiplake RG9 . . . . .36 A2
Slough SL3 . . . . .44 A2

New Rd continued
Twyford RG10 . . . . .61 B4
Windlesham GU19,GU20 . .146 A2
Wokingham RG41 . . . . .115 A4
New Road Hill RG7 . . . . . . .108 A2
New Scotland Hill
Prim Sch GU47 . . . . .143 A1
New Sq East Bedfont TW14 . . .98 B4
Slough SL1 . . . . .42 C2
New St Beech Hill RG7 . . . .138 A1
Henley-on-T RG9 . . . . .15 C1
Staines TW18 . . . . .97 A2
New Town Prim Sch RG1 . .86 B4
New Way RG7 . . . . .82 A1
New Wickham La TW20 . . . .96 A1
New Wokingham Rd
RG45 . . . . .143 A3
New Zealand Ave KT12 . . .125 C1
Newall Rd TW6 . . . . .71 B3
Newalls Rise RG10 . . . . .36 C1
Newark Rd GU20 . . . . .146 A3
Newark St RG1 . . . . .86 A3
Newbery Cres SL4 . . . . .66 B3
Newbery Cl RG31 . . . . .57 B1
Newbery Way SL1 . . . . .42 B2
Newbold Coll RG42 . . . . . . .90 B1
Newbold Rd RG14 . . . . .104 B3
Newbold Sch RG42 . . . . .90 B1
Newbolt Cl RG18 . . . . .106 B3
Newbury Cl RG18 . . . . .61 A2
Newbury Coll RG14 . . . . . . .104 C2
Newbury District Hospl
RG14 . . . . .104 C1
Newbury District Mus
RG14 . . . . .105 A2
Newbury Dr SL6 . . . . .40 A3
Newbury Hill RG18 . . . . .52 C3
Newbury La RG20 . . . . .31 B2
Newbury Ret Pk
Great Shefford RG17 . . . . . . .48 A1
Harmondsworth TW6 . . . . . . .70 C3
Hermitage RG18 . . . . .79 A3
Lambourn RG17 . . . . .25 B1
Newbury Ret Pk RG14 . . . .131 A4
Newbury St
Kintbury RG17 . . . . .102 A1
Lambourn RG17 . . . . .25 A1
Newbury Sta RG14 . . . . . . .105 A1
Newcastle Rd RG2 . . . . .86 C1
Newchurch Rd Slough SL2 . .41 C4
Tadley RG26 . . . . .135 A1
Newell Gn RG42 . . . . .91 B2
Newfield Gdns SL7 . . . . .1 C2
Newfield Rd SL6 . . . . .39 C4
Newfield Way SL7 . . . . .1 C2
Newhaven Cres TW15 . . . . .98 B2
Newhaven Spur SL2 . . . . . . .22 A1
Newhurst Gdns RG42 . . . . . .91 B2
Newlands Ave RG4 . . . . .59 A3
Newlands Cl SL6 . . . . .64 B4
Newlands Dr
Maidenhead SL6 . . . . .39 A4
Poyle SL3 . . . . .69 C2
Newlands Rd GU15 . . . . . . .151 A1
Newlands Sch SL6 . . . . .39 A4
Newlyn Gdns RG31 . . . . .86 A1
Newmarket Cl 10 RG6 . . . . .87 B1
Newport Cl 11 RG14 . . . . . .105 A2
Newport Dr RG42 . . . . .91 B2
Newport Rd
Harmondsworth TW6 . . . . . . .71 A3
Newbury RG14 . . . . .105 A2
Reading RG1 . . . . .59 A1
Slough SL2 . . . . .21 C1
Newquay Dr RG6 . . . . .87 A1
Newstead Rise RG2 . . . . . . .86 C1
Newton Ave RG4 . . . . .59 B3
Newton Cl SL3 . . . . .43 C2
Newton Ct SL4 . . . . .68 A1
Newton La SL4 . . . . .68 A1
Newton Side Orch SL4 . . . .68 A1
Newtonside SL4 . . . . .68 A1
Newtown RG26 . . . . .135 A1
Newtown Gdns RG9 . . . . . . .35 C4
Newtown Rd
Henley-on-T RG9 . . . . .35 C4
Marlow SL7 . . . . .1 C2
Newbury RG14 & RG20 . . . .130 A4
Sandhurst GU47 . . . . .150 A4
Niagara Rd RG9 . . . . .35 C4
Nicholas Cl 22 RG41 . . . . . .85 C4
Nicholas Gdns SL1 . . . . .41 C3
Nicholas Rd RG9 . . . . .35 A4
Nicholls SL4 . . . . .66 B2
Nicholls Wlk SL4 . . . . .66 B2
Nicholson Wlk 3 TW20 . . . .96 A2
Nicholsons Ctr 5 SL6 . . . . .39 C4
Nicholsons La SL6 . . . . .39 C4
Nideggen Cl RG19 . . . . .106 B2
Nightingale Cres RG12 . . . .118 A2
Nightingale Gdns GU47 . . .150 A4
Nightingale Ho 3 RG1 . . . . .85 C3
Nightingale La
Maidenhead SL6 . . . . .19 B2
Mortimer RG7 . . . . .137 B3
Nightingale Pk SL2 . . . . . . .21 C3
Nightingale Pl SL6 . . . . .19 B2
Nightingale Rd RG18 . . . . . .87 B2
Nightingale Wlk SL4 . . . . . .67 B2
Nightingales The
Newbury RG14 . . . . .131 A4
Stanwell TW19 . . . . .97 C4
Nimrod Cl RG5 . . . . .88 A4
Nimrod Way RG2 . . . . .86 A3
Nine Acres SL1 . . . . .41 C3

Nine Elms Cl TW14 . . . . .98 C4
Nine Mile Ride
Bracknell RG12, RG40 . . . . .117 C1
Crowthorne RG40 . . . . .142 B4
Nine Mile Ride Prim Sch
RG40 . . . . .141 C3
Nire Rd RG4 . . . . .59 C1
Nixey Cl SL1 . . . . .42 B3
No 4 RG30 . . . . .85 B3
Noakes Hill RG8 . . . . .54 A4
Nobel Dr UB3 . . . . .71 C4
Noble Rd RG9 . . . . .35 C4
Nobles Way TW20 . . . . .95 C1
Nodmore RG20 . . . . .49 A4
Norcot Rd RG30 . . . . .84 C4
Norden Cl SL6 . . . . .39 B2
Norden Mdws SL6 . . . . .39 B3
Norden Rd SL6 . . . . .39 B3
Nores Rd RG2 . . . . .113 B4
Norfolk Ave SL1 . . . . .42 B4
Norfolk Chase RG42 . . . . . . .91 C1
Norfolk Cl RG41 . . . . .115 C3
Norfolk Park Cotts SL6 . . . .39 C4
Norfolk Rd Maidenhead SL6 . .85 B4
Reading RG30 . . . . .85 B4
Norland Dr HP10 . . . . .3 B4
Norland Nursery
Training Coll RG17 . . . . . . .101 B4
Norlands RG18 . . . . .106 B3
Norlands La TW18, TW20 . .123 C4
Norman Ave RG9 . . . . .15 C1
Norman Cl TW18 . . . . .97 A2
Norman Ho TW17 . . . . .125 A1
Norman Keep RG42 . . . . . . .118 C4
Norman Pl RG1 . . . . .59 A1
Norman Rd Ashford TW15 . .98 B1
Caversham RG4 . . . . .59 B2
Normandy Cl SL6 . . . . .96 B2
Normanhurst TW15 . . . . . . .98 A1
Normans The SL2 . . . . .43 A4
Normanstead Rd RG31 . . . . .84 B4
Normay Rise RG14 . . . . .130 B3
Normoor Rd RG7 . . . . .110 C1
Norreys Ave RG40 . . . . .116 B4
Norreys Dr SL6 . . . . .39 A2
Norris Field RG20 . . . . .49 A4
Norris La RG20 . . . . .49 A4
Norris Rd Reading RG6 . . . . .87 A3
Staines TW18 . . . . .96 C2
North Burnham Cl SL1 . . . . .22 A1
North Cl East Bedfont TW14 . .71 B1
Medmenham SL7 . . . . .18 C4
Windsor SL4 . . . . .67 A4
North Cotts SL2 . . . . .22 B1
North Croft HP10 . . . . .3 C3
North Dr Sulhamstead RG7 . .110 B4
Wentworth GU25 . . . . .121 C2
North End La SL5 . . . . .121 A1
North Farm Cl RG17 . . . . . . .25 B2
North Fryerne GU46 . . . . . .149 B4
North Gn Bracknell RG12 . .118 B4
3 Maidenhead SL6 . . . . .19 C1
Slough SL1 . . . . .42 C3
North Gr KT16 . . . . .123 C2
North Hatton Rd TW6 . . . . .71 B3
North Links Rd HP10 . . . . . . .3 A4
North Lodge Dr SL5 . . . . . .119 B4
North Lodge Mews RG30 . . .85 B2
North Pk SL0 . . . . .44 B2
North Rd
East Bedfont TW14 . . . . .71 B1
Maidenhead SL6 . . . . .39 C4
Moulsford OX10 . . . . .13 C2
Winkfield SL5 . . . . .119 A4
North Row SL3 . . . . .44 C3
North St Caversham RG4 . . .59 A1
Egham TW20 . . . . .95 C2
Reading RG1 . . . . .85 C4
Winkfield SL4 . . . . .93 A3
North Standen Rd RG17 . .100 A2
North Star La SL6 . . . . .39 B3
North Town Cl 1 SL6 . . . . . .19 C1
North Town Mead 4 SL6 . . .19 C1
North Town Moor SL6 . . . . .19 C1
North Town Rd SL6 . . . . . . .19 C1
North View Gdns 8
RG14 . . . . .105 A2
North Wlk RG7 . . . . .83 C2
Northam Cl RG6 . . . . .87 C2
Northampton Ave SL1 . . . . .42 B4
Northampton Cl RG12 . . . .118 C3
Northborough Rd SL2 . . . . .22 A1
Northbourne Cl RG2 . . . . . . .87 A1
Northbrook Copse RG12 . .118 C2
Northbrook Rd RG4 . . . . . . .59 B3
Northbrook St RG14 . . . . . .105 A2
Northbury Ave RG10 . . . . . .61 C3
Northbury La RG10 . . . . .61 C3
Northcott RG12 . . . . .118 A3
Northcott Cl TW20 . . . . .95 A2
Northcroft SL2 . . . . .22 A1
Northcroft Cl TW20 . . . . . . .95 A2
Northcroft Gdns TW20 . . . .95 A2
Northcroft La RG14 . . . . . . .104 C2
Northcroft Rd TW20 . . . . . . .95 A2
Northcroft Terr RG14 . . . . .104 C2
Northcroft Villas RG14 . . . .95 A2
Northdean 5 SL6 . . . . .39 A1
Northend RG12 . . . . .118 A3
Northern Hts SL6 . . . . .19 C4
Northern Perimeter Rd
TW6 . . . . .71 B3
Northern Perimeter Road
(W) TW6 . . . . .70 C3
Northern Rd SL2 . . . . .22 B1

Northern Woods HP10 . . . . . .3 B4
Northfield GU18 . . . . .153 A4
Northfield La RG9 . . . . .36 A2
Northfield Cr
Henley-on-T RG9 . . . . .15 B2
Staines TW18 . . . . .124 A4
Northfield End RG9 . . . . .15 B2
Northfield Rd Eton SL4 . . . . .41 C1
Maidenhead SL6 . . . . .39 B3
Reading RG1 . . . . .59 A1
Shiplake RG9 . . . . .36 A2
Staines TW18 . . . . .124 A4
Thatcham RG18 . . . . .106 A2
Northfields Cheveley RG20 . .51 A2
Lambourn RG17 . . . . .25 B2
Northfields Terr RG17 . . . . .25 B2
Northgate Dr GU15 . . . . . . .152 A4
Northington Cl RG12 . . . . . .118 C2
Northlands Dr SL1 . . . . .21 B2
Northmead Rd SL2 . . . . .41 C4
Northolt Rd TW6 . . . . .70 C3
Northrop Rd TW6 . . . . .71 C3
Northumberland Ave RG2 . .86 B2
Northumberland Cl
Bracknell RG42 . . . . .91 C1
Stanwell TW19 . . . . .70 C1
Northumberland Cres
TW14 . . . . .71 C1
Northumbria Rd SL6 . . . . . . .39 A2
Northview RG17 . . . . .100 B3
Northview Hts RG17 . . . . . .100 B3
Northway Newbury RG14 . .105 A1
Thatcham RG18 . . . . .106 B3
Wokingham RG41 . . . . .115 C4
Northwood Dr RG14 . . . . . .105 B2
Northwood Rd TW6 . . . . . . .70 C3
Norton Cl RG14 . . . . .130 B3
Norton Pk SL5 . . . . .120 B2
Norton Rd Frimley GU15 . .152 B2
Reading RG1 . . . . .86 C4
Swallowfield RG7 . . . . .139 B2
Wokingham RG40 . . . . .116 B3
Woodley RG5 . . . . .87 C3
Norway Dr SL2 . . . . .43 A4
Norwich Ave GU15 . . . . . . .151 C2
Norwich Dr RG5 . . . . .87 B4
Norwich Ho SL6 . . . . .39 C4
Norwood Cres TW6 . . . . . . .71 B3
Norwood Rd RG2 . . . . .86 C4
Notley End TW20 . . . . .95 B1
Notton Way RG6 . . . . .113 C4
Nuffield Dr GU47 . . . . .143 C1
Nuffield Rd Barkham,
Arborfield Garrison RG2 . . . .140 C1
Barkham, Langley Common
RG2 . . . . .141 A4
Nugee Ct RG45 . . . . .143 A3
Nugent Cl SL7 . . . . .1 C2
Nuneaton RG12 . . . . .118 C2
Nunhide La RG8, RG31 . . . . .83 C3
Nuns Acre RG8 . . . . .34 A4
Nuns Wlk GU25 . . . . .122 B2
Nuptown La RG42 . . . . .91 C4
Nursery Cl Hurst RG10 . . . . .88 C4
Shiplake RG9 . . . . .36 A2
Nursery Gdns
Purley on T RG8 . . . . .57 A3
Staines TW18 . . . . .97 A1
Sunbury TW16 . . . . .125 C4
Nursery La
North Ascot SL5 . . . . .119 C4
Slough SL3 . . . . .43 B3
Nursery Rd Burnham SL1 . . .41 A4
Staines TW16 . . . . .125 C4
Nursery Way TW19 . . . . .68 B1
Nursery Wlk SL7 . . . . .1 A1
Nut La RG10 . . . . .62 C3
Nutbean La RG7 . . . . .139 C3
Nutbourne Ct TW18 . . . . . . .96 C1
Nutfield Ct GU15 . . . . .151 B4
Nuthatch Dr RG6 . . . . .87 A2
Nuthurst RG12 . . . . .118 A1
Nutley Cl GU46 . . . . .149 B3
Nutmeg Cl RG6 . . . . .86 C1
Nutter's La RG2 . . . . .140 A4
Nuttings RG20 . . . . .49 C3
Nutty La TW17 . . . . .125 B3

O

O' Bee Gdns RG26 . . . . . . .134 C1
Oak Ave Egham TW20 . . . . . .96 B1
Sandhurst GU47 . . . . .143 B1
Oak Dr
Burghfield Common RG7 . . .111 A2
Newbury RG14 . . . . .104 C1
Woodley RG5 . . . . .88 B3
Oak End Way RG7 . . . . .109 B2
Oak Farm Cl GU17 . . . . . . .150 B3
Oak Gn RG2 . . . . .113 B4
Oak Grove Cres GU15 . . . .150 C3
Oak Hill SN8 . . . . .99 B2
Oak La
Englefield Green TW20 . . . . .95 B3
Windsor SL4 . . . . .67 A3
Oak Leaf Ct SL5 . . . . .119 B4
Oak Lo 13 TW16 . . . . .98 C1
Oak Tree Ave SL7 . . . . .1 B2
Oak Tree Cl Marlow SL7 . . . .1 B2
Tadley RG26 . . . . .135 A1

Oak Tree Cl continued
Wentworth GU25 ....122 B2
Oak Tree Copse RG31 ....57 C2
Oak Tree Dr TW20 ....95 B2
Oak Tree Rd Marlow SL7 .....1 B2
  Reading RG31 ....57 C1
  Thatcham RG19 ....106 C1
Oak Tree Wlk RG8 ....57 B3
Oak View RG31 ....84 B4
Oak Way
  East Bedfont TW14 ....98 C4
  Woodley RG5 ....87 B2
Oakdale RG12 ....118 B2
Oakdale Cl RG31 ....84 B4
Oakdale Wlk RG5 ....88 A4
Oakdene
  Burghfield Common RG7 ....111 A1
  Sunningdale SL5 ....120 C2
Oaken Copse GU15 ....152 B4
Oaken Gr Maidenhead SL6 ...19 B1
  Newbury RG14 ....130 B4
Oakengates RG12 ....118 A1
Oakes Ct RG17 ....100 B3
Oakfield RG1 ....86 B3
Oakfield Ave SL3 ....42 A3
Oakfield Cl RG41 ....116 A3
Oakfield Cty Fst Sch SL4 ...67 A3
Oakfield Rd Ashford TW15 ...98 A2
  Blackwater GU17 ....150 C2
  Bourne End SL8 ....3 A2
  Silchester RG26 ....135 C1
Oakfields GU15 ....151 A3
Oakhall Ct TW16 ....98 C2
Oakhall Dr TW16 ....98 C2
Oakham Dr RG31 ....57 B1
Oakhurst SL6 ....20 A2
Oaklands Reading RG1 .....86 B3
  Yateley GU46 ....149 B3
Oaklands Cl SL5 ....92 C1
Oaklands Cty Jun Sch
  RG45 ....143 A3
Oaklands Dr
  North Ascot SL5 ....92 C1
  Wokingham RG41 ....116 A3
  Wokingham RG41 ....116 A3
Oaklands Inf Sch RG45 ....143 A3
Oaklands La RG45 ....143 A4
Oaklands Pk RG41 ....116 A2
Oaklea Dr RG27 ....140 C1
Oakleigh GU18 ....153 B4
Oakley HP10 ....3 C4
Oakley Cres SL1 ....42 C3
Oakley Green Rd SL4 .....66 A3
Oakley Rd
  Camberley GU15 ....151 A2
  Caversham RG4 ....58 C2
  Newbury RG14 ....105 B2
Oakmede Pl RG42 ....90 B1
Oakridge GU24 ....153 C3
Oaks Rd Shiplake RG9 .....36 A2
  Stanwell TW19 ....2 B3
Oaks The Bracknell RG12 ..118 B4
  Staines TW18 ....96 C2
  Yateley GU46 ....149 B3
Oakside Way RG2 ....113 C4
Oaktree Way GU47 ....143 A1
Oakway Dr GU16 ....151 C1
Oakwood Rd
  Bracknell RG12 ....118 C4
  Virginia Water GU25 ......122 B2
  Windlesham GU20 ....146 C2
Oareborough RG12 ....118 C2
Oast Ct TW18 ....96 C2
Oast House Cl TW19 ......95 C4
Oatlands Dr Slough SL1 ....42 B4
  Walton-on-T KT12 ....125 C1
Oatlands Rd RG2 ....113 C3
Oban Ct SL6 ....42 B2
Oban Gdns RG5 ....87 C2
Obelisk Way GU15 ....151 B3
Oberon Way TW17 ....124 C3
Ockwells Rd SL6 ....39 B1
Octavia RG12 ....118 A1
Octavia Way TW18 ....96 C1
Oddfellows Rd RG14 ......104 C1
Odell Cl RG6 ....114 A4
Odencroft Rd SL2 ....22 A1
Odiham Ave RG4 ....59 C3
Odiham Rd RG2 ....139 B1
Odney La SL6 ....20 A4
Ogmore Cl RG30 ....84 C4
Okingham Cl GU47 ....143 B1
Old Acre La RG10 ....61 A3
Old Barn Cl RG4 ....59 A3
Old Bath Rd Charvil RG10 ...61 A3
  Newbury RG14 ....104 C2
  Sonning RG4 ....60 B1
Old Bisley Rd GU16 ....152 B3
Old Bothampstead Rd
  RG20 ....51 B3
Old Bracknell Cl RG12 .....118 A3
Old Bracknell La E RG12 ..118 A3
Old Bracknell La W
  RG12 ....118 B3
Old Charlton Rd TW17 .....125 B2
Old Court Cl SL6 ....39 A2
Old Crown ⬛ SL1 ....42 C2
Old Dean Rd GU15 ....151 B4
Old Elm Dr RG30 ....84 B4
Old Farm Cres RG31 ......57 B1
Old Farm Dr RG12 ....91 B1
Old Ferry Dr TW19 ....68 B1
Old Fives Ct SL1 ....21 A1
Old Forest Rd RG41 ......88 C1

Old Forge Cl SL6 ....40 A2
Old Forge Cres TW17 .....125 A4
Old Forge End GU47 ......150 A4
Old Green La GU15 ....151 B4
Old Hayward La RG17 .....73 B1
Old House Ct SL3 ....43 B4
Old Kennels Ct RG30 .....85 A3
Old Kiln Rd HP10 ....3 A4
Old La
  Hamstead Marshall RG20 ..102 C1
  Headley RG19 ....133 C1
Old La The RG1 ....85 C3
Old Lands Hill RG12 ....118 B4
Old Marsh La SL6 ....40 C2
Old Mill Ct RG10 ....61 B3
Old Mill La SL6 ....40 B2
Old Moor La HP10 ....3 C4
Old Newtown Rd RG14 ....104 C1
Old Nursery Pl TW15 ......98 A2
Old Orchard The RG31 ....84 C2
Old Palace Ct SL3 ....69 B3
Old Pasture Rd
  GU16, GU15 ....151 C2
Old Pharmacy Ct RG45 ...143 B2
Old Pond Cl GU15 ....151 B1
Old Portsmouth Rd
  GU15 ....152 A3
Old Post Office La ⓪ SL6 ..39 C2
Old Priory La RG42 ....91 B1
Old Sawmill La RG43 ......143 B3
Old Sawmills The SL17 ....127 C3
Old School Ct TW19 ......95 C4
Old School La GU46 ......149 B3
Old School The
  Hampstead Norreys RG18 ...52 C3
  Wooburn Green HP10 ......3 B2
Old School Yd The RG17 ...25 A1
Old Slade La SL0 ....44 C1
Old St Cherveley RG18 ....51 C1
  Cherveley, Beedon
  Common RG20 ....51 B3
  Penge Hermitage RG18 ....78 C4
Old Station Bsns Pk RG20 .31 C2
Old Station Way HP10 ......3 C3
Old Station Yd The RG17 ..25 A1
Old Vicarage Way HP10 ....3 B2
Old Watery La HP10 ....3 C4
Old Well Ct RG4 ....60 B2
Old Welmore GU46 ....149 C3
Old Whitley Wood La
  RG2 ....113 B3
Old Wokingham Rd
  RG40,RG45 ....143 B4
Old Wooseehill La RG41 ...115 C4
Oldacre GU24 ....153 C4
Oldacres SL6 ....40 A4
Oldbury RG12 ....117 C3
Oldbury Rd KT16 ....123 C1
Oldcorne Hollow GU46 ...149 A3
Olde Farm Dr GU17 ......150 A3
Oldean Cl RG21 ....57 B1
Oldershaw Mews SL6 .....39 A4
Oldfield Cl RG6 ....87 A4
Oldfield Prim Sch SL6 .....40 A3
Oldfield Rd SL6 ....40 A4
Oldfield Rd Ind Est SL6 ...40 A4
Oldhouse La GU18 ....146 B1
Oldstead RG12 ....118 B2
Oldway La SL1 ....41 B3
Oleander Cl RG45 ....143 A4
Oliver Dr RG31 ....84 B3
Oliver Rd SL5 ....120 A3
Oliver's Paddock SL7 ......1 B3
Ollerton RG12 ....118 A1
Omega Way RG30 ....123 B4
Omer's Rise RG7 ....110 C2
One Pin La SL2 ....22 B4
Onslow Dr SL5 ....93 A1
Onslow Gdns RG4 ....59 C3
Onslow Lodge TW18 ......96 C1
Onslow Mews KT16 ......124 A2
Onslow Rd SL5 ....121 A1
Opal Ct SL3 ....23 B1
Opal Way RG41 ....115 C4
Opendale Rd SL1 ....41 A4
Opladen Way RG12 ....118 C2
Oracle Ctr The RG1 ....86 A4
Oracle Parkway
  Reading RG6 ....86 C4
  Sonning RG6 ....60 A1
Orbit Cl RG40 ....141 C3
Orchard Ave Ashford TW15 .98 B1
  Hatton TW14 ....71 C1
  Slough SL1 ....41 A4
  Windsor SL4 ....67 A3
Orchard Chase RG10 .....88 C3
Orchard Cl Ashford TW15 ...98 B1
  Farnborough (Hants) GU17 .150 C1
  Henley-on-T RG9 ....15 C1
  Maidenhead SL6 ....40 A2
  Newbury RG14 ....105 B3
  Purley on T RG31 ....57 B2
  Shinfield RG7 ....113 A1
  Shiplake RG9 ....35 C1
  West End GU24 ....85 B3
  Wokingham RG40 ....116 B3
  Wolverhampton RG7 .....108 B1

Orchard Gate
  Farnham Common SL2 ....22 B4
  Maidenhead SL6 ....39 B4
Orchard Gr Caversham RG4 .59 C2
  Flackwell Heath HP10 ......3 A4
  Maidenhead SL6 ....39 B4
Orchard Hill Bourne End SL8 .3 A1
  Windlesham GU20 ....146 B2
Orchard Ho ⑥ SL8 ....3 A2
Orchard Park Cl RG17 ....100 B2
Orchard Pl RG40 ....116 B3
Orchard Rd Hurst RG10 ...88 C4
  Mortimer RG7 ....137 A3
  Old Windsor SL4 ....68 A1
Orchard St RG1 ....86 A3
Orchard The
  Flackwell Heath HP10 ......3 A4
  Lightwater GU18 ....153 A4
  Marlow SL7 ....2 C2
  Theale RG7 ....83 C2
  Virginia Water GU25 .....122 C2
Orchard Way
  Ashford TW15 ....97 C3
  Camberley GU15 ....151 A1
  Slough SL3 ....43 C3
Orchardene RG14 ....105 A2
Orchards The TW18 ......98 B2
Orchardville SL1 ....21 A1
Orchids The OX11 ....10 B4
Oregon Ave RG31 ....57 B2
Oregon Wlk RG40 ....141 C4
Oriel Hill GU15 ....151 B3
Oriental Rd SL5 ....120 B3
Orion RG12 ....118 A1
Orkney Cl RG31 ....84 C2
Orkney Ct SL6 ....20 C3
Ormathwaites Cnr RG42 ..91 C1
Ormonde Rd RG41 ....116 A3
Ormsby St RG1 ....85 C4
Orrin Cl RG30 ....84 C4
Orts Rd Newbury RG14 ...105 A1
  Reading RG1 ....86 B4
Orville Cl RG5 ....88 A4
Orwell Cl Caversham RG4 ..58 C2
  Windsor SL4 ....67 B2
Osborne Ave TW19 ......97 C4
Osborne Dr GU18 ....153 A4
Osborne La RG42 ....91 B2
Osborne Mews SL4 ......67 B3
Osborne Rd Egham TW20 .95 C1
  Reading RG30 ....85 A4
  Windsor SL4 ....67 B3
  Wokingham RG40 ....116 B3
Osborne St SL1 ....42 C2
Osbourne Ct SL4 ....67 B3
Osier Pl TW20 ....96 B1
Osman's Cl RG42 ....92 A1
Osnaburgh Hill GU15 ....151 A3
Osney Rd RG14 ....19 C1
Osprey Cl ⑧ RG1 ....86 B4
Osterley Cl RG40 ....116 C3
Osterley Dr RG4 ....59 C3
Ostler Gate SL6 ....19 B1
Oswald Cl RG42 ....117 C4
Otter Cl RG45 ....143 A4
Our Lady of Peace
  RC Inf Sch SL1 ....41 B4
Our Lady of Peace
  RC Jnr Mix & Inf Sch SL1 .41 B4
Our Lady of the Rosary
  RC Sch TW18 ....97 A1
Our Lady's Prep Sch
  RG45 ....143 A3
Ouseley Lodge TW19 .....95 B4
Overbridge Sq RG14 .....105 C2
Overbury Ave RG41 ......88 C1
Overdale Rise GU16 ......151 C2
Overdown Rd RG31 ......57 B2
Overlanders End RG31 ...57 C2
Overlord Cl GU15 ....151 B4
Owen Rd Newbury RG14 ..105 A3
  Windlesham GU20 ....146 B3
Owl Cl RG41 ....115 C4
Owlsmoor Cty Prim Sch
  GU47 ....143 C1
Owlsmoor Rd GU47 .....143 C1
Owston RG6 ....87 B1
Oxenhope RG12 ....117 C3
Oxford Ave Burnham SL1 ..21 A2
  Harlington UB3 ....71 C4
  Slough SL1 ....42 A1
Oxford Cl TW15 ....98 B1
Oxford Rd Marlow SL7 .....1 B1
  Newbury RG14 ....104 C3
  Reading RG30 ....58 A1
  Sandhurst GU47 ....143 C1
  Windsor SL4 ....67 B3
  Wokingham RG41 ....116 A4
Oxford Rd E SL4 ....67 B3
Oxford Road Prim Sch
  RG1 ....85 C4
Oxford St Caversham RG4 ..59 A1
  Hungerford RG17 ....100 C4
  Lambourn RG17 ....25 A2
  Newbury RG14 ....104 C2

P

Pacific Cl TW14 ....98 C4
Pack & Prime La RG9 .....15 B1
Packman Dr RG10 ....61 A3
Padbury Cl TW14 ....98 B4
Padbury Oaks UB7 ....70 A3
Paddick Cl RG6 ....60 C2
Paddick Dr RG6 ....87 B1

Paddock Cl
  Camberley GU15 ....152 A3
  Maidenhead SL6 ....39 B4
Paddock Cotts SL6 ....39 A1
Paddock Hts RG10 ....61 C2
Paddock Rd
  Caversham RG4 ....59 B1
  Newbury RG14 ....130 C4
Paddock The
  Bracknell RG12 ....118 B3
  Crowthorne RG45 ....143 A3
  Datchet SL3 ....68 A3
  Maidenhead SL6 ....19 B1
  Newbury RG14 ....105 B1
Paddocks The HP10 ....3 A4
Padley E ⑦ RG40 ....87 C2
Padstow Cl SL3 ....43 C2
Padstow Gdns RG2 ......86 C1
Padstow Wlk TW14 ......98 C4
Padworth La RG7 ....109 C2
Padworth Prep Sch RG7 .109 C1
Padworth Rd RG14 ......136 B4
Page Rd TW14 ....71 B1
Page's Croft RG40 ....116 B3
Pages La SL6 ....38 A2
Pagoda The SL6 ....39 A2
Pagoda The SL6 ....39 A2
Paices Hill RG7 ....135 A3
Pakenham Rd RG12 .....118 B1
Palace Cl SL1 ....41 C3
Paley St SL6 ....64 A2
Palmer CE Jun Sch The
  RG40 ....116 B4
Palmer Cl
  Crowthorne RG40 ....143 A4
  Peasemore RG20 ....50 B4
Palmer Park Ave RG6 ....87 A3
Palmer School Rd RG40 .116 B3
Palmera Ave RG31 ....84 B2
Palmerstone Ave RG6 ....87 A4
Palmerstone Rd RG6 .....87 A3
Pamber Heath Rd RG26 .135 C1
Pamber Rd RG7 ....136 A1
Pamela Row ⑴ SL6 ......65 A4
Pangbourne Coll RG8 ....56 B3
Panbourne Hill RG8 ......56 B3
Pangbourne Coll RG8 ....56 B3
Pangbourne Prim Sch
  RG8 ....56 C3
Pangbourne St ⑵ RG30 ..85 A4
Pangbourne Sta RG8 ....56 B3
Pankhurst Dr RG12 ......118 B2
Pannells Ct KT16 ....123 C1
Pantile Row SL3 ....44 A1
Papist Way OX10 ....13 C4
Papplewick Sch SL5 .....120 A1
Paprika Cl RG6 ....86 C1
Par The SL2 ....22 C2
Parade The Ashford TW16 ..98 C1
  Bourne End SL8 ....3 A2
  Earley RG6 ....87 A2
  Egham TW18 ....96 B2
  Reading RG30 ....85 B2
  Windsor SL4 ....66 B3
  Woodley RG5 ....87 C4
Paradise Mews RG9 .....15 B1
Paradise Rd RG9 ....15 B1
Paradise Way RG7 ......108 B4
Park Ave Camberley GU15 .151 B2
  Egham TW20 ....96 B1
  Staines TW18 ....97 A1
  Thatcham RG18 ....106 B2
  Upper Halliford TW17 ....125 C3
  Wraysbury TW19 ....68 B2
Park Cl SL4 ....67 B3
Park Close Cotts TW20 ...94 C2
Park Cnr SL4 ....66 C2
Park Cres Reading RG30 ..85 B3
  Sunningdale SL5 ....120 C2
Park End GU41 ....116 A3
Park Farm Ind Est GU15 .151 B1
Park Ho RG30 ....85 B3
Park Ho SL6 ....39 C3
Park House Sch RG14 ...130 C3
Park La Barkham RG40 ...141 A3
  Beech Hill RG7 ....137 B1
  Binfield RG42 ....90 C4
  Burnham SL1 ....21 C4
  Camberley GU15 ....151 B3
  Charvil RG10 ....61 A2
  Horton SL3 ....69 A2
  Newbury RG14 ....105 A2
  Reading RG31 ....84 B2
  Slough SL3 ....43 A2
  Stockcross RG20 ....103 A1
  Thatcham RG18 ....106 B2
  Wickham cum
  Welford SL4 ....93 A4
Park Lane Prim Sch RG31 .84 B2
Park Lane Prim Sch
  Annexe RG31 ....84 B2
Park Lawn SL2 ....22 B1
Park Mews TW15 ....97 C4
Park Rd Ashford TW15 ....98 A2

Park Rd continued
  Bracknell RG12 118
  Camberley GU15 151
  Egham TW20 96
  Henley-on-T RG9 15
  Lower Halliford TW17 125
  Sandhurst GU47 150
  Stanwell TW19 70
  Stoke Poges SL2 22
  Wokingham RG40 116
Park St Bagshot GU19 ...145
  Camberley GU15 151
  Hungerford RG17 100
  Newbury RG14 105
  Newbury RG14 105
  Poyle SL3 43
  Slough SL1 42
  Windsor SL4 67
Park Terr RG14 105
Park View RG31 57
Park View Bagshot GU19 ..145
Park View Dr N RG10 61
Park View Dr S RG10 61
Park Wall La RG8 34
Park Way
  Hungerford RG17 100
  Newbury RG14 105
Park Wlk RG8 57
Parkcorner La RG41 114
Parker's La RG42 92
Parkers Ct SL1 145
Parkgate SL1
Parkhill Cl GU17 150
Parkhill Dr RG31 57
Parkhill Rd GU17 150
Parkhouse La RG30 85
Parkhouse Mews ⑨ RG30 .85
Parkhurst ⑩ RG30 85
Parkland Ave SL3 43
Parkland Dr RG12 118
Parkland Gr TW15 98
Parkland Rd TW15 98
Parkside Henley-on-T RG9 .15
  Maidenhead SL6 19
Parkside Rd Reading RG30 .85
  Sunningdale SL5 121
  Thatcham RG18 106
Parkside Wlk SL1 43
Parkstone Dr GU15 151
Parkview
  Flackwell Heath HP10 3
  Maidenhead SL6 39
Parkview Chase SL1 41
Parkway Camberley GU15 .151
  Crowthorne RG45 143
  Marlow SL7 2
Parkway Dr RG4 60
Parlaunt Park Comb Sch
  SL3 43
Parlaunt Rd SL3 43
Parliament La SL1 20
Parnham Ave GU18 153
Parry Gn N SL3 43
Parry Green S SL3 44
Parsley Cl RG6 86
Parson's Wood La SL2 ...22
Parsonage La
  Farnham Common SL2 22
  Hungerford RG17 100
  Windsor SL4 67
Parsonage Pl RG17 25
Parsonage Rd TW20 95
Parsonage Way GU16 ...151
Parsons Cl Barkham RG2 .141
  Newbury RG14 104
Parsons Down
  Jun & Inf Sch RG19 106
Parsons Field GU47 150
Parsons La RG6
Part La RG7 86
Parthia Cl RG1 86
Partridge Ave GU46 149
Partridge Cl GU16 151
Partridge Dr RG31 84
Partridge Mead SL6 39
Paschal Rd GU15 151
Pasture Cl RG6 114
Patches Field SL7 1
Paterson Cl GU16 152
Pates Manor Dr TW14 ...98
Patricia Cl SL1 42
Patrick Gdns RG42 91
Patrick Rd RG4 59
Patriot Pl RG1 86
Patten Ash Dr RG40 116
Patten Ave GU46 149
Pavenham Cl RG6 114
Pavilion Gdns TW18 97
Pavilions End The GU15 .151
Paxton Ave SL1 42
Payley Dr RG40 116
Paynesdown Rd RG19 ..106
Peace La SL6 19
Peach St RG40 116
Peachy Dr RG19 106
Peacock Ave TW14 98
Peacock Cotts RG12 ...117
Peacock La RG12 117
Peacock Rd SL7 2
Pear Ave TW17 125
Pear Tree Ct GU15 152
Pear Tree La RG14 105
Pear Tree Rd TW15 98
Pearce Cl SL6 19
Pearce Dr SL6 19

earce Rd SL6 .... 19 C1
earce Orch RG9 .... 15 B2
earl Gdns SL1 .... 42 A3
earmain Cl TW17 .... 125 A2
earmans Glade RG2 ...... 113 C4
earson Rd RG4 .... 60 B2
earson Way RG5 .... 87 C3
eartree Cl SL1 .... 43 C3
eascod Pl ⑪ SL4 .... 67 B3
eascod St SL4 .... 67 B3
ease Hill RG7 .... 107 C4
easemore Hill RG20 .... 50 A4
ebble Hill RG17 .... 128 A3
eckmoor Dr RG19 .... 131 B4
eddlars Gr GU46 .... 149 C3
eel Cl Caversham RG4 ...... 59 B1
  Windsor SL4 .... 66 C2
  Woodley RG5 .... 88 A4
eel Ct SL1 .... 42 A4
eel Ctr The RG12 .... 118 A4
eel Ho TW20 .... 95 C1
egasus Cl RG19 .... 106 A2
egasus St RG21 .... 84 B4
eggotty Pl GU47 .... 143 C1
egs Green Cl RG30 .... 85 A3
eket Cl TW18 .... 123 C4
elham Ct Maidenhead SL6 ... 39 C4
  Reading RG30 .... 85 B3
  Staines TW18 .... 97 A2
elican La RG4 .... 105 A2
elican Rd RG26 .... 135 C1
ell St RG1 .... 86 A3
elling Hill SL4 .... 95 A4
emberton Gdns RG31 ...... 84 B3
emberton Rd SL2 .... 21 C2
embroke RG12 .... 118 A1
embroke Broadway
  GU15 ....
embroke Cl Ascot SL5 ..... 120 B2
  Burghfield Common RG30 . 111 B2
embroke Ho ⑯ RG4 .... 59 B1
embroke Mews SL5 .... 120 B2
embroke Pl SL2 .... 22 A1
embroke Rd ㉒ RG14 ...... 105 A2
embury Ct UB3 .... 71 B4
endals Cl RG18 .... 79 C1
endeen Ct SL1 .... 42 A3
endell Ave UB3 .... 71 C4
endennis Ave RG4 .... 59 C3
endine Pl RG12 .... 118 A1
endlebury RG12 .... 118 A1
endragon Ct RG30 .... 85 B3
endragon Way GU15 ...... 152 B2
endred Rd RG2 .... 113 B3
eninsular Cl GU15 .... 152 A4
eninsular Cl TW14 .... 71 C1
ennfield Cl SL6 .... 19 C3
enn Cl RG4 .... 59 A3
enn Ct ⑧ SL7 .... 1 C2
enn Mdw SL2 .... 22 B1
enn Rd Newbury RG14 ..... 104 B3
  Slough SL2 .... 22 B1
ennfields RG10 .... 61 C3
ennine Cl RG31 .... 84 A3
ennine Rd SL2 .... 21 A2
ennine Way Charvil RG10 .. 61 A2
  Harlington UB3 .... 71 B4
enny La TW17 .... 125 C1
ennylets Grn SL2 .... 23 A3
ennypiece RG8 .... 34 B4
ennyroyal Ct RG1 .... 86 A3
enroath Ave RG30 .... 85 B3
enrose Ave RG5 .... 87 C2
enrose Ct RG44 .... 104 C3
enrose Ct TW20 .... 95 B1
ensford RG45 .... 143 A4
enshurst Rd SL6 .... 39 B3
entangle The ⑯ RG14 .... 105 A2
entland Ave TW17 .... 125 A2
entland Cl RG30 .... 84 C3
entland Pl RG19 .... 106 B1
entland Rd SL2 .... 22 A2
enthands The RG17 .... 102 B1
enton Cl TW18 .... 124 A4
enton Ct TW18 .... 96 C1
enton Hall TW18 .... 124 A4
enton Hall Dr TW18 .... 124 A4
enton Hook Marina
  TW18 .... 124 A4
ertbersey KT16 .... 124 A4
egham TW18 .... 123 C4
enton Hook Rd TW18 ...... 124 A4
enton Rd TW18 .... 96 C1
enwood Cl SL6 .... 39 A4
enwood Gdns RG12 .... 117 B2
enwood La SL7 .... 1 B1
enwood Rd RG20 .... 130 B2
enyston Rd SL6 .... 39 A4
enzance Spur SL2 .... 22 A1
epler Cl RG4 .... 35 C4
eppard Rd RG4 .... 59 A2
epper La RG2 .... 86 C2
epys Cl SL3 .... 69 A4
erch Cl SL1 .... 21 C1
ercival Rd TW13 .... 98 B3
ercy Ave TW15 .... 98 A2
ercy Bryant Rd TW16 .... 98 C1
ercy Pl SL3 .... 68 A3
eregrine Cl
  Bracknell RG12 .... 118 A2
  Wokingham RG41 .... 115 C1
eregrine Rd TW16 .... 125 C4
eriam Cl RG9 .... 35 B4
erkins Ct TW15 .... 97 C2
erkins Way RG41 .... 116 A3
errin Cl TW15 .... 97 C2
erry Ho SL1 .... 21 C1
erry Oaks SL3 .... 118 C4
erry Oaks Dr TW6, UB7 .. 70 B3

Perry Way Bracknell RG12 .. 118 C4
  Lightwater GU18 .... 152 C4
Perrycroft SL4 .... 66 C2
Perryfields Way SL1 .... 21 A1
Perryhill Dr GU47 .... 142 C1
Perryman Way SL2 .... 21 C1
Perserverance Hill RG9 .... 35 A3
Perth Ave SL1 .... 42 A4
Perth Cl RG5 .... 61 A1
Perth Trad Est SL1 .... 42 A4
Peterhead Mews SL3 .... 44 C1
Peterhouse Cl GU47 .... 143 C1
Petersfield Ave Slough SL2 . 43 A3
  Staines TW18 .... 97 B1
Petersfield Rd TW18 .... 97 B2
Petrel Cl RG41 .... 115 C3
Petts La TW17 .... 125 A3
Petty Pl SL6 .... 39 B2
Petworth Ave RG30 .... 84 C2
Petworth Ct Reading RG1 . 85 C3
  Windsor SL4 .... 67 A3
Pevensey Ave RG4 .... 59 C3
Pevensey Cl RG2 .... 86 C1
Pevensey Rd SL2 .... 42 A4
Pewsey Vale RG12 .... 118 C2
Pheasant Cl RG41 .... 88 B1
Pheasant La RG20 .... 131 C2
Pheasants Croft SL6 .... 39 A2
Pheasants Ridge SL7 ...... 1 B4
Philbye Mews SL1 .... 41 C2
Philip Dr HP10 .... 3 B8
Philip Rd TW18 .... 97 B1
Phillimore Rd RG4 .... 59 B4
Phillips Cl RG5 .... 61 A1
Phipps Cl SL6 .... 39 A1
Phipps Rd SL1 .... 41 C4
Phoebe Ct RG1 .... 86 A3
Phoenix Bsns Pk RG12 .... 117 B4
Phoenix Cl RG41 .... 115 C3
Phoenix La SL6 .... 39 B2
Phoenix Pk TW18 .... 97 A2
Phoenix Wlk RG14 .... 130 B3
Phyllis Court Dr RG9 ...... 15 C2
Pickering RG12 .... 118 A3
Picket Post Cl RG12 .... 118 C3
Picketts La RG8 .... 55 C2
Pickford Dr SL3 .... 43 C3
Pickins Piece SL3 .... 69 A3
Pickwell Cl RG6 .... 87 B1
Pickwick Gdns GU15 ...... 152 A2
Picton Cl GU15 .... 152 A2
Picton Way RG4 .... 59 A2
Piercefield RG31 .... 84 B1
Pierces Hill RG31 .... 57 B1
Pierson Rd SL4 .... 66 B3
Pigeonhouse La SL4, SL5 . 92 C2
Pigeons Farm Rd RG19 ... 131 B4
Piggott Sch The RG10 ..... 61 B4
Piggotts Rd ④ RG4 .... 59 B1
Pightle The RG7 .... 111 C2
Pigott Rd RG40 .... 116 B3
Pigott Rd RG40 .... 116 C4
Pile Cl SL7 .... 18 B4
Pike St RG14 .... 105 A2
Pikeshaw Way RG31 .... 57 B1
Pimento Dr RG6 .... 86 C1
Pimpernel Pl RG18 .... 106 C2
Pincents Kiln Ind Est
  RG31 .... 84 A2
Pincents La RG31 .... 84 A3
Pinchcut RG7 .... 111 A2
Pinchington La
  RG14 & RG19 .... 131 A4
Pindar Pl RG40 .... 105 C3
Pine Ave GU15 .... 151 A2
Pine Cl Maidenhead SL6 .. 39 A4
  Sandhurst GU15 .... 150 C4
Pine Croft Rd RG41 .... 116 A1
Pine Ct RG12 .... 118 C3
Pine Dr Blackwater GU17 .. 150 C2
  Mortimer RG7 .... 136 C3
  Wokingham RG40 .... 142 A4
Pine Gr Twyford RG10 ..... 61 B4
  Windlesham GU20 .... 146 B2
Pine Mount Rd GU15 ...... 151 B2
Pine Ridge RG14 .... 105 B3
Pine Ridge Golf Ctr
  GU16 .... 151 A4
Pine Ridge Rd RG7 .... 111 A2
Pine Trees Bsns Pk TW18 . 96 C2
Pine Way TW20 .... 95 A1
Pinecote Dr SL5 .... 120 C1
Pinecroft SL7 .... 2 A2
Pinefields Cl RG45 .... 143 A2
Pinehill Rd RG45 .... 143 B2
Pinehill Rise GU47 .... 150 B4
Pinehurst SL5 .... 120 B2
Pinel Cl GU25 .... 122 C3
Piner Cotts SL4 .... 66 C2
Pineridge Cty Inf Sch
  GU15 .... 145 A1
Pineridge Gdns ⑩ RG31 .. 85 A3
Pines Cty Inf Sch RG12 ... 118 A1
Pines Cty Jun Sch RG12 .. 118 A1
Pines The
  Camberley GU15 .... 151 C4
  Twyford RG10 .... 61 C1
Pinetree Ct RG4 .... 59 A3
Pinewood Cl RG45 .... 143 A2
Pinewood Cl RG26 .... 134 B1
Pinewood Dr
  Caversham RG4 .... 58 C3
  Newtown RG20 .... 131 A1
Pinewood Gdns GU19 ..... 145 B2
Pinewood Mews TW19 ..... 70 B1
Pinewood Rd SL3 .... 122 A3
Pingewood Cl RG30 .... 114 B4

Pingewood Rd RG30 .... 85 A1
Pingewood Rd S
  RG7, RG30 .... 112 B4
Pinglestone Cl TW6, UB7 . 70 C4
Pink La SL1 .... 21 A2
Pinkneys Dr SL6 .... 38 C4
Pinkneys Rd SL6 .... 39 A4
Pinks La RG26 .... 134 C1
Piper's End GU25 .... 122 B3
Pipers Cl SL1 .... 21 B1
Pipers Ct Burnham SL1 .... 21 B1
  Thatcham RG19 .... 107 A1
Pipers Way RG9 .... 107 A1
Pipit Cl RG19 .... 106 A2
Pippins Cl TW15 .... 98 A1
Pippins The SL3 .... 43 C3
Pipsons Cl GU46 .... 149 B3
Pitch Pl RG42 .... 90 B2
Pitcroft Ave RG6 .... 87 A3
Pitfield La RG7 .... 137 B2
Pitford Rd RG5 .... 88 A4
Pitts Cl RG42 .... 90 B1
Pitts La RG6 .... 87 A4
Pitts Rd SL1 .... 42 B3
Plackett Way SL1 .... 41 B3
Plaines Cl SL1 .... 41 C3
Plaitinson Rd RG2 .... 113 B3
Planes The KT16 .... 124 A1
Plantagenet Pk RG42 ..... 118 C4
Plantation Cl RG18 .... 78 C3
Plantation Rd Chilton OX12 . 9 C4
  Tadley RG26 .... 134 C1
Plantation Row GU15 ...... 151 A3
Platt Cl RG17 .... 100 C2
Platt La RG17 .... 45 B3
Play Platt RG7 .... 84 B4
Players Grn RG5 .... 87 C3
Playhatch Rd RG4 .... 60 A4
Plough La Shiplake RG9 ... 35 C1
  Wokingham RG40 .... 116 C3
Plough Rd GU46 .... 149 C4
Ploughlands RG42 .... 117 C4
Ploughlees La SL1 .... 42 C3
Plover Cl Staines TW18 ... 96 C3
  Wokingham RG41 .... 115 C3
Plover La RG27 .... 140 C1
Plowden Way RG9 .... 35 C1
Plummery The ⑪ RG1 ..... 86 B4
Plumpton Rd RG14 .... 105 B1
Plumtrees RG6 .... 87 A1
Pluto Cl SL1 .... 41 C2
Pluto Rd OX11 .... 9 C4
Plymouth Ave RG5 .... 87 B3
Plymouth Rd SL1 .... 41 C4
Plympton Cl RG6 .... 87 C2
Pocket Cl RG12 .... 117 B4
Pococks La SL4 .... 42 C1
Poffley Pl RG19 .... 107 A2
Point (L Ctr) The RG12 ... 118 A4
Point Royal RG12 .... 118 A2
Pointers Cl RG20 .... 31 A1
Points The SL9 .... 39 A2
Polehampton CE Inf Sch
  RG10 .... 61 B2
Polehampton Cl RG10 ..... 61 B2
Polehampton Jun Sch
  RG10 .... 61 B2
Pollard Cl SL4 .... 68 A1
Pollard Gr GU15 .... 152 B2
Pollardrow Ave RG42 ..... 117 C4
Pollards Way RG31 .... 84 B2
Polsted Rd RG31 .... 57 B1
Polyanthus Way RG45 .... 143 A4
Polygon Bsns Ctr SL3 .... 69 C3
Pond Cl RG14 .... 130 B4
Pond Croft GU46 .... 149 C3
Pond Head La RG6 .... 114 A1
Pond La Hermitage RG18 .. 79 B4
  Maplenham RG4 .... 58 A3
Pond Moor Rd RG12 ...... 118 A2
Pond Rd TW20 .... 96 B1
Pondside Cl UB3 .... 71 B4
Pool End Cl TW17 .... 125 A2
Pool La Slough SL1 .... 42 C3
  Waltham St Lawrence RG10 .. 63 A3
Poole Cl RG30 .... 85 A1
Pooley Ave TW20 .... 96 B2
Pooley Green Cl TW20 .... 96 B2
Pooley Green Rd TW20 .... 96 B2
Poolmans Rd SL4 .... 66 B3
Pope Cl TW14 .... 98 C4
Popes Cl SL3 .... 43 B4
Popes La SL4 .... 19 B4
Popeswood Rd RG42 ..... 117 B4
Popham Cl RG12 .... 118 C2
Poplar Ave Reading RG30 . 84 C2
  Windlesham GU20 .... 146 A3
Poplar Cl SL4 .... 43 C1
Poplar Gdns RG2 .... 86 C1
Poplar Ho SL3 .... 43 C1
Poplar La Hurst RG10 ..... 62 A1
  Winnersh RG41 .... 88 B2
Poplar Pl RG14 .... 105 A3
Poplar Rd TW15 .... 98 A3
Poplars Gr SL6 .... 20 A1
Poplars The SL3 .... 120 A2
Poppy Dr RG18 .... 106 C2
Poppy Pl RG40 .... 116 A3
Poppy Way RG31 .... 84 B3
Poppyhills Rd RG12 ...... 118 C4
Porchester SL5 .... 120 A4
Porchester Rd RG14 ..... 105 A1
Porchfield Cl RG6 .... 87 A1
Porlock Cl RG19 .... 106 B1
Porlock Pl RG31 .... 84 B2
Port Down RG17 .... 100 C3
Porter Cl RG6 .... 114 B4

Porter End RG14 .... 131 A4
Portesbery Hill Dr GU15 .. 151 C3
Portesbery Rd GU15 ...... 151 C3
Portesbery Sch GU15 ..... 151 B3
Portia Gr RG42 .... 118 C4
Portland Bsns Ctr SL3 .... 68 A3
Portland Cl SL2 .... 21 B1
Portland Cres TW13 .... 98 B2
Portland Gdns RG30 ...... 84 B4
Portland Rd TW15 .... 97 C3
Portland Mews ⑧ SL7 .... 1 B1
Portlock Rd SL6 .... 39 B4
Portman Cl ⑧ RG42 ...... 118 A4
Portman Rd RG30 .... 58 B1
Portmeirion Gdns RG30 .. 57 C1
Portnall Dr GU25 .... 121 C2
Portnall Rd GU25 .... 121 C2
Portnall Rise GU25 .... 121 C2
Portrush Rd RG5 .... 87 C3
Portsmouth Ct SL1 .... 42 C3
Portsmouth Rd GU15 ..... 152 A4
Portway Swallowfield RG7 . 139 B1
  Tadley RG26 .... 134 C1
Portway Cl RG1 .... 85 C3
Post Horn Pl RG31 .... 84 C2
Post Office Cotts SL2 ..... 23 A3
Post Office La
  Burghfield Common RG30 . 111 B3
  Slough SL3 .... 43 B3
Post Office Rd RG17 ...... 127 C3
Posting House Mews
  RG14 .... 130 C4
Potley Hill Cty Prim Sch
  GU46 .... 150 A3
Potley Hill Rd GU46 ...... 149 C3
Pottery La RG17 .... 127 C3
Pottery Rd RG30 .... 57 C1
Poulcott TW19 .... 68 C1
Pound Cres SL7 .... 1 B1
Pound La Hurst RG10 ..... 89 A3
  Little Marlow SL7 .... 2 B4
  Newbury RG20 .... 104 B2
  Sonning RG4 .... 60 C1
  Thatcham RG19 .... 106 A2
  Windlesham GU20 .... 146 B2
Pound Piece RG17 .... 100 B3
Pound Rd KT16 .... 124 A1
Pound St RG14 .... 104 C1
Pound The Cookham SL6 .. 20 A3
  Slough SL1 .... 21 B1
Poundfield La SL6 .... 19 B4
Poundfield Way RG10 ..... 61 C2
Powis Cl SL6 .... 39 A2
Powney Rd SL6 .... 39 B4
Poyle 14 Trad Est SL3 .... 69 C2
Poyle Cty Fst Sch SL3 .... 69 C2
Poyle Gdns RG12 .... 118 B4
Poyle La SL1 .... 21 A2
Poyle New Cotts SL3 ..... 69 C2
Poyle Rd SL3 .... 69 C2
Poyle Tech Ctr The SL3 .. 69 C2
Poynings SL1 .... 44 C1
Prancing Horse Cl RG19 . 106 C2
Precinct The TW20 .... 96 A2
Precincts The SL1 .... 21 B1
Prescott RG12 .... 117 C1
Prescott Rd SL3 .... 69 C2
Presentation Coll RG30 .. 85 B3
Preston Pl RG14 .... 105 B3
Preston Rd Littleton TW17 . 125 A2
  Reading RG2 .... 86 B3
  Slough SL2 .... 43 B3
Prestwick Ct ㉚ RG1 ...... 86 B4
Prestwood SL2 .... 43 A4
Pretoria Rd KT16 .... 123 C1
Price Gdns RG42 .... 91 A1
Prides Crossing SL5 ...... 93 A1
Priest Ave RG40 .... 116 C3
Priest Hill Caversham RG4 . 59 C2
  Egham TW19, SL4 .... 95 B3
Priest La GU24 .... 153 B3
Priestwood Ave RG42 .... 117 C4
Priestwood Court Rd
  RG42 .... 118 A4
Priestwood Sq ⑪ RG42 .. 118 A4
Primrose Cl RG3 .... 84 A2
Primrose La RG41 .... 88 B2
Primrose Walk GU46 ..... 149 A3
Primrose Way GU47 ...... 143 A1
Primrose Wlk RG12 ...... 118 B2
Prince Albert Dr SL5 ..... 119 B2
Prince Andrew Cl SL6 .... 20 A1
Prince Andrew Way SL5 .. 119 B4
Prince Consort Cotts SL4 . 67 B3
Prince Consort Dr SL5 ... 119 B3
Prince Consort's Dr
  Old Windsor SL4 .... 94 A3
  Winkfield SL4 .... 93 C2
Prince Dr GU47 .... 143 A1
Prince Hold Rd RG19 .... 106 A2
Prince of Wales Ave RG30 . 85 B3
Prince of Wales Wlk ⑪
  GU15 .... 151 B3
Prince William Ct TW15 .. 97 C2
Prince William Dr RG31 .. 57 C2
Princes Cl Bagshot GU19 . 145 C1
  Eton SL4 .... 41 C1
Princes Ct SL1 .... 42 C2
Princes La RG20 .... 22 B3
Princes Rd Ashford TW15 . 97 C2
  Bourne End SL8 .... 3 B2
  Egham TW20 .... 95 C3
  Feltham TW13 .... 98 C3
Princes St Reading RG1 ... 86 B4
  Slough SL1 .... 43 A2

Princess Ave SL4 .... 67 A2
Princess Christians Hospl
  SL4 .... 67 B3
Princess Margaret Hospl
  The SL4 .... 67 B3
Princess Margaret Royal
  Free Sch The SL4 .... 67 B2
Princess Marina Dr
  Barkham, Arborfield
  Garrison RG2 .... 140 C4
  Barkham, Langley
  Common RG2 .... 115 A1
Princess Sq RG12 .... 118 A4
Princess St SL6 .... 39 C3
Princess Way GU15 .... 151 B3
Prior Croft Cl GU15 ...... 152 A2
Prior End GU15 .... 152 A2
Prior Heath Cty Inf Sch
  GU15 .... 152 A3
Prior Rd GU15 .... 152 A3
Prior's La GU17 .... 150 A3
Priors Cl Maidenhead SL6 . 40 A1
  ⑧ Slough SL1 .... 43 A2
Priors Court Rd RG18 .... 78 C4
Priors Court Specl Sch
  RG18 .... 78 B4
Priors Rd Tadley RG26 ... 135 A1
  Windsor SL4 .... 66 B2
Priors Way SL6 .... 40 A1
Priors Way Ind Est SL6 .. 40 A1
Priory Ave Caversham RG4 . 59 A1
  Hungerford RG17 .... 100 B2
Priory Cl Hungerford RG17 . 100 B2
  Sunningdale SL5 .... 121 A1
Priory Ct Camberley GU15 . 150 C2
  Caversham RG4 .... 59 A1
  Egham TW20 .... 96 B3
  Winnersh RG41 .... 88 B2
Priory Cty Jun & Inf Sch
  SL1 .... 41 B4
Priory Gn TW18 .... 97 A2
Priory La RG42 .... 91 B1
Priory Mews TW18 .... 97 A2
Priory Pl Greenham RG19 . 131 A3
  Hungerford RG17 .... 100 B2
Priory Rd Burnham SL1 ... 41 B4
  Hungerford RG17 .... 100 B2
  Newbury RG14 .... 105 A1
  Sunningdale SL5 .... 121 A1
  Winkfield SL5 .... 119 A4
Priory The RG41 .... 88 B2
Priory Way Datchet SL3 ... 68 A4
  Harmondsworth UB7 ...... 70 C3
Priory Wlk RG12 .... 118 C3
Priscilla Ho ⑮ TW16 ..... 98 C1
Pritchard Cl RG19 .... 131 B4
Privet Cl RG6 .... 87 A1
Proctors Rd RG40 .... 117 A3
Progress Bsns Ctr SL1 ... 41 B4
Promenade SL4 .... 67 B4
Promenade Rd RG4 .... 59 A1
Prospect Ct Camberley GU15 . 150 C2
Prospect Ct RG30 .... 84 C2
Prospect La TW20 .... 95 A2
Prospect Pl Hurley SL6 .. 17 C2
  Newbury RG14 .... 105 A1
  Staines TW18 .... 96 C2
  Windsor SL4 .... 67 A3
Prospect Rd
  Hungerford RG17 .... 100 B3
  Marlow SL7 .... 1 B1
Prospect St
  Caversham RG4 .... 59 A1
  Reading RG1 .... 85 C4
Providence Ho GU19 ..... 145 C2
Providence La UB3 .... 71 B4
Providence Pl SL6 .... 39 C4
Prudential Bldgs ⑧ SL1 . 42 C2
Prune Hill TW20 .... 95 B2
Prunus Cl GU24 .... 153 C3
Pudding Hill RG10 .... 37 B3
Pudding La RG20 .... 28 C1
Puffers Way RG14 .... 104 C1
Pullmans Pl TW18 .... 97 A2
Pump La Ascot SL5 .... 120 C4
  Shinfield RG7 .... 112 B1
Pump La N SL7 .... 1 C3
Pump La S SL7 .... 2 A2
Pumpkin Hill SL1 .... 21 C3
Pundles La SL3 .... 63 B3
Purbrook Ct RG12 .... 118 C2
Purcell Rd RG45 .... 143 A4
Purfield Dr RG10 .... 36 C1
Purley CE Inf Sch RG8 .. 57 B3
Purley La RG8 .... 57 B3
Purley Rise RG8 .... 56 C3
Purley Village RG8 .... 57 B3
Purley Way RG8 .... 56 C3
Pursers Farm RG7 .... 113 A2
Purslane RG40 .... 116 B3
Pursall Cl SL6 .... 39 A2
Purton Ct SL2 .... 22 B3
Purton La SL2 .... 22 B3
Putman Pl RG9 .... 15 C1
Pycroft Ct KT16 .... 123 C1
Pyegrove Chase RG12 .... 118 C1
Pyke Cl RG40 .... 116 B3
Pykes Hill RG8 .... 54 B2
Pyle Hill RG14 .... 105 B3
Pyrcroft Grange Prim Sch
  KT16 .... 123 C1
Pyrcroft Rd KT16 .... 123 C1

Q

Quadrant Ct RG12 . . . . .118 C3
Quadrant The SL6 . . . . .40 A3
Qualitas RG12 . . . . .117 C1
Quantock Ave RG4 . . . . .59 B3
Quantock Cl Charvil RG10 . . . .61 A2
   Harlington UB3 . . . . .71 B4
   Slough SL3 . . . . .44 A1
Quantocks The RG19 . . . . . .106 B1
Quarrington Cl RG19 . . . . . .106 C1
Quarry Bank GU18 . . . . .153 A4
Quarry La Shiplake RG9 . . . . .36 A2
   Yateley GU46 . . . . .149 C2
Quarry Wood Rd SL6,SL7 . . .19 A4
Quarrydale Dr SL7 . . . . .1 C1
Quartz Cl RG41 . . . . .115 B4
Quaves Rd SL3 . . . . .43 B2
Quebec Gdns GU17 . . . . .150 B2
Quebec Rd RG9 . . . . .35 C4
Queen Anne Fst Sch The
   SL4 .67 B2
Queen Anne's Cl SL4 . . . . . . .94 A3
Queen Anne's Ct [?] SL4 . . . .67 B3
Queen Anne's Rd SL4 . . . . . . .67 B2
Queen Anne's Rd RG4 . . . . . .59 A2
Queen Annes Gate RG4 . . . . .59 B2
Queen Charlotte St [?] SL4 . .67 B3
Queen Cl RG9 . . . . .15 C1
Queen Elizabeth Rd
   GU15 . . . . .144 B1
Queen Mary Ave GU15 . . . . .151 A3
Queen Mary Rd TW17 . . . . . .125 B4
Queen St Caversham RG4 . . . .59 A2
   Chertsey KT16 . . . . .124 A1
   Henley-on-T RG9 . . . . .15 C1
   Maidenhead SL6 . . . . .39 C4
Queen Victoria
   Cross Roads GU15 . . . . . .151 A3
Queen Victoria Ho RG40 . . .116 B3
Queen Victoria St RG1 . . . . . .86 A4
Queen's Acre SL4 . . . . .67 B2
Queen's Cl
   North Ascot SL5 . . . . .119 C4
   Old Windsor SL4 . . . . .68 A1
Queen's Ct Slough SL1 . . . . . .42 C3
   Staines TW18 . . . . .97 B1
Queen's Gate SL4 . . . . .67 B2
Queen's La [?] SL6 . . . . .39 C4
Queen's Pl SL5 . . . . .120 A3
Queen's Rd Ascot SL5 . . . . . .120 B4
   Datchet SL3 . . . . .68 A4
   Egham TW20 . . . . .95 C1
   Marlow SL7 . . . . .1 B1
   Newbury RG14 . . . . .105 A1
   Slough SL1 . . . . .42 C3
   Windsor SL4 . . . . .67 B2
Queen's Terr [?] SL4 . . . . .67 B2
Queens Acre Ho [?] SL4 . . . . .67 B2
Queens Cotts RG1 . . . . .86 A4
Queens Ct [?] RG14 . . . . .105 A1
Queens Dr The RG2 & RG6 . . .86 C2
Queens Hill Rise SL5 . . . . . . .120 B3
Queens Keep GU15 . . . . .151 B3
Queens Lawns RG1 . . . . .86 A4
Queens Rd Bisley GU24 . . . . .153 C1
   Camberley GU15 . . . . .151 A2
   Caversham RG4 . . . . .59 B1
   Eton SL4 . . . . .41 C1
   Reading RG1 . . . . .86 A4
Queens Ride RG45 . . . . .143 A4
Queens Way RG17 . . . . .102 B1
Queens Wlk TW15 . . . . .97 B2
Queens Wlk Mall [?] SL6 . . . .39 C4
Queensborough Dr RG4 . . . . .58 C3
Queensbury Pl GU17 . . . . . . .150 B2
Queenshill Lodge SL5 . . . . . .120 A3
Queensmead
   Ashford TW15 . . . . .97 C2
   Camberley GU15 . . . . .152 A4
   Datchet SL3 . . . . .68 A3
Queensmere Rd SL1 . . . . .43 A2
Queensway Caversham RG4 . .59 B3
   Maidenhead SL6 . . . . .19 C1
Quentin Rd RG5 . . . . .87 B4
Quincey Way GU25 . . . . .122 A3
Quinbrookes SL2 . . . . .23 A4
Quince Cl SL5 . . . . .120 B3
Quincy Rd TW20 . . . . .96 A2
Quinn St RG30 . . . . .85 A4
Quintilis RG12 . . . . .117 C1
Quoiting Sq SL7 . . . . .1 B1
Quoitings Dr SL7 . . . . .1 B1

R

R.E.M.E Mus RG2 . . . . .141 A4
Race Course Rd RG14 . . . . . .105 B1
Race Course Sta RG14 . . . . . .105 B1
Raceview Bsns Ctr RG14 . . . .105 A1
Rachaels Lake View RG42 . . .91 C1
Rackstraw Rd GU47 . . . . .143 B1
Radbourne Rd RG31 . . . . .84 B2
Radcliffe Way RG42 . . . . .117 C4
Radcot Ave SL3 . . . . .44 A2
Radcot Cl Maidenhead SL6 . . .39 A4
   Woodley RG5 . . . . .60 C1
Radical Ride RG40 . . . . .141 C4
Radius Pk TW6 . . . . .71 C2
Radley Bottom
   Hungerford Newtown RG17 101 B4

Radley Bottom continued
   Hungerford Newtown RG17 . .74 A2
Radley Cl TW14 . . . . .98 C4
Radnor Cl RG9 . . . . .15 C1
Radnor Ho [?] RG1 . . . . .85 C3
Radnor Rd Bracknell RG12 . .118 C3
   Earley RG6 . . . . .87 B2
Radnor Way SL3 . . . . .43 C1
Radstock La RG6 . . . . .87 A1
Radstock Prim Sch RG6 . . . . .87 A1
Radstock Rd RG1 . . . . .86 C4
Raeburn Way GU47 . . . . .150 B3
RAF Staff Coll RG12 . . . . . . .118 B3
Ragdale RG7 . . . . .111 A2
Raggleswood Cl RG6 . . . . .87 B2
Raghill RG7 . . . . .135 B3
Raglan Cl RG2 . . . . .86 B1
Raglan Gdns RG4 . . . . .59 B3
Ragley Mews RG4 . . . . .59 B3
Ragmans Cl SL7 . . . . .1 B4
Ragstone Rd SL1 . . . . .42 C2
Railside RG7 . . . . .108 C1
Railton Cl RG2 . . . . .113 B4
Railway App KT16 . . . . .123 C1
Railway Rd RG14 . . . . .105 A1
Railway Terr Egham TW18 . . .96 B2
   Slough SL3 . . . . .42 C3
Railways Cotts RG8 . . . . .34 B3
Rainbow Pk RG41 . . . . .88 A1
Rainsborough Chase SL6 . . . .39 A2
Rainworth Cl RG6 . . . . .114 A4
Raleigh Cl Slough SL1 . . . . . . .42 A3
   Woodley RG5 . . . . .87 C3
Raleigh Ct TW18 . . . . .97 A2
Raleigh Rd TW13,TW14 . . . . .98 C3
Raleigh Way GU16 . . . . .151 A3
Ralphs Ride RG12 . . . . .118 C3
Rambler Cl SL6 . . . . .41 A4
Rambler La SL3 . . . . .43 B2
Ramptons La RG7 . . . . .136 A3
Ramsay Rd GU20 . . . . .146 C3
Ramsbury Cl RG12 . . . . .117 C2
Ramsbury Dr Earley RG6 . . . .87 A2
   Hungerford RG17 . . . . .100 C3
Ramsey Cl
   Camberley GU15 . . . . .152 A4
   Earley RG6 . . . . .87 B2
Ramsey Ct SL2 . . . . .21 B1
Ramslade Rd RG12 . . . . .118 B3
Rances La RG40 . . . . .116 C3
Randall Cl SL3 . . . . .43 C1
Randall Ct SL4 . . . . .68 A1
Randall Mead RG42 . . . . .90 A1
Randell Cl GU17 . . . . .150 C1
Randolph Rd Reading RG1 . . .59 A1
   Slough SL3 . . . . .42 C3
Ranelagh Cres SL5 . . . . .119 B4
Ranelagh Dr RG12 . . . . .118 B3
Ranelagh Sch RG12 . . . . .118 B3
Range Rd RG40 . . . . .142 A4
Range Rde GU15 . . . . .150 C4
Range View GU47 . . . . .150 C4
Range Villas TW17 . . . . .124 C1
Range Way TW17 . . . . .125 A1
Rangewood Ave RG30 . . . . . .84 B3
Ranikhet Prim Sch RG30 . . . .85 A4
Rapley Cl GU15 . . . . .151 C4
Rapley Gn RG12 . . . . .118 B2
Ratby Cl RG6 . . . . .87 B1
Raven Cl GU46 . . . . .149 A3
Ravendale Rd TW16 . . . . . . .125 C4
Ravenglass Cl RG6 . . . . .87 B2
Ravens Field SL3 . . . . .43 B2
Ravensbourne Ave TW19 . . . .97 C4
Ravensbourne Dr RG5 . . . . . .61 A2
Ravenscote Cty Jun Sch
   GU16 . . . . .152 A2
Ravenscourt Marlow SL7 . . . . .2 A2
   Sunbury TW16 . . . . .125 C4
Ravenscroft Rd RG9 . . . . .15 B1
Ravensdale Mews TW18 . . . .97 A1
Ravensdale Rd SL5 . . . . .120 A2
Ravensfield TW20 . . . . .95 B1
Ravenshoe Ct SL8 . . . . .3 A2
Ravenstone Rd GU15 . . . . . .152 A4
Ravenswing Mobile Home
   Pk RG7 . . . . .135 B1
Ravenswood Ave RG45 . . . . .142 C3
Ravenswood Dr GU15 . . . . . .152 A3
Ravenswood Village
   Settlement RG45 . . . . . . .142 C3
Ravensworth Rd
   Mortimer RG7 . . . . .136 C3
   Slough SL2 . . . . .22 A1
Rawcliffe Ho SL6 . . . . .40 A4
Rawdon Rise GU15 . . . . .152 A3
Rawlinson Rd GU15 . . . . . . .150 C3
Ray Dr SL6 . . . . .40 A4
Ray Ho RG [?] SL6 . . . . .3 A2
Ray Lea Cl SL6 . . . . .40 A4
Ray Lea Rd SL6 . . . . .40 A4
Ray Lodge SL6 . . . . .40 A4
Ray Lodge Mews SL6 . . . . . . .40 A4
Ray Mdw SL6 . . . . .20 A1
Ray Mead Ct SL6 . . . . .20 B1
Ray Mead Rd SL6 . . . . .20 B1
Ray Mill Rd E SL6 . . . . .20 B1
Ray Mill Rd W SL6 . . . . .40 A4
Ray Park Ave SL6 . . . . .40 A4
Ray Park La SL6 . . . . .40 A4
Ray Park Rd SL6 . . . . .40 A4
Ray St SL6 . . . . .40 A4
Rayfield SL6 . . . . .40 A4
Raymond Cl SL3 . . . . .43 B2
Raymond Rd
   Maidenhead SL6 . . . . .39 B4
   Slough SL3 . . . . .44 A2
Rayners Cl SL3 . . . . .69 B4

Rays Ave SL4 . . . . .66 C4
Raywood Cl UB3 . . . . .71 B4
Reade Ct SL2 . . . . .22 B3
Reading Alternative Sch
   RG4 . . . . .60 B2
Reading Blue Coat Sch
   RG1 . . . . .86 C3
Reading Bridge RG1 . . . . .59 A1
Reading Coll of Tech RG1 . . .86 A2
Reading Coll of Arts & Tech
   RG1 . . . . .86 C3
Reading Gate Ret Pk RG2 . . .85 C1
Reading Girls Sch RG1 . . . . . .86 B2
Reading Grim Sch RG1 . . . . .86 B2
Reading Link Ret Pk RG2 . . . .86 A3
Reading Rd Aldworth RG8 . . .33 A1
   Arborfield RG2 . . . . .114 B2
   Blackwater GU17 . . . . .150 B2
   Burghfield Common RG7 . .111 A1
   Finchampstead RG27 . . . . .140 C2
   Goring RG8 . . . . .34 C3
   Henley-on-T RG9 . . . . .15 C1
   Moulsford OX10 . . . . .14 A4
   Pangbourne RG8 . . . . .56 B3
   Streatley RG8 . . . . .34 A3
   Wargrave RG10 . . . . .36 C1
   Woodley RG5 . . . . .87 B4
   Yateley GU46 . . . . .149 B3
Reading St Michael
   Cty Prim Sch RG30 . . . . . .85 A4
Reading Sta RG1 . . . . .86 A4
Reading West Sta RG30 . . . . .85 C4
Recreation Cl GU14 . . . . .150 C1
Recreation La RG7 . . . . .113 A1
Recreation Rd
   Bourne End SL8 . . . . .3 A2
   Burghfield Common RG7 . .111 A1
   Reading RG30 . . . . .84 C4
   Wargrave RG10 . . . . .36 C1
Rectory Cl Bracknell RG12 . .118 B3
   Farnham Common SL2 . . . .22 B2
   Littleton TW17 . . . . .125 A3
   Newbury RG14 . . . . .104 C1
   Sandhurst GU47 . . . . .149 C4
   Windsor SL4 . . . . .67 A3
   Wokingham RG40 . . . . .116 B3
Rectory La
   Aston Tirrold OX11 . . . . . . .12 C4
   Bracknell RG12 . . . . .118 A3
   Letcombe Bassett OX12 . . . .6 C4
   Windlesham GU20 . . . . . . .146 B2
Rectory Rd Caversham RG4 . .59 A1
   Padworth RG7 . . . . .135 C4
   Streatley RG8 . . . . .33 B4
   Taplow SL6 . . . . .20 C1
   Wokingham RG40 . . . . .116 B3
Rectory Row RG12 . . . . .118 A3
Rectory Terr SL2 . . . . .22 B2
Red Cottage Dr RG31 . . . . . . .84 B2
Red Cottage Mews SL3 . . . . .43 B2
Red Cross Rd RG8 . . . . .34 B3
Red Ct SL1 . . . . .42 C3
Red Hill RG9 . . . . .35 A3
Red House Cl RG6 . . . . .114 A4
Red La RG7 . . . . .135 B3
Red Leaf Cl SL3 . . . . .43 C3
Red Lion Cotts SL2 . . . . .23 A1
Red Lion Way HP10 . . . . .3 C3
Red Rd RG18, GU24, GU15 . .153 B4
Red Rose RG42 . . . . .91 B2
Red Shute Hill RG18 . . . . . . .79 A2
Red Shute Ind Est RG18 . . . . .79 A2
Redberry Cl RG4 . . . . .59 B3
Redcrest Gdns GU15 . . . . . . .151 C3
Reddington Dr SL3 . . . . .43 C1
Redditch RG12 . . . . .118 B1
Redfield Ct RG14 . . . . .105 B2
Redford Ct TW13 . . . . .98 C3
Redford Rd SL4 . . . . .66 B4
Redgauntlet RG40 . . . . .141 B3
Redgrave Pl SL7 . . . . .1 C2
Redhatch Dr RG6 . . . . .87 A2
Redlake La RG40 . . . . .116 C1
Redlands Pl RG40 . . . . .115 C1
Redlands Prim Sch RG1 . . . . .86 C3
Redlands Rd RG1 . . . . .86 C3
Redlane Hill RG7 . . . . .135 B3
Redleaves Ave TW15 . . . . . . .98 A1
Redmayne GU15 . . . . .152 B2
Redriff Cl SL6 . . . . .39 B3
Redruth Gdns RG2 . . . . .86 A1
Redshots Cl SL7 . . . . .1 C2
Redvers Rd RG12 . . . . .118 A2
Redwood Burnham SL1 . . . . . .21 A2
   Egham TW20 . . . . .123 C4
Redwood Ave RG5 . . . . .88 A3
Redwood Dr
   Frimley GU15 . . . . .152 B2
   Sunningdale SL5 . . . . .121 A2
Redwood Gdns SL1 . . . . .42 B3
Redwood Mews TW15 . . . . . .98 B1
Redwood Way RG31 . . . . .57 B2
Redwoods The SL4 . . . . .67 B2
Reed Cl SL6 . . . . .44 C4
Reed Place Bsns Pk
   TW17 . . . . .124 C1
Reed Wlk RG14 . . . . .105 B2
Reed's Hill RG12 . . . . .118 A2
Reeds Ave RG6 . . . . .87 A2
Reedsfield Cl TW15 . . . . .98 A3
Reedsfield Rd TW15 . . . . .98 A3
Reeve Rd SL6 . . . . .44 C4
Reeves Way RG41 . . . . .116 A2
Reform Rd SL6 . . . . .40 A4
Regal Ct SL6 . . . . .40 A4
Regatta Ho TW18 . . . . .96 C2
Regency Hts RG4 . . . . .59 B4

Regent Cl Earley RG6 . . . . . . .87 B1
   Hungerford RG17 . . . . .100 B3
Regent Ct Bagshot GU19 . . .145 C1
   [?] Maidenhead SL6 . . . . . .39 C4
   Reading RG1 . . . . .86 A4
   Slough SL1 . . . . .42 C4
   Windsor SL4 . . . . .67 B3
Regent St RG1 . . . . .86 C4
Regent Way GU16 . . . . .152 A1
Regents Cl RG14 . . . . .104 C2
Regents Pl GU47 . . . . .150 B4
Regents Wlk SL5 . . . . .120 B1
Regis Cl RG2 . . . . .113 B4
Regis Ct TW14 . . . . .71 B1
Regnum Dr RG14 . . . . .105 A3
Reid Ave SL6 . . . . .19 C4
Rembrandt Cl RG41 . . . . .115 B3
Rembrandt Way RG1 . . . . . . .85 C3
Remembrance Rd RG14 . . . .104 C1
Remenham Church La
   RG9 .16 A2
Remenham La RG9 . . . . .15 C2
Remenham Terr RG9 . . . . . . .16 B1
Renault Rd RG2 . . . . .88 A3
Renfree Way TW17 . . . . .125 A1
Rennie Cl TW15 . . . . .97 B3
Repton Cl SL6 . . . . .39 B2
Repton Rd RG6 . . . . .87 B2
Restwold Cl RG30 . . . . .85 B2
Retford Cl RG5 . . . . .60 C1
Retreat The
   Englefield Green TW20 . . . .95 C2
   Holyport SL6 . . . . .65 B4
Revel Rd HP10 . . . . .3 B4
Revesby Cl Maidenhead SL6 . .39 B2
   West End GU24 . . . . .153 B3
Rex Ave TW15 . . . . .98 A2
Reynards Cl RG41 . . . . .88 B1
Reynolds Ct SL6 . . . . .106 B2
Reynolds Gn GU47 . . . . .150 B3
Rhigos RG4 . . . . .58 C3
Rhine Cl RG4 . . . . .59 B1
Rhodes Cl Earley RG6 . . . . . . .87 B2
   Egham TW20 . . . . .96 A2
Rhodes Ct TW20 . . . . .96 A2
Rhododendron Cl SL5 . . . . . . .92 C1
Rhododendron Rd GU16 . . .152 C1
Rhododendron Ride
   SL4,TW20 . . . . .94 C2
Rhododendron Wlk SL5 . . . . .92 C1
Ribbleton Cl RG6 . . . . .87 B2
Ribstone Rd SL6 . . . . .39 A2
Ricardo Rd SL4 . . . . .68 A2
Richard Ct TW15 . . . . .97 C2
Richard Nevill Ct [?] RG4 . . . .59 B1
Richards Cl UB3 . . . . .71 B4
Richards Way SL1 . . . . .21 C1
Richardson's Lawn Cotts
   SL4 .94 A3
Richborough Cl RG6 . . . . .87 A1
Richfield Ave RG1 . . . . .58 C1
Richmond Ave
   Feltham TW14 . . . . .71 C1
   Thatcham RG19 . . . . .106 A2
Richmond Cl GU16 . . . . .151 C1
Richmond Cres Slough SL1 . .43 A3
   Staines TW18 . . . . .96 C2
Richmond Dr TW17 . . . . .125 B2
Richmond Ho GU47 . . . . .150 C4
Richmond Rd
   Caversham RG4 . . . . .58 C2
   Reading RG30 . . . . .85 B4
   Sandhurst GU47 . . . . .150 C4
   Staines TW18 . . . . .96 C2
Richmond Rise RG41 . . . . . .115 C4
Richmondwood SL5 . . . . . . .121 A1
Rickman Cl
   Arborfield RG2 . . . . .114 C1
   Bracknell RG12 . . . . .118 B2
   Woodley RG5 . . . . .87 B3
Rickman's La SL2 . . . . .22 C3
Riddings La RG19 . . . . .133 B1
Riders La RG7 . . . . .112 A2
Ridgeway Cl GU15 . . . . .151 A2
Ridge Hall Cl RG4 . . . . .58 C2
Ridge Mount Rd SL5 . . . . . . .121 A3
Ridge The Cold Ash RG18 . .106 B4
   Lower Basildon RG8 . . . . . . .34 C1
   Upper Basildon RG8 . . . . . .54 C4
Ridge Way Iver SL0 . . . . .44 C3
Ridgeway Water GU25 . . . . .122 C2
Ridgebank SL1 . . . . .41 C3
Ridgemead Rd TW20 . . . . . . .95 A3
Ridgemount Cl RG31 . . . . . . .57 A1
Ridgeway
   Walton-on-T KT12 . . . . . . .125 C1
   Wokingham RG40 . . . . .36 C1
Ridgeway Cl
   Hermitage RG18 . . . . .79 A4
   Lightwater GU18 . . . . .153 A4
   Marlow SL7 . . . . .1 C2
Ridgeway Prim Sch RG2 . . . .86 B1
Ridgeway Sch SL6 . . . . .38 C3
Ridgeway The
   Bracknell RG12 . . . . .118 B3
   Caversham RG4 . . . . .59 A4
   Letcombe Bassett OX12 . . . .6 C4
   Lightwater GU18 . . . . .146 A1
   Marlow SL7 . . . . .1 C2
   Woodley RG5 . . . . .87 C3
Ridgeway Trad Est The
   SL6 .44 C3
Ridgewood Ctr (Hospl)
   GU16 . . . . .152 A2
Ridgewood Dr GU16 . . . . . . .152 B2
Riding Court Rd SL3 . . . . .68 B4
Riding Ct SL3 . . . . .68 B4

Riding Way RG41 . . . . .115 C
Ridings The
   Caversham RG4 . . . . .59 B
   Frimley GU16 . . . . .152 A
   Iver SL0 . . . . .44 C
   Maidenhead SL6 . . . . .39 A
Ridleigh Ct TW15 . . . . .98 A
Ridlington Cl RG6 . . . . .87 C
Rigby Lodge SL1 . . . . .42 C
Righton Cl RG10 . . . . .61 A
Riley Rd Marlow SL7 . . . . .1 B
   Reading RG30 . . . . .85 B
Ring The RG12 . . . . .118 B
Ringmead Bracknell,
   Great Hollands RG12 . . . . .117 C
   Bracknell, Hanworth RG12 .118 A
Ringwood RG12 . . . . .117 C
Ringwood Cl SL5 . . . . .120 A
Ringwood Rd
   Blackwater GU17 . . . . .150 B
   Reading RG30 . . . . .85 A
Ripley Ave TW20 . . . . .95 C
Ripley Cl SL3 . . . . .43 C
Ripley Rd RG30 . . . . .58 A
Ripon Cl GU15 . . . . .152 B
Ripplesmere RG12 . . . . .118 B
Ripplesmore Cl GU47 . . . . . .150 A
Ripston Rd TW15 . . . . .98 B
Risborough Rd SL6 . . . . .39 C
Rise Rd SL5 . . . . .120 A
Rise The Caversham RG4 . . . .59 A
   Cold Ash RG18 . . . . .106 B
   Crowthorne RG45 . . . . . . .142 C
   Finchampstead RG40 . . . . .141 A
   Maidenhead RG41 . . . . . . .116 A
   Wokingham RG40 . . . . .116 A
   Riseley Rd SL6 . . . . .40 B
Rissington Cl RG31 . . . . .57 C
River Ct SL6 . . . . .40 A
River Gdns Maidenhead SL6 . .40 B
   Purley on T RG8 . . . . .57 B
River Mount KT12 . . . . .125 C
River Park Ave TW18 . . . . . . .96 B
River Pk RG14 . . . . .105 B
River Rd Caversham RG4 . . . .58 C
   Reading RG1 . . . . .86 A
   Staines TW18 . . . . .123 C
   Taplow SL6 . . . . .40 B
   Yateley GU46 . . . . .149 A
River & Rowing Mus RG9 . . . .15 C
River Side Cotts HP10 . . . . . . .3 C
River St SL4 . . . . .67 B
River View HP10 . . . . .3 B
River Wlk RG14 . . . . .105 A
Riverbank TW18 . . . . .96 C
Riverdene Dr RG41 . . . . .88 A
Riverfield Rd TW18 . . . . .96 C
Rivermead Cl SL7 . . . . .1 B
Rivermead Ind Est RG19 . . .106 C
Rivermead Prim Sch RG5 . . . .87 C
Rivermead Rd
   Camberley GU15 . . . . .151 A
   Woodley RG5 . . . . .87 C
Riverpark Dr SL7 . . . . .1 C
Riversdale SL8 . . . . .3 A
Riversdale Ct RG1 . . . . .86 C
Riversdell Cl KT16 . . . . .123 C
Riverside Bradfield RG7 . . . . .82 B
   Egham TW20 . . . . .96 A
   Lower Halliford TW17 . . . .125 C
   Wraysbury TW19 . . . . .95 B
Riverside Ave RG5 . . . . .153 B
Riverside Cl SL1 . . . . .21 C
Riverside Ct [?] RG4 . . . . .59 A
Riverside Dr Egham TW18 . . .96 C
   Staines TW18 . . . . .96 C
Riverside Pl TW19 . . . . .70 C
Riverside Rd Staines TW18 . . .96 C
   Stanwell TW19 . . . . .70 C
Riverside Way GU15 . . . . . . .151 A
Riverside Wlk SL4 . . . . .67 B
Riverview TW17 . . . . .125 B
Riverview Rd RG8 . . . . .56 B
Riverway
   Great Shefford RG17 . . . . . .48 A
   Staines TW18 . . . . .123 C
Riverwood Cl SL7 . . . . .18 C
Riverwoods Ave SL7 . . . . .2 A
Riverwoods Dr SL7 . . . . .2 A
Rixman Cl SL6 . . . . .39 B
Rixon Cl SL3 . . . . .43 C
Robert Piggott CE Inf Sch
   RG10 . . . . .36 C
Robert Piggott CE Jun Sch
   RG10 . . . . .36 C
Robert Sandilands
   Prim Sch RG14 . . . . .104 C
Roberts Cl TW19 . . . . .70 B
Roberts Gr RG41 . . . . .115 C
Roberts Rd GU15 . . . . .151 A
Roberts Way RG10 . . . . .95 B
Robertsfield RG19 . . . . .105 C
Robertson Cl RG14 . . . . .131 A
Robin Cl RG7 . . . . .111 A
Robin Hill Dr GU15 . . . . .152 A
Robin Hood Cl SL1 . . . . .41 C
Robin Hood Way RG41 . . . . . .88 B
Robin La Newtown RG20 . . .131 C
   Sandhurst GU47 . . . . .143 B
Robin Par SL5 . . . . .22 B
Robin Way Reading RG31 . . . .84 A
   Staines TW18 . . . . .96 C
Robin Willis Way SL4 . . . . . . .66 B
Robin's Bow GU15 . . . . .151 A
Robindale Ave RG6 . . . . .87 B
Robinhood La RG41 . . . . .88 B
Robins Cl RG14 . . . . .130 C
Robins Grove Cres GU46 . . .149 A
Robins Hill RG17 . . . . .127 C

Robinson Cl OX11 12 A4
Robinson Ct RG6 87 A1
Roby Dr RG12 118 B1
Rochester Ave
Feltham TW13 98 C3
Woodley RG5 60 C1
Rochester Rd TW20 96 B1
Rochford Way SL6 41 A4
Rochfords Gdns SL2 43 B3
Rockall Ct SL3 44 A2
Rockbourne Gdns RG30 58 A1
Rockfel Rd RG17 25 A1
Rockfield Way 7 GU47 150 B4
Rockingham Rd RG14 104 C1
Rockmoor La SP11 147 A1
Rodd Est TW17 125 B2
Rodney Ct 11 RG1 86 A3
Rodney Way SL3 69 C3
Rodway Rd RG30 57 C1
Roebuck Est RG42 90 B1
Roebuck Gn SL1 41 C3
Roebuck Rise RG31 57 B2
Roebuts Cl RG14 130 C4
Rogers La SL2 22 C2
Rogers's La RG17 47 B3
Rogosa Rd GU24 153 C3
Rokeby Cl Bracknell RG12 118 B4
Newbury RG14 131 A4
Rokeby Dr RG4 58 B4
Rokes Pl GU46 149 A3
Rokesby Rd SL2 21 C1
Rolls La SL6 64 C4
Roman Field RG7 136 A1
Roman Lea SL6 19 C4
Roman Ride RG45 142 B3
Roman Way Bourne End SL8 3 A2
Earley RG6 87 B2
Thatcham RG18 106 A2
Winkfield RG42 118 C4
Romana Ct TW18 97 A2
Romano Ct 9 RG14 105 A1
Romans Gate RG26 135 C1
Romany Cl RG30 58 A1
Romany La RG30 58 A1
Romeo Hill RG42 118 C4
Romney Cl TW15 98 B2
Romney Ct 11 SL7 1 C2
Romney Ho RG12 118 C3
Romney Lock Rd SL4 67 B4
Romsey Cl
Blackwater GU17 150 B3
Slough SL3 43 C2
Romsey Rd RG30 58 A1
Rona Ct RG30 85 A4
Ronaldsay Spur SL1 42 C4
Ronita Ct RG1 86 C3
Rood Hill RG20 76 B2
Rook Cl RG41 115 C3
Rook Rd HP10 3 B2
Rookery Ct SL7 1 B1
Rookery Rd TW18 97 A2
Rookery The RG20 50 B4
Rooksfield RG20 132 A1
Rooksmead Rd TW16 125 C4
Rooksnest La RG17 128 A3
Rookswood Bracknell RG42 91 A1
Stockcross RG20 103 C3
Rookwood Ave GU47 143 C1
Rope Wlk RG19 106 B2
Rosa Ave TW15 98 A2
Rosary Gdns Ashford TW15 98 A2
Yateley GU46 149 B3
Rose Cl RG5 88 A4
Rose Cotts SL6 39 B2
Rose Ct RG40 116 B3
Rose Gdns TW19 97 B4
Rose Hill Binfield RG42 90 B2
Burnham SL1 21 A3
Rose Ind Est
Bourne End SL8 3 A2
Marlow Bottom SL7 1 B3
Rose Kiln La RG1 & RG2 86 A2
Rose La Hurley RG9 17 A1
Knowl Hill RG10 37 A4
Rose St RG40 116 B3
Rose Wlk Reading RG1 86 A4
Slough SL2 42 A4
Roseacre Cl TW17 125 A2
Rosebank Cl SL6 19 C4
Rosebay RG40 116 C4
Rosebery Rd RG4 58 B4
Rosecroft Way RG2 113 C3
Rosedale RG42 90 B2
Rosedale Cres RG6 87 A4
Rosedale Gdns
Bracknell RG12 118 A2
Thatcham RG19 106 B1
Rosedene La GU47 150 B4
Rosefield Rd TW18 97 A2
Rosehill Ct SL1 43 A2
Rosehill Ho RG4 59 B4
Rosehill Pk RG4 59 B4
Roseleigh Cl SL6 39 A4
Rosemary Ave RG6 86 C1
Rosemary Gdns GU17 150 B3
Rosemary La
Blackwater GU17 150 B3
Thorpe TW20 123 A3
Rosemary Terr RG14 104 C1
Rosemead KT16 124 A1
Rosemead Ave
Feltham TW13 98 C3
Purley on T RG31 57 A2
Rosen Ct RG19 106 C2
Rosery The SL8 3 A2
Roses La SL4 66 B3
Rosewood RG5 87 B2
Rosewood Dr TW17 124 C2
Rosewood Way
Farnham Common SL2 22 B4
West End GU24 153 C3
Rosier Cl RG19 106 C1
Rosken Gr SL2 22 A2
Roslyn Rd RG5 87 B3
Ross Ho 2 RG30 85 B3
Ross Rd Maidenhead SL6 39 C2
Reading RG1 59 A1
Rossendale Rd RG4 59 B2
Rossett Cl RG12 118 A3
Rossey Pl SL4 42 B1
Rossington Pl RG2 113 B4
Rossiter Cl SL3 43 C1
Rosslea GU20 146 A3
Rosslyn Cl TW16 98 C1
Rothbury Wlk GU15 152 B2
Rother Cl GU47 150 B4
Rotherfield Ave RG41 116 A4
Rotherfield Cl RG7 83 C2
Rotherfield Rd RG9 35 C4
Rotherfield Way RG4 59 A2
Rothwell Gdns RG5 61 A1
Rothwell Ho RG45 143 B2
Rothwell Wlk RG4 59 B1
Rotten Row Hill RG7 81 C2
Roughgrove Copse RG42 90 A1
Rounce La GU24 153 B3
Round Cl GU46 149 C3
Round End RG14 130 B3
Roundabout La RG41 115 B4
Roundfield RG7 107 A3
Roundhead Rd RG7 83 B2
Roundshead Dr RG12 118 B4
Roundway Egham TW20 96 B2
Frimley GU15 152 B3
Roundway Cl GU15 152 B3
Routh Ct TW14 98 B4
Routh La RG30 84 C3
Row La RG4 59 C4
Rowallan Cl RG4 59 B3
Rowan 2 RG12 118 C2
Rowan Ave TW20 96 B2
Rowan Cl Camberley GU15 151 C4
Wokingham RG41 115 C3
Rowan Ct RG6 87 A1
Rowan Dr
Crowthorne RG45 143 B3
Newbury RG14 105 A3
Woodley RG5 87 C4
Rowan Ho 1 SL8 3 A2
Rowan Way
Burghfield Common RG30 111 A3
Slough SL2 42 A4
Rowanhurst Dr SL2 22 B4
Rowans Cl GU14 150 C1
Rowans The TW16 98 C2
Rowcroft Rd RG2 140 C4
Rowdell Dr RG2 86 B1
Rowdown RG17 24 C3
Rowe Ct RG30 85 A4
Rowland Cl SL4 66 B2
Rowland Hill Almshouses
TW15 98 A2
Rowland Way Earley RG6 86 C1
Littleton TW15 98 B1
Rowland's Cl RG7 136 B3
Rowles Paddock RG20 10 A1
Rowley Cl RG12 118 C3
Rowley La SL3 23 B2
Rowley Rd RG2 86 A2
Roxborough Way SL6 38 C2
Roxburgh Cl GU15 152 B2
Roxeth Ct TW15 98 A2
Roxford Cl TW17 125 C2
Roxwell Cl SL1 41 C3
Roy Cl RG18 78 C3
Royal Ascot Golf Club
SL5 120 A4
Royal Ave RG31 84 B3
Royal Berkshire Hospl The
RG1 86 B3
Royal Cotts SL6 19 B4
Royal Ct 10 RG1 86 B4
Royal Free Ct 22 SL4 67 B3
Royal Holloway Univ
of London TW20 95 B1
Royal Hunt Ho SL5 119 B4
Royal Mans RG9 15 C1
Royal Military Acad
GU15 150 C3
Royal Military Acad Hospl
GU15 151 A4
Royal Oak Cl GU46 149 C3
Royal Oak Dr RG45 143 A4
Royal Prim Sch The SL4 94 B2
Royal Victoria Gdns SL5 120 A2
Royal Way RG2 112 C4
Royal Windsor
Race Course SL4 66 C4
Roycroft La RG40 141 C4
Royston Cl RG30 84 C4
Royston Way SL1 41 B4
Rubus Cl GU24 153 C3
Ruby Cl Slough SL1 42 A2
Wokingham RG41 115 C4
Rudd Hall Rise GU15 151 C2
Ruddlesway SL4 66 B3
Rudland Cl RG19 106 B1
Rudsworth Cl SL3 69 B4
Rufus Isaacs Rd RG4 59 A1
Rugby Cl GU47 143 C1
Ruggles-Brise Rd TW15 97 B2
Rumseys La OX11 12 A4
Runnemede Rd TW20 96 A2
Runnymede Cotts TW19 96 B4
Runnymede Ct TW20 96 A2
Runnymede Rdbt TW20 96 A2
Rupert Cl RG9 15 C2
Rupert House Sch RG9 15 C1
Rupert Rd RG14 130 C4
Rupert Sq 19 RG1 86 B4
Rupert St RG1 86 B4
Rupert Wlk 17 RG1 86 B4
Rupert's La RG9 15 C2
Ruscombe Gdns SL3 68 A4
Ruscombe La RG10 61 C3
Ruscombe Pk RG10 61 C3
Ruscombe Rd RG10 61 C3
Ruscombe Way TW14 98 C4
Rushall Cl RG6 113 C4
Rusham Park Ave TW20 96 A1
Rusham Rd TW20 95 C1
Rushbrook Rd RG5 87 B4
Rushburn HP10 3 C3
Rushden Dr RG2 86 C1
Rushes The
Maidenhead SL6 40 B3
Marlow SL7 18 B4
Rushey Way RG6 87 B1
Rushington Ave SL6 39 C3
Rushmere Pl TW20 95 C2
Rushmoor Gdns RG31 84 A2
Rushy Ho 7 RG12 118 C3
Ruskin Ave TW14 71 C1
Ruskin Ct RG45 142 C2
Ruskin Rd TW18 96 C1
Ruskin Way RG41 115 B3
Russel Cl RG12 118 B1
Russell Ct
Blackwater GU17 150 B3
Maidenhead SL6 39 C4
Russell Dr TW19 70 B1
Russell Ho 3 SL8 3 A2
Russell Rd
Lower Halliford TW17 125 B1
Mapledurham RG4 58 B4
Newbury RG14 104 C1
Russell St Reading RG1 85 C4
Windsor SL4 67 B3
Russell Way RG41 88 A1
Russet Ave TW16,TW17 125 C3
Russet Cl TW19 69 C1
Russet Gdns GU15 151 B2
Russet Glade
Burghfield Common RG7 111 A1
Caversham RG4 59 B4
Russet Rd SL6 39 B2
Russington Rd TW17 125 B2
Russley Gn RG40 116 A1
Rustington Cl 5 RG6 87 A1
Ruston Way SL5 119 C4
Rutherford Cl SL4 66 C3
Rutherford Wlk RG31 84 A4
Rutherwyk Rd KT16 123 C1
Rutland Ave SL1 42 B4
Rutland Gate SL6 39 B3
Rutland Pl SL6 39 B3
Rutland Rd Maidenhead SL6 39 B3
Reading RG30 85 B4
Ruxbury Ct TW15 97 C3
Ruxbury Rd KT16 123 B2
Ryan Mount GU47 150 A4
Ryans Mount SL7 1 B1
Rycroft SL4 66 C2
Rydal Ave RG30 57 C1
Rydal Cl GU15 152 B3
Rydal Dr RG19 106 A2
Rydal Pl GU18 153 A4
Rydal Way TW20 96 A1
Ryde Gdns GU46 149 A3
Ryde The TW18 124 A4
Rydings SL4 66 C2
Rye Cl Maidenhead SL6 39 A2
Newell Green RG12 91 B1
Winkfield RG12 118 B4
Rye Ct 1 SL1 43 A2
Rye Gr GU18,GU20 146 C1
Ryecroft Cl Wargrave RG10 36 C1
Woodley RG5 60 C1
Ryecroft Gdns GU17 150 C2
Ryehurst La RG42 90 C3
Ryeish Green Comp Sch
RG7 113 B2
Ryeish La RG7 113 B2
Ryemead La RG42, SL4 92 B3
Ryhill Way RG6 113 C4
Ryland Cl TW13 98 C2
Rylstone Cl SL6 39 B2
Rylstone Rd RG30 85 B4
Ryvers Ave GU46 149 A3
Ryvers End SL3 43 C2
Ryvers Rd SL3 43 C2
Ryvers Sch SL3 43 B2

S

Sabah Ct TW15 98 A2
Sackville St RG1 86 A4
Sacred Heart Coll SL5 121 B2
Sacred Heart RC Prim Sch
The RG9 15 B1
Saddleback Rd GU15 151 C4
Saddlebrook Pk TW16 98 C1
Saddler Cnr GU47 150 A4
Saddlewood GU15 151 B2
Sadlers Ct RG41 88 B1
Sadlers End RG41 115 B4
Sadlers La RG41 115 B4
Sadlers Mews SL6 40 A4
Sadlers Rd RG17 127 A3
Saffron Cl Datchet SL3 68 A3
Earley RG6 87 B2
Newbury RG14 104 C2
Saffron Ct TW14 98 B4
Saffron Rd RG12 118 A3
Sage Cl RG6 87 A1
Sage Rd RG31 57 B2
Sage Wlk RG42 91 B1
Sagecroft Rd RG18 106 B3
Sailing Club Rd SL8 3 A2
Sainsbury Ctr The KT16 124 A1
St Adrian's Cl SL6 39 A2
St Agnes Mews RG2 86 B1
St Agnes Terr RG17 25 A1
St Alban's St SL4 67 B3
St Albans Cl 16 SL4 67 B3
St Andrew's Ave SL4 66 C3
St Andrew's Cl
Old Windsor SL4 68 A1
Upper Halliford TW17 125 B3
Wraysbury TW19 68 C1
St Andrew's Cres SL4 66 C3
St Andrew's Sch RG8 55 B1
St Andrew's Way SL1 41 B3
St Andrews RG12 117 C2
St Andrews Cl
Bradfield RG7 82 B3
Crowthorne RG45 142 C3
St Andrews Cotts 1 SL4 67 A3
St Andrews Ct Ascot SL5 120 B2
Colnbrook SL3 69 B4
35 Reading RG1 86 B4
23 Slough SL1 42 C2
St Andrews Rd
Caversham RG4 58 C2
Henley-on-T RG9 35 B4
St Ann's Cl KT16 123 C2
St Ann's Heath Cty Mid
Sch GU25 122 C2
St Ann's Hill Rd KT16 123 B2
St Ann's Rd KT16 123 C2
St Anne's Ave TW19 97 B4
St Anne's Cl RG9 15 B1
St Anne's Prim Sch TW19 97 C4
St Anne's RC Prim Sch
Caversham RG4 59 A1
Chertsey KT16 124 A1
St Annes Glade GU19 145 B2
St Annes Rd RG4 59 A1
St Anthony's RC Prim Sch
SL2 22 B1
St Anthony's Way TW14 71 C2
St Anthonys Cl RG42 118 A4
St Augustine's
RC Prim Sch GU16 151 C1
St Barnabas Rd
Caversham RG4 59 A3
Earley RG2 86 C1
St Bartholemew's Sch
RG14 104 C1
St Bartholomews Rd RG1 86 C4
St Bernard's Convent Sch
SL3 43 B2
St Bernard's Prep Sch
SL1 43 A2
St Bernards Rd SL3 43 B2
St Birinus Rd RG31 84 B3
St Catherine's Sch GU15 151 B2
St Catherines Cl RG41 88 A1
St Catherines Ct
Staines TW18 97 A2
3 Windsor SL4 67 A3
St Catherines Hill RG7 136 C3
St Catherines Rd GU16 152 A1
St Cecelia Ct RG2 86 B2
St Chad's Rd SL6 39 A2
St Christophers Gdns
SL5 119 B4
St Clements Cl RG6 87 B1
St Columba's Cl SL6 39 A2
St Crispin's Comp Sch
RG40 116 C3
St Cuthbert's Cl TW20 95 B1
St Cuthbert's RC Prim Sch
TW20 95 B1
St David's Cl SL6 39 A2
St David's Jun Sch TW15 97 C3
St David's Rd RG14 104 C1
St Davids Cl RG4 58 C3
St Davids Dr TW20 95 B1
St Dominic Savio
RC Prim Sch RG5 87 B4
St Donats Pl RG14 105 A1
St Dunstan's Rd TW13 98 C3
St Edmund Campion
RC Prim Sch SL6 39 A3
St Edward's RC Sch
Reading RG30 85 B4
Windsor SL4 67 A3
St Edward's Royal Free
Ecumenical Mid Sch
Reading RG30 85 B4
Windsor SL4 67 A3
St Edwards Rd RG6 87 A3
St Elizabeth Cl RG2 113 A4
St Elmo Cl SL2 22 B1
St Elmo Cres SL2 22 B1
St Ethelbert's RC Sch SL2 43 A4
St Finian's RC Prim Sch
RG18 106 B4
St Francis RC Sch SL5 120 A2
St Gabriel's Sch RG20 131 A3
St George's Ave RG14 104 C1
St George's Cl SL4 66 C3
St George's Cres SL1 41 B3
St George's La SL5 120 A3
St George's Rd GU15 151 B3
St George's Sch
Ascot SL5 120 A3
Windsor SL4 67 B4
St Georges Ct GU47 143 C1
St Georges Ind Est GU15 151 A2
St Georges Rd RG30 85 B4
St Georges Terr RG30 85 A4
St Giles Cl RG1 86 A3
St Giles Ct 14 RG1 86 A3
St Helens Cres GU47 150 A4
St Helier Cl RG41 116 A2
St Hilda's Ave TW15 97 C2
St Ives Cl RG7 83 B1
St Ives Rd SL6 40 A4
St James Cl
Pangbourne RG8 56 B3
Twyford RG10 61 C3
St James Ctyd 4 SL7 1 C1
St James Pl SL1 41 B4
St James Rd RG40 141 C4
St James Wlk SL0 44 C2
St John the Evangelist
CE Sch RG14 104 C1
St John's Beamont
Prep Sch SL4 95 A3
St John's CE Prim Sch
RG1 86 B4
St John's Gdns RG14 104 C1
St John's Rd
North Ascot SL5 92 C1
Sandhurst GU47 150 B4
St Johns Cl RG5 87 C4
St Johns Ct TW20 96 A2
St Johns Dr SL4 67 A3
St Johns Hill RG1 86 B4
St Johns Inf Sch RG7 137 A3
St Johns Rd
Caversham RG4 59 B1
Mortimer RG7 137 A3
Newbury RG14 105 A1
Reading RG1 86 B4
Slough SL2 43 A3
Thatcham RG19 106 B2
Windsor SL4 67 A3
St Johns St
Crowthorne RG45 143 A2
Reading RG1 86 B4
St Johns Way KT16 124 A1
St Joseph's Convent Sch
RG1 86 C3
St Joseph's Convent Sch
Prep Sch RG1 86 C3
St Joseph's Ct 7 RG14 105 A2
St Joseph's RC Prim Sch
Bracknell RG12 118 B4
Newbury RG14 105 A2
St Joseph's RC Sec Sch
SL2 43 A4
St Jude's CE Sch TW20 95 B1
St Jude's Cl TW20 95 B2
St Jude's Cotts TW20 95 B2
St Jude's Rd TW20 95 B2
St Katherines Rd RG9 35 B4
St Laurence Way SL1 43 A2
St Lawrence Sq RG17 100 B3
St Leger Ct RG14 104 C2
St Leonard's Ave 29 SL4 67 B3
St Leonard's Rd
Windsor SL4 67 B2
Windsor, Clewer Green SL4 66 B1
St Leonards Hill SL4 66 C2
St Leonards Wlk SL0 44 C2
St Luke's CE Prim Sch
SL6 39 C4
St Luke's Rd
Maidenhead SL6 39 C4
Old Windsor SL4 68 A1
St Lukes Ct RG4 59 A2
St Lukes Way RG4 59 A3
St Margaret Clitherow
RC Prim Sch RG12 117 C1
St Margaret's Rd SL6 39 A4
St Margarets Ave TW15 98 A2
St Mark's Cl RG7 83 A3
St Mark's Cres SL6 39 A4
St Mark's Hospl SL6 39 B4
St Mark's Pl SL4 67 B3
St Mark's Rd
Binfield RG42 117 B4
Henley-on-T RG9 15 C1
Maidenhead SL6 39 B4
Windsor SL4 67 B3
St Marks Cl RG19 106 B2
St Marks Rd Binfield RG42 90 B1
Henley-on-T RG9 35 B4
St Martin's Ct TW15 97 B2
St Martins Cl 3 RG6 87 B1
St Martins RC Prim Sch
RG4 59 C3
St Mary's All Saints
CE Prim Sch RG1 85 C3
St Mary's Ave TW19 97 B4
St Mary's CE Comb Sch
SL3 68 A3
St Mary's CE Jun Sch
RG18 106 B2
St Mary's CE Prim Sch
Kintbury RG17 102 A1
Slough SL1 43 A2
Winkfield RG42 92 A2
St Mary's CE Sch TW19 97 C4
St Mary's Cl
Maidenhead SL6 40 A4
Stanwell TW19 97 B4
St Mary's Cres TW19 97 B4
St Mary's Ct 6 RG14 105 A2
St Mary's Dr TW14 98 B4
St Mary's Gdns GU19 145 C2
St Mary's Hill SL5 120 B2
St Mary's Jun Sch RG7 137 B3

St Mary's Pl 🄸 RG14 . . . . . . .105 A2
St Mary's RC Prim Sch
SL6 . . . . .19 C1
St Mary's Rd Ascot SL5 . . . .120 A2
Camberley GU15 . . . . .151 B3
Slough SL3 . . . . .43 C2
St Mary's Sch SL5 . . . . .120 A1
St Mary's Wlk SL6 . . . . .39 C4
St Marys Ave RG8 . . . . .57 B3
St Marys Butts RG1 . . . . .86 A4
St Marys Cl
Henley-on-T RG9 . . . . .35 A4
Sandhurst GU47 . . . . .150 B4
St Marys La SL4 . . . . .92 B3
St Marys Rd
Mortimer RG2 . . . . .137 A3
Newbury RG14 . . . . .105 A2
Wokingham RG41 . . . . .88 A1
St Marys Way RG7 . . . . .111 A2
St Matthew's Ct TW15 . . . . . .98 A2
St Michael's CE Prim Sch
RG12 . . . . .118 A2
St Michael's Ct SL2 . . . . .21 B1
St Michael's RC Prim Sch
TW15 .98 A2
St Michael's Rd
Newbury RG14 . . . . .104 C1
Reading RG30 . . . . .84 B4
St Michaels CE Prim Sch
GU47 . . . . .149 C4
St Michaels Cl RG17 . . . . .25 A1
St Michaels Cotts RG40 . . . .143 B4
St Michaels Ct RG10 . . . . . . .61 C3
St Michaels Rd
Ashford TW15 . . . . .98 A2
Camberley GU15 . . . . .151 A3
Sandhurst GU47 . . . . .149 C4
St Michael's Ct St Sch5 . . . .120 B2
St Nazaire Cl TW20 . . . . .96 B2
St Nicholas CE Comb Sch
SL6 . . . . .20 C1
St Nicholas CE Prim Sch
Hurst RG10 . . . . .88 C3
Shepperton TW17 . . . . .125 A2
St Nicholas Dr TW17 . . . . . .125 A2
St Nicholas' Rd RG14 . . . . . .104 C1
St Nicolas CE Jun Sch
RG14 . . . . .105 A1
St Olave's CE Inf Sch SL4 . . .96 C1
St Patrick's Ave RG10 . . . . . .61 A3
St Patrick's Cl SL6 . . . . .39 A2
St Paul's CE Comb Sch
HP10 . . . . .3 B2
St Paul's CE Jun Sch
RG41 . . . . .116 A3
St Paul's Cl TW15 . . . . .98 B2
St Paul's Ct SL5 . . . . .39 C3
St Paul's Gate RG41 . . . . . . .116 A3
St Paul's RC Prim Sch
RG31 .84 B4
St Paul's Rd TW18 . . . . .96 B1
St Pauls Ave SL2 . . . . .43 A3
St Pauls Ct RG1 . . . . .86 A3
St Peter St SL7 . . . . .1 B2
St Peter's CE Comb Sch
SL1 . . . . .21 A1
St Peter's CE Mid Sch
SL4 . . . . .67 C1
St Peter's CE Prim Sch
RG6 . . . . .87 A3
St Peter's Cl
Burnham SL1 . . . . .21 A1
Old Windsor SL4 . . . . .68 A1
St Peter's RC Comb Sch
SL7 . . . . .1 B2
St Peter's Rd SL6 . . . . .19 B1
St Peters Ave RG4 . . . . .58 C2
St Peters Gdns GU46 . . . . . .149 B3
St Peters Hill RG4 . . . . .58 C2
St Peters Rd RG6 . . . . .87 A3
St Pinnock Ave TW18 . . . . . .124 A4
St Pirans Ind Day Sch
SL6 . . . . .19 C1
St Richards Rd RG4 . . . . .105 A2
St Ronans Rd RG30 . . . . .85 A4
St Saviour's Terr 🄹
RG1 . . . . .86 A3
St Saviours Rd RG1 . . . . .85 C3
St Sebastian Cl RG40 . . . . . .142 C4
St Stephens Cl RG4 . . . . .59 A1
St Swithins Cl RG20 . . . . .75 B2
St Swithuns Ct RG10 . . . . . . .61 B2
St Swithuns RC Prim Sch
RG40 . . . . .116 B3
St Theresa's Rd TW14 . . . . . .71 C2
St Thomas Ct RG18 . . . . .106 C2
St Thomas Wlk SL3 . . . . .69 B4
St-Cloud Way SL6 . . . . .40 A4
Salamanca RG45 . . . . .142 C3
Salcombe Dr RG6 . . . . .114 C4
Salcombe Rd
Ashford TW15 . . . . .97 C3
Newbury RG14 . . . . .104 C1
Reading RG2 . . . . .86 B2
Sale Garden Cotts
RG40 . . . . .116 B3
Saleby Cl RG6 . . . . .87 C1
Salesian Gdns KT16 . . . . . . .124 A1
Salesian Sch KT16 . . . . .124 A1
Salford Cl RG2 . . . . .113 B4
Salisbury Ave SL2 . . . . .42 B4
Salisbury Cl RG41 . . . . .116 A1
Salisbury Ct SL6 . . . . .39 C3
Salisbury Mews SL2 . . . . . . .22 B1

Salisbury Rd
Blackwater GU17 . . . . .150 B3
Harlington TW6 . . . . .71 B1
Hungerford RG17 . . . . .100 B2
Reading RG30 . . . . .85 C4
Salmon Cl RG2 . . . . .113 A1
Salmond Rd RG2 . . . . .113 B3
Salt Hill Ave SL1 . . . . .42 B3
Salt Hill Dr SL1 . . . . .42 B3
Salt Hill Mans SL1 . . . . .42 B3
Salt Hill Way SL1 . . . . .42 B3
Salters Cl SL6 . . . . .40 A4
Salters Rd SL6 . . . . .40 A4
Saltersgate Cl RG6 . . . . .87 B1
Saltire Gdns 🄴 RG42 . . . . . .118 A4
Salva Ct 🄹 RG1 . . . . .86 B3
Salwey Cl RG12 . . . . .118 A2
Samarkand Cl GU15 . . . . . . .152 A2
Samian Pl RG42 . . . . .90 C1
Sampage Cl RG2 . . . . .113 B3
Sampson Bsns Pk GU15 . . .151 A2
Sampson Ct TW17 . . . . .125 B2
Sampson Pk RG42 . . . . .117 B4
Sampsons Gn SL2 . . . . .21 C1
Sanctuary Cl RG30 . . . . .84 C4
Sanctuary Rd TW19, TW6 . . .71 A1
Sandcroft Rd RG4 . . . . .58 C3
Sanden Cl RG17 . . . . .100 B3
Sandford Down RG12 . . . . . .118 C2
Sandford Dr RG5 . . . . .60 C1
Sandford La RG5, RG10 . . . . .88 B3
Sandgate Ave RG30 . . . . .57 C1
Sandhills Ct GU25 . . . . .122 C2
Sandhills La GU25, TW20 . . .122 C2
Sandhills Mdw TW17 . . . . . .125 B1
Sandhills Way RG31 . . . . .84 C2
Sandhurst La GU17 . . . . .150 A3
Sandhurst Rd
Crowthorne RG45 . . . . .143 A2
Wokingham RG40 . . . . .116 A4
Yateley GU46 . . . . .149 C4
Sandhurst Sch GU47 . . . . . .150 B4
Sandhurst Sta GU47 . . . . . .150 A4
Sandisplatt Rd SL6 . . . . .39 A3
Sandleford Cl RG2 . . . . .113 B3
Sandleford Hospl RG14 . . . .131 A4
Sandleford Rise RG14 . . . . .131 A4
Sandlers End SL2 . . . . .22 A1
Sandow Ave RG31 . . . . .84 A2
Sandown Cl GU17 . . . . .150 B3
Sandown Dr GU16 . . . . .151 C1
Sandown Rd SL2 . . . . .41 C4
Sandown Way RG14 . . . . . . .105 B4
Sandpit Hill RG14,RG20 . . . .130 B2
Sandpit La RG7 . . . . .140 A3
Sandringham La SL1 . . . . .41 B4
Sandringham Dr TW15 . . . . . .97 B2
Sandringham Rd
Maidenhead SL6 . . . . .19 C1
Stanwell TW19, TW6 . . . . . . .70 C1
Sandringham Way RG31 . . . .84 A2
Sands Farm Dr SL1 . . . . .21 B1
Sandstone Cl RG41 . . . . .88 B1
Sandy Cl RG18 . . . . .79 A2
Sandy Dr TW14 . . . . .98 C4
Sandy La Bracknell RG12 . . .118 B4
Camberley GU15 . . . . .151 C3
Hermitage RG18 . . . . .78 C2
North Ascot SL5 . . . . .119 B4
Sandhurst GU47 . . . . .143 A1
Sunningdale SL5 . . . . .121 A2
Virginia Water GU25 . . . . . . .122 C3
Wokingham RG41 . . . . .115 B2
Sandy Lane Inf Sch RG42 . . .91 B1
Sandy Lane Jun Sch RG42 . . .91 B1
Sandy Mead SL6 . . . . .40 B1
Sandy Ride SL5 . . . . .120 C3
Sandy Way RG12 . . . . .125 C1
Sandygate Cl SL7 . . . . .1 B2
Sandygate Rd SL7 . . . . .1 B2
Sapgood Cl RG19 . . . . .106 C1
Sapphire Cl RG41 . . . . .115 B2
Sarsby Dr TW19 . . . . .96 A3
Sarum Cl SL4 . . . . .117 C1
Sarum Cres RG40 . . . . .116 B4
Sarum Ct RG30 . . . . .85 B3
Sarum Rd RG26 . . . . .135 A1
Sarum Way RG17 . . . . .100 B2
Satis Ho SL3 . . . . .68 B4
Saturn Cl RG41 . . . . .115 C3
Saturn Croft RG42 . . . . .92 A1
Saunders Cl RG10 . . . . .61 C2
Saunders Ct RG8 . . . . .57 A3
Saunton Ave UB3 . . . . .71 C4
Savernake Cl RG30 . . . . .84 C4
Savernake Way RG12 . . . . . .118 C2
Savill Gardens The TW20 . . .94 C1
Savill Way SL7 . . . . .1 C1
Saville Cres TW15 . . . . .98 B1
Saville Gdns GU15 . . . . .152 A3
Savory Wlk RG42 . . . . .90 B1
Savoy Gr GU17 . . . . .150 B2
Sawmill Rd RG18 . . . . .79 A2
Sawpit Rd RG10 . . . . .88 C4
Sawtry Cl RG6 . . . . .87 C1
Sawyer's Cl SL4 . . . . .66 C4
Sawyers Cl SL6 . . . . .39 A1
Sawyers Cres SL6 . . . . .39 A1
Saxby Cl RG12 . . . . .111 A2
Saxon Cl SL3 . . . . .43 C2
Saxon Ct 🄹🄹 Reading RG1 . . .86 B4
Stanwell TW19 . . . . .70 A1
Saxon Dr RG42 . . . . .118 C4
Saxon City Jun Sch
TW17 . . . . .125 A2
Saxon Dr RG42 . . . . .118 C4
Saxon Gdns SL6 . . . . .20 B1
Saxon Rd TW15 . . . . .98 B1

Saxon Way
Harmondsworth UB7 . . . . . . .70 B4
Old Windsor SL4 . . . . .68 A1
Saxons Acre RG20 . . . . .28 B2
Sayers Cl RG14 . . . . .131 A4
Scafell Cl RG31 . . . . .57 A1
Scafell Rd SL2 . . . . .41 C4
Scampton Rd TW6 . . . . .70 C1
Scania Wlk RG42 . . . . .92 A1
Scarborough Rd TW6 . . . . . . .71 B1
Scarborough Way SL1 . . . . . .42 A2
Scarlet Oaks GU15 . . . . .151 C2
Scarletts La RG10 . . . . .37 B1
Sch of Electronic
Engineering RG12 . . . . .114 C1
Scholars Cl Caversham RG4 . .58 C2
Great Shefford RG17 . . . . .48 A2
School Cl GU24 . . . . .153 C2
School Hill
Crowthorne RG45 . . . . .143 B2
Sandhurst GU47 . . . . .143 A1
Wargrave RG10 . . . . .36 B1
Woolhampton RG7 . . . . .107 C2
School Ho TW19 . . . . .70 B1
School La Bagshot GU19 . . .145 C1
Bradford RG20 . . . . .76 C2
Burghfield Common RG7 . . .111 A1
Caversham RG4 . . . . .59 A1
Caversham, Emmer
Green RG4 . . . . .59 A3
Cookham SL6 . . . . .20 A4
Cookham, Cookham
Dean SL6 . . . . .19 A4
East Garston RG17 . . . . .47 B3
Egham TW20 . . . . .96 A2
Frohfield SN8 . . . . .99 A1
Little Marlow SL7 . . . . .2 B3
Littlewick Green SL6 . . . . .38 A2
Lower Halliford TW17 . . . . . .125 A1
Maidenhead SL6 . . . . .40 A1
Medmenham SL7 . . . . .17 A3
Silchester RG7 . . . . .136 A1
Stoke Poges SL2 . . . . .23 A2
Swallowfield RG7 . . . . .139 C2
Wargrave RG10 . . . . .36 B1
Windlesham GU20 . . . . .146 B4
Yateley GU46 . . . . .149 A3
School of Military Survey
RG18 .78 C4
School Rd Arborfield RG2 . . .114 C1
Ascot SL5 . . . . .120 B2
Ashford TW15 . . . . .98 A1
Burghfield Common RG30 . .111 B3
Chieveley RG20 . . . . .78 A4
Compton RG20 . . . . .31 C2
Harmondsworth UB7 . . . . . . .70 B4
Hurst RG10 . . . . .88 B4
Padworth RG7 . . . . .109 C1
Reading RG31 . . . . .84 B4
Swallowfield RG7 . . . . .139 C2
Waltham St Lawrence RG10 . .62 C2
Windlesham GU20 . . . . .146 B4
Wooburn Green HP10 . . . . . . .3 C3
School Terr RG1 . . . . .86 C4
Schroder Ct TW20 . . . . .95 A2
Scotland Hill GU47 . . . . .150 A4
Scotlands Dr SL2 . . . . .22 A3
Scots Cl TW19 . . . . .97 B4
Scots Dr RG41 . . . . .115 C4
Scott Cl Caversham RG4 . . . . .59 A3
Farnham Common SL2 . . . . . .22 C4
Woodley RG5 . . . . .88 A4
Scott Terr RG12 . . . . .118 C4
Scott's Ave TW16 . . . . .98 C1
Scott's Way TW16 . . . . .98 C1
Scottalls La RG18 . . . . .52 A3
Scours La RG30 . . . . .58 A1
Scratchface La RG7 . . . . .81 C3
Scrivens Mead RG19 . . . . . .106 C2
Scylla Cres TW6&TW14 . . . . .98 A4
Scylla Rd TW14, TW6 . . . . . . .71 A1
Seacourt Rd SL3 . . . . .44 A1
Seafield Cl 🄹🄴 RG1 . . . . .86 B4
Seaford Gdns RG5 . . . . .87 C3
Seaford Rd
Stanwell TW19, TW6 . . . . . . .70 B1
Wokingham RG40 . . . . .116 B3
Sealand Rd TW6 . . . . .71 A1
Searing Way RG26 . . . . .135 A1
Searles Farm La RG30 . . . . .85 A1
Seaton Gdns RG2 . . . . .86 B1
Seaton Rd GU15 . . . . .151 A3
Second Ave RG7 . . . . .135 B1
Second Cres SL1 . . . . .42 B4
Second St RG7 . . . . .132 A3
Second St W RG19 . . . . .131 C2
Seddon Hill RG42 . . . . .91 A1
Sedge Gr RG18 . . . . .106 C2
Sedgefield Rd RG14 . . . . . . .131 B4
Sedgmoor Cl HP10 . . . . .3 A4
Sedgmoor Gdns HP10 . . . . . .3 A4
Sedgmoor La HP10 . . . . .3 A4
Sedgmoor Rd HP10 . . . . .3 A4
Seebys Oak GU47 . . . . .150 C3
Sefton Cl Stoke Poges SL2 . .22 C2
West End GU24 . . . . .153 C3
Sefton Paddock SL2 . . . . . . .23 A3
Sefton Park Cotts SL2 . . . . . .23 A3
Segsbury Gr RG12 . . . . .118 C3
Seilborne Cl GU17 . . . . .150 B3
Selborne Ct 🄹 RG1 . . . . .86 B4
Selborne Gdns SL2 . . . . .22 A2
Selby Rd TW15 . . . . .98 B1
Selcourt Cl RG5 . . . . .87 B4
Sellafield Way RG6 . . . . .87 C1
Selsdon Ave RG5 . . . . .87 C4

Selsey Way RG6 . . . . .114 A4
Selwood Cl TW19 . . . . .70 B1
Selwood Gdns TW19 . . . . . . .70 B1
Selwyn Cl SL4 . . . . .66 C3
Selwyn Dr GU46 . . . . .149 A3
Selwyn Pl 🄹 SL1 . . . . .41 C3
Sen Cl RG42 . . . . .91 B1
Send Rd RG4 . . . . .59 B1
Servite Ho SL6 . . . . .40 B4
Setley Way RG12 . . . . .118 C3
Seton Dr RG31 . . . . .84 C3
Sett The GU46 . . . . .149 A3
Sevenoaks Dr RG7 . . . . .113 A2
Sevenoaks Rd RG6 . . . . .87 A2
Seventh St RG19 . . . . .131 C3
Severalls The SN8 . . . . .126 B2
Severn Cl Sandhurst GU47 . .150 B4
Thatcham RG18 . . . . .106 A3
Severn Cres SL3 . . . . .69 A4
Severn Way RG30 . . . . .84 C4
Sewell Ave RG41 . . . . .116 A4
Sewell Cl RG18 . . . . .79 A1
Seymour Ave RG2 . . . . .113 C4
Seymour Cl SL6 . . . . .39 A2
Seymour Court La SL7 . . . . . . .1 A3
Seymour Court Rd SL7 . . . . . . .1 B2
Seymour Dr GU15 . . . . .152 A4
Seymour Ho SL3 . . . . .43 A4
Seymour Park Rd SL7 . . . . . . .1 B2
Seymour Plain SL7 . . . . .1 A3
Seymour Rd SL1 . . . . .42 B4
Seymour Way TW16 . . . . .98 C1
Shackleton Cl 🄴 TW19 . . . . . .70 C1
Shackleton Rd SL1 . . . . .42 C3
Shackleton Way RG5 . . . . . . .88 A4
Shafer Cl RG14 . . . . .105 A1
Shaftesbury Cl RG12 . . . . . .118 B2
Shaftesbury Cres TW18 . . . . .97 B1
Shaftesbury Ct
Maidenhead SL6 . . . . .19 C1
🄹 Slough SL1 . . . . .42 C2
Wokingham RG40 . . . . .116 B3
Shaftesbury Mount
GU17 . . . . .150 B2
Shaftesbury Rd
Bisley GU24 . . . . .153 C2
Reading RG30 . . . . .85 A4
Shaggy Calf La SL2 . . . . .43 A3
Shakespeare Cl RG4 . . . . .59 B3
Shakespeare Rd RG18 . . . . .106 B2
Shakespeare Way RG42 . . . .118 C4
Shalbourne Cl RG17 . . . . . . .100 A3
Shalbourne Rise GU15 . . . . .151 B3
Sharney Ave SL3 . . . . .44 A2
Sharnwood Dr RG31 . . . . .84 C3
Sharonelle Cl RG40 . . . . .116 A3
Sharpethorpe Cl 🄹🄹 RG6 . . . .87 C1
Shaw Ct SL4 . . . . .66 C4
Shaw Farm Rd RG14 . . . . . .105 A3
Shaw Hill RG14 . . . . .105 A3
Shaw Hill RG14 . . . . .105 A3
Shaw Pk RG45 . . . . .143 A2
Shaw Rd Newbury RG14 . . .105 A2
Reading RG5 . . . . .85 C3
Shaw The SL6 . . . . .19 C3
Shaw-Cum-Donnington
Parochial Prim Sch
RG14 . . . . .105 A3
Shears Ct TW16 . . . . .98 C1
Sheehy Way SL2 . . . . .43 A4
Sheep Fair Way RG17 . . . . . .25 A1
Sheep Leaze La RG20 . . . . . .29 B1
Sheep Wlk RG4 . . . . .59 A2
Sheepcote La
Bourne End SL1 . . . . .3 C1
Holyport SL6 . . . . .64 B2
Sheepcote Rd Eton SL4 . . . . .42 A1
Windsor SL4 . . . . .66 C3
Sheepdrove Rd RG17 . . . . . . .25 B2
Sheephouse Rd SL6 . . . . .20 B3
Sheephouse Way GU24 . . . . .49 A3
Sheepleaze La SL7,HP10 . . . .2 C3
Sheeps Ditch Cl TW18 . . . . . .96 C2
Sheepwalk Littleton TW17 . .125 A2
Shepperton TW17 . . . . .124 C2
Sheepwash RG20 . . . . .131 A1
Sheepways La RG4 . . . . .58 A4
Sheerlands Rd RG2 . . . . .140 C4
Sheet St SL4 . . . . .67 B3
Sheet Street Rd SL4 . . . . .94 A4
Sheffield Rd
Harlington TW14,TW6 . . . . . .71 B1
Slough SL1 . . . . .42 B4
Shefford Cl RG7 . . . . .48 C2
Shefford Cres RG40 . . . . . . .116 B4
Shefford Lodge 🄴 RG14 . . . .105 A1
Sheldon Gdns RG2 . . . . .86 B1
Shelgate Wlk RG5 . . . . .87 B3
Shelley Ave RG12 . . . . .118 B4
Shelley Cl Medmenham SL7 . .17 B4
Slough SL3 . . . . .43 C2
Wooburn Green HP10 . . . . . . .3 C4
Woodley RG5 . . . . .87 C3
Shelley Ct
Camberley GU15 . . . . .151 B3
🄴 Reading RG1 . . . . .86 B4
Shelley Rd 🄴 Marlow SL7 . . . .1 C2
Thatcham RG18 . . . . .106 B2
Shelley Wlk GU46 . . . . .149 A3
Shelson Ave TW13 . . . . .98 C2
Shelton Ct SL3 . . . . .43 B3
Shenstone Cl RG40 . . . . .142 A4
Shenstone Dr SL1 . . . . .22 A2
Shenstone Pk SL5 . . . . .120 C3
Shenstone Rd RG2 . . . . .86 A2
Shephards La RG42 . . . . .91 A1
Shepherd's Hill RG2 . . . . . . .86 C2

Shepherds Ave RG6 . . . . .87 A4
Shepherds Chase GU19 . . . .145 C1
Shepherds Cl Hurley SL6 . . . .17 C2
Shepperton TW17 . . . . .125 A2
Shepherds Ct SL4 . . . . .66 C3
Shepherds Hill
Bracknell RG12 . . . . .118 B4
Compton RG20 . . . . .31 C2
Earley RG6 . . . . .87 B4
Woodley RG5 . . . . .60 B3
Shepherds House La RG6 . . .87 A4
Shepherds La
Caversham RG4 . . . . .58 B3
Hurley SL6 . . . . .17 C2
Shepherds Mount RG20 . . . . .31 C2
Shepherds Rise RG20 . . . . . . .31 C2
Shepherds Way RG45 . . . . . .142 C2
Shepherds Wlk RG6 . . . . .87 A4
Shepley Dr Reading RG30 . . .85 B2
Wentworth SL5 . . . . .121 B2
Shepley End SL5 . . . . .121 B2
Shepperton Bsns Pk
TW17 . . . . .125 A2
Shepperton Court Dr
TW17 . . . . .125 A2
Shepperton Ct TW17 . . . . . .125 A2
Shepperton Rd
TW17,TW18 . . . . .124 B3
Shepperton Sta TW17 . . . . .125 B2
Shepperton Studios
TW17 . . . . .124 C2
Sheraton Cl GU17 . . . . .150 C2
Sheraton Dr RG13 . . . . .57 A1
Sherborne Cl SL3 . . . . .69 C3
Sherborne Dr SL5 . . . . .121 B2
Sherborne Rd TW14 . . . . .98 B4
Sherbourne Dr
Maidenhead SL6 . . . . .39 B2
Wentworth SL5 . . . . .121 B2
Windsor SL4 . . . . .67 C2
Woodley RG5 . . . . .87 C4
Sherbourne Gdns TW17 . . . .125 C3
Sherbourne Wlk SL2 . . . . . . .22 B4
Sherfield Cl RG2 . . . . .86 B2
Sherfield Dr RG2 . . . . .86 B2
Shergold Way SL6 . . . . .19 C3
Sheridan Ave RG4 . . . . .58 C2
Sheridan Cres RG26 . . . . . . .134 C2
Sheridan Ct
Maidenhead SL6 . . . . .40 A4
Newbury RG14 . . . . .105 B2
🄹 Slough SL1 . . . . .42 C3
Sheridan Way RG41 . . . . . . .116 A3
Sheringham Ct 🄹 RG1 . . . . . .86 B3
Sherman Rd Reading RG1 . . .86 B3
Slough SL1 . . . . .42 C4
Sherrardmead RG14 . . . . . . .105 A3
Sherring Ct RG42 . . . . .91 B3
Sherwood Cl
Bracknell RG12 . . . . .119 A4
Slough SL3 . . . . .43 C2
Sherwood Ct
Colnbrook SL3 . . . . .69 B4
Slough SL1 . . . . .43 C1
Sherwood Dr SL6 . . . . .39 A2
Sherwood Gdns RG9 . . . . . . .35 B4
Sherwood Ho 🄹🄹 RG1 . . . . . .85 C2
Sherwood Pl RG8 . . . . .34 B3
Sherwood Rd RG41 . . . . .88 B1
Sherwood Rise RG8 . . . . .34 B3
Sherwood St RG30 . . . . .85 B4
Shield Rd TW15 . . . . .98 B3
Shifford Cres SL6 . . . . .19 C2
Shildon Cl GU15 . . . . .152 B2
Shilling Cl RG30 . . . . .85 A3
Shinfield CE Jun Sch
RG2 .113 C2
Shinfield Rd RG2 . . . . .86 C2
Shinfield Rise RG2 . . . . .86 C1
Shiplake Coll RG9 . . . . .35 C3
Shiplake Ho
Bourne End SL8 . . . . .3 A2
Bracknell RG12 . . . . .118 C3
Shiplake Sta RG9 . . . . .36 A2
Shipley Cl RG5 . . . . .61 A3
Shipton Cl RG31 . . . . .57 B3
Shire Cl GU19 . . . . .145 C3
Shire's Head Cl RG30 . . . . . . .85 B3
Shires The RG41 . . . . .115 B2
Shires Way GU46 . . . . .149 B4
Shirley Ave Reading RG2 . . .113 B4
Windsor SL4 . . . . .66 C2
Shirley Rd SL3 . . . . .43 C3
Shoesmiths Ct 🄴 RG1 . . . . . . .86 A4
Sholto Rd TW6 . . . . .71 A1
Shooters Hill RG8 . . . . .56 B3
Shooters Way RG2 . . . . .112 C4
Shop La
Leckhampstead RG20 . . . . . . .49 C3
Newbury RG14 . . . . .104 C3
Shoppenhanger's Rd SL6 . . .39 C2
Shoreham Rd (E) TW6 . . . . . .70 A1
Shoreham Rd (W) TW6 . . . . .70 A1
Shoreham Rise SL2 . . . . .21 B1
Shorland Oaks RG42 . . . . . . .91 B3
Short La TW15, TW19 . . . . . .97 C4
Short The RG8 . . . . .57 B2
Shortfern SL2 . . . . .22 B4
Shortheath La RG7 . . . . .110 C2
Shortlands Hill OX10 . . . . . . .71 B4
Shortlands Hill OX10 . . . . . . .71 A4
Shortwood Ave TW18 . . . . . . .97 A3

Shortwood Cty Inf Sch TW18 .... 97 A3
Shrewbury Terr RG14 .... 104 C1
Shrewsbury Rd TW14,TW6 .... 71 B1
Shrivenham Cl 3 GU47 .150 B4
Shropshire Gdns RG42 ... 91 C1
Shrubbs Hill La SL5 ..... 121 B2
Shrubland Dr RG30 .... 85 A2
Shrublands Dr GU18 .... 153 A4
Shute End RG40,41 ...... 116 A3
Shyshack La RG26 .... 134 C1
Sibley Park Rd RG6 ...... 87 A1
Sibson RG0 .... 87 B1
Sidbury Ct SL5 .... 121 A2
Sidestrand Rd RG14 ..... 130 C4
Sidings The TW18 .... 97 A2
Sidmouth Ct 3 RG1 ...... 86 B4
Sidmouth Grange Rd RG6 .87 A4
Sidmouth Grange Rd RG6 .87 A4
Sidmouth St RG1 .... 86 B4
Sidney Rd Staines TW18 ..97 A2
Windsor SL4 .... 66 B2
Silbury Cl RG21 .... 88 A2
Silchester CE Prim Sch RG7 .... 136 A1
Silchester Ct TW15 ...... 97 C3
Silchester Ho SL6 .... 40 A4
Silchester House Sch SL6 .40 B4
Silchester Rd Reading RG30 .... 85 B2
Tadley RG26 .... 135 B1
Silco Dr SL0 .... 39 C3
Silk La RG10 .... 61 B2
Silver Birches RG41 ..... 115 B2
Silver Cl SL6 .... 39 A3
Silver Dr GU15 .... 152 B2
Silver Fox Cres RG5 ..... 87 B3
Silver Hill GU47 .... 150 C4
Silver La RG7 .... 136 A4
Silver St RG1 .... 86 A3
Silver Street Flats RG1 ..86 A3
Silverdale Rd Earley RG6 .87 B2
Tadley RG26 .... 135 A1
Wargrave RG10 .... 36 C1
Silverglades GU46 ...... 149 B2
Silverthorne Dr RG4 ..... 58 C3
Silvertrees Dr SL4 ...... 39 A3
Silverwood Dr GU15 .... 152 A4
Silwood RG12 .... 117 C1
Silwood Cl SL5 .... 120 B4
Silwood Pk (Imperial Coll) SL5 .... 120 C3
Silwood Rd SL5 .... 120 C3
Simkins Cl RG42 .... 92 A1
Simmonds Cl RG42 ...... 117 C4
Simmonds St RG1 .... 86 A4
Simmons Cl SL3 .... 44 A1
Simmons Field RG18 .... 106 C2
Simmons Fields RG10 .... 61 A2
Simmons Pl TW18 .... 96 C2
Simmons Rd RG9 .... 15 B2
Simms Farm La RG7 .... 136 C2
Simod Ct RG30 .... 85 B4
Simons Cl RG31 .... 57 B2
Simons La RG41 .... 115 B4
Simons Wlk TW20 .... 95 B1
Simpson Cl SL6 .... 40 A4
Sindle Cl RG41 .... 88 A1
Sindlesham Rd RG2 .... 114 C2
Sindlesham Specl Sch RG41 .... 114 C4
Singer La RG9 .... 15 C1
Singers Cl RG9 .... 35 C4
Singers La RG9 .... 35 C4
Sinhurst Rd GU15 ...... 151 A2
Sipson La UB3,UB7 ...... 71 A4
Sipson La UB3, UB7 ..... 71 A4
Sipson Rd UB7 .... 71 A4
Sipson Way UB7 .... 71 A4
Sir Sydney Camm Ho SL4 .67 A3
Sir William Borlase's Gram Sch SL7 .... 1 B1
Sir William Perkin's Ind Sch for Girls KT16 .... 123 C1
Sirius Cl RG41 .... 115 C3
Sirl Cotts SL5 .... 120 B3
Six Acre La RG17 .... 25 A3
Sixth St RG19 .... 131 C3
Skarries View RG4 .... 58 B4
Skeffling Cl RG4 .... 87 C1
Skelmersdale Way RG6 ...87 C2
Skelton Fields RG42 ..... 91 B1
Skerries Ct SL3 .... 44 A1
Skerrit Way RG8 .... 57 B2
Skillman Dr RG19 ...... 106 C2
Skilton Rd RG31 .... 57 B2
Skimpedhill La RG12 ... 118 A4
Skinners Green La RG14 .130 A4
Skippons Cl RG14 ...... 130 B3
Sky Bsns Pk TW20 ..... 123 B4
Skydmore Path SL2 ...... 21 C1
Skye Cl RG43 .... R4 C2
Skyes Dr TW18 .... 97 A2
Skylings RG14 .... 105 B2
Skyport Dr UB7 .... 70 B4
Skyway 14 Trad Est SL3 ..69 C2
Slade Hill Gdns RG20 ... 129 C1
Sladburn Gn RG12 ...... 116 C1
Slanting Hill RG18 .... 79 A2
Sledmere Ct TW14 ...... 98 C4
Sleets Rd RG4 .... 59 B1
Slopes The RG4 .... 59 B1
Sloane & Eton CE Sec Sch SL1 .... 42 B2
Slough Gram Sch SL3 ... 43 A2
Slough Mus SL1 .... 43 A2

Slough Rd Datchet SL3 ...68 A4
Slough Sta SL1 .... 42 C1
Slough Sta SL1 .... 42 C3
Slough Trad Est SL1 ..... 42 A4
Smallmead Rd Burghfield Common RG2 ...85 B1
Reading RG2 .... 86 A1
Smallridge RG14 .... 130 B2
Smith Hospl RG9 .... 15 A3
Smith Sq RG12 .... 118 B4
Smith's La SL4 .... 66 A3
Smitham Bridge Rd RG17 .... 100 B3
Smithfield Cl SL6 .... 38 C2
Smithfield Rd SL6 .... 39 A2
Smiths Hill OX12 .... 6 C3
Smithy's Gn GU20 ...... 146 B2
Snake La RG20 .... 104 A4
Snape Spur SL1 .... 42 C4
Snelsmore Common Ctry Pk RG18 .... 77 C1
Snipe La RG20 .... 131 C1
Snowball Hill Maidenhead SL6 .... 39 A1
White Waltham SL6 ...... 64 A4
Snowberry Cl RG41 ..... 115 C3
Snowden Cl SL4 .... 66 B2
Snowden Dr RG31 .... 84 A3
Snowden Rd RG19 ...... 106 B1
Snowden Rd TW6 .... 71 B1
Snowdrop Copse RG18 .. 106 C2
Snowdrop Gr RG41 ...... 88 B2
Snows Paddock GU20 ... 146 A4
Snows Ride GU20 ...... 146 A3
Soane End RG4 .... 59 A4
Soham Cl RG6 .... 114 B4
Soho Cres HP10 .... 3 B2
Soho Mills Ind Est HP10 ...3 B2
Soke Rd RG7 .... 135 C2
Soldiers Rise RG40 ..... 142 B4
Soldern Cl 3 RG1 .... 86 A3
Solent Rd TW6 .... 70 C1
Somerford Cl SL6 .... 40 A4
Somersby Cres SL6 ...... 39 C2
Somerset Cl Hungerford RG17 ...... 100 B3
Wokingham RG41 .... 115 B3
Somerset Gr RG42 .... 91 C1
Somerset Hospital SN8 ...99 A3
Somerset Lodge 3 SL6 ...39 C3
Somerset Way SL0 .... 44 C2
Somerset Wlk RG31 ...... 84 A3
Somerton Gdns RG6 ..... 87 A1
Somerton Gr RG19 ..... 106 B1
Somerville Cres GU46 .. 149 C3
Somerville Gr RG41 ..... 115 B2
Somerville Rd SL4 .... 42 B1
Sonning CE Prim Sch RG4 .... 60 B2
Sonning La RG4 .... 60 B1
Sonning Mdws RG4 ..... 60 B1
Sonning Way SL6 .... 39 B1
Sopwith Cl RG5 .... 88 A4
Sorrel Cl Burghfield Common RG7 .111 A2
Newbury RG14 .... 105 B3
Wokingham RG40 ...... 116 C4
Sorrel Dr GU18 .... 152 C4
Sospel Ct SL2 .... 22 B2
South Ave Egham TW20 ..96 B1
Henley-on-T RG9 .... 35 C4
South Bank RG8 .... 14 B2
South Close Green RG42 ..91 A3
Medmenham SL7 .... 17 B4
Wokingham RG40 ...... 116 B2
South Dr Reading RG2 ...86 C1
Sonning RG4 .... 60 B1
Sulhamstead RG7 ...... 110 B4
Wentworth GU25 ...... 122 A1
Wokingham RG40 ...... 116 B3
South End Rd RG7 .... 82 A1
South Farm La GU19 ... 146 A1
South Field Cl SL4 .... 41 B2
South Gate Ave TW13 ....98 B2
South Gn SL1 .... 42 C3
South Gr KT16 .... 123 C2
South Groves RG17 ...... 73 A1
South Hill Rd RG12 .... 118 B3
South Hill Rd RG12 .... 118 A2
South Lake Cres RG5 .....87 C3
South Lake Inf Sch RG5 ..87 C3
South Lake Jun Sch RG5 .87 B3
South Lynn Cres RG12 .. 118 A2
South Mdw RG45 ...... 143 B2
South Meadow La SL4 ....67 A4
South Oak Way RG2,RG7 .112 C4
South Path SL4 .... 67 B3
South Rd Bisley GU24 ... 153 C2
Bracknell RG40,RG12 ... 117 C1
Crowthorne RG45 ...... 143 C2
Englefield Green TW20 ...95 B1
Maidenhead SL6 .... 39 C3
South Row Chilton OX11 ..10 B4
Fulmer SL3 .... 23 C4
South St Blewbury OX11 ..12 A4
Caversham RG4 .... 59 A1
Reading RG1 .... 86 B4
Staines TW18 .... 96 C2

South View Pk RG4 ...... 59 B1
Southampton Cl GU17 .. 150 B3
Southampton Rd TW19,TW6 .... 70 C1
Southampton St RG1 ..... 86 A3
Southbank Gdns RG17 ...25 B1
Southbourne Dr SL8 ...... 3 A2
Southbury La RG10 ...... 61 C3
Southcote Dr GU15 .... 152 A2
Southcote Farm La RG30 ..85 B2
Southcote La RG30 ...... 85 A2
Southcote Lodge RG30 ...85 A2
Southcote Prim Sch RG30 .85 B2
Southcote Rd RG30 ...... 85 B3
Southcroft Englefield Green TW20 ...95 A2
Slough SL2 .... 22 B1
Southdown Rd Caversham RG4 .... 59 A3
Tadley RG26 .... 135 A1
Southdown Rd RG12 ... 105 C2
Southend RG18 .... 106 B3
Southern Cl RG41 ...... 115 C3
Southern Ct 10 RG1 ..... 86 A4
Southern Hill RG1 ...... 86 B3
Southern Ind Area RG12 .117 C3
Southern Perimeter Rd East Bedfont TW14 ...... 71 A1
Harlton TW14,TW6 ...... 71 B1
Stanwell TW19,TW6 ..... 70 B1
Southern Rd GU15 ..... 151 B3
Southerndene Cl RG31 ...57 B1
Southfield Gdns SL1 ..... 41 A4
Southfields Boxford RG20 .76 B2
Chieveley RG20 .... 78 A4
Southfields Ave TW15 ...98 A1
Southfields Sch RG40 .. 116 B3
Southgate Ho SL1 .... 39 C4
Southglade RG12 ...... 113 B4
Southlake Ct RG5 .... 87 B3
Southlands Cl RG40 .... 116 B3
Southlands Rd RG40 .... 116 B2
Southlea Rd SL3 .... 68 A3
Southview Cl RG10 ...... 61 C3
Southview Rd SL7 .... 1 C2
Southville Cl TW14 ...... 98 C4
Southville Cres TW14 ....98 C4
Southville Jun & Inf Schs TW14 .... 98 C4
Southville Rd TW14 ..... 98 C4
Southwark Cl GU46 .... 149 B3
Southwark Ct 3 SL6 ..... 39 C4
Southway SL1 .... 151 A2
Southwell Park Rd GU15 .151 B3
Southwick Ct 3 RG12 .. 118 C2
Southwold Cl 3 RG12 .. 117 C1
Southwold Rd RG7 ...... 87 B1
Southwood Spur SL3 ..... 44 B2
Southwood RG40 .... 116 B2
Southwood Gdns Burghfield Common RG7 .111 A2
Cookham SL6 .... 19 C3
Southwood Rd SL6 ...... 19 C3
Sovereign Dr GU15 .... 152 A4
Sovereign Ho TW15 ...... 97 C2
Sovereign Way RG31 .... 84 B3
Sowbury Bank RG20 .... 78 A4
Spackman Cl RG19 ..... 106 B1
Spackmans Way SL1 ..... 42 B2
Spade Oak Mdw SL8 ...... 2 C2
Span Hill RG4 .... 60 A4
Sparrow Cl RG41 ...... 115 C3
Sparrow Rd RG18 ...... 106 B1
Sparvell Way GU15 .... 151 B3
Speedbird Way UB7 ..... 70 B4
Speedwell Way RG18 .. 106 C2
Speen Hill Cl RG14 .... 104 C2
Speen La RG14 .... 104 B2
Speen Lodge Ct RG14 .. 104 C2
Speen Pl RG14 .... 104 C2
Speenhamland Ct 5 RG14 .... 105 A2
Speenhamland Prim Sch RG14 .... 104 C2
Spelthorne Coll TW17 ...97 C2
Spelthorne Cty Inf Sch TW15 .... 98 C1
Spelthorne Gr TW16 ..... 98 C1
Spelthorne La TW15,TW17 .... 125 B4
Spelthorne Mus TW16 ...96 C2
Spelthorne Sports Club TW18 .... 97 A1
Spencer Cl Silchester RG26 .... 135 C1
Wokingham RG41 ...... 115 B3
Spencer Gdns SW20 ..... 95 B1
Spencer Rd Bracknell RG42 .... 90 C2
Newbury RG14 .... 130 B3
Reading RG2 .... 113 A4
Slough SL3 .... 43 C3
Spencers Cl SL6 .... 39 B4
Spencers La SL6 .... 19 C1
Spencers Rd SL6 .... 39 B4
Spenwood Cl RG7 ...... 113 A1
Sperling Rd SL6 .... 39 B4
Spey Rd RG30 .... 85 A4
Spinfield Cty Comb Sch SL7 .... 1 A1
Spinfield La W SL7 .... 1 A1
Spinfield Mount SL7 ...... 1 A1
Spinfield Pk SL7 .... 1 A1
Spinis RG12 .... 117 C1
Spinner Gn RG12 ...... 118 A2
Spinners Wlk Marlow SL7 ..1 A1
Windsor SL4 .... 67 B3
Spinney SL1 .... 42 A3

Spinney Cl RG4 .... 59 A4
Spinney Dr TW14 .... 98 B4
Spinney La SL4 .... 93 A4
Spinney The Ascot SL5 . 120 C2
Frimley GU15 .... 152 B3
Reading RG31 .... 84 C2
Wokingham RG40 ...... 141 C4
Yateley GU46 .... 149 B4
Spinningwheel La RG42 ...90 B4
Spitfire Way RG5 .... 88 A4
Spittal St SL7 .... 1 B1
Splash The RG42 .... 91 A1
Spode Cl RG30 .... 84 C4
Spout La TW19 .... 70 A2
Spout La N TW19 .... 70 A2
Spray La RG20 .... 28 B1
Spray Rd Ham SN8 ...... 126 C2
Inkpen RG17 .... 127 A2
Spriggs Cl RG19 .... 106 B1
Spring Ave TW20 .... 95 C1
Spring Cl Maidenhead SL6 ..39 C3
Pangbourne RG8 .... 56 C3
Spring Cnr TW13 .... 98 C3
Spring Gdns Ascot SL5 . 120 A3
Bourne End SL8 .... 3 A2
Frimley GU15 .... 152 A3
Marlow SL7 .... 1 C2
Shinfield RG7 .... 113 A1
Wooburn Green HP10 ..... 3 C4
Spring Gr RG1 .... 86 A3
Spring Hill SL6 .... 39 C2
Spring Ho SL7 .... 1 C2
Spring La Aldermaston RG7 ...... 135 B4
Aston Tirrold OX11 ..... 12 C4
Caversham RG4 .... 60 A3
Cold Ash RG18 .... 106 B4
Cookham SL6 .... 19 C2
Farnham Common SL2 ....22 B3
Mortimer RG7 .... 137 A3
Slough SL1 .... 41 C3
Swallowfield RG7 ..... 139 B2
Spring Mdw RG12 ..... 118 B4
Spring Mdws RG12 ...... 48 A2
Spring Rd TW13 .... 98 C3
Spring Rise TW20 .... 95 C1
Spring Terr 2 RG1 .... 86 A3
Spring Wlk RG10 .... 36 B1
Spring Woods Sandhurst GU47 .... 143 B1
Virginia Water GU25 ... 122 A3
Springate Field SL3 ..... 43 C2
Springcross Ave GU17 .. 150 B2
Springdale Earley RG6 ...87 A1
Wokingham RG40 ...... 141 C4
Springfield Lightwater GU18 ...... 153 B4
Slough SL1 .... 42 A3
Springfield Cl SL4 .... 67 A3
Springfield La Marlow SL7 ..1 A1
Newbury RG14 .... 131 A4
Springfield Park Ave RG4 ..59 A2
Springfield Pk Maidenhead SL6 .... 40 B1
Twyford RG10 .... 61 C2
Springfield Prim Sch RG31 .... 84 A4
Springfield Rd Ashford TW15 .... 97 C2
Bracknell RG12 .... 117 B4
Brands Hill SL3 .... 69 A4
Frimley GU15 .... 152 A3
Silchester RG26 .... 135 C1
Windsor SL4 .... 67 A3
Springfields Cl KT16 ... 124 A1
Springhill Ct RG12 .... 118 A3
Springhill Rd RG8 .... 34 B4
Springmead Ct GU47 .. 143 C1
Spruce Ct 3 SL2 .... 22 B2
Spruce Ct GU47 .... 153 A4
Spruce Rd RG5 .... 88 A3
Spur The Slough SL1 ..... 41 B4
Wargrave RG10 .... 36 C3
Spurcroft Prim Sch RG19 .... 106 B1
Spurcroft Rd RG19 ..... 106 B1
Square The Bagshot GU19 .145 C2
Bracknell RG12 .... 118 C2
Earley RG6 .... 114 A4
Harmondsworth TW6 .... 70 A3
Lightwater GU18 ...... 146 B1
Pangbourne RG8 .... 56 B3
Shinfield RG7 .... 113 A1
Squire's Bridge Rd TW17 .125 A3
Squire's Bridge Rd KT17 .124 C3
Squires Ct Camberley GU15 ...... 151 B2
Chertsey KT16 .... 124 A1
Squires Wlk TW15 .... 98 B1
Squirrel Cl GU47 ...... 150 B4
Squirrel Dr SL4 .... 93 A4
Squirrel Rise SL7 .... 1 C3
Squirrels Drey RG45 ... 142 C3
Squirrels Way RG6 .... 87 A1
Stable Cl RG7 .... 111 A2
Stable Cotts SL7 .... 17 B2
Stable Croft GU19 ..... 145 B1
Stable Ct RG14 .... 105 A4
Stable View GU46 ..... 149 B4
Stables Ct SL7 .... 1 A1
Stacey's Ind Est RG26 . 135 B1
Staddlestone Cl RG31 ...57 B1

Stadium Way RG30 .... 58 A1
Staff Coll GU15 .... 151 B4
Staff College Rd GU15 . 151 A3
Stafferton Way SL6 ...... 40 A3
Stafford Ave SL2 .... 22 B1
Stafford Cl Burnham SL6 ..21 A4
Woodley RG5 .... 87 C4
Stafford Lake GU21,GU24 .153 C1
Staffordshire Cl RG30 ...84 C4
Staffordshire Croft RG42 .91 C1
Stag Hill RG17 .... 73 A1
Stainash Cres TW18 ..... 97 A2
Stainash Par TW18 ...... 97 A2
Staines By-Pass TW15,TW18 .... 97 B2
Staines Central Trad Est SL1 .... 96 C2
Staines La KT16 .... 124 A3
Staines Lane Cl KT16 .. 123 C2
Staines Prep Sch The TW18 .... 97 A2
Staines Rd Chertsey KT16 .124 A3
East Bedfont TW14 ...... 98 B4
Laleham TW18 .... 124 A3
Wraysbury TW19 .... 95 C4
Staines Rd W TW15,TW16 .98 B1
Staines Sta TW18 .... 97 A2
Stainford Cl TW15 .... 98 B2
Stamford Ave GU46 .... 151 C1
Stamford Rd SL6 .... 39 B3
Stanbrook Cl RG7 .... 82 A1
Stanbury Gate RG7 .... 113 A2
Stanfield RG26 .... 135 A1
Stanford Dingley Circular Wlks RG18 ..... 80 C4
Stanham Rd RG30 .... 84 C4
Stanhope Heath TW19 ...70 B1
Stanhope Rd Camberley GU15 ...... 150 C2
Reading RG2 .... 86 B2
Slough SL1 .... 41 B4
Stanhope Way TW19 .... 70 B1
Stanlake La RG10 .... 61 C2
Stanley Cl SL7 .... 1 C2
Stanley Cotts SL2 .... 42 C3
Stanley Gn E SL3 .... 43 C1
Stanley Gn E SL3 .... 43 C1
Stanley Gn W SL3 .... 43 B1
Stanley Rd SL4 .... 68 A1
Stanley Rd Ashford TW15 .97 C2
Wokingham RG40 ...... 116 C3
Stanley St RG1 .... 85 C4
Stanmore Gdns RG7 ... 136 C3
Stanmore Rd Beedon RG20 .30 B1
East Isley RG20 .... 30 C3
Stanshawe Rd RG1 ...... 86 A4
Stansted Rd TW6 .... 70 C1
Stanton Cl RG6 .... 87 B2
Stanton Way SL3 .... 43 C1
Stanway Cotts 7 Chertsey KT16 ...... 124 A1
Reading RG1 .... 86 C3
Stanwell Cl TW19 .... 70 B1
Stanwell Gdns TW19 .... 70 B1
Stanwell Moor Rd TW19,TW6, UB7 .... 70 A2
Stanwell New Rd TW18,TW19 .... 97 A3
Stanwell Rd Ashford TW15 .97 C2
East Bedfont TW14, TW19 .... 98 A4
Horton SL3,TW19 .... 69 B2
Stapleford Rd RG30 ..... 85 B2
Staplehurst RG12 ...... 117 C1
Stapleton Cl Marlow SL7 ...1 C2
Star La Knowl Hill RG10 ...37 C2
Reading RG1 .... 86 A4
Star Post Rd GU15 .... 151 C4
Star Rd RG4 .... 59 B1
Starling Cl RG41 ...... 115 C3
Starlings Dr RG31 .... 84 A3
Starmead Dr RG40 .... 116 C3
Starting Gates RG14 ... 105 B1
Startins La SL6 .... 19 B4
Starwood Ct SL3 .... 43 B2
Statham Ct RG42 .... 117 C4
Station App Ashford TW15 .97 C2
Maidenhead SL6 .... 39 C3
Reading RG1 .... 86 A4
Shepperton TW17 .... 125 B3
Staines TW18 .... 97 A2
Virginia Water GU25 ... 122 B3
Station Cres TW15 ...... 97 C2
Station Flats SL5 ...... 121 A1
Station Hill Ascot SL5 . 120 C4
Cookham SL6 .... 19 C4
Hampstead Norreys RG18 .52 C3
Reading RG1 .... 86 A4
Station Ind Est RG40 .. 116 A3
Station Par Ashford TW15 .97 C2
Virginia Water GU25 ... 122 C2
Station Path SL4 .... 96 C2
Station Rd Ashford TW15 .97 C2
Bagshot GU19 .... 145 C2
Bourne End SL8 .... 3 A2
Bracknell RG12 .... 118 C3
Chertsey KT16 .... 124 A1
Cookham SL6 .... 19 C4

Station Rd continued
Earley RG6 ....87 B2
East Garston RG17 ....47 B3
Egham TW20 ....96 A2
Frimley GU16 ....151 B1
Goring RG8 ....34 B3
Great Shefford RG17 ....48 A2
Henley-on-T RG9 ....15 C1
Hungerford RG17 ....100 B3
Kintbury RG17 ....102 A1
Marlow SL7 ....1 C1
Newbury, City RG14 ....105 A1
Newbury, Speen RG14 .....104 B3
Pangbourne RG8 ....56 B3
Reading RG1 ....86 A4
Shepperton TW17 ....125 B2
Shiplake RG9 ....26 A2
Slough SL1 ....41 C4
Slough, Langley SL3 ......44 A2
Sunningdale SL5 ....121 A2
Taplow SL6 ....40 C4
Thatcham RG19 ....106 C1
Theale RG7 ....83 C2
Twyford RG10 ....61 B2
Wargrave RG10 ....36 B1
Wokingham RG40 ....116 A3
Woolhampton RG7 ....109 A1
Wraysbury TW19 ....68 A1
Station Rd 🖾 RG30 ......96 A2
Station Rise SL7 ....1 C1
Station Road Ind Est
RG19 ....106 C1
Station Yard Ind Est
RG17 ....100 C3
Staunton Rd SL2 ....42 B4
Staveley Rd TW15 ....98 B1
Staverton Cl
Bracknell RG42 ....91 A1
Wokingham RG40 ....116 C3
Staverton Rd RG2 ....86 B2
Stayne End GU25 ....122 A3
Steam Farm La TW14 ....71 C2
Steeple Wlk RG6 ....113 C4
Steerforth Copse GU47 ..143 C1
Steggles Cl RG5 ....87 B4
Stepgates KT16 ....124 A1
Stepgates Cl KT16 ......124 A1
Stepgates Prim Sch
KT16 ....124 A1
Stephanie Chase Ct
RG40 ....116 B4
Stephen Cl Egham TW20 ..96 B1
Twyford RG10 ....61 C2
Stephen's Rd RG7 ....136 C3
Stephens Cl RG7 ....136 C3
Stephens Firs RG7 ......136 C3
Stephenson Ct RG18 ....106 B2
Stephenson Dr SL1 ......42 C2
Stephenson Dr SL4 ......67 A4
Stephenson Rd RG2 .....141 A4
Sterling Ave TW17 ......125 C3
Sterling Ctr The RG12 ..118 B3
Sterling Ind Est RG14 ..105 A1
Sterling Gdns GU47 .....150 C4
Sterling Way RG18 ....58 A1
Stevens Hill GU46 ....149 C3
Stevenson Dr RG42 ....90 B2
Stewart Ave
Littleton TW17 ....125 A3
Slough SL1 ....42 C4
Stewart Cl SL3 ....65 B3
Stewarts Dr SL2 ....22 A4
Stewarts Way SL7 ....1 B4
Stile Rd SL3 ....43 B2
Stilton Cl RG6 ....87 C1
Stilwell Cl GU46 ....149 C3
Stirling Cl Caversham RG4 .59 B3
Frimley GU16 ....151 C1
Windsor SL4 ....66 B3
Stirling Rd Slough SL1 ..42 A4
Stanwell TW19, TW6 ....70 C1
Stirling Way RG18 ....106 B2
Stirrup Cl RG14 ....131 A4
Stockbridge Way GU46 ..149 B2
Stockbury Cl RG6 ....87 C1
Stockcross CE Prim Sch
RG20 ....103 C3
Stockdales Rd SL4 ....41 C1
Stockton Rd RG2 ....86 B3
Stockwells SL6 ....20 B1
Stockwood Rise GU15 ...151 C3
Stoke Common Rd SL3 ....23 A4
Stoke Court Dr SL2 ......22 C2
Stoke Gdns SL1 ....42 C3
Stoke Gn SL2 ....22 A2
Stoke Park Ave SL2 ......22 B1
Stoke Poges La SL1, SL2 .42 C4
Stoke Poges Sch SL2 ....22 B3
Stoke Poges Sch The SL2 .22 C3
Stoke Rd SL2 ....42 C4
Stoke View SL1 ....22 A2
Stoke Wood SL2 ....22 C4
Stokeford Cl 🖾 RG12 ....118 C2
Stokes La RG26 ....134 B1
Stokes View RG8 ....56 B3
Stokesay SL2 ....42 C3
Stokesley Rise HP10 ......3 B3
Stomp Rd SL1 ....41 B4
Stompits Rd Holyport SL6 .65 B4
Maidenhead SL6 ....65 A4
Stone Copse RG14 ....105 C4
Stone Cres TW14 ....98 C4
Stone House La SL6 ......2 B1
Stone St RG30 ....58 A1
Stonea Cl RG6 ....114 B4

Stonebridge Field SL4 ...42 A1
Stonecroft Ave SL0 ......44 C4
Stonefield Pk SL6 ....39 B4
Stonegate GU15 ....152 B3
Stoneham Cl RG30 ....85 A3
Stonehaven Dr RG5 ....88 A3
Stonehill Rd GU18 .....146 A1
Stonehouse Rise GU16 ..151 C1
Stoneleigh Ct GU16 ....151 C1
Stoney Cl GU46 ....149 B2
Stoney La Burnham SL2 ..22 A2
Newbury RG14, RG18 ....105 B3
Thatcham RG19 ....106 C2
Stoney Meade SL1 ....42 A3
Stoney Rd RG42 ....118 A4
Stoney Ware SL7 ....16 C4
Stoney Ware Cl SL7 ......16 B3
Stoneyfield RG7 ....109 A3
Stoneyland Cl 🖾 TW20 ..95 C2
Stoneylands Rd TW20 .....95 C2
Stookes Way GU46 ......149 A2
Stornaway Rd SL3 ....44 B1
Stour Cl Reading RG30 ..85 A4
Slough SL1 ....42 A2
Stovell Rd SL4 ....62 A4
Stow Rd RG9 ....35 C4
Stowe Rd SL1 ....41 C3
Strachey Cl RG8 ....56 B1
Straight Bit HP10 ....3 A4
Straight La RG17 ....46 C2
Straight Mile The
Hurst RG10 & RG40 ....89 B3
Waltham St Lawrence RG10 .62 C1
Straight Rd SL4 ....68 A1
Strand La SL6 ....19 C3
Strand View Wlk SL6 .....19 C3
Strand Way RG6 ....87 B1
Stranraer Gdns SL1 ......42 C3
Stranraer Way 🖾 TW6 ...70 C1
Stratfield RG12 ....117 C1
Stratfield Ct SL6 ....40 A4
Stratfield Rd SL1 ....43 A2
Stratford Cl SL2 ....21 B1
Stratford Dr HP10 ....3 B2
Stratford Gdns SL6 ......39 C2
Stratford Rd TW6 ....71 B1
Stratford Way RG31 ......84 A3
Strathcona Cl HP10 ....3 B4
Strathcona Way HP10 .....3 B4
Strathearn Ave UB3 ......71 C4
Strathenden Pl 🖾 RG41 .116 A3
Strathmore Ct GU15 ....151 B3
Strathmore Dr RG10 .....61 A2
Strathy Cl RG30 ....85 A4
Stratton Gdns RG2 ....86 B1
Stratton Rd TW16 ......125 C4
Strawberry Hill
Newbury 104 C2
Newell Green RG42 ....91 C1
Streamside SL1 ....41 C3
Streatley CE Sch RG8 ....33 C2
Streatley & Goring Bridge
RG8 ....34 A3
Streatley Hill RG8 ....33 C3
Street The
Aldermaston RG7 ....135 A4
Bradfield RG7 ....83 A3
Mortimer RG7 ....137 B3
Moulsford OX10 ....14 A3
South Stoke RG8 ....14 A2
Swallowfield RG7 ....139 B4
Tidmarsh RG8 ....56 B1
Waltham St Lawrence RG10 .62 A3
Streets Heath GU24 .....153 C4
Stretton Cl RG7 ....82 A1
Strode St TW20 ....96 A2
Strode's Coll TW20 ....95 C2
Strode's Cres TW18 ......97 B2
Strodes College La TW20 .95 C2
Stroller Cl RG19 ....105 C2
Stroma Cl SL1 ....41 B3
Strongrove Hill RG17 ...100 B3
Strood La SL5 ....92 C1
Stroud Cl SL4 ....66 B2
Stroud Farm Rd SL6 .....65 A4
Stroud Way TW15 ....98 A1
Stroude Rd Egham TW20 ..96 A1
Virginia Water
GU25, TW20 ....122 C3
Strouds Mdw RG18 ....106 B4
Strouds The RG7 ....108 B3
Stuart Cl Caversham RG4 .59 B3
Windsor SL4 ....66 C3
Stuart Ho RG42 ....117 C4
Stuart Rd RG14 ....130 B3
Stuart Way Staines TW18 .97 A1
Virginia Water GU25 .....122 A3
Windsor SL4 ....66 C3
Stubbington House Sch
SL5 ....120 A1
Stubbles La SL6 ....19 A3
Stubbs Folly GU47 ......150 B4
Studios Rd TW17 ....124 C3
Studland Cl RG2 ....113 B4
Studland Ind Est RG20 ..129 A2
Sturbridge Cl RG6 ....87 B1
Sturdee Cl GU16 ....151 C1
Sturges Rd RG40 ....116 B3
Sturt Gn SL6 ....64 C4
Styventon Pl KT16 ......123 C1
Sucks La RG8 ....54 B2
Suffolk Cl Bagshot GU19 .145 C1
Slough SL1 ....41 C4
Wokingham RG41 ....115 B3
Suffolk Combe RG42 .....91 C1
Suffolk Ct SL6 ....19 C2
Suffolk Rd Maidenhead SL6 .39 B2
Reading RG30 ....85 B4

Sulham La RG8 ....56 C2
Sulham Wlk RG30 ....85 A2
Sulhamstead Hill RG7 ...110 B3
Sulhamstead La RG7 .....110 B2
Sulhamstead Rd
RG7,RG30 ....111 A3
Sulhamstead & Ufton
Nervet Prim Sch RG7 ....110 B2
Sulham Gdns GU15 ......151 A3
Sumburgh Way SL1 ......42 C4
Summer Gdns GU15 ......152 B3
Summerfield Cl RG41 ....88 C1
Summerfield Rise RG8 ....34 B4
Summerlea SL1 ....43 A3
Summerleaze Rd SL6 .....20 A1
Summers Rd SL1 ....21 B1
Summit Cl RG40 ....141 C4
Summit Ctr UB7 ....70 B4
Sun Cl SL4 ....67 B4
Sun Gdns RG7 ....111 A1
Sun La Maidenhead SL6 ..39 C4
Swallowfield RG7 ....139 A1
Sun Pas SL4 ....67 B3
Sun Ray Est GU47 ......150 C4
Sun St RG1 ....86 B4
Sunbury Cres TW13 ......98 C2
Sunbury Cross Ctr 🖾
TW16 ....98 C1
Sunbury Ct SL4 ....67 B4
Sunbury Int'ness Ctr
TW16 ....125 C4
Sunbury Manor Sch
TW16 ....125 C4
Sunbury Rd Eton SL4 ....67 B4
Feltham TW13 ....98 C2
Sunderland Cl RG5 ....88 A4
Sunderland Ct 🖾 TW19 ..70 C1
Sunderland Rd RG18 ....106 B2
Sunderland Rd SL6 ....39 A4
Sundew Cl
Lightwater GU18 ....153 B4
Wokingham RG40 ....116 C4
Sundial Cl RG30 ....85 A3
Sundon Cres GU25 ......122 B2
Sundown Rd TW15 ....98 B2
Sundry Cl RG41 ....130 B3
Sunning Ave SL5 ....120 C1
Sunning Ho Ascot SL5 ...120 B3
Windlesham SL5 ....146 C4
Sunningdale Pk (Civil
Service Coll) SL5 ....120 C2
Sunningdale Sch SL5 ....120 C2
Sunningdale Sta SL5 ....121 A1
Sunninghill Cl SL5 ......120 B3
Sunninghill Ct SL5 ....120 B3
Sunninghill Lodge SL5 ..120 B4
Sunninghill Rd Ascot SL5 .120 B3
Windlesham GU20 ....146 A4
Winkfield SL4, SL5 ....93 C1
Sunnybank Ascot SL5 ...120 A3
Marlow SL7 ....1 B2
Sunnymeads Sta TW19 ...68 C2
Sunnymede Cotts SL6 ....20 A1
Sunnyside RG14 ....104 C3
Surbiton Rd GU15 ......145 A1
Surley Row RG4 ....59 A3
Surly Hall Wlk SL4 ....66 C3
Surrey Ave
Camberley GU15 ....151 A2
Slough SL2 ....22 B1
Surrey Ct RG42 ....91 A1
Surrey Heath Mus GU15 .151 B3
Surrey Rd RG2 ....86 A2
Surridge Ct GU19 ......145 C1
Sussex Cl SL1 ....43 A2
Sussex Gdns RG5 ....87 C4
Sussex Ho SL2 ....22 B3
Sussex Keep SL1 ....43 A2
Sussex La RG7 ....113 B1
Sussex Lodge 🖾 RG1 ....39 C3
Sutcliffe Ave RG6 ....87 B2
Sutherland Ave TW16 ...125 C4
Sutherland Chase SL5 ...119 C4
Sutherland Gdns TW16 ..125 C4
Sutherland Ct RG31 ......84 C2
Sutherland Grange SL4 ..66 A4
Sutherlands RG14 ......130 C4
Sutherlands Ave RG1 .....86 B3
Sutton Ave SL3 ....43 B2
Sutton Cl Cookham SL6 ..20 A4
Maidenhead SL6 ....39 B3
Sutton La Brands Hill SL3 .69 A4
Slough SL3 ....44 B1
Sutton Pl SL3 ....69 A4
Sutton Rd
Camberley GU15 ....145 A1
Cookham SL6 ....20 A3
Newbury RG14 ....104 B3
Sutton Wlk RG1 ....86 B3
Suttons Park Ave RG6 ...86 C4
Swabey Rd SL3 ....44 A1
Swainstone Rd RG2 ......86 A3
Swaledale RG12 ....118 A2
Swallow Cl Reading RG31 .84 B3
Staines TW18 ....96 C2
Swallow La GU46 ....149 A3
Swallow Ho SL7 ....1 B2
Swallow St SL0 ....44 B4
Swallow Way RG41 ......115 C3
Swallowfield TW20 ....95 A1
Swallowfield Dr RG2 ....113 B3
Swallowfield Gdns RG7 ..137 C2
Swallowfield Pk RG7 ....139 C4
Swallowfield Rd RG2 ....114 B1
Swan Cl RG14 ....104 C2
Swan Dr RG7 ....109 A3

Swan Ho GU47 ....150 A1
Swan La GU47 ....150 A1
Swan Pl 🔟 RG1 ....86 A4
Swan Rd SL0 ....44 C4
Swan Wlk TW17 ....125 C1
Swancote Gn RG12 ......118 A2
Swandrift TW18 ....96 C1
Swangate RG17 ....100 B4
Swanholm Gdns RG5 .....84 C2
Swanmore Cl RG6 ....87 C1
Swanscourt RG12 ....61 C2
Swansdown Wlk RG10 ...106 A2
Swansea Rd
Harlington TW4, TW6 .....71 B1
Reading RG1 ....59 A1
Swansea Terr RG31 ......84 C1
Swanston La RG8 ....54 B2
Sweeps Ditch Cl TW18 ..97 A1
Sweeps La TW20 ....95 C2
Sweet Briar Dr RG31 .....84 B2
Sweetbriar RG45 ....143 A4
Sweetzer's Piece RG7 ...136 C3
Swepstone Cl RG6 ....87 B1
Swift Cl RG41 ....115 C3
Swift Dr SL7 ....1 C1
Swift La RG19 ....2 A1
Swift La GU19 ....146 A4
Swinbrook Cl RG31 ......57 B2
Swindon Rd TW6 ....71 B1
Swinley County Prim Sch
SL5 ....120 A2
Swinley Rd SL5 ....119 B2
Swiss Cottage Cl RG31 ..84 B4
Switchback Rd N SL6 ....19 B1
Switchback Rd S SL6 .....19 B2
Switchback St SL6 ....19 B1
Switchback The SL6 .....19 B1
Swithin Chase RG42 .....91 C1
Sycamore Cl
🖾 Bourne End SL8 ....3 A2
Burghfield Common RG30 .111 A2
Frimley GU16 ....151 C1
Maidenhead SL6 ....39 B2
Sandhurst GU47 ....150 A4
Newbury RG5 ....87 B3
Sycamore Ct SL4 ....67 B2
Sycamore Dr
Frimley GU16 ....151 C1
Marlow Bottom SL7 ....1 B3
Twyford RG10 ....61 B3
Sycamore Lo 🖾 TW16 ...98 C1
Sycamore Rd RG2 ....86 C1
Sycamore Rise
Bracknell RG12 ....118 B3
Newbury RG14 ....105 B3
Sycamore Wlk
Englefield Green TW20 ....95 A1
Slough SL3 ....43 C4
Sycamores The GU17 ...150 A3
Sydings The RG14 ....104 B3
Sydney Cl
Crowthorne RG45 ....143 B4
Thatcham RG19 ....106 C2
Sydney Cres TW15 ....98 A1
Sydney Gr SL1 ....42 B4
Sydney Lodge RG19 ....106 C2
Syke Clue SL0 ....44 C2
Syke Ings SL0 ....44 C2
Sykes Cotts GU15 ......118 C1
Sykes Rd SL1 ....42 A4
Sylvan Edge GU47 ......143 A1
Sylvan Wlk RG30 ....85 B2
Sylvanus RG12 ....117 C1
Sylverns Ct RG42 ....91 B1
Sylvester Cl
Newbury RG14 ....104 C3
Winnersh RG41 ....88 B2
Sylvester Rd SL6 ....19 C1
Symondson Mews RG42 ..90 B2
Sympson Rd RG26 ......135 B1

T

Tachbrook Rd TW14 ......98 C4
Tadcroft Wlk RG31 ......84 C2
Tadham Pl RG19 ....106 B1
Tadley Common Rd
RG26 ....135 B1
Tadmor Cl TW16 ....125 C3
Taff Way RG30 ....85 A4
Tag La RG10 ....37 B1
Talbot Ave SL3 ....43 C2
Talbot Cl Caversham RG4 .59 B1
Newbury RG14 ....104 C3
Talbot Ct 🖾 Reading RG1 .86 A4
Talbot Pl Bagshot GU19 .145 C2
Datchet SL3 ....68 B3
Talbot Rd TW15 ....97 C2
Talbot Way RG31 ....57 B2
Talbots Dr SL6 ....39 B3
Talfourd Ave RG6 ....87 A3
Talisman Cl RG45 ......142 B3
Tall Trees SL3 ....69 A2
Tallis La RG30 ....85 A3
Tamar Cl RG23 ....85 B3
Tamar Gdns RG2 ....87 A1
Tamar Way Slough SL3 ...44 A1
Wokingham RG41 ....115 C4
Tamarind Ct 🖾 TW20 ....95 C2
Tamarind Way RG6 ......87 B1
Tamarisk Ave RG2 ....86 C1
Tamarisk Rise RG40 ....116 B4
Tamarisk Way SL1 ....42 A2
Tamarisk Ct RG18 ......106 C2
Tamesis Ho TW17 ......125 A1

Tamesis Pl RG4 ....59 A1
Tamworth RG12 ....118 B3
Tamworth Cl 🖾 RG6 .....87 B1
Tangier Cl SL4 ....67 B4
Tangier La SL4 ....67 B4
Tanglewood RG40 ......143 A4
Tanglewood Ride GU24 ..153 B4
Tangley Dr RG41 ....116 A2
Tanglyn Ave TW17 ......125 A2
Tanhouse La RG41 ......116 A2
Tank Rd GU15 ....150 C2
Tanner Cl RG14 ....105 A2
Tanners Cl RG4 ....110 C3
Tanners La RG4 ....58 C4
Tanners Yd GU19 ....145 C2
Tape La RG10 ....88 C4
Tapestries The SL4 ......68 A3
Taplow Common Rd SL6 ..21 A2
Taplow Rd SL6 ....41 A4
Taplow Sta SL6 ....40 C4
Tarbat Ct 🖾 GU47 ......150 B4
Tarbay La SL4 ....66 A3
Target Cl TW14 ....71 C3
Target Hill RG42 ....91 B3
Targett Ct RG41 ....88 A3
Tarlton Ct RG30 ....84 C2
Tarmac Way UB7 ....70 A4
Tarn Howes Cl RG19 ....106 A2
Tarn La RG14 ....130 C4
Tarnbrook Way RG12 ...118 C2
Tarragon Cl Earley RG6 ..86 C1
Newell Green RG42 ....91 B3
Tarragon Way RG42 .....111 A2
Tarrant Gn RG42 ....91 B3
Tarrants Hill RG17 ......100 B3
Tasker Cl UB3 ....71 B4
Tasman Cl 🖾 TW16 ......98 C4
Tatchbrook Cl SL6 ....40 A4
Tattersall Cl RG40 ......116 C3
Tavistock Cl
Maidenhead SL6 ....39 A4
Staines TW18 ....97 B3
Tavistock Rd RG2 ....86 A2
Tawfield RG12 ....117 C1
Tay Rd RG30 ....85 A4
Taylor Cl 🖾 RG1 ....85 C4
Taylor's Cl SL7 ....1 B2
Taylors Cl SL6 ....39 A4
Taynton Wlk 🖾 RG1 ......86 A3
Tazewell Ct RG1 ....85 C3
Tebbit Cl RG12 ....118 B4
Teesdale Rd SL2 ....21 B3
Teikyo Sch (UK) SL3 .....23 A3
Tekels Ave GU15 ....151 B2
Tekels Ct GU15 ....151 C2
Tekels Way GU15 ....151 C2
Telford Ave RG45 ....143 A4
Telford Cres RG5 ....60 C3
Telford Dr SL1 ....42 A2
Telston Cl SL8 ....3 A3
Tempest Rd TW20 ....96 B1
Templar Cl GU47 ....150 A4
Templars Pl 🔟 SL7 ......1 C1
Temple Gdns TW18 .....123 C4
Temple La SL7 ....18 B3
Temple Mews RG1 ....87 C4
Temple Mill Cotts SL7 ...18 B3
Temple Mill Island SL7 ..18 B3
Temple Pk SL7 ....17 C2
Temple Pl RG1 ....86 A3
Temple Rd SL4 ....67 A4
Temple Way Binfield RG42 .90 C1
Farnham Common SL2 ....22 B4
Templecroft TW15 ....98 B1
Templedene Ave TW18 ..97 B1
Templeton Gdns RG2 ....86 B1
Templewood La SL2 ......22 B4
Ten Acre La TW20 ......123 B4
Tenaplas Dr RG8 ....54 C3
Tenby Ave RG4 ....59 B3
Tenby Dr SL5 ....120 B2
Tennyson Rd
Ashford TW15 ....97 C2
Thatcham RG18 ....106 B2
Woodley RG5 ....87 C2
Tennyson Way SL3 ....21 C1
Tensing Ct TW19 ....97 C4
Teresa Vale RG42 ....91 C1
Tern Cl RG30 ....85 A3
Terrace Rd N RG42 ......90 B2
Terrace Rd S RG42 ......90 B1
Terrace The Ascot SL5 ..120 B2
Camberley GU15 ....151 A3
Crowthorne RG45 ....143 B3
Maidenhead SL6 ....40 B2
Wokingham RG40 ....116 A3
Terrent Ct SL4 ....67 A3
Terrington Hill SL7 ....1 A1
Terry's La SL6 ....19 C4
Tesimond Dr GU46 .....149 A3
Tessa Rd RG1 ....58 C1
Test Cl RG30 ....85 A4
Testwood Rd SL4 ....66 B3
Tetbury Ct 🖾 RG1 ....85 C4
Teviot Rd RG30 ....84 C4
Thackery Lodge TW14 ....71 B1
Thakerays The RG19 ....106 B1
Thames Ave
Chertsey KT16 ....124 A3
Pangbourne RG8 ....56 B3
Reading RG1 ....59 A1
Windsor SL4 ....67 B4
Thames Cl
Bourne End SL8 ....3 A2
Chertsey KT16 ....124 B1
Thames Cres SL6 ....20 A1
Thames Dr RG10 ....60 C4
Thames Ind Est SL7 ....1 C1

hames Mdw
KT12,TW17 ....125 C1
hames Mead SL4 ....66 C3
hames Rd Goring RG8 .....34 A3
Slough SL3 ....44 A2
Thatcham RG18 ....106 A3
hames Reach
Medmenham SL7 ....17 B3
Purley on T RG8 ....57 B3
hames Side
Henley-on-T RG9 ....15 C1
Laleham KT16,TW18 ......124 B2
Reading RG1 ....59 A1
Staines TW18 ....96 C1
Walton SL4 ....67 B4
hames Side Prom RG1 .....59 A1
hames St Sonning RG4 .....60 B2
Staines TW18 ....96 C2
Walton-on-T KT12 ....125 C1
Windsor SL4 ....67 B4
hames Valley Bsns Pk
RG6 ....60 A1
hames Valley Univ SL1 ....32 C3
hamesbourne Mews SL8 .....3 A2
hamesfield Ct TW17 ......125 B1
hamesfield Gdns SL7 ....1 C1
hamesgate TW18 ....124 A4
hameside Prim Sch RG4 ....59 A1
hamesmead Sch TW17 ....125 B2
hanington Way RG4 ....87 A1
hatcham Nature
Discovery Ctr RG19 ......106 A1
hatcham Sta RG19 ....106 C1
hatchers Dr SL6 ....39 A3
heale Ct SL4 ....150 B4
heale CE Prim Sch RG7 ....83 B2
heale Green Com Sch
RG7 ....83 B2
heale Rd RG30 ....111 B3
heale Sta RG7 ....83 C1
heobald Dr RG31 ....57 C2
hetford Mews RG4 ....59 B3
hetford Rd TW15 ....97 C3
hibet Rd GU47 ....150 B4
hicket Gr SL6 ....38 C4
hicket Rd RG30 ....84 C4
hickthorne La TW18 ......97 B1
hird Ave Marlow SL7 ......1 C1
Tadley RG7 ....135 B1
hird Cres SL1 ....42 B4
hird St Greenham RG19 ...131 C3
Newtown RG19 ....132 A3
hirkleby Cl SL1 ....42 B3

Three Gables La RG8 ......34 A4
Three Post La RG17 ....25 A1
Threshfield RG12 ....118 A2
Thrift La Holyport SL6 ....64 B4
Throat Handpost Cnr The
RG40 ....62 A4
Throgmorton Rd GU46 ....149 A3
Thrush Cl RG7 ....111 A2
Thurlby Way SL6 ....39 B2
Thurlestone Cl TW17 .....125 B2
Thurlestone Gdns RG2 .....86 B1
Thurlestone Par TW17 ....125 B2
Thurleys Cotts SL3 ....23 A2
Thurnscoe Cl RG6 ....113 C4
Thurso Cl RG30 ....85 A4
Thurston Rd SL1 ....42 C4
Thyme Cl RG6 ....87 C4
Tichborne Cl GU17 ....115 C3
Tichbourne Cl GU16 ......151 C2
Tickenor Dr RG40 ....141 C4
Tickhill Cl RG6 ....113 C4
Tickleback Row RG42 ......91 A4
Tidmarsh La RG8 ....56 A1
Tidmarsh Rd RG8 ....56 B2
Tidmarsh St ■ RG30 ......85 A4
Tidwells Lea RG12 ....118 C4
Tierney Ct ■ SL1 ....1 C1
Tiffany Cl RG41 ....115 B3
Tiger Cl RG5 ....88 A4
Tigerseye Cl RG41 ....115 C4
Tilbury Cl RG4 ....59 B2
Tilbury Wlk SL3 ....44 A2
Tile Barn Row RG20 .....129 C1
Tilebarn Cl RG9 ....15 B3
Tilecotes Cl SL7 ....1 B1
Tilehurst La RG42 ....90 B2
Tilehurst Rd RG1 & RG30 ..85 B4
Tilehurst Sta TW18 ....57 C2
Tilling Cl RG31 ....57 A1
Tilly's La TW18 ....96 C2
Tilney Way RG6 ....113 C4
Tilstone Ave SL4 ....41 C1
Tilstone Cl SL4 ....41 C1
Timbers Wlk SL6 ....39 A3
Timline Gn RG12 ....118 C4
Timsway TW18 ....96 C2
Tindal Cl GU46 ....149 B3
Tinkers La SL4 ....66 B3
Tinsey Cl TW20 ....96 A2
Tinsley Cl RG6 ....113 C4
Tintagel Dr GU16 ....151 C1
Tintagel Ho SL1 ....42 B3
Tintagel Rd RG40 ....142 A4
Tintern Cl SL1 ....42 B3
Tintern Cres RG1 ....85 C3
Tinwell Cl RG6 ....87 C4
Tippett Rise RG2 ....86 A3
Tippings La RG5 ....88 A4
Tippits Mead RG42 ......117 B4
Tiptree Cl RG6 ....113 C4
Tiree Ho SL2 ....42 A4
Titcombe Way RG17 .....102 A1
Tite Hill TW20 ....69 A1
Tithe Barn Dr SL6 ....40 C1
Tithe Cl Maidenhead SL6 ..40 B1
Wentworth GU25 ....122 B2
Tithe Ct Slough SL3 ....44 A1
Tithe La TW19 ....69 A1
Tithe Mdws GU25 ....122 B2
Tithebarn Gr RG31 ....84 C2
Titlarks Hill Rd SL5 .....121 A1
Tiverton Cl RG5 ....88 B4
Tiverton Way GU16 ......151 C1
Toad La GU17 ....150 C2
Tocker Gdns RG42 ....91 A1
Tockley Way SL1 ....21 A1
Tofrek Terr RG30 ....85 B4
Tokers Green Rd RG4 .....58 C4
Tokersgreen La RG4 ......58 B3
Toll Gdns RG12 ....118 C4
Tollgate SL5 ....39 A3
Tolpuddle Way GU46 ....149 C3
Tomlin Cl RG19 ....106 C1
Tomlin Rd SL2 ....22 A1
Tomlins Ave GU16 ....151 C1
Tomlinscote Sch GU16 ...152 A1
Tomlinscote Way GU16 ...152 A1
Tomlinson Dr RG40 ......142 A4
Toogood Pl RG42 ....91 B2
Top Common RG42 ....91 B1
Topaz Cl Slough SL1 ......42 A3
Wokingham RG41 ....115 C4
Tope Cres RG2 ....140 C4
Tope Rd RG2 ....140 C4
Torcross Gr RG31 ....84 A2
Torin Ct TW20 ....95 B3
Torquay Spur SL2 ....22 C1
Torridge Rd SL3 ....69 A4
Torrington Rd RG2 ....86 B1
Toseland Way RG6 ....87 C2
Totale Rise RG42 ....91 A1
Totnes Rd RG2 ....86 B1
Tottenham Wlk GU47 ....143 B1
Totterdown RG7 ....110 C1
Toulouse Cl GU17 ....150 C1
Toutley Cl RG41 ....88 C1
Toutley Rd RG41 ....88 B3
Toutly Works RG41 ....89 A1
Tower Cl Caversham RG4 ..59 B4
Flackwell Heath HP10 .....3 B4
Tower Ho Iver SL0 ....49 A4
Tower Ho Twr SL0 ....49 A4
■ Slough SL1 ....42 C2
Towers Dr RG45 ....143 A2
Town Farm Cty Prim Sch
TW19 ....97 B4

Town Farm Way TW19 .....97 B4
Town La Stanwell TW19 ....97 B4
Wooburn Green HP10 ......3 B2
Town Mills ■ RG14 ......105 A2
Town Quay TW18 ....124 B3
Town Sq Bracknell RG12 ..118 B4
Camberley GU15 ....151 B3
■ Slough SL1 ....42 C2
Town Tree Rd TW15 ....98 A2
Townlands Hospl RG9 .....15 B1
Townsend Cl RG12 ....118 C2
Townsend Rd
Aldworth RG8 ....32 C2
Ashford TW15 ....97 C2
Streatley RG8 ....34 A4
Townside Pl GU15 ....151 B3
Towpath TW17 ....124 C1
Tozer Wlk SL4 ....66 B2
Trafalgar Cl RG41 ....115 C3
Trafalgar Ct SL1 ....115 C3
Trafalgar Way GU15 .....150 C2
Trafford Rd RG1 ....85 C3
Transport & Road
Research Laboratory
RG45 ....143 B4
Travic Rd SL1 ....21 C1
Travis Ct SL2 ....22 A1
Travis La GU47 ....150 B4
Treble Ho Terr OX11 ......9 C4
Tredegar Rd RG4 ....59 A3
Trees Cl RG30 ....84 B4
Tree Tops Ave GU15 .....152 A4
Trees Rd SL8 ....3 A3
Treesmill Dr SL6 ....39 B2
Trefoil Cl RG6 ....113 C4
Trefoil Ct RG40 ....116 C4
Trefoil Dro RG18 ....106 C2
Treforgan RG4 ....58 C3
Trelawney Ave SL3 ....43 C2
Trelawney Dr RG31 ....84 A3
Trelleck Rd RG2 ....85 C3
Tremayne Wlk GU15 .....152 B2
Trenchard Rd SL6 ....65 A4
Trenches La SL3,SL3 ......44 A3
Trent Cl RG41 ....115 C4
Trent Cres RG8 ....106 A3
Trent Rd SL3 ....69 A4
Trent Villas Est SL3 ......68 A3
Trenthams Cl RG8 ....57 B3
Trenton Cl GU16 ....149 A3
Tresham Cres GU46 ......149 A3
Tressel The SL4 ....66 B3
Trevelyan RG12 ....117 C1
Trevelyan Mdw Sch SL4 ..67 A3
Trevithick Ct TW14 ....70 C1
Trevor Cl TW19 ....70 A1
Trevor Ho ■ RG40 ....116 C1
Trevose Ho SL2 ....22 A1
Treyarnon Ct RG2 ....86 B3
Triangle The
Greenham RG14 ....131 A4
Reading RG30 ....84 B4
Trident Ind Est SL3 ....69 C2
Trilakes Ctry Pk
GU46,GU47 ....149 C4
Trindledown RG42 ....91 A1
Tring Rd RG31 ....57 B1
Trinity GU47 ....143 C1
Trinity Ave SL7 ....1 B2
Trinity Cl TW19 ....70 A1
Trinity Cres SL5 ....121 A2
Trinity Ct RG7 ....83 B2
Trinity Ho SL6 ....19 C3
Trinity Pl Reading RG1 ....85 C4
Windsor SL4 ....67 B3
Trinity Rd SL1 ....43 B3
Trinity Sch RG14 ....105 A3
Trinity St Stephens
CE Fst Sch SL4 ....67 A3
Triumph Cl Harlington UB7 .71 B3
Triumph Rd RG45 ....87 C3
Troon Ct Ascot SL5 ......120 B2
■ Reading RG1 ....86 B4
Troston Ct TW18 ....97 A4
Trotsworth Ave GU25 ...122 C3
Trotsworth Ct GU25 .....122 B3
Trotwood Cl GU47 ......143 C1
Trout Cl Earley RG6 ....87 A4
Marlow SL7 ....18 B4
Trout Wlk RG14 ....105 B2
Troutbeck Cl Slough SL2 ..43 A3
Twyford RG10 ....61 B3
Troutbeck Wlk GU15 ....152 B2
Trowes La Beech Hill RG7 ..138 B2
Swallowfield RG7 ....139 B3
Trumball Rd RG42 ....91 A1
Trumper Way SL1 ....41 C3
Trumps Green Cl GU25 ..122 C2
Trumps Green Cty Fst Sch
GU25 ....122 B2
Trumps Hill La Chavey D ...122 B2
Trumpsgreen Ave GU25 ..122 B2
Trumpsgreen Rd GU25 ...122 B2
Truro Cl SL6 ....39 A4
Truss Hill Rd SL5 ....120 B2
Trust Cnr RG9 ....35 C4
Trusthorpe Cl RG6 ....87 C1
Tubbs Farm Cl RG17 .....25 A1
Tudor Ave RG30 ....85 C3
Tudor Cl RG20 ....23 A2
Tudor Dr RG12 ....118 A2
Tudor Ct Ashford TW15 ...97 C2
Wokingham RG40 ....116 C3
Tudor Ct Maidenhead SL6 ..39 B1
Stanwell TW19 ....70 C1
Tudor Dr
Wooburn Green HP10 .....3 B4
Yateley GU46 ....149 B2

Tudor Ho RG12 ....118 A2
Tudor La SL4 ....95 B4
Tudor Mill HP10 ....3 C3
Tudor Rd Ashford TW15 ...98 B1
Newbury RG14 ....105 A1
Reading RG1 ....86 A4
Tudor Way SL4 ....66 C3
Tull Way RG14 ....105 C3
Tunnel Link Rd TW6 ......71 A1
Tunnel Rd E TW6 ....71 A3
Tunnel Rd W TW6 ....71 A3
Tuns Hill Cotts RG6 ......87 A3
Tuns La Henley-on-T RG9 ..15 C1
Slough SL1 ....42 B2
Tupsley Rd RG1 ....85 C3
Turbary Gdns RG26 .....135 A1
Turf Hill Rd SL5 ....151 C4
Turks Head Ct SL4 ....67 B4
Turks La RG7 ....132 A4
Turmeric Cl RG6 ....86 C1
Turnberry RG12 ....117 C1
Turnberry Ct ■ RG1 ......86 B4
Turnbridge Cl RG6 ......114 A4
Turner Pl GU47 ....150 B3
Turner Rd SL3 ....43 B2
Turners Cl TW18 ....97 A2
Turners Dr RG19 ....106 C1
Turnery The RG19 ......106 B2
Turnfields RG19 ....106 B2
Turnoak Pk SL4 ....66 C2
Turnpike Comp Sch
RG14 ....105 B2
Turnpike Ind Est RG14 ..105 B3
Turnpike Rd
Brackenll RG42 ....117 B4
Newbury RG14, RG19 ...105 C2
Turnstone Cl RG41 ......115 A3
Turnstone End GU46 ....149 A3
Turnville Cl GU18 ......146 A1
Turpin Rd TW14 ....71 C1
Turpins Gn SL6 ....39 A3
Turpins Rise GU20 ......146 A3
Turton Way SL1 ....42 B2
Tuscam Way GU15 ......150 C2
Tuscan Cl RG30 ....57 C1
Tuxford Mews RG30 ......85 A4
Tweed Cl RG30 ....85 A4
Tweed Rd SL3 ....69 A4
Twin Oaks RG4 ....59 A3
Twinches La SL1 ....42 A4
Twinwoods RG20 ....49 A2
Two Mile Dr SL1 ....41 C2
Two Rivers Sh Ctr TW18 ..96 C2
Two Rivers Way RG42 .....90 A4
Two Tree Hill RG9 ....35 A4
Twycross Rd RG40 ......116 C4
Twyford
Binfield RG10 & RG42 .....90 B4
Waltham St Lawrence RG10 ..62 C3
Wokingham RG40 ....89 A1
Twyford Sta RG10 ....61 C3
Twynersh Ave KT16 ......123 C2
Twynham Rd SL6 ....39 A4
Tyberton Pl RG1 ....85 C3
Tydehams RG14 ....130 C4
Tyle Pl SL4 ....68 A1
Tyle Rd RG30 ....84 B4
Tyler Cl RG4 ....58 C3
Tyler Dr RG2 ....140 C4
Tylers La RG42 ....80 A1
Tylers Pl RG30 ....84 B4
Tylorstown RG4 ....58 C3
Tyne Way RG18 ....106 A3
Tyrell Gdns SL4 ....66 B4
Tyrrel Ct ■ RG1 ....86 B4
Tytherton RG12 ....118 B4

U

Uffington Cl RG31 ....84 B4
Uffington Dr RG12 ......118 C3
Uffcott Cl RG12 ....113 C4
Ufton Court Yd SL8 ....3 A2
Ufton Ct SL8 ....3 A2
Ullswater RG12 ....117 C1
Ullswater Cl Burnham SL1 ..41 B4
Lightwater GU18 ....146 A1
Thatcham RG19 ....106 C1
Ullswater Dr RG31 ....57 B2
Ullswater Rd GU18 ......146 A1
Ulster Cl RG4 ....59 B3
Umberville Way GU47 .....21 C1
Underhill OX10 ....14 A2
Underhill Cl SL6 ....39 C3
Underwood RG12 ....117 C2
Underwood Ct RG42 ......90 B1
Underwood Rd RG30 ......85 A2
Union Cl GU47 ....143 C1
Union Rd RG2 ....82 B2
Union St RG1 ....86 A4
Unity Cl RG4 ....59 A3
Unity Ct RG4 ....59 A3
Univ of Reading
Earley RG6 ....87 A3
Reading, Whiteknights RG6 ..86 C2
Unwin Ave TW14 ....71 B1
Upavon Dr RG1 ....85 C3
Upavon Gdns RG12 .....118 C2
Upcroft SL4 ....67 A3
Upcroft Prim Sch RG30 ...84 C4
Updown Hill GU20 ....46 B4
Upland Rd GU15 ....151 B4
Uplands
Hungerford RG17 ....100 B3
Marlow Bottom SL7 ......1 B3
Uplands Cl GU47 ....150 A4

Uplands Cty Prim Sch
GU47 ....150 A4
Uplands Rd RG4 ....58 C3
Upper Bray Rd SL6 ....40 B2
Upper Broadmoor Rd
RG45 ....143 B3
Upper Charles St GU15 ..151 B3
Upper Chobham Rd
GU15 ....152 A2
Upper College Ride
GU15 ....151 C4
Upper Crown St RG1 ......86 A3
Upper Eddington RG17 ...100 C4
Upper End RG20 ....49 A4
Upper Gordon Rd GU15 ..151 B3
Upper Halliford Rd
TW17 ....125 C3
Upper Halliford Sta
TW16 ....125 C4
Upper Lambourn Rd
RG17 ....25 A2
Upper Lees Rd SL2 ....22 A1
Upper Meadow Rd RG2 ...86 B1
Upper Nursery SL5 ....121 B3
Upper Park Rd GU15 ....151 C3
Upper Red Cross Rd RG8 ..34 B4
Upper Redlands Rd RG1 ...86 C3
Upper Verran Rd GU15 ...151 B2
Upper Village Rd SL5 ....120 B2
Upper Warren Ave RG4 ...58 B2
Upper Wlk GU25 ....122 C3
Upper Woodcote Rd RG4 ..58 B3
Uppingham Dr RG5 ....60 C1
Uppingham Gdns RG4 .....59 B3
Upshire Gdns RG12 .....118 C3
Upton Cl Henley-on-T RG9 ..15 C1
Slough SL1 ....42 C2
Upton Court Rd SL3 ......43 A2
Upton Hospl SL1 ....42 C2
Upton House SL4 ....67 B3
Upton Lea Par SL2 ....43 A3
Upton Pk SL1 ....42 C2
Upton Rd Reading RG30 ...85 A4
Slough SL1 ....43 A2
Urquhart Rd RG19 ......106 C1
Usk Rd RG30 ....84 C3
Uxbridge Rd SL1, SL2, SL3 ..43 B3

V

Vachel Rd RG1 ....86 A4
Vale Cres RG30 ....57 C1
Vale Gr SL1 ....42 C2
Vale Rd Camberley GU15 ..151 A2
Windsor SL4 ....66 C3
Vale View RG10 ....61 A2
Valentia Cl RG30 ....85 B4
Valentia Rd RG30 ....85 B4
Valentine Cl RG6 ....87 A3
Valentine Cres RG4 ....59 B2
Valentine Wood Ind Est
RG7 ....135 C2
Valeview Dr RG7 ....138 B3
Valley Cl Caversham RG4 ..59 B2
Goring RG8 ....34 B3
Valley End RG45 ....34 B4
Valley Gdns TW20,GU25 ..121 C4
Valley Rd
Burghfield Common RG7 ..111 A2
Frimley GU16 ....152 B1
Henley-on-T RG9 ....35 A4
Newbury RG14 ....130 C4
Valley Road Prim Sch
RG9 ....35 B4
Valley View GU47 ......150 A4
Valley Way RG26 ....135 C1
Valon Rd RG2 ....140 C4
Valpy St RG1 ....86 A4
Valroy Cl GU15 ....151 B3
Vanburgh Ct RG1 ....86 B4
Vandyke RG12 ....117 C2
Vanguard Ho ■ TW19 .....70 C1
Vanlore Way RG31 ....84 B3
Vanners La RG20 ....129 B3
Vansittart Est SL4 ....67 A4
Vansittart Rd Bisham SL7 ..18 C4
Windsor SL4 ....67 A3
Vantage Rd SL1 ....42 A3
Vanwall Bsns Pk SL6 ......39 B2
Vanwall Rd SL6 ....39 B2
Vastern Rd RG1 ....59 A1
Vaughan Almshouses
TW15 ....98 A2
Vaughan Copse SL4 ....48 B1
Vaughan Gdns SL4 ....41 C1
Vaughan Way SL2 ....21 C1
Vauxhall Dr RG5 ....88 B3
Vegal Cres TW20 ....95 B3
Venetia Cl RG4 ....59 B4
Venning Rd RG2 ....113 B4
Ventnor Rd RG31 ....57 B1
Ventura Cl RG6 ....113 C3
Venus Cl RG41 ....115 C3
Verdon Ct SL2 ....22 A1
Verey Cl RG10 ....61 A3
Vermont Rd SL2 ....21 C1
Vermont Woods RG40 ...141 C4
Verney Cl SL7 ....1 B1
Verney Mews RG30 ....85 A4
Vernon Cres RG2 ....113 A4
Vernon Dr SL5 ....119 C4

Vernon Rd TW13 ....98 C3
Verran Rd GU15 ....151 B2
Viburnum Cl GU24 ....153 C3
Vicarage Ave TW20 ....96 A2
Vicarage Cl Cookham SL6 ....20 A4
　Wokingham RG40 ....141 C3
Vicarage Cres TW20 ....96 A2
Vicarage Ct
　East Bedfont TW14 ....98 B4
　Egham TW20 ....96 A1
Vicarage La SL6 ....40 B2
Vicarage Flats SL4 ....67 B3
Vicarage Gdns Ascot SL5 ....120 A2
　White Waltham SL6 ....63 C4
Vicarage La
　Cold Ash RG18 ....106 B4
　Laleham TW18 ....124 B3
　Wraysbury TW19 ....95 C4
　Yateley GU46 ....149 B4
Vicarage Rd Ashford TW16 ....98 C1
　Bagshot GU19 ....145 B2
　Blackwater GU17 ....150 C2
　Egham TW20 ....96 A2
　Henley-on-T RG9 ....35 C4
　Maidenhead SL6 ....39 C4
　Reading RG2 ....86 B3
　Staines TW18 ....96 C2
　Yateley GU46 ....149 B4
Vicarage Way SL3 ....69 B4
Vicarage Wlk SL6 ....40 B2
Vicarage Wood Way
　RG31 ....57 A1
Vickers Cl Shinfield RG2 ....113 C2
　Woodley RG5 ....88 A4
Vickers Ct 🖪 TW19 ....70 C1
Victor Cl SL6 ....39 A4
Victor Rd Thatcham RG19 ....106 C2
　Windsor SL4 ....67 B2
Victor Way RG5 ....88 A4
Victoria Ave GU15 ....151 A3
Victoria Ct Bagshot GU19 ....145 C1
　Henley-on-T RG9 ....15 C1
　🖬 Marlow SL7 ....1 C1
　Slough SL1 ....42 C3
Victoria Dr GU17 ....150 B2
Victoria Gdns RG14 ....105 A2
Victoria Ho SL4 ....68 A1
Victoria La UB3 ....71 B4
Victoria Mews RG30 ....85 A4
Victoria Rd Ascot SL5 ....120 A2
　Caversham RG4 ....59 A2
　Eton SL4 ....41 C1
　Farnham Common SL2 ....22 B3
　Marlow SL7 ....1 C1
　Mortimer RG7 ....136 C3
　Reading RG31 ....84 B4
　Sandhurst GU47 ....149 B2
　Slough SL2 ....43 A3
　Staines TW18 ....96 C3
　Wargrave RG10 ....36 C1
Victoria St
　Englefield Green TW20 ....96 B1
　Reading RG1 ....86 B4
　🖩 Slough SL1 ....42 C2
　Windsor SL4 ....67 B3
Victoria Way 🖪 RG1 ....86 B4
Victory Rd KT16 ....124 A1
Vigo La GU46 ....149 B2
Viking RG12 ....117 C2
Villa Mews RG1 ....86 C4
Village Cl RG2 ....113 A3
Village Ct SL5 ....120 B2
Village Gate SL7 ....125 A2
Village Rd Dorney SL4 ....41 A2
　Thorpe TW20 ....123 B3
Village Sh Ctr The 🖪
　SL1 ....42 C2
Village The
　Finchampstead RG40 ....141 C2
　Old Windsor SL4 ....94 A3
Village Way Ashford TW15 ....98 A2
　Yateley GU46 ....149 B4
Villiers Ct SL4 ....67 A4
Villiers Mead RG41 ....116 A4
Villiers Rd SL2 ....42 B4
Villiers Way RG14 ....130 B3
Villiers Wlk RG14 ....130 B3
Vincent Cl Chertsey KT16 ....123 C1
　Harmondsworth UB7 ....71 A4
　Woodley RG5 ....87 C3
Vincent Dr TW17 ....125 C3
Vincent Ho 🖩 RG1 ....85 C4
Vincent Rd Chertsey KT16 ....123 C1
　Thatcham RG18 ....106 C2
Vincent Rise RG12 ....118 C3
Vine Cl TW19 ....70 A1
Vine Cres RG30 ....85 A2
Vine Ct Newbury RG14 ....105 A1
　Stoke Poges SL2 ....22 C3
Vine Rd SL2 ....22 C3
Vineries Cl UB7 ....71 A4
Vinery The RG10 ....36 B1
Vines The RG41 ....115 B2
Vineyard Dr SL8 ....3 A3
Vinter Ct TW17 ....125 A2
Viola Ave TW19 ....97 C4
Viola Croft RG42 ....118 C4
Violet Gr RG18 ....106 C3
Virginia Ave GU25 ....122 C2
Virginia Beeches GU25 ....122 B3
Virginia Cl TW18 ....124 B3
Virginia Ct Ashford TW15 ....97 C3
　Virginia Water GU25 ....122 B3
Virginia Dr GU25 ....122 B3
Virginia Water SL5 ....121 C3

Virginia Water Prep Sch
　GU25 ....122 B3
Virginia Water Sta GU25 ....122 C2
Virginia Way RG30 ....85 A3
Viscount Cl 🖪 SL4 ....67 B3
Viscount Ind Est SL3 ....69 C2
Viscount Rd TW19 ....97 C4
Viscount Way Hatton TW6 ....71 C2
　Woodley RG5 ....88 A4
Vivien Cl SL6 ....19 C3
Vivienne Ho TW18 ....97 A2
Vo-Tec Ctr RG14 ....105 C1
Voller Dr RG31 ....84 B3
Volunteer Rd RG2 ....83 B1
Vulcan Cl Sandhurst GU47 ....150 A4
　Woodley RG5 ....61 A1
Vulcan Way GU47 ....150 A4

W

Waborne Rd SL6 ....3 A2
Wade Dr SL1 ....42 A3
Wadham GU47 ....143 C1
Wadham Cl TW17 ....125 B1
Wagbullock Rise RG12 ....118 B2
Waggoners Hollow GU19 ....145 C1
Wagner Cl SL6 ....38 C2
Wagtail Cl RG10 ....61 C2
Waingel's Copse Sch
　RG10 ....61 A1
Waingels Rd RG5, RG10 ....61 A1
Wainscot Sl 120 C2
Wakefield Cres SL2 ....22 C3
Wakeford Cl RG26 ....135 C1
Wakeford Ct RG26 ....135 C1
Wakelins End SL6 ....19 C4
Wakeman Rd SL8 ....3 A2
Wakemans RG8 ....55 B2
Walbury RG12 ....118 B2
Waldeck Rd SL6 ....40 A4
Waldeck St RG1 ....86 A3
Waldegrave Pl RG14 ....105 A2
Walden Ave RG2 ....114 B2
Waldens Cl SL8 ....3 A2
Waldorf Hts GU17 ....150 B2
Waldron Hill RG12 ....118 C4
Waldrons The RG17 ....47 B3
Waleys Pl 🖪 RG4 ....59 B1
Walgrove Gdns SL6 ....63 C4
Walk The Ashford TW16 ....98 C1
　Eton SL4 ....41 C2
Walker Cl TW14 ....98 C4
Walker Rd SL6 ....40 A2
Walker's Ridge GU15 ....151 C3
Walkers La RG17 ....25 A2
Walkers Pl RG30 ....85 B4
Wall La RG7 ....136 B1
Wallace Cl Marlow SL7 ....1 C2
　Upper Halliford TW17 ....125 B3
　Woodley RG5 ....87 B3
Wallace Wlk SL4 ....42 C1
Wallcroft Cl RG42 ....90 C1
Walled Gdn The RG10 ....36 B1
Waller Ct RG4 ....59 A1
Waller Dr RG14 ....105 C3
Wallingford Cl RG12 ....118 C3
Wallingford Rd
　Compton RG20 ....31 C3
　Goring RG8 ....34 B4
　South Stoke RG8 & OX10 ....14 B3
Wallington Rd GU15 ....145 A1
Wallington's Rd RG17 ....101 C1
Wallis Cl SL1 ....43 A2
Wallner Way RG40 ....116 C3
Walmer Cl
　Crowthorne RG45 ....143 B3
　Reading RG30 ....85 A3
Walmer Rd RG5 ....60 C1
Walnut Cl
　Wokingham RG41 ....115 C3
　Yateley GU46 ....149 B2
Walnut Tree Cl
　Bourne End SL8 ....3 C2
　Twyford RG10 ....61 C3
Walnut Tree Ct RG8 ....34 B3
Walnut Tree Ho TW20 ....95 C2
Walnut Tree Rd TW17 ....125 B4
Walnut Way Bourne End SL8 ....3 A1
　Reading RG30 ....84 B4
Walpole Rd
　Old Windsor SL4 ....95 A3
　Slough SL1 ....41 B4
Walrus Cl RG5 ....60 C1
Walsh Ave RG42 ....91 C1
Walter Inf Sch RG41 ....116 A3
Walter Jun Sch RG41 ....116 A3
Walters Cl RG18 ....106 C2
Waltham Cl
　Maidenhead SL6 ....38 C1
　Sandhurst GU47 ....143 B1
Waltham Rd Twyford RG10 ....62 A3
　White Waltham SL6 ....62 A4
Waltham St Lawrence
　Cty Prim Sch RG10 ....62 C2
Walton Ave RG9 ....35 C4
Walton Bridge Rd
　KT12, TW17 ....125 C1
Walton Cl RG5 ....87 B4
Walton Dr SL5 ....119 C4
Walton Gdns TW13 ....98 B4
Walton La Burnham SL2 ....21 C2
　Lower Halliford KT12,TW17 ....125 B1
　Walton-on-T TW17 ....125 C1
Walton Way RG14 ....105 B2
Wandhope Way RG31 ....57 B1
Wansey Gdns RG14 ....105 B3
Wanstraw Gr RG12 ....118 C1

Watermans Bsns Pk The
　TW18 ....96 C2
Watermans Rd RG9 ....35 C4
Watermans Way RG10 ....36 B1
Watermead TW14 ....98 C4
Watermeadows The
　RG14 ....105 A2
Watermill Ct RG7 ....108 B1
Waters Dr TW18 ....96 C2
Watersfield Cl 🖪 RG6 ....87 A1
Waterside HP10 ....3 C2
Waterside Ct RG14 ....105 B2
Waterside Dr
　Purley on T RG8 ....57 B3
　Slough SL3 ....43 C2
　Theale RG7 ....83 C2
Waterside Gdns 🖪 RG1 ....86 A4
Watersplash La RG42 ....91 A1
Watersplash Rd TW17 ....125 A3
Watery La Kintbury RG20 ....128 C3
　Wooburn Green HP10 ....3 C4
Watkins Cl RG40 ....141 C4
Watlington St RG1 ....86 B4
Watman La RG41 ....88 B1
Watson Cl RG40 ....115 C1
Watts La OX11 ....12 A4
Wavell Cl RG2 ....86 C1
Wavell Gdns SL2 ....21 C1
Wavell Rd SL6 ....39 A3
Wavendene Ave TW20 ....96 B1
Waverley RG12 ....117 C2
Waverley Cl GU15 ....151 C2
Waverley Ct 🖪 RG30 ....85 B3
Waverley Dr
　Camberley GU15 ....151 C3
　Virginia Water GU25 ....122 A3
Waverley Rd
　Bagshot GU19 ....145 C2
　Reading RG30 ....85 B4
　Slough SL1 ....42 B2
Waverley St RG40 ....115 C1
Waverley Way RG40 ....115 C1
Waverleys The RG18 ....106 B2
Waybrook Cres RG1 ....86 C3
Wayland Cl RG12 ....118 C3
Waylands TW19 ....68 C1
Waylands Cl RG7 ....82 B2
Waylen St RG1 ....85 C4
Ways End GU15 ....151 C2
Wayside Mews SL6 ....39 C4
WC Lee's Resthouses
　GU20 ....146 B2
Weald Rise RG30 ....57 C1
Wealden Way RG30 ....84 C4
Weardale Cl RG2 ....86 B2
Weaver Mews GU47 ....150 A4
Weavers Ct 🖪 RG1 ....86 B4
Weavers La RG17 ....127 B3
Weavers Way RG10 ....61 B2
Weavers Wlk 🖪 RG14 ....105 A1
Webb Cl Bagshot GU19 ....145 C1
　Binfield RG42 ....90 C2
　Slough SL3 ....43 B1
Webb Ct RG40 ....116 C4
Webb's Acre RG19 ....106 C1
Webbs Acre RG19 ....106 C1
Webbs La RG7 ....109 A4
Webster Cl SL6 ....39 A3
Wedderburn Cl RG41 ....88 B1
Wedgewood Way RG30 ....57 C1
Weir Cl RG31 ....84 C2
Weir Pl TW18 ....123 C4
Weir Rd KT16 ....124 A1
Weirside Ct 🖪 RG1 ....86 B4
Welbeck RG12 ....117 C2
Welbeck Rd SL6 ....39 A2
Welby Cl SL6 ....39 A2
Welby Cres RG41 ....88 A1
Weldale St RG1 ....85 C4
Welden SL2 ....43 A4
Welford Ho RG20 ....75 C4
Welford Rd RG5 ....60 A1
Welford & Wickham
　CE Prim Sch RG20 ....75 B2
Well Cl GU15 ....151 A2
Well House La RG17 ....140 A2
Well Mdw RG14 ....105 B3
Welland Cl Brands Hill SL3 ....69 A4
　Reading RG31 ....57 B1
Wellbank SL6 ....20 C2
Wellburn Cl GU47 ....150 A4
Wellcroft Rd SL1 ....42 A3
Weller Dr Barkham RG40 ....141 A3
　Camberley GU15 ....151 B2
Wellers La RG42 ....91 B4
Wellesley Ave SL4 ....44 C2
Wellesley Cl GU19 ....145 B2
Wellesley Dr RG45 ....142 C3
Wellesley Path SL1 ....43 A2
Wellesley Rd SL1 ....43 A2
Welley Ave TW19 ....68 C1
Welley Rd TW19 ....68 C1
Wellfield Cl RG31 ....84 B4
Wellhill Rd OX12 ....7 B3
Wellhouse La RG18 ....79 C3
Wellhouse Rd SL6 ....19 C1
Wellington Ave
　Reading RG2 ....86 B2
　Virginia Water GU25 ....122 A2
Wellington Bsns Pk
　RG45 ....142 C2
Wellington Cl
　Newbury RG14 ....105 B3
　Sandhurst GU47 ....150 B4
　Walton-on-T KT12 ....125 C1

Wellington Coll RG45 ....143 A3
Wellington Cotts
　Ball Hill RG20 ....129 A4
　Heath End RG20 ....37 B1
Wellington Cres RG26 ....134 B3
Wellington Ct
　Ashford TW15 ....97 C3
　Shinfield RG7 ....113 A4
　Stanwell TW19 ....97 C2
Wellington Dr RG12 ....118 C2
Wellington Dr RG12 ....118 C2
Wellington Gdns RG7 ....82 A4
Wellington Rd
　Ashford TW15 ....97 C3
　Crowthorne RG45 ....143 B3
　Hatton TW14 ....71 C1
　Maidenhead SL6 ....39 B4
　Sandhurst GU47 ....150 B4
　Wokingham RG40 ....116 A1
　Woodley RG5 ....61 A3
Wellington St SL1 ....43 A3
Wellington Terr RG17 ....150 B4
Wellingtonia Ave
　RG45,RG40 ....142 B3
Wells Cl SL4 ....67 A4
Wells La SL5 ....120 A4
Welsh La RG7, RG7 ....139 A4
Welshmans Rd RG7 ....136 A4
Welwick Cl RG6 ....87 C1
Welwyn Ave TW14 ....71 C3
Wendan Rd RG14 ....130 C3
Wendover Ct TW18 ....96 B3
Wendover Dr RG10 ....152 B3
Wendover Pl TW18 ....96 B3
Wendover Rd
　Bourne End SL8 ....3 A3
　Burnham SL1 ....41 A4
　Egham TW18, TW19 ....96 B3
Wendover Way RG30 ....84 B3
Wenlock Edge RG10 ....61 A3
Wenlock Way RG19 ....106 B3
Wensley Cl RG10 ....61 B3
Wensley Rd RG1 ....85 C3
Wensleydale Dr GU15 ....152 B3
Wentworth Ave
　North Ascot SL5 ....119 B3
　Reading RG2 ....113 B3
　Slough SL2 ....22 A3
Wentworth Cl
　Ashford TW15 ....98 A3
　Crowthorne RG45 ....142 C3
　Yateley GU46 ....149 B3
Wentworth Club GU25 ....122 A3
Wentworth Cres SL6 ....39 B3
Wentworth Ct RG14 ....105 A3
Wentworth Dr GU25 ....121 C3
Wentworth Way SL5 ....119 B3
Wescott Inf Sch RG40 ....116 B3
Wescott Rd RG40 ....116 B3
Wesley Dr TW20 ....96 A1
Wesley Pl SL4 ....93 A4
Wessex Cl RG17 ....100 B3
Wessex Ct ④ TW19 ....70 C2
Wessex Gdns RG14 ....61 C2
Wessex Inf Sch SL6 ....39 A4
Wessex Jun Sch SL6 ....39 A4
Wessex Rd Harmondsworth TW19, TW6 ....70 C2
Wessex Road Ind Est SL3 ....3 A
Wessex Way SL6 ....39 A4
Wessons Hill SL6 ....19 B
West Cl Ashford TW15 ....97 C
　Medmenham SL7 ....12 A
West Cres SL4 ....66 C
West Ct RG40 ....39 C
West Dean SL6 ....39 C
West Dr Reading RG31 ....84 C
　Sonning RG4 ....60 B
　Wentworth GU25 ....121 C
West End Ct SL2 ....22 C
West End La
　Harlington UB3 ....71 B
　Newell Green RG42 ....91 A
　Stoke Poges SL2 ....22 C
West End Rd RG7 ....136 C
West Fryerne GU46 ....149 B
West Gn GU46 ....149 A
West Green Ct RG1 ....85 C
West Hill RG1 ....86 A
West Ilsley Ho RG20 ....10 A
West La RG9 ....15 B
West Mead SL6 ....39 C
West Mead Sch RG40 ....116 B
West Mills RG14 ....104 C
West Mills Yd RG14 ....104 C
West Point SL1 ....41 B
West Ramp TW6 ....71 A
West Rd Bracknell RG40 ....117 B
　Camberley GU15 ....151 C
　East Bedfont TW14 ....98 B
　Maidenhead SL6 ....39 C
West Ridge SL8 ....3 A
West St
　Henley-on-T RG9 ....15 B
　Maidenhead SL6 ....39 C
　Marlow SL7 ....1 C
　Newbury RG14 ....104 C
　Reading RG1 ....86 A
West Surrey Est 🖪 TW15 ....125 B
West View
　East Bedfont TW14 ....98 B
　Peasemore RG20 ....50 B
West View Cl RG5 ....60 C
West Way TW17 ....125 B
Westacott Bsns Ctr SL6 ....38 C
Westacott Way SL6 ....38 B
Westborough Ct SL6 ....39 B
Westborough Rd SL6 ....39 A

estbourne Rd
eltham TW13 . . . . .98 C3
sandhurst GU47 . . . . .150 C4
eston TW18 . . . . .97 A1
estbourne Terr
3 Newbury RG14 . . . . .105 A2
Reading RG6 . . . . .85 B4
estbrook SL6 . . . . .40 C1
estbrook Ct RG12 . . . . .100 B3
estbrook Gdns RG12 . . . . .118 B4
estbrook Gn OX11 . . . . .11 C4
estbrook Rd
Reading RG30 . . . . .58 B1
Staines TW18 . . . . .96 C2
estbrook St OX11 . . . . .11 C4
estbury Cl
Crowthorne RG45 . . . . .143 A3
Shepperton TW17 . . . . .125 A2
estbury La RG8 . . . . .57 A3
estcombe Cl RG12 . . . . .118 C1
estcote Rd RG30 . . . . .85 B3
estcotts Gn RG42 . . . . .91 B1
estcroft SL2 . . . . .22 A1
estdene Cres RG14 . . . . .104 C2
estende WG40 . . . . .116 B3
estende Jun Sch RG40 . . . . . . .116 B3
esterdale RG10 . . . . .36 A4
esterdale Dr GU16 . . . . .152 A2
esterham TW16 . . . . .98 C4
estern Ave
Chertsey KT16 . . . . .124 A3
Henley-on-T RG9 . . . . .35 C4
Newbury RG14 . . . . .104 C2
Thorpe TW20 . . . . .123 A3
Woodley RG5 . . . . .60 C1
estern Cl KT16 . . . . .124 A3
estern Ctr The RG12 . . . . .117 C4
estern Dr
Shepperton TW17 . . . . .125 B3
Wooburn Green HP10 . . . . .3 C3
estern Elms Ave RG30 . . . . .85 C4
estern End RG14 . . . . .104 C1
estern House Inf Sch
SL1 . . . . .42 A3
estern Ind Area RG12 . . . . . . .117 C4
estern Oaks RG41 . . . . .57 C1
estern Perimeter Rd
TW19, TW6, UB7 . . . . .70 A3
estern Perimeter Rd Rdbt
TW19 . . . . .70 B1
estern Rd
Bracknell RG12 . . . . .117 C4
Henley-on-T RG9 . . . . .35 C4
Reading RG1 . . . . .85 B3
estfield Bglws SL7 . . . . .16 C3
estfield Cotts SL7 . . . . .16 C3
estfield Cres
Chiplake RG9 . . . . .36 A2
Thatcham RG18 . . . . .106 A2
estfield Inf Sch SL8 . . . . .3 A2
estfield Jun Sch
SL1 . . . . .42 A3
estgate Rd RG14 . . . . .104 C1
esthatch Cnr RG42 . . . . .91 B3
esthatch La RG42 . . . . .91 B3
esthead Dr RG14 . . . . .131 A4
esthorpe Rd SL7 . . . . .1 C2
estland RG18 . . . . .106 A2
estland Cl TW19 . . . . .70 C1
estlands Ave Earley RG2 . . . . . .86 C1
Slough SL1 . . . . .41 A4
estlands Cl SL1 . . . . .41 A4
estlands Inf Sch SL1 . . . . .41 B4
estlyn Rd RG26 . . . . .135 C1
estmacott Dr TW14 . . . . .98 C4
estmead SL4 . . . . .67 A2
estmead Dr RG14 . . . . .130 C4
estminster Way RG40 . . . . .88 B1
estmorland Cl RG41 . . . . .115 B3
estmorland Dr
Bracknell RG42 . . . . .91 C1
Frimley GU15 . . . . .152 A2
eston Rd GU19 . . . . .145 C1
eston Rd SL1 . . . . .41 C4
estonbirt Dr RG4 . . . . .58 C2
estons RG20 . . . . .51 B4
estridge Ave RG8 . . . . .57 B3
estview Dr RG10 . . . . .61 C3
estward Rd RG41 . . . . .115 C4
estwates Cl RG12 . . . . .118 B4
estway RG8 . . . . .34 B4
estwood Farm Jun
& Inf Schs RG31 . . . . .57 B2
estwood Glen RG31 . . . . .57 B2
estwood Gn SL6 . . . . .19 C3
estwood Rd Marlow SL7 . . . . . . .1 B1
Newbury RG14 . . . . .104 C1
Reading RG31 . . . . .57 B2
estwood Row RG31 . . . . .57 B2
etherby Cl RG4 . . . . .59 B3
etherby Ho GU15 . . . . .151 B4

Wethered Dr SL1 . . . . .41 A4
Wethered Pk SL7 . . . . .1 B1
Wethered Rd SL7 . . . . .1 B1
Wetton PI TW20 . . . . .95 C2
Wexford Ct SL6 . . . . .40 A4
Wexham Court Comb Sch
SL2 . . . . .43 B4
Wexham Cty Sec Sch SL2 . . . . .43 B4
Wexham Park Hospl SL3 . . . . . .23 B1
Wexham Park La SL3 . . . . .23 B1
Wexham PI SL2 . . . . .23 B3
Wexham Rd SL1, SL2 . . . . .43 A3
Wexham St SL3 . . . . .23 A2
Wexham Woods SL3 . . . . .43 B4
Wey Ave KT16 . . . . .124 A3
Wey Cl GU15 . . . . .151 A3
Weybridge Mead GU46 . . . . . . .149 C4
Weycrofts RG42 . . . . .90 C1
Weymead Cl KT16 . . . . .124 B1
Whaley Rd RG40 . . . . .116 B4
Wharf La Bourne End SL8 . . . . . . .3 A2
Henley-on-T RG9 . . . . .15 C2
Wharf Rd SL6 . . . . .39 C4
Wharf St SL4 . . . . .67 C4
Wharf The Newbury RG14 . . . . .105 A2
Taplow SL6 . . . . .40 C4
Wharfedale Rd RG41 . . . . .88 A2
Wharfside RG7 . . . . .109 B2
Whatley Gn RG12 . . . . .118 A2
Whatmore Cl TW19 . . . . .70 A1
Wheatash Rd KT15 . . . . .124 A1
Wheatbutts The SL4 . . . . .41 C1
Wheatfield Cl SL6 . . . . .39 A2
Wheatfields Rd RG2 . . . . .113 C3
Wheatlands Cl RG31 . . . . .84 C2
Wheatlands La RG14 . . . . .130 A3
Wheatlands Rd SL3 . . . . .43 B2
Wheatley RG12 . . . . .117 C2
Wheatley Cl RG2 . . . . .86 C1
Wheatsheaf La
Newbury RG14 . . . . .105 A2
Staines TW18 . . . . .96 C1
Wheatsheaf Par SL4 . . . . .68 A1
Wheble Dr RG5 . . . . .87 B4
Wheeler Cl
Burghfield Common RG7 . . . . . .111 A2
Wokingham RG41 . . . . .115 C3
Wheeler Ct SL1 . . . . .41 C4
Wheelers Green Way
RG19 . . . . .106 C1
Wheelton Cl RG6 . . . . .87 C1
Wheelwrights PI SL3 . . . . .69 B4
Whins Cl GU15 . . . . .151 A2
Whins Dr GU15 . . . . .151 A2
Whinshill Ct SL5 . . . . .121 A1
Whistler Gr GU47 . . . . .150 B3
Whistlers La RG7 . . . . .136 A1
Whistley Cl RG12 . . . . .118 C3
Whitakers Cl RG18 . . . . .106 A2
Whitamore Row RG9 . . . . .35 C4
Whitby Cl RG4 . . . . .59 A1
Whitby Dr 7 RG1 . . . . .86 B3
Whitby Gn RG4 . . . . .59 A1
Whitby Rd SL1 . . . . .42 B3
Whitchurch Cl SL6 . . . . .39 A2
Whitchurch Prim Sch
RG8 . . . . .56 C4
Whitchurch Rd RG8 . . . . .56 C4
White Bridge Cl TW14 . . . . .71 C1
White City RG45 . . . . .143 A3
White Cl Hermitage RG18 . . . . . .78 C3
Slough SL1 . . . . .42 B3
White Gates Rd SL6 . . . . .21 B4
White Hart Ind Est GU17 . . . . .150 C2
White Hart Rd
2 Maidenhead SL6 . . . . .39 C4
Slough SL3 . . . . .42 B2
White Hart Row 3 KT16 . . . . . .124 A1
White Hill
Remenham Hill RG9 . . . . .16 A1
Shiplake RG9 . . . . .35 A3
Windlesham GU20 . . . . .146 A3
Wooburn Moor HP9 . . . . .3 C4
White Horse La RG40 . . . . .141 B3
White Horse Rd SL4 . . . . .66 B3
White House Gdns RG40 . . . . . .149 B4
White House Prep Sch
RG41 . . . . .116 A3
White House Rd OX10 . . . . .14 C4
White Lilies Island SL4 . . . . .67 A4
White Lion Way GU46 . . . . .149 B4
White Lodge Cl
Marlow Bottom SL7 . . . . .1 B3
Purley on T RG31 . . . . .57 A2
White Paddock SL6 . . . . .39 A1
White Rd Chilton OX11 . . . . . . .10 B4
White Rock SL6 . . . . .20 A1
White Shoot OX11 . . . . .12 A3
White Waltham
CE Prim Sch SL6 . . . . .39 A4
Whiteacres Dr SL6 . . . . .40 A1
Whitebeam Cl RG41 . . . . .115 B2
Whiteford Rd SL2 . . . . .42 C4
Whitegates La RG6 . . . . .87 A4
Whitegrove Prim Sch
RG42 . . . . .91 C1
Whitehall SL5 . . . . .20 A1
Whitehall Dr RG2 . . . . .140 C4
Whitehall Farm La GU25 . . . . .122 C2
Whitehall La Egham TW20 . . . . .95 C1
HORTON SL3 . . . . .69 A3
Whitehaven SL1 . . . . .42 C3
Whitehill Cl GU15 . . . . .151 B4
Whitehill PI GU25 . . . . .122 C2
Whitehills Cl SL7 . . . . .1 B3
Whitehills Gn RG8 . . . . .34 B3

Whitehouse Way SL3 . . . . .43 B2
Whiteknights Prim Sch
RG6 . . . . .86 C1
Whiteknights Rd RG6 . . . . .86 C2
Whitelands Dr SL5 . . . . .119 B4
Whitelands Park Prim Sch
RG18 . . . . .106 B3
Whitelands Rd RG18 . . . . .106 B2
Whitelocke Inf Sch
RG40 . . . . .116 B4
Whitelocks Piece RG17 . . . . . . .73 A1
Whitemoor La
Lower Basildon RG8 . . . . .34 B1
Upper Basildon RG8 . . . . .54 C3
Whitepit La HP10 . . . . .3 A4
Whites Hill RG7 . . . . .110 B3
Whites La Beenham RG7 . . . . . .109 A4
Datchet SL3 . . . . .68 A4
Whitestone Cl RG6 . . . . .87 A1
Whitewell Cl RG2 . . . . .114 C1
Whiteways CI TW17 . . . . .97 A1
Whitewell Cl RG2 . . . . .114 C1
Whitley Cl TW19 . . . . .70 C1
Whitley Park Inf Sch RG2 . . . . .86 A1
Whitley Park La
RG2 . . . . .86 A1
Whitley Park Rd RG2 . . . . .86 B2
Whitley Rd GU46 . . . . .149 B2
Whitley St SL6 . . . . .86 A3
Whitley Wood La RG2 . . . . .113 B4
Whitley Wood Rd RG2 . . . . .113 B4
Whitmoor Rd GU19 . . . . .145 C1
Whitmore Cl GU47 . . . . .143 B1
Whitmore La SL5 . . . . .121 B4
Whitstone Gdns RG2 . . . . .86 B1
Whittaker Rd SL2 . . . . .21 C1
Whittenham Cl SL2 . . . . .43 A3
Whittle Cl
Sandhurst GU47 . . . . .143 A1
Wokingham RG40 . . . . .141 C4
Whittle Parkway SL1 . . . . .41 B4
Whitton Cl 6 RG6 . . . . .87 B1
Whitton Rd RG12 . . . . .118 C3
Whitworth Rd RG2 . . . . .141 A4
Whurley Way SL6 . . . . .19 C1
Whynstones Rd SL5 . . . . .120 A2
Whyteladyes La SL6 . . . . .19 C3
Wick Hill La RG40 . . . . .142 A3
Wick La TW20 . . . . .94 A4
Wick Rd TW20 . . . . .95 A1
Wickets The Ashford TW15 . . . .97 C2
Maidenhead SL6 . . . . .39 B4
Wickford Way RG6 . . . . .113 C4
Wickham La TW20 . . . . .96 A1
Wickham Rd
Camberley GU15 . . . . .151 C4
Earley RG6 . . . . .87 C1
Wickham Vale RG12 . . . . .117 C2
Wickhurst Cotts SL6 . . . . .38 A3
Wicks Gn RG42 . . . . .90 A2
Widbrook Rd SL6 . . . . .20 A2
Widecroft Rd SL0 . . . . .44 C4
Widmere La SL7 . . . . .1 A3
Wield Ct RG6 . . . . .87 C1
Wiggett Gr RG42 . . . . .90 B1
Wigmore La Reading RG30 . . . . .58 A1
Theale RG7 . . . . .83 B1
Wigmore Rd RG26 . . . . .134 C1
Wilberforce Mews SL6 . . . . .39 C4
Wilberforce Way RG12 . . . . . . .118 B2
Wilcox Gdns TW17 . . . . .124 C3
Wild Briar RG40 . . . . .141 C4
Wild Cl RG6 . . . . .114 B4
Wildcroft Dr RG40 . . . . .116 A1
Wilde Theatre RG12 . . . . .118 B1
Wilder Ave RG8 . . . . .56 C3
Wilderness Cl RG6 . . . . .87 A2
Wilderness Rd Earley RG6 . . . . .87 A2
Frimley GU16 . . . . .152 A1
Wilders Cl Bracknell RG42 . . . . .91 A1
Frimley GU16 . . . . .151 C1
Wildgreen N SL3 . . . . .44 A1
Wildgreen S SL3 . . . . .44 A1
Wildridings Cty Prim Sch
RG12 . . . . .118 A3
Wildridings Rd RG12 . . . . .118 A3
Wildridings Sq RG12 . . . . .118 A3
Wildwood Dr RG26 . . . . .134 B1
Wildwood Gdns GU46 . . . . .149 B2
Wilford Cl RG12 . . . . .118 B3
Wilfred Way RG19 . . . . .107 A2
Wilfrids Wood Cl HP10 . . . . .3 A3
Willats Cl KT16 . . . . .124 A2
William Byrd Sch UB3 . . . . .71 B4
William Cl RG19 . . . . .106 B1
William Ellis Cl SL4 . . . . .68 A1
William Gray Cty Inf Sch
The RG5 .87 B4
William Gray Cty Jun Sch
The RG5 .87 B3
William Penn Comb Sch
SL2 . . . . .22 B1
William Sim Wood
RG42 . . . . .92 C3
William St Reading RG1 . . . . . . .85 C3
Slough SL1 . . . . .42 C3
Windsor SL4 . . . . .67 B3
Williant Cl SL6 . . . . .38 C1
Willington Cl GU15 . . . . .151 A3
Willink Sch The RG7 . . . . .110 C1
Willis Cl RG18 . . . . .79 A2
Willoners SL2 . . . . .42 A4
Willoughby Rd
Bracknell RG12 . . . . .117 C3
Slough SL3 . . . . .44 A2
Willow Bank SL7 . . . . .1 B3

Willow Bank Jun & Inf Schs
RG5 . . . . .87 A4
Willow Cl
Burghfield Common RG30 . . . . .111 A3
Colnbrook SL3 . . . . .69 B4
Flackwell Heath HP10 . . . . .3 B2
Newbury RG14 . . . . .104 C1
Willow Cotts OX10 . . . . .13 C3
Willow Court La OX10 . . . . .13 C3
Willow Ct 2 Charlton TW16 . . . .98 C1
Frimley GU16 . . . . .151 B1
Wokingham RG41 . . . . .116 A3
Willow Dr Bracknell RG12 . . . . .118 B4
Maidenhead SL6 . . . . .40 A1
Twyford RG10 . . . . .61 B3
Willow Gdns
Purley on T RG31 . . . . .57 A1
Reading RG2 . . . . .86 C1
Willow Gn GU24 . . . . .153 C3
Willow Gr SL4 . . . . .67 A2
Willow La
Blackwater GU17 . . . . .150 B2
Wargrave RG10 . . . . .36 B2
Willow Lo 10 TW16 . . . . .98 C1
Willow Par SL3 . . . . .23 A3
Willow PI SL4 . . . . .67 B4
Willow Rd Newtown RG20 . . . . .131 C1
Poyle SL3 . . . . .69 C3
Willow St 3 RG1 . . . . .86 A3
Willow Tree Glade RG31 . . . . . . .84 B2
Willow Way GU47 . . . . .142 C1
Willow Wlk
Chertsey KT16 . . . . .124 A1
Englefield Green TW20 . . . . .95 B2
Willow Wood Cl SL1 . . . . .21 A2
Willowbrook SL4 . . . . .66 A3
Willowbrook Rd TW19 . . . . .97 C3
Willowdale RG40 . . . . .141 C4
Willowford GU46 . . . . .149 B4
Willowherb Cl RG40 . . . . .116 C4
Willowmead TW18 . . . . .124 A4
Willowmead Cl
10 Marlow SL7 . . . . .1 C2
Newbury RG14 . . . . .130 B3
Willowmead Gdns SL7 . . . . .1 C2
Willowmead Rd 8 SL7 . . . . .1 C2
Willowmead Sq 9 SL7 . . . . .1 C2
Willows Ct RG8 . . . . .56 B3
Willows End GU47 . . . . .150 A4
Willows Rd SL8 . . . . .3 A2
Willows The
14 Bourne End SL8 . . . . .3 A2
9 Bracknell RG12 . . . . .118 C3
Caversham RG4 . . . . .59 A1
Lightwater GU18 . . . . .146 A1
Windsor SL4 . . . . .66 B4
Willowside RG5 . . . . .60 C1
Willson Rd TW20 . . . . .95 A2
Wilmington CI RG5 . . . . .87 C4
Wilmot Cl RG42 . . . . .90 A2
Wilmot Rd SL1 . . . . .21 A1
Wilmot Way GU15 . . . . .151 C2
Wilmot Wlk RG14 . . . . .130 B3
Wilsford Cl RG6 . . . . .113 C4
Wilson Ave SL6 . . . . .19 C1
Wilson Cl RG20 . . . . .31 C2
Wilson Ct RG41 . . . . .88 A1
Wilson Prim Sch RG30 . . . . .85 B4
Wilson Rd RG30 . . . . .85 B4
Wilson Valkenburg Ct
RG14 . . . . .104 C2
Wilstrode Ave RG42 . . . . .90 C1
Wilton Cl UB7 . . . . .70 B4
Wilton Cres SL1 . . . . .66 B2
Wilton Rd
Camberley GU15 . . . . .151 A2
Reading RG30 . . . . .85 B4
Wiltshire Ave
Crowthorne RG45 . . . . .143 A3
Slough SL2 . . . . .22 B1
Wiltshire Cl RG17 . . . . .100 B3
Wiltshire Dr RG40 . . . . .116 B4
Wiltshire Gr RG42 . . . . .91 C1
Wiltshire Lodge 2 SL6 . . . . . . .39 C3
Wiltshire Rd Marlow SL7 . . . . . . .2 A2
Wokingham RG40 . . . . .116 B4
Wiltshire Wlk RG31 . . . . .84 B4
Wilwood Rd RG42 . . . . .117 C4
Wilwyne Cl RG4 . . . . .59 B2
Wimbledon Cl GU15 . . . . .144 C1
Wimbledon Rd GU15 . . . . .144 C1
Wimblington Dr RG6 . . . . .114 B4
Wimbourne Gdns RG30 . . . . . . .58 A1
Wimbushes RG40 . . . . .141 B3
Winbury Ct SL6 . . . . .39 C4
Winbury Sch SL6 . . . . .40 A2
Wincanton Rd RG2 . . . . .113 B4
Winch CI RG42 . . . . .90 B2
Winchbottom La SL7 ,HP10 . . . .2 A4
Winchcombe Cty Jun
& Inf Schs RG14 . . . . .105 A2
Winchcombe Rd
Newbury RG14 . . . . .105 A2
Twyford RG10 . . . . .61 C2
Winchester Cl SL3 . . . . .69 C3
Winchester Dr SL6 . . . . .39 A2
Winchester Ho 7 RG14 . . . . . .105 A1
Winchester Rd
Harlington UB3 . . . . .71 C4
Reading RG2 . . . . .86 A4
Winchester Way SL1 . . . . .150 B3
Winchgrove Rd RG42 . . . . .91 A1
Winchstone CI TW17 . . . . .124 C3
Wincroft Rd RG4 . . . . .58 C3
Windermere Cl
East Bedfont TW14 . . . . .98 C4
Stanwell TW19 . . . . .97 B3

Windermere Cl continued
Thorpe Lea TW20 96
Winnersh RG41 . . . . .88 B2
Windermere Rd
Lightwater GU18 . . . . .146 A1
Reading RG2 . . . . .86 B2
Windermere Way
Slough SL1 . . . . .41 B4
Thatcham RG19 . . . . .106 A2
Windermere Wlk GU15 . . . . . . .152 A3
Winding Wood Dr GU15 . . . . . .152 A2
Windle Cl GU20 . . . . .146 B2
Windlebrook Gn 3 RG42 . . . . .118 A4
Windlemere Golf Ctr
GU24 . . . . .153 C4
Windlesham Ct GU20 . . . . .146 A3
Windlesham Rd
Bracknell RG42 . . . . .117 C4
West End GU24 . . . . .153 C4
Windlesham Village
Cty Inf Sch GU20 . . . . .146 A3
Windmill Ave RG41 . . . . .115 C4
Windmill Bsns Village
TW16 . . . . .125 C4
Windmill Cl Charlton TW16 . . . .98 C1
Windsor SL4 . . . . .67 A3
Wokingham RG41 . . . . .115 C4
Windmill Cnr RG7 . . . . .137 A3
Windmill Ct RG27 . . . . .152 A2
Windmill Field RG20 . . . . .146 B2
Windmill La RG7 . . . . .108 A3
Windmill Lodge TW16 . . . . .125 C4
Windmill Rd
Bracknell RG42 . . . . .118 A4
Charlton TW16 . . . . .125 C4
Cookham SL6 . . . . .19 C3
Fulmer SL3 . . . . .23 B4
Mortimer RG7 . . . . .137 A3
Slough SL1 . . . . .42 B3
Windmill Rd W TW16 . . . . .125 C4
Windmill Terr TW17 . . . . .125 C3
Windmill Trad Est TW16 . . . . .125 C4
Windrush Ave SL3 . . . . .44 A2
Windrush Ct 8 RG30 . . . . .85 A4
Windrush Ho SL3 . . . . .3 A2
Windrush Hts GU47 . . . . .150 A4
Windrush Way
Maidenhead SL6 . . . . .39 C4
Reading RG30 . . . . .85 A4
Windsor Boys Sch SL4
Windsor Bsns Ctr The
SL4 . . . . .67 B4
Windsor Castle SL4 . . . . .67 C4
Windsor Cl SL1 . . . . .21 B1
Windsor Ct 16 RG1 . . . . .85 C4
Windsor Dr TW15 . . . . .97 B2
Windsor & Eton
Central Sta SL4 . . . . .67 B4
Windsor & Eton
Riverside Sta SL4 . . . . .67 B4
Windsor Forest Ct SL5 . . . . . . .119 B4
Windsor Girls Sch SL4 . . . . .67 A2
Windsor Great Pk SL4 . . . . .94 B2
Windsor Hill HP10 . . . . .3 C2
Windsor Ho RG9 . . . . .35 C4
Windsor L Ctr SL4 . . . . .67 A4
Windsor La SL1 . . . . .21 B1
Windsor Park Rd UB3 . . . . .71 C4
Windsor PI KT16 . . . . .124 A2
Windsor Rd Datchet SL3 . . . . . .68 A4
Englefield Green
TW19, TW20 . . . . .95 C3
Fulmer SL2 . . . . .23 A4
Holyport SL6 . . . . .40 B1
North Ascot SL5 . . . . .120 A4
Slough SL1 . . . . .42 C2
Wraysbury TW19 . . . . .68 C1
Windsor Ride
Bracknell SL5 . . . . .119 B2
Sandhurst GU15 . . . . .151 A4
Wokingham RG40 . . . . .142 A4
Windsor Rise RG14 . . . . .131 B4
Windsor Sq 2 RG1 . . . . .86 A3
Windsor St KT16 . . . . .124 A2
Windsor Way RG31 . . . . .84 B3
Windsor Youth Hostel
SL4 . . . . .67 A4
Wing Cl SL7 . . . . .1 B1
Wingate Rd RG5 . . . . .87 C3
Wingfield Gdns GU16 . . . . .152 B2
Wingrove Rd RG30 . . . . .85 A3
Winkfield Cl RG41 . . . . .116 A2
Winkfield La
Oakley Green SL4 . . . . .66 A1
Winkfield SL4 . . . . .92 B4
Winkfield Row Ascot SL5 . . . . . .120 A4
Windsor SL4 . . . . .66 C1
Winkfield Row RG42 . . . . .92 A2
Winkfield St SL4 . . . . .92 B3
Winkworth La RG7 . . . . .135 B1
Winnersh Gate RG41 . . . . .88 B1
Winnersh Gr RG41 . . . . .88 B1
Winnersh Prim Sch RG41 . . . . .88 B2
Winnersh Sta RG41 . . . . .88 B1
Winnersh Triangle Ind Est
RG41 . . . . .88 A2
Winnersh Triangle Sta
RG41 . . . . .88 A2
Winscombe RG12 . . . . .117 C2
Winser Dr RG30 . . . . .85 B3
Winston Cl RG7 . . . . .113 B1
Winston Way
Purley on T RG8 . . . . .57 A3
Thatcham RG19 . . . . .105 C2
Winter Hill SL6 . . . . .2 B1

Winter Hill Rd SL6 ....19 A2
Winterberry Way RG4 ....58 C3
Winterbourne Ct RG12 ...118 B4
Winterbourne Rd RG20 ...76 C2
Winterton Dr RG14 ......104 B3
Winton Cres GU46 ....149 B3
Winton Rd RG2 ....113 B4
Wintoun Path SL2 ....21 C1
Wintringham Way RG8 ....57 B3
Winvale SL1 ....42 C2
Winwood Slough SL2 ......43 B4
Windsor SL4 ....66 C3
Wisdom Ct 12 RG30 ....85 B3
Wises Firs RG7 ....110 B2
Wishmoor Cl GU15 ....151 C4
Wishmoor Rd GU15 ......151 C4
Wispington Cl RG6 ....87 B1
Wistaria La GU46 ....149 B3
Wisteria Cl RG41 ....115 C3
Wiston Terr RG1 ....86 A4
Witcham Cl RG6 ....114 B4
Withey Cl SL4 ....66 C3
Witheygate Ave TW18 .....97 A1
Withy Cl Lightwater GU18 ..146 B1
Reading RG31 ....84 B3
Withybed La RG17 ....101 C2
Withybed Way RG18 .....106 C3
Withycroft SL3 ....43 C4
Withys The RG40 ....53 C1
Wittenham Ave RG31 .....84 A4
Wittenham Rd RG12 .....118 C4
Wittington Cotts SL7 .....17 B3
Woburn Cl Caversham RG4 .58 C2
Frimley GU16 ....152 A1
Wokefield Row RG7 .....137 B4
Wokingham Hospl RG41 ..116 A3
Wokingham Rd
Bracknell RG12 ....117 C4
Earley RG6 ....87 B2
Hurst RG10 ....88 C4
Sandhurst RG45,GU47 ...142 C1
Wokingham Sta RG40 ....116 A3
Wokingham Theatre
RG40 ....116 A4
Wolf La SL4 ....66 C2
Wolseley St RG1 ....86 A3
Wolsey Rd Ashford TW15 ..97 C2
Ashford, Felthamhill TW16 ..98 C1
Caversham RG4 ....59 A1
Wolsingham Way RG19 ..106 B1
Wondesford Dale RG42 ...90 B2
Wooburn Grange HP10 .....3 B2
Wooburn Manor Pk HP10 ..3 C3
Wooburn Mews HP10 ......3 C3
Wood Cl SL4 ....67 B2
Wood End RG45 ....142 C4
Wood Gn RG2 ....113 B4
Wood Green Cl RG30 .....85 C4
Wood La Arborfield RG41 .114 C2
Beech Hill RG7 ....138 C3
Binfield RG42 ....90 B1
Iver SL0 ....44 B4
Slough SL1 ....42 A2
Wood Moor RG40 ....141 C1
Wood Rd Camberley GU15 .151 A1
Littleton TW17 ....125 A3
Wood Ridge RG14 ....130 C4
Woodbery Cl RG14 ....59 A3
Woodborne Cl Earley RG6 ..87 B1
Sandhurst GU47 ....150 B4
Woodbine Cotts TW20 ....95 C1
Woodbine La RG20 ......130 C1
Woodbourne Cl GU46 ...149 B3
Woodbridge Dr GU15 ...151 B4
Woodbridge Rd
Blackwater GU17 ....150 A3
Reading RG31 ....84 A3
Woodbury RG17 ....25 B1
Woodbury Cl SL8 ....3 B2
Woodby Dr SL5 ....120 C1
Woodcock Ct RG7 ....113 A2
Woodcock SL6 ....39 B3
Woodcote House Sch
GU20 ....146 A3
Woodcote Pl SL5 ....119 C4
Woodcote Rd
Caversham RG4 ....58 C2
South Stoke RG8 ....14 C2
Woodcote Way RG4 ......58 B3
Woodend Cl SL5 ....119 C4
Woodend Dr SL5 ....120 A2
Woodenhill RG12 ....117 C1
Woodenhill Cty Prim Sch
RG12 ....117 C1
Woodfield Dr SL6 ....39 A3
Woodfield Way RG7 ......83 C2
Woodford Cl RG4 ....58 C2
Woodford Gn RG12 .....118 C3
Woodford Way SL2 ....22 A1
Woodhall La SL5 ....146 C4
Woodhaw TW20 ....96 A2
Woodhouse La RG19 ....133 C1
Woodhouse St RG42 .....90 C1
Woodhurst La RG41 ....115 C4
Woodhurst Rd SL6 ....20 A1
Woodhurst South SL6 ....20 B1
Woodies Cl RG42 ....90 B1
Woodland Ave
Slough SL1 ....42 B3
Windsor SL4 ....66 C2
Woodland Cl SL7 ....1 C2
Woodland Cres RG42 .....91 B1
Woodland Dr RG30 ....84 B4
Woodland Way SL7 ....1 C2
Woodlands GU46 ....149 B2
Woodlands Ave
Burghfield Common RG7 ..111 A2
Wokingham RG41 ....116 A3
Woodley RG5 ....87 B4
Woodlands Bsns Pk SL6 ..39 A1
Woodlands Cl Ascot SL5 ..119 C2
Farnborough (Hants)
GU17 ....150 C1
Hermitage RG18 ....78 C3
Woodlands Cotts 4 SL2 ..22 B4
Woodlands Ct GU47 ....143 C1
Woodlands Gr RG4 ......59 C2
Woodlands La
GU20,GU24 ....146 C2
Woodlands Par TW15 ....98 B1
Woodlands Park Ave SL6 ..39 A1
Woodlands Park Prim Sch
SL6 ....39 A1
Woodlands Park Rd SL6 ..39 A2
Woodlands Rd
Camberley GU15 ....151 A3
Shiplake RG9 ....35 C2
Tadley RG26 ....134 B1
Virginia Water GU25 ...122 B3
Woodlands Rd E GU25 ..122 B3
Woodlands Rd W GU25 ..122 B3
Woodlands Ride SL5 ....120 A2
Woodlands The RG41 ...115 B3
Woodlands Wlk GU17 ...150 C1
Woodley CE Prim Sch
RG5 ....88 A4
Woodley Gn RG5 ....87 C4
Woodley Park Est RG5 ...87 B4
Woodman Cl RG2 ....113 B3
Woodmancott Cl RG12 ..118 C2
Woodmans La RG7 ......110 C2
Woodmere RG12 ....118 C3
Woodmere Cl RG6 ....87 A1
Woodmoor End SL6 ......20 A4
Woodpecker Cl RG10 ....61 C2
Woodpeckers RG12 .....118 A3
Woodridge Cl RG12 ....118 B3
Woodrow Dr RG40 ......116 C3
Woods Rd RG4 ....59 C2
Woodsend Cl RG6 ....113 C4
Woodshore Cl GU25 ....122 A2
Woodside
Blackwater GU17 ....150 B2
Cold Ash RG18 ....79 B1
Flackwell Heath HP10 ....3 B3
Newbury RG14 ....130 B4
Sandhurst GU15 ....150 C4
Woodside Ave HP10 ......3 B4
Woodside Bsns Pk RG2 ..113 A4
Woodside Cl
Bucklebury RG7 ....107 B3
Mortimer RG7 ....137 A3
Wokingham RG40 ....141 C4
Woodside Dr RG18 ....79 A3
Woodside La SL4,SL5 ....93 B2
Woodside Rd SL5 ....93 A1
Woodside Way
Reading RG2 ....113 B4
Virginia Water GU25 ...122 A3
Woodstock Rd40 ....116 B3
Woodstock Ave SL3 ......43 B1
Woodstock Cl SL6 ....19 C1
Woodstock St RG1 ....86 C4
Woodthorpe Rd TW15 ....97 B2
Woodview Rd RG8 ....56 B3
Woodward Cl GU17 ....150 A3
Woodward Cl RG41 ......88 B1
Woodway GU15 ....151 A3
Woodway Rd OX11 ....12 A4
Woodwaye RG5 ....87 B4
Woodyer Cl RG5 ....87 C3
Woolacombe Dr RG6 ....86 C1
Woolf Dr RG40 ....116 A4
Woolford Cl RG42 ....92 B1
Woolhampton
CE Prim Sch RG7 ......108 B2
Woolhampton Hill RG7 ..108 B2
Woolhampton Way
RG12 ....118 B2
Woolton Lodge Gdns
RG20 ....129 C1
Woosehill RG41 ....115 C3
Woosehill Cl RG41 ......115 C4
Woosehill La RG41 .....115 C3
Wootton Cl RG31 ....84 B4
Wootton Dr HP10 ....3 C4
Wootton Rd RG9 ....35 B4
Wootton Way SL6 ....39 B3
Worcester Cl
Maidenhead SL6 ....39 B2
Reading RG30 ....85 A3
Worcester Ct
Ashford TW15 ....98 A2
Staines TW15 ....97 A2
Worcester Dr TW15 ......98 A2
Worcester Gdns SL1 .....42 B2
Worcestershire Lea RG42 ..91 C1
Wordsworth RG12 ....117 C2
Wordsworth Ave GU46 ..149 A2
Wordsworth Ct RG4 ......59 A4
Wordsworth Rd
Slough SL2 ....21 B1
Thatcham RG18 ....106 B2
Worlds End Hill RG12 ...118 C2
Wormersley Rd RG19 ...131 B4
Worple Ave TW18 ....97 A1
Worple Rd TW18 ....97 A1
Worple The TW19 ....68 C1
Worrall Way RG6 ....113 C4
Worsley Pl RG7 ....83 C2
Worster Rd SL6 ....19 C3
Worton Dr RG2 ....113 A4
Worton Grange Ind Est
RG2 ....113 A4
Wrabness Way TW18 ...124 A4
Wraysbury Cty Comb Sch
TW19 ....68 C1
Wraysbury Rd TW18,TW19 .96 B3
Wraysbury Sta TW19 .....69 A1
Wren Cl
Burghfield Common RG7 ..111 A2
Wokingham RG41 ....115 C3
Yateley GU46 ....149 A3
Wren Ct Egham TW20 ....96 A2
Slough SL3 ....44 A2
Wrenfield Dr RG4 ....58 C3
Wrens Ave TW15 ....98 B2
Wrensfield SL7 ....1 B1
Wrenswood Cl RG2 .....113 A4
Wright SL4 ....66 B2
Wright Cl RG5 ....88 A4
Wright Gdns TW17 .....125 A2
Wright Sq SL4 ....66 B2
Wright Way SL4 ....66 B2
Wroxham RG12 ....117 C2
Wroxham Rd RG5 ....87 B4
Wyatt Rd Staines TW18 ..97 A2
Windsor SL4 ....66 B2
Wychcotes RG4 ....58 C2
Wychelm Rd
Lightwater GU18 ....153 B4
Shinfield RG2 ....113 C3
Wychwood Ave RG12 ...118 C3
Wychwood Cl RG6 ....86 C2
Wychwood Cres RG6 .....86 C2
Wycombe La HP10 ....3 A4
Wycombe Rd SL7 ....1 C2
Wye Cl Ashford TW15 ....98 A2
Reading RG30 ....84 C3
Wye Rd HP10 ....3 B4
Wye Valley Sch SL8 ......3 A2
Wykeham Cl UB7 ....71 A4
Wykeham Rd RG6 ....87 A3
Wylam RG12 ....117 C2
Wylands Rd SL3 ....44 A1
Wyld Court Hill RG18 ...53 A3
Wyld Court Rainforest
RG18 ....53 B3
Wymers Cl SL1 ....21 A2
Wymers Wood Rd SL1 ...21 A2
Wyncote Cl RG2 ....86 C1
Wyndale Cl RG9 ....15 C1
Wyndham Cl GU46 .....149 B4
Wyndham Cres
Burnham SL1 ....21 A2
Woodley RG5 ....60 B1
Wyndham Rd RG14 ....105 B3
Wynford Cl RG30 ....85 B2
Wynnstay Gdns SL7 ......1 C3
Wynsham Way GU20 ...146 A3
Wyre Ct RG31 ....57 B2
Wyresdale RG12 ....118 C1
Wyther Mead RG42 ......90 A1
Wythegate TW18 ....96 C1
Wyvern Cl RG12 ....118 A3
Wyvern Ct TW15 ....97 C3

Yale Cl GU47 ....143 C1
Yard Mead TW20 ....96 A3
Yardley RG12 ....117 C2
Yarmouth Rd SL1 ....42 B3
Yarnold Cl RG40 ....116 C
Yarnton Cl RG4 ....59 B
Yateley Common Ctry Pk
GU17,GU46 ....149 C
Yateley Inf Sch GU46 ...149 B
Yateley Manor Prep Sch
GU46 ....149 B
Yateley Rd GU47 ....149 C
Yateley Sch GU46 ......149 A
Yates Copse RG14 ......105 A
Yattendon CE Prim Sch
RG18 ....53 C
Yattendon Ct RG18 ......53 C
Yattendon La RG8,RG18 ..54 B
Yattendon Rd RG18 ......79 B
Yaverland Dr GU19 .....145 B
Ye Meads SL6 ....40 C
Yelverton Rd RG2 ....86 B
Yeomans La RG20 ......131 A
Yeomans Way GU15 ....151 C
Yeosfield RG7 ....139 B
Yeoveney Cl TW19 ....96 B
Yeovil Ent Ctr SL1 ....41 C
Yeovil Rd Sandhurst GU47 .143 C
Slough SL1 ....41 C
Yew Cl RG41 ....115 C
Yew Gate RG14 ....104 C
Yew La RG1 ....85 C
Yew Tree Cl SL6 ....39 C
Yew Tree Ct RG8 ....34 C
Yew Tree Rd SL1 ....43 A
Yew Tree Rise RG31 .....84 A
Yew Tree Stables RG20 ..31 C
Yew Tree Wlk GU16 ....151 C
Yew Trees TW17 ....124 C
Yewhurst Cl RG10 ....61 B
Yews The TW15 ....98 A
Yewtrees TW20 ....123 B
Yield Hall La 11 RG1 ....86 A
Yield Hall Pl RG1 ....86 A
Yockley Cl GU15 ....152 B
Yoreham Cl RG6 ....87 C
York Ave Slough SL1 .....42 B
Windsor SL4 ....67 A
York Cl RG14 ....105 A
York Ho RG42 ....117 C
York Rd Binfield RG42 ...90 B
Camberley GU15 ....151 B
Henley-on-T RG9 ....15 E
Hungerford RG17 ....100 B
Maidenhead SL6 ....40 A
Marlow SL7 ....1 B
Newbury RG14 ....105 A
Reading RG1 ....59 A
Windsor SL4 ....67 A
York Town Ind Est GU15 .151 A
York Way GU47 ....150 A
Yorkshire Pl RG42 ....91 C
Yorktown Rd
Sandhurst GU47 ....150 A
Sandhurst GU47 ....150 C
Youlden Cl GU15 ....152 A
Youlden Dr GU15 ......152 A
Young Cres RG19 ....131 B
Young's Ind Est RG7 ...134 C

Z

Zealand Ave UB7 ....70 C
Zenith Ct GU47 ....143 E
Zetland Ct SL6 ....40 A
Zinnia Cl RG41 ....115 E
Zinzan St RG1 ....85 C